Music, Health, and Wellbeing

This book is dedicated to Tony Wigram.

Shortly after the final submission of the completed manuscript Tony Wigram very sadly passed away. We would like to pay tribute to Tony who was one of the most respected and influential music therapists working today. He was also an inspirational friend and colleague to countless people around the world and he will be enormously missed.

Music, Health, and Wellbeing

Edited by

Raymond A. R. MacDonald
Glasgow Caledonian University, UK

Gunter Kreutz
Carl von Ossietzky University, Germany

Laura Mitchell
Bishop's University, Canada

OXFORD
UNIVERSITY PRESS

OXFORD

UNIVERSITY PRESS

Great Clarendon Street, Oxford OX2 6DP
United Kingdom

Oxford University Press is a department of the University of Oxford.
It furthers the University's objective of excellence in research, scholarship,
and education by publishing worldwide. Oxford is a registered trade mark of
Oxford University Press in the UK and in certain other countries

© Oxford University Press 2012

The moral rights of the authors have been asserted

First Edition published 2012
First published in paperback 2013

Impression: 1

British Library Cataloguing in Publication Data
Data available

Library of Congress Cataloging in Publication Data
Library of Congress Control Number: 2011944046

ISBN 978–0–19–958697–4
ISBN 978–0–19–968682–7 (pbk)

Printed in Great Britain on acid-free paper by
Ashford Colour Press Ltd, Gosport, Hampshire

Contents

Acknowledgements

This book began with a brief conversation between the three of us at the *10th International Conference on Music Perception and Cognition* in Sapporo, Japan, in 2008. By coincidence, we had this discussion next to the Oxford University Press book stall where commissioning editor Martin Baum was working. Straight away, we discussed with him the possibility of a proposal around music, health, and wellbeing, and, with some very encouraging comments from Martin, the genesis of this book happened very quickly. Our aim was to bring together an international and multidisciplinary group of articles that reflected the breadth and depth of interest in the link between music, health, and wellbeing echoing the huge interest there currently is in this relationship.

Each chapter in this book has been read and reviewed by at least one external reader and we would like to thank the following esteemed academics who all gave their time freely to read and comment on the chapters: Gary Ansdell, Lars Ole Bonde, Leslie Bunt, Olle Bygren, Gordon Cox, Franziska Degé, Tia DeNora, Denise Erdonmez, Alasdair Forsyth, Alinka Greasley, Noola Griffiths, David Hargreaves, Gary MacPherson, Wendy Magee, Björn Merker, Dorothy Miell, Helen Mitchell, Nikki Moran, Ian Morrison, Emery Schubert, Fred Schwartz, Katie van Buren, and Victoria Williamson.

The staff at Oxford University Press have been approachable, friendly, and encouraging throughout the whole process of editing this book and we would like to thank in particular Martin Baum and Charlotte Green who have provided expert and timely advice throughout. A number of other people have provided valuable insights and support and we would like to thank: Tracy Ibbotson, Maria and Eva MacDonald, Dorothy Miell, David Hargreaves, Martel Ollerenshaw, David Bell, James Cox, William Connolly, Sonja Bayerlein, Daniel Levitin, Martin Sharp, and Paul Flowers.

Raymond MacDonald
Gunter Kreutz
Laura Mitchell
June 2011

List of Contributors

Eckart Altenmüller
Institute of Music Physiology and
Musicians' Medicine,
Hannover University of Music,
Drama and Media,
Hannover, Germany

Gary Ansdell
Nordoff Robbins Centre,
London, UK

Günther Bernatzky
Department of Organismic Biology,
Neurosignaling Unit,
University of Salzburg,
Salzburg, Germany

Lars Ole Bonde
Institute for Communication,
Aalborg University,
Aalborg, Denmark

Stephan Bongard
Department of Psychology,
Goethe-University,
Frankfurt am Main,
Germany

Stephen Clift
Sidney De Haan Research Centre
for Arts and Health,
Canterbury Christ Church University,
Folkestone, Kent, UK

Eugenia Costa-Giomi
School of Music,
The University of Texas at Austin,
Austin, TX, USA

Jane Davidson
School of Music,
University of Western Australia,
Crawley, WA, Australia

Norma Daykin
Department of Health and Applied
Social Sciences,
Faculty of Health and Social Care,
University of the West of England,
Bristol, UK

Régine Debrosse
Department of Psychology,
McGill University, Montreal, QC,
Canada

Tia DeNora
Department of Sociology & Philosophy,
SSIS Exeter University,
Exeter, UK

David J. Elliott
Department of Music & Performing
Arts Professions,
New York University,
New York, NY, USA

Andrea Emberly
School of Music,
University of Western Australia,
Crawley, WA, Australia

Paul Flowers
Department of Psychology,
Glasgow Caledonian University,
Glasgow, UK

Patrick Gaudreau
School of Psychology,
University of Ottawa,
Ottawa, ON, Canada

Heiner Gembris
Institute for Research on Music Ability,
University of Paderborn,
Paderborn, Germany

Jane Ginsborg
Centre for Music Performance Research,
Royal Northern College of Music,
Manchester, UK

Christian Gold
GAMUT, Uni Health,
Uni Research,
Bergen, Norway

Susan Hallam
Institute of Education,
University of London,
London, UK

David J. Hargreaves
Applied Music Research Centre,
Roehampton University,
London, UK

Terry Hartig
Department of Psychology,
Uppsala University,
Uppsala, Sweden

Patrik N. Juslin
Department of Psychology,
Uppsala University,
Uppsala, Sweden

Vicky Karkou
Division of Nursing, Occupational
Therapy and Arts Therapies,
School of Health Sciences,
Queen Margaret University,
Edinburgh, UK

Laurence J. Kirmayer
Department of Psychiatry,
Division of Social & Transcultural
Psychiatry,
McGill University,
Montreal, QC, Canada

Stefan Koelsch
Cluster Languages of Emotion,
Freie Universität Berlin,
Berlin, Germany

Gunter Kreutz
Department of Music,
School of Linguistics and Cultural Studies,
Carl von Ossietzky University Oldenburg,
Oldenburg, Germany

Werner Kullich
Ludwig Boltzmann Institut,
Cluster for Rheumatology,
Balneology and Rehabilitation,
Saalfelden, Austria

A. Blythe LaGasse
Center for Biomedical Research in Music,
Colorado State University,
Fort Collins, CO, USA

Alexandra Lamont
School of Psychology,
Dorothy Hodgkin Building,
Keele University, Keele, UK

Raymond MacDonald
Department of Psychology,
Glasgow Caledonian University,
Glasgow, UK

Kyproulla Markou
Applied Music Research Centre,
Southlands College,
Roehampton University,
London, UK

Dave Miranda
Department of Psychiatry,
Division of Social & Transcultural
Psychiatry,
McGill University,
Montreal, QC, Canada

Laura Mitchell
Department of Psychology,
Bishop's University,
Sherbrooke QC, Canada

Julien Morizot
School of Psychoeducation,
University of Montreal,
Montreal, QC, Canada

Michael Murray
School of Psychology,
Dorothy Hodgkin Building,
Keele University,
Keele, UK

Adrian C. North
School of Life Sciences,
Heriot-Watt University,
Edinburgh, UK

Adam Ockelford
Applied Music Research Centre
Southlands College,
Roehampton University,
London, UK

Mercédès Pavlicevic
Nordoff Robbins Centre,
London, UK

Maria Pothoulaki
Department of Psychology,
Glasgow Caledonian University,
Glasgow, UK

Michaela Presch
Department of Organismic Biology,
Neurosignaling Unit,
University of Salzburg,
Salzburg, Austria

Cynthia Quiroga Murcia
Department of Psychology,
Goethe-University,
Frankfurt am Main,
Germany

Even Ruud
Department of Musicology,
University of Oslo,
Oslo, Norway

Suvi Saarikallio
Department of Music,
University of Jyväskylä,
Jyväskylä, Finland

E. Glenn Schellenberg
Department of Psychology,
University of Toronto Mississauga,
Mississauga, ON, Canada

Gottfried Schlaug
Department of Neurology,
Music and Neuroimaging Laboratory,
Beth Israel Deaconess Medical Center and
Harvard Medical School,
Boston, MA, USA

Marissa Silverman
John J. Cali School of Music,
Montclair State University,
Montclair, NJ, USA

Claudia Spahn
Freiburg Institute for Musicians' Medicine,
University of Music Freiburg and
University Clinic Freiburg,
Freiburg, Germany

Ralph Spintge
Institute for Music Therapy,
University for Music and
Drama HfMT Hamburg,
Sportklinik Hellersen,
Lüdenscheid, Germany

Thomas Stegemann
Department of Music Therapy,
University of Music and
Performing Arts Vienna,
Wien, Austria

Brynjulf Stige
The Grieg Academy Music Therapy
Research Centre,
Bergen, Norway

Simon Strickner
Lichtenbergstrasse 3,
Saalfelden, Austria

Michael H. Thaut
Center for Biomedical Research in Music,
Colorado State University,
Fort Collins, CO, USA

Töres Theorell
Stress Research Institute,
University of Stockholm,
Stockholm, Sweden

Gro Trondalen
Centre for Music and Health,
Norwegian Academy of Music,
Oslo, Norway

Daniel Västfjäll
Department of Psychology,
University of Gothenburg,
Gothenburg, Sweden

Franz Wendtner
Department of Oncology,
Privat Paracelsus University,
Salzburg, Austria

Tony Wigram
Institute for Communication,
Aalborg University,
Aalborg, Denmark

Aaron Williamon
Centre for Performance Science,
Royal College of Music,
London, UK

Section 1

Introductory Chapters:
Setting the Scene

Chapter 1

What is *Music, Health, and Wellbeing* and Why is it Important?

Raymond MacDonald, Gunter Kreutz,
and Laura Mitchell

The origins of *Music, Health, and Wellbeing*

The great saxophonist Charlie Parker once proclaimed 'if you don't live it, it won't come out of your horn'. This quote has often been used to explain the hedonistic lifestyle of many jazz greats; however, it also signals the reciprocal and inextricable relationship between music and wider social, cultural, and psychological variables. This link is complex and multifaceted and is undoubtedly a central component of why music has been implicated as a therapeutic agent in vast swathes of contemporary research studies. Music is always about more than just acoustic events or notes on a page. Moreover, music's universal and timeless potential to influence how we feel and think lies at the heart of our motivation to produce this edited volume.

Music has been imbued with curative, therapeutic, and other medical value throughout history. Musicians, therapists, philosophers, as well as other artists and scholars alike have documented its physical, mental, and social effects in treatises from as early as 4000 BC to the present (Spintge and Droh 1992). Clearly, the relationship between music, health, and wellbeing is complex and involves numerous facets and challenges. To begin with, there is considerable debate on all three of the key terms in the title of this volume. Leaving aside the intricacies of etymology and translation in various languages, one significant challenge is the establishment of causal links between musical activities on the one hand and specific individual health and wellbeing benefits on the other. This book is conceived to accept this challenge by means of building evidence-bases in different areas of music and health research and we hope that this collection of chapters will further our understanding of music as a part of both human nature and human culture.

The integration of different academic disciplines presented throughout this text reflects recent developments in music research where multidisciplinary approaches are viewed as vital to the development of our understanding of musical behaviour. It is also important to note that the profession of music therapy dates back to the early twentieth centenary and music therapists have been researching and delivering therapeutic interventions across a vast range of clinical settings for a considerable amount of time (Bunt and Hoskyns, 2002). Moreover, interest in the social psychology of music and evolutionary origins of music have emerged as key themes in music psychology research. Consequently, the effects of musical activities on individuals in both clinical and non-clinical settings are now being studied. These approaches place emphasis on variables including psychological, physiological, cultural and behavioural effects which may have implications for health and wellbeing. In brief, music therapy and music psychology research complement each other while maintaining traditions that are specific to each of these areas.

Research into the relationship between music, health, and wellbeing necessitates novel approaches from right across the academic spectrum, including arts and humanities as well as the social and natural sciences (Pothoulaki et al. in press). From engineers endeavouring to develop new technology to help individuals with physical disabilities explore their creativity, to music graduates seeking to use their skills and training within a community music context, through to surgeons playing recorded music for patients in hospital to alleviate pain and anxiety. Musical activities and responses are also considered as potent preventative measures to enhance psycho-physiological wellbeing reaching into almost every aspect of life.

What is understood now as a multidisciplinary interest in the relationship between music, health, and wellbeing has captured the public's imagination as well as sparking a wealth of academic research (Cassidy and MacDonald 2010). Witness the huge growth in community singing. Singing is now viewed as being more accessible than in previous times, and many community singing groups explicitly state that the health benefits of community singing are a primary reason for participation (Clift, Chapter 9). One reason for this growing recognition of the potential benefits of music interventions in the general population, irrespective of the individual level of musical training, is the considerable advance in research that investigates the benefits of music on various health measures (Wosch and Wigram 2007). Indeed, in recent years there have been an increasing number of studies that investigate the relationship between music, wellbeing, and health. Importantly, this heightened interest is influenced by developments in research methodologies (qualitative and quantitative) in many contexts including laboratory, clinical, educational, and community settings. The current book presents many of these contexts and research designs.

Why music?

What are, if any, the special reasons to consider music in contexts of wellbeing and health? Many authors in this volume rightfully address the lack of coherence of research in this field. The diversity of approaches and findings, the heterogeneity of methods, participants, outcomes, and interpretations of findings which are reflected in this text may be serious obstacles in theory building and could well compromise progress in the field. But by the same token, this heterogeneity of research is also indicative of an undercurrent suggesting broad support of basic ideas, which run throughout the chapters. The fact that music is implicated in so many different types of interventions relating to health and wellbeing underscores the belief that being moved or touched by music cannot be held purely as a metaphor, which renders music as mere embellishment of our daily lives. Presented below are a number of possible reasons as to why music could produce these beneficial effects.

Music is ubiquitous

Now more than at any other time in history, music is pervasive. The technological revolution that has taken place in terms of music listening means that we can now listen to our own musical choices 24 hours a day. Cheap, discreet, and easily operated digital music devices with large storage capacities facilitate selecting music to accompany household chores, driving, a romantic meal, a bus journey, shopping, a long walk, etc. Indeed, these devices are so discreet that we can, in effect, listen to our own music in virtually every context imaginable.

Music is emotional

There is no doubt that music affects our emotions (Juslin and Sloboda 2010). When selecting music to listen to in any particular situation we make a number of sophisticated and highly nuanced psychological assessments in an instant. This type of assessment may include questions such as: how do I feel right now? How do I want to feel in five minutes or one hour and what music will help me achieve this goal? Which music suits me for this very moment, or a certain period of time? Is anybody else listening and what will they think? Within and beyond these assessments we also make very specific musical decisions about how particular pieces will change the environment and the psychological states of other individuals around us. This capacity of music to affect our mood and emotions may be one of the key features that facilitate musical activities producing positive effects.

Music is engaging

When we play or listen to music we are involved in various different levels of processing. A number of chapters within the book demonstrate to what extent engaging in music may produce positive neurological effects in the brain. Indeed it has been suggested that music can influence the plasticity of the brain in specific ways, which can translate into changes, for example, of the human motor system (LaGasse and Thaut, Chapter 12).

Music is distracting

When we are listening to, or playing music we can be distracted from aspects of our lives that are distressing: a painful stimulus, a very emotional event. Certainly there is evidence that music can distract the listener and performer in many ways, e.g. possibly through the immersive state of 'flow' (Csíkszentmihályi 1996), and in doing so can provide health benefits.

Music is physical

In addition to the entwined relationship of music and dance, musical performance can be physically demanding. Drummers, for example, are required to have high levels of stamina, coordination, and dexterity across all four limbs. Specifically in a health context, coupling music with physiotherapy can help stroke patients undertake rehabilitation exercises that may facilitate development in arm and leg function more quickly (van Wijck et al. in press).

Music is ambiguous

Another reason why music can evoke such strong emotions is that music is ambiguous in meaning. Regardless of what specific emotion a composer attempts to imbue a piece of music with, or no matter what specific emotion a performer wants to convey in any given performance, as listeners we filter everything we hear though our own listening histories, experiences, and preferences. We are therefore free to interpret what we hear in an infinite number of ways (Mitchell and MacDonald 2011). While there is a significant amount of research investigating the effects of specific structural parameters upon musical communication, it is clear that preference and structure interact in a number of sophisticated ways to produce meaning for the listener (Knox et al. in press).

Music is social

Music, by its very nature, is a social activity. Indeed it may be possible to define music through its social function, i.e. any sound, action, or silence can be termed 'music' if the social context labels it as such. The social functions of music are numerous and vastly important to society, linking people whether one-to-one, in large gatherings, or connecting through technology.

Music is communicative

One of the primary functions of music is to communicate (Miell et al. 2005). Indeed, music can be viewed as a fundamental channel of communication, providing a means by which emotions and ideas can be expressed, communicated, and shared, both locally and globally, even when communicating by language may be impossible (Hargreaves et al. 2005). Taking the specific example of investigating the link between music and health, the profession of music therapy is predicated upon a deep and sophisticated understanding of the process of musical communication. In order to develop a trusting and effective clinical relationship, a music therapist must utilize this knowledge of musical communication to produce positive effects for clients. The communicative potential of music is undoubtedly linked to its therapeutic potential.

Music affects behaviour

There is now a considerable amount of research highlighting how music affects our behaviour in very deep and sophisticated ways (North and Hargreaves 2008). Whether in a personal, social, consumer, educational, or motivational context there is clear and unequivocal evidence that music affects behaviour. This capacity of music to affect our behaviour has been harnessed in numerous contexts to change behaviours in beneficial ways (Hallam and MacDonald 2008).

Music affects identities

There is no doubt that music also has an important part to play in our constantly evolving and socially negotiated identities (MacDonald et al. 2002). There is evidence that music listening is the most important recreational activity for young people, influencing clothing preferences, magazines read, places to socialize, and even friendship groups (Zillman and Gan 1997). For many young people, music is key to how they orient themselves in their lives and their music tastes are often employed as a 'badge of identity' or way of signalling to the world key aspects of their personality (Hargreaves and North 1997).

What is health?

One of the most widely discussed contemporary definitions of health from the World Health Organization (WHO) reveals it as 'a state of complete physical, mental, and social well-being and not merely the absence of disease or infirmity'. This definition embraces, although indirectly, a salutogenetic approach to health (e.g. Antonovsky 1987). This perspective suggests that every individual can activate intrinsic and personal psychological resources that can help to cope with illness without relying exclusively on extrinsic support to overcome health problems. Therefore health is, to some extent, in our own hands rather than being granted from any health system surrounding us. Moreover, health practices are rooted in everyday activities and many of those are related to the arts and culture. One important consequence of this view is that the term 'wellbeing' has now become an integral part of health. In other words, what matters is not only how poorly we feel, but it is of no less importance how well we feel and which cultural resources are available to sustain and develop our sense of coherence.

Some commentators, however, have suggested that the WHO definition of health also has some pitfalls. For example, it falls short of suggesting the critical importance of economic resources that are available to individuals and the society in which they live. Also, it does not address specific cultural activities as prominent resources. In numerous strands of research following the WHO and other definitions and models of health, there is significant focus on nutrition, physical activities, and environmental conditions. These are certainly major influences on individual health in the most direct sense. However, it is still surprising that the value of cultural and arts practices are, by and large, absent from any key discussions surrounding health and health promotion. In summary, approaches to health and wellbeing place different emphasis on the extent to which individuals can influence their own health condition. There is evidence to show that music is an intrinsic and important part of human development. Thus, it needs to be considered as a universal resource, from which implications for health and wellbeing emerge.

Given this broad definition of health that stresses wellbeing in all its manifestations, and given the various qualities of music outlined above, it is perhaps not surprising that there has been an upsurge in interest in the relationship between arts in general and specifically music and health. Various countries have instigated national bodies to investigate the relationship between the arts and healthcare, for example, The Arts and Health (Australia), The Society for the Arts in Healthcare (USA), and Artful (Scotland). There are also a number of dedicated international journals such as *Arts and Health: An International Journal for Research, Policy and Practice*.

How is the relationship between music and health assessed?

A specific aim of this book is to overview the multitudinous ways in which the relationship between music and health is assessed. One way of conceptualizing these approaches is to classify different research methodologies as either qualitative or quantitative. Quantitative methodologies include physiological and neurological measures, observation of behaviour, and assessment of task performance, self-report questionnaires, and the use of rating scales. In contrast, qualitative methodologies include focus groups, interviews, real-life interactions, and web-based resources. This work can include informal situations such as investigating music listening in everyday life or experimental contexts where the effects of music are investigated in more controlled environments. A key point here is that the relationships between outcome measures assessed by these various techniques and 'music' are complex, and developing causal links is a fundamental challenge for this area of study. In particular there is a need to develop 'evidence-based practice', a concept which, as Wigram and Gold discuss in Chapter 13, must be defined broadly and with subtle consideration for the different epistemologies that underlie each approach to 'evidence'. Along with this heightened interest in music, health, and wellbeing there is significant spurious postulating about the benefits of music. Therefore, one challenge for researchers is to sensitively evaluate the evidence available in this area where there are a multitude of approaches and many different epistemologies. Our contention, which we hope that this book helps demonstrate, is that when music is utilized in knowledgeable ways, evidence suggests it can have positive effects.

Conceptual framework

One of the main reasons for wanting to bring together a collection of chapters such as those in the present volume is to attempt to integrate a number of related disciplines that all utilize music for reasons of positive outcome. Figure 1.1 displays one possible way of integrating these related approaches.

The area with the most explicit remit and longest history relating to health and wellbeing is music therapy, and there are a number of chapters that utilize a music therapy approach. Music therapy can be defined in a number of ways but fundamental to all approaches is an emphasis on the therapeutic relationship between the client and the therapist, using music as a primary means of establishing and maintaining this relationship and producing positive benefit for the client. Another group of chapters within this volume originate from a music education perspective. There is considerable interest in the possibility that music education can produce benefits in other areas for participants, for example, the question of whether attending piano lessons improves pupils' maths ability or if violin lessons enhance general cognitive capacities. The key point here is that these interventions are not primarily aimed at wider psychological benefits. The purpose of a piano lesson is to improve piano skills; but there may be secondary benefits for participants relating to health and wellbeing and it is these psychological benefits of music education that

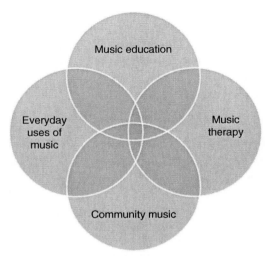

Fig. 1.1 Conceptual framework for music, health, and wellbeing.

overlap with music therapy. Additionally, in Chapter 21, Ockelford outlines how music education for individuals with special needs can also have beneficial effects on wider psychological variables. This type of work is another overlap between music therapy and music education.

A more recent field of study is community music, which can be defined as organized music interventions that take place outside of formal education contexts. One of the most popular of these is community singing, but there are many different types of community music interventions, often with educational objectives; running music lessons in community centres where groups get together to perform pop music is a good example of an intervention that allows people to develop their creativity through music but also to develop instrumental skills. These community interventions will sometimes have therapeutic objectives as secondary goals, such as the running of music classes in a psychiatric hospital where patients can develop percussion skills. Here the emphasis is on the development of specific skills but the intervention (which is social, enjoyable, and rewarding) may afford the participants other non-musical benefits, illustrating how community music overlaps with both music education and music therapy.

The fourth subsection in the Venn diagram in Figure 1.1 is 'everyday uses of music'. While this is not a distinct field of practice and there are a number of professional practitioners developing interventions within an 'everyday uses of music context', there is considerable interest in the effects of listening to music in real-world informal settings. For example, does listening to preferred music while driving enhance mood and can music listening while doing housework reduce feelings of pain and anxiety? Once again these musical situations are not explicitly clinical or therapeutic but there is significant interest in these contexts in terms of how they can positively affect health and wellbeing.

Structure of the book

This book presents issues for researchers and practitioners across a variety of fields including music, therapy, public health, and medicine. It does this by bringing together a range of chapters to provide a multidisciplinary and pluralistic account of recent research advances and applications in both clinical and non-clinical contexts. Some of the areas explored include: the nature of the scientific evidence to support the relationship between music and health; the current views from different disciplines on empirical observations and methodological issues concerning the effects of musical interventions on health-related variables; the mechanisms which drive these effects and how they can be utilized for building robust theoretical frameworks.

While covering a wide range of diverse yet complementary areas, there is a definite focus on evidence-based approaches as well as critical reviews of recent published research. One innovative and important aspect of this book is that research from the contrasting but related disciplines of music therapy, community music, and music education is presented and synthesized. This strategy aims to ensure that closely-related strands of research in different disciplines are brought together.

The book is structured in five sections with each section delineating one particular approach to music health and wellbeing. Section 1 provides an introductory context by presenting neurological (Chapter 2, Altenmüller and Schlaug) and cultural (Chapter 3, Elliot and Silverman) overviews relating to music health and wellbeing. The significant contribution made by the music therapy profession to music, health, and wellbeing is also signalled here in Chapter 4 (Trondalen and Ole Bonde).

Section 2 covers issues in community music and public health. The growing recognition of community music as an important musical activity is very much in keeping with current thinking that supports the integration of social, educational, medical, and therapeutic practices. In this section there is discussion around the different approaches that provide evidence of the relationship between music-making and potential positive effects on public health. Chapter 5 (Daykin) discusses the role of music in the development of healthy communities while Murray and Lamont (Chapter 6) investigate community music across a range of contexts. Two Chapters, 7 (Ruud) and 8 (Ansdell and DeNora), present a relatively new approach to music therapy that explicitly recognizes the importance of community music. Community music therapy has a prominent position within the text, as this approach is a significant attempt to investigate clinical practice within a community context that is very much in keeping with the aims of the book. Another term that appears in these chapters and across a number of other chapters in the book is 'health musicking'; a term that is highly relevant here as it relates to musical activities across a range of contexts that have implications for health. Chapter 9 by Clift provides a summary of his empirical and practical work in the area of psychological effects of group singing while Chapter 10 (Quiroga Murcia and Kreutz) and Chapter 11 (Davidson and Emberly) explore the relationship between dancing and music within a heath context.

In Section 3, the relationship between music and health is investigated in clinical and therapeutic contexts. This section again takes into account both biological (Chapter 12 by LaGasse and Thaut) and cultural perspectives (Chapter 14 by Stige, and Chapter 15 by Pavlicevic). Some of the chapters within the book have relevance across a number of sections. For example, Chapter 14 also relates to section 2. Wigram and Gold reflect on the continued need for case studies and in-depth qualitative methods as well as quantitative assessment within quasi-experimental and experimental research paradigms in Chapter 13. Chapters 17–20 include clinical and experimental examples of how music can be used to alleviate pain and anxiety, with a key theme of the relationship between musical preference and musical structure. The final chapters in this section highlight the important dichotomy of music listening and musical participation.

Section 4 focuses on educational contexts and the widely-discussed relationship between music education and psychological and social benefits. This section examines the notion that musical participation (both listening and performing) and musical skill development may influence mental and physical wellbeing in a variety of educational settings across different social environments and music cultures. The relationship between music education and music therapy is discussed in

Chapter 21 (Ockelford) and 26 (Ockleford and Markou). Musicians' health, with some emphasis on health prevention in contemporary music conservatory education, is discussed in Chapter 24 by Ginsborg, Spahn, and Williamon while music education across the life span is examined in Chapter 25 by Gembris.

Section 5 looks at everyday uses of music related to health and wellbeing and presents chapters dealing with the positive effect of music listening in non-clinical everyday contexts. Västfjäll, Juslin, and Hartig (Chapter 27) highlight the importance of music's capacity to provoke strong emotional responses in listeners as a possible key component relating to health and wellbeing while Koelsch and Stegemann (Chapter 29) discuss neurological effects of musical activities and their therapeutic implications. Theorell and Kreutz (Chapter 28) summarize epidemiological work around music and health, a scarcely developed, but highly fertile field of future research. Kreutz, Quiroga Murcia, and Bongard (Chapter 30) summarize psychoneuroendocrine research on music to provide some ground for further exploration. Cross-cultural approaches to music and health are presented by Saarikallio in Chapter 31. Hallam reviews the very important issue of the possible positive effects of background music in Chapter 32, and this final section also contains two chapters discussing the possible deleterious effects of music listening.

In summary, aligned with the explosion of interest in the relationship between music and health are considerable advances in the quality and quantity of research investigating the ways in which music and health are related. The text attempts to be innovative in the way in which it brings together research from a wide variety of academic and applied backgrounds to add to our understanding of the many ways in which music and health are related. The book provides an opportunity for such interdisciplinary critiques and for a wide-ranging consideration of the processes and outcomes of musical participation as it relates to health and wellbeing.

While any book about music about is ultimately trying to translate into words a process where the fundamental characteristics are non-verbal, the attempt to try and understand more fully the process and outcomes of musical engagement is of vital importance. This is particularly crucial if we are to further our knowledge about the beneficial effects of music. Of course music is not an ultimate panacea, a magic bullet that can cure all ills, but there is a growing body of evidence suggesting that when utilized in knowledgeable ways music can have significant positive effects upon our health and wellbeing. Victor Hugo's observation that 'music expresses that which cannot be put into words and cannot remain silent' highlights both the power of music and the paradox of trying to write about music (Hugo 1864). Regardless of this paradox there is much to be gained from attempting to translate into words the crucial relationship that exists between music and health improvements. In times of socio-economic turmoil, questions as to how to respond to the vast challenges of demographic change have remained unanswered. We believe there is a clear need to bring back more culture and humanity into medical systems, which have replaced doctors, nurses and patients by providers, customers and clients (Hartzband & Groopman, 2011). In conclusion, the creative potentials of music and art are needed more than ever.

References

Antonovsky, A. (1987). *Unraveling the mystery of health*. San Francisco, CA: Jossey-Bass.

Bunt, L. and Hoskyns, S. (2002). *The Handbook of Music Therapy*. London: Routledge.

Cassidy, G.G., MacDonald, R.A.R. (2010). The effects of music on time perception and performance of a driving game. *Scandinavian Journal of Psychology*, **51**(6), 455–64.

Csíkszentmihályi, M. (1996). *Creativity: Flow and the Psychology of Discovery and Invention*. New York: Harper Perennial.

Hallam, S. and MacDonald, R.A.R. (2008). The effects of music in educational and community settings. In: S. Hallam, J. Sloboda, M. Thault (eds.) *The Handbook of Music Psychology*, pp. 471–80. Oxford: Oxford University Press.

Hargreaves, D.J. and North, A. (eds.) *The Social Psychology of Music*. Oxford: Oxford University Press.

Hargreaves, D.J., MacDonald, R.A.R., and Miell, D. (2005). How do people communicate using music. In: D. Miell, R.A.R. MacDonald, and D.J. Hargreaves (eds.) *Musical Communication*, pp. 1–26. Oxford: Oxford University Press.

Hartzband, P. and Groopman, J. (2011). The new language of medicine. *New England Journal of Medicine*. **365**(15), 1372–1373.

Hugo, V. (1864). *William Shakespeare*. London: Hauteville House.

Juslin, P.N. and Sloboda, J.A. (eds.) (2010). *Handbook of music and emotion: Theory, research, applications*. Oxford: Oxford University Press.

Knox, D., Beveridge, S., Mitchell, L.B., and MacDonald, R.A.R. (2011). Acoustic analysis and mood classification of pain-relieving music. *Journal of the Acoustical Society of America*, **130**, 1673–82.

MacDonald, R.A.R., Miell, D., and Hargreaves, D.J. (eds.) (2002). *Musical Identities*. Oxford: Oxford University Press.

Miell, D., MacDonald, R.A.R., and Hargreaves, D.J. (eds.) (2005). *Musical Communication*. Oxford: Oxford University Press.

Mitchell, H.F. and MacDonald, R.A.R. (2011). Remembering, recognising and describing singers' sound identities. *Journal of New Music Research*, **40**(1), 75–80.

North, A.C. and Hargreaves, D.J. (2008). *The Social and Applied Psychology of Music*. Oxford: Oxford University Press.

Pothoulaki, M., MacDonald, R.A.R., and Flowers, P. (in press). An interpretative phenomenological analysis of an improvisational music therapy program for cancer patients. *Journal of Music Therapy*.

Spintge, R. and Droh, R. (1992). *Music Medicine*. Saint Louis, MO: MMB.

van Wijck, F., Knox, D., Dodds, C., Cassidy, G., Alexander, G., and MacDonald, R. (in press). Making music after stroke: using musical activities to enhance arm function. *Annals of the New York Academy of Sciences*.

Wosch, T. and Wigram, T. (2007). *Microanalysis: methods, techniques and applications for clinicians, researchers, educators and students*. London: Jessica Kingsley.

Zillman, D. and Gan, S. (1997). Musical taste in adolescence. In: D.J. Hargreaves and A. North (eds.) *The Social Psychology of Music*, pp. 161–87. Oxford: Oxford University Press.

Chapter 2

Music, Brain, and Health: Exploring Biological Foundations of Music's Health Effects

Eckart Altenmüller and Gottfried Schlaug

Introduction: music as an immensely rich experience

Making music is a powerful way of engaging a multisensory and motor network and inducing changes and linking brain regions within this network. These multimodal effects of music-making together with music's ability to tap into the emotion and reward system in the brain can be used to facilitate therapy and rehabilitation of various brain disorders. In this chapter, we review short- and long-term effects of listening to music and making music on functional networks and structural components of the brain. The specific influence of music on the developing brain is emphasized and possible transfer effects on emotional and cognitive processes are discussed. Furthermore we present some data on the potential of music-making to serve as a supportive and facilitative therapy in rehabilitation from motor disorders and aphasia following brain injury.

Musical experience is probably the richest human emotional, sensorimotor, and cognitive experience. It involves listening, watching, feeling, moving and coordinating, remembering, and expecting. It is frequently accompanied by profound emotions resulting in joy, happiness, bittersweet sadness, or even in overwhelming peak experiences which manifest themselves in bodily reactions like tears in the eyes or shivers down the spine. A large number of brain regions across various domains contribute to this musical experience (for reviews see Tramo 2001; Altenmüller and McPherson 2007).

Primary and secondary regions in the cerebral cortex, for example, are critical for any conscious perception of sensory information, be it auditory, visual, or somatosensory. However, music also changes activity in multisensory and motor integration regions in the frontal and parietal lobes. The frontal lobe is involved in guidance of attention, in planning and motor preparation, in integrating auditory and motor information, and in specific human skills such as imitation and empathy which play an important role into the acquisition of musical skills and in the emotional expressiveness of music. Multisensory integration regions in the parietal lobe and temporo-occipital regions integrate different sensory inputs, from the ear, eyes, and touch sensors into a combined sensory impression; it is this combined sensory impression which constitutes the typical musical experience. The cerebellum is another important part of the brain that plays a critical role in the musical experience. It is important for motor coordination and in various cognitive tasks especially when aspects of timing play a role, for example, in rhythm processing and tapping in synchrony with an external pacemaker such as a metronome. Finally, the extended emotional network (comprising the base and the inner surfaces of the two frontal lobes, the cingulate gyrus, and brain structures in the evolutionarily old parts of the brain such as the amygdala, the hippocampus, and the midbrain) is crucial for the emotional perception of music and hitherto for an individual's motivation to listen to or to engage in any musical activity.

The brain as a highly dynamically organized structure can change and adapt as a result of activities and demands imposed by the environment. Musical activity has proven to be a powerful stimulus for this kind of brain adaptation, or brain plasticity, as pointed out by Wan and Schlaug (2010). Effects of plasticity are not restricted to musical prodigies, they occur in children learning to play a musical instrument (Hyde et al. 2009) and in adult musical amateurs (Bangert and Altenmüller 2003), albeit to a lesser extent. Thus, with the main topic of our chapter in mind, we suggest that music-induced brain plasticity may produce benefits for wellbeing in general and may influence neurohormonal status as well as cognitive and emotional processes in healthy and diseased individuals, helping to improve various sensory, motor, coordinative, or emotional disabilities.

In the following sections, we will first briefly review mechanisms of music-induced brain plasticity. We will than clarify the impact of music on emotion and neurohormones. Subsequently, we will briefly demonstrate transfer effects of music exposure and making music to other cognitive and emotional domains, and finally show examples of the potential of music to serve as a supportive and facilitative therapy in rehabilitation from motor impairment and aphasia following brain injury.

Mechanisms of music-induced brain plasticity

During the past decade, brain imaging has provided important insights into the enormous capacity of the human brain to adapt to complex demands. These adaptations are referred to as brain plasticity and do not only include the quality and extent of functional connections of brain networks, but also fine structure of nervous tissue and even the visible gross structure of brain anatomy (Bangert and Schlaug 2006). Brain plasticity is best observed in complex tasks with high behavioural relevance causing emotional arousal and motivational activation. Furthermore, plastic changes are more pronounced when the specific activities have started early in life and require intense training. Obviously, continued musical activities provide in an ideal manner these prerequisites of brain plasticity. It is therefore not astonishing that the most dramatic effects of brain plasticity have been demonstrated in professional musicians (for a review see Münte et al. 2002).

Our understanding of the molecular and cellular mechanisms underlying these adaptations is far from complete. Brain plasticity may occur on different time axes. For example, the efficiency and size of synapses may be modified in a time window of seconds to minutes, the growth of new synapses and dendrites may require hours to days. An increase in grey matter density, reflecting either an enlargement of neurons, a change in synaptic density, more support structures such as capillaries and glial cells, or a reduced rate of physiological cell death (termed apoptosis) needs up to several weeks. White matter density also changes as a consequence of musical training. This effect seems to be primarily due to an enlargement of myelin cells: the myelin cells, wrapped around the nerve fibres (axons), are contributing essentially to the velocity of the electrical impulses travelling along the nerve fibre tracts. Under conditions requiring rapid information transfer and high temporal precision, these myelin cells are growing and as a consequence nerve conduction velocity will increase. Finally, brain regions involved in specific tasks may also be enlarged after long-term training due to the growth of structures supporting the nervous function, for example, blood vessels that are necessary for the oxygen and glucose transportation sustaining nervous function.

Comparison of the brain anatomy of skilled musicians with that of non-musicians shows that prolonged instrumental practice leads to an enlargement of the hand area in the motor cortex

(Amunts et al. 1997) and to an increase in grey matter density corresponding to more and/or larger neurons in the respective area (Gaser and Schlaug 2003). These adaptations appear to be particularly prominent in all instrumentalists who have started to play prior to the age of ten and correlate positively with cumulative practice time. Furthermore, in professional musicians, the normal anatomical difference between the larger, dominant (mostly right) hand area and the smaller, non-dominant (left) hand area is less pronounced when compared to non-musicians. These results suggest that functional adaptation of the gross structure of the brain occurs during training at an early age.

Similar effects of specialization have been found with respect to the size of the corpus callosum. Professional pianists and violinists tend to have a larger anterior (front) portion of this structure, especially those who have started prior to the age of seven (Schlaug et al. 1995a). Since this part of the corpus callosum contains fibres from the motor and supplementary motor areas, it seems plausible to assume that the high demands on coordination between the two hands, and the rapid exchange of information may either stimulate the nerve fibre growth—the myelination of nerve fibres that determines the velocity of nerve conduction—or prevent the physiological loss of nerve tissue during the typical pruning processes of adolescence or during aging. These between-group differences in the midsagittal size of the corpus callosum were recently confirmed in a longitudinal study comparing a group of children learning to play musical instruments versus a group of children without instrumental music experience (Hyde et al. 2009).

It is not only motor areas, however, that are subject to anatomical adaptation. By means of magnetoencephalography (MEG), the number of nerve cells involved in the processing of sensory stimulation in individual fingers can be monitored. Using this technique, professional violinists have been shown to posses enlarged sensory areas corresponding to the index through to the small (second to fifth) fingers of the left hand (Elbert et al. 1995) even though their left thumb representation is no different from that of non-musicians. Again, these effects were most pronounced in violinists who started their instrumental training prior to the age of ten.

A further example of functional specialization reflected by changes in gross cortical anatomy can be found in musicians possessing absolute pitch. In musicians who possess this ability, the upper back portion of the left temporal lobe, the part of the Wernicke region termed planum temporale (PT) is larger in comparison to those musicians without absolute pitch (Schlaug et al. 1995b). Although the precise role of the PT in the phenotypical expression of absolute pitch is not quite clear, it is possible that the PT only serves as a hub for auditory information that is directed to categorization centres in the superior temporal sulcus (Loui et al. 2011) which would be responsible for what uniquely characterizes absolute pitch, the ability to categorize pitches as belonging to unique and fixed categories. Using MEG, the functional specialization of the auditory cortex has been demonstrated by Pantev et al. (1998). When compared to participants who had never played an instrument, the number of auditory nerve cells involved in the processing of piano tones, but not of pure sinusoidal tones, was about 25% greater in pianists. Similarly, Sarah Bengtsson and her colleagues (2005) have found structural differences in the corticospinal tract, particularly in the posterior limb of the internal capsule, between musicians and non-musicians. This difference was related to measures of training intensity.

It is not only cortical structures that are enlarged by early and prolonged instrumental training. Subcortical structures also seem to be highly affected. In professional musicians, the cerebellum, which contributes significantly to the precise timing and accuracy of motor commands, is also enlarged (Gaser and Schlaug 2003; Hutchinson et al. 2003).

In summary, when training starts at an early age (before about 7 years), these plastic adaptations of the nervous system affect brain anatomy by enlarging the brain structures that are involved in different types of musical skills. When training starts later, it modifies brain organization by rewiring neuronal webs and involving adjacent nerve cells to contribute to the required tasks. These changes result in enlarged cortical representations of, for example, specific fingers or sounds within existing brain structures. In the following we will more closely examine the emotional prerequisites for brain plasticity and the impact of music on emotions and neurohormones.

Why is making music such an effective stimulus for brain plasticity?

An intriguing question is why music is such a powerful means to produce these effects on brain physiology and anatomy. This brings us to the specific motivational and emotional role of musical experience. Here, we will first discuss the implications of dopamine on brain adaptations and than focus on the biological basis of the potential of music in emotional activation.

It is a well-established fact that expert musicians have consistently invested high amounts of time during their childhood and adolescence—about 10,000 hours of dedicated practice over 10 or more years—to attain eminence on their instrument (Ericsson 1996; Ericsson et al. 1993). Of course, this '10,000 hours—10 years rule' of expertise is a necessary, not a sufficient, condition to succeed. What causes children and adolescents to dedicate so many hours of their lives to deliberate practice at their instrument instead of having fun with their schoolmates? Motivational factors and the ability to think in sound, to improvise, and to transpose pieces will lead to a rewarding playful atmosphere during skill acquisition (McPherson and Renwick 2011). It is important that children learn to represent music in multiple ways, so that they are, on the one hand, able to develop their sensitivity to the expressive properties of music and, on the other hand find continuous interest in their activity (McPherson 2005). In consequence, the quality of deliberate practice is critical and may depend largely on strategies, which allow the children to monitor, control, and reflect their own progress in a self-rewarding manner.

This behaviour, which is characterized by curiosity, stamina, and the ability to strive for rewarding experiences in the future and which results in incentive goal-directed activities such as deliberate practice, is to a large extent mediated by the transmitter substance dopamine. Most nerve cells sensitive to this neurotransmitter are found in a small part of the brain which is localized behind the base of the frontal cortex, the so-called mesolimbic system, an important part of the 'emotional' brain. Dopamine is widely recognized to be critical to the neurobiology of reward, learning, and addiction. Virtually all drugs of abuse—including heroin, alcohol, cocaine, and nicotine—activate dopaminergic systems. So-called 'natural' rewards such as musical experiences and other positive social interactions likewise activate dopaminergic neurons and are powerful aids to attention and learning (Keitz et al. 2003). There is ample evidence that the sensitivity to dopamine in the mesolimbic brain regions is largely genetically determined, resulting in the enormous variability in reward-dependent behaviour. The genetic 'polymorphism' of dopaminergic response explains the different motivational drives we observe in children with a similar social and educational background. It is intriguing that there is a strong link of dopaminergic activity to learning and memory, which in turn promote plastic adaptations in brain areas involved in the tasks to be learned.

Other neurobiological effects of music relevant for health and wellbeing

Emotional responses to music are often cited when people describe why they value music and why they ascribe certain effects of music on wellbeing and health. Music is known to have a wide range of physiological effects on the human body, including changes in heart rate, respiration, blood pressure, skin conductivity, skin temperature, muscle tension, and biochemical responses (e.g. Bartlett 1996; for a review see also Kreutz et al., Chapter 30, this volume). Responses to music that influence hormonal status have been of great interest in the medical field for their therapeutic benefits. A small but intriguing body of research suggests that musical experiences combined with imagery strengthen the immune system by promoting the release of stress-reducing peptide hormones such as interleukin-1 (Bartlett et al. 1993) or by controlling the release of stress-related hormones such as cortisol (Tanioka et al. 1987) and peptide antibodies, such as immunoglobulin A (Tsao et al. 1991; Kreutz et al. 2004). Furthermore, the use of music is proving very successful for alleviating pain in patients, speeding up recovery time, and reducing drug dosages up to 50% (e.g. Spintge and Droh 1992; Spintge, Chapter 20, this volume).

Here, we will focus on music's effect on the release of neurotransmitters in the brain. Serotonin is a neurotransmitter commonly associated with feelings of satisfaction from expected outcomes, whereas dopamine is associated with feelings of pleasure based on novelty or newness. In a study of neurochemical responses to pleasant and unpleasant music, serotonin levels were significantly higher when participants were exposed to music they found pleasing (Evers and Suhr 2000). In another study with participants exposed to pleasing music, functional and effective connectivity analyses showed that listening to music strongly modulated activity in a network of mesolimbic structures involved in reward processing including the dopaminergic nucleus accumbens and the ventral tegmental area, as well as the hypothalamus and insula. This network is believed to be involved in regulating autonomic and physiological responses to rewarding and emotional stimuli (Menon and Levitin 2005).

Blood and Zatorre (2001) determined changes in regional cerebral blood flow (rCBF) with positron emission tomography (PET)-technology during intense emotional experiences involving sensations such as goose bumps or shivers down the spine whilst listening to music. Each participant listened to a piece of their own favourite music to which they usually had a chill experience. Increasing chill intensity correlated with rCBF decrease in the amygdala as well as the anterior hippocampal formation. An increase in rCBF correlating with increasing chill intensity was observed in the ventral striatum, the midbrain, the anterior insula, the anterior cingulate cortex, and the orbitofrontal cortex: again, these latter brain regions are related to reward and positive emotional valence.

In a recently published study by the same group, the neurochemical specificity of [(11)C]raclopride PET scanning was used to assess dopamine release on the basis of the competition between endogenous dopamine and [11C]raclopride for binding to dopamine D_2 receptors (Salimpoor et al. 2011). They combined dopamine-release measurements with psychophysiological measures of autonomic nervous system activity during listening to intensely pleasurable music and found endogenous dopamine release in the striatum at peak emotional arousal during music listening. To examine the time course of dopamine release, the authors used functional magnetic resonance imaging (fMRI) with the same stimuli and listeners, and found a functional dissociation: the caudate was more involved during the anticipation and the nucleus accumbens was more involved during the experience of peak emotional responses to music. These results indicate that intense pleasure in response to music can lead to dopamine release in the striatal system. Notably, the anticipation of an abstract reward can result in dopamine release in an anatomical pathway distinct from that associated with the peak pleasure itself. Such results may well help to explain why music is of such high value across all human societies.

Even if individuals do not have intense 'chill experiences', music can evoke activity changes in the amygdala, the ventral striatum, and the hippocampus. Investigating the emotional valence dimension with music, Koelsch et al. (2006) compared brain responses to joyful instrumental tunes to those evoked by electronically manipulated, permanently dissonant counterparts of these tunes. During the presentation of pleasant music, increases in brain activation were observed in the ventral striatum and the anterior insula. Dissonant music, by contrast, elicited increased brain activity in the amygdala, the hippocampus, and the parahippocampal gyrus—regions linked to the processing of negative affect and fear.

In another study, musically untrained participants listened to unfamiliar music that they reported as having enjoyed (Brown et al. 2004). Bilateral activations were distributed widely throughout limbic and paralimbic regions. These were stronger in the left hemisphere, which is consistent with hypotheses about positive emotions being more strongly registered on the left (Altenmüller et al. 2002).

Taken together, these powerful music-induced modulations of neurohormonal status may not only account for intense pleasurable experiences but may also play a role in transfer effects with music influencing cognitive functions, such as guided attention and memory (see below). Furthermore, many beneficial effects of music therapy may be related to these hormonal central nervous changes. Since music can change activity in brain structures that function abnormally in patients suffering from depression—such as amygdala, hippocampus, and nucleus accumbens— it seems plausible to assume that music can be used to stimulate and regulate activity in these structures either by listening to or by making music, and thus ameliorate symptoms of depression. However, so far the scientific evidence for effectiveness of music therapy on depression is surprisingly weak, mainly because of the lack of high-quality prospective randomized controlled studies (Koelsch 2010; see also Koelsch and Stegemann, Chapter 29, this volume).

The neurobiological basis of transfer effects of music to other cognitive and emotional domains

It has long been assumed that an increase in brain connectivity or in grey matter density or the release of neurohormones such as dopamine or serotonin and the reduction of stress hormones can at least temporarily improve general cognitive abilities. Typically, this is investigated with intervention studies assessing the effect of music on performance in other cognitive domains. Probably the most controversial of these transfer effects is the 'Mozart effect'. In the original study, college students who listened to the first 10 minutes of Mozart's Sonata K. 448 for two pianos scored higher afterwards on a spatiotemporal reasoning task than after they listened to relaxation instructions or silence (Rauscher et al. 2003). Based on an extensive meta-analysis, Chabris (1999) stated that any cognitive enhancement following listening to this sonata is small, transient, and does not reflect any change in intelligence quotient (IQ) or reasoning ability in general, but instead derives entirely from performance on one specific type of cognitive task and has a simple neuropsychological explanation called 'enjoyment arousal'. Positive emotional arousal facilitating spatiotemparal reasoning can also be produced by non-musical stimuli, such as listening to Shakespeare's sonnets or to short stories of Steven King.

More substantial effects of cognitive transfer are found in children and adults learning to play a musical instrument. The intervention studies of Eugenia Costa-Giomi who compared IQs in children with and without piano lessons are an interesting example (Costa-Giomi 1999, see also Chapter 23, this volume). Sixty-seven 9-year-old children from a rather poor social stratum were given weekly piano lessons for 3 years; the control group of 50 children had no piano lessons. At the beginning of the study all the children showed the same IQ for language, spatial, and mathe- matical performance. After 2 years, the piano students were ahead in all three tested IQ domains; however, after 3 years, the children in the control group had caught up. Similar enhancements in IQ were shown in more recent studies. In an intervention study led by Schellenberg, 144 6-year-old children were given piano lessons, singing lessons, drama lessons, or none of these for a period of

36 weeks. After these 9 months, the IQ values for the children with piano and singing lessons were 3–3.5 higher than for the other children (Schellenberg 2006; for a critical discussion see Schellenberg, Chapter 22, this volume).

Such effects of music lessons on cognition are apparently not restricted to children. Bugos and colleagues (2007) gave piano lessons for 6 months to 20 senior citizens aged between 60 and 85 years and compared their cognitive skills with those of 18 similarly elderly people. After the piano lessons, the piano group showed significant improvements in memory performance, working memory, planning memory, and strategy management.

Perhaps the most promising transfer effects can be found in a domain related to emotional competence. Music education, for example, improves the ability to decode affective states in spoken language (Thompson et al. 2004) and musical activity encourages prosocial cooperative behaviour in nursery school children (Kirschner and Tomasello 2010).

How does music improve cognition? Music listening and especially music-making is stimulating many psychological functions; however, core functions addressed by musical activities are executive functions. These include attention, working memory, planning, and motor control, all relying on networks predominantly located in the frontal cortex. As has been exemplified in the previous paragraphs, musical engagement was found to increase grey matter density in frontal brain areas involved in controlling the practised task (e.g. Gaser and Schlaug 2003; Bangert and Schlaug 2006; Hyde et al. 2009; Jäncke 2009). Further evidence that musical practice involve the frontal cortex in elderly adults has been provided by Sluming et al. (2002). These authors demonstrated that musicians who practise beyond 60 years of age show less or no degeneration of grey matter density in the frontal cortex. Thus, practising a musical instrument seems to prevent degeneration of frontal cortex and deterioration of the above mentioned executive functions. Results of Verghese et al. (2003) hint in the same direction, demonstrating that Alzheimer's dementia is less common in the elderly who are regularly involved in musical activities.

Brain mechanisms of neurological music therapy: music-supported training in motor and language disorders in stroke patients

Studies on neurological applications of music therapy have so far mainly dealt with basal ganglia disorders, such as Parkinson's disease and with therapy of stroke patients. Since the former will be mentioned in Chapter 12 (this volume) by Lagasse and Thaut, we will concentrate on a series of new studies utilizing active musical interventions to improve rehabilitation of motor and language disorders in stroke patients.

Music-supported therapy (MST) in the rehabilitation of fine motor hand skills was first systematically investigated by Schneider et al. in 2007. Patients were encouraged to play melodies either with the paretic hand on a piano, or to tap with the paretic arm on eight electronic drum pads that emitted piano tones. It was demonstrated that these patients regained their motor agility faster, and improved in timing, precision, and smoothness of fine motor skills. Along with fine motor recovery, an increase in neuronal connectivity between sensorimotor and auditory regions was demonstrated by means of electroencephalography-coherence measures (Altenmüller et al. 2009; Schneider et al. 2010). Therefore, establishing an auditory-sensorimotor corepresentation may support the rehabilitation process. This notion is corroborated by findings in a patient who underwent music-supported training 20 months after suffering a stroke. Along with clinical improvement, fMRI follow-up provided evidence for the establishment of an auditory-sensorimotor network due to the training procedure (Rojo et al. 2011).

Undoubtedly, MST is efficient and seems to be even more helpful than functional motor training using no auditory feedback, but otherwise similar fine motor training. A randomized prospective study comprising all three groups is presently underway and will clarify the differential effects of functional motor training and MST. With respect to the underlying mechanisms, there still remain a number of open questions. First, the role of motivational factors must be clarified. From the patients` informal descriptions of their experience with MST, it appears that this was highly enjoyable and a highlight of their rehabilitation process. Thus, motivational and emotional factors might have contributed to the success of the training programme. Furthermore, according to a recent study by Särkämö and colleagues (2008), music listening activates a widespread bilateral network of brain regions related to attention, semantic processing, memory, motor functions, and emotional processing. Särkämö and colleagues showed that music exposure significantly enhances cognitive functioning in the domains of verbal memory and focused attention in a music group compared to a control group. The music group also experienced less depressed and confused mood than the control groups. These mechanisms may also hold true for the MST we applied.

Another issue is related to the auditory feedback mechanisms. Up to now it has not been clear whether any auditory feedback (e.g. simple beep tones) would have a similar effect on fine motor rehabilitation or whether explicit musical parameters such as a sophisticated pitch and time structure are prerequisites for the success of the training. This will be addressed in a planned study comparing the effects of musical feedback compared to simple acoustic feedback. With respect to the latter, according to a study by Thaut and colleagues (2002), simple rhythmic cueing with a metronome significantly improves the spatiotemporal precision of reaching movements in stroke patients. Finally, the stability of improvements needs to be assessed in further studies, and the length and number of training sessions might be manipulated in future research. Additionally, the effect of training in chronic patients suffering from motor impairments following a stroke for more than a year will be assessed.

From singing to speaking: facilitating recovery from non-fluent aphasia

The ability to sing in humans is evident from infancy, and does not depend on formal vocal training but can be enhanced by training. Given the behavioural similarities between singing and speaking, as well as the shared and distinct neural correlates of both, researchers have begun to examine whether forms of singing can be used to treat some of the speech-motor abnormalities associated with various neurological conditions (Wan et al. 2010).

Aphasia is a common and devastating complication of stroke or other brain injuries that results in the loss of ability to produce and/or comprehend language. It has been estimated that between 24–52% of acute stroke patients have some form of aphasia if tested within 7 days of their stroke; 12% of survivors still have significant aphasia at 6 months after stroke (Wade et al. 1986). The nature and severity of language dysfunction depends on the location and extent of the brain lesion. Accordingly, aphasia can be classified broadly into fluent or non-fluent. Fluent aphasia often results from a lesion involving the posterior superior temporal lobe known as Wernicke's area. Patients who are fluent exhibit articulated speech with relatively normal utterance length. However, their speech may be completely meaningless to the listener, and littered with jargon, as well as violations to syntactic and grammatical rules. These patients also have severe speech comprehension deficits. In contrast, non-fluent aphasia results most commonly from a lesion in the left frontal lobe, involving the left posterior inferior frontal region known as Broca's area. Patients who are non-fluent tend to have relatively intact comprehension for conversational speech, but have marked impairments in articulation and speech production.

The general consensus is that there are two routes to recovery from aphasia. In patients with small lesions in the left hemisphere, there tends to be recruitment of both left-hemispheric, peri-lesional cortex with variable involvement of right-hemispheric homologous regions during the recovery process (Heiss et al. 1999; Rosen et al. 2000; Heiss and Thiel 2006; Hillis 2007). In patients with large left-hemispheric lesions involving language-related regions of the frontotem-poral lobes, the only path to recovery may be through recruitment of homologous language and speech-motor regions in the right hemisphere (Rosen et al. 2000; Schlaug et al. 2008). It has been suggested that recovery via the right hemisphere may be less efficient than recovery via the left hemisphere (Heiss and Thiel 2006; Heiss et al. 1999), possibly because patients with relatively large left-hemispheric lesions are generally more impaired and recover to a lesser degree than patients with smaller left-hemisphere lesions. Nevertheless, activation of right-hemispheric regions during speech/language fMRI tasks has been reported in patients with aphasia, irrespec-tive of their lesion size (Rosen et al. 2000). For patients with large lesions that cover the language-relevant regions on the left, therapies that specifically engage or stimulate the homologous right-hemispheric regions have the potential to facilitate the language recovery process beyond the limitations of natural recovery (Hillis 2007; Schlaug et al. 2008, 2009). Based on clinical obser-vations of patients with severe non-fluent aphasia and their ability to sing lyrics better than they can speak the same words (Gerstman 1964; Geschwind 1971; Keith and Aronson 1975), an into-nation-based therapy called Melodic Intonation Therapy (MIT) that would emphasize melody and contour and engage a sensorimotor network of articulation on the unaffected hemisphere through rhythmic tapping was developed (Albert et al. 1973; Sparks and Holland 1976; Schlaug et al. 2010). The two unique components of MIT are: (1) the intonation of words and simple phrases using a melodic contour that follows the prosody of speech, and (2) the rhythmic tapping of the left-hand which accompanies the production of each syllable and serves as a catalyst for fluency.

To date, studies using MIT have produced positive outcomes in patients with non-fluent apha-sia. These outcomes range from improvements on the Boston Diagnostic Aphasia Examination (BDAE; Goodglass and Kaplan 1983; see also Bonakdarpour et al. 2000), to improvements in articulation and phrase production (Wilson et al. 2006) after treatment. The effectiveness of this intervention is further demonstrated in a recent study that examined transfer of language skills to untrained contexts. Schlaug et al. (2008) compared the effects of MIT with a control intervention (speech repetition) on picture naming performance and measures of propositional speech. After 40 daily sessions, both therapy techniques resulted in significant improvement on all outcome measures, but the extent of this improvement was far greater for the patient who underwent MIT compared to the one who underwent the control therapy.

The therapeutic effect of MIT also is evident in neuroimaging studies that show reorganization of brain functions. MIT resulted in increased activation in a right-hemisphere network involving the premotor, inferior frontal, and temporal lobes (Schlaug et al. 2008), as well as increased fibre number and volume of the arcuate fasciculus in the right hemisphere (Schlaug et al. 2009). These findings demonstrate that intensive experimental therapies such as MIT—when applied over a longer period of time in chronic stroke patients—can induce functional and structural brain changes in a right-hemisphere vocal-motor network, and these changes are related to speech output improvements.

Conclusions

Emerging research over the last decade has shown that long-term music training and the associated sensorimotor skill learning can be a strong stimulant for neuroplastic changes in the developing as well as in the adult brain, affecting both white and grey matter as well as cortical and subcortical structures. Making music including singing and dancing leads to a strong coupling of perception and action mediated by sensory, motor, and multimodal brain regions and affects either in a top-down or bottom-up fashion important sound relay stations in the brainstem and thalamus. Furthermore, listening to music and making music provokes motions and emotions, increases between-subject communications and interactions, and—mediated via neurohormones such as serotonin and dopamine—is experienced as a joyous and rewarding activity through activity changes in amygdala, ventral striatum, and other components of the limbic system. Making music makes rehabilitation more enjoyable and can remediate impaired neural processes or neural connections by engaging and linking brain regions with each other that might otherwise not be linked together.

Music-based experimental interventions similar to other experimental interventions need to be grounded on a neurobiological understanding of how and why particular brain systems could be affected. The efficacy of these experimental interventions should be assessed quantitatively and in an unbiased way as one would require with any other experimental intervention. A neuroscientific basis for music-based interventions and data derived from randomized clinical trials are important steps in establishing neurologically-based music therapies that might have the power to enhance brain recovery processes, ameliorate the effects of developmental brain disorders, and neuroplasticity in general.

Acknowledgements

G.S. gratefully acknowledges support from NIH (1RO1 DC008796, 3R01DC008796–02S1, R01 DC009823–01), the family of Rosalyn and Richard Slifka, and the Matina R. Proctor Foundation.

References

Albert, M.L., Sparks, R.W., and Helm, N.A. (1973). Melodic intonation therapy for aphasia. *Archives of Neurology*, **29**, 130–1.

Altenmüller, E. and McPherson, G. (2007). Motor learning and instrumental training. In: W. Gruhn and F. Rauscher (eds.) *Neurosciences in Music Pedagogy*, pp. 145–55. New York: Nova Science Publisher.

Altenmüller, E., Schürmann, K., Lim, V., and Parlitz, D. (2002). Hits to the left – flops to the right. Different emotions during music listening are reflected in cortical lateralisation patterns. *Neuropsychologia*, **40**, 2242–56.

Altenmüller, E., Schneider, S., Marco-Pallares, P.W., and Münte, T.F. (2009). Neural reorganization underlies improvement in stroke induced motor dysfunction by music supported therapy. *Annals of the New York Academy of Sciences*, **1169**, 395–405.

Amunts, K., Schlaug, G., Jäncke, L., Steinmetz, H., Schleicher, A., Dabringhaus, A., *et al.* (1997). Motor cortex and hand motor skills: structural compliance in the human brain. *Human Brain Mapping*, **5**, 206–15.

Bangert, M. and Altenmüller, E. (2003). Mapping perception to action in piano practice: A longitudinal DC-EEG-study. *BMC Neuroscience*, **4**, 26–36.

Bangert, M. and Schlaug, G. (2006). Specialization of the spezialized in features of external brain morphology. *European Journal of Neuroscience*, **24**, 1832–4.

Bartlett, D.L. (1996). Physiological responses to music and sound stimuli. In: D.A. Hodges (ed.) *Handbook of Music Psychology, Second edition*, pp. 343–85. San Antonio TX: IMR Press.

Bartlett, D.L., Kaufman, D., and Smeltekop, R. (1993). The effects of music listening and perceived sensory experiences on the immune system as measured by interleukin-1 and cortisol. *Journal of Music Therapy*, **30**, 194–209.

Bengtsson, S.L., Nagy, Z., Skare, S., Forsman, L., Forssberg, H., and Ullen, F. (2005). Extensive piano practicing has regionally specific effects on white matter development. *Nature Neuroscience, 8*, 1148–50.

Blood, A.J. and Zatorre, R.J. (2001). Intensely pleasurable responses to music correlate with activity in brain regions implicated in reward and emotion. *Proceedings of the National Academy of Sciences USA, 198*, 11818–23.

Bonakdarpour, B., Eftekharzadeh, A., and Ashayeri, H. (2000). Preliminary report on the effects of melodic intonation therapy in the rehabilitation of Persian aphasic patients. *Iranian Journal of Medical Sciences, 25*, 156–60.

Brown, S., Martinez, M.J., and Parsons, L.M. (2004). Passive music listening spontaneously engages limbic and paralimbic systems. *Neuroreport, 15*, 2033–7.

Bugos, J., Perlstein, W.M., McCrae, C.S., Brophy, T.S., and Bedenbaugh, P. (2007). Individualized piano instruction enhances executive functioning and working memory in older adults. *Aging & Mental Health, 11*, 464–71.

Chabris, C.F. (1999). Prelude or requiem for the 'Mozart-effect'. *Nature, 400*, 826–7.

Costa-Giomi, E. (1999). The effects of three years of piano instruction on children's cognitive development. *Journal of Research in Music Education, 47*, 198–212.

Elbert, T., Pantev, C., Wienbruch, C., Rockstroh, B., and Taub, E. (1995). Increased cortical representation of the fingers of the left hand in string players. *Science, 270*, 305–7.

Ericsson, K.A. (1996). *The road to excellence: The acquisition of expert performance in the arts and sciences, sports, and games.* Mahwah, NJ: Lawrence Erlbaum.

Ericsson, K.A., Krampe, R.T., and Tesch-Römer, C. (1993). The role of deliberate practice in the acquisition of expert performance. *Psychological Review, 100*, 363–406.

Evers, S. and Suhr, B. (2000). Changes of the neurotransmitter serotonin but not of hormones during short time music perception. *European Archives in Psychiatry and Clinical Neurosciences, 250*, 144–7.

Gaser, C., and Schlaug, G. (2003). Brain structures differ between musicians and non-musicians. *Journal of Neuroscience, 23*, 9240–5.

Gerstman, H.L. (1964). A case of aphasia. *Journal of Speech and Hearing Disorders, 29*, 89–91.

Geschwind, N. (1971). Current concepts: aphasia. *New England Journal of Medicine, 284*, 654–6.

Goodglass, H. and Kaplan, E. (1983). *Boston diagnostic aphasia examination* (2nd edn.) Philadelphia, PA: Lea & Febiger.

Heiss, W.D. and Thiel, A. (2006). A proposed regional hierarchy in recovery of post-stroke aphasia. *Brain and Language, 98*, 118–23.

Heiss, W.D., Kessler, J., Thiel, A., Ghaemi, M., and Karbe, H. (1999). Differential capacity of left and right hemispheric areas for compensation of poststroke aphasia. *Annals of Neurology, 45*, 430–8.

Hillis, A.E. (2007). Aphasia: progress in the last quarter of a century. *Neurology, 69*, 200–123.

Hutchinson, S., Lee, L.H.L., Gaab, N., Schlaug, G. (2003). Cerebellar volume: gender and musicianship effects. *Cerebral Cortex, 13*, 943–9.

Hyde, K.L., Lerch, J., Norton, A., Forgeard, M., Winner, E., Evans, A.C., *et al.* (2009). Musical training shapes structural brain development. *Journal of Neuroscience, 29*, 3019–25.

Jäncke, L. (2009). The plastic human brain. *Restoration in Neurology and Neurosciences, 27*, 521–38.

Keith, R.L. and Aronson, A.E. (1975). Singing as therapy for apraxia of speech and aphasia: report of a case. *Brain and Language, 2*, 483–8.

Keitz, M., Martin-Soelch, C., and Leenders, K.L. (2003). Reward processing in the brain: a prerequisite for movement preparation? *Neural Plasticity, 10*, 121–8.

Kirschner, S. and Tomasello, M. (2010). Joint music making promotes prosocial behavior in 4-year-old children. *Evolution and Human Behavior, 31*, 354–64.

Koelsch, S., Fritz, T., V Cramon, D.Y., Müller. K., and Friederici, A.D. (2006). Investigating emotion with music: an fMRI study. *Human Brain Mapping, 27*, 239–50.

Koelsch, S. (2010). Towards a neural basis of music-evoked emotions. *Trends in Cognitive Sciences, 14*, 131–7.

Kreutz, G., Bongard, S., Grebe, D., Rohrmann, S., Hodapp, V. (2004). Effects of choir singing or listening on secretory IgA, cortisol, and emotional state. *Journal of Behavioral Medicine*, **27**, 623–34.

Loui, P., Li, H.C., Hohmann, A., and Schlaug, G. (2011). Enhanced cortical connectivity in absolute pitch musicians: a model for local hyperconnectivity. *Journal of Cognitive Neuroscience*, **23**, 1015–26.

McPherson, G.E. (2005). From child to musician: skill development during the beginning stages of learning an instrument. *Psychology of Music*, **33**, 5–35.

McPherson, G.E. and Renwick, R.J. (2011). Self-regulation and the mastery of musical skills. In B.J. Zimmermann and D.H. Schunck (eds.) *Handbook of self-regulation of learning and performance*, pp 234–48. New York: Routledge.

Menon, V. and Levitin, D.J. (2005). The rewards of music listening: response and physiological connectivity of the mesolimbic system. *Neuroimage*, **28**, 175–84.

Münte, T.F., Altenmüller, E., and Jäncke, L. (2002). The musician's brain as a model of neuroplasticity. *Nature Neuroscience*, **3**, 473–8.

Pantev, C., Oostenveld, R., Engelien, A., Ross., B., Roberts, L.E., and Hoke, M. (1998). Increased auditory cortical representation in musicians. *Nature*, **392**, 811–14.

Rauscher, F., Shaw, G.L., and Ky, K.N. (2003). Music and spatial task performance. *Nature*, **365**, 611.

Rojo, N., Amengual, J., Juncadella, M., Rubio, F., Camara, E., Marco-Pallares, J., *et al.* (2011). Music-Supported Therapy induces plasticity in the sensorimotor cortex in chronic stroke: A single-case study using multimodal imaging (fMRI-TMS). *Brain Injury*, **25**, 787–93.

Rosen, H.J., Petersen, S.E., Linenweber, M.R., Snyder, A.Z., White, D.A., Chapman, L., *et al.* (2000). Neural correlates of recovery from aphasia after damage to left inferior frontal cortex. *Neurology*, **55**, 1883–94.

Särkämö, T., Tervaniemi, M., Laitinen, S., Forsblom, A., Soinila, S., Mikkonen, M., *et al.* (2008). Music listening enhances cognitive recovery and mood after middle Cerebral artery stroke. *Brain*, **131**, 866–76.

Salimpoor, V.N., Benovoy, M., Larcher, K., Dagher, A., and Zatorre, R.J. (2011). Anatomically distinct dopamine release during anticipation and experience of peak emotion to music. *Nature Neuroscience*, **14**, 257–62.

Schellenberg, E.G. (2006). Exposure to Music: The truth about the consequences. In G.E. McPherson (ed.) *The child as musician: A handbook of musical development*. pp. 111–34. Oxford: Oxford University Press.

Schlaug, G., Jäncke, L., Huang, Y., and Steinmetz, H. (1995a). Increased corpus callosum size in musicians. *Neuropsychologia*, **33**, 1047–55.

Schlaug, G., Jäncke, L., Huang, Y., and Steinmetz, H. (1995b). In vivo evidence of structural brain asymmetry in musicians. *Science*, **267**, 699–71.

Schlaug, G., Marchina, S., and Norton, A. (2008). From singing to speaking: Why patients with Broca's aphasia can sing and how that may lead to recovery of expressive language functions. *Music Perception*, **25**, 315–23.

Schlaug, G., Marchina, S., and Norton, A. (2009). Evidence for plasticity in white-matter tracts of patients with chronic Broca's aphasia undergoing intense intonation-based speech therapy. *Annals of the New York Academy of Sciences*, **1169**, 385–94.

Schlaug, G., Norton, A., Marchina, S., Zipse, L., and Wan, C.Y. (2010). From singing to speaking: facilitating recovery from nonfluent aphasia. *Future Neurology*, **5**, 657–65.

Sluming, V., Barrick, T., Howard, M., Cezayirli, E., Mayes, A., and Roberts, N. (2002). Voxel-based morphometry reveals increased gray matter density in Broca's area in male symphony orchestra musicians. *Neuroimage*, **17**, 1613–22.

Schneider, S., Schönle, P.W., Altenmüller, E., Münte, T.F. (2007). Using musical instruments to improve motor skill recovery following a stroke. *Journal of Neurology*, **254**, 1339–46.

Schneider, S., Münte, T.F., Rodriguez-Fornells, A., Sailer, M., Altenmüller, E. (2010). Music supported training is more efficient than functional motor training for recovery of fine motor skills in stroke patients. *Music Perception*, **27**, 271–80.

Sparks, R.W. and Holland, A.L. (1976). Method: melodic intonation therapy for aphasia. *Journal of Speech and Hearing Disorders,* **41**, 287–97.

Spintge, R. and Droh, R. (1992). Toward a research standard in musicmedicine/music therapy: A proposal for a multimodal approach. In R. Spintge and R. Droh (eds.) *MusicMedicine*, pp. 345–49. St. Louis, MO: MMB.

Tanioka, F., Takazawa, T., Kamata, S., Kudo, M., Matsuki, A. and Oyama, T. (1987). Hormonal effect of anxiolytic music in patients during surgical operations under epidural anesthesia. In: R. Spintge and R. Droh (eds.) *Music in Medicine,* pp. 199–204. Berlin: Springer-Verlag.

Thaut, M.H., Kenyon, G.P., Hurt, C.P., McIntosh, G.C., and Hoemberg, V. (2002). Kinematic optimization of spatiotemporal patterns in paretic arm training with stroke patients. *Neuropsychologia,* **40**, 1073–81.

Thompson, W.F., Schellenberg, E.G., and Husain, G. (2004). Decoding speech prosody: Do music lessons help? *Emotion,* **4**, 46–64.

Tramo, M.J. (2001). Biology and music. Music of the hemispheres. *Science,* **291**, 54–6.

Tsao, C.C., Gordon, T.F., Maranto, C.D., Lerman, C. and Murasko, D. (1991). The effects of music and directed biological imagery on immune response S-IgA. In: C.D. Maranto (ed.) *Applications of Music in Medicine,* pp. 85–121. Washington, DC: National Association for Music Therapy.

Verghese, J., Lipton, R.B., Katz, M.J., Hall, C.B., Derby, C.A., Kuslansky, G., *et al.* (2003). Leisure activities and the risk of dementia in the elderly. *New England Journal of Medicine,* **348**, 2508–16.

Wade, D.T., Hewer, R.L., David R.M., and Enderby, P.M. (1986). Aphasia after stroke: natural history and associated deficits. *Journal of Neurology, Neurosurgery and Psychiatry,* **49**, 11–16.

Wan, C.Y. and Schlaug, G. (2010). Music making as a tool for promoting brain plasticity across the life-span. *The Neuroscientist,* **16**, 566–77.

Wan, C.Y., Rüber, T., Hohmann, A., and Schlaug, G. (2010). The therapeutic effects of singing in neurological disorders. *Music Perception,* **27**, 287–95.

Wilson, S.J., Parsons, K., and Reutens, D.C. (2006). Preserved singing in aphasia: A case study of the efficacy of the Melodic Intonation Therapy. *Music Perception,* **24**, 23–36.

Chapter 3

Why Music Matters: Philosophical and Cultural Foundations

David J. Elliott and Marissa Silverman

Music, health, and wellbeing—what these concepts mean, why it may be important to link them, and how their linkages ought to be investigated are just a few of the complex issues addressed in this volume by a wide array of experts, including psychologists, physicians, neuroscientists, therapists, educators, musicians, and sociologists. What may go unnoticed, however, is that music, health, and their cognates have been the focus of innumerable philosophical theories and debates throughout history. There are several reasons for this philosophical concern.

First, since these concepts and practices are among the most important pursuits and concerns of human beings everywhere, they are 'contested concepts': experts in different fields and people in different cultures have disparate views on the natures, values, and 'best practices' of music, health, therapy, education, and so forth. For example, philosophers of medicine argue that common medical terms and concepts are not uniform but contingent: health, disease, condition, normal, abnormal, treatment, intervention, diagnosis—all these terms have cultural and evaluative dimensions. Thus, 'for all its scientific base, medicine must be a value-laden practice guided by the values of its practitioners and its public' (Zucker 2006, p. 465). Indeed, and in addition to details of individual physiology, concepts of health and wellness are related to time, place, culture, age, gender, social status, ethnicity, and self-efficacy.

Second, and because music and health-related issues are so complex, any serious reflection on one or more of these issues leads inevitably to deeper questions about knowledge, meaning, being, and ethics, as well as such normative concepts as culture, beauty, freedom, happiness, and social justice. Consequently, instead of investigating direct connections between (say) music and health, music and the brain, or music and education, a philosopher is likely to begin by asking: What is music? What is health? What is education? What is culture? And what is the nature of the human 'self' that music is being engaged to heal?

What goes unnoticed also is that philosophy, rightly understood, has an ancient connection to issues of health and wellness. For in addition to being a process that examines why some people's ways of thinking about concepts and practices might be more rationally defensible than others (depending on the quality of arguments for and against them), many early thinkers conceived philosophy as 'a deliberative life-practice that brings beauty and happiness to its practitioners' (Shusterman 1997, p. 3). Indeed, some of history's most eminent philosophers (e.g. Socrates) communicated their teachings and beliefs not through their theoretical writings, but through the critically reflective and purposeful conduct of their admirable lives—through modelling inspiring modes of life (and death) in the pursuit of self-knowledge about and for their own and others' wellbeing. Many contemporary philosophers might scorn the concept of philosophy as the life-long contemplation and practice of 'artful living'—of virtuous and healthy living for oneself, for the health and happiness of others, and for society as a whole. Yet care for one's self and others was philosophy's primary aim for centuries. It remains an admirable one.

Following from the above, this chapter casts a philosophical eye on selected concepts at the heart of this book, especially music and selfhood. Our first premise is that what people assume and believe about concepts, ideas, and practices affects dramatically what people (e.g. musicians, physicians, psychologists) envision and seek to do 'rightly' for others. Our second premise is that 'music for health and wellbeing' ought to be debated, conceived, and applied in relation to human beings considered holistically, as selves or persons, not simply distressed, unwell, or 'diseased' individuals. Otherwise, healers and researchers may assume too little about music's potencies and potentials for improving the quality of human life.

Explaining music

What is music? Although music is a word, and although most people have some sense of what it means, the question of what music *is* will not be answered satisfactorily by a concise definition. For one thing, different cultures, historical eras, scholars, musicians, and laypeople have widely divergent ideas about the natures and values of music; thus, a universally acceptable definition of music is impossible. For another thing, and from a philosophical perspective, requests to reduce complex phenomena like music to simple descriptions are as absurd as they are common; they ignore the fact that things to which we assign words do not all take the same form. Although language makes it seem so, there is no single way to capture everything in our verbal nets by applying clear-cut rules of classification. As Wittgenstein (1966) said in his *Philosophical Investigations*, words such as 'music' have no single, 'essentialist' meaning. Thus, what people mean by 'music' is always pluralistic, even fluid and contradictory, as dictated by the situated circumstances of its use. Put another way: some things, like an apple, have a core; some, like an onion, do not. Some things, like a tree, follow branching patterns; some, like a butterfly, transform. Some, like music, are conceptually delicate and intricate, like branching trees and transforming butterflies. However, and again, not everyone would accept these comparisons.

Notwithstanding its diverse meanings, it is both possible and important to unravel two ways of conceptualizing music that have exerted a powerful influence on the musical thinking and doing of scholars and laypeople past and present. It is also possible and important to explain why these two concepts hold very different implications for anyone interested in music and health, music and education, music and emotion, and so forth. To set the stage for these explanations, let us unpack some of today's most commonsense assumptions about the nature and value of music.

Many Westerners tend to assume that music is a matter of humanly organized sounds and silences. But as Jerrold Levinson (1990) points out, while sounds and silences are necessary conditions of music, they are not sufficient. The reason is that although your speaking voice and the ticking of a clock (and the throbbing of an engine and the babbling of a 2-year-old) are all instances of humanly organized sounds and silences, they are not examples of what most people count as music. A slight variation on this first assumption is that music is a matter of humanly organized 'musical' sounds and silences, in the sense of deliberately designed patterns of melody, harmony, rhythm, tone colour, and texture. But while melody, harmony (and so on) may be typical features of many musical products or 'pieces', they are not necessary features of all musical products. For example, the *Kete* drumming of the Ewe people has nothing Westerners would call melody, but it surely counts as music. The same holds for *Ionization* by Varese. Also, a typical lullaby sung by the Zuni Indians has nothing we would call harmony, but it counts as music to the Zuni people. Besides, not every musical culture in the world conceives of music in terms of musical products, pieces, or 'works' of music. In short, the sonic features of 'music' around the world are inherently unstable. Moreover, these features often evolve to the point of producing new ways of thinking about the nature of music and new means of music-making. As a result, thinking of music in terms of musical features and products is, at best, incomplete.

Another popular assumption is that music is a matter of humanly organized sounds that evoke or express emotions or feelings. The problem with this idea is that while our experiences of music often involve affect, so do many other aural experiences, including the sounds of a child in pain and the sorrowful words of a bereaved father. Accordingly, neither the evocation nor the expression of emotions/feelings is a necessary or sufficient feature of all works of music. As Levinson (1990) suggests, something like George Crumb's *Makrokosmos* 'seems neither the embodiment of a creator's inner state nor a stimulus to emotional response in hearers, but rather an abstract configuration of sounds in motion and/or a reflection of some non-individual—or even nonhuman—aspect of things' (p. 271). Whether Levinson is correct about *Makrokosmos*, his basic point remains: 'music cannot be defined [entirely] by some special relation to emotional life; no such relation holds for *all* music and *only* for music' (p. 271).

The strongest and most persistent assumption during the past 250 years is that music is 'aesthetic' in its nature and value. At root, the aesthetic concept of music is an elaborate combination of the problematic assumptions outlined above. Because the aesthetic concept has dominated many people's ideas about music for so long, it is important to examine it more carefully. Doing so will also explain our contention that people concerned with music and health, music and education, and so forth, are ill-served by adopting (or assuming) the aesthetic concept, or what others often call the work-centred or 'fine art' concept of music. To begin, let us consider the aesthetic concept in historical perspective and alongside the second concept of music we will consider here: namely, the praxial concept.

Music: philosophical and cultural concepts

The Greeks used *mousiké* to catch a wide array of creative and theoretical activities in their net. Mousiké referred mainly to a type of song—poetry, rhythm, and melody—and dance, accompanied by gestures and poses performed by amateur actors (Wright 1969, pp. 37–41). In Greek society, music was not for contemplation. Music was considered a social praxis that existed for social uses: music was praxial. Everything 'musical' was integrated with ceremonies, celebrations, entertainments, feasts, rituals, education, and therapy. Bards, who held significant social status, sang to their own accompaniment on the lyre. They 'sang about gods, heroes, historical events, and praised families in whose service one was bound' (Edström 2008, p. 39), whereas ordinary men and women sang and danced at parties, processions, and rites, or during work (e.g. weaving and shepherding) and exercise. Mousiké was highly valued, instrumental music was not. Overall, then, Greek music was a social-playful pastime 'that nonetheless possessed ethical, moral, metaphysical and practical significance' (Regelski 1996, p. 27).

As part of Greek musical praxis, Plato and Aristotle argued that music had a unique social-ethical power: music was capable of imitating and arousing specific emotions in listeners, so much so that the state should limit modes and rhythms to those that had a positive ethical influence. Thus, Plato's *Republic* argues that the Lydian mode (among others) should be avoided because it makes people 'drunk and soft and idle' and certain rhythms are dangerous because they encourage 'meanness and promiscuity or derangement' (Waterfield 1993, p. 116). In contrast, Aristotle's *Politics* argues that 'in rhythms and melodies there are . . . close imitations of anger and gentleness and of courage and moderation and of all their opposites . . . we experience change in our soul when we hear such things' (1340a).

For the next 1800 years or so, music was dominantly praxial across all levels of society. This changed gradually with the dawn of the Enlightenment, when 'reason' became the primary source of authority in all matters of intellectual, scientific, and cultural life. By the mid-eighteenth century a new concept of music began to emerge: the concept of music as 'aesthetic', as a 'fine art', or Art (Kristeller 1990). Some theorists argue that the idea of music as a fine art emerged as early as the Italian Renaissance, when there was 'a self-conscious and concerted effort on the part of workers in certain media to raise the status of their efforts by means of reconceptualizing their products' as 'liberal, free, "intellectual" endeavors serving the higher calling of the mind' and redefining themselves as 'artists', as opposed to mere artisans or craftsmen (Korsmeyer 2004, p. 27). Korsmeyer argues, however, that the emergence of the aesthetic and/or fine art concept of music was more likely 'gradual and uneven, and . . . took several centuries to accomplish' (p. 27).

According to the aesthetic concept that matured in the early nineteenth century, the value of music lies entirely in the beauty or 'meaning' of its sonorous forms—in the 'music itself'. Several corollaries attach to this view: composers are fully autonomous individuals who have special access to human subjectivity. In virtue of their exceptional gifts and superhuman seriousness of purpose, composers are able to capture subjectivity in the formal/syntactical structures of sonic creations. By means of notated scores, performers communicate a composer's 'knowledge of feeling' to listeners, who are (allegedly) humanized or 'improved' intellectually during their experiences of sonic forms.

There have been many variations on the premises and corollaries of the aesthetic concept during the last 250 years or so. Most notably, aesthetic doctrine argues that musical works are 'aesthetic objects' that exist to be perceived with a so-called pure, context-free, 'aesthetic attitude'—with distanced and disinterested attention to the complexity, novelty, and beauty of a work's formal properties or 'aesthetic qualities'. When listeners listen aesthetically, they (allegedly) undergo a transformational kind of intellectual-emotional pleasure called 'aesthetic experience'. Aesthetic musical meaning is mentalist, rational, and non-discursive. Musical 'emotion' is often conceived as cognitive, un-felt, symbolized, 'aesthetic emotion'. In one form or another, these premises anchor many philosophical writings about musical affective experience, past and present (e.g. Hanslick 1891; Langer 1942, 1953, 1958; Reimer 1970, 1989; Kivy 1980, 1989, 1990).

Not surprisingly, concepts of 'aesthetic-this and aesthetic-that' led to, and still underpin, a theoretical and practical division between the fine arts that exist for their aesthetic value alone—'art for art's sake'—and products and actions that are useful or beneficial in practical and social ways (Korsmeyer 2004, p. 26; Bowman 2005, p. 5). The notion of aesthetic value, says Korsmeyer, was attached to a new concept of aesthetic pleasure and 'good taste' (p. 28), as opposed to pleasures, enjoyments, satisfactions, and social benefits that arise from music as praxis—music as/for social, educational, ethical, spiritual, and healthful ends. Establishing criteria for the proper apprehension of aesthetic objects by socially privileged, male connoisseurs was a major preoccupation of the time (Korsmeyer 2004, p. 48). This theory-practice cult of aesthetic appreciation fostered an 'us–them', listener–work separation that privileged an abstract and disembodied relationship with musical syntax, rather than a concrete, embodied, sensual, visceral, practical, 'moving', participatory relationship with musical-social sounds and group experiences of music-making.

The aesthetic emphasis on separating music from life has had a dramatic effect on what counts as Western musical values and 'culture'. In addition to the idea that music, properly construed, is non-utilitarian or practically useless, the aestheticization of music includes several theoretical and operational principles: (1) a certain repertoire of music—European 'classical', instrumental music—is highbrow, Art, fine art, serious music, great music or, simply, music itself; (2) classical music is transhistorical, unsituated, and pure; (3) everything that is not serious music is popular, ethnic, lowbrow, entertainment, or mass music; and (4) classical music is for a privileged social group of 'classy' people who have excellent 'taste', either innately or in virtue of 'higher' education (Levine 1988; Martin 1995; Regelski 2006). However, as Bourdieu (1993) says, what past and present followers of the aesthetic concept of music neglect naively to consider is that their taken-for-granted, class-based notions of aesthetic-this and aesthetic-that are, themselves, historical and institutional inventions.

Given the cultural hegemony of the aesthetic concept, the mere suggestion that music is, or could be, 'good for' anything 'extramusical', such as health and wellness, may surprise or disturb many of today's classically trained musicians, scholars, music educators, and healthcare workers who simply assume that the value of all music or some music is intrinsic, that music exists 'for is own sake'. Put another way, what needs careful consideration is whether the aesthetic concept of music is, or should be, the assumed or practical paradigm among scholars and practitioners in the field of music and health. Considering the limitations of aesthetic doctrine, and the problematic musical attitudes and behaviours it requires and excludes, can its claims about the nature, value, and universality of music be sustained? Our answer is 'no'. The differences between conceiving music in aesthetic terms and conceiving music as a social praxis have profound implications for anyone committed to the beneficial integration of music, health, and wellness.

Music as social praxis

If the aesthetic concept of music is fundamentally problematic, what alternatives do we have? To begin with, there is a straightforward principle underlying all human involvements with music that promises a more comprehensive and socially beneficial concept of music: that is, without some form of intentional human activity, there can be neither musical sounds nor 'works' of musical sound. Put another way, 'music is not simply a collection of products, or objects. Fundamentally, music is something that people do' (Elliott 1995). Several things follow from this premise. First, taking the vast expanse of human culture into consideration (and without any prejudices in terms of age, 'talent', instruments, and technologies), musical 'doing' includes an extremely wide range of actions, mediums, situations, and uses. For example, 'music'—as a form of intentional, social, sound-related action—includes listening, and 'musicing' (Elliott 1995) in all its productive forms (i.e. all forms of performing, improvising, composing, arranging, conducting, record producing), and integrations of (for example) music and dance/movement, music and worship/ritual, and of course the musical products that eventuate from music-making and listening. Also, the concept of music-as-action acknowledges and welcomes any and all forms of musical-social participation included in Small's (1998) concept of musicking.

The next step in this line of reasoning is to emphasize that in any situation in which people use the term 'music' or its equivalents (e.g. musique, música, musikk, muzyka, musiqi, musakazo, hudba, glazba), or describe actions akin to what we outlined above, the nature of music becomes more specific when we understand the musical aims, values, uses, functions, beliefs, and skills/understandings (informal or formal) of the people who make and partake of 'their' musical sounds and actions. In other words, music is a social practice; music is *praxial* in its nature and value (Elliott 1995). As Kramer (1990) says, 'music . . . is a form of activity: a practice. If we take it in these terms, we should be able to understand it less as an attempt to say something than as an attempt to do something' (Kramer 1990, p. xii).

The concept of praxis originates with Aristotle. Praxis is a matter of skilled, intentional, and ethical action or 'doing' that is judged as 'good' according to the benefits it provides to specific groups of people who are situated in specific contexts. From this viewpoint, any world 'culture' is an elaborate web of interconnected social practices (Bauman 1999; Tuomela 2002; Regelski 2006). A social practice is something that a particular group of people organizes toward some kind of practical end; a social practice is 'a set of doings and sayings organized by a pool of understandings, a set of rules and a teleoaffective structure' (Schatzki 2001, pp. 52–53). Social practices (e.g. medicine, clinical psychology, education, law, farming) are shared interactional patterns of human effort that people organize and develop to meet specific needs or achieve certain 'goods'.

In praxial terms, music is vital to all societies and cultures because its doings-and-makings help to define, embody, and reflect a society's values by fulfilling a wide range of divergent and evolving needs. Thus the 'world of music' includes thousands and thousands of specific socio-musical practices or musical communities (e.g. Indian bhangra, Bebop jazz, Irish fiddling, Baroque singing, Bluegrass gospel, ad infinitum) that thrive at local and regional levels, and across national borders, and overlap for a variety of reasons and purposes. We would also include, of course, instances of social-musical practices such as mother–infant musical interactions, or musical trancing, which are always specified according to cultural norms and aims. Of course, in any case of a musical practice or musical style-community, the people who make and partake of 'their music' will inevitably differ about how or whether to maintain the traditional means and ends of their music, or allow their music to evolve or cross-pollinate with the means and ends of other musics.

More specifically, a praxial concept of music posits that 'music' exists and is defined in relation to an infinite range of social needs and practices. For example, this volume's focus on relationships between music and health testifies to the praxial nature of music, as do documentations of music's deep connections with self identification (Hargreaves et al. 2002; O'Neill 2002; DeNora 2008, 2010), music education as praxis (Elliott 1995; Regelski 2006), music and emotional regulation (DeNora 2000; Bicknell 2009; Hallam 2010), music in the workplace (Prichard et al. 2007), and so on.

In praxial terms, sound is deemed to be music according to any personal, social, and cultural functions it serves. Sounds are 'musical' not simply because of their sonic characteristics, but because of the functions people assign them in specific social-cultural situations. Without shared understandings of tonal-rhythmic systems and their socially-related behaviours and uses, music would not be understood as anything more than random sounds. In short, music is made by human beings for other human beings. The existence and continuance of musical practices depends on human transmission, or various forms of informal and formal education that are also matters of social-musical praxis. Thus, musical values and meanings are not intrinsic, they are not 'fixed-in' sonic forms or captured in notated scores; musical values are socially assigned to sounds according to how sounds are used, experienced, and understood as being 'good for' various purposes in personal and social life (Kramer 1995; Martin 1995; Regelski 2004, 2009; Clayton 2009; Cross and Tolbert 2009). Thus, and far from being strictly individual or 'interior', musical experiences are socially constructed and socially shared phenomena, and musical experiences invariably include many dimensions beyond so-called aesthetic qualities—specific voices, instruments, situations, places, processes, people, and so forth. In other words, there is not such thing as 'music itself', or 'art for art's sake', or 'pure' or 'absolute' music. Music can only be understood and experienced in relation to contexts of socio-musical practice; musical meanings and experiences are never disinterested or distanced from social, cultural, historical, and personal needs and functions. From a praxial perspective, 'music' has meaning only in relation to, and in recognition of, distinct human aims and needs. Given that human beings are inherently and necessarily social beings, none of this should be surprising. Plato and Aristotle were adamant in their belief that the nature of humankind lies in our social relationships. Indeed, Aristotle emphasized that anything living outside a social community would simply not be human.

Because music depends on active doing (music-making and partaking of any kind) music involves *embodied* knowledge and experience (Bourdieu 1990; Regelski 2006). In contrast to the dualistic separation of mind and body that grounds the aesthetic concept of disinterested contemplation, the praxial concept reunites the dualisms implicit in the 'fine art' concept of music: body and mind become body-mind; thinking and feeling become thinking-feeling; likewise with knowing/doing, classical/pop, reflection/practice, musical/extramusical. Conceived as praxis, the musical body-mind is holistically integrated. Human corporeality is a constitutive dimension of all music played, danced to, listened for, felt, enjoyed, and so forth.

The praxial realignment of music has profound implications for education. For example, whereas the American 'aesthetic education' philosophy (e.g. Reimer 1970, 1989) emphasizes the aesthetic perception of musical structures for disembodied aesthetic experience, praxial music education (Elliott 1995; Elliott and Silverman, forthcoming) emphasizes social, ethical, embodied musical 'particip-action' in musicing and listening for deeply felt musical experiences, experienced self-growth, happiness, health, democratic fellowship, intercultural understanding, and the construction and reconstruction of self-efficacy in broader social-cultural-political affairs.

Musical sounds, then, do not act on us; musical sounds are not 'stimuli'. Rather, music's powers are determined by music-makers and listeners themselves; musical effects and affects derive from the ways in which social beings interact with musical sounds and situations (DeNora 2000, p. 41); music's force is found in 'the ways in which an individual appropriates that music, the things she brings to it, the context in which it is set' (p. 42). Indeed, everything individuals bring to musical encounters—their personal and collective bodies, minds, emotions, fantasies, memories—are intrinsically musical and distinctive, not extrinsic or extramusical, as aesthetic ideology maintains. 'Music is not about life but is rather implicated in the formulation of life; it is something that gets into action, something that is a formative, albeit often unrecognized resource of social agency' (DeNora 2000, pp. 152–53). Regelski (2004) concurs and emphasizes that focusing on music as praxis 'is the key to observing music's sociality in action' (p. 28). Regelski then points to Martin (1995) who says that if we privilege 'the ways in which it is created, performed and heard by specific people in specific social contexts' (Martin 1995, p. 166)—that is, the ways in which music is praxial—then we will be in a better position to understand why music exists, why it is practised in such diverse and ever changing ways, and why its values are unfolding and unending.

Musical praxis and selfhood

Implicit in all questions related to music, health, wellness, therapy, and education is a more fundamental question: what or where is 'the self' that we are concerned to heal, revitalize, rehabilitate, or educate? Who am I, me, you, and us? The concepts embedded in social practice theory provide pathways to an improved understanding of the self and music–self relationships.

Taken in broad perspective, social practice theory (Schatzki et al. 2001) posits that social-cultural practices are the building blocks of society (Tuomela 2002). It is by individual and collective 'doings and makings' that culture, society, and all human institutions, knowledge, and meanings are socially constructed (Regelski 2004). From this standpoint, 'culture' is an intricate web of social practices (Bauman 1999) that are propelled, sustained, and advanced by embodied actions. This prioritization of social-cultural practices and embodiment over the Enlightenment ideals of reason and disembodied contemplation lead to a transformed conception of the human self. The concept of embodiment argues that it's not possible to understand the self or consciousness independent of the body and the human organism's relationship to its social-cultural environment. This complexity further suggests that an individual may be more than 'one self'.

Indeed, Neisser (1988) argues that the individual self may be thought of as a combination of several simultaneous selves or dimensions: an ecological self (the self in its physical environment), an interpersonal-self, an extended self (defined by its personal memories), a conceptual-cultural self, a private self (I-awareness), and a narrative self (the self-portrait one creates about oneself over time). Similarly, Strawson reasons that a human being consists of numerous selves, 'each of which lasts as long as the conscious experience of which it is the subject' (cited in McLaughlin et al. 2009, p. 19). Ledoux (2002) concurs with these viewpoints and posits the concept of a working self, 'an on-the-fly construction about who we are that reflects who we've been (past selves), and who we want and don't want to be (future selves)' (p. 255). More broadly, Ledoux sees the self as 'a dynamic and mutable construction' that changes in relation to social and environmental circumstances: 'One's working self is thus a subset of the universe of possible self-concepts that can occur at any one time' (p. 255).

Self-consciousness is arguably the most fundamental component of the self. Selfhood seems to involve a unique, first-person experience of the world. Although this idea has a long and illustrious history in both Western and Eastern thought (Williford 2009), the connection between conscious experience and selfhood is not obvious, partly because there is no consensus on what 'consciousness' actually involves and partly because 98% of what we do and know is unconscious (LeDoux 2002). Indeed, there remains a huge 'explanatory gap' (Levine 2001) between what is most salient about the self and self-consciousness—the phenomenal character of (say) the auditory–visual experience of *Rigoletto*, the unique sounds of Miles Davis on *Kind of Blue*, the sensation of warm sunlight, the feeling of joy or love—and the activity of billions of neurons that make trillions of synaptic connections in our numerous brain systems at any given moment (Ledoux 2002, p. 49). What is it that connects our subjective 'I-experiences' of the world and the physical nature of our brains? Recent developments in neuroscience have advanced dramatically our understandings of the neural underpinnings of many aspects of consciousness. And yet, as Tsakiris and Firth (2009) point out, current neurocognitive data does not support the existence of a specialized neural centre or system underlying selfhood as a whole. Instead, 'multiple specialized processes underlie distinct aspects of selfhood, such as the affective and sensory motor self, the autobiographical self, [and] the social self' (p. 588), all of which operate at an unconscious level.

In other words, the nature of the self seems to lie at the nexus of many continuous and constantly changing systems and processes. By 'systems and processes' we do *not* mean brain systems and processes alone. We mean (a) the combined body-brain-mind-conscious-and-unconscious systems and processes that contribute to the self as an integrated whole and (b) the fluid systems and processes of our unique environments (our physical-social-gendered-cultural-historical contexts) that we interact with constantly and that shape and re-shape all our 'self-processes'. Implicit in this view is our resistance to a widespread belief that human beings are essentially 'brains', that music is 'in the brain', that musical experiences are 'just brain processes', and so forth. We do not mean to deny that the brain is *necessary* for human being. Of course a healthy self requires a healthy brain, of course a seamless sense of phenomenal experience depends on the seamless operation of conscious and unconscious brain processes. However, we challenge the claim (as do several contemporary philosophers) that the brain is *sufficient* for the existence of self and consciousness. As Thompson (2007) says, 'the brain is an organ, not an organism, and it is the organism, animal, or person [as a whole] that has conscious access to the world' (p. 242). Noë (2009) agrees and extends the point: 'we have been looking for consciousness where it isn't' (p. xii); 'the locus of consciousness is the dynamic life of the whole, environmentally plugged-in person' (p. xiii).

Thus, as we argue in more detail elsewhere (Elliott and Silverman, forthcoming), the self might be compared to a huge jazz ensemble whose many millions of players (self-processes) are so expert at improvising collaboratively in relation to continuous changes in environmental circumstances that 'beautiful music'—meaning *you* and your unique experience of reality—flows continuously. The players in the ensemble create *your experience of you* as the arranger and performer of your life's music 'in all its complexity, emotional nuance, crescendo and diminuendo—the ballad that is the you-ness of you' (Blakeslee and Blakeslee 2007, pp. 207–8). Indeed, Dewey (1925/1981) argued that our psychological, emotional, cognitive, and spiritual lives are integrated and inseparable from our body's biological and physical functions and actions. What people commonly refer to as 'body and mind' or 'physical and mental' are just different dimensions of an ongoing process of experience. Thus, Dewey preferred the term 'mind-body' to emphasize his resistance to common but deeply inaccurate talk of 'mind and body'. Johnson (2006) emphasizes that 'our bodies determine both what we can experience and think, and also how we think, that is, how we conceptualize and reason' (p. 51). Like Noë, Dewey argued that the human body-mind-self is not private but fundamentally social because our survival, development, and wellbeing depend on transactions with our environmental and cultural situations. The centre of human experience—all experience, including musical experience—is our multilayered selfhood, always constructed and under reconstruction in relation to the fluid details of our physical, biological, social, and cultural circumstances.

It follows from this that musical-emotional experiences occur in multiple ways when 'music'—conceived as praxis, as a multilayered, social phenomenon—is 'taken in, up, and through' by the multilayered, embodied-experiential self, not 'music cognition' alone. It also follows that music contributes to health and wellbeing in numerous ways because it interconnects with the self as a unity—as a fluid and integrated matrix of body-brain-mind-conscious-and-unconscious systems that are continuously sculpted by cultural, social, and environmental processes.

Johnson (2007) supports this view when he argues that human understanding begins with bodily structures, processes, and actions that have many dimensions, such that the body is far more than a 'fleshy thing'. Johnson (2007) conceives the body as five-dimensional (pp. 275–78). Our embodied selves are simultaneously biological, ecological, phenomenological, social, and cultural. Of course, we must also add the gendered body/self. So, for example, the living musical self of a classical cellist or a teenage hip-hop listener is 'inscribed' with the distinctive embodied dispositions, understandings, values, and expectations of a classical cellist (and her listeners), or a teenage hip-hop listener, his/her peer group, and his/her favourite hip-hop artists. 'Fleshed out' in musical terms, our biological bodies give us the living organs, muscles, breath, brain tissues, limbs, and energy we need to activate our voices and instruments and respond to musical sounds and situations; our ecological bodies are penetrated by, and shaped in relation to, our culture's musical sounds; our phenomenological bodies provide us with a constant awareness of our sonic, musically active, tactile-kinaesthetic selves-in-music; our social-musical bodies (our musical preferences, ideas, and so forth) are shaped by our relationships with other music makers and listeners; and our cultured-gendered musical bodies are engrained with our musical identities, abilities, and motivations to communicate with other music makers and listeners in our musical communities.

An explanation of the human brain and its relationship to the self is far beyond the scope of this chapter. Suffice it to say that the brain has a particular function: 'it is the part of the body toward which every other body part is communicating, and that can communicate to every other' (Damasio and Damasio 2006, p. 16). Moreover, our brain is the locus of many embodied systems: we have multiple perception and memory systems, multiple memory and cognition systems, and so forth. To make our way in the world, we must generate continuous updates about our embodied systems, including ways to locate and adjust to everything in our immediate situations. How does this occur? Part of the answer is that our integrated body-brain communication processes rely on chemical and neural processing systems flowing to and from the brain, and on *body-mapping* and *mirror neuron systems*. Body maps are mental representations of a huge range of our body states that occur moment to moment—changes in breathing, temperature, emotions, perceptions, thoughts, and so on—as we do everything in life, including listening to music and/or watching and listening to others make music. We feel joy, sadness, disgust, satisfaction, shame, and so forth largely because of our body maps (Blakeslee and Blakeslee 2007, p. 11).

Mirror neuron systems help explain a wide range of phenomena, including the human tendency to respond emotionally to other people's expressions of emotions (Gallese 2003). For example, it is often the case that 'anger is contagious', or that a person's smile can 'light up a room', or that audiences at large pop concerts 'move as one to the music'. Mirror neurons 'are cells within certain high-level body maps that represent actions performed both by oneself and others' (Blakeslee and Blakeslee 2007, p. 213). We simulate others' movements and emotional expressions 'automatically, without logic, thinking, analyzing' (Risolatti quoted in Blakeslee and Blakeslee 2007, p. 167). Mirror neurons might also explain Finnegan's observation (2003) that 'we learn how to feel, and how to deploy particular emotions in ways and contexts appropriate to your situation' (p. 183). The same holds for musical expressions and experiences of happiness, anger, distress, as Davies (2010) suggests. But this begs the question of what 'things' like happiness, anger, and sadness really are.

Although there is no consensus about the precise nature of 'emotion', a broad range of contemporary philosophical, psychological, and neurological research (e.g. Robinson 2005; Bicknell 2009; LeDoux 1996, 2002; Juslin and Västfjäll 2008) strongly suggests that an emotion is not a thing but a process. An emotion seems to involve an intense, momentary, cyclical process consisting of: (1) a non-cognitive appraisal of a situation that causes (2) physiological responses (e.g. changes in heart rate, skin temperature), (3) brainstem and cortical activation, (4) action tendencies (you run away, or relax, and so on), (5) overt expressions of emotions (e.g. crying, smiling, frowning), (6) subjective feeling, (7) self-regulation (attempts to control reactions), (8) synchronization among all these components, and (9) more discriminating cognitive monitoring of felt emotions and the circumstances triggering the emotional process. An emotion is a process by which the brain instantly, unconsciously, and automatically assesses and responds to the qualities of all types of events and patterns in our environment: sounds, sights, threats, objects, social interactions, music, and so on, ad infinitum. Our sensory systems process our environmental and bodily changes and activate the chemical-neural brain systems responsible for emotional processing. Emotional responses cause an avalanche of profound changes in our body-brain 'landscapes'; the body-brain 'changes quite remarkably over the ensuing hundreds of milliseconds', seconds, and, in some cases, minutes (Damasio 2000, p. 2). Feelings occur when we become consciously aware of changes in our unconscious emotional states. A feeling is a conscious perception of an emotional process: 'feelings emerge after all processes of emotional arousal run their course' (Damasio 2003, p. 88). Whereas emotions can display themselves outwardly in public, feelings are private. Thus we display and interpret (we see, hear, and 'read') people's emotions in the details of their facial expressions, gait, and posture, and in the qualities of their voices.

Because of the multifaceted nature of the self and our many 'self-systems', listening to music can arouse, be expressive of, and be perceived as expressing a wide range of human emotions in many ways (Juslin and Västfjäll 2008; Elliott and Silverman, forthcoming). This view challenges several major philosophical theories of musical and emotion that claim emotions are not important in musical experience (Hanslick 1891/1974); that music can only provide a cognitive representation of un-felt patterns of feeling (Langer 1942/1976, 1953, 1958); and that music can be expressive of a few 'garden variety emotions' (e.g. sadness, happiness), without arousing these emotions, by resembling the contours of everyday movements and speech and by musical-historical convention (Kivy 1980, 1989, 1990); or that musical expressions of emotions can be expressive of, and thereby arouse, a reasonably wide range of musical emotions (Davies 1994), though Davies does not explain the mechanisms underlying such arousal. That said, the existence of body mapping and mirror neuron systems may affirm the thrust of Davies's theory: listeners and performers are able to map, mirror, and feel the emotions that musical patterns are expressive of. Specifically, based on numerous studies that use a variety of research techniques, researchers now argue that the most prevalent musical-emotional experiences reported by listeners (in laboratory and everyday situations) are happiness, sadness, excitement, calm, nostalgia, love, pleasure, awe, pride, anxiety, and anger, as well as 'thrills, chills, and shivers' (Juslin and Västfjäll 2008; Juslin et al. forthcoming).

In contrast to most past and present music philosophy, extensive research in music psychology affirms that 'music can induce just about any emotion that may be felt in other realms of human life' (Huron 2006; Juslin and Västfjäll 2008; Juslin et al. 2009, p. 133). For example, music can arouse emotions through a variety of mechanisms and their combinations: brainstem reactions (Juslin and Västfjäll 2008); synchronization (Patel 2008; Juslin and Västfjäll 2008); conditioning (Juslin et al. 2009); mirror neurons and emotional contagion (De Waal 2007; Elliott and Silverman, forthcoming); emotional memory (LeDoux 2002); personal associations and autobiographical memory (Juslin et al. 2009; Schulkind et al. 1999); expectancy (Meyer 1956; Huron 2006); cognitive monitoring (Robinson 2005); visual-musical interactions (Juslin and Västfjäll 2008); imaginative projection (Cone 1974); socio-musical interactions (Preston and de Waal 2002; Lakin et al. 2003; Penn and Clarke 2008); and musical 'flow' conditions (Csikszentmihalyi 1990; Elliott 1995).

Conclusion

Accepting that music is a socially embedded and embodied praxis commits musicians, researchers, educators, and healers to healthy and healthful musical actions and the ethical deployment of music for health and wellbeing. Since this volume provides, describes, and testifies to hundreds of examples, we will only highlight a few by way of conclusion.

Based on his work with people in Uganda, where HIV/AIDS is rampant and patients are in desperate need of individual and collective empowerment, Barz (2008) posits that musical involvements (i.e. making, listening, moving, dancing, and so forth) offer powerful ways to activate and maintain the process of 're-memorying'—the process of revitalizing the hope and health of individuals and communities in dire need of healing. A key to understanding this process traces to the fact that emotions can be strongly influenced by the memories, associations, and beliefs that we attach to musical patterns (Meyer 1956; Juslin et al. 2009) and songs. Underlying this phenomenon is the finding that our non-cognitive, bodily-emotional reactions to events are stored in emotional memory, ready to be called up automatically when we see or hear something significant to us (LeDoux 2002). Emotional memories cause immediate physiological changes without us knowing why or how. We may forget the details of a pleasant or unpleasant incident or stimulus, but a cue (e.g. a melody, a song) can trigger an instant emotional reaction.

Because cultural memory in Uganda is frequently maintained within music and musical responses, Barz engaged the community in composing, performing, and listening to their own songs about HIV/AIDS and the efforts of traditional healers and medical doctors in their midst. Gradually, the community became more hopeful as their songs moved from musical expressions of profound grief, stress, and despair to expressions of hope for a more positive life. As Barz says, music was able to 're-memory' the community—to 'change the memory of AIDS among listeners and thus shift the attitude that accompanies disease toward one of positive living' (p. 165). It was the people's embodied musical-emotional engagements, expressions, and experiences that helped to shift their community's identity and associations with AIDS and to reframe their autobiographical selves.

Clift and Hancox (2001) report direct health benefits of embodied, praxial engagements in choral singing. In their study of a university choir, they found that 84% of the singers noted improvements in such areas as lung function, breathing, mood, and stress reduction. Additional benefits of singing included enhanced social and emotional wellbeing. Similarly, reviews of research with adult singers (Stacey et al. 2002; Clift et al. 2008) reported a range of benefits including an enhanced sense of happiness, joy, and emotional and physical wellbeing; heightened energy, cognitive focus, and self-confidence; and a sense of being involved in meaningful activity.

Finally, in a more unusual example of music as praxis, Bakan (2008) describes how Balinese Gamelan beleganjur music is central to daily Hindu-Balinese life, in *ngaben* processions linked to mortuary rituals: 'the performance of belenganjur music is a major component of this ritual preventive care protocol and functions on multiple levels to ensure the best possible outcomes of a *ngaben*' (p. 260). That is, belenganjur music is a key part of caring for souls who are perceived as being in transition from life and an afterlife. Bakan makes a crucial point: 'the benefits of preventive care *for* the living need not necessarily be limited to practices of care and treatment dedicated *to* the living' (p. 261). For Balinese people, caring for departed souls in communal musical-social rituals is crucial for maintaining 'strong bonds of solidarity within their communities' (p. 261). Bakan's last point about belenganjur music applies across all musical cultures and affirms a central point of this chapter: 'music provides all members . . . with a shared sense of purpose and the opportunity to make productive contributions to their community . . . music is used to help people help each other, and in very practical and functional ways' (pp. 261–262).

References

Bakan, M. (2008). Preventative care for the dead: Music, community, and the protection of souls in Balinese cremation ceremonies. In: B.D. Koen, J. Lloyd, G. Barz, and K. Brummel-Smith (eds.) *The Oxford handbook of medical ethnomusicology,* pp. 246–64. Oxford: Oxford University Press.

Barz, G. (2008). The performance of HIV/AIDS in Uganda: Medical ethnomusicology and cultural memory. In: B.D. Koen, J. Lloyd, G. Barz, and K. Brummel-Smith (eds.) *The Oxford handbook of medical ethnomusicology,* pp. 164–84. Oxford: Oxford University Press.

Bauman, Z. (1999). *Culture as praxis.* London: Sage Publications.

Bicknell, J. (2007). Explaining strong emotional responses to music: Sociality and intimacy. *Journal of Consciousness Studies,* **14**(12), 5–23.

Bicknell, J. (2009). *Why music moves us.* Houndmills: Palgrave Macmillan.

Blakeslee, S. and Blakeslee, M. (2007). *The body has a mind of its own: How body maps in your brain help you do (almost) everything better.* New York: Random House.

Bourdieu, P. (1984). *Distinction: A social critique of the judgment of taste.* Cambridge, MA: Harvard University Press.

Bourdieu, P. (1990). *The logic of practice.* Stanford, CA: Stanford University Press.

Bourdieu, P. and Johnson, R. (1993). *The field of cultural production: Essays on art and literature.* New York: Columbia University Press.

Bowman, W. (2005). Music, beauty, and privileged pleasures: Situating fine art and 'Aesthetic' experience. *Action, Criticism & Theory for Music Education,* **5**(1). Available at: http://act.maydaygroup.org/articles/Bowman5_1.pdf (accessed 15 February 2010).

Clayton, M. (2009). The social and personal functions of music in cross-cultural perspective. In: S. Hallam, I. Cross, and M. Thaut (eds.) *The Oxford handbook of music psychology,* pp. 35–44. Oxford: Oxford University Press.

Clift, S. and Hancox, G. (2001). The perceived benefits of singing: Findings from preliminary surveys of a university college choral society. *Journal of the Royal Society for the Promotion of Health,* **121**(4), 248–56.

Clift, S., Hancox, G., Staricoff, R., and Whitmore, C. (2008). *Singing and health: A systematic mapping and review of non-clinical research.* Canterbury: Sidney de Haan Research Centre for Arts and Health, Canterbury Christ Church University.

Cone, E.T. (1974). *The composer's voice.* Berkeley, CA: University of California Press.

Cross, I., and Tolbert, E. (2009). Music and meaning. In: S. Hallam, I. Cross, and M. Thaut (eds.) *The Oxford handbook of music psychology,* pp. 24–34. Oxford: Oxford University Press.

Csikszentmihalyi, M. (1990). *Flow: The psychology of optimal experience.* New York: Harper and Row.

Damasio, A. (2000). Emotion, consciousness, and decision making. Lecture at the London School of Economics and Political Science, 24 January. Available at: http://www2.lse.ac.uk/PublicEvents/events/2000/20001124t1343z001.aspx (accessed 10 August 2009).

Damasio, A. (2003). *Looking for Spinoza: Joy, sorrow, and the feeling brain.* Orlando, FL: Harcourt.

Damasio, A. and Damasio, H. (2006). Minding the body. *Daedalus,* **135**(3), 15–22.

Davies, S. (2010). Emotions expressed and aroused by music. In: P.N. Juslin, and J.A. Sloboda (eds.) *Handbook of Music and Emotion: Theory Research, Applications,* pp. 15–43. Oxford: Oxford University Press.

De Waal, F. (2007). The 'Russian doll' model of empathy and imitation. In: S. Braten (ed.) *On being Moved: From mirror neurons to empathy,* pp. 49–69. Amsterdam: John Benjamins.

DeNora, T. (2001). Aesthetic agency and musical practice: New directions in the sociology of music and emotion. In: P.N. Juslin and J.A. Sloboda (eds.) *Music and emotion,* pp. 161–80. Oxford: Oxford University Press.

DeNora, T. (2008). Culture and music. In: T. Bennett and J. Frow (eds.) *The Sage handbook of cultural analysis,* pp. 145–62. London: Sage Publications.

DeNora, T. (2010). Emotion as social emergence: Perspectives from music sociology. In: P.N. Juslin, and J.A. Sloboda (eds.) *Handbook of music and emotion,* pp. 159–83. Oxford: Oxford University Press.

DeNora, T. (2000). *Music in everyday life.* Cambridge: Cambridge University Press.

Dewey, J. (1981). *The later works: 1925–1953* (J.A. Boydston, ed.). Carbondale, IL: Southern Illinois University Press.

Edström, K., and Speerstra, J. (2008). *A different story: Aesthetics and the history of western music* [Annan berättelse om den västerländska musikhistorien, och det estetiska projektet.]. Hillsdale, NY: Pendragon Press.

Elliott, D.J. (1995). *Music matters: A new philosophy of music education.* New York: Oxford University Press.

Elliott, D.J. and Silverman, M. (Forthcoming). Rethinking philosophy, re-viewing musical-emotional experiences. In: W. Bowman and A. L. Frega (eds.) *The Oxford handbook of music education philosophy.* New York: Oxford University Press.

Elliott, D.J. and Silverman, M. (Forthcoming). *Music matters: A praxial philosophy of music education,* 2nd ed. New York: Oxford University Press.

Finnegan, R. (2003). Music, experience, and the anthropology of emotion. In: M. Clayton, T. Herbert, and R. Middleton (eds.) *The cultural study of music,* pp. 181–92. New York: Routledge.

Gallese, V. (2003). The manifold nature of interpersonal relations: The quest for a common mechanism. *Philosophical Transactions of the Royal Society of London,* **358**, 517–28.

Hallam, S. (2010). Music education: The role of affect. In: J.N. Juslin and J.A. Sloboda (eds.) *Handbook of music and emotion,* pp. 791–818. Oxford: Oxford University Press.

Hanslick, E. (1974/1891). *The beautiful in music; a contribution to the revisal of musical aesthetics* [Vom Musikalisch-Schönen.]. New York: Da Capo Press.

Hanslick, E. and Payzant, G. (1986). *On the musically beautiful: A contribution towards the revision of the aesthetics of music* [Vom Musikalisch-Schönen.]. Indianapolis, IN: Hackett Pub. Co.

Hargreaves, D.J., Miell, D., and MacDonald, R.A. (2002). What are musical identities, and why are they important? In: D.J. Hargreaves, D. Miell, and R.A. MacDonald (eds.) *Musical identities,* pp. 1–20. Oxford: Oxford University Press.

Huizinga, J. (1955). *Homo ludens; a study of the play-element in culture.* Boston, MA: Beacon Press.

Huron, D. (2006). *Sweet anticipation: Music and the psychology of expectation.* Cambridge MA: MIT Press.

Johnson, M. (2006). Mind incarnate: From Dewey to Damasio. *Daedalus,* **135**(3), 46–54.

Johnson, M. (2007). *The meaning of the body: Aesthetics of human understanding*. Chicago, IL: The University of Chicago Press.

Juslin, P.N. and Västfjäll, D. (2008). Emotional responses to music: The need to consider underlying mechanisms. *Behavioral and Brain Sciences*, **31**, 559–621.

Juslin, P.N., Liljeström, S., Laukka, P., Västfjäll, D., and Lundqvist, L. (forthcoming). A nationally representative survey study of emotional reactions to music: Prevalence and causal influences. *Journal of Personality and Social Psychology,*

Kivy, P. (1980). *The corded shell: Reflections on musical expression*. Princeton, NJ: Princeton University Press.

Kivy, P. (1989). *Sound sentiment: An essay on the musical emotions*. Philadelphia, PA: Temple University Press.

Kivy, P. (1990). *Music alone: Philosophical reflections on the purely musical experience*. Ithaca, NY: Cornell University Press.

Korsmeyer, C. (2004). *Gender and aesthetics: An introduction*. New York: Routledge.

Kramer, L. (1990). *Music as cultural practice, 1800–1900*. Berkeley, CA: University of California Press.

Kramer, L. (1995). *Classical music and postmodern knowledge*. Berkeley, CA: University of California Press.

Kristeller, P.O. (1990). *Renaissance thought and the arts: Collected essays*. Princeton, NJ: Princeton University Press.

Langer, S.K. (1942/1976). *Philosophy in a new key: Third edition*. Cambridge, MA: Harvard University Press.

Langer, S.K. (1953). *Feeling and form*. New York: Charles Scribner's Sons.

Langer, S. (1958). The cultural importance of the arts. In: R.A. Smith (ed.) *Aesthetics and problems of education*, pp. 86–94. Urbana, IL: University of Illinois Press.

LeDoux, J. (1996). *The emotional brain*. New York: Simon & Schuster.

LeDoux, J. (2002). *Synaptic self: How our brains become who we are*. New York: Viking.

Levine, J. (2001). *Purple haze: The puzzle of consciousness*. Oxford: Oxford University Press.

Levine, L.W. (1988). *Highbrow lowbrow: The emergence of cultural hierarchy in America*. Cambridge, MA: Harvard University Press.

Levinson, J. (1990). *Music, art, and metaphysics: Essays in philosophical aesthetics*. Ithaca, NY: Cornell University Press.

Martin, P.J. (1995). *Sounds and society: Themes in the sociology of music*. Manchester: Manchester University Press; Distributed exclusively in the USA and Canada by St. Martin's Press.

McLaughlin, B.P., Beckermann, A., and Walter, S. (2009). Introduction. In: B.P. McLaughlin, A. Beckermann, and S. Walter (eds.) *The Oxford handbook of philosophy of mind*, pp. 1–28. Oxford: Oxford University Press.

Meyer, L.B. (1956). *Emotion and meaning in music*. Chicago, IL: University of Chicago Press.

Neisser, U. (1988). Five kinds of self-knowledge. *Philosophical Psychology*, **1**, 35–59.

Noë, A. (2009). *Out of our heads: Why you are not your brain, and other lessons from the biology of consciousness*. New York: Hill and Wang.

O'Neill, S.A. (2002). The self-identity of young musicians. In: D.J. Hargreaves, D. Miell, and R.A. MacDonald (eds.) *Musical identities*, pp. 79–96. Oxford: Oxford University Press.

Patel, A.D. (2008). *Music, language, and the brain*. Oxford: Oxford University Press.

Pitcher, G. (1966). *Wittgenstein: The philosophical investigations* (1st edn.). Garden City, NY: Anchor Books.

Prichard, C., Korczynski, M. and Elmes, M. (2007). Music and work: An introduction. *Group and Organization Management*, **32**, 4–21.

Regelski, T.A. (1996). Taking the 'art' of music for granted: A critical sociology of the aesthetic philosophy of music. In: L.R. Bartel and D.J. Elliott (eds.) *Critical reflections on music education*, pp. 23–57. Toronto, ON: Canadian Music Education Research Center.

Regelski, T. (2004). Social theory, and music and music education as praxis. *Action, Criticism, and Theory for Music Education*, **3**(3), Available at: http://act.maydaygroup.org/articles/Regelski3_3.pdf (accessed 15 February 2010).

Regelski, T. (2006). Music appreciation as praxis. *Music Education Research,* **8**(2), 281–310.

Regelski, T. (2009). Curriculum Reform: Reclaiming 'Music' as Social Praxis. *Action, Criticism, and Theory for Music Education,* **8**(1), 66–84. Available at: http://act.maydaygroup.org/articles/Regelski8_1.pdf (accessed 26 June 2010).

Reimer, B. (1970). *A philosophy of music education* (First edn.). Englewood Cliffs, NJ: Prentice Hall.

Reimer, B. (1989). *A philosophy of music education* (Second edn.). Englewood Cliffs, NJ: Prentice Hall.

Reimer, B. (2003). *A philosophy of music education: Advancing the vision* (Third edn.). Upper Saddle River, NJ: Prentice Hall.

Robinson, J. (2005). *Deeper than reason: Emotion and its role in literature, music, and art.* Oxford: Oxford University Press.

Schatzki, T.R., Knorr-Cetina, K., and von Savigny, E. (2001). *The practice turn in contemporary theory.* New York: Routledge.

Schulkind, M., Hennis, L., and Rubin, D. (1999). Music, emotion, and autobiographical memory: They are playing our song. *Memory and Cognition,* **27**, 948–55.

Shusterman, R. (1997). *Practicing philosophy: Pragmatism and the philosophical life.* New York: Routledge.

Shusterman, R. (2000). *Pragmatist aesthetics: Living beauty, rethinking art* (Second edn.). Lanham, MD: Rowman and Littlefield Publishers.

Small, C. (1998). *Musicking: The meanings of performing and listening.* Hanover, NH: University Press of New England.

Stacey, R., Brittain, K., and Kerr, S. (2002). Singing for health: an exploration of the issues. *Health Education,* **102**(4), 156–62.

Thompson, E. (2007). *Mind in life.* Cambridge, MA: Harvard University Press.

Tsakiris, M. and Frith, C.D. (2009). Self: Scientific perspectives. In: T. Bayne, A. Cleeremans, and P. Wilken (eds.) *The Oxford companion to consciousness,* pp. 585–88. Oxford: Oxford University Press.

Tuomela, R. (2002). *The philosophy of social practices: A collective acceptance view.* Cambridge: Cambridge University Press.

Williford, K. (2009). Self-representational theories of consciousness. In: T. Bayne, A. Cleeremans, and P. Wilken (eds.) *The Oxford companion to consciousness,* pp. 583–85. Oxford: Oxford University Press.

Wittgenstein, L. and Barrett, C. (1966). *Lectures & conversations on aesthetics, psychology, and religious belief.* Berkeley, CA: University of California Press.

Wright, F.A. (1969/1923). *The arts in Greece; three essays.* Port Washington, NY: Kennikat Press.

Zucker, A. (2006). Philosophy of medicine. In: D. Borchert (ed.) *Encyclopedia of philosophy* (2nd edn.), pp. 465–67. Detroit, MI: Macmillan Reference USA.

Chapter 4

Music Therapy: Models and Interventions

Gro Trondalen and Lars Ole Bonde

Introduction

In the present book music therapy is contextualized within a larger framework of theories and models applying music, music experiences, and music interventions for health and wellbeing purposes. We acknowledge the concept 'health musicking' (Stige 2003) to describe the vast and composite field of health technologies and practices based on music and understand music therapy as one of many ways to promote health through music.

This chapter takes as its point of departure a descriptive theoretical model (Bonde 2011) to give an overview of the field of health musicking, in order to discuss the position and rationale of music therapy (and music medicine) in a wider context. Then follows a section defining music therapy and music medicine as disciplines within the area before the chapter focuses more closely on music therapy. A number of internationally well-known models of music therapy are described in succession and placed in the model, based on an interpretation of their theoretical foundations and practical procedures. The discussion part focuses on recent developments within the models and their current relationship to each other and to 'health musicking' as a field in development. In addition, there is an elaboration on music therapy as a multilayered phenomenon, which allows for a variety of experiences at different levels.

Bonde (2011) suggests that 'health musicking' can be understood as the common core of any use of music experiences to regulate emotional or relational states or to promote wellbeing, be it therapeutic or not, professionally assisted or self-made. Over the last 10–15 years many social science based studies have documented some of the many ways in which music is used to promote health by 'lay people' in their daily life (DeNora 2000, 2007). Thus, the field of music and health covers lay-therapeutic musicking in everyday life as well as community musicking and the more specific professional practices of music medicine and music therapy. Bonde's model (2011) describes how health musicking is related to four major purposes or goals:

1. The development of communities and values through musicking.

2. The shaping and sharing of musical environments.

3. The professional use of music(king) and sound(ing) to help individuals.

4. The formation and development of identity through musicking.

On this basis, he suggests a quadrant model to illustrate how professional practices are positioned in the field and this is shown in Figure 4.1.

In the model, music therapy and music medicine are described very broadly as belonging to three of the four quadrants and related to some of the major paradigms. In the following sections we will focus on specific models and finally place them in the health musicking model (see Figure 4.3).

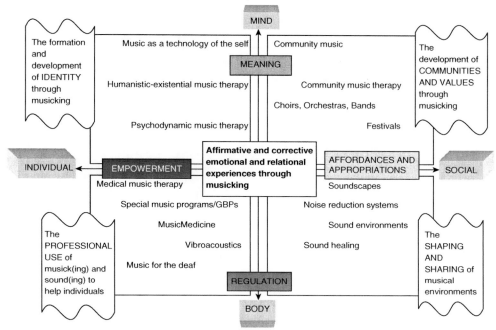

Fig. 4.1 Health musicking: a theoretical model. Adapted from Ansdell, G. (2001). Musicology: Misunderstood guest at the music therapy feast? In: D. Aldridge, G. Di Franco, E. Ruud, and T. Wigram (eds.) *Music Therapy in Europe. The 5th European Music Therapy Congress (Napoli, April 2001)*, pp. 1–33. Rome: Ismez, and K. Wilber (2000). *Integral Psychology: Consciousness, Spirit, Psychology, Therapy.* Boston, MA: Shambhala.

Music medicine and music therapy

Music medicine—sometimes also labelled music in medicine or musicmedicine—is the use of pre-recorded music to improve patient status and medical care. Music medicine is employed in a variety of settings within a hospital, directed towards many medical conditions and procedures, i.e. medical interventions, to enhance or facilitate the treatment and to assist rehabilitation. Music is used to influence the patient's physical, mental, or emotional states before, during, or after medical, dental, or paramedical treatment (Bruscia 1998; Dileo 1999). There is usually no therapeutic relationship established through music involved in such a procedure. From a paradigmatic point of view, Music medicine might be seen as a cognitive-behaviourally oriented intervention model.

The fundamental difference between music medicine and music therapy is that while music medicine is based on a stimulus–response paradigm, the latter is relational and always involves the triad of music, client, and therapist. Such a music therapeutic *relationship* also includes assessment, treatment, and evaluation. Music medicine is most often administered by a nurse or other member of the medical staff. The music used may have been chosen or developed by a music therapist, but this is usually not the case. Most music medicine protocols have been developed by medical doctors, nurses, or music psychologists and often the music is composed by musicians or composers who may or may not have medical or therapeutic training. In music therapy the music experience is always embedded in the therapeutic relationships that are both interpersonal and intermusical. The difference between the two practices is illustrated in Figure 4.2.

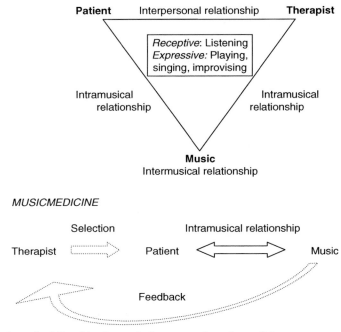

Fig. 4.2 Elements and relationships in music therapy and music medicine.

Music medicine is quite well established in North American hospital treatment and care, but only on its way in other continents. Apart from palliative care, music therapy is less included in somatic care worldwide; however, there is evidence that both practices are effective. Dileo and Bradt (2005) examined the therapeutic effects of the two practices in 11 medical areas, based on 183 controlled studies. Their conclusions were: (1) that both practices have a significant effect in 10 of the 11 areas, and (2) that the effect of music therapy in most areas was almost the double of the effect of music medicine (effect size measured as Cohen's *d*). A conclusion on the relative effectiveness of the two practices will demand further studies and meta-analyses in both fields. But it can be concluded that both music medicine and music therapy are effective and can serve as complementary practices in somatic care.

Models and methods of music therapy[1]

Introduction

In international music therapy there are many methods, schools, models and techniques and different ways of practising and understanding music therapy. In an extensive anthology Maranto (1993) identified 14 models of schools in the USA alone, including more than 100 different techniques. Similar information is continuously updated in the 'Country of the Month' column of the

---

[1] The present chapter is based on Chapter 3 in Wigram et al. (2002), but is, however, updated on new research literature, in addition to an introduction to Benenzon Music Therapy and Community Music Therapy.

e-journal *Voices*.[2] Before selecting models for presentation in this chapter, there is a need for an outline of our understanding of some core concepts. Bruscia's definition of what constitutes a method, variation, procedure, technique, and model is a point of departure in connection with understanding terminology in theoretical descriptions (Bruscia 1998, p.115) as he summarizes:

> A *method* is a particular type of music experience that the client engages in for therapeutic purposes; a *variation* is the particular way in which that music experience is designed; a *procedure* is everything that the therapist has to do to engage the client in that experience; a *technique* is one step within any procedure that a therapist uses to shape the client's immediate experience; and a *model* is a systematic and unique approach to method, procedure and technique based on certain principles.

In some countries and languages, especially European, there does not seem to be a sharp distinction between the words method, approach, and model, and this may cause linguistic confusion and communication challenges. However, what we describe in this chapter are internationally well-known and acknowledged models of music therapy today.

The 9th World Congress of Music Therapy in Washington (1999) had 'five internationally known models of music therapy' as a concurrent theme (Wigram et al. 2002). These five models were introduced and illustrated from many different perspectives: history, therapy theory, clinical practice, research, and training, and included *Guided Imagery and Music, Analytical Music Therapy, Creative Music Therapy, Benenzon Music Therapy*, and *Behavioural Music Therapy*. In addition to the models mentioned above, we would like to add *Community Music Therapy*. This is an approach first presented clinically and theoretically in the 1980s (Ruud 1980a), but internationally acknowledged and theorized as a method mainly during the last few decades.

The selected six models are presented in the same format: (1) a historical outline and definitions from the literature; (2) the session format; (3) clinical applications; (4) documentation; and (5) classification (using the system of Bruscia (1998) with four levels of practice: auxiliary, augmentative, intensive, and primary).

The Bonny Method of Guided Imagery and Music (GIM)

(1) In receptive music therapy the most important procedure is active music listening. There are several models and procedures within receptive music therapy (Grocke and Wigram 2007), for example 'Regulative Music Therapy' (Schwabe 1987). However, the most internationally renowned model is the *Bonny Method of Guided Imagery and Music* (hereafter GIM). GIM was developed in the early 1970s by the violinist and music therapist Helen Lindquist Bonny, while she worked at Maryland Psychiatric Research Center in the United States (Bonny and Savary 1973; Summer 1988; Bonny 2002). Gradually (and especially after the prohibition of LSD in 1972) Bonny developed a session format in five phases and a series of music programmes. Throughout the years, GIM has grown significantly and is currently practised worldwide (Bruscia and Grocke 2002; Parker 2010).

According to the founder, Helen Lindquist Bonny, 'GIM is a process, where imagery is evoked during music listening' (Bonny 1990), while a more in-depth definition is offered by Frances Goldberg (1995, pp. 112–114):

> GIM is a depth approach to music psychotherapy in which specifically programmed classical music is used to generate a dynamic unfolding of inner experiences... (it is) holistic, humanistic and transpersonal, allowing for the emergence of all aspects of the human experience: psychological, emotional, physical, social, spiritual, and the collective unconscious.

---

[2] http://www.voices.no

In GIM specifically *sequenced classical music programmes* are used to stimulate and sustain a dynamic unfolding of inner experiences. Facilitators who conduct sessions in this one-to-one modality have backgrounds in the helping professions and are formally trained in the Bonny Method. The music is Western classical and ranges from the Baroque period to the twentieth century, both instrumental and vocal (Bonny 1976). Twelve of the programmes are created by Helen Linquist Bonny and are often referred to as 'core programmes'. In 1995–96 Ken Bruscia developed a set of 10 CDs, *Music for the Imagination*, and he published a manual describing the story of the programmes, their revisions, and the new collection based on Naxos recordings. In 2002 there were 66 programmes available (Bruscia and Grocke 2002), and in 2010 over 100 (Bonde 2009), and new programmes are continually being produced.

The music programmes last from 30–50 minutes and are composed of three to eight longer or shorter selected movements or single pieces from the classical music heritage. The music is sequenced in order to support, generate, and deepen experiences related to various psychological (or physiological) needs. GIM combines listening to music with relaxation, visualization, drawing, and verbal conversation and allows for experiences at different levels of consciousness. In the music travel the client has the opportunity to experience aspects of his/her life as *imagery* in many modalities, i.e. inner pictures, bodily experiences, sensations, feelings, thoughts, memories, and noetic experiences (Grocke 1999; Goldberg 2002). From a philosophical point of view, the model implies music *as* therapy (Bruscia 1998).

(2) In GIM there is a set of protocols—procedures and techniques—for conducting a listening session: a) prelude; b) induction, relaxation, and focusing; c) music travel; d) return and drawing; and e) verbal conversation.

In the *prelude*, or preliminary discussion, the music therapist and the client together discuss the focus of the session and potential imagery that may provide a useful point of departure for the musical journey, as related to the client's life world and conscious experience of his/her challenges in life. With this in mind, the therapist selects the music programme.

The *induction* (relaxation-based or autogenic) focuses on the release of tension throughout the different muscle groups of the body, as the subject lies down on a mat and closes his/her eyes. The purpose of the induction is to facilitate a transition from ego-dominated to deeper levels of consciousness and to surrender to a more flexible experience of time and space. The therapist may suggest a start image related to the focus of the session.

During the *music travel*, the client verbally describes his/her experience while listening to the music. The therapist listens intensively and periodically makes non-directive verbal interventions to 'help the client to describe the experience, to stay close to it, and to feel the full impact of it' (Grocke 2005, p. 46). During this stage, which lasts from 30–50 minutes, the therapist takes written notes about the client's experience and narrative as well, and a copy of the written transcript is given to the client after each session.

When the music is over, there is a *return* phase where the therapist guides the client back to a non-altered state of consciousness. He/she is then encouraged to make a drawing—a 'mandala' (Kellogg 1984), a sculpture (clay work) or a poem to capture what stands out as important experiences and images emerging during the music travel.

In the *postlude*, these 'visible' experiences in the form of a mandala work as a focal point for further *verbal conversation*, where the therapist helps the client to connect the experience to his/her daily life and the session focus. The client's own interpretation of the experience is acknowledged as authoritative.

(3) GIM has been used in a number of clinical settings and many different populations: self-development and transpersonal work of neurotypical people, music healing, training therapy, drug addiction, abuse, neurotic disturbances, and in the somatic field clients suffering from heart

problems or cancer, and people living with HIV and other life-threatening diseases. Modifications of the format—e.g. shorter music travels—have been developed for other clinical populations (e.g. psychiatric patients or patients in end-of-life care), and also different group formats are common (Summer 2002; Moe 2007; Bonde 2010).

(4) The GIM literature covers clinical studies, clinical therapy, and research studies in both process and effect and research is conducted in quantitative, qualitative, and mixed designs (e.g. Wrangsjö and Körlin 1995; Körlin and Wrangsjö 2001; Bonde 2005; Grocke 2010). Over the years, devotees of GIM have concentrated increasingly upon metaphors and narratives in their work (Bonde 2007), and personal development has become linked to personal empowerment (Trondalen 2009–2010). Research demonstrates that GIM can change counterproductive behaviour patterns, increase self-understanding, empower people to solve problems, reduce stress, and increase access to personal creative resources (see e.g. Grocke 1999; Abrams 2002; Bruscia and Grocke 2002; Martin 2007). In 2010, *Voices* published an online commemorative issue, dedicated to the life and work of Helen Bonny.[3]

(5) In Bruscia's systematic account of music therapy models (Bruscia 1998), GIM is placed at the *intensive level* as a transformative music psychotherapy, because in GIM 'the music experience is therapeutically transformative and complete in, of, and by itself, independent of any insights gained through verbal exchange' (Bruscia 1998, p. 219).

Analytically Oriented Music Therapy (AOM)

(1) From the early twentieth century there was within psychoanalysis a tradition of exploring music and music experiences (Nass 1971; Bonde 2009) and also the Jungian tradition of analytical psychology had some affinity with music (Wärja 1994). However, an analytical tradition in music therapy developed quite late, with Juliette Alvin and especially Mary Priestley as contributors. From the early 1970s Priestley developed 'Analytical Music Therapy' as an active, psychotherapeutic method based on the symbolic use of musical and non-verbal improvisations followed by an interpretive therapeutic dialogue between therapist and client. The client would sing and/or play on self-chosen instruments in musical dialogue with the therapist, often with a 'playing rule' (or 'given') as point of departure. A 'playing rule' is a symbolic theme related to the client's conscious problem sphere, decided before the improvisation. In the improvisation, unconscious energy connected with the problem, is activated and expressed, and this is discussed and reflected upon after the musical part. Mary Priestley, a professional violinist, combined insights and experiences from her personal psychoanalysis and her music therapy training to a unique model. The transference phenomena between client and therapist (and music) were considered a core element in training as well as in theory (Priestley 1975, 1994). Priestley's own definition is as follows:

> Analytical Music Therapy is the name that has prevailed for the analytically-informed symbolic use of improvised music by the music therapist and client. It is used as a creative tool with which to explore the client's inner life so as to provide the way forward for growth and greater self-knowledge
>
> (Priestley 1994, p. 3).

Priestley's model has influenced training and clinical practice in the UK and in central Europe. In Denmark, Germany, UK, and USA the term Analytical Music Therapy has been replaced by

---

[3] See vol. 10, issue 3. The issue contains articles in all categories including perspectives on practice, reports, examples of research, essays, stories, a Refshare document with links to the huge research materials on GIM, archival texts, and a keynote speech by Helen Bonny that appears for the first time as a written text (http://www.voices.no).

'Analytically Oriented Music Therapy' (AOM) in order to reflect a psychoanalytically informed, but broader theoretical base including developmentally informed psychology and communication theories (Pedersen 2002; Scheiby 2002, 2010; Austin 2008).

(2) There is no specific session format in AOM, but the session will often start with a verbal dialogue on what is meaningful and important for the client here and now. This leads to the formulation of 'a playing rule' as inspiration for the musical improvisation. The rule/topic is explored non-verbally, and the music therapist can be supportive or creative, or play a given role decided beforehand. After the improvisation the client and therapist will discuss the meaning of the music.

Priestley also used recordings of the improvisation. The client and therapist can listen to the recording together and talk about it, and this may lead to a second improvisation at the end of the session. Music making and verbal processing has equal weight, thus from a philosophical point of view it is music *in* therapy.

(3) Priestley primarily developed her model in work with psychiatric patients and in counselling work with private clients. Today AOM is still an important model within psychiatry and mental health care, but it is also used with a large range of other clinical population, including patients in medical care and rehabilitation, and in the training of music therapy students. The training discipline *intertherapy*, where one music therapy student is the therapist, the other the client (and vice versa) under direct supervision, has been developed into an advanced training methodology, aimed at developing the students sensitivity and awareness of transference and countertransference to a level so that they can better resonate with the problems of their clients.

In AOM, with all client populations the focus is on stimulating the client's self-healing forces and mental resources through musicking and verbal dialogue. In AOM work with multiply disabled clients who cannot verbalize, improvisations with simple musical playing rules can be used to enhance contact and develop communication at very basic levels of what Malloch and Trevarthen (2009) call 'communicative musicality', where tiny nuances and changes mean a lot to the client and not least to the relatives (Holck 2004).

(4) The basic documentation emerging from the analytical model is presented by Priestley (1975, 1994). Over the last 20 years, however, AOM has been growing in the USA, where Scheiby has introduced the training and documented her own work with students and with patients in neurological rehabilitation in several publications (Scheiby 1998, 2002, 2005). Many chapters in international publications document processes in, and treatment effects of, AOM, especially in psychiatry (Langenberg 1988; Bruscia 1998; Pedersen 1999, 2002, 2007; Wigram and De Backer 1999; Hannibal 2001; Eschen 2002; Mahns 2004).

(5) In Bruscia's systematic account of music therapy models (Bruscia 1998) AOM is placed as 'Insight Music Therapy' at the *intensive level* (p. 219) when it has re-educative goals (behaviour change, goal modification, self-actualization), and at the *primary level* when it has reconstructive goals (in-depth changes in the client's personality structure).

Creative Music Therapy—Nordoff–Robbins music therapy (CMT)

(1) The Nordoff–Robbins approach, called Creative Music Therapy, is one of the most famous improvisational models of music therapy developed over the last 50 years. Paul Nordoff, an American composer and pianist, and Clive Robbins, a British trained special education teacher, collaborated to pioneer the model which is known worldwide and has been taught in a variety of countries over the world. Most of the early development of Creative Music Therapy was aimed at children with learning disabilities, from the mild end of the spectrum to the severe (Aigen 1998). Paul Nordoff died in 1976 and Clive Robbins further expanded the work together with his wife, Carol Robbins, including a new focus on children with hearing-impairment (Robbins and Robbins 1980).

In the early years of developing their method, Nordoff and Robbins were influenced by the ideas of Rudolf Steiner and the anthroposophic movement in humanistic psychology. From this influence emerged the idea that within every human being there is an innate responsiveness to music, and within every personality one can reach a 'music child' or a 'music person'. The idea was vital in their approach to the handicapped population, as they believed in the potentially normal and natural responsiveness to music and the power of music to enable self-expression and communication, in spite of severe degrees of learning-and physical disabilities. Later Nordoff and Robbins related their therapeutic goals to the humanistic concepts of Abraham Maslow, including in their framework the aspiration towards self-actualization and peak experiences (Maslow 1962).

(2) The relationship with the client is built on a warm, friendly approach, accepting the child as he/she is, recognizing, reflecting, and respecting the child's feeling, allowing the child to make choices, and a non-directive approach to give the child autonomy, and the therapist the role of following and facilitating. The style is unique and often easily recognizable. The therapists are usually highly skilled musicians, as the style of a harmony instrument is central to their working style. During training the music therapists develop a sophisticated use of piano (and in some cases guitar) in improvised music making. In individual therapy, clients are typically offered a limited channel for their musical material, mainly the cymbal and drum, together with strong encouragement to use their voice. In group work, other instruments are involved—pitched instruments, reed horns, wind instruments, and various string instruments.

In much of the individual work Nordoff–Robbins therapists (where at all possible), work in a pair. One person establishes a musical relationship from the piano, while the other therapist facilitates the child's responses and engagement. In most cases, the therapist, who often plays in a tonal style, uses creative improvisation, and creates an engaging musical atmosphere from the moment the client enters the room to the moment he/she leaves. In Creative Music Therapy the approach comes within the conceptual framework of *music as therapy*, where the music provides the therapeutic catalyst through which change will take place. The relationship itself is formed *in* the music. The therapists work through different phases in their therapy: 'Meet the child musically [...] Evoke musical response [...] develop musical skills, expressive freedom, and interresponsiveness' (Bruscia 1987, p. 45).

(3) Nordoff and Robbins offered a significant perspective on how music can be used in music therapy from musical play songs (e.g. Nordoff and Robbins 1966, 1969) to pure improvisation. Examples are: the improvisational style of music must be free from musical conventions, and flexible. Intervals are considered important and represent different feelings, when used in melody. Triads and chords can be used in special ways and improvised music should also include 'musical archetypes', such as organum, exotic scales (Japanese, Middle Eastern), Spanish idioms, and modal frameworks.[4]

The therapist often provides a musical frame, frequently establishing clear rhythm and pulse, and particularly, singing about what the client is doing while they are doing it, in order to bring into focus the experience that is occurring. Any musical expression produced by the client—vocal or instrumental—is incorporated into a frame, and encouraged.

The clinical application of Creative Music Therapy has been introduced in wide-ranging and in diverse ways, including work with adult patients in the areas of neurology, psychiatry, and terminal illness. The model has been developed through research and extension of application (Aigen 1991, 1996b, 1998, 2005; Pavlicevic and Trevarthen 1994; Ansdell 1995, 1996, 1997a; Pavlicevic 1995,

---

[4] For an extensive elaboration see Nordoff and Robbins (1977). For a historical record and analysis of the development of the model see Aigen (1998).

1997; Lee 1996, 2000; Neugebauer and Aldridge 1998; Brown 1999; Streeter 1999; Næss and Ruud 2008; Stensæth 2008).

(4) This model of music therapy has also developed methods of analysing what is going on and how therapy is progressing. A number of rating scales have been generated including: thirteen categories of response, child–therapist relationship, musical communicativeness, musical response scales (instrumental rhythmic responses, singing responses).

So far, case studies are the most typical way by which therapist working in the Nordoff–Robbins tradition document their work (e.g. Howat 1995; Etkin 1999; Aigen 2002, 2005).

Piano-based improvisation still forms the foundation, but guitar-based improvisation developed by Dan Gormley in the USA, jazz and blues improvisational styles more culturally effective with some populations in New York developed by Alan Turry, and Aesthetic Music Therapy recently defined by Colin Lee in Canada (Lee 2003), amongst others, have emerged from the initial foundations of Creative Music Therapy. Among the Scandinavian pioneers are the Danish music therapist Claus Bang (http://www.clausbang.com) and the Norwegian music therapist Tom Næss (Næss 1989) and Unni Johns (Johns 1996).

Creative Music Therapy has lasted the test of time. This is visible in the increasing number of music therapists using this approach and not least due to the extensive publications of case studies on the basis of Creative Music Therapy. Also some very important writings have been published by Paul Nordoff, and Clive and Carol Robbins (Nordoff and Robbins 1971/83, 1971a, 1977; Robbins and Robbins 1980). There is also an extensive literature on case studies in books (see, for example, Bruscia 1991; Ansdell 1995; Aigen 1996a; Pavlicevic 1997; Wigram and de Backer 1999).

(5) In Bruscia's systematic account of music therapy models (Bruscia 1998) Creative Music Therapy is placed as either 'Developmental Music Therapy' or 'Music Therapy in Healing' or 'Transformative Music Psychotherapy' at the *intensive level* (pp. 189, 210, 219).

Benenzon Music Therapy

(1) Psychiatrist, musician, and composer Rolando Benenzon founded the first music therapy training programme in South America in 1966. This was in Buenos Aires, Argentina, and over the next decades Benenzon participated in the development of training programmes and professional associations in several countries, not only in South America, but also in southern Europe (Wagner 2007).

Benenzon's model is mainly known and practised in South American countries and in Spain and Italy. Theoretically it is an eclectic model inspired by many different psychological and psychotherapeutic theories, including psychoanalysis and psychodrama. Some of Benenzon's texts are available in English (Benenzon 1982, 1997, 2007). A recent definition of the model can be found in the last reference given:

> The aim of this model of music therapy is to enable clients to direct their creative energies into opening channels of communication between people, a process that is dependent upon the ability to establish relationships and connections. In music therapy, these connections are developed within the non-verbal context
>
> (Benenzon 2007, p. 149).

The key concept is 'Musical Sound Identity (ISO)'. The ISO principle was originally defined by Altschuler (1948/2001) as a crossmodal similarity between internal psychological states and external sound expressions. Benenzon understands ISO as the infinite set of sound energy, acoustic, and movement that belongs to an individual and characterizes it; all in all they comprise his identity. 'The mental time of the patient must coincide with the sound and musical time executed by the therapist' (Benenzon 1982, p. 33). Four sub-concepts describe different aspects of this individual energy field that can be activated by music: Universal ISO, Cultural Iso, Complementary or Group ISO, and Gestalt ISO. Fundamental for the person, patient as well as therapist, is the Gestalt ISO, the dynamic mosaic of sound features characterizing the individual. The Complementary ISO is 'the momentary fluctuation of the Gestalt ISO induced by specific cir-cumstances', e.g. in the music therapy session. The Group ISO needs time to be established within the social system of the group, be it a therapy group or a musical ensemble. In a music therapy group it is a dynamic synthesis of each patient's identity. The group ISO is always part of and influenced by the Cultural ISO, defined by Grebe as 'the sound identity proper to a community of relative cultural homogeneity', in a dynamic interchange with subcultures or groups. From his work with psychotic children Benenzon developed the concept of a Universal ISO—the 'sound identity that characterizes or identifies all human beings (…) including the specific characteristics of the heartbeat, the sound of inhaling and exhaling, the mother's voice during birth, and the first days of the infant.' (Benenzon 1982, p. 36). There are similarities and differences between this concept and Nordoff–Robbins' concept of 'The Music Child'.

From psychoanalysis and psychodrama Benenzon imports two other important theoretical concepts: the intermediary object and the integrating object. Music instruments and sounds can have the function of intermediary objects, but unlike, for example, puppets, they have a life of their own, and the music therapist can explore together with the patient(s) what instruments and sounds resonate best with the Gestalt ISO and thus may have an integrative function. Musical instruments can be more or less dominating, thus enabling leading instruments in a group to link distinct Gestalt ISOs to both Group and Cultural ISO.

(2) In Benenzon's Music Therapy Manual three session stages are described: 1) warming up and catharsis, 2) perception and observation, and 3) sonorous dialogue. In the first stage the aim is to discharge stress (for Benenzon equivalent to 'catharsis'), and this is primarily done through rhythmic playing on selected instruments. The second stage is 'limited to the moments when the therapist discovers or elaborates a hypothesis about the patient's complimentary ISO' (Benenzon 1982, p. 70). Based on the therapist's personal ISO reflection a communication channel is opened, and the third stage unfolds. Benonzon makes it clear that the duration of each stage is unpredict-able and that there is no guarantee for a sound dialogue to occur. From a philosophical point of view, music is understood *as* therapy.

(3) From the very beginning Benenzon concentrated on specific clinical areas: autism (defined as early childhood psychosis), vegetative states (coma), and states dominated by hypertension. The major problem of the autistic person according to Benenzon is the isolation ('like a fetal psychic system living outside the womb'). As an intermediary object music may enable commu-nication between that autistic person and the therapist who primarily uses the ISO principle to engage her patient in dyadic work.

(4) Benenzon has published mostly in Spanish, but his books on music therapy for children within the autistic spectrum are translated into English, Portuguese, and Italian. The Benenzon model is described by di Franco in the Italian edition of Wigram et al. (2004).

(5) In Bruscia's systematic account of music therapy models (Bruscia 1998), Benenzon music therapy is not listed. Benenzon himself describes his model as psychotherapy that can be used as a model on its own (i.e. intensive) or as an adjunct to medical treatment (i.e. augmentative).

Cognitive-Behavioural Music Therapy (CBMT)

(1) From the very beginning, modern music therapy was closely related to behavioural theory. The therapeutic work with American veterans of the Second World War was based on behavioural

principles, and Behavioural Music Therapy (BMT) has probably been the most influential theoretical reference of American music therapy education (Ruud 1980; Bunt 1994). The model is defined as follows:

> …the use of music as contingent reinforcement or stimulus to increase or modify adaptive behaviours and extinguish maladaptive behaviours
>
> (Bruscia 1998).

One of the pioneers in BMT was Clifford Madsen. In 1981 he published a book called *Music therapy: a behavioral guide for the mentally retarded*, and he is still contributing to the literature. Another researcher from the tradition of natural science who has contributed to the understanding of music therapy as a modern, cognitive-behavioural science-based treatment model is Michael Thaut (Thaut 1990, 2005; Davis et al. 1999; Leins et al. 2010).

In 1966 Madsen and colleagues described BMT in an article as a form of cognitive-behaviour modification using music: 1) as a cue, 2) as a time structure and body movement structure, 3) as a focus of attention, 4) as a reward (Madsen et al. 1966). Music is used to modify behaviour through conditioning, and the results can be measured by applied behaviour analysis. The therapeutic process is based on a stimulus–response paradigm, and as a dependent variable the music must be controlled. This explains why specific music, often recorded, is preferred to, for example, improvisation in the treatment of patients.

(2) Many types of behaviours are manipulated in CBMT: physiological, motor, psychological, emotional, cognitive, perceptual, and autonomic. A patient-preferred music stimulus can be given or withdrawn as related to the patient's target behaviour, e.g. increase of attention span.

Music-assisted reinforcement in its purest form is used in Standley's research with premature infants (Standley and Moore 1995). Music was used to stimulate sucking, and when the infant stopped sucking, music was withdrawn. Standley documented a positive effect of music stimulation on sucking time, weight gain, and health of the infants.

The session format depends on the cognitive or behaviour modification goals, but it always has a firm structure and strict protocol. Predictability and control of the musical stimulus is necessary. When participation in musical activities is used as stimulus there is a given relationship between the activity, e.g. singing, playing, or dancing, as a means, and non-musical goals and objectives, such as enhanced social engagement, increased physical activity, improved communication, development of cognitive processing, increased attention and concentration, enjoyment and self-expression, reduction or elimination of antisocial or self-damaging behaviour.

CBMT is an example of music *in* therapy, because the music acts as a reinforcing stimulus of non-musical behaviour. Music and musical activities are means to achieve cognitive and behavioural changes.

(3) CBMT is used with a wide variety of clinical populations, including children and adolescents with development disability, geriatric populations, and psychiatric patients; however, most often patients have physiological problems and belong to a somatic patient group. Premature infants have been mentioned as an example, people with Parkinson's disease (Myskja 2004) or autism are other typical patient groups. Neurological rehabilitation is a major field in current music therapy, and Michael Thaut has developed a specific training in 'neurological music therapy', based on the principles of CBMT (Thaut 2000, 2005).

(4) CBMT was, from the beginning, based on the rigorous standards and procedures of natural science, ensuring the possibilities of replication and standardization and thus leading to recognition in the scientific community. Research has been used to define what types of music will promote specific therapeutic and treatment objectives. Thaut has shown that pulsed, rhythmical

music can promote good walking patterns in patients with Parkinson's disease. In fact, the rhythm in itself can be more effective in gait training, and a metronome can be sufficient to produce the right stimulation (Thaut and Abiru 2010). Music with slower tempos is used when older adults are prompted to move or dance.

Applied behaviour analysis allows the CBMT therapist or researcher to measure the effect over time of the music medicine or music therapy intervention. It can measure, for example, the number of defined asocial behaviours targeted during periods with or without music therapy, utilizing the patient's preferred music or activity. Using reversal designs and multiple baselines, the researcher can evaluate the efficacy of the music intervention over time when compared with periods of non-intervention.

(5) In Bruscia's systematic account of music therapy models (Bruscia 1998, p. 184), BMT is placed as a 'Didactic Practice' at the augmentative level, because this model works with limits and goals that specifically address symptoms and (maladaptive or inappropriate) behaviours, and, to a lesser degree, with the client's personality or general development.

Community Music Therapy

(1) The term Community Music (Therapy) has been used in American literature since 1960 and there have been community-oriented practices for decades. However, today's *Community Music Therapy* is something more than and different from music therapy in community settings (Stige 2010). Initial traces of the recent emergence of Community Music Therapy are found in some early publications from Even Ruud, where he does not only relate music therapy to different treatment theories (Ruud 1980), but also emphasizes, for example, handicapped people's *right to music* (our italics) (Ruud 1990, 2010). Such a socially engaged practice—music as a situated activity within a context—is theoretically elaborated on in depth by Stige in his doctoral dissertation (Stige 2003) and *Invitation to Community Music Therapy* (Stige and Aarø 2011).

An international scholarly discourse on Community Music Therapy is a relatively new phenomenon involving theories from fields such as systems theory, anthropology, sociology, community psychology, and new musicology (e.g. Ansdell 1997b, 2001; Small 1998; DeNora 2000). The movement of Community Music Therapy addresses mechanisms of exclusion and inclusion in a broader context and requires a more socially engaged practice, as is the case in a setting of a more traditional clinical practice within clinical/professional or institutionalized settings (Ruud 2004a; Stige 2010). Community Music Therapy (post 2000) 'goes beyond conceptions of music therapy in community settings to also embrace music therapy *as* community and music therapy *for* community development' (Stige 2010, p.10). It aims to engage directly with problems and possibilities of music and health in society—towards a psychosociocultural model concerned with the musical cultivation of personal and social wellbeing (empowerment). Accordingly, it concerns how music may afford and appropriate therapeutic experiences and processes of change, through collaborative musicking to mobilize resources (cf. Rolvsjord 2010) for the benefit of individuals and communities.

There is no common definition of Community Music Therapy. Ansdell (2002) has even called it an 'anti-model'. Stige suggests Community Music Therapy may operate as a 'cultural critique' informed by sociocultural processes of change both in society at large and in the academic discourse on music, and suggests that we discuss music therapy as a discipline, a profession, and a practice (Stige 2003, p.11). During an ongoing discussion (Ansdell 2002; Garred 2002; Kenny and Stige 2002b; Stige 2002; Ansdell 2005), Ruud suggests 'Community Music Therapy is the reflexive use of performance-based music therapy within a systemic perspective' (Ruud 2004b, p. 33). While Stige takes a broader position:

> Community Music Therapy as an arena of professional practice is situated health musicking in community, as a planned process of collaboration between client and therapist with a special focus upon promotion of sociocultural and communal change through a participatory approach where music as ecology of performed relationships is used in non-clinical and inclusive settings
>
> (Stige 2003, p. 454).

However, definitions of Community Music Therapy are still a topic of debate (Stige et al. 2010).

(2) There are no common established procedures or techniques in Community Music Therapy. Community Music Therapy sessions are related to ordinary everyday contexts and practices, where people engage in music regularly. Every single setting requires a procedure adapted to the context, either at an individual, group, or community scenery, where music can reveal its transforming power. This means that a community music therapist often works in ways similar to those of a community musician, accompanying participants and promoting community singing (DeNora 2000, 2007; Stige et al. 2010). The main difference is that the community music therapist has the needs and potentials of participants with health problems as point of departure.

(3) Community music therapy is always seen in relation to health, human development, and social change and coherence in some way or another and may offer its potential to marginalized individuals of groups, or to communities at a more general level aiming at creating a cultural and social link between music therapy and music (and health) in everyday life.

(4) There is an extensive literature on Community Music Therapy practices. One early example is a project on community integration in and through music in the mid 1980s in Norway (Kleive and Stige 1988). During the last decade, however, there has been an extensive publication of a variety of examples on Community Music Therapy from female adults recreating their identity varying from criminal band member to music band members (e.g. Nielsen 1996) to *Music for Life* with young men in a South African context, exploring music therapy as social activism (Pavlicevic 2010). Several national contexts are currently published, discussed, and explored in a wide range of theoretical orientations, however, always focusing on *health musicking* (Stige 2002) as it focuses on the relationship between individual experiences and the possible creation of musical community (Kenny and Stige 2002a; Stige 2002; Aigen 2004; Pavlicevic and Andsdell 2004; Stige et al. 2010).

(5) The current Community Music Therapy movement is included in Bruscia's systematic account of music therapy models and labelled as 'ecological' music therapy (1998). A similar view is also at the forefront of Aasgaard's 'milieu' music therapy (Aasgaard 2002, 2004). Community Music Therapy is suggested at the *intensive level*, as this level incorporates ecological aims and values into the client's music therapy, or combining traditional form of therapy with community work. Such an approach may also lead to significant and enduring changes in the individual or community, when the goals and processes extend across several areas of practice (Aasgaard 2002, 2004).

Discussion: recent developments and orientations of the models

Music therapy theories and models are closely related to the development of psychological theories and paradigms, as stated early by Ruud (1980). The behavioural 'wave' in psychology was the theoretical foundation of the first clinical models of music therapy in modern time (Madsen et al. 1966), and this tradition has developed into a modern cognitive-behavioural model leaning heavily on neuroscientific evidence of 'the music effect' (Schneck and Berger 2006; Thaut and Abiru 2010). Psychoanalysis had from the early twentieth century a tradition of exploring music and music experiences (Nass 1971; Bonde 2009) and also the Jungian tradition of analytical psychology had some affinity with music (Wärja 1994).

However, an analytical tradition in music therapy developed quite late (from the 1970s), with especially Mary Priestley as a contributor and Benenzon as a pioneer quite closely related to psychodynamic thinking. During the last 25 years Priestley's 'Analytical Music Therapy' has been developed into a more eclectic dynamic tradition focusing on the therapeutic relationship as the primary agent of change i.e. 'Analytically Oriented Music therapy'.[5]

The third wave in psychology—the humanistic-existential—is reflected in both Creative Music Therapy and GIM, the latter also influenced by the fourth: transpersonal wave. GIM has evolved towards an integrative foundation (referring to Wilber's (1999) use of the concept 'Integrative'), while the Nordoff–Robbins tradition has influenced the newest 'model', Community Music Therapy, strongly. The influence of Positive psychology, Recovery theory and New musicology on CMT is obvious. In other words, all the international models of music therapy presented here are still alive and developing in order to meet health needs of people in the twenty-first century. In graphic form this can be illustrated by placing the models in the earlier presented Figure 4.1 (see Figure 4.3).

Music therapy is both a science and an art form (Wigram et al. 1995). And as a discipline, a profession, and a clinical practice (Stige 2003), no matter which theoretical or clinical orientation, music therapy shares some common core values. There is still an urgent need for a specialized music therapy degree/training—and in some countries, a board-certification (BC) is required to

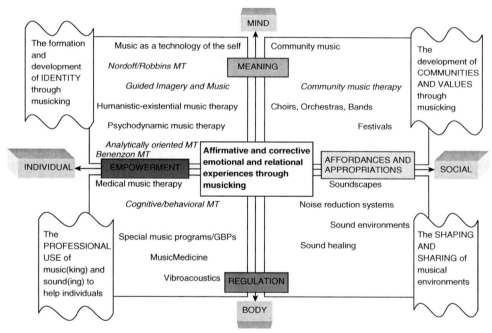

Fig. 4.3 Health musicking: a theoretical model - with the six models of music therapy inserted. Adapted from Ansdell, G. (2001). Musicology: Misunderstood guest at the music therapy feast? In: D. Aldridge, G. Di Franco, E. Ruud, and T. Wigram (eds.) *Music Therapy in Europe. The 5th European Music Therapy Congress (Napoli, April 2001)*, pp. 1–33. Rome: Ismez, and K. Wilber (2000). *Integral Psychology: Consciousness, Spirit, Psychology, Therapy*. Boston, MA: Shambhala.

---

[5] Therefore it is a small paradox that the edited book by Eschen (2002) bears the traditional title *Analytical Music Therapy*, when most of the contributors belong to the second or third generation normally using the term AOM.

be titled 'music therapist'. Music therapy can be considered a complementary or an integrative practice, or as a primary means of treatment—as illustrated by Bruscia's categorizations (1998).

In music therapy the therapeutic relationship is established and developed through musicking. Music as a relational phenomenon may be interpreted in different theoretical perspectives. In this context we want to underline the intersubjective perspective, which views communication as an ongoing process at different levels (Stern 2000). The basic assumption is that everybody has an inherent human ability to give and share thoughts, experiences, and actions. Such a sharing allows for recognition and partaking in one another's life at an existential level (Trondalen 2008).

At the very heart of the 'Health Musicking Model' (Bonde 2011) is the 'affirmative and corrective emotional and relational experiences through musicking'. A meaningful musical relationship is based on the client's experience of being empowered (at a non-verbal and/or verbal level) as the musicking affords and appropriates a variety of interpretations. From a therapeutic point of view, there may be a need for verbal processing to contextualize, develop, and interpret the musical journey at a symbolic level. Such a reworking is, however, not necessary in order to experience and recognize the power of the non-verbal musical relationship per se (Malloch and Trevarthen 2009). At the core of such an affirmative or appreciative recognized relationship is *music*. Music, a multilayered phenomenon that unfolds in time and space and allows for a variety of experiences at different levels, while supporting creation of new life stories over and over again.

In the article, 'Improvisation in Music Therapy Practice: tradition–art–technique', Trondalen (2005) elaborates on music therapy improvisation as a multilayered phenomenon (cf. Figure 4.4). The musicking (cf. the curled line) as a multilayered experience is presented through three dimensions: a) *Being*: an existential awareness b) *Doing*: an aesthetic participation and c) *Transformation*: as a symbol. Hence, the presentation of these layers also includes GIM, i.e. receptive music therapy. Musicking (more specifically here: experiencing and doing musical utterances) is primarily related to an individual perspective, however, it does not exclude the transfer to a broader cultural context. Such a musicking is associated to both the musical theme and the moving along process at an interpersonal level.

Being in the musicking is related to a primary consciousness (a procedural representation) in a present moment. From a phenomenological point of view, such a primary or emerging awareness

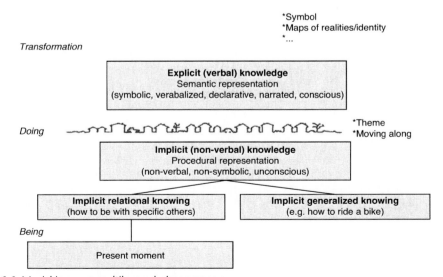

Fig. 4.4 Musicking as a multilayered phenomenon.

is always intentional and connected to the living and perceiving body, i.e. 'the embodied mind' (Damasio, 1994). Stern suggests a developmental working model, based on the infant's subjective experience towards a 'sense of self' (Stern 2000). The mental signals, i.e. inner intensities of arousal, emerging from the body are always present and available for interaction. Stern calls these inner intensities of vital existence 'dynamic forms of vitality' (previously named 'vitality affects', Stern 2000) and describes them in terms like 'exploding, swinging, fading' etc. (Stern 2010, p. 7). 'Dynamic forms of vitality are part of episodic memories and give life to the narratives we create about our lives', he says (Stern 2000, p. 11). From a (psycho)therapeutic point of view, they form another path of connecting to non-verbal and non-conscious past experiences, not least to the 'implicit relational knowing', i.e. how we specifically know how 'to be with' specific other (Lyons-Ruth 1998; Boston Change Process Study Group 2010) and the emergence of a 'present moment' (Stern 2004).

In music therapy, there is always use of a vitality form and some sort of affect attunement (Trondalen and Skårderud 2007), including multiple variations in duration, force, and temporal contour of the musical utterance. In expressive musical improvisation (Wigram 2004)—and in receptive music therapy as well—the non-verbal attunement through respectively instrument or voice is most striking and related to the domain of implicit knowing. Such non-verbal knowledge is not self-reflexive and not verbalized, however, and is experienced as an existential awareness (being) in the musicking. Accordingly, also people without a verbal language can experience such an appreciative *being* in the musical presence of another person (Trolldalen 1997). Paradoxically, such an appreciative recognition in the music, allows for recognition both for the client and the therapist.

Doing is understood as *aesthetic*[6] *participation* through musicking. Many music therapists focus on the aesthetic dimension in music therapy. An example is Kenny, who in her book *Field of Play* (1989) put 'beauty' (i.e. 'the act of listening, playing and creating') in the centre for 'aesthetic' understanding and practice. By linking aesthetic to a doing or a bodily sensing participation in musicking, there is a movement beyond the classical meta-physical interpretation of aesthetics as a highway towards truth (cf. Plato). Through the *doing*—the aesthetic participation—inner senses of self may be explored through musical expression and practical actions, which promote an experience of personal empowerment. Such a position promotes a possible transformation *process*, as opposed to a complete aesthetic product. In a keynote in 2001 'Music Therapy Aesthetic Dimensions' the German music therapist Isabelle Frohne-Hagemann states: '... the process of transformation is more important than the created product'. She relates to the phenomenological concept of 'the living body' (in German 'Leib' as opposed to 'Körper') as a starting point for the aesthetic experience. In modern music therapy this is an experience characterized by an exchange between *thinking* as sensed and felt, and a *feeling* which is reflected through thoughts and actions (cf. levels of knowledge). The French philosopher Merleau-Ponty (1945/1994) also concentrates on the living body—experiencing, acting, and seeking towards meaning through reflection and actions. Another aspect is connected to the *living body* and such a phenomenal body's capacity of 'double-sensing' i.e. the living body's ability to grasp (psychically) and perceive (mentally) at the same time from an inside perspective (Merleau-Ponty 1945/1994). There is a point here that the aesthetic participation does not materialize independently of mundane categories and contexts. Everything has a certain pattern and frame, a certain 'order' (cf. Kant's 'aesthetic turn', elaborated on by Nietzsche, in Storheim (1993)). Transferred to music therapeutic practice, whatever the client and music therapist carry with them into the joint musicking,

---

6 *Aisthetikos* from Greek.: aware/perceive/sense/remember

their stories will only function as a starting point and be interpreted in the forever present context. Accordingly, the doing—the aesthetic participation in the musicking—is the living and sensing participation itself during musicking.

The third layer is *transformation* and the musicking may be interpreted as a sign or as a *symbol*. With reference to the historian Kjeldstadli's What are symbols? (1997), the musicking may be able to store and mediate meaning. The musicking can be interpreted as a representation that refers to developmentally earlier interacting experiences. Due to the music's ambiguity, the client (and the music therapist) can put any meaning they want into the musicking, with the music representing both similarities and differences between them and acting as an open symbol. All musicking is about 'modeling personal subjectivity by giving form to body, gestures and emotion—in short making tacit self knowledge audible' (Ruud 1996, p.146), i.e. a form of identity performance (Ruud 1997). Ruud is referring to the philosopher Wittgenstein, as he suggests that a word does not have a meaning, however, it acquires meaning in practice within a context. Transferred to music this allows for understanding music as an open symbol, that the musical participation creates meaning in context as a 'flexible map of realities' (in Ruud 1992, p.114). Hence, the client and music therapist may position different values, thoughts, and meaning into the musicking. Such a view allows for a procedural understanding of the relationship between the music and its interpretation (or representation) of this phenomenon. From this follows, that expressive and receptive musicking allows for experiences at different levels through a present aesthetic participation within a multilayered frame of interpretation (Trondalen, 2005).

Concluding remarks

In this text we have elaborated on an overview chapter covering some of the major international music therapy orientations/models, their theoretical foundations, and practical approaches to health and wellbeing or 'health musicking'. Music therapy is most commonly defined as an intervention where the therapist helps the client to promote health, using music experiences and the relationships developing through them. Some music approaches use music for health-related goals, in ways that, however, do not qualify as music therapy, but are described as, for example, Music medicine. The very essence of music therapy is the therapeutic *relationship*, which is *established through music*, and it is interactive in nature. The relational context—the interplay of (expressive as well as receptive) music experiences (musicking), the therapeutic or broader social relationship, and the specific participants in their environment—is discussed and compared between the models.

Expressive and receptive musicking allows for experiences at different levels through a present aesthetic participation within a multilayered frame of interpretation. Such a musical relationship, based on empowerment and attunement supports affirmative, corrective, emotional, and relational experiences through musicking, and it defines music therapy as a specific health promoting practice. Elaborating music therapy as a health promoting practice is an ongoing story.

References

Aasgaard, T. (2002). Song Creations by Children with Cancer: Process and Meaning. PhD dissertation, Aalborg University, Denmark.

Aasgaard, T. (2004). A Pied Piper among white coats and infusion pumps. In: G. Ansdell and M. Pavlicevic (eds.) *Community Music Therapy - International Initiatives*, pp. 147–166. London: Jessica Kingsley Publishers.

Abrams, B. (2002). Definitions of transpersonal BMGIM experience. *Nordic Journal of Music Therapy*, **11**(2), 103–26.

Aigen, K. (1991). The Roots of Music Therapy: Towards an Indigenous Research Paradigm. Doctoral dissertation, New York University.

Aigen, K. (1996a). *Being in Music: Foundations of Nordoff-Robbins Music Therapy*. St. Louis, MI: MMB.

Aigen, K. (1996b). *Here We are in The Music: One Year With an Adolescent, Creative Music Therapy Group*. St. Louis, MI: MMB Music.

Aigen, K. (1998). *Path of Development in Nordoff-Robbins Music Therapy*. Gilsum, NH: Barcelona Publishers.

Aigen, K. (2002). *Playin' in the band: a qualitative study of popular music styles as clinical improvisation*. New York: Parkway Book Service.

Aigen, K. (2005). *Music-centered Music Therapy*. Gilsum, NH: Barcelona Publishers.

Aigen, K. (Ed.) (2004). *Conversation on Creating Communities: Performance as Music Therapy in New York City*. In: M. Pavlicevic and G. Andsdell (eds.) *Community Music Therapy*, pp. 186–213. London: Jessica Kingsley.

Aigen, K. (2005). Being who you aren't; doing what you can't. Community music therapy & the paradoxes of performance. *Voices. A World Forum for Music Therapy*, **5**(3).

Altschuler, M. (1948/2001). A psychiatrist's experience with music as a therapeutic agent. *Nordic Journal of Music Therapy*, **10**(1), 69–76.

Ansdell, G. (1995). *Music for Life – Aspects of Creative Music Therapy with Adults Clients*. London: Jessica Kingsley Publishers.

Ansdell, G. (1996). Talking about music therapy. A dilemma and a qualitative experiment. *British Journal of Music Therapy*, **11**(2), 4–15.

Ansdell, G. (1997). Musical elaborations. What has the new musicology to say to music therapy? *British Journal of Music Therapy*, **11**(2), 36–44.

Ansdell, G. (2001). Musicology: Misunderstood guest at the music therapy feast? In: D. Aldridge, G. Di Franco, E. Ruud and T. Wigram (eds.) *Music Therapy in Europe. The 5th European Music Therapy Congress (Napoli, April 2001)*, pp. 1–33. Rome: Ismez.

Ansdell, G. (2002). Community music therapy and the winds of change - A discussion paper. *Voices: A Worlds Forum for Music Therapy*, **2**(2).

Ansdell, G. (2005). Being who you aren't; doing what you can't. Community music therapy & the paradoxes of performance. *Voices. A World Forum for Music Therapy*, **5**(3).

Austin, D. (2008). *The Theory and Practice of Vocal Psychotherapy: Songs of the Self*. London: Jessica Kingsley Publishers.

Benenzon, R.O. (1982). *Music Therapy in Child Psychosis*. Springfield, IL: Charles C. Thomas.

Benenzon, R.O. (1997). *Music Therapy and Theroy and Manual: Contributions to Knowledge of Nonverbal Contexts*. Springfield, IL: Charles C. Thomas.

Benenzon, R.O. (2007). The Benenzon model. *Nordic Journal of Music Therapy*, **16**(2), 148–59.

Bonde, L.O. (2005). The Bonny Method of Guided Imagery and Music (BMGIM) with Cancer Survivors. A Psychosocial Study with Focus on the Influence of BMGIM on Mood and Quality of Life. PhD dissertation, Musikkterapi og Musik, Aalborg Universitetet, Aalborg.

Bonde, L.O. (2007). Music as metaphor and analogy. *Nordic Journal of Music Therapy*, **16** (1), 60–81.

Bonde, L.O. (2009). *Musik og menneske. Introduktion til musikpsykologi*. Copenhagen: Samfundslitteratur.

Bonde, L.O. (2010). Music as support and challenge. Group music and imagery with psychiatric outpatients. In: H. Schirmer (ed.) *Music Therapy Annual vol. 6*, pp. 89–118. Wiesbaden: Reichert.

Bonde, L.O. (2011). Health music(k)ing – Music therapy or music and health? A model, eight empirical examples and some personal reflections. *Music and Arts in Action* (Special Issue: Health promotion and wellness) 120–40.

Bonny, H. (1976). Music and Psychotherapy. Doctoral Thesis, Union Graduate School.

Bonny, H. (1990). Music and change. *Journal of the New Zealand Society for Music Therapy*, **12**(3), 5–10.

Bonny, H. (2002). *Music & Consciousness: The Evolution of Guided Imagery and Music* (L. Summer ed.). Gilsum, NH: Barcelona Publishers.

Bonny, H. and Savary, L. (1973). *Music and Your Mind: Listening with a new consciousness*. New York: Harper & Row.

Boston Change Process Study Group. (2010). *Change in Psychotherapy. A unifying paradigm*. New York: W. W. Norton & Company.

Brown, S. (1999). The music, the meaning, and the therapist's dilemma. In: T. Wigram and J. De Backer (eds.) *Clinical Applications of Music Therapy in Developmental Disability, Paediatrics and Neurology*, pp. 183–200. London: Jessica Kingsley Publishers.

Bruscia, K.E. (1987). *Improvisational Models of Music Therapy*. Springfield, IL: Charles C. Thomas Publishers.

Bruscia, K.E. (1998). *Defining Music Therapy*. Second Edition ed. Lower Village: Barcelona Publishers.

Bruscia, K.E. (Ed.) (1991). *Case Studies in Music Therapy*. Philadelphia, PA: Barcelona Publishers.

Bruscia, K.E. and Grocke, D.E. (Eds.) (2002). *Guided Imagery and Music: The Bonny Method and Beyond*. Gilsum, NH: Barcelona Publishers.

Bunt, L. (1994). *Music Therapy - An Art beyond Words*. London: Routledge.

Damasio, A.R. (1994). *Descartes Error: Emotion, Reason and the Human Brain*. New York: G.P. Putnam's Sons.

Davis, A., Gfeller, K.E., and Thaut, M. (1999). *An Introduction to Music Therapy. Theory and Practice*. Boston, MA: McGraw-Hill College.

DeNora, T. (2000). *Music in Everyday Life*. Cambridge: Cambridge University Press.

DeNora, T. (2007). Health and music in everyday life - a theory of practice. *Psyke & Logos*, **28**(1), 271–87.

Dileo, C. (ed.) (1999). *Music Therapy and Medicine: Clinical and Theoretical Applications*. Silver Spring, MD: American Music Therapy Association.

Dileo, C. and Bradt, J. (2005). *Medical Music Therapy: A Meta-Analysis of the Literature and an Agenda for Future Research*. Cherry Hill, NJ: Jeffrey Books.

Eschen, J. Th. (ed.) (2002). *Analytical Music Therapy*. London: Jessica Kingsley Publishers.

Etkin, P. (Ed.) (1999). The use of creative improvisation and psychodynamic insights in music therapy wtih an abused child. In: T. Wigram and J. De Backer (eds.) *Clinical Applications of Music Therapy in Developmental Disability, Paediatrics and Neurology, pp.* 155–65. London: Jessica Kingsley Publishers.

Frohne-Hagemann, I. (2001). Music Therapy Aestetic Dimensions. Sub-keynote. Music Therapy in Europe. The 5th European Congress for Music Therapy, 22nd April, Naples, Italy.

Garred, R. (2002). The Ontology of Music in Music Therapy. *Voices. A World Forum For Music Therapy*, **1**(3).

Goldberg, F. (1995). The Bonny method of guided imagery and music. In: T. Wigram, B. Saperston and R. West (eds.) *The Art & Science of Music Therapy: A Handbook, pp.* 112–28. Chur: Harwood Academic Publishers.

Goldberg, F.S. (2002). A holographic field theory model of the Bonny method of guided imagery and music (BMGIM). In: K.E. Brusica and D.E. Grocke (eds.) *Guided Imagery and Music. The Bonny Method and Beyond*, pp. 359–77. Gilsum, NH: Barcelona Publishers.

Grocke, D.E. (1999). A Phenomenological Study of Pivotal Moments in Guided Imagery and Music Therapy. Doctoral Thesis, Faculty of Music, University of Melbourne, Victoria, Australia, CD-Rom. (D. Aldridge, ed.)

Grocke, D.E. The role of the therapist in the Bonny method of guided imagery and music (BMGIM). *Music Therapy Perspectives*, **23**(1), 45–52.

Grocke, D.E. (2010). An overview of research in the Bonny method of guided imagery and music. *Voices. A World Forum For Music Therapy*, **10**(3).

Grocke, D. and Wigram, T. (Eds.) (2007). *Receptive Methods in Music Therapy*. London: Jessica Kingsley.

Hannibal, N.J. (2001). Præverbal overføring i musikterapi–kvalittaiv undersøgelse af overføringsprocesser i den musikalske interaktion. PhD dissertation, Aalborg University.

Holck, U. (2004). Turn-taking in music therapy with children with communication disorders. *British Journal of Music Therapy*, **18**(2), 45–54.

Howat, R. (1995). Elisabeth: A case study of an autistic child with individual music therapy. In: T. Wigram, B. Saperston and R. West (eds.) *The Art and Science of Music Therapy*, pp. 238–57. London: Harwood Academic.

Johns, U. (1996). *Songs we can share - Sanger mellom oss*. Nesoddtangen: Musikkpedagogisk Forlag a/s.

Kellogg, J. (1984). *Mandala: Path of Beauty*. Williamsburg, VA: Mari Institute.

Kenny, C.B. (1989). *The Field of Play*. Atascadero, CA: Ridgeview Publishing Company.

Kenny, C. and Stige, B. (eds.) (2002). *Contemporary voices in music therapy: communication, culture and community*. Oslo: UniPub.

Kjeldstadli, K. (1997). Hva er symboler? En introduksjon. *Tidsskrift for etnologi. Dugnad*, **23**(3), 3–25.

Kleive, M. and Stige, B. (1988). *Med lengting liv og song. Prøveordning med musikktilbod for funksjonshemma i Sogn og Fjordane*. Oslo: Samlaget.

Körlin, D. and Wrangsjö, B. (2001). Gender differences in outcome of guided imagery and music. *Nordic Journal of MusicTherapy*, **10**(2), 132–43.

Langenberg, M. (1988). *Vom Handeln zum Behandeln*. Stuttgart: Fischer.

Lee, C. (1996). *Music at The Edge. Music Therapy Experiences of a Musician with AIDS*. London: Routledge.

Lee, C. (2000). A method of analyzing improvisations in music therapy. *Journal of Music Therapy*, XXXVII(2), 146–67.

Lee, C. (2003). *The Architecture of Aesthetic Music Therapy*. Gilsum, NH: Barcelona Publishers.

Leins, A.K., Spintge, R., and Thaut, M. (2010). Music therapy in medical and neurological rehabilitation settings. In: S. Hallam, I. Cross, and M. Thaut (eds.) *The Oxford Handbook of Music Psychology*, pp. 526–35. Oxford: Oxford University Press.

Lyons-Ruth, K. (1998). Implicit relational knowing: Its role in development and psychoanalytic treatment. *Infant Mental Health Journal*, **19**(3), 282–9.

Madsen, C. (1981). *Music Therapy: A Behavioral Guide for the Mentally Retarded*. Washington DC: National Association of Music Therapy.

Madsen, C.K., Cotter, V. and Madsen, C.H. Jr. (1966). A behavioral approach to music therapy. *Journal of Music Therapy*, **5**, 69–71.

Mahns, W. (2004). *Symbolbildung in der analytischen Kindermusiktherapie. Eine qualitative Studie über die Bedeutung der musikalischen Improvisation in der Musiktherapie mit Schulkindern*. Reihe Materialien zur Musiktherapie, Band 6. Münster: LIT-Verlag.

Malloch, S. and Trevarthen, C. (eds.) (2009). *Communicative Musicality. Exploring the basis of human companionship*. Oxford: Oxford University Press.

Maranto, C.D. (Ed.) (1993). *Music Therapy, International Perspectives*. Pipersville, PA: Jeffrey Books.

Martin, R. (2007). *The Effect of a Series of Short GIM Sessions on Music Performance Anxiety*. Master. Music Therapy Department, University of Melbourne, Melbourne.

Maslow, A. (1962). Lessons from the peak experiences. *Journal of Humanistic Psychology*, **2**, 9–18.

Merleau-Ponty, M. (1945/89). *Phenomenology and perception*. London: Routledge.

Moe, T. (2007). Receptiv musikterapi med misbrugspatienter–et pilotprojekt. *Psyke & Logos*, **28**(1), 478.

Myskja, A. (2004). Kan musikkterapi hjelpe pasienter med nevrologiske sykdommer? *Tidsskrift for den norske lægeforening*, **124**(24), 3229–323.

Nass, R. (1971). Some considerations of a psychoanalytic interpretation of music. *Psychoanalytical Quarterly*, **40**, 303–16.

Neugebauer, L. and Aldridge, D. (1998). Communication, heart rate and the musical dialogue. *British Journal of Music Therapy*, **12**(2), 46–52.

Nielsen, V.R. (1996). Musikk i fengsel og frihet. *Nordisk Tidsskrift for musikkterapi*, **5**(2), 111–16.

Nordoff, P. and Robbins, C. (1966). *The Three Bears*. Bryn Mawr, PA: Thedore Presser Company.

Nordoff, P. and Robbins, C. (1969). *Pif-Paf-Poltrie*. Bryn Mawr, PA: Theodore Presser Company.

Nordoff, P. and Robbins, C. (1971/83). *Music Therapy in Special Education* (Second Edition). St. Louis MO: Magnamusic-Baton.

Nordoff, P. and Robbins, C. (1971a). *Therapy in Music for Handicapped Children*. London: Victor Gollancz.

Nordoff, P. and Robbins, C. (1977). *Creative Music Therapy. Individual Treatment for the Handicapped Child*. New York: John Day.

Næss, T. (1989). *Lyd og vekst. En innføring i metoden terapeutisk improvisasjon*. Nesodden: Musikkpedagogisk Forlag.

Næss, T. and Ruud, E. (2008). Fra terapeutisk improvisasjon til samfunnsmusikkterapi. In: G. Trondalen and E. Ruud (eds.) *Perspektiver på musikk og helse. 30 år med norsk musikkterapi*, pp. 465–80. Oslo: Skriftserie fra Senter for musikk og helse. Norges Musikkhøgskole.

Parker, A. (2010). Report on the association for music and imagery: The development of guided imagery and music around the world. *Voices. A World Forum For Music Therapy*, **10** (3).

Pavlicevic, M. (1995). Interpersonal processes in clinical improvisation: Towards a subjectivity objective systematic definition. In: T. Wigram, B. Saperston and R. West (eds.) *The Art and Science of Music Therapy, pp.* 167–80. London: Harwood Academic Publishers.

Pavlicevic, M. (1997). *Music Therapy in Context. Music, Meaning and Relationship*. London: Jessica Kingsley Publishers Ltd.

Pavlicevic, M. (2010). Music in an ambiguous place: Youth development outreach in Eersterust, South Africa. In: B. Stige, G. Andsdell, C. Elefant, and M. Pavlicevic (eds.) *Where Music Helps. Community Music Therapy in Action adn Reflection*, pp. 219–22. Farnham: Ashgate.

Pavlicevic, M. and Andsdell, G. (eds.) (2004). *Community Music Therapy*. London: Jessica Kinglsey Publishers.

Pavlicevic, M. and Trevarthen, C. (1994). Improvisational music therapy and the rehabilitation of persons suffering from chronic schizophrenia. *Journal of Music Therapy*, **31**(2), 86–201.

Pedersen, I.N. (1999). Music therapy as holding and re-organising work with schizophrenic and psychotic patients. In: T. Wigram and J. De Backer (eds.) *Clinical Applications of Music Therapy in Psychiatry*, pp. 24–43. London: Jessica Kingsley Publishers.

Pedersen, I.N. (2002). Analytical music therapy with adults in mental health and in counselling work. In: J. Th. Eschen (ed.) *Analytical Music Therapy*, pp. 64–84. London: Jessica Kingsley Publishers.

Pedersen, I.N. (2007). Counter transference in music therapy: A phenomenological study of counter transference used as a clinical concept by music therapists working with musical improvisation in adult psychiatry. PhD dissertation. Dept. of Communication and Psychology, Aalborg University.

Priestley, M. (1975/85). *Music Therapy in Action*. St. Louis, MO: Magnamusic Baton.

Priestley, M. (1994). *Essays on Analytical Music Therapy*. Phoenixville, PA: Barcelona Publishers.

Robbins, C. and C. Robbins. (1980). *Music for the Hearing Impaired and other Special Groups*. St. Louis, MO: Magnamusic-Baton.

Rolvsjord, R. (2010). *Resource Oriented Music Therapy in Mental Health Care*. Phoenixville, PA: Barcelona Publishers.

Ruud, E. (1980). *Hva er musikkterapi?* Oslo: Gyldendal Norsk Forlag A/S.

Ruud, E. (1980a). *Music Therapy and its Relationship to Current Treatment Theories*. St. Louis, MO: Magnamusic-Baton Inc.

Ruud, E. (1990). *Musikk som kommunikasjon og samhandling*. Oslo: Solum Forlag.

Ruud, E. (1992). *Innføring i systematisk musikkvitenskap*. Oslo: Universitet i Oslo.

Ruud, E. (1996). *Musikk og verdier*. Oslo: Universitetsforlaget.

Ruud, E. (1997). Music and identity. *Nordic Journal of Music Therapy*, **6**(1), 3–13.

Ruud, E. (2004a). *Foreword*. In: G. Ansdell and M. Pavlicevic (eds.) *Community Music Therapy – International Initiatives*. London: Jessica Kingsley Publishers.

Ruud, E. (2004b). Systemisk og framføringsbasert musikkterapi. *Musikkterapi*, **4**, 28–34.

Ruud, E. (2010). *Music therapy – A perspective from the humanities*. Gilsum, NH: Barcelona Publishers.

Scheiby, B. (1998). The role of musical countertransference in analytical music therapy. In: K. Bruscia (ed.) *The Dynamics of Music Psychotherapy*, pp. 213–47. Gilsum, NH: Barcelona Publishers.

Scheiby, B. (2002). Improvisation as a musical healing tool and life approach – theoretical and clinical applications of analytical music therapy improvisation in a short- and long-term rehabilitation facility. In: J. Th. Eschen (ed.) *Analytical Music Therapy*, pp. 115–53. London: Jessica Kingsley Publishers.

Scheiby, B. (2005). An intersubjective approach to music therapy: identification and processing of musical countertransference in a music psychotherapeutic context. *Music Therapy Perspectives, 23*, 8–17.

Scheiby, B. (2010). Analytical music therapy and integrative medicine: The impact of medical trauma on the psyche. In: K. Stewart (ed.) *Music Therapy & Trauma: Bridging Theory and Clinical Practice*, pp. 74–87. New York: Satchnote Press.

Schneck, D.J. and Berger, D.S. (2006). *The Music Effect*. London: Jessica Kingsley Publishers.

Schwabe, C. (1987). *Regulative Musiktherapie. 2. Überarbeitete*. Leipzig: Thieme/Stuttgart: Fischer.

Small, C. (1998). *Musicking : the meanings of performing and listening*. Hanover, NH: University Press of New England.

Standley, J. and Moore, R. (1995). Therapeutic effects of music and mothers voice on premature infants. *Pediatric Nursing, 21*(6), 509–12, 574.

Stensæth, K. (2008). *Musical Answerability. A Theory on the Relationship between Music Therapy Improvisation and the Phenomenon of Action*. PhD. Norwegian Academy of Music. Oslo: Norges musikkhøgskoles publikasjoner 2008:1.

Stern, D.N. (2000). *The Interpersonal World of the Infant. A View from Psychoanalysis & Developmental Psychology*. New York: Basic Books.

Stern, D.N. (2004). *The Present Moment In Psychotherapy and Everyday Life*. New York: W.W. Norton & Company.

Stern, D.N. (2010). *Forms of Vitality: Exploring Dynamic Experience in Psychology, the Arts, Psychotherapy, and Development*. New York: Oxford University Press.

Stige, B. (2002). *Culture-centered Music Therapy*. Gilsum, NH: Barcelona Publishers.

Stige, B. (2003). Elaborations towards a Notions of Community Therapy. Doctoral dissertation. Faculty of Arts, University of Oslo, Oslo.

Stige, B. (Ed.) (2010). Introduction. In: B. Stige, G. Andsdell, C. Elefant and M. Pavlicevic (eds.) *Where Music Helps. Community Music Therapy in Action and Reflection*, pp. 3–16. Farnham: Ashgate.

Stige, B., Ansdell, G., Elefant, C., and Pavlicevic, M. (eds.) (2010). *Where Music Helps. Community Music Therapy in Action and Reflection*. Farnham: Ashgate.

Stige, B. and Aarø, L.E. (2011). *Invitation to Community Music Therapy*. New York, London: Routledge. Taylor and Francis Group.

Storheim, E. (1993). Immanuel Kant. In: T.B. Eriksen (ed.) *Vestens tenkere. Fra Descartes til Nietzsche*. Oslo: Aschehoug.

Streeter, E. (1999). *Definition and use of the musical transference relationship*. In: T. Wigram and J. De Backer (eds.) *Clinical Applications of Music Therapy in Psychiatry*, pp. 84–101. London: Jessica Kingsley Publishers.

Summer, L. (1988). *Guided Imagery and Music in the Institutional Setting*. Saint Louis, MO: Magnamusic-Baton.

Summer, L. (2002). Group music and imagery therapy: Emergent receptive techniques in music therapy practice. In: K.E. Bruscia, and D.E. Grocke (eds.) *Guided imagery and music: The Bonny method and beyond*, pp. 297–306. Gilsum, NH: Barcelona Publishers.

Thaut, M.H. (1990). *Physiological Responses to Music Stimuli. Music Therapy in the Treatment of Adults with Mental Disorders*. New York: Schikerne Books.

Thaut, M.H. (2000). *A scientific model of music in therapy and medicine*. St. Louis, MO: MMB Music.

Thaut, M.H. (2005). Rhythm, human temporality, and brain function. In: D. Miell, R. MacDonald, and D.J. Hargreaves (eds.) *Musical Communication*, pp. 171–92. Oxford: Oxford University Press.

Thaut, M. and Abiru, M. (2010). Rhythmic auditory stimulation in rehabilitation of movement disorders: A review of current research. *Music Perception: An Interdisciplinary Journal, 27*(4), 263.

Trolldalen, G. (1997). Music therapy and interplay. A music therapy project with mothers and children elucidated through the concept of 'appreciative recognition'. *Nordic Journal of Music Therapy*, **6**(1), 14–27.

Trondalen, G. (2005). Improvisasjon i musikkterapipraksis: tradisjon–kunst–teknikk. In: E. Nesheim, I.M. Hanken, and B. Bjøntegaard (eds.) *Flerstemmige Innspill. En artikkelsamling*, pp. 123–43. Oslo: NMH-publikasjoner.

Trondalen, G. (2009–2010). Exploring the rucksack of sadness: Focused, time-limited bonny method of guided imagery and music with a female executive. *Journal of the Association for Music and Imagery*, **12**, 1–20.

Trondalen, G. (2008). Musikkterapi – et relasjonelt perspektiv. In: G. Trondalen and E. Ruud (eds.) *Perspektiver på musikk og helse. 30 år med norsk musikkterapi*, pp. 29–49. Oslo: Norges Musikkhøgskole.

Trondalen, G. and F. Skårderud. (2007). Playing with affects. And the importance of 'affect attunement'. *Nordic Journal of Music Therapy*, **16**(2), 100–11.

Wagner, G. (2007). The Benenzon model of music therapy. *Nordic Journal of Music Therapy*, **16**(2), 146–7.

Wärja, M. (1994). Sounds of music through the spiraling path of individuation: A Jungian approach to music psychotherapy. *Music Therapy Perspectives*, **12**(2), 75–83.

Wigram, T. (2004). Improvisation. *Methods and Techniques for Music Therapy Clinicians, Educators and Students*. London: Jessica Kingsley Publishers.

Wigram, T. and de Backer, J. (Eds.) (1999). *Clinical Applications of Music Therapy in Developmental Disability, Paediatrics and Neurology*. London: Jessica Kingsley Publishers.

Wigram, T., Saperston, B., and West, R. (eds.) (1995). *The Art and Science of Music Therapy*. London: Harwood Academic Publishers.

Wigram, T., Pedersen, I.N., and Bonde, L.O. (2002). *A Comprehensive Guide to Music Therapy. Theory, Clinical Practice, Research and Training*. London: Jessica Kingsley Publishers.

Wilber, K. (1999). *Integral Psychology. The Collected Works of Ken Wilber, Vol. 4*, pp. 423–718. Boston, MA: Shambhala.

Wrangsjö, B. and Körlin, D. (1995). Guided Imagery and Music (GIM) as a psychotherapeutic method in psychiatry. *Journal of the Association for Music and Imagery*, **4**, 79–92.

Section 2

Community Music and Public Health

Chapter 5

Developing Social Models for Research and Practice in Music, Arts, and Health: A Case Study of Research in a Mental Health Setting

Norma Daykin

Introduction

This chapter explores the role of music in promoting health and wellbeing, drawing on social models of health and locating music within the broad field of arts and health. This has been defined as a diverse, multidisciplinary field dedicated to promoting health and wellbeing by connecting people with the power of the arts (State of the Field Committee 2009). This definition encompasses a wide range of art forms, including music, literary and visual arts, as well as arts therapies. Artists from a range of disciplines are increasingly engaged in a wide range of healthcare and community settings in a variety of roles including supporting clinical care, enhancing healthcare environments, and promoting community wellbeing. To date, most research on arts and health focuses on the first two areas, with relatively little research on the impacts of community arts. Further, relatively little research within clinical settings has addressed the social context of participation in arts. Understanding these issues requires different research models and approaches than those used to identify clinical outcomes, and at present, such approaches are relatively underdeveloped. This chapter surveys some of the conceptual frameworks that might support research in addressing the social dimensions of music and arts in healthcare, including perspectives on social capital and empowerment.

This chapter also considers professional development issues for musicians who are engaged in promoting health and wellbeing. As artists they are not necessarily therapists and neither are they assumed to be specialists in healthcare. Their practice falls between several defined fields and professions, including community music, music therapy, and community music therapy. There is an ongoing debate about the definitions and boundaries between these groupings (Ansdell 2002; O'Grady and McFerran 2007). This chapter seeks to contribute to the debate by highlighting some of the professional issues that can arise for artists and staff in participatory arts projects. It draws on qualitative research on an arts project in a UK mental healthcare setting.

The notion of the hospital as a healthy community influenced the research study discussed here. Although concerned with health, the study did not seek to identify clinical outcomes, partly because this was beyond the scope of this small project but also because there is as yet little consensus about what clinical outcomes should be measured and what methodologies should be used to evaluate arts for health activity. Rather, the study focused on the role of participation in promoting subjective experiences of wellbeing as well as enhancing communication and relationships, including interprofessional relationships, within the hospital.

Research on music and health: beyond the medical model

Since the review of evidence on arts and health by Rosalia Staricoff (2004) there has been a growth in the volume of research that seeks to understand the role of music and creativity in health. Much of this work has been focused on clinical outcomes, with several reviews of music and music and arts therapy now included in the Cochrane Library, which is generally regarded as the gold standard for evidence from clinical trials (Sonke et al. 2009). Findings from this body of work have guided policy, with arts therapies now included in national guidelines for the care of patients with schizophrenia in the UK. Within the UK, senior policy makers have recognized the evidence base for arts in healthcare (Cayton 2007).

Despite these advances, arts and health research is still an underdeveloped field, which currently faces many challenges deriving from the complex nature of arts interventions and the diversity of art forms, settings, participants, goals, and health issues to be explored (Clift et al. 2009). These challenges are pronounced within the community-focused arts and health field where there is widespread uncertainty about what research and evaluation methods to use (White 2009).

A further challenge relates to the development of suitable theoretical frameworks for researching the role of music and arts. Historically, healthcare provision and research in the developed countries has been shaped by the doctrine of Western scientific medicine (WSM). The consequent problems of biological reductionism, individualism, medicalization, and a failure to fully understand the social and material conditions that create ill health have been documented (Nettleton 2006). While WSM has been increasingly under challenge since the 1970s (Kelleher et al. 2005), the medical model has continued to shape research, including research on music and arts.

One attempt to redress this has been through the development of qualitative research, since many aspects of music and arts are not amenable to measurement (White and Angus 2003; Hacking et al. 2008). On the whole, however, developments in qualitative research on arts and health have not kept pace with those in quantitative research. A recent review found that outside of arts therapies research, much available qualitative evidence for arts and health is from project evaluations that often fail to engage with appropriate analytic frameworks and procedures. For example, there is a tendency to rely on face value reporting rather than interpretation of participants' accounts of their experiences of arts projects. There remains for many practitioners an underlying confusion about the purpose of qualitative research, with a conflation of research and advocacy, and a tendency to report 'outcomes' using language and frameworks more appropriate for quantitative research (Daykin et al. 2008a). A key challenge facing both quantitative and qualitative research on arts in healthcare is the development of appropriate conceptual frameworks. Concepts such as empowerment and social inclusion are often alluded to, and many claims are made for arts in respect of these. However, these concepts are seldom well elaborated or critically discussed in arts and health research.

Music and health: social models

Social research on health and wellbeing incorporates diverse perspectives and approaches but overall it draws attention to three domains in which the health and wellbeing of individuals are constituted: the economic and political domain, which shapes access and distribution of resources necessary to sustain wellbeing; the discourses and discursive practices that sustain social relationships and within a particular field; and the micro-level interactions through which individuals generate meaning and make sense of their world.

When music and arts are examined in terms of these economic, discursive, and reflexive domains, a number of paradoxes and challenges become apparent. One issue is the impact of

social inequalities: unequal access to music and arts may mediate people's experiences of participation. A further problem relates to the role of discourses of music and creativity in constructing
social relationships and hierarchies (Williams 2001; Ruud 2008).

A key challenge is addressing elitist and hierarchical notions surrounding creativity as well as
cultural essentialism and the impact of stereotypes, such as the association between creativity and
suffering (Daykin 2005). These are often reinforced through phenomena such as celebrity culture
and media representations that influence many people's perceptions of the arts. This partly
explains why participants in arts projects sometimes express initial reluctance to take part.
Common responses include anxiety about not being 'musical' or 'talented', qualities that are
often assumed to be inherent rather than socially constructed (Daykin et al. 2007b, 2008b).

As well as notions of creativity, broader sociopolitical discourses can influence experiences of
participation in arts at a micro-level. In a recent study of hospital arts, funding mechanisms and
notions of modernization were found to influence perceptions of aesthetics (Daykin et al. 2010).
On one level, arts were constructed within a discourse of 'prestige' as adding value and quality to
healthcare environments. This was welcomed by some stakeholders as helping to de-stigmatize
these settings. On the other hand, it created tension with the goal of 'authenticity,' which privi-
leges the notion that arts projects and the works they produce should reflect and validate the
identities of the members of a given community. This is reinforced by notions of patient and
public involvement which have been strongly emphasized in health policy in recent years
(Crawford et al. 2002; Daykin et al. 2007a). A key challenge for projects that involve professional
musicians is defining the roles of participants, who are variously constructed: as 'patients' with
needs that can be met by arts; as 'stakeholders' who should be consulted about the development
of strategies; and as 'artists.'

Social capital, empowerment, and social action

Participatory music making is often viewed as empowering. In relation to empowerment, there
are different models to consider, such as consumerism, which emphasizes the notion of informed
choice, and liberationism, which focuses on self-advocacy and voice (Starkey 2003). This suggests
that notions of empowerment need to be more closely defined and differentiated in relation to
specific social contexts. For example, empowerment may be shaped by social forces including age,
gender, and ethnicity. Hence research on young people's experiences of performing arts has identified the negative impact of stereotypical representations of youth that mediate these experiences
(Mattingly 2001). Empowerment in this context means generating alternative forms of community representation as well as intervention at the individual level.

Linked to empowerment is the concept of social capital, which has had a significant influence
on the development of community arts. Most definitions follow Putnam (1995, 2000), viewing
social capital in terms of connections, networks, norms and trust. High levels of participation in
community activity are seen to encourage shared norms and the development of trusting relationships that facilitate reciprocity. The consequent development of networks is seen as a particularly strong marker of social capital. Hence participation in arts may be a means of generating
positive social capital leading to positive health outcomes such as increased access to services and
health promotion, reduced inequalities and disadvantage, meaningful social roles and purpose,
and a greater sense of control (Osborne et al. 2009).

Although these positive outcomes are difficult to demonstrate in empirical research, evidence
suggests that there may be a positive effect on mortality and morbidity of participation in cultural
activities. A recent study of over 7000 industrial employees in Finland followed-up over 18 years
found improved survival rates of those employees who were culturally engaged. These differences
were found to exist even when other variables such as education and income are controlled.

These effects were attributed to the fact that culturally engaged employees face reduced risk of death from external causes such as accidents, violence, and suicide (Vaananen et al. 2009). Mixed methods research by Secker et al. (2007) see also Hacking et al. (2008) found that participation in arts led to significant improvements in a quantitative measure of empowerment, particularly self-efficacy and positive outlook. The study researched projects that were open to people with and without mental health conditions, but the changes in empowerment and mental health were strongest for participants with 'clinically significant' mental health problems.

Research on social capital during the last decade has tended to follow Putnam's normative approach (Fulkerson 2008). However, some researchers have followed what is regarded as the more critical approach of Bourdieu (1986). These researchers emphasize the fact that social capital is, like economic, cultural, and symbolic capital, unequally distributed (Osborne et al. 2009). Further, they view social capital as a resource that can be used to create or maintain social inequality, reinforcing power relationships within and between communities and enabling people both to advance their own position and to exclude and obstruct the goals of others (Muntaner and Lynch 2002; Navarro 2002; Osborne et al. 2009,). This body of research suggests that social capital is neither an 'asset' that can be acquired or conferred nor a straightforward cure for social divisions (Kawachi and Berkman, 2001; Osborne et al. 2009). The acquisition of social capital is a constant struggle rather than a straightforward outcome of participation.

Empirical research has explored the barriers to acquiring social capital, which include social position, social processes that define 'normality' and micro-level group dynamics that reinforce unequal power relationships (Campbell and McLean 2002; Fulkerson 2008; Osborne et al. 2009). All of these barriers potentially limit music and arts participation and need to be addressed in models of empowerment. Campbell and McClean's study of the factors shaping African-Caribbean participation in local community networks in the UK highlights the gap between, on the one hand, the widespread adoption by young people of music, language, and style associated with Afro-Caribbean culture with, on the other, the lack of integration and the exclusion of Afro-Caribbean people at the level of the country's political and economic mainstream (Campbell and McLean 2002). Osborne et al. (2009) present a detailed analysis of the way in which social processes that generate social capital reinforce gender inequalities: by excluding women from powerful networks; by naturalizing expectations and assumptions about gender appropriate activities; and through group dynamics, including conflict and tension, which can devalue women's participation.

This suggests that positive impacts of music and arts participation cannot be assumed: these forms of practice may also have negative or unintended consequence of increasing social inequalities rather than reducing them. Participation, as well as leading to health-enhancing social capital, can be potentially damaging for health. Projects that fail to recognize these aspects risk disengagement, frustration, and disappointment (Bolam et al. 2006).

Critics of Bourdieu have identified as somewhat deterministic his focus on social stratification and the reproduction of inequalities (Franklin et al. 2006). These authors draw attention to the possibility that inequalities can be contested as well as reproduced, through processes of resistance. This suggests that participatory music making for health can serve as a form of social action, allowing participants to challenge limiting discourses and reconstruct creativity in ways that are beneficial. In this context, music-making can be seen as a potential resource for networking and community building, offering opportunities to redress inequalities and increase status through participation in valued activities such as performance (Procter 2004, 2006). As Campbell and McClean (2002) suggest, one way in which marginalized groups can challenge their status, improve their life circumstances, or raise the levels of social recognition they receive from other groups is through identity construction. Rather than drawing on fixed and predetermined notions of identity, these authors view identity construction as a reflexive process. They also recognize the importance of collective identity in relation to processes such as social capital.

The notion of identity construction offers a useful tool for understanding the impact of music and arts on health. Participatory arts projects can offer opportunities for engagement with creative identities and this has been recognized as a form of empowerment, particularly for those whose identities have been stigmatized, for example, following diagnosis and treatment of a mental health condition (Secker et al. 2007; Hacking et al. 2008). Understanding the role of music and arts in constructing meaning and shaping identity in everyday life has been given impetus by the work of sociologists such as Tia Denora, who has explored the role of music as a technology of the self (DeNora 1995, 2000). Within this perspective activities such as music listening offer a means of taking care of oneself at many levels, balancing energies and moods, as well as physical activity during periods of wellness and ill health (Batt-Rawden et al. 2005).

Narrative approaches in particular have explored identity and biography construction in relation to illness and health. Narrative analysis takes as its starting point the notion that individuals seek to impose order on experience and that when faced with disruptions to the life course, such as ill health, personal stories and reflexive biographies play a restorative role (Bury 1982, 2001; Riessman 1993; Frank 1995; Becker 1997). More recently, notions of disruption have been challenged by research that has emphasized the non-disruptive nature of some experiences of diagnosis of serious illness (Sinding and Wiernikowski 2008).Nevertheless, these perspectives are of value in that they recognize narratives and identity construction as processes that go beyond the personal, attending to cultural scripts and discourses that mediate experiences of arts, health, and participation.

Professional issues

Musicians and artists are increasingly engaged in healthcare settings and their work is seen as contributing to a wide range of goals including clinical outcomes, wellbeing, empowerment, satisfaction, and enhanced healthcare environments. The emergence of artists in healthcare as a nascent professional grouping has stimulated reflection in the related professions of music and art therapy, with some therapists arguing that these professions have been too strongly influenced by the medical model and that they need to revisit their artistic roots.

One professional challenge is the risk of medicalization. The occupational strategies of emergent healthcare professionals have historically fluctuated between medicalized and non-medicalized discourses. For example, in nursing, ambiguity and tension has sometimes been caused by the adoption of different strategies of professionalization. On the one hand, nurses have gained status, prestige, and financial rewards by following the strategy of role-extension in which they increasingly take on tasks previously restricted to doctors. However, this strategy has to some extent confounded the development of practice on the basis of autonomous forms of knowledge such as the discourse on holism favoured by some nurse educators during the 1980s (Witz 1992; Daykin and Clarke 2000). Similar tensions characterize the debate about the development of arts therapy professions in the UK where they have recently been included in healthcare regulatory frameworks (Davis 1995). For example, some music therapists have suggested that a negative consequence of professionalization is the dominance of perspectives from medicine and psychiatry (Ansdell 2002; Procter 2004, 2006). Developments such as community music therapy represent an attempt to shift the balance. Hence community music therapists are seen as crossing a boundary between 'therapy' and 'community music' at the same time as reclaiming an earlier radical vision of music therapy as a social movement that can contribute to social change as well as a treatment provision (Ruud 2008).

The role of artists working in healthcare settings is sometimes ambiguous, falling between established boundaries. Outside of music and arts therapies, there are relatively few formal training programmes for participatory artists. There is as yet no consensus about the prerequisites for this work in terms of education, training, and professional development. Too often, artists report experiences of moving from project to project with few formal opportunities for professional development or reflection.

The impact of participatory music and arts on a hospital community: a case study

The remainder of this chapter discusses findings from research on a participatory arts project in a mental health setting (Daykin and Feldtkeller 2009). As well as process evaluation, the study sought to encourage reflective practice by supporting artists using an action–learning approach. It also provided an opportunity to document the skills, strategies, and support structures the artists found useful in their attempts to deliver safe and satisfying experiences of music and arts in a complex mental healthcare setting.

The project involved four artists working in collaboration to provide participatory arts activity for adults and older adults in a large campus-style hospital. A musician, a poet, and a two-dimensional visual artist offered participatory workshops while a fourth, reflective artist worked across the residencies, producing drawings and other outputs that sought to capture and illuminate the experiences of the project. The artists were engaged as freelance artists and not as therapists: they were not specialists in mental health and they were not party to detailed clinical information about individuals such as diagnosis or care plans. They did not work with participants unaccompanied but were supported by staff from the occupational therapy and arts therapy departments who co-facilitated sessions. Showcasing and performance elements distinguished this project from existing arts therapy activities within the hospital. Participants' work was shown and performed at a final showcase event in April 2009, which was attended by service users, staff, carers, and external stakeholders.

Evaluation research sought to explore the impact of the project using qualitative methods including participant observation and focus groups. Observation of seven sessions across the art forms was undertaken by two researchers, one (this author) a university academic and the other a hospital-based researcher who is also a dance and movement therapist. It was designed to be unobtrusive: the observers participated fully in the arts activity and wrote up field notes afterwards. If any individual in the group objected to a researcher being present, or retrospectively to the notes being written up, the policy was that the research would not go ahead. In practice, no such objections were raised.

As well as a project evaluation, the research incorporated a professional development element in which the four artists and the project manager met with the university researcher in a series of three reflective learning cycles. Thematic analysis of field notes and audio recordings of focus group discussions was inductive, iterative, and informed by principles of constructivist grounded theory (Charmaz 2000). All participants gave informed consent for the research, which was reviewed by the local NHS Research Ethics Committee and the University Research Ethics Committee.

A key focus of the research was on the nature of participation. In this particular setting, forms of participation were complex and diverse. While some participants were able to engage with arts activities such as drumming for sustained periods, the presence of others was more fleeting. Some individuals were clearly able to 'shine'. However, participation in group activity was affected by individuals' healthcare needs including mental health conditions, severity of symptoms, and the impact of medication on mood, concentration and energy levels. In this context, the artists demonstrated a wide range of skills. As well as arts-specific and generic facilitation skills, these were identified as empowerment for arts and health. The artists worked with the therapies staff to facilitate choice, demystify arts processes, affirm identities, and support health and wellbeing, for instance, by adapting to participants' impairments.

The goal of showcasing work distinguished this project which was culture-centred rather than individualistic in its focus (O'Grady and McFerran 2007). Some participants were very keen to take part and many took a real pride in showing their work. While not everyone was well enough to take part, some participants whose mental health needs were relatively acute were able to connect with the arts processes, often through biographical stories and snippets. In music sessions, people often mentioned previous experiences of playing or singing: many of these were positive, linked with the valued ability 'to do' something.

Issues of empowerment arose from the beginning of the project. For some participants choosing whether or not to take part, both in the project and the research, was the first time they had been able to exercise choice and control over what happened to them since they were admitted to hospital. Some participants expressed apprehension about taking part. Doubts were also sometimes expressed during the sessions, usually focused on the question of whether participants' art was 'good enough'. Wider cultural notions of creativity were often invoked in participants' responses. These included notions of 'fame', reflected in questions such as 'Are we going to release this on YouTube?' and fears about exploitation, reflected in questions about whether someone might appropriate the recorded music and use it for their own purposes.

The formality of some processes heightened issues of power and control. Participants needed to give written consent for their work to be shown or performed. All participants needed to agree, no matter how fleeting their engagement had been, and this could potentially disappoint some people. Some staff expressed unease about the consent process, stating that this could interfere with the creative process and anticipating that participants would not want to sign forms. These issues were compounded by the need for research consent. Some participants did not want to sign documents. On the other hand, the experience of giving consent sometimes reinforced participants' positive experiences of choice and decision-making.

A key issue that arose was that of safe practice. Working with support was a key skill demonstrated by the artists. Clinical and therapy staff played a crucial role in ensuring successful delivery of the workshops. They mentored artists, supported workshops, encouraged participation, and helped to facilitate showcase events. They also contributed to research and project management, managing risk and establishing boundaries in order to frame safe practice. Before each session, the artists met with a member of staff to discuss their session plan, and they met again afterwards to review the session. These 'up-brief' and 'down-brief' sessions were seen as key to identifying potential issues of risk and safety as well as enabling clinical and therapy staff to follow-up any issues and support needs that might have arisen during the activity for particular participants. In general, artists and staff found this process extremely beneficial, however, artists sometimes found themselves confused by a lack of consensus between the professionals about what constituted 'safe' practice. The professionals themselves came from different backgrounds and this was reflected in their different ways of working and different perspectives on risk and boundaries. This highlights the need for reflexivity. While artists who are not therapists may need to be guided by professionals, they also need to develop the capacity for sensing the impact of their work and minimizing potentially negative impacts.

As well as exploring the impact of the study on participants, the research examined the impact of arts and research on relationships between staff, researchers, and artists. Issues of power and control also emerged here. The artists needed to demonstrate high level skills in communication and negotiation with these different groups. Interprofessional relationships can be an issue in such projects, which potentially challenge the roles of existing therapy staff, some of whom may feel that their creative skills and professional experience are being overlooked. Some staff seemed initially ambivalent about the project as this introduced unknown elements, potentially adding to their workloads. The research project generated a further challenge in the form of the presence of researchers, another variable to be managed. These tensions reduced as staff took control over decision-making, for example, deciding when to schedule research observations, which to some extent limited the methodology. On the other hand, once their own role was more certain, staff felt more in control and were enthusiastic participants, with some demonstrating huge commitment to making the project a success. Overall, the project and the research both stimulated a heightened sense of stake, with many people wanting to contribute to discussions about both elements as these developed.

The therapies staff identified many benefits from the project for participants and on this basis they were keen to repeat the experience. A key strength identified was the project's contained nature: the focus on an endpoint was motivating and invigorating. They also described themselves as having gained from the project in a number of ways: expanding horizons; working with new people and groups; reflecting and learning; developing new skills and techniques; rekindling enthusiasm for work and mitigating burnout; engendering a sense of wellbeing; and increasing confidence.

The project also stimulated collaboration and connection, with senior staff from different parts of the hospital making unprecedented visits to find out what was going on in the therapies department. This created a heightened sense of visibility among therapies staff as well as a strong sense of their work being valued. One manager commented that the project had challenged accepted hierarchies, making working relationships more equal. A key perception of staff was that the project brought together professionals and patients from different units, creating a sense of community within the hospital. Further, the project allowed new connections and external partnerships to be formed.

Implications for research and practice

This chapter has argued for a broadening of current research agendas in arts and health. Understanding of the impacts of arts in healthcare can be advanced by rigorous study, not just of outcomes and impacts on individuals but of the social contexts that mediate these effects. This chapter has highlighted the complexity of issues such as participation and the need for situated research in order to understand its impact on empowerment and social capital. This discussion raises key issues for those involved in delivering or developing arts provision in mental healthcare settings. It points towards the potential role of arts activity in promoting participation and engagement, perhaps signalling a role for arts in policy and service development as well as clinical practice. It also highlights the resources needed to underpin effective and sustainable participatory arts activity including support for all those involved in programme delivery.

This chapter has also addressed some practice issues. Participatory arts practice is an emergent area of healthcare practice for which appropriate protocols are still in development. While the results of small studies such as the one discussed here cannot necessarily be generalized they do highlight some of the potential benefits, impacts, and challenges of using music and arts to promote participation and inclusion in particular contexts.

A key challenge is to define and understand the role and impact of arts beyond medicalized discourse. In this project staff and service users valued the fresh perspectives and approaches the artists brought to hospital life. These enlivened and invigorated the hospital as a community.

The issue of whether mental healthcare experience was a prerequisite for successful arts practice was considered and the consensus was that this was of less importance than the artists' ability to inspire and include people through their art. The recent growth of arts in healthcare as an area of practice signals that there is an appetite for arts-based as well as therapeutic approaches to complex health challenges.

One issue is the provision of professional development opportunities for artists, who, while maintaining an arts-based focus, nevertheless need to adapt to healthcare agendas and complex frameworks of governance in order to work safely and effectively. Further challenges are inter-professional working and appropriate use of strategies such as critical reflection to support sustainable development. While it would be unrealistic to expect artists to be experts in all of these areas, it seems important that they are able to understand and respond to these broad agendas that impinge on their work.

Finally, research and evaluation is a key issue. Those competing for scarce healthcare resources are under pressure to justify the effectiveness and impact of their work, but to evaluate rigorously requires resources and skills that are beyond the scope of most arts projects. One of the dangers is overclaiming the impact of arts in response to demands for 'magic bullets' and quick solutions to complex problems. Greater knowledge and understanding of research and evaluation, including social models of research, is therefore needed across the emergent arts and health field.

References

Ansdell, G. (2002). Community Music therapy & the winds of change. *Voices: A World Forum for Music Therapy,* **2**(2).

Batt-Rawden, K.B., DeNora, T., and Ruud, E. (2005). Music listening and empowerment in health promotion: A study of the role and significance of music in everyday life of the long-term ill. *Nordic Journal of Music Therapy,* **14**(2), 120–35.

Becker, G. (1997). *Disrupted Lives: How people create meaning in a chaotic world.* London: University of California Press.

Bolam, B., McClean, C., Pennington, A., and Gillies, P. (2006). Using new media to build social capital for health: a qualitative process evaluation study of participation in the CityNet project. *Journal of Health Psychology,* **11**(2), 297–308.

Bourdieu, P. (1986). The forms of capital. In: J.G. Richardson (ed.) *The handbook of theory and research for the sociology of education,* pp. 241–58. New York: Greenwood.

Bury, M. (1982). Chronic illness as biographical disruption. *Sociology of Health and Illness,* **4**(2), 167–82.

Bury, M. (2001). Illness narratives: fact or fiction? *Sociology of Health and Illness,* **23**(3), 263–85.

Campbell, C. and McLean, C. (2002). Ethnic identities, social capital and health inequalities: factors shaping African-Caribbean participation in local community networks in the UK. *Social Science and Medicine,* **55**, 643–57.

Cayton, H. (2007). *The report of the review of arts and health working group.* London: Department of Health.

Charmaz, C. (2000). Grounded theory: Objectivist and constructivist methods. In: N. Denzin and Y. Lincoln (eds.) *Handbook of Qualitative Research (2nd edn.),* pp. 509–35. London: Sage.

Clift, S., Camic, P.M., Chapman, B., Clayton, G., Daykin, N., Eades, G., *et al.* (2009). The state of arts and health in England. *Arts and Health,* **1**(1), 6–35.

Crawford, M.J., Rutter, D., Manley, C., Weaver, T., Bhui, K., Fulop, N., *et al.* (2002). Systematic review of involving patients in the planning and development of healthcare. *British Medical Journal,* **325**(7375), 1263–5.

Davis, C. (1995). *Gender and the Professional Predicament in Nursing.* Buckingham: Open University Press.

Daykin, N. (2005). Disruption, dissonance and embodiment, creativity, health and risk in music narratives. *Health: An Interdisciplinary Journal for the Social Study of Health, Illness and Medicine,* **9**(1), 67–87.

Daykin, N. and Clarke, B. (2000). They'll still get the bodily care. Discourses of care and relationships between nurses and health care assistants in the NHS. *Sociology of Health and Illness,* **22**(3), 249–363.

Daykin, N. and Feldtkeller, B. (2009). *Arts @ Callington Rd: Project Evaluation Report.* Bristol: University of the West of England.

Daykin, N., Evans, D., Petsoulas, C., and Sayer, A. (2007a). Evaluating the impact of patient and public involvement initiatives on UK health services: a systematic review. *Evidence and Policy,* **3**(1), 47–65.

Daykin, N., McClean, S., and Bunt, L. (2007b). Music Therapy in Cancer Care: Participants' Accounts. *Health: An Interdisciplinary Journal for the Social Study of Health, Illness and Medicine,* **11**(3), 349–70.

Daykin, N., Orme, J., Evans, D., and Salmon, D. (2008a). The impact of participation in performing arts on adolescent health and behaviour: a systematic review of the literature. *Journal of Health Psychology,* **13**(2), 251–64.

Daykin, N., McClean, S., and Pilkington, P. (2008b). *Evaluation of Art-Lift: A Partnership Arts and Health Project.* Bristol: University of the West of England.

Daykin, N., Byrne, E., Soteriou, T., and O'Connor, S. (2010). Using arts to enhance mental healthcare environments: findings from qualitative research. *Arts and Health, an International Journal of Research, Policy and Practice,* **2**(1), 33–46.

DeNora, T. (1995). The musical composition of social reality? Music, action and reflexivity. *Sociological Review,* **43**(2), 295–315.

DeNora, T. (2000). *Music in Everyday Life.* Cambridge: Cambridge University Press.

Frank, A.W. (1995). *The Wounded Storyteller: Body, Illness and Ethics.* London: University of Chicago Press.

Franklin, J., Holland, J., and Edwards, R. (2006). W(h)ither Social Capital? In: R. Edwards, J. Franklin, and J. Holland (eds.) *Assessing Social Capital: Concept, Policy and Practice,* pp. 1–13. Newcastle: Cambridge Scholars Press.

Fulkerson, G.M. (2008). The evolution of a contested concept: a meta-analysis of social capital definitions and trends (1988–2006). *Sociological Inquiry,* **78**(4), 536–57.

Hacking, S., Secker, J., Spandler, H., Kent, L., and Shenton, J. (2008). Evaluating the impact of participatory art projects for people with mental health needs. *Health and Social Care in the Community,* **16**(6), 638–48.

Kawachi, I. and Berkman, L.F. (2001). Social cohesion, social capital and health. In: L. Berkman and I. Karachi (eds.) *Social epidemiology,* pp. 174–90. New York: Oxford University Press.

Kelleher, D., Gabe, J., and Williams, G. (2005). *Challenging Medicine.* London: Routledge.

Mattingly, D. (2001). Place, teenagers and representations: lessons from a community theatre project. *Social and Cultural Geography,* **2**(4), 445–59.

Muntaner, C. and Lynch, J. (2002). Social capital, class gender and race conflict, and population health: An essay review of Bowling Alone's implications for social epidemiology. *International Journal of Epidemiology,* **31**, 261–7.

Navarro, V. (2002). A critique of social capital. *International Journal of Health Services,* **32**, 423–32.

Nettleton, S. (2006). *The Sociology of Health and Illness.* Cambridge: Polity.

O'Grady, L. and McFerran, K. (2007). Community music therapy and its relationship to community music: where does it end? *Nordic Journal of Music Therapy,* **16**(1), 14–16.

Osborne, K., Baum, F. and Zeirsch, A. (2009). Negative consequences of community group participation for women's mental health and well-being: implications for gender aware social capital building. *Journal of Community and Applied Social Psychology,* **19**, 212–24.

Procter, S. (2004). Playing politics: Community music therapy and the therapeutic redistribution of music capital for mental health. In: M. Pavlicevic and G. Ansdell (eds.) *Community Music Therapy,* pp. 214–230. London: Jessica Kingsley Publishers.

Procter, S. (2006). What are we playing at? Social capital and music therapy. In: R. Edwards, J. Franklin, and J. Holland (eds.) *Assessing Social Capital: Concept, Policy and Practice,* pp. 146–62. Newcastle: Cambridge Scholars Press.

Putnam, D.R. (1995). Bowling alone: America's declining social capital. *Journal of Democracy,* **6**(1), 65–78.

Putnam, R. (2000). *Bowling Alone: the collapse and revival of American community*. New York: Simon and Schuster.

Riessman, C.K. (1993). *Narrative Analysis*. London: Sage.

Ruud, E. (2008). Music in therapy: increasing possiblities for action. *Music & Arts in Action,* **1**(1), 46–60.

Secker, J., Hacking, S., Spandler, H., Kent, L., and Shenton, J. (2007). *Mental Health, Social Inclusion and Arts. Developing the evidence base Final Report.* Chelmsford: Anglia Ruskin University/Department of Health.

Sinding, C. and Wiernikowski, J. (2008). Disruption foreclosed: older women's cancer narratives. *Health: An Interdisciplinary Journal for the Social Study of Health, Illness and Medicine,* **12**(3), 389–411.

Sonke, J., Rollins, J., Brandman, R., and Graham-Pole, J. (2009). The state of the arts in healthcare in the United States. *Arts and Health, an International Journal of Research, Policy and Practice,* **1**(2), 107–3.

Staricoff, R.L. (2004). *Arts in health: a review of the medical literature*. London: Arts Council England.

Starkey, F. (2003). The 'empowered debate': Consumerist, professional and liberational perspectives in health and social care. *Social Policy and Society,* **2**, 273–84.

State of the Field Committee. (2009). *State of the field report: Arts in healthcare 2009*. Washington, DC: Society for the Arts in Healthcare.

Vaananen, A., Murray, M., Koskinen, A., Vahtera, J., Kouvonen, A., and Kivimaki, M. (2009). Engagement in cultural activities and cause-specific mortality: prospective cohort study. *Preventive Medicine,* **49**, 142–7.

White, M. (2009). *Arts Development in Community Health, a social tonic*. Oxford: Radcliffe.

White, M. and Angus, J. (2003). *Arts and Adult Mental Health Literature Review*. Centre for Arts and Humanities in Health and Medicine: University of Durham.

Williams, A. (2001). *Constructing Musicology*. Aldershot: Ashgate.

Witz, A. (1992). *Professions and Patriarcy*. London: Routledge.

Chapter 6

Community Music and Social/Health Psychology: Linking Theoretical and Practical Concerns

Michael Murray and Alexandra Lamont

Music is an inherently social act, and one which contains enormous potential to bring people together and to facilitate various forms of social action. The process of engaging with other people through music has been applied to a wide range of health-related functions, including: communication and emotional sharing for those with disabilities and special needs; maintaining healthy brain activity and counteracting cognitive decline in the elderly; alleviating depression and anxiety by raising spirits; providing regular commitments to attend events which combat inactivity; and providing social support which reduces feelings of isolation and loneliness (Clift et al. 2010).

However, despite this intrinsic sociability, much of the research on the effects of music for health and wellbeing has focused on the individual in one way or another, particularly through the use of individual psychological measures of constructs such as quality of life, satisfaction, or emotional wellbeing (e.g. Bailey and Davidson 2005; Clift et al. 2010) as well as more direct measures of physical health such as levels of cortisol (Kreutz et al. 2004). This draws on a tradition of individual and largely positivist research arguing that health and subjective wellbeing can be simply predicted by various individual characteristics and activities. For example, it has been demonstrated that being more physically active can help redress many lifestyle stresses and lead to greater levels of subjective wellbeing (Biddle and Ekkekakis 2005). Similarly, choral singing has been shown to reduce tension and increase hedonic tone (Valentine and Evans 2001). The *group* in this kind of approach functions simply as an enabling context in which musical activity can take place.

A different approach to music-making in groups is that of community music, a form of musical activity that is designed to transform and mobilize communities. This approach has many similarities to other forms of community art, and has considerable potential to achieve more than purely musical goals in terms of identity, health, and wellbeing (e.g. Faulkner and Davidson 2006). The aim of this chapter is to consider in more detail what is meant by the term community and how it connects with community music, to explore a number of examples from diverse settings, and to consider the short- and long-term impact of community music on the participants and the wider community.

Dimensions of community

Community is very much a contested term, theoretically, politically and practically. Hillery (1955) identified 94 different definitions of community in the research literature and after reviewing these concluded that there is 'no complete agreement as to the nature of community' (p. 119). A number of different social scientific approaches to understanding the concept have been put forward over the past few years, including those informed by critical perspectives on social capital, empowerment, and community action (e.g. Campbell and Murray 2004; Ledwith 2005; Arneil 2006; see also Daykin, Chapter 5, this volume). To complement Daykin's chapter we focus here on approaches drawing on social representation and narrative theory.

Social representation theory is concerned with exploring the shared and dynamic nature of social knowledge that develops in everyday social interaction and provides people with an orientation to their social and material world. As Moscovici (1973) explained, social representations 'do not represent simply "opinions about", "images of" or "attitudes towards", but "theories" or "branches of knowledge" in their own right, for the discovery and organisation of reality' (p. xiii). A community can be defined as a group or collective with a common social representation and a common identity (Howarth 2001). It is the common assumptions which provide coherence to a community and distinguishes it from another. Communities can also be a resource for empowerment whereby they can take action as a collective to access resources and to challenge negative social representations of them held by outsiders (e.g. Murray and Crummett 2010). It is through this process of challenge and counter-challenge that a community becomes more aware of its strengths.

A related concept is that of narrative, which can be defined as an organized interpretation of events (Sarbin 1986). Research on narrative has often focused on the individual story, but we can analyse narrative at different social levels from the individual to the societal (Murray 2000). A community narrative is the shared story held by members of a community. It defines the community's history and how it is distinguished from neighbouring communities. As such narrative provides a temporal and historical dimension to social representations. It is not only concerned about past events but can also be concerned about future possibilities. The narrative can thus become an organizing framework to facilitate social change.

Community psychology and community arts

Much of the concerns of community psychology focus on the process of working with communities to promote such social change. This involves challenging established restrictive social representations and promoting a new narrative that offers potential for something different. In participating in community action the residents of a community have the opportunity of challenging established power and also of growing in power themselves (cf. Campbell and Jovchelovitch 2000). This process of *empowerment* has been central to community action (Ledwith 2005). It is a much debated concept, particularly with regard to the extent to which it is real or symbolic. As with the individualistic approach looking at subjective wellbeing, much of the research on empowerment has concentrated on feelings or a sense of empowerment rather than actual changes in power relationships. Community psychology offers the potential of promoting real social change.

Community health psychology attempts to work with groups or communities to identify how they see their worlds and to explore opportunities for change. The initial focus is on exploring their worlds in a collaborative manner, rather than imposing a particular agenda. As Jovchelovitch (2007) explained:

> Contrary to the idea that local representational systems need to be changed or improved as a matter of course, the first task of researchers [and, we would add, of community musicians] is to 'understand the understandings' of local people and listen to the other (p. 165).

It is through this process of listening and support that residents can be encouraged to reflect upon their practices and to grow in confidence through collective action.

One form of collective action is that promoted through community arts. Webster (2005, p. 2) has distinguished community arts from other forms of art on three criteria:

1) It promotes participation, regardless of the existing level of skill or 'talent';
2) It is undertaken by a group who either have the same collective identity, or a goal greater than the art form itself, or both;
3) It is developed primarily to provide opportunities for people who through economic or social circumstance have little access to the means to participate in the Arts.

Webster further argued that community art is 'not defined by art form but by process' (Webster 2005, p. 2). The success of community arts is thus not in the classic sense of its aesthetic quality, but rather the extent that it can contribute to some form of personal and social transformation. As Meade and Shaw (2007) articulate, the power of community arts lies in its capacity to

> enter attentively into the experience of others, excavating and exploring causes of flaws and wounds in society, thinking critically about structures and relations of power and acting creatively and collectively to transform the world for the better (p. 414).

As with other forms of community psychology, work in community arts can be compromised to serve the interests of the state more so than that of the community. Meade and Shaw (2007) caution that the arts can provide 'a convenient means of political displacement, distracting attention from the real causes of social problems' (p. 416). In this sense we can contrast art as anaesthetic, by which it dulls awareness of the state, with art as aesthetic, which can enable people to see through the hidden veils of control and also assert a new agenda. This tension between accommodation and critique is played out in the everyday practice of community art. It is why it is necessary for community arts workers to reflect upon the process and to consider who are the main beneficiaries of the actions. The same tensions are apparent in community music.

Community music

Sound Sense, a UK agency that promotes community music, defines it as a practice that

> involves musicians from any musical discipline working with people to develop active and creative participation in music. It is concerned with putting equal opportunities into practice, can happen in all types of communities (whether based on place, institution, interest, age or gender group) and reflects the context in which it takes place… [it] helps people to make music – on their own terms. It reflects their lives and experiences. And, as well as providing an enjoyable and fulfilling experience, community music brings people together through music… it can help people express things, empower them, create positive attitudes, build confidence, provide skills and open up routes to new opportunities (http://www.soundsense.com).

A more extensive definition is provided by Veblen (2004) under five different headings:

♦ **Kinds of music**: community music includes all forms of music. A central theme is active music-making, which includes performance, creating, and improvising.

♦ **Intention:** community music emphasizes lifelong learning and open access. It stresses that 'the social and personal well being of all participants is as important as their musical learning (if not more important)'. Furthermore, it brings people together and promotes individual and collective identity.

♦ **Participants:** it can include a very wide range of participants, including the marginalized and disadvantaged, immigrants, and other kinds of clients seeking aesthetic experiences.

+ **Teaching:** it focuses on active learning and participation, with learners directing their own progress towards personal satisfaction and self-expression. '[A] reoccurring theme in musical communities concerns their fluidity of knowledge, expertise, and roles, with individuals participating in various ways from observer, to participants, to creator, to leader.'

+ **Context:** community music interplays between informal and formal contexts. Thus, community is defined in an expansive manner to include 'geographically situated, culturally based, artistically concerned, re-created, virtual, imagined or otherwise'.

Together, these definitions not only define what is particular about community music but highlight the similarities and differences with community arts. Whereas community arts downplays the formal aesthetic quality of the arts product with a greater emphasis on process, community music attempts to ensure that both product and process are intertwined. It is through the enjoyment of developing skills that the community music participants can grow in confidence and challenge the negative social representation of their community. They can begin to build a narrative of strength and one of change.

In their review of arts and health initiatives, Macnaughton et al. (2005) developed what they termed the Arts and Health Diamond (see Figure 6.1). On the right-hand side of the diamond are those activities that are focused on the individual and are concerned with either enhancing creativity and wellbeing or supporting healthcare. On the left-hand side of the diamond are those arts activities that focus on the collective and are concerned with promoting community wellbeing or engaging the collective more actively with healthcare. In this chapter we use a similar model. Our attention is more on those musical activities on the left-hand side of the model that contribute to enhancing social wellbeing and also promote some more specific health-relevant action in communities.

Key dimensions of arts/health

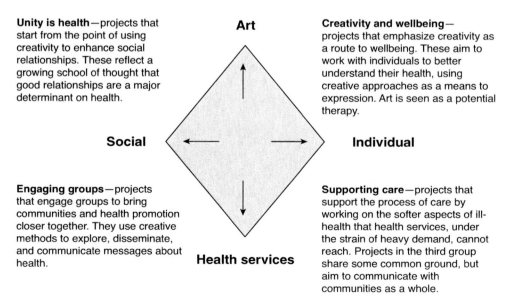

Unity is health—projects that start from the point of using creativity to enhance social relationships. These reflect a growing school of thought that good relationships are a major determinant on health.

Creativity and wellbeing—projects that emphasize creativity as a route to wellbeing. These aim to work with individuals to better understand their health, using creative approaches as a means to expression. Art is seen as a potential therapy.

Engaging groups—projects that engage groups to bring communities and health promotion closer together. They use creative methods to explore, disseminate, and communicate messages about health.

Supporting care—projects that support the process of care by working on the softer aspects of ill-health that health services, under the strain of heavy demand, cannot reach. Projects in the third group share some common ground, but aim to communicate with communities as a whole.

Fig. 6.1 Arts and Health diamond. From Macnaughton, R.J., White, M., and Stacy, R. (2005). Researching the benefits of arts in health. *Health Education*, **105**, 332–9.

Combining these ideas of community health psychology with the focus on the more social axis of the Health and Arts diamond, we can identify two primary orientations of community music initiatives:

♦ **Promoting social wellbeing:** this orientation is concerned with promoting greater identification with the community and greater participation in community activities.

♦ **Promoting health behaviour change:** this orientation is concerned with working with community members to identify particular health challenges and strategies of taking action to combat these and to promote health.

In the remainder of this chapter we provide examples of recent work in community music that falls into these two categories.

Promoting community wellbeing and action

Urban community festival

Craigmillar is a large public housing project on the outskirts of Edinburgh. The early buildings were constructed in the 1930s and the original residents were families who were moved by the local council from decaying and crowded accommodation in the inner city. Although the residents had high expectations when they moved there, they soon found that the estate had very few facilities. By the 1960s the population of the area had grown to 25,000 but it had also developed a very unsavoury reputation in the wider region. For example, it had the highest local level of juvenile delinquency, children taken into care, overcrowding and pulmonary tuberculosis. It also had very high levels of infant mortality and stillbirths.

Despite sustained political pressure by local councillors and various local campaigns, there was little municipal action to enhance the housing stock or to improve facilities. In the early 1960s a group of women in the area decided to organize a community festival. This was in some ways a retort to the world renowned Edinburgh International Festival which had no connection with the residents. After overcoming many local obstacles, the first Craigmillar Festival of Music, Art and Drama was launched in 1964. There were a total of 11 items on the programme—most being musical, including a choir and a percussion band. A leading person in this initiative was the local resident Helen Crummy who subsequently wrote a detailed history of the festival (Crummy 1992). Her account has been described by the arts promoter Richard Demarco as 'a life-enhancing account of an almost miraculous story'. In her account Crummy vividly details how a small determined group of women spearheaded the original festival. Crummy herself was an activist in the local Labour Party and not only had a large number of contacts and informal training in how to negotiate with bureaucracy but also an awareness of the political dimensions of the festival.

Initially, local politicians were dismissive of the festival as being a distraction from more serious campaigns. However, Crummy notes that not only did the festival grow in size and quality but the organizing committee began to take up a wide range of local issues. As she comments:

> Little by little we were making links between politics (with a small 'p') and local culture. And in doing so we were challenging the way in which Politics (with a capital 'P') seemed to be the province of men (p. 48).

Thus the Festival Society began to take up a wide range of social issues.

Participation in the various festival activities had an energizing effect on the core members and groups. Crummy describes how this energizing effect grew and widened:

> At first they saw the Festival Society just as somewhere they could find the opportunity to meet socially and do their own thing. But gradually as they began to realise how the lack of amenities and resources affects community life, they came to see that perhaps only political action would ever bring about change (p. 53).

She continued:

> The annual festival had proved to be the key to tapping and releasing the community's creative imagi-
> nation and talent. Once released, men and women's horizons widened. They became aware of the
> restrictive and damaging effect on family life, of living in an area where there are only houses, scarce
> community facilities, little work and second class education (p. 58).

Thus the project moved from initial small steps in building community confidence, in challenging the dominant social representation of the community as worthless, to developing a new narrative of strength and confidence to transform their local neighbourhood. As Jovchelovitch
(2007) stressed, 'without experiencing and feeling their power as a community of people, there is
little or no disposition to participate and to engage in the hard battles associated with obtaining
resources' (p. 164).

Rural community festival

A contrast to the urban festival was a rural community festival organized in a small isolated village
in Newfoundland, Canada. This village had been the subject of substantial outmigration and the
residents were generally older people. Again, there were limited local facilities. In this setting the
Tramore Arts Festival was established (further details can be found at http://www.tramore.ca).
A driving force behind this was Agnes Walsh, a former resident of the area who had subsequently
trained in anthropology. She teamed up with a local community activist, Arlene Morrisey, and
together they established the festival, which comprised a summer-long series of dramatic and
musical events. A feature of these events was the central position given to music and song. In
particular, there was a deliberate aim to recapture the traditional songs of the region and the style
of singing. In doing so, the emphasis was not on importing professional musicians into the community but rather on working with local residents to develop their own talents, providing them
with an opportunity to recognize their own strengths and their own history. Here the contrast was
highlighted between music as a commodity that could be purchased and enjoyed in a passive
manner and music as a community resource which conveyed local stories, reaffirmed a sense of
community history, and could be enjoyed collectively.

The performances proved extremely popular. The local residents were enthused and in addition, the performances began to attract the attention of people further afield and they also began
to attract tourists. This attention led to greater publicity (e.g. Dragland 2005) and the exchange of
performers with similar groups in Ireland. The festival also began to take up health issues. Initially,
this was in collaboration with one of the authors in a project on safety in the fisheries (Murray and
Tilley 2006, see further below), but it also included issues about loneliness and social isolation,
which were common experiences among the residents.

Through the process of collective music-making the residents reaffirmed their community
identity, its history, and traditions which they felt were being ignored or disparaged by the wider
society. By making connections with outside agencies and taking their songs to other settings they
began to challenge the negative social representation of themselves as being inward looking and
resistant to change that they felt were held by outsiders.

Music-making in favelas

The third example of the role of music in community building is provided by Abrahams (2005).
He described his visit to a number of *favelas* or shanty towns that exist around large cities in
Brazil. In many of these *favelas* he found examples of community music projects. He was particu-
larly interested in the extent to which they operated on the principles of Freire's critical pedagogy
(Freire 1970).

In his survey Abrahams found that the character of the music projects in the *favelas* differed substantially. Some had been in existence for many years and involved large numbers of the residents whereas others were smaller scale and had few participants. However, all of them were premised upon the Freirean active model of learning. In contrast to formal music education, the community music projects engaged in an active process of learning and building upon the participants' knowledge of music:

> Students attained a level of *conscientization* outside of formal schooling. While formal training on instruments, or participation in vocal and instrumental ensembles, broadened their experiences, students brought an inner knowing to the learning experience and did not attain it as a result (p. 15).

In addition, participation in the music projects led to broader changes:

> There was clear evidence that the perceived benefits of music instruction stretched beyond a well-produced sound in performance... there was also the belief that singing in the choir would teach folks how to work together, rather than to make music that was artistic or of high standards (p. 16).

Here again we see the tension between the aesthetic quality of the musical production and the process of producing the music. The participants were themselves aware of its aesthetic limitations but they were also aware that by practice they could enhance its quality and their own confidence. Again, it was through the collective music-making that they grew in confidence and challenged negative social representations of *favelas*.

Promoting health action

Safety education

The first example, of using community music as a means of promoting community health action is taken from a study of promoting safety in the fishing industry. Commercial fishing is one of the world's most dangerous industries. The Food and Agriculture Organization (FAO) estimate that every year thousands of fish harvesters are killed and hundreds of thousands injured worldwide. This has led to the introduction of a wide range of safety measures to improve the working conditions aboard fishing vessels but the very nature of the industry which means working on a very unstable platform in changeable weather conditions means that it will remain a dangerous occupation. One strategy to reduce the rate of accidents has been to require fish harvesters to undergo compulsory safety training. However, this approach is not only unpopular among fish harvesters but it tends to individualize the problem.

The eastern seaboard of Canada has historically been a very rich fishing ground. There are two main types of fishing—the inshore fishery which is conducted from small boats not far from shore and the offshore fishery which uses larger industrial vessels. The fish harvesters for both fisheries usually come from small hamlets that are relatively isolated. The tradition has been for children in these hamlets to leave school early to start working in the fisheries.

In the 1990s one of the authors began conducting interviews with residents of these hamlets about their lives. These interviews confirmed not only the high rate of accidents but also the resistance of the fish harvesters to what they perceived as outside interference by government safety agencies (Murray 2007). One of the consequences of this research was the development of a community safety education programme (Murray and Tilley 2006). The aim of this programme was to increase awareness of the importance of safety throughout the hamlets using a variety of community arts activities. All of these activities were developed and enacted by the local people themselves. An important feature was the role of music and song. Local people wrote and performed a series of songs about the importance of safety. Again, the lyrics and the musicianship could be criticized as lacking sophistication but the performers were immensely proud and enthused by them. In addition, the performances attracted substantial local interest with large numbers of residents attending them coupled with reports in local newspapers and on radio and television.

Throughout this project there were certain key individuals who played a central role. These included not just the performers but also those who helped behind the scenes organizing the events. Each of them did so because they realized that the project was addressing real social issues—residents of their communities were seriously injured and drowned not infrequently.

Together, the local song-making and musicianship provided the basis for a narrative of hope and possibility rather than one of fatalism and acceptance of the high rate of accidents. Admittedly, in itself the community music events did not contribute to a reduction in accidents, but it provided the basis for further action to involve the residents in a process of social action to promote safety awareness and safety routines.

Music listening and health promotion

The second example of a project explicitly addressing health concerns through music is an innovative study by Batt-Rawden and DeNora (2005) exploring music listening as a tool for health promotion. This study started from the perspective that music listening can be just as engaging an activity as music performance, drawing on Small's concept of musicking as meaning:

> to take part, in any capacity, in a musical performance, whether by performing, by listening, by rehearsing or practicing, by providing material for performance (what is called composition) or by dancing
>
> (Small 1998, p. 9).

Batt-Rawden and DeNora were inspired also by Antonovsky's (1996) concept of salutogenetics (factors that heighten health through enhancing individuals' sense of coherence and continuity) and Ruud's (2002) idea from music therapy of using music as a technology of health. In their study, adult participants with chronic illness and prior experience of music-making took part in a series of musical exchanges and interviews where they were encouraged to tell their life stories and stories of being well and being ill through a process of 'musical narratives and metaphors' (Batt-Rawden and DeNora 2005, p. 293). Although the primary form of data collection was individual interviews between researcher and participant, all participants were aware of the group nature of the project as the music that was used at varying points was shared within the group, creating a virtual participant community. As well as this sense of community, the stimulation to engage with music listening for health promotion actively inspired participants to connect or reconnect with others. One male participant suffering from depression highlighted musicking as a way of connecting with others:

> What I have gained through this project is to reinforce my belief that the strongest effect I gain from music is through playing and singing with other people, this synergy effect is like an encounter of love, it is so mysterious, just like somebody connects you to heaven, it is so strong this playing together, you know… (Batt-Rawden and DeNora 2005, p. 295).

The project served to highlight for individuals the ways in which music could make them feel, giving them a repertoire of self-care activities and self-knowledge which could then lead to even more active types of musicking. One female suffering from depression and back pain explained this process:

> It has been very important to me that I have been able to focus on my resources and the kind of resources I have through music… huge contrast to my feelings of weariness and tiredness. This project

has actually made me make contact with a folk-music group in my community and now I am feeling so good. I have regained control and well-being in my life. It is great (pp. 295–296).

This kind of participatory project is able to inspire people, often with severe health problems, to learn more about themselves and others, and to provide a resource. As one participant noted: 'it is rare I am so ill that I can't listen to music' (p. 301). Such engagement with music listening is a means of providing a positive self-narrative and a different but very effective setting for health promotion.

Common features

Although each of these musical activities took place in different settings, several common features can be identified as follows.

1) **Developing challenge** Through participating in a range of different musical activities the community residents become involved in a process challenging the perceived negative social representations of the communities held by outsiders and of developing a narrative of change. They begin to develop a new positive community identity. The ability to show the outsider that they have certain talents provides added energy to the participants.

2) **Focus on local** Practically there is a focus on local musicianship. Rather than importing professional players from outside the community, the emphasis is on identifying and supporting local talent or in supporting people to engage with music at their own level of interest and expertise. To the outsider, the performances could be seen in many ways as amateurish but it is the working with the community rather than imposing something on the community which is the key to the success. Residents gain great satisfaction at the achievements of their neighbours.

3) **Energizing impact** In all of the projects a common consequence was the energizing impact of the music and other arts activities on the participants (cf. Matarasso 1997). It is not uncommon for many musical 'performers' (whether performing or listening) to describe the experience as being the most exciting event in their lives and as being personally transformative. Through public performances and media reports this impact spreads to a much larger audience. However, while these obvious positive benefits are apparent in the short term, there is a greater challenge in terms of the sustainability of the projects.

4) **Role of organizers** The prospects of short-term success being sustained often fall on a small number of individuals. These individuals often have previous experience of local politics or community organizing. Underlying their involvement is a drive to improve the quality of life of residents in the area. Although initially concerned about organizing a limited number of musical activities it is not unusual for the organizers to begin to consider community action to address broader social issues.

5) **Importance of social values** This final point is one of the most important issues to consider when developing community music activities. In many cases, a central role is played by a limited number of individuals who have limited access to support and resources. Funding is often provided for limited time periods to set up new initiatives. After the initial enthusiasm around the community music events participants can often withdraw and the key leaders may feel frustrated or demoralized. To continue to promote action requires a commitment to the community and to improving the quality of life locally. This is underpinned by a belief system that is infused with social values often informed by political and/or religious ideals about justice and transcendence. It is these ideals that convince the community leaders to continue despite adversity and the lack of any recognition by outsiders.

References

Abrahams, F. (2005). Critical pedagogy in the community music education programs in Brazil. *International Journal of Community Music*, B(1).

Antonovsky, A. (1996). The salutogenetic model as a theory to guide health promotion. *Health Promotion International*, **11**, 11–18.

Arneil, B. (2006). *Diverse communities: The problem with social capital.* Cambridge: Cambridge University Press.

Bailey, B.A. and Davidson, J.W. (2005). Effects of group singing and performance for marginalized and middle-class singers. *Psychology of Music*, **33**(3), 269–303.

Batt-Rawden, K. and DeNora, T. (2005). Music and informal learning in everyday life. *Music Education Research*, **7**(3), 289–304.

Biddle, S.J.H. and Ekkekakis, P. (2005). Physically active lifestyles and well-being. In: F.A. Huppert, N. Baylis, and B. Keverne (eds.), *The science of well-being*, pp. 141–68. Oxford: Oxford University Press.

Campbell, C. and Jovchelovitch, S. (2000). Health, community and development: towards a social psychology of participation. *Journal of Community and Applied Social Psychology*, **10**, 255–70.

Campbell, C. and Murray, M. (2004). Community health psychology: definitions and challenges. *Journal of Health Psychology*, **9**(2), 179–88.

Clift, S., Hancox, G., Morrison, I., Hess, B., Kreutz, G., and Stewart, D. (2010). Choral singing and psychological wellbeing: Quantitative and qualitative findings from English choirs in a cross-national survey. *Journal of Applied Arts and Health*, **1**(1), 19–34.

Crummy, H. (1992). *Let the people sing: A story of Craigmillar.* Newcraighall, Edinburgh: Author.

Dragland, S. (2005). The right intelligence of home: Agnes Walsh and Tramore Theatre troupe. *Newfoundland Quarterly*, **97**, 201–3.

Faulkner, R. and Davidson, J.W. (2006). Men in chorus: collaboration and competition in homo-social vocal behaviour. *Psychology of Music*, **34**(2), 291–37.

Freire, P. (1970). *Pedagogy of the oppressed.* New York: Continuum.

Hillery, G. (1955). Definitions of community: areas of agreement. *Rural Sociology*, **20**, 111–23.

Howarth, C.S. (2001). Towards a social psychology of community: a social representations perspective. *Journal for the Theory of Social Behaviour*, **31**, 223–38.

Jovchelovitch, S. (2007). *Knowledge in context: Representations, community and culture.* London: Routledge.

Kreutz, G., Bongard, S., Rohrmann, S., Hodapp, V., and Grebe, D. (2004). Effects of choir singing or listening on secretory immunoglobulin A, cortisol, and emotional state. *Journal of Behavioural Medicine*, **27**, 623–35.

Ledwith, M. (2005). *Community development: A critical approach.* Bristol: Policy Press.

Matarasso, F. (1997). *Use or ornament?: The social impact of participation in the arts.* Stroud: Comedia.

Macnaughton, R.J., White, M., and Stacy, R. (2005). Researching the benefits of arts in health. *Health Education*, **105**, 332–9.

McLeroy, K.R., Norton, B.L., Kegler, M.C., Burdine, J.N., and Sumaya, C.V. (2003). Community-based interventions. *American Journal of Public Health*, **93**(4), 529–33.

Meade, R. and Shaw, M. (2007). Community development and the arts: reviving the democratic imagination. *Community Development Journal*, **42**, 413–21.

Moscovici, S. (1973). Foreword. In: C. Herzlich: *Health and illness: A social psychological analysis.* London: Academic Press.

Murray, M. (2000). Levels of narrative analysis in health psychology. *Journal of Health Psychology*, **5**(3), 331–42.

Murray, M. (2007). 'It's in the blood and you're not going to change it': Fish harvesters' narrative accounts of injury and disability. *WORK: A Journal of Prevention, Assessment and Rehabilitation*, **28**, 165–74.

Murray, M. and Crummett, A. (2010). 'I don't think they knew they knew we could do these sorts of things': Social representations of community and participation in community arts by older people. *Journal of Health Psychology*, **15**, 777–85.

Murray, M. and Tilley, N. (2006). Using community arts to promote awareness of safety in fishing communities: an action research study. *Safety Science*, **44**, 797–808.

Ruud, E. (2002). Music as a cultural immunuogen–three narratives on the use of music as a technology of health. In: I.M. Hanken, S. Graabræk Nielsen and M. Nerland (eds.) *Festschrift for Harald Jøregensen: Research in and for Higher Music Education (2)*. Oslo: NMH-Publications.

Sarbin, T.R. (1986). The narrative as a root metaphor for psychology. In: T.R. Sarbin (ed.) *Narrative psychology: the storied nature of human conduct*. New York: Praeger.

Small, C. (1998). *Musicking: The meanings of performing and listening*. Middletown, CT: Wesleyan University Press.

Valentine, E. and Evans, C. (2001). The effects of solo singing, choral singing and swimming on mood and physiological indices. *British Journal of Medical Psychology*, **74**(1), 115–20.

Veblen, K.K. (2004). The many ways of community music. *International Journal of Community Music*, **1**, 8–16.

Webster, M. (2005). Warming up. In: M. Webster and G. Buglass (eds.) *Finding voices, making choices: Creativity for social change*, pp. 1–8. Nottingham: Educational Heretics Press.

Chapter 7

The New Health Musicians

Even Ruud

The field of music and health has undergone major changes within the last decade. New areas of practice, new roles and identities for music therapists, music educators, and community musicians, and, not least, new theoretical discourses have both expanded our existing knowledge and suggested new areas for research as well. Those who benefit from the field have also increased in number; among recent target groups and services are choirs for the homeless (Bailey and Davidson 2003), rock bands with female prisoners (Ruud Nilsen 1996), music for homeless children (Barcellos 2005), music with immigrant workers (Schwantes, in progress), and community music among young people living in a refugee camp (Storsve et al. 2010). Within the arts and health movement more generally, music is being increasingly recognized as a 'cultural immunogen' (Ruud 2002)—that is, the act of making or even simply listening to music, or 'musicking', appears to have specific disease-preventative or health-promoting qualities (Cohen 2009; Clift et al. 2010). Research on the effects of attendance at cultural events upon longevity and self-rated health (Bygren et al. 2009) also supports this trend toward health-related musicking. In music psychology, recent research likewise documents examples of individual musicking as an applied 'technology of health' (see DeNora 2007), including the purposeful everyday use of MP3 players (Skånland 2009; Skarpeid 2009), or music's role in evoking strong emotional experiences related to health (Gabrielsson 2008). Recent community music therapy work has also embraced new areas of application, including choirs for the elderly, the sharing of music among marginalized children and adolescents, and music's effect upon outpatient groups of the mentally ill (Stige et al. 2010).

A general shift in emphasis toward more community-based musicking practices, coupled with an interest in health-promoting rather than curative activities within the field of music and health, gives rise to a new set of questions best addressed by the broadest possible cultural, theoretical, or sociological perspective. Some of these questions concern the ethical and political dimensions of musicking—for instance, should we describe communal musicking activities as ultimately educational, cultural, therapeutic, or health promoting? Other questions concern the traditional boundaries that distinguish music therapists from community musicians or health workers, for example. Should these boundaries be blurred, perhaps via the new role of *health musician*? What competencies should be required for doing health work using musical activities? Which musical, social and theoretical skills would best accommodate health-related musical interventions?

I will propose some answers to these questions by reporting briefly on a community music project presently being conducted among young Palestinians living under adverse conditions in a refugee camp in South Lebanon. But first, I will give some theoretical background on and conceptual clarification to the field of music and health and the concept of musicking.

Music as a cultural immunogen

While there is unquestionably a link between music and health, both theoretical arguments *and* empirical evidence are required to expose it. First of all, we need to conceptualize the areas in question. In brief, I understand *music* here in terms of Christopher Small's take on 'musicking'. That is, I see no inherent qualities, or internal mechanics, in music that act to improve the health of our minds and bodies in any sort of direct or one-to-one relationship. Instead, 'healthful' musical meaning arises from an active engagement with music via a *situated* practice whose outcome is in fact the result of a 'person–situation–music' dynamic. Musicking is a performed activity, and its health-related affordances arise solely from that basic fact.

In keeping with this expansive definition of music, I likewise understand 'health' in this particular context to include the subjective interpretation of our relation to the 'world'—to ourselves (and our bodies), to other people, and to our existential situation. At the risk of downplaying the importance of specific physical condition, health in this case must incorporate larger issues of overall quality of life. I have previously identified four dimensions or categories of quality of life that benefit from musicking (Ruud 1997, 1998): vitality (emotional life, aesthetic sensibility, pleasures), agency (sense of mastery and empowerment, social recognition), belonging (network, social capital), and meaning (continuity of tradition, transcendental values, hope) (see also Ruud 2010; Storsve et al. 2010).

In the literature we find a range of other generative factors that transform simple engagement with music into health-promoting musicking. For instance, Clift and his colleagues (2010) identified six generative mechanisms linking singing with the fortification of one's wellbeing: attendant positive emotions, focused concentration, controlled breathing, social bonding, education and learning, and active participation. When considering how music therapists or community music educators can contribute to or promote health or life quality, we must engage with the communal practice of musicking as a way of seeking to maintain vitality, exercise personal agency, build networks and communities, and engage in a meaningful activity. When musicking fulfils these functions, it begins to resemble a sort of *immunogen behaviour* (Ruud 2002, 2010), along the same lines as the many other technologies we presently employ to prevent disease and promote health.

The music project in Rashedie

The following case study, based upon ongoing work with young Palestinian refugees in a camp in Lebanon, will illustrate some of the political, ethical, methodological, and disciplinary challenges we face in the promotion of community-based health musicking. A professor at the Norwegian Academy of Music in Oslo run this project, and my role has been to advise upon potential music therapy efforts, co-write and publish reports, and, lately, do interviews with the children and adolescents who have been taking part in it. Space prohibits a detailed discussion of our research methodology here.

I visited the camp on two occasions (in January and November 2009) and did some participant observation while attending rehearsals and other activities that were taking place at the camp's cultural centre. I also interviewed six children (three girls and three boys, ages 12–18 years) with different overall lengths of participation in the project. The project leader and the leader of the local cultural centre chose the children I interviewed, based upon their availability on the weekend in question. In addition, interviews with local community and organizational leaders, videos, and in-depth discussions with project leaders have provided information about the project. A Lebanese teacher facilitated my interviews with the children and adolescents in Arabic and translated the replies into English on the spot. (Later, in Norway, an Arab- and Norwegian-speaking translator prepared a fresh translation of the exchange into Norwegian as well.) The Lebanese interviewer was asked to focus upon qualitative content (Kvale 1997) and to 'lead the respondent into discussion of actual happenings and practices' (DeNora 2010, p. 172). Data analysis after the interviews focused specifically upon some of the variables that linked participation in the project with aspects of experienced health. Techniques like 'get a sense of the whole, making case notes, culling the raw data, segment, format and collaborate' (cf. Bruscia 2005) helped to process the data. In the interest of an inductive approach, or a phenomenological perspective, 'grounded theory' began the process of analysis (Strauss and Corbin 1995)—to identify units of meaning, researchers combined open coding with their preunderstanding of the data in order to create categories and subcategories.

The following discussion of community music activities and their promotion of health will engage these questions, among others: Can musical activities influence the health situation of individuals or groups? What is the nature of a successful musical intervention? What are the most salient experiences of the participants? What are some of the links between cultural participation and our conception of health?

First, I will briefly present the project, in terms of its method of organizing musical learning in a community of practice, and the related identity work that is taking place at the same time (Wenger 1998); the nature of the musical material and arrangements it uses; and the potential health-related outcomes that participants have noted. I will focus especially upon experiences of self-identity, mastery, belonging, dignity and 'recognition' as fundamental to the experience of health. I will also explore how the concept of recognition, with its roots in Hegelian philosophy and its recent elaboration within critical philosophy by German social philosopher Axel Honneth (2003), among others, introduces an important dimension to the new role of the health musician.

Since 2002, the Norwegian Academy of Music has been involved in a music project in the Palestinian refugee camp Rashedie in the South Lebanese city of Tyr. This 'community music project for health and cultural cooperation' has been run by Associate Professor Vegar Storsve. For a detailed report about the musical programme and the theories behind it, see Storsve et al. (2009, 2010).[1]

To this day, Lebanon remains host to 368,000 Palestinian refugees, who are placed together in 12 official camps and sadly denied rights to healthcare, education, and job prospects within a whole range of professions in Lebanese society. Obviously, then, unemployment, social problems, and mental health problems are common within the camps. Blaxter (2004) has pointed to the link between adverse social conditions and our health situation, drawing upon the model of 'socio-biologic translation': children and adolescents living in these camps experience psychological distress that may then surface in feelings of shame, a lack of self-esteem, or an absence of dignity or self-respect (see also Gandour 2001, p. 157). Among the refugees there persists an overwhelming need for practical coping and buffering strategies that might alleviate the effects of this distress.

The music project seeks to reach as many children and young Palestinians as possible through communal musicking, instrumental activity, and dancing. Today, about 40 children and adolescents are participating in the project. Over the years, Norwegian contributors have brought many instruments from Norway, and the project's orchestra presently boasts three synthesizers, microphones and public address systems, electric guitars, violins, guitars, saxophones, Orff instruments, drumsets, hand drums, an accordion, and melodicas. This blend of instruments, of course, creates its own challenges regarding any musical arrangements to be made for shared performances.

---

[1] See http://voices.no/mainissues/mi4001099158.ph.

Project leaders visit the camp five or six times a year to teach, organize, and advise on musical programming. Once a year, students from the Norwegian Academy of Music also visit the camp, both to teach and to give concerts. This recurrent combination of Norwegian instructors and students and Palestinian children and adult instructors creates a truly unique musical community of practice.

From the outset of the academy's project in 2002, local musicians were engaged to teach music, and the social workers and leaders of the organization Beit Atfal Assumoud, [2] a Lebanese non-governmental organization soon lent their support to these activities. Music teaching has since become a permanent aspect of the camp's cultural centre, and local musicians have adopted many of the project's methods, described further below, in their own work. Two local instructors, with the support of a group of eight to ten adolescents, now run weekly programmes throughout the year. The local instructors are responsible for teaching both instrumental skills and individual musical parts to the younger participants. When the Norwegian music educators are present, they suggest new pieces to be performed and new riffs or ostinatos to be practised. All of this musical material is orally transmitted, and melodies, harmonies and rhythmic patterns are repeated until they are mastered.

The methodological principle behind project-related performances was developed by Storsve (1991) and conceptualized as the 'multi-use arrangement', whereby everyone is given the opportunity to take part in the performance. Arrangements include everything from simple rhythmic figures and two-tone melodies to more complex riffs or ostinatos as well as more challenging harmonic textures. Repetition and variation are likewise employed to create a good flow and changing musical texture to a performance, and the same parts must be able to be played on different instruments. This approach to musical arrangement recalls that of music therapists working in special education, but the sheer assortment of instruments and number of participants in this case still allows for quite sophisticated musical challenges.

This type of music project is clearly representative of a 'community of practice' (Wenger 1998; Ansdell 2010), in that it creates a unique possibility for musical interaction by providing children with the status of legitimate participants. Musical learning and changes in identity go hand-in-hand. Because these young musicians may take on different roles within the project, they participate in a learning process that leads directly to more involvement with, responsibility for and even influence upon the negotiations that ultimately define this musical community. According to Wenger (1998, pp. 153–155), a community of practice in fact accommodates many different 'strategies of belonging', as people are forced to navigate among social alignments that might be described as *peripheral, inbound, insider, boundary* or *outbound.* One's musical capacity increases as participants go from a peripheral role to an apprentice or journeyman role to full participation. At the same time, one's confidence grows. For Lave and Wenger (1991), a diverse field of relations among 'old-timers' and newcomers is vital to this process.

For example, in situations where learning-in-practice takes the form of apprenticeship, succeeding generations of participants give rise to what in its simplest form is a triadic set of relations: The community of practice encompasses apprentices, young masters with apprentices, and masters, some of whose apprentices have themselves become masters. But there are other inflection points as well, where journey folk, not yet masters, are *relative* old-timers with respect to newcomers (pp. 56–57).

Lave and Wenger emphasize the relevance of this blend of roles to the circulation of knowledge and skills, as opposed to more dyadic forms of conventional learning.

---

[2] http://www.socialcare.org/

Cultural work as health promotion

The community music project at Rashedie has resulted in much more than musical learning. The adolescents who have participated have experienced a markedly positive effect upon their sense of vitality, agency and belonging, as well as their felt meaning and hope for the future—in other words, they have experienced positive health effects.

Bonding and belonging

First, in light of my prior conviction that musicking is linked to health and quality of life (Ruud 1997), I wanted to examine the ways in which the project contributed to participants' sense of belonging in general, and to a strengthening of the network among participants. Interestingly, this sense of connectedness went beyond the notion of community itself. Ansdell (2010) has observed that communities may have different qualities—some offer a more mechanical or superficial bridging among people, while others have a more 'organic' character, as we see in musical communities, for example, that have existed for some time. To most of the participants in the Rashedie project, the community was experienced intensely, almost as a second family. The other children were regarded not as co-players, fellow members of the orchestra, or even friends but as brothers and sisters, while the older leaders were regarded as big brothers or even fathers. 'Everybody here at Assumoud is like my second family', Mona (age 15) said. 'We are like a big group, with one name, as a family', Hamsa (age 19) said. 'They are not my friends, they are my brothers and sisters', another participant agreed.

Vitality and pleasure

When I analysed the interviews, I also found many statements to support my understanding of how musical experiences relate to both our emotions and our bodies—specifically, to our energy level and sense of vitality. 'When I play I am lost in the music', Khaled (age 14) told me. 'To be engaged in music is "soft and nice", and I feel good when I am playing'. To Mahmud (age 20), musical participation helped him to forget about all of his worries and relax: 'All the time I have a lot of problems. Usually I think about how I will get money in order to learn how to help my parents and my brothers and sisters. But when I come to the centre, I forget about my problems and feel relaxed'. Hamsa (age 19) reported that 'music had influenced his soul and made people happy'.

Agency and recognition

As I described earlier, this particular music community of practice gave adolescents the opportunity to experience the role of teacher or instructor as well as performer. As they fulfilled these responsibilities, they were mentored via occasional meetings with Norwegian students and master teachers. Their sense of agency among their peers and with the younger children grew as their musical skills grew. In addition, their concert performances contributed to their sense of recognition within the wider local community.

Khaled, for instance, described his pride in himself: 'I feel special and privileged because I learned to play a difficult instrument'. Through the project, girls were also given the opportunity to play instruments like guitar or saxophone, which was unusual in Palestinian culture. 'I like the idea that a girl can play the guitar', Mona (age 15) stated. All of the adolescents who were part of the instructor-assistant group also expressed pride and joy in their new role. 'Teaching is a very beautiful experience', said Mahmud, in English. The teaching responsibilities had a deeper significance for these young Palestinians as well, given their ongoing experience of captivity. Their loyalty to their historical tradition and culture made them especially aware of the need to maintain community morale and transmit their values to the next generation. When Hamsa (age 19) was asked if he liked to teach, he said: 'Yes, I am born here. We have to continue because the younger have to continue'. It also became strikingly clear from the interviews that participants' visits to Norway had given them a new perspective on their sense of identity or value as people. Living with a Norwegian host family, as a family member, left a lasting impression. Mahmud stated, 'People in Norway deal with others in a respectful way. Not like here. I can't blame people because of the situation they live in'.

It became evident through such statements that a sense of 'recognition' had arisen from the respectful treatment these young Palestinians had experienced, in contrast to how they felt they were treated both inside and outside the refugee camp. Such experiences of self-identity, dignity, and recognition are fundamental to good health, and community-based music therapy efforts must engage recognition at the societal as well as the individual level. Recognition should inform our entire critical perspective, in fact, particularly where social inclusion and human rights play an important role. Honneth observes that recognition has its roots in the relationship between the caregiver and the infant. However, in order to fully accept and value ourselves, we also need to have our human rights recognized in our roles as grown (or growing) citizens. If this recognition is denied, we will not be able to experience social solidarity or any sense of our common norms and values.

Meaning: tradition and hope

Meaning comprises the last category of music's relationship to health. This project's significance to its participants informed all of their replies to the question, 'What would you have been doing today if you were not coming to the centre?' Many of the children said they would probably be sleeping, watching television, or being bored. Sara (age 16) observed, 'If it had not been for the centre, my life had been empty. It keeps me busy'. Some of the children also indicated that this opportunity to play music had become a means of expressing Palestinian traditions: 'I would like to play traditional Palestinian music on the saxophone, then I can show my tradition through the music', Khaled said. This loyalty to traditional Palestinian values and musical culture also appeared in their indication of musical preferences. Only Khaled said that he liked all kinds of music; the others dismissed even popular commercial music, whether Western or Arabic. Even Khaled added, 'I love the Palestinian music the most, since I can represent my country through this music'. Mahmud extended his affection for the traditional to other cultures as well: 'I love the traditional music, so I love the traditional music from other countries. I listen to Norwegian music, like *Reven, rotta og grisen*' (a traditional Norwegian folk tune).

By cultivating positive emotions and a belief in one's own skills, the Rashedie project attempts to contribute to the development of the participant's sense of identity and empowerment. We also asked the musicians about their hopes for the future—recent theories on the development and maintenance of hope indicate the relevance here of one's sense of self-mastery, increased self-esteem, and ability to prepare for and realize solutions. In addition, the act of hoping is a health-promoting process in itself, observe Snyder et al. (2002, p. 257): 'Hopeful thought reflects the belief that one can find pathways to desired goals and become motivated to use those pathways'. To be able to create goals (short- or long-term), to formulate possible strategies or routes for reaching the goals, and to engage a motivational component—that is, a belief in self-agency—are central components to the process of hoping. Within this complex psychological picture, *meaning* becomes crucial, and it must be a very present sense of meaning as well.

For these young Palestinian participants, the future is uncertain. Opportunities for higher education are sparse, and even when they acquire a professional qualification, they are not allowed to work in Lebanon. 'It is very difficult to become something. If I become good enough, I will teach the younger children', Sara said. While the cultural centre itself has become a possible route to a meaningful job for some of them, others continue to worry about their prospects. Mahmud, despite his ongoing university studies, would not admit to much faith in the future: 'I will be lying if I tell you yes. I hope that I can do that, be optimistic, yes.'

Despite these bitter truths, there are many important reasons to promote this musical community of practice, which encourages the participant's sense of belonging, pride in one's skills, and mastery of instruments, hope and plans for the future, and motivation for school, whatever the extenuating circumstances. Attendance at the cultural centre, in short, replaces boredom and empty leisure time with aesthetic and pleasurable experiences of flow and happiness while maintaining Palestinian values in a marginal social situation. As Mariam Sleiman, the leader of the cultural centre Beit Atfal Assumoud, observed in January 2009, 'The young who take part in this music project are friendlier, more social and more curious that other youngsters in the camp'. Many of these musicians are later chosen to participate in leadership programs in the local community as well, she noted.

Music therapy, community music, or health musicking?

Project leaders join local authorities like Sleiman in acknowledging that many of the health challenges and problems facing the young Palestinian refugees are connected to their political and social situation. A life of oppression and poverty, with its attendant lack of healthcare, adequate housing, and sanitary conditions, will in itself create health problems that are beyond the reach of a music project. The marginalization and lack of social recognition that also stem from a life outside of the surrounding Lebanese society likewise inhibit good health, as refugees are forbidden to own land, buy a house, or pursue higher education or many professions. Despite the complexities of the international origins of this unfortunate situation, Amnesty International recommends that all Lebanese laws that discriminate against Palestinian refugees be banned.[3]

From the perspective of community psychology, it is apparent that the psychosocial problems that arise under such conditions cannot be solved through initiatives aimed at the individual (Nelson and Prilleltensky 2005). However, because this music project offers concrete opportunities for learning and the growth of personal identity, it may well promote mental health in general, given that 'health' must be seen to encompass more than just the absence of somatic or mental illness (Ruud 2006, 2010). From a salutogenetic perspective (Antonovsky 1987), or as a subjectively experienced phenomenon, health has everything to do with our experience of meaning and continuity in life—how we experience control and mastery, belongingness and supportive relations with others, and a sense of vitality and emotional flexibility, accompanied by possibilities for emotional expression (Ruud 2001). We should also add that, in this context, health includes a sense of our political rights or opportunity to engage in social and political processes. At a societal level, it further includes rights to an education and the acquisition of basic skills, as well as rights to employment, income and housing (see also Nelson and Prilleltensky 2005, p. 28).

Finally, we want to emphasize again that this is a *community* music project—that is, a cultural effort with health-promoting consequences. It therefore has the qualities (and admits to the limitations of) a music therapeutical (or community music therapy) project. But it is different as well. It is centred upon musical learning and performance, whatever its possible consequences for health and quality of life. It should not fall into the 'treatment' trap that appears too often when we seek individualistic explanations and solutions to collective problems that in fact arise from

---

[3] See http://www.amnestyusa.org/document.php?lang=e&id=ENGMDE180062007.

oppression and the maintenance of asymmetrical power relations. Through the development of a musical *community* of practice and the encouragement of participants' cooperation in realizing a common goal, we may avoid those sorts of individualizing actions that lead to what community psychologists call 'blaming the victim'—that is, saddling the victims with responsibility for a situation that they were forced into in the first place. This is not to say that either community music therapy or community psychology is irrelevant to projects like ours. Rather, it may be that our project can contribute something unique to the literature concerning the links between cultural work and the promotion of mental health.

The New Health Musicians

As we observed in the introduction, when music is introduced to places where people are marginalized, have left (or been rejected from) communities, or live in a 'space between', both community music therapists and community musicians have important roles. As Brynjulf Stige states in *Where Music Helps* (Stige et al. 2010, p. 11), the labelling of health musicking as 'community music therapy' may not be sufficient: 'Alternative labels for some of these projects could be prevention, health promotion, non-medical care, community development, or just music' (p. 11). As we have seen in this project, both educators and participants can benefit from musicking—not only those for whom the 'therapy' is intended—provided both groups display the kinds of skills and values that are necessary to make things work.

Today, community music making and community music therapy employ different agents with distinct qualifications, educational training, and professional identities. However, their practices are much the same. Community music can even be so broadly defined (Veblen, 2004) that almost any project outside of the classroom applies to the category. Often traditional community music projects tend to imitate mainstream professional music life and its emphasis on notated music, hierarchic organization, a music-centred goal, a philosophical conception of music as autonomous and so on. On the other hand, we also find community music projects like the one I have discussed in this article. In these cases the goals might be both musical *and* extramusical and include explicit health goals; the instruction methods might be exclusively oral; the arrangements might be individually tailored; and the participants might be found within a marginalized or disadvantaged group.

While the work of community music therapists can range from special educational settings aimed at social integration to choir work with the elderly or outpatient work with mental health patients, all of these efforts rely upon the same sorts of competencies as other community music projects. Traditional musical competencies in teaching, performing and arranging music are very important. Musicking for health also demands a sensitivity to musical forms of *communication*— an ability to engage participants in communal musicking and create a sense of communal belonging (Ansdell 2010). In the toolbox of musical intervention skills, we must also find a knack for sensitive and flexible musical leadership—the ability to adjust to participants' individual skills, pace, and comfort level. In fact, one of the core musical competencies of the music therapist or community music leader involves arranging for adapted instruments and creating scores based on participants' individual performance skills. Furthermore, skills in musical improvisation are necessary in order to engage participants in constructive musical exchange. Bruscia (1984) analysed models of music therapy improvisations and identified categories of improvisational techniques that included empathy, structuring, intimacy, elicitation, and redirection. The mastery of such skills and improvisational techniques is basic to much music therapy work.

With regard to health interventions through musicking, additional knowledge about group dynamics, communication skills and participants' backgrounds (health problems, cultural background, social situation) is relevant. I would also advocate for the communication and social skills necessary to network and collaborate with other organizations and individuals in the community in order to foster greater social integration, as underscored by Stige (2002, p. 328) in his analysis of community music therapy.

In short, there is no reason to believe that the health impact of this community music project would have been any different if it had been carried out by music therapists, or other health workers, as opposed to community music educators and musicians. I would suggest, however, that in the near future, we will need a new kind of musician, therapist, community musician, and music educator—a *health musician*, if you will—with the necessary musical and performative skills, the methodological equipment, and theoretical familiarity, and, not least, the personal, ethical, and political values to best carry out these health-musicking projects.

References

Ansdell, G. (2010). Reflection: Belonging through musicking: Explorations of musical community. In: B. Stige, G. Ansdell, C. Elefant, and M. Pavlicevic (eds.) *Where Music Helps: Community Music Therapy in Action and Reflection,* pp. 41–62. Farnham: Ashgate.

Antonovsky, A. (1987). *Unravelling the Mystery of Health: How People Manage Stress and Stay Well.* San Francisco, CA: Jossey-Bass Publishers.

Bailey, B. and Davidson, J. (2003). Amateur group singing as a therapeutic instrument. *Nordic Journal of Music Therapy,* **12**(1), 18–33.

Barcellos, L.R. (2005). Juggling with life. *Voices. A World Forum for Music Therapy,* February 14. Available at: http://www.voices.no/?q=fortnightly-columns/2005-juggling-life

Baxter, M. (2004). *Health.* Cambridge: Polity Press.

Bruscia, K. (1984). *Improvisational Models of Music Therapy.* Springfield, IL: Charles C. Thomas Publisher.

Bruscia, K. (2005). Data analysis in qualitative research. In: B. Wheeler (ed.) *Music Therapy Research (2nd edn.),* pp.179–87. Gilsum, NH: Barcelona Publishers.

Bygren, L.O., Johansson, S-E., Konlaan, B.B. Grjibovski, M.,Wilkinson, A.V., and Sjöström, M. (2009). Attending cultural events and cancer mortality: A Swedish study. *Arts and Health,* **1**(1), 64–74.

Clift, S., Hancox, G., Morrison, I., Hess, B., Kreutz, G., and Stewart, D. (2010). Choral singing and psychological wellbeing: Quantitative and qualitative findings from English choirs in a cross-national survey. *Journal of Applied Arts and Health,* **1**(1), 19–34.

Cohen, G. (2009). New theories and research findings on the positive influence of music and art on health with aging. *Arts and Health,* **1**(1), 48–63.

DeNora, T. (2007). Health and music in everyday life—a theory of practice. *Psyke and Logos,* **28**, 271–87.

DeNora, T. (2010). Emotion as social emergence: Perspectives from music sociology. In: P.N. Juslin and J.A. Sloboda (eds.), *Handbook of Music and Emotion: Theory, Research, Applications,* pp. 15–87. Oxford: Oxford University Press.

Gabrielsson, A. (2008). *Starka musikopplevelser.* Hedemora: Gidlunds Förlag.

Ghandour, N. (2001). Meeting the Needs of Palestinian Refugees in Lebanon. In: N. Aruri (ed.) *Palestinian Refugees: The Right of Return,* pp. 123–61. London: Pluto Press.

Honneth, A. (2003). *Behovet for anerkjennelse.* København: Hans Reitzels Forlag.

Karam, E.G., Mneimneh, Z.N., Karam, A.N., Fayyad, J.A., Nasser, S.C., Chatterji, S., *et al.* (2006). Prevalence and Treatment of Mental Disorders in Lebanon: A National Epidemiological Survey. *Lancet,* **367**, 1000–6.

Kvale, S. (1997). *Det kvalitative forskningsintervju* [An introduction to qualitative research interviewing]. Oslo: Gyldendal.

Lave, J. and Wenger, E. (1991). *Situated Learning: Legitimate Peripheral Participation.* Cambridge: Cambridge University Press.

Nelson, G., and Prilleltensky, I. (2005). *Community Psychology: In Pursuit of Liberation and Well-Being*. New York: Palgrave Macmillan.

Nilsen, V.R. (1996). Musikk i fengsel og frihet. *Nordic Journal of Music Therapy*, **5**(2), 113–18.

Ruud, E. (1997). Music and quality of life. *Nordic Journal of Music Therapy*, **6**(2), 86–92.

Ruud, E. (1998). *Music Therapy: Improvisation, Communication, and Culture*. Gilsum, NH: Barcelona Publishers.

Ruud, E. (2001). *Varme øyeblikk. Om musikk, helse og livsvalitet*. Oslo: Unipub.

Ruud, E. (2002). Music as a cultural immunogen—three narratives on the use of music as a technology of health. In: I.M. Hanken, S.G. Graabræk Nielsen, and M. Nerland (eds.) *Research in and for Higher Music Education*, pp. 109–20. Oslo: NMH Publications.

Ruud, E. (2006). *Musikk gir helse*. In: T. Aasgaard (ed.) *Musikk og helse*. Oslo: Cappelen akademisk.

Ruud, E. (2010). *Music Therapy—A Perspective from the Humanities*. Gilsum, NH: Barcelona Publishers.

Skarpeid, G. (2009). Daglig musikklytting. In: E. Ruud (ed.) *Musikk i psykisk helsearbeid med barn og unge*, pp. 131–53. Oslo: Skriftserie fra Senter for musikk og helse, NMH-publikasjoner.

Skånland, M.S. (2009). (Mobil) musikk som mestringsstrategi, in E. Ruud (ed.), *Musikk i psykisk helsearbeid med barn og unge*, pp.113–31. Oslo: Skriftserie fra Senter for musikk og helse, NMH-publikasjoner.

Snyder, C.R., Rand, K.L., and Sigmon, D.R. (2002). Hope theory: A member of the positive psychology family. In: C.R. Snyder and S.J. Lopez (eds.) *Handbook of Positive Psychology*, pp. 257–76. New York: Oxford University Press.

Stige, B. (2002). *Culture-Centered Music Therapy*. Gilsum, NH: Barcelona Publishers.

Stige, B. (2010). Introduction: Music and Health in Community. In: B. Stige, G. Ansdell, C. Elefant, and M. Pavlicevic (eds.) *Where Music Helps: Community Music Therapy in Action and Reflection*, pp. 3–16. Farnham: Ashgate.

Storsve, V. (1991). *Pop/rock samspill: Et aksjonsforskningsprosjekt i ungdomsskolen*. Oslo: Hovedoppgave ved Norges musikkhøgskole.

Storsve, V. (2008). Kulturen som brobygger og arena for livsutfoldelse: Erfaringer fra et musikkprosjekt i en flyktningleir i Libanon. In: S. Rodin and G. Gjestrud (eds.) *Flyktning i Libanon: Fra al-Nakba til Nahr el-Bared*. Oslo: Forum for kultur og internasjonalt samarbeid.

Storsve, V., Westby, I.A., and Ruud, E. (2009). Håp og anerkjennelse: Om et musikkprosjekt blant ungdommer i en palestinsk flyktningleir. In: E. Ruud (ed.) *Musikk i psykisk helsearbeid med barn og unge*, pp. 187–204. Oslo: Skriftserie fra Senter for musikk og helse, NMH-publikasjoner.

Storsve, V., Westby, I.A., and Ruud, E. (2010). Hope and recognition. *Voices. A World Forum for Music Therapy*, **10**(1).

Strauss, A.J. and Corbin, J. (1995). *Grounded Theory in Practice*. London: Sage.

Veblen, K.K. (2004). The many ways of community music. *International Journal of Community Music*, **1**(1), 5–21.

Wenger, E. (1998). *Communities of Practice: Learning, Meaning, and Identity*. Cambridge: Cambridge University Press.

Chapter 8

Musical Flourishing: Community Music Therapy, Controversy, and the Cultivation of Wellbeing

Gary Ansdell and Tia DeNora

Health – a resource for everyday life, not the objective of living. Health is a positive concept emphasizing social and personal resources, as well as physical capacities.

WHO Ottawa Charter for Health Promotion (1986)

To create flourishing and connected communities through the promotion of well-being and resilience and the reduction of inequalities.

New Horizons [UK Department of Health mental health strategy, 2010]

Music triggered a healing process from within me… I started singing for the joy of singing myself… and it helped me carry my recovery beyond the state I was in before I fell ill nine years ago…to a level of well-being that I haven't had perhaps for thirty years…

Cleo

Introduction: a Lord, a singer, and three controversies around music's help

On Thursday 6 March 2008 Lord Howarth rose to speak in a House of Lords debate on the arts in healthcare. As part of his speech, in the service of his call for increasing government support for this area, he quoted Cleo's words (see above in the epigraph) about how her experiences of singing had radically enhanced her wellbeing. A week previously Cleo had also been heard on a BBC Radio 3 edition of the *Music Matters* programme devoted exclusively to the subject of the emerging 'music and health' movement. Cleo and another member of a Community Music Therapy project in West London spoke eloquently of how their musical participation had helped forge a pathway for their gradual recovery from mental illness.

In this chapter we will use our ongoing research involvement in the project that Cleo was part of to help us reflect on the growing recognition of music's potential as a resource in health and social care. We will suggest how a growing interdisciplinary understanding of health and wellbeing as 'ecological' phenomena meshes perfectly with a similarly developing ecological understanding of people, music, and context. Together these perspectives show how music can provide a resource for cultivating wellbeing, understood as the positive flourishing of identity, relationship, and community (regardless of 'objective' health status).

We will also highlight in this chapter some of the dilemmas, controversies, and ironies associated with this current fashionable applause for 'music and health'. We take this tack not to undermine the applause, but to subject some current assumptions and confusions to a degree of scrutiny appropriate to this volume. As the sociologist Bruno Latour (2005) has pointed out, we should learn to 'feed off controversies' as they often focus broader dimensions of a given phenomenon. Here our phenomenon is 'music's help', and its current shifting practice, discipline, and profession dimensions. We hope our discussion and analysis will help with ongoing attempts to clarify this field—intellectually and politically.

Firstly, a controversy of practice concerns what forms of musical/therapeutic practice are necessary and suitable for what kinds of people and places[1], and how to provide appropriate 'evidence of effectiveness' for such practices.

Secondly, a controversy of discipline concerns what (inter)disciplinary understanding should inform, justify, or explain music/health practices. Music therapy seems currently to be developing in two different and, at first glance, seemingly incommensurable disciplinary directions—towards either 'music medicine' (or 'music therapy in integrative medicine') grounded in a biomedical treatment model (Hanser 2009), or alternatively towards Community Music Therapy within a psychosociocultural model more concerned with the musical cultivation of personal and social wellbeing (Stige et al. 2010). What more inclusive theoretical models might help future consilience?

Thirdly, a controversy of profession concerns the interests of varying professional groups providing music services across an increasingly diverse arena of professional practice, and how these link with policy, strategy, and governance dimensions of health and social care providers and legislators. The language and *realpolitik* of this controversy highlights an interesting new coalition between cultural and healthcare politics.

We hope that discussion of these broad themes will bring to the fore both the exciting potential of an invigorating field, but also some of the areas where careful analysis, discrimination and conceptual care are urgent. During our argument we will continually touch base with an empirical case study of Community Music Therapy to illustrate what we understand by 'musical flourishing'.

A Community Music Therapy project

In January 2005 Gary[2] initiated a Community Music Therapy project in London aiming to strengthen collaboration between two adjacent mental health facilities: a medium-sized psychiatric unit run by the NHS, and (next door in an older building) a community-based day centre for people with enduring mental health problems run by a charity with funding from the local Social Services. Between 1999–2004 Gary had worked as a music therapist in the hospital setting, doing individual sessions, small groups, and larger communal musical events with patients from the wards and day hospital. During this period he'd been increasingly developing a Community Music Therapy approach, both in his thinking and practice.[3] This took its inspiration from the original broad-based work of the Nordoff–Robbins approach to music therapy he was trained in (Nordoff and Robbins 1977/2007; Aigen 2005), but also evolved from simply following the varying musical needs of the patients in the hospital, and of the 'circumstantial community' where patients and staff find themselves. His key question was always simply: 'How can music help here, in this often emotionally challenging and socially isolating context?'

---

[1] 'People and places' is a rather weak descriptor, but we are trying to avoid foreclosing the discussion in terms of 'patients', 'clients', 'service users', or set delivery domains such as social care, healthcare, education, since these very variables are currently changing as part of the complex field we discuss.

[2] In this article we will use the convention of referring to ourselves as practitioners (music therapist, researcher) by our first names, and as researchers or scholars by our surnames.

[3] For accounts of the evolving thinking and practice of Community Music Therapy see Ansdell (2002), Stige (2003), Pavlicevic and Ansdell (2004), Stige et al. (2010), and Aigen (in press).

He found how 'traditional' individual sessions in a private setting were often needed to establish musical communication and relationship with patients in an acute phase of their illness. But as they recovered, small group sessions were also necessary to help foster musical community between patients through playing and singing together. Talented musicians emerged amongst the patients, whose illness had disrupted their health-promoting relationship to music. These people needed to perform again, and to be witnessed as musicians by both fellow patients and staff. Small performance events in the hospital aided their musical needs, but also provided staff with a temporary respite from the 'them/us' hierarchy of medical settings. The music therapy service developed a fluid pattern of 'formats' of music therapy—with patients often showing and talking about how music therapy helped them to re-establish a healthy relationship to music, and to use the musical relationship with the therapist as a trusted one that could accompany them through progressive stages of their recovery. Colleagues told Gary that his work helped them work more pleasurably in this environment and helped cultivate more positive perceptions and relationships with patients.

In 2005 Gary handed over this work in the hospital to colleague Sarah Wilson and moved to the day centre one minute's walk away on the same site. The intention was to find a practical solution to the oft-asked questions: 'What happens after formal music therapy?'; 'When people are discharged from acute medical care how can the benefits of music and music therapy continue for them?'

In January 2005 Gary established a weekly music group in the day-centre café. This ongoing group called BRIGHT Music is a cross between a music therapy session and an open-mic session, and is billed as a weekly 2-hour music afternoon open to anyone attending (which includes both regular members and members of the public just dropping in for a coffee). Between 2005–2010 there have been 200 sessions—comprising of all kinds of musicking: solos and group singing based on an evolving song-book repertoire, but also spontaneous individual 'turns'. There is also improvisation with percussion instruments, spontaneous dancing, celebrations of birthdays and festive occasions. Gradually a 'backing band' built up from talented musicians who belong to this community (guitars, drums, violin, harmonica, trombone, clarinet). The session includes a variety of people of varying ages, backgrounds, and levels of musical training and experience—including staff and visitors.

As this event established itself explicit links were made between the two venues. Sarah (now working in the hospital) could encourage patients also to use BRIGHT Music when well enough, or when discharged they could 'graduate' to BRIGHT. The project was enhanced one stage further when funding was found for Sarah to co-facilitate the afternoon café group. Sarah was able now to physically accompany people across from the hospital to BRIGHT Music, and provide moral support through her established musical relationship with hospital patients, helping them 'bridge the gap' in several ways: between an acute and a community setting; between an individual-focused medical model and a socially-focused wellbeing and empowerment model; between specialist music therapy attention and the looser and more socially normalized feel of music in BRIGHT.

Sarah also set up two 'spin-off' groups at BRIGHT for more specialist musical needs on a second afternoon. The BRIGHT Music group had identified a group of men who had previously played in bands, and who needed help to set up a proper band together. Equally, another group wanted to sing together, but in a more intimate group than the open group, and with more of a learning focus. Both groups have established identities—BRIGHT Band and BRIGHT Singers—and have both provided 'home-grown' entertainment for BRIGHT occasions and parties, and have also been booked for external gigs in the area.

This project has developed in fascinating ways in its five years. In 2008 it won the Royal Society for Public Health 'Arts & Health Award' and was featured on a BBC Radio 3 programme on music and health. The Director of BRIGHT comments: 'BRIGHT Music lights up this organisation and the lives of the people who participate in it. It is one of the most important things we do here. . .'.

A parallel research arm to the project has trailed its developments and participants in the hope of understanding better the factors contributing to its success. After a year of the project an ethnographic interview project explored participation in the music project in the context of more general relationships to music of members and staff of BRIGHT. Four overall themes emerged from this work—which have subsequently acted as orientating concepts for the following 3 years of varying ethnographic study:

♦ **Musical participations and collaborations**: the project was seen to enhance people's capacity (in both sites) to participate socially through participating musically—and to enhance collaboration. It also fostered increased collaboration between the two sites/services.

♦ **Musical narratives:** confirming Ansdell and Meehan's earlier (2010) research in the hospital setting, members' narratives of their musical experiences within BRIGHT connected with their everyday and historical relationships with music, their everyday uses of music, and their access (or not) to local cultural resources. These narratives suggested a strong relationship between members' musical participations (often mediated by the new possibilities of BRIGHT Music) in relation to their overall wellbeing, identity, social mobility, and 'social capital' as they lived with the effects of long-term mental illness. We call these stories 'music-health-illness narratives' (after Ansdell and Meehan (2010)).

♦ **Musical environments and networks:** the project and its various musical activities enhanced the physical, emotional, social and cultural environment and helped people build or expand social and cultural networks.

♦ **Musical pathways:** the project helped forge and develop pathways between the two sites; between acute and community care, and between experienced states of illness and health.

The ongoing study (2005–2010) has attempted to form a grounded and detailed longitudinal study of the project, informed by an interdisciplinary understanding coming from music therapy and a cultural sociology of health perspective. Its focus has been on how people can use music as a key resource for enhancing their personal, social and environmental wellbeing, how professional music therapy can help with this, and how such outcomes can be studied.

Two 'musical pathways'

The concept of 'musical pathways' has proved central to exploring the project as a whole, and to understanding the key associations between people, music, health, and wellbeing. A second stage of the research project has tracked ten willing participants who best illustrate this phenomenon. These are people who have in different ways used music to help forge a pathway both between the physical sites of their care, but also between experiential states of illness and health.

For this chapter we will introduce just two of these 'pathway cases'—two women[4] whose eloquent testimonies on the Radio 3 broadcast we quote from in this section.

Sophie describes her early life as filled with music, and music has remained central to her personal and social identity. She also has a diagnosis of personality disorder, and for a period in her twenties was either in acute or day care of the psychiatric unit. During this period she also stopped being involved in music. Sophie occasionally attended hospital music therapy groups, but found the new

---

[4] Their names and details are anonymized here, but these participants have given full permission for their words and stories to be used as part of the research process of this project, and subsequent published accounts.

performance group that Sarah set up suited her better. Whilst still an inpatient, but just before her discharge, she managed to perform a song to fellow patients and staff, a moment she describes as a key moment—'I did it!'. Sophie was able to move seamlessly after discharge over to BRIGHT Singers, which Sarah also ran. Music, music therapy and Sarah were able to accompany Sophie through a difficult transition in the location of her care, and in her personal journey to health. Subsequently Sophie has flourished, with music and singing providing a pathway for her recovery. She has performed both in the group, and externally, built new social networks and found a job.

> Sophie: I suffer with personality disorder. . . so often interacting with people can be quite diffi-cult. . . my mood changes very rapidly. . . so when I'm using music to help me it's a stabilizing influence. . . because it's something very constant and very stable. . . that I can enjoy and build something around.
>
> Interviewer: So has it had an effect then. . .in the rest of your life, in negotiating those relationships with people. . .the experience of making music with other people, and what's happening at BRIGHT today, has helped?
>
> Sophie: Yes, definitely. . . it really is. . . this is so crucial. Without the music groups I probably wouldn't have got out yesterday at all. . . had it not been for the music group. And like-wise today. . . I probably wouldn't have been able to get out of the house had I not had this group to actually want to come to, and enjoy, and meet people and talk to people, and have contact with the outside world. . . which is so crucial in recovering and main-taining recovery. Mental health can be incredibly lonely. . . it's an incredibly isolating condition in its broad spectrum. . . so to have something that everybody can come together and have contact with a couple of people twice a week, once a week. . . whatever it is. . . is absolutely crucial to maintaining it. . .

Sophie later gave the researchers the following statement, saying that she wanted to sum up what the music therapy project had meant for her:

> Music and music therapy has been the support and driving force of my treatment and continuing recovery. The continuity, unconscious nurturing and support to my confidence and mental health has been a key to where I am now. It has bridged and supported every step to enable me to progress – in a way that no other therapy has managed in such an all-inclusive way.

Cleo also describes the problems of living with enduring mental health problems. She, too, has always used music to help herself, but at points of acute illness finds she can no longer access this resource for herself. As a long-term patient in the hospital, Cleo had individual and group music therapy and sang in the inpatient performance group. On discharge she enthusiastically partici-pated in both BRIGHT Music and BRIGHT Singers, and then 'graduated' to music courses and a choir at a local adult education centre. She has now moved area and is helping set up music activi-ties there for people with mental health problems. Cleo commented on her 'musical pathway':

> Cleo: I have bi-polar affective disorder, otherwise known as manic depression. And it presents in me originally as mild mania, then extremely severe suicidal depressions, for months at a time. . . People think that mental health somehow affects your intelligence. . . it doesn't! It may affect your ability to remember things, or to function. . . but your innate intelligence never goes away. . . and your innate music doesn't go either. So once it's been triggered. . . it's a life-enhancing thing, overtaking the illness. It's the stronger force in me. . . it's the wellness in me. . .
>
> Interviewer: What part did music play in your recovery?
>
> Cleo: I think that. . . not just music. . . but what Gary and Sarah offered. . . that triggered in me the wish to sing. . . and that triggered in me a healing process from within me. So that, yes, it was being facilitated by them. . . and needed to be facilitated by them for quite some time. . . before I could stand on my own. . . little vocal chords, if you like, . . . and

> start singing for the joy of singing myself. . . and carry my recovery beyond the state I
> was in before I fell ill nine years ago. . . to a level of wellbeing that I haven't had perhaps
> for thirty years. . .

These two brief but conceptually-rich vignettes characterize the 'musical flourishing' that we have identified as a key aspect of the Chelsea Community Music Therapy Project. This work, however, has also served to highlight some broader current dilemmas and controversies over the identity, provision, evaluation and potential of music when connected to domains of health and wellbeing. In the remainder of this chapter we will consider aspects of the project (and of Cleo and Sophie's experiences) alongside three areas of controversy.

First controversy: practice and evidence

Practice

Cleo and Sophie's accounts present us with a topical dilemma. They talk both of their relationship to music and how it helps them, but also how the specialist provision of music therapy mediates this. But exactly what such 'facilitation' involves opens out the first of our controversies, both within the music therapy profession, and between it and other contenders offering 'music's help'. There's often an ambiguity between what clients think they are getting, what music therapists and other musicians think they are doing, and what employers are seeking or needing to justify.

With other comparable Allied Health Professions[5] such as physiotherapy or speech and language therapy the professional aim and role is often clearer. Few would suggest an amateur be substituted for a professional. With music therapy it is not quite so simple. Some 'patients' will already use music as a 'therapeutic' resource for themselves. So what is a 'therapist' adding?

'A theory' might be one answer given. But there is a problem here. The vast history of 'music therapy' (ancient and modern) could be characterized broadly as either a theory in search of a practice, or a practice in search of a theory (Ansdell 2003). Firm connection between practice and theory has never really stabilized. The situation for the last 60 years have been rather like the protagonist of Woody Allen's film *Zelig*, who pathologically adapts to fit in his immediate context— changing colour, size, or personality accordingly. Music therapy practice has equally adapted practice and theory to both treatment context and client group (Ruud 1980, 2010). Music therapists working in various medical settings have striven to demonstrate and talk of symptomatic change; those in psychiatric units have adapted practice to follow the psychotherapeutic agenda of patients developing reflective insight; those working with autistic children have invoked developmental/psychodynamic theory to guide and legitimate communication practices initiating developmental processes. Such pragmatism is of course welcome in one way—it could be said to be catering to the particular needs of particular clients. It has also, however, bred the current controversy of practice.

An alternative and probably more fruitful answer to the question 'What is a music therapist adding?' could be 'a tailored craft practice'. Instead of aligning to a medical or psychological theory, music therapists are seen primarily to contribute craft expertise, working both like midwives and surgeons (that is, as accompanists and interveners). The music therapist's professional expertise in this regard involves variously: knowing how to be personally sensitive in relation to the client's problems or illness; knowing how to be musically sensitive, and how to use music in

---

5 In the UK music therapy has been a state-registered health profession since 1999, professionally organized within the 'allied health professions' umbrella of the NHS. Other countries have varying degrees of professional registration and organization for music therapy (see http://www.voices.no for country profiles).

sensitive ways (based on know how to attend to and understand clients' musical practices); knowing how to use music strategically to instigate and support musicking in a variety of formats.

This praxial answer (of 'doing things with music') is at the heart of what has become known as a 'music-centred' approach to music therapy (Ansdell 1995; Aigen 2005; Verney and Ansdell 2010) and it is a hallmark of the Nordoff–Robbins tradition in which the aims, techniques, and possible benefits of music have to do with the specific features and affordances of the art-form itself. A music therapist working from this perspective asks:

- How can I help this client to be 'a musician';[6] help this place to become musicalized?
- How can I help them overcome the barriers to full musical participation, or loosen the hindrances to full, creative, relational musicking?
- What strategies and techniques can I use to mobilize the specific qualities and affordances of music for this particular person/situation and their particular needs?
- What diverse benefits could flow from such 'full musicking'?

The music therapist's expertise is then how she musically addresses these questions in practice. This way of thinking and working has several advantages. It avoids practice being inappropriately co-opted within treatment models which ill fit with music. It nevertheless orientates professional aims relevant to working musically with people, cultivates precise craft practices, and allows the practitioner to remain their identity both as a musician and a 'health professional' or equivalent. It enables 'therapeutic outcomes' to be defined in terms of possible musical entailments, rather than direct non-musical effects or therapeutic transformations.

Community Music Therapy has grown out of this music-centred tradition and principle (Ansdell 2002; Stige 2003; Pavlicevic and Ansdell 2004; Garred 2006; Stige et al. 2010; Aigen in press). The project we characterize in this chapter shows many of the above characteristics of practice. Gary 'listened' for how music could help patients, and the psychiatric hospital itself. He worked to try to locate and ease the barriers and hindrances to musicking for people there. Sometimes the work was 'specialist' (Ansdell et al. 2010), using particular music-therapeutic techniques, whilst sometimes it was more general and needed the help of other staff and musicians. Overall the professional competences were: to attend to and accompany people musically; to be sensitive to people's own relationships to music; to foster musical communication and musical community.

But an important aspect of our argument here is also that this professional help is only part of the picture. Cleo and Sophie organize some of the therapeutic help of music for themselves. What music therapy provides is rather a specialist 'bridge' between this and their further accessing of music's help in the community. Of course not all client groups that music therapists work with can articulate their needs this clearly, and a music therapist may sometimes have to provide nearly all of their 'access to music'.

A further aspect of the controversy over practice and expertise involves the relationship between music therapists and other musicians who work in the growing 'music and health' field, and who are beginning to challenge the music therapist's monopoly on 'therapeutic' work. A health service with diminishing resources may be reluctant to keep employing expensive music therapists when they can employ others cheaper. A clinician may be suspicious of a music therapist claiming only to 'facilitate full access to musicking' rather than deliver common team-based clinical outcomes. A quick glance at a music therapy group may see no difference between an amateur and a professional's work.

---

[6] By 'musician' we mean not that someone assumes a professional identity, but that they act from their innate personal and social musicality.

So for music therapists the 'practice dilemma' involves a precarious tight-rope walk. Firstly in balancing a confidence in their specialist craft skill and professional knowledge whilst acknowledging the equal and complementary abilities of clients and other musicians. Secondly, retaining a confidence in their often tacit praxial knowledge of people, music, illness and health, and not falling into a cosy association with the 'wrong' professional theory in the search for occupational approval and legitimation.

Evidence

How effective is music therapy practice? The controversy of evidence has brewed over what is appropriate as evidence, and how this might be demonstrated. This controversy highlights how we register people and their wellbeing, what kind of thing music is to offer them help, and what 'proof' of such help might be acceptable. Music therapists increasingly need to account for the effectiveness of what they do in a manner commensurate with the evidence-based medicine movement (EBM) in medical research (Pavlicevic et al. 2009; Wigram and Gold, Chapter 13, this volume). But inevitably, EBM (or evidence-based practice, EBP) discourse bears traces of the medical model and the predominance within medical research of certain notions of health and illness—pathology, an aetiology lodged in biopsychological terms, and a conception of treatment as a specific (and typically pharmacological or surgical) intervention. And yet, perhaps especially in relation to mental health or other psychosocial 'conditions', meaning, emotion and social fit come into play, and in ways that are poorly catered to by the protocol of the randomized control trial (RCT).

We suggest that the current situation is too procrustean. We believe the time has come to think critically about the 'fit' or appropriateness of assessment methods and their purported hierarchy since the 'gold standard' of these methods, the RCT, was designed for testing physical matter (and physiological reactions) and not wellbeing, let alone 'community health'. Just how applicable, in other words, is the RCT for music therapy, a mode of activity that is, essentially, a form of human cultural interaction (more than physical reaction)? And if we use it, will we, like Procrustes, find ourselves either stretching or cutting off the truth of just how music works?

For example, music may not make the symptoms of illness 'go away'—for example, music therapy is unlikely to 'cure' cancer. What it can do, however, is alert us to the ways in which the cancer identity may be mediated, transcended, elided, or mollified through collective activity such that it might even become possible to speak of how, even at the very end of life, it is possible to 'be well', for example by dwelling in a meaningful state with others. With psychosocial 'conditions' such as those associated with mental health there is yet more grey area since the very process of assessment can contribute to the condition it is meant merely to describe. What we are getting at here is that mental health is as much an identity as a condition, and as such, mental health can never be fully extricated from the culture in which it is performed and recognized.

If that is indeed the case, then the question of how to create cultures capable of eliding mental illness and magnifying, to return to Cleo whom we quoted earlier, the 'wellness in me'. If Cleo's pathway to wellbeing is ecologically grounded in musical practice, then it is in relation to that practice that we will be able to see, and document, the 'wellness in her' and that passage-work will not occur according to a RCT imagery of some administration of a treatment variable. Rather it will be observable only over the long term and in her situated practices, as she herself and in collaboration with others goes forward into different patterns of action and world making, ones that displace patterns associated with illness, replace her in a world of 'health-musicking' (Stige, Chapter 14, this volume).

This process involves multidimensional change: skills, practices, relations, new habits, embodied stances and styles, activities, and forms of occupation. There is no 'one' way of measuring this form of wellbeing since it emerges from so many things at once. It is not about what is 'done to'

Cleo but about what Cleo is able to 'do to/do with' her worlds, a two-way interaction of client and world, one in which the 'variables' that help her are constantly being modified by her so as to make a better 'fit' between her capacities and what her social habitat affords and expects. She is, in short, active in the production of the 'variables' that she then appropriates as part of a wider project of interactive musicking. And here the music therapist's job is, as we described above, to be musically sensitive, to facilitate this process. Simple measurement is just not up to the job of comprehending what is happening. To assess this practice there is only one thing to be done: we have to consult the clients themselves, and trust their self-insight. Thus at its core, Community Music Therapy is truly client-centred, and poses a radical challenge to conventional modes of EBM.

This challenge consists of two key shifts. Firstly, away from a coarse dichotomy of health–illness in favour of the mechanisms and processes of moving along a continuum from wellness to illness, sometimes back and forth within a single day or hour! And that means a focus on how these shifts are effected, by clients and therapists in tandem. And that means a theoretical conception that enables us to perceive the most minute of changes, as a composite of social/musical/psychological. For example, within a social setting, how do clients/users learn (and can be informally encouraged) to craft narratives of self that enhance psychosocial development? How is that process collaborative and how is investigating that process simultaneously active in its constitution (Procter 2004, 2006; Rolvsjord 2010; Batt-Rawden and DeNora 2005; Batt-Rawden 2006).

The second shift is professional. If there is currently a move in favour of, for example, randomized clinical trials, reliability, and transparent procedure, this is in great part linked to the shift in power between medical and managerial personnel. The drive towards regularization and accountability (as produced by findings that can be abstracted and upheld as justification for particular ways of doing) is always a move that favours managerial sectors; it moves criteria of evaluation away from the valuing of individual expert (in this case clinical-practical) opinion and in favour of documentable evidence.

Music therapy has, as we discussed above, been somewhat timorous in relation to calls for 'hard' evidence. And yet the irony of music therapy is that it is precisely poised to show those who demand evidence that they need to broaden the terms of what counts as evidence and from whom. This touches on our third controversy—profession. For we think that music therapy's influence lies precisely in its 'underdog' status as a 'para-medical' profession. It can serve to open up our understanding of how music 'really' works through how its powers are negotiated in and through musical interaction, and how musical activity works often because it supplants practices and habits linked to illness or pathology by offering things that medicalized forms of treatment rarely if ever touch (and RCTs find difficult to measure)—pleasure, communality, conviviality, trust. The conundrum over 'measuring' things such as 'enhanced confidence' or 'heightened trust' revolves around a paradox. On the one hand, the health-policy needs for reliable modes of assessment (i.e. if a programme is to be funded as general provision—e.g. 'music on the NHS'—it needs to deliver effectiveness to many[7]). On the other hand, the very things that need to be measured are only 'real' in the ways they emerge from individual and collective experience, from the personal and 'lay' forms of expertise that surround individuals' senses of 'wellbeing' as opposed to health. This conundrum leads us into our second controversy—the area of professional 'discipline' which provides the ground for conceptualizing music work, its meanings and effects.

---

[7] See Wigram and Gold, Chapter 13, this volume

Second controversy: discipline

'What is the theory behind your work?' Whilst this question is often asked innocently enough it opens up both an ongoing dilemma and a realm of controversy for music therapy and music and health practices. Theoretical perspectives used variously to guide practice, explain effects, and seek occupational justification have seldom proved compatible bed-fellows with the realities of practice!

Music and healing practices have been linked to cosmological, metaphysical, and scientific concepts of the day (Schullian and Schoen 1948; Ruud 1980; Gouk 2000; Horden 2000). In 'modern' music therapy theoretical alliances continue to be shadowed by these discourses, while also ingesting biological, psychological and cultural terminologies, depending on who a therapist works with, and where. As such, music therapy can appear a pre-paradigmatic (or possibly non-paradigmatic) endeavour.

Community Music Therapy's contribution to this meta-theoretical dilemma has been to attempt to reframe what theory can and should do in relation to music therapy practice. The perspective we have been building up in this chapter suggests that what is required is not a theory that specifically directs or explains practice 'non-musically', but one which can orientate practice within a broader theoretical territory in which flexible musical-social practice can 'explain itself', without being reduced to the instrumentalization of a single theory of any type. This is nearest to the original Goethean idea of a 'delicate empiricism', part of a 'qualitative science' that attempts to 'preserve the phenomenon' whilst putting this in a context of theory which allows it to be seen ecologically.[8]

In the service of this aim two interrelated disciplinary shifts have conveniently arrived in recent years to help us understand the varying relationships between music, health, disability and well-being—and consequently the role and 'mechanisms' of more specialist practices such as music therapy within such an understanding.

Firstly, a shift in 'music studies' is emerging from a synthesis of the insights of the 'new musicology', anthropological studies of cross-cultural and sub-cultural musics, popular music studies, social psychology of music, and the 'new' sociology of music (see Ansdell 2004; Ruud 2010). Together these provide a vital reorientation to thinking about music essentially as 'music-in-action' or 'musicking' in relation to people, context, and culture.

Overall this evolving understanding could be characterized a performative or ecological one (Small 1998; DeNora 2000, 2003; Hennion 2003; Clarke 2005)—acknowledging musick(ing) as the outcome of the dynamic interdependence of human and 'non-human' phenomena and resources (sounds, agents, actions, forms, processes, purposes, 'habitats').

The second necessary disciplinary shift has been a parallel ecological understanding of health, illness, disability, and wellbeing. Together, these two streams could form a useful confluence, which we outline in the following preliminary sketch for an ecological model for music and health.

An ecological model of health, wellbeing, and music

We have suggested that health and wellbeing are multidimensional phenomena. These included matters biochemical, psycho-motor, cognitive, emotional, social, and cultural (moral, spiritual, aesthetic). It is possible to enjoy 'good health' according to some of these measures, while being 'ill' according to others. There is in short no 'one form' of health. Moreover, all forms of

---

[8] For more on Goethe's theory of science see Bortoft (1996), Naydler (1996), Hoffmann (2007), and in relation to Nordoff–Robbins music therapy practice, theory and research see Ansdell and Pavlicevic (2010).

health-promoting practice not only seek to 'treat' a condition, they simultaneously perform particular conceptions of what it is to be 'well'—to be 'cancer-free', to be 'free of drug-dependency', 'pain free', 'without anguish', 'loved and loving', 'with grace' or 'together'. How would or could one choose between these things?

Thinking about this question highlights some of the ways that our notions of being well are cultural constructions, linked to matters that take shape or emerge in relation to sociocultural practices. To speak of this matter is to recognize the ecological basis of what we take at face value to be health and wellbeing. And to make this recognition is to remind ourselves of the knowledge-based controversies discussed above in relation to evidence. Who is to say what health is and how is that definitional process characterized by a relations of production?

For example, from one corner, health consists of our ability to perform various conventional functions in everyday life. For example, are we able to eat and digest a meal, walk up stairs or hold a conversation. From another corner, these abilities (or their absence) may be read as presentational symptoms of 'conditions', for example when we are told that the pain and burning sensation we experience after a rich meal is an ulcer, the inability to climb stairs an indication of an arthritic condition, the inability to speak in public a feature of pathological shyness (Scott 2009). A condition is an official inscription, a lodging or matching of performance factors with discursive categories of health/illness. From yet another corner, however, health consists of the ways that our abilities/disabilities are mediated, transcended, magnified or diminished by the ways they articulate with what we and others do, and with aspects of our material cultural environments (Carel 2008). So, for example, if I relax more while eating or alter my diet, the symptoms may disappear without ever having made it to the level of official diagnosis; if I am in a social setting where my taciturn conduct is 'not a problem' I may become less self-conscious; if I never bother with stairs and live in a ground floor flat I might never notice I had mobility issues. Needless to say, the interaction between 'health' and social ecology becomes yet more interesting when we realize that there are ways, therefore, of 'getting better' that involve adaptations of environment to the needs and abilities of its inhabitants, and that health/illness identities can be seen to emerge in relation to these environments.

In recent years, scholars from a range of backgrounds have begun to explore how the manifestation of health states is mediated by particular and institutional configurations of the built environment and cultural practices. This work points to the ways in which health as a state may be seen to emerge from couplings between individuals, practices and modes of experience. As Clarke and Chalmers (1998)[9] suggest, 'if we remove the external component the system's behavioural competence will drop, just as it would if we removed part of the brain [or body]' (pp. 8–9). Of course, 'couplings' may include any number of humans, any number of materials. Similarly, recent research in the area of human/non-human interaction emphasizes the environmental affordances that are found within physical and/or conceptual spaces. Each of these bodies of work emphasize the interdependence of identities (including health identity, as known to self and other) and materials outside individuals.

From such an ecological understanding what we have observed in BRIGHT makes increasing sense in terms of the relationships between music, illness/health, disability and wellbeing. The 'musical-social resources' available through this project are not specific and static but various and 'in flow'. They are not targeted to just symptomatic relief or rehabilitation, but are ready to be appropriated individually and collectively to what suits people at a particular time, in a particular location—and in relation to what they need, then and there.

---

[9] http://consc.net/papers/extended.html

In her 'pathway interview' Cleo uses a conventional ecological analogy to describe her emergence from the worst year of her illness:

> … it's a bit like a plant… it's under the earth… you've sown a seed in the ground… and it's germinating… but you have no idea what's going on there, because it's invisible. But once that shoot comes up through the earth, you can begin to see things visibly growing… so if you take that year… in the last year… and you consider that I'm a little shoot… [both laugh]… and I've actually appeared… visibly… and I'm developing a bit here and there… with a little bit of water and a little bit of sunshine… you know… it's part of a whole context […] [S]o it's this [participating in the music project]… that gives me the platform for me to come out of myself… to emerge… that's the best way I can put it… and, um… . and this is actually hugely important to me… and it's not just through music… it's through personal confidence… being able to go up to a microphone and sing… to get myself back into mainstream life… and it's all helped… it's probably been the single most therapeutic catalyst… for my recovery… that I can actually name… and I really mean that!

The controversy within the disciplinary dimension of music therapy will creatively continue—with new and varying inputs from emerging interdisciplinary theory. What it must strive for, however, is to take evidence like Cleo's seriously, to follow its implications and to develop a theoretical understanding adequate to dealing with the following interdependent variables:

- Of people within their immediate context, community, and culture.

- In relation to their history, taste, and preferences.

- Along with their personhood, particular health/illness, disability, individual needs and preferences, ambitions, and hopes.

- In relation to the total available ecological resources comprising 'music's help'—mediated variously by professional, semi-professional, and 'lay' expertise.

Third controversy: profession

One rather dramatic early response to Community Music Therapy described it as 'professional suicide' (Erkkilä 2003). This was said against a background of increasing flux in the professional status of professional music therapy in Europe—where a challenge to medical-model music therapy was seen to be undermining half a century of theoretical and professional progress and consolidation. A further controversy flared in the *British Journal of Music Therapy* in 2008 when a lead article by Alison Barrington critiqued Community Music Therapy and was answered in a series of responses (Ansdell and Pavlicevic 2008; Procter 2008). Such local professional skirmishes have usefully directed attention to a broader situation for which Community Music Therapy is arguably being treated as a straw man for (Ansdell 2008).

This broader (increasingly international) situation concerns the current practice, disciplinary and professional developments in the area of music therapy/music and health. Recent research into the professionalization of music therapy in the UK (Barrington 2008)[10] has charted the rise to the point of perhaps maximum professional gain. But this has ironically appeared coincidentally with several factors threatening this. Firstly the de-institutionalization of many of the former medical-model services in which music therapy found both a home and a professional legitimacy

---

[10] Whilst music therapy in the UK is still a small profession, it has the longest professional history of development after the US (which Aigen (in press) confirms as having a largely parallel pattern of development in this area). Its professional and disciplinary phases are arguably of direct relevance to other less developed international music therapy communities.

and justification, and secondly the rise of the 'music and health' movement which now poses a challenge to music therapists' monopoly in key areas (Moss and O'Neill 2009; Clift 2010), but seems to be reinventing the wheel in terms of practice, discipline, and professional development.

Such professional patterns are too complex to deal with in any detail in this chapter, but would merit attention from a sociology of professions perspective. Overall perhaps what we see happening is what Stige et al. (2010, p. 304) have termed not a de-professionalization but a re-professionalization. This is turn involves aspects of the other two controversies we've outlined in this chapter—of practice and discipline. We could summarize the professional controversy in terms of two dilemmas. Firstly, a question concerning the professional: Who best does what for whom, where, and how? Secondly, a question concerning the shifting profession: What professional structures best support emerging necessary changes in practice and discipline?

But we must not forget our ongoing emphasis on what people can do for themselves! Our evidence from the Chelsea project (and the studies that informed this) has allowed us to trace the continuum between people's lay-expertise in using music as a helpful resource, through to the necessity for professionally-trained mediation, intervention and facilitation—at certain times, and in certain places. This continuum of experience of music and music therapy is clear in both Cleo and Sophie's accounts of their 'musical pathways'. They describe a permeable but definable border between the experience of music itself, the use of music as a self-therapy, and access to music as an organized therapy format provided within professional structures.

We would like to suggest the possibility of rethinking professionalism in the light of such examples, and in relation to the attitude Community Music Therapy takes. It is perhaps a case of cultivating permeable borders between experiences, activities and roles. This contrasts with the sharp boundaries which the institutionalization and professionalization of music therapy has attempted to impose, but which seems increasingly to limit its possibilities—for users and professionals alike.

Inconclusion

The situation we have outlined in this chapter is currently an inconclusive one on several levels. We could summarize the controversies and dilemmas as the following 'inconclusives':

- Firstly, how do we help people with music, but also help them to help themselves? What works best—for whom, for where, with what?
- Secondly, what (inter)disciplinary perspectives serve as the best guide to the further exploration, development and legitimation of a range of 'music and health' practices?
- Thirdly, what professional structures serve to best organize, educate, monitor, coordinate, and promote such a range of practices?

Our inclusion is, however, no council of despair! The controversies and dilemmas we've sketched also indicate new orientations within the currently shifting field.

A first pointer is perhaps to consider a broader spectrum of 'music's help'—acknowledging people's own capacity to mobilize their own 'music therapy', but also the need for a broader spectrum of professional and semi-professional facilitation too—at different times, and in different places for varying purposes. We hope that the case material in this chapter—from Sophie, Cleo, and BRIGHT Music—has shown just this. For too long the natural continuum of musical help has been artificially cut up and sequestered by professional and disciplinary restrictions.

A second pointer is towards a more ecological understanding of 'music's help'. A view of wellbeing as culturally and socially emergent provides a useful organizing idea for a psychosociocultural understanding of what music can offer people and situations. We have seen through the examples from BRIGHT how agents (clients, patients, musicians) can create—with support—bespoke resources for health promotion, in and through the creation of cultural/musical environments that permit them to assume the mantle of wellness—understood as an ecologically emergent identity. This helps release our thinking about music and health from a solely pathogenic focus and reorientates it towards the salutogenic landscape we have sketched in this chapter.

This is probably why 'wellbeing' is increasingly an organizing concept at policy, theory, and practice levels in contemporary health and social care domains.[11] Wellbeing derives from Aristotle's concept of *eudaimonia*, variously translated as 'an activity of the soul in accordance with excellence', or more simply, 'higher flourishing' (Vernon, 2008, p.43). Mike White (2005) reminds us that that as early as 1975 Michael Wilson was questioning our contemporary attitudes to health in his famous book *Health is for People*, in which he stated: 'It is difficult to describe what we mean by wellbeing without asking the question: What is health for?' Health, as we've been outlining in this chapter, is not separable from the varying ecological relationships we have to others, to the contexts we live in, the projects we have, and our beliefs, hopes and resources.

The philosopher Havi Carel writes about her own chronic illness and her finding health within illness.

> Wellbeing is the invisible context enabling us to pursue possibilities and engage in projects. It is the condition of possibility enabling us to follow through aims and goals, to act on our desires, to become who we are.
>
> (Carel 2008, p.53).

This sense of wellbeing is exactly what we have witnessed in the various musical activities in BRIGHT, and through the 'pathway narratives' of its members about music, illness, health, and wellbeing—exemplified in this chapter through the words of Cleo and Sophie. Cleo says that through her renewed musical participation she has 'reached a level of wellbeing that I haven't had perhaps for thirty years. . .'.

We suggest that Cleo's words about 'musical wellbeing' should be taken in accord with Aristotle's original insight: that we need a shift from an excessive attention to health as 'cure', towards a consideration of wellbeing cultivated through care and the cultivation of broader human flourishing. Here both illness and health are reconfigured within a more spacious social and cultural landscape. Wellbeing involves our flourishing together, within our sociocultural community.

This notion brings together a further necessary relationship, between ethics and aesthetics. Questions of justice, equity, and access are focused within the question that John Carey (2005) entitled his book with: *What Good are the Arts?* The time has come to open up the agenda of the relationship between healthcare and cultural politics—to what the arts as resources and activities can offer to the cultivation of greater wellbeing.

Aristotle, unlike Plato, did not think that music helped because of metaphysical correspondences with the planets, but because it promoted earthbound conviviality and communality ('wine, women, and song' to paraphrase!) (Horden 2000). Wellbeing is not just the absence of illness, or just an individual matter, or just the result of the provision of 'health technology'. It is, as Mark Vernon suggests, part of our pursuit of the 'spirit level', part of our seeking the 'good life'— through which we may find wellbeing together.

---

[11] See UK Dept of Health *Commisioning framework for health and well-being* (2007); UK Dept of Health Mental Health Strategy, *New Horizons*, 2009.

For many people wellbeing emerges in the spaces made between people and music. This was after all an insight that the pioneer music therapists Paul Nordoff and Clive Robbins came to 50 years ago through their work: that when music flourishes people flourish too.

References

Aigen, K. (2005). *Music-centered music therapy*. Gilsum, NH: Barcelona.

Aigen, K. (in press). Community music therapy. In G. McPherson, G. Welch (eds.) *Oxford handbook of music education*. Oxford: Oxford University Press.

Ansdell, G. (1995). *Music for life – Aspects of creative music therapy with adult clients*. London: Jessica Kingsley.

Ansdell, G. (2002). Community music therapy and the winds of change. [online] *Voices: A World Forum for Music Therapy*, 2(2).

Ansdell, G. (2003). The stories we tell: Some metatheoretical reflections on music therapy. *Nordic Journal of Music Therapy*, **12**(2), 152–9.

Ansdell, G. (2004). Rethinking music and community: Theoretical perspectives in support of Community Music Therapy. In: M. Pavlicevic, G. Ansdell (eds.) *Community Music Therapy*, pp. 91–113. London: Jessica Kingsley.

Ansdell, G. and Pavlicevic, M. (2008). Responding to the challenge: Converting boundaries into borders? A response to Alison Barrington's article 'Challenging the Profession'. *British Journal of Music Therapy*, **22**(2), 73–7.

Ansdell, G. and Meehan, J. (2010). 'Some light at the end of the tunnel': Exploring users' evidence for the effectiveness of music therapy in adult mental health settings. *Music and Medicine*, 2(1), 41–7.

Ansdell, G., Davidson, J., Magee, W., Meehan, J., and Procter, S. (2010). From 'this f***ing life' to 'that's better'. . . in four minutes: An interdisciplinary study of music therapy's 'present moments' and their potential for affect modulation. *Nordic Journal of Music Therapy*, **19**, 3–28.

Ansdell, G. and Pavlicevic, M. (2010). Practising gentle empiricism: The Nordoff-Robbins research heritage. *Music Therapy Perspectives*, **28**(2).

Barrington, A. (2008). Challenging the profession. *British Journal of Music Therapy*, **22**(2), 65–73.

Batt-Rawden, K. and Aasgaard, T. (2006). Music–a key to the Kingdom? A qualitative study of music and health in relation to men and women with long-term illnesses. *Electronic Journal of Sociology* http://www.sociology.org/content/2006/tier1/batt-rawden.html

Batt-Rawden, K. and DeNora, T. (2005). Music and informal learning in everyday life. *Music Education Research*, **7**, 3.

Batt-Rawden, K., Trythall, S., and DeNora, T. (2007). Health musicking as cultural inclusion. In: J. Edwards (eds.) *Music: Promoting Health & Creating Community in Healthcare Contexts*, pp. 64–82. Newcastle: Cambridge Scholars Publishing.

Bortoft, H. (1996). *The wholeness of nature: Goethe's way of science*. Edinburgh: Floris Books.

Carel, H. (2008). *Illness*. Stocksfield: Acumen.

Carey, J. (2005). *What Good Are The Arts?* London: Faber.

Clarke, E. (2005). *Ways of listening: An ecological approach to the perception of musical meaning*. Oxford: Oxford University Press.

Clarke, A. and Chalmers, D.J. (1998). The extended mind. *Analysis* **58**, 10–23.

Clift, S. (2010). Let the music play. *British Journal of Wellbeing*, **1**(1), 15–17.

DeNora, T. (2000). *Music in everyday life*. Cambridge: Cambridge University.

DeNora, T. (2003). *After Adorno. Rethinking music sociology*. Cambridge: Cambridge University.

Erkkilä, J. (2003). Book review of *Contemporary voices in music therapy: Communication, culture and community* (eds C. Kenny and B. Stige). [online] *Nordic Journal of Music Therapy*, Retrieved from www.njmt.no/bookreview_2003029.html

Garred, R. (2006). *Music as therapy: A dialogical perspective*. Gilsum, NH: Barcelona.

Gouk, P. (2000). *Musical healing in cultural contexts*. Aldershot: Ashgate.

Hanser, S. (2009). From ancient to integrative medicine: models for music therapy. *Music Medicine*, **1**, 87–96.

Hennion, A. (2003). Music and mediation: Towards a new sociology of music. In: M. Clayton, T. Herbert and R. Middleton (eds.) *The cultural study of music*, pp. 80–91. London: Routledge.

Hoffmann, N. (2007). *Goethe's science of living form: the artistic stages*. Hillsdale, NY: Adonis Press.

Horden, P. (2000). *Music as medicine: The history of music therapy since Antiquity*. Aldershot: Ashgate.

Latour, B. (2005). *Reassembling the social: an introduction to Actor-Network-Theory*. Oxford: Oxford University Press.

Moss, H. and O'Neill, D. (2009). What trainings do artists need to work in healthcare settings? *Medical Humanities*, **35**, 101–5.

Naydler, J. (1996). *Goethe on science: An anthology of Goethe's scientific writings*. Edinburgh: Floris Books.

Nordoff, P. and Robbins, C. (1977/2007). *Creative Music Therapy*. Gilsum, NH: Barcelona Publishers.

Pavlicevic, M. and Ansdell, G. (2004). *Community Music Therapy*. London: Jessica Kingsley.

Pavlicevic, M., Ansdell, G., Heaney, S. and Procter, S. (2009). *Presenting the Evidence: A Guide for Music Therapists Responding to the Demands of Clinical Effectiveness and Evidence-Based Practice*. London: Nordoff Robbins.

Procter, S. (2004). Playing politics: Community Music Therapy and the therapeutic redistribution of musical capital for mental health. In: M. Pavlicevic and G. Ansdell (eds) *Community Music Therapy*, pp. 214–32. London: Jessica Kingsley.

Procter, S. (2006). What are we playing at? Social capital and music therapy. In: R. Edwards, J. Franklin and J. Holland (eds). *Assessing social capital: Concept, policy, and practice*. Cambridge: Scholars Press.

Procter, S. (2008). Premising the challenge: A response to Alison Barrington's article 'Challenging the Profession'. *British Journal of Music Therapy*, **22**(2), 77–83.

Rolvsjord, (2010). *Resource-Oriented Music Therapy in Mental Health Care*. Gilsum, NH: Barcelona Publishers.

Ruud, E. (1980). *Music therapy and its relationship to current treatment theories*. Gilsum, NH: Barcelona Publishers.

Ruud, E. (2010). *Music Therapy: A Perspective from the humanities*. Gilsum, NH: Barcelona Publishers.

Schullian, D. and Schoen, M. (1948). *Music and medicine*. New York: Henry Schuman.

Scott, S. (2009). *Shyness and Society: The Illusion of Competence*. London: Palgrave Macmillan.

Small, C. (1998). *Musicking: The meanings of performing and listening*. Hanover, NH: Wesleyan University Press.

Stige, B. (2003). *Elaborations toward a notion of Community Music Therapy*. [Doctoral thesis] University of Oslo: Unipub.

Stige, B., Ansdell, G., Elefant, C., and Pavlicevic, M. (2010). *Where music helps: Community Music Therapy in action and reflection*. Aldershot: Ashgate.

Verney, R. and Ansdell, G. (2010). *Conversations on Nordoff-Robbins Music Therapy*. Gilsum, NH: Barcelona Publishers.

Vernon, M. (2008). *Wellbeing*. Stocksfield: Acumen.

White, M. (2005). Well being or well meaning? *Animated Dance Magazine*, Spring, 1–5.

Chapter 9

Singing, Wellbeing, and Health

Stephen Clift

Introduction

Since the early 1990s the questions of health benefits associated with singing, and the role of singing as a form of music therapy for people with compromised health, have attracted increasing international attention. Clift et al. (2008a) report a systematic mapping and review of research on singing, wellbeing, and health, focusing on non-clinical research (i.e. excluding music therapy). Clift et al. (2010a) have updated this review focusing specifically on studies of group or choral singing, and extending the scope to include music therapeutic interventions for specific health conditions. Skingley and Vella-Burrows (2010) have also reviewed research on the value of music and singing for older people in the context of healthcare. These reviews are drawn upon here to provide a selective and critical overview of research studies on the possible benefits of singing in groups.

The need to be critical is highlighted by the many unsubstantiated claims about singing and health made in newspaper reports and postings on the web, and by eminent musicians and distinguished academics. Thomas (2010), for example, claims that singing can prevent colds and flu, and Pomfret (2009) states that singing leads to endorphin release. The UK Singing Ambassador, Howard Goodall, suggests that singing can help childhood asthma[1] and Levitin (2008) claims that oxytocin is released when people sing together, giving rise to feelings of 'group spirit'. Unfortunately, however, none of these claims is supported by a robust body of research.

More research is needed before strong evidence-based claims can be made for the value of singing for health. The existing corpus of research on this issue lacks a common approach to health and wellbeing and little attention has been given to developing a coherent model of the mechanisms by which singing could affect health. Many studies are exploratory and involve very small samples and very few well-controlled experimental studies have been undertaken. Little attempt has been made to build a body of knowledge in a coherent way. Nevertheless, the research published so far does give promising indications in support of the hypothesis that 'singing is good for health'.

This chapter begins with an overview of non-clinical studies involving existing community choirs and singing groups or which have established singing groups for purposes of research. The focus then shifts to therapeutically oriented research investigating the value of singing for people with specific health or social care needs. The chapter will conclude with a brief outline of the work of the Sidney De Haan Research Centre for Arts and Health, and its efforts to develop an integrated and progressive programme of research on singing, wellbeing, and health.

---

[1] See: http://women.timesonline.co.uk/tol/life_and_style/women/body_and_soul/article1714652.ece

Non-clinical research on singing, wellbeing, and health

Qualitative studies of singing and health

A number of small-scale qualitative studies and larger-scale descriptive surveys have identified a range of social, psychological, and health benefits which singers feel they gain from singing (Clift et al. 2008a, 2010a). While such studies are difficult to synthesize to draw precise conclusions, similar themes appear repeatedly. Most studies, for example, report that singing can be mood enhancing (Clift and Hancox 2001; Bailey and Davidson 2002, 2005; Palmer 2008; Clift et al. 2008b, 2010b; Bungay et al. 2010; Clift and Hancox 2010), even to the point of producing feelings of 'euphoria' or a 'singer's high' (Jacob et al. 2009). Singing brings people together and helps to create a sense of group identity, social support and friendship (Clift and Hancox 2001; Latimer 2008; Lally 2009; Southcott 2009, Bungay et al. 2010). Singing can help to develop skills, self-confidence, self-esteem, and a sense of achievement (Bailey and Davidson 2002, 2005; Silber 2005). Singing is also a physical activity which is both 'energizing and relaxing' and can help to relieve stress and tension (Bailey and Davidson 2003; Tonneijck et al. 2008; Jacob et al. 2009). Singers commonly believe that singing helps to improve breathing and lung capacity, improves voice quality, and promotes good posture (Clift and Hancox 2001; Clift et al. 2009). Because of the cognitive demands associated with singing, the activity can also serve to distract attention from personal worries (Clift and Hancox 2010; Clif et al. 2010b). Several studies also identify a strong spiritual dimension to singing (Clift and Hancox 2001; Latimer 2008; Tonneijck et al. 2008).

'Experimental' studies of singing and health

Five studies have measured mood, emotional state, or wellbeing of participants before and after singing, using standardized instruments (Valentine and Evans 2001; Unwin et al. 2002; Kreutz et al. 2004, Cohen 2007; Sandgren 2009). In each case, the broad hypothesis being tested was that singing enhances positive mood/emotions and a sense of wellbeing. There is some support for this hypothesis, but effects sizes are generally smaller than might be expected from the evidence of qualitative studies (Kreutz et al. 2004; Clift et al. 2008a), and those studies employing listening controls have found that singing and listening can have similar effects in changing mood and subjective wellbeing (Unwin et al. 2002; Cohen 2009). Sangren (2009) reports that positive emotional changes associated with singing are stronger for women than for men, a finding consistent with evidence on sex differences in the experience of choral singing (Clift and Hancox 2001, 2010; Clift et al. 2010b)

Physiological changes associated with singing

Some studies have undertaken physiological monitoring of individuals, before, during, and after singing, to assess bio-markers assumed to have relevance to wellbeing and health (Beck et al. 2000; Grape et al. 2003; Kreutz et al. 2004). These studies vary substantially in terms of measures used, participants, and character of singing, and consequently general conclusions are difficult to draw (Clift et al. 2008a). It is remarkable, for example, that only single studies have measured heart rate and blood pressure (Valentine and Evans 2001), and heart rate variability in response to singing (Grape et al. 2003), despite the fact and that energetic singing undoubtedly serves to 'exercise' the cardiovascular system.

Five studies, however, have measured the effect of singing on salivary immunoglobulin A (sIgA), an antibody which is part of the immune system defending against respiratory infections. Four studies report an increase in sIgA in response to singing (Beck et al. 2000; Kuhn 2002; Kreutz et al. 2004; Beck et al. 2006) whereas one study found a decline (Rider et al. 1991). While significant increases in sIgA suggest increased immune system activity it is unclear whether such changes have any significance for health. Firstly, studies report shifts in average values over periods ranging from a few minutes to a couple of hours, and no data are presented on how long such changes are sustained after singing. Secondly, no evidence is presented to show that the level of changes has any real clinical significance with respect to an individual's resistance to infection. And thirdly, in studies of group singing, the change may have come about because singers are breathing in close proximity to one another. In other words, the heightened immune response may be a direct response to an increased risk of respiratory infection.

Effects of group singing on measures of physical and mental health

Cohen et al. (2006, 2007) report the only study to assess the value of group singing over time, using standardized measures of health and indicators of health service utilization. In a controlled but non-randomized study, healthy elderly people engaged in singing activities for 30 weeks a year over 2 years, were compared with a 'comparison group' who received no form of intervention except the assessments involved.

The outcomes of the study appear quite remarkable:

> Results obtained from utilizing established assessment questionnaires and self-reported measures, controlling for any baseline differences, revealed positive findings for the intervention such that the intervention group (*chorale*) reported a higher overall rating of physical health, fewer doctor visits, less medication use, fewer instances of falls, and fewer other health problems than the comparison group. The intervention group also evidenced better morale and less loneliness than the comparison group. In terms of activity level, the comparison group experienced a significant decline in total number of activities, whereas the intervention group reported a trend toward increased activity
>
> (Cohen et al. 2006, p. 726).

Despite the admirable features of this study, Clift et al. (2008a) identify a range of significant problems with data presentation, analysis, use of significance levels, and the way in which conclusions were drawn from the results. For example, no account was taken of substantial attrition rates over 2 years. Apparent floor effects on some of the measures employed were not acknowledged. Furthermore, a very liberal 10% level was used for judging significance of changes, raising the risks of falsely rejecting the null hypothesis (type 1 error). In addition to these technical issues, Cohen et al. do not address the possible role of participants' and researchers' expectations of benefit (i.e. study demand characteristics) which may have substantially biased questionnaire completion. Thus, while the study does provide some evidence of health benefits for older people from choral singing, Clift et al. (2008a) caution against accepting Cohen et al.'s findings at face value.

Singing and lung function

Four studies have investigated the hypothesis that singing has a beneficial effect on aspects of 'pulmonary function' among trained and amateur singers. The two earliest studies, Heller et al. (1960) and Gould and Okamura (1973) are at variance with one another, and have been strongly criticized by Schorr-Lesnick et al. (1985), for methodological weaknesses due to small sample sizes and inappropriate controls. In a larger and better controlled investigation, Schorr-Lesnick et al. compared professional singers with professional wind and string instrumentalists on seven measures of pulmonary function. No significant differences were found between groups when compared directly or when controlling for potentially confounding variables such as weight, smoking, and years of performing.

Only one further research study has assessed the lung function of classically trained singers using standard spirometric measures (Carroll et al. 1996). Comparison with published norms for a general population, revealed higher values for singers, and Carroll et al. conclude that there is a need for 'separate normative data' in assessing the performance of 'the vocal athlete'. The study was uncontrolled, however, and had no longitudinal dimension, so the alternative hypothesis that singers were already higher on measures of pulmonary function prior to training could not be ruled out.

Clinical investigations of the benefits of group singing

The notion that singing can promote health in a holistic sense is an attractive one. Most qualitative studies offer a convincing story that group singing can be beneficial for psychological and social wellbeing. But robust objective evidence on the value of singing for physical wellbeing is virtually non-existent, even in relation to lung function, where intuitively, singing might be expected to show benefits. There is, however, a growing literature on the value of singing for individuals with chronic health problems. Attention is given here to research on singing and breathing problems, singing in the context of social care for elderly people with dementia and singing and Parkinson's disease. One study concerned with chronic pain (Kenny and Faunce 2004) found no convincing evidence that group singing helped with pain control. Racette et al. (2006) show that group singing can help aphasics regain speech; Giaquinto et al. (2006) explore the value of group singing in combating postoperative depression, and Pavlakou (2009) reports on the benefits of group singing for people with eating problems. In a discussion paper, Young (2008) considers the potential value of community singing groups for people with cancer.

Singing and breathing problems

In a rather complex design, Wade (2002) compared the value of vocal exercises and singing with music-assisted relaxation for nine children with asthma. She reports that exercises and singing improved peak expiratory flow rates, especially when singing followed relaxation. However, the number of participants was small, and the study ran over a very short period of time. In addition, no statistical analysis was undertaken and the significance of the changes reported is unknown.

Eley and Gorman (2008, 2010) assessed the effects of weekly singing lessons for nine Aboriginal girls with asthma, over a period of 6 months and significant improvements were observed for peak expiratory flow (PEF), but not for forced expiratory flow (FEV_1) and forced vital capacity (FVC). However, the sample size is small, and the intervention uncontrolled. While FEV_1 data for individual participants are reported, similar tables for PEF and FVC values are not given. In addition, raw FEV_1 values are reported and as a percentage relative to sex/age norms. The mean percentage at baseline for the girls was 105%, indicating above average performance. This may have been a factor which restricted the potential for improvement in response to the singing intervention. These limitations make it difficult to reach any firm conclusions about the value of singing for asthma in girls, despite the reported significant improvement in PEF values.

Engen (2005) studied the impact of vocal exercise and group singing on the lung function and breathing patterns of seven patients with emphysema. None of the physical health and quality of life measures showed improvements over the 6 weeks of the study, but counting as a measure of breath control and voice intensity both improved significantly. In addition, breathing mode changed from being 'predominantly clavicular to 100% diaphragmatic that was maintained in all but one subject 2 weeks after the treatment sessions ended'. Again, this study is very small scale and uncontrolled.

Bonilha et al. (2009) report a small randomized controlled trial to assess the impact of singing groups on lung function and quality of life among patients with chronic obstructive pulmonary disease (COPD). The major finding was that while the control group showed a decline in measures of maximal expiratory pressure, the group involved in singing showed a small improvement. No improvements were found, however, on a range of additional spirometric measures. Both groups showed increased quality of life scores but with no statistically significant difference. While the study is small, it represents an admirable development in being controlled and clinically focused.

A small trial examining the effects of singing lessons for patients with COPD is reported by Lord et al. (2010). Thirty-six COPD patients (mean FEV 37.2% predicted) were randomized to either 12 one-hour sessions of singing lessons over 6 weeks, or usual care. Following attrition 15 patients in the singing group were compared with 13 controls. Significant improvements were found in levels of anxiety and self-assessed physical wellbeing in the singing group. No differences were found between the groups for single breath counting, incremental shuttle walking test (ISWT) scores, or recovery time following ISWT and intriguingly breath-hold time increased more in the control group than the singing group.

Singing, elderly people in care, and dementia

Singing and musical activity are commonly referred to as 'non-pharmacological interventions' in the context of elderly care and dementia. The potential advantages of using music therapeutically, including listening to recorded music and singing by caregivers, are supported by research evidence (Skingley and Vella-Burrows 2010). Group singing, however, does not emerge as an effective intervention for people with dementia in recent systematic reviews (e.g. Hulme et al. 2008; O'Connor et al. 2009a,b). Indeed, Brown et al. (2001) caution that with the decline in cognitive function associated with late-stage dementia, the capacity to engage in coordinated group singing becomes more difficult, and may have little benefit. Nevertheless, two recent studies have explored the value of group singing for elderly people with dementias in residential care, and provide some indications of positive benefits.

Myskyja and Nord (2008) considered the impact of re-introducing active participation in group singing and music making in a nursing home catering for residents with dementia. Musical activities in the home ceased when the music therapist took leave of absence, and staff reported increased depression among residents. The return of the music therapist gave an opportunity for a 'natural experiment' to assess the effects of singing. Residents were assessed for depression, using the Montgomery Aasberg Depression Rating Scale before the musical activity started and again after 2 months of twice-weekly group singing. A significant reduction in depression was found over the period of the intervention with greater improvement among residents showing highest levels of engagement with singing. While the study has limitations, it has strengths in being conducted in a care setting, and is perhaps the best that can be achieved in research terms given the challenges of investigating interventions with people who are very elderly, frail, and cognitively impaired.

Svansdottir and Snaedel (2006) conducted a small controlled trial on the value of group singing for elderly patients with moderate to severe dementia. The intervention involved small groups of participants, encouraged by a music therapist to sing and use instruments in 30-minute sessions, three times a week for 6 weeks. The findings revealed that 'activity disturbances' were significantly reduced in the singing group over the 6-week intervention, and scores for 'activity disturbances, aggressiveness, and anxiety' when combined also showed a significant reduction. These beneficial changes were not maintained after a 4-week follow-up, however. While this study had the strength of being controlled with blind-assessment, the sample size was small and the drop-out rate was high. In addition, only a few of the participants had substantial symptoms as assessed by the rating scales used, and the intervention was unlikely to show a significant change in symptoms due to a 'floor effect'. In addition, some participants did not actively sing, but were able to participate in the session through listening, supporting the point made by Brown et al. (2001) that group singing can be too challenging for people with late-stage dementia.

Singing and Parkinson's disease

Di Benedetto et al. (2009) report a small-scale, uncontrolled study of choral singing for patients with Parkinson's disease. The rationale was that group singing could be a cost-effective form of intervention to help improve speech quality. Twenty patients were recruited into the study, and over a period of 5 months participated in vocal exercises and choral singing. Significant improvements were found in maximum phonation time, measured by asking the patient to sustain the vowel 'a' for as long as possible and improved quality of prosody and reduced fatigue when reading a short passage. In addition, improvements were found in respiratory variables measured by standard spirometry, including increases in maximal inspiratory and expiratory pressure. While the study was small and uncontrolled, these findings indicate that singing may be useful for people with Parkinson's in maintaining speech quality. In addition, it is clear that the activity was highly valued in contributing to overall wellbeing and quality of life. This is convincingly demonstrated by the fact that the choral group formed for research purposes continued to meet after the study and has gained new members. The 'Corale Gioconda' has gone on to give many public performances.[2]

The work of the Sidney De Haan Research Centre for Arts and Health

The Sidney De Haan Research Centre for Arts and Health was established in 2004. The first priority was to undertake a systematic mapping and review of non-clinical research on singing and health (Clift et al. 2008a), which has recently been updated and extended (Clift et al. 2010a). These reviews have shown clearly that research on singing and health is in an early stage of development with a range of limitations noted in the introduction to this chapter. The Centre is now in the fifth year of a planned 12-year programme of research on singing and health to address the challenges the reviews have identified. Two empirical projects have been undertaken to date and further projects are in process (see Clift 2010).[3]

A cross-national survey of choral singing, wellbeing, and health

The cross-national survey involved over a thousand members of choirs in Australia, England, and Germany, and included more singers than all of the previous published research on choral singers combined (Clift et al. 2008b, 2009, 2010b; Clift and Hancox 2010). The principal aims were to build on the earlier study by Clift and Hancox (2001) to document definitively the perceived benefits of singing held by choristers, and to describe the demographic and health profile of singers in established community singing groups. The survey included three open questions about singing and health and a specially constructed set of 24 statements on a range of potential effects

---

[2] See: http://www.coralegioconda.org/home.html
[3] See the Centre's website for up-to-date details: http://www.canterbury.ac.uk/centres/sidney-de-haan-research/

and benefits associated with singing. It also made use of the WHOQOL-BREF, which measures four domains of life quality, to place findings on perceptions of choral singing in the context of a conceptually strong and empirically grounded model of health and wellbeing.

A majority of choral singers were well-educated (over half have experienced Higher Education, and around a quarter Further Education). Many choir members were in retirement, with an average age of 58 across the three countries and there were between two to three times as many women as men. Choristers had been singing on average for 25 years, and had been loyal members of their present choir for an average of 6 years. Generally speaking, self-assessed health was high in each of the three national samples, but a significant minority of respondents reported less than satisfactory health. Long-term health problems were reported by approximately half of all participants. Not surprisingly, such problems were more common among older members of choirs. In order to construct a summary scale or scales to assess the benefits of choral singing, the 24 items in the singing questionnaire were subject to factor analysis. A strong first component with substantial loadings from 12 items emerged (e.g. improved mood, enhanced quality of life, greater happiness, stress reduction, and emotional wellbeing) and these were used to create a single, highly reliable measure of the perceived effects of singing on wellbeing. Women scored more highly on this scale, confirming the finding of Clift and Hancox (2001) that women report stronger wellbeing effects from singing than men. Sandgren (2009) has also reported stronger emotional impacts from singing among women compared with men.

Answers given to the open questions about singing and health produced many examples of the benefits choral singers believe they gain from singing and also provided a range of intuitive hypotheses employed by singers to explain how singing can be beneficial. Six mechanisms have been identified in a preliminary model of how singing can impact on health and wellbeing through encouraging: positive affect, focused concentration, deep controlled breathing, social support, cognitive stimulation, and regular commitment. Each of these mechanisms serves to counter factors and processes that are potentially detrimental to wellbeing and health.

Establishing and evaluating the Silver Song Club Project

From the outset the Sidney De Haan Research Centre has sought to help promote and evaluate community singing projects, and helped to establish a charitable organization called 'Sing For Your Life' to develop a programme of 'Silver Song Clubs' for older people. Now in its fourth year, Sing For Your Life runs over 50 Silver Song Club sessions monthly across the south east of England.[4]

At an early stage in the work of Sing For Your Life, researchers in the Sidney De Haan Research Centre undertook a 'formative evaluation' based on six Silver Song Clubs formed in the early stages of the project (Bungay and Skingley 2008; Skingley and Bungay 2010). Given the rapid expansion of the network of song clubs following this initial study, the evaluation was followed-up with a larger-scale survey of club participants (Bungay et al. 2010).

The initial formative evaluation sought to identify the key characteristics and processes of a Silver Song Club and to gain the views of participants, facilitators, volunteers, and centre managers regarding the health and social benefits of attending the clubs. Semi-structured interviews were conducted with 17 participants from three of the clubs. Participants valued the opportunity to sing with others, they liked the organization of the clubs, including the ways in which different facilitators presented the materials and choice of songs. Approximately three-quarters of those

---

[4] See: http://www.singforyourlife.org.uk/. A short film illustrating song clubs can be viewed through this site.

interviewed had quite extensive previous musical experience either as members of choirs or singing groups or playing musical instruments. The following themes were identified as potential benefits for the participants of attending Silver Song Clubs: enjoyment, promotion of wellbeing and mental health, social interaction, physical improvement, and cognitive stimulation.

On the basis of the formative evaluation participants in all the clubs (32 in the South East of England at the time) were surveyed to gather information on the age, gender, and living circumstances of participants, and to assess whether the views of those interviewed in the qualitative phase were held more widely. A total of 369 members of 26 clubs completed the questionnaire. Ages ranged from 60–99, with an average age of 79 years. Most were female (77%) living in their own homes (88%) as opposed to living in nursing or residential care. More than half lived on their own (52%), and a third received some external support (33%). In general, large majorities of the participants enjoyed the clubs, looked forward to them, and felt that singing helped to make them feel better in themselves. Interestingly, however, previous experience of music and singing was an important factor in this respect. Most people with lower previous musical experience enjoyed the clubs (86%), and looked forward to them (82%), but to a lesser extent than those with higher previous experience (98% and 96% respectively).

Current developments in the Sidney De Haan Research Centre

Recently, the Centre has secured funding from the National Institute for Health Research to conduct a community pragmatic randomized trial to assess the benefits of singing groups for older people. The trial commenced in spring 2010, with randomization of participants to five new song clubs and non-treatment control groups. Standardized measures of health and wellbeing (the SF-12 (see Iglesias et al. 2001) and the EQ-5D[5]) and monitoring of health and social care service utilization will allow an assessment of the cost-effectiveness of the intervention.

Following the model developed in research on singing groups for older people, the Centre is pursuing further project development on the value of singing for people with enduring mental health issues, chronic breathing problems (COPD), and Parkinson's disease.

The Centre has established a network of singing groups across the East Kent geographic area for people with enduring mental health issues (Clift and Morrison 2011). At the time of writing, eight singing groups are part of the network involving over 100 mental health service users. These groups came together to form a large chorus for two public performances during 2010. The project is being evaluated qualitatively on the basis of questionnaires, observation and interviews, and more systematically employing the Clinical Outcomes in Routine Evaluation (CORE) questionnaire, an instrument widely used in clinical practice within the NHS in the UK.[6] Over an 8-month period from November 2009 to June 2010, significant improvements in mental wellbeing have been found on the CORE. This is the first time that substantial and clinically meaningful changes have been found in the wellbeing of people with a history of mental ill-health as a result of participation in group singing.[7]

With respect to singing and chronic respiratory illness, the Centre has established a pilot singing group which currently has over 20 members with a range of breathing problems. The group

---

[5] EQ-5D is a standardized instrument which has been very widely used in health research as a measure of health outcome. For details of its development and applications see: http://www.euroqol.org/

[6] The CORE System is a UK instrument to measure outcomes from clinical interventions. For details see: http://www.coreims.co.uk/

[7] A film based on the second public performance of the network choirs can be viewed at: http://www.youtube.com/watch?v=MIsoii8pxO4

is being monitored through qualitative feedback and the use of the St George's Respiratory Questionnaire, a very widely used instrument used in clinical practice and research with COPD patients. The Centre plans to establish singing groups in association with British Lung Foundation Breathe Easy Groups in East Kent for research purposes. Participants will be systematically monitored through spirometry, standardized measures used in the trial with older people, and the St George's questionnaire (SGRQ).[8] This study is intended to provide the foundation for proceeding to a larger, robust randomized controlled trial, which will allow the cost effectiveness of group singing as an intervention to be carefully evaluated.

Finally, the Centre has also established a singing group for people with Parkinson's disease in association with a local branch of the Parkinson's disease society. This will be supported through links with three existing singing and Parkinson's groups operating in different parts of the UK.

A concluding thought

An early reference to the idea that singing can be good for health and wellbeing is found in the writings of William Byrd (1543–1623). In the preface to his *Psalmes, Sonnets & Songs*, published in 1588, Byrd outlined eight reasons 'to perswade every one to learne to sing'. Four of these reasons resonate with contemporary views on the 'therapeutic' benefits of singing. Singing, he asserted, helps to maintain health, by being 'delightfull to Nature' (i.e. giving pleasure and joy), by exercising the musculature of the chest, by expanding the lungs and by helping to reduce stammering and improve voice quality.

Byrd summed up his advocacy for singing in a well-known couplet:

> Since singing is so good a thing,
>   I wish all men would learne to sing.

Remarkably, it is only now, over 400 years later, that scientific attention has begun to assess the merits of Byrd's insights. Some useful research has been undertaken, but there is some way to go before the real significance and limitations of singing for health and wellbeing is fully understood and widely acted upon in the practical contexts of health and social care.

References

Bailey, B.A. and Davidson, J.W. (2002). Adaptive characteristics of group singing: perceptions from members of a choir for homeless men. *Musicae Scientiae*, VI(2), 221–56.

Bailey, B.A. and Davidson, J.W. (2003). Perceived holistic health effects of three levels of music participation. In: R. Kopiez, A.C. Lehmann, I. Wohther, and C. Wolf (eds.) *Proceedings of the 5th Triennial ESCOM Conference*, pp. 220–3 (8–13 September 2003, Hanover University of Music and Drama, Germany).

Bailey, B.A. and Davidson, J.W. (2005). Effects of group singing and performance for marginalized and middle-class singers. *Psychology of Music*, **33**(3), 269–303.

Beck, R.J., Cesari, T.C., Yousefi, A., and Enamoto, H. (2000). Choral singing, performance perception, and immune system changes in salivary immunoglobulin A and cortisol. *Music Perception*, **18**(1), 87–106.

Beck, R.J., Gottfried, T.L., Hall, D.J., Cisler, C.A., and Bozeman, K.W. (2006). Supporting the health of college solo singers: the relationship of positive emotions and stress to changes in salivary IgA and cortisol during singing. *Journal of Learning through the Arts: A Research Journal on Arts Integration in Schools and Communities*, **2**(1), article 19.

---

[8] For further information on the SGRQ see: http://www.healthstatus.sgul.ac.uk/

Bonhila, A.G., Onofre, F., Vieira, M.L., Prado, M.Y.A., and Martinez, J.A.B. (2009). Effects of singing classes on pulmonary function and quality of life in COPD patients. *International Journal of COPD*, **4**(1), 1–8.

Brown, S., Gotell, E., and Ekman, S-L. (2001). 'Music-therapeutic caregiving': The necessity of active music-making in clinical care. *The Arts in Psychotherapy*, **28**, 125–35.

Bungay, H. and Skingley, A. (2008). *The Silver Song Club Project: A Formative Evaluation*. Canterbury: Canterbury Christ Church University.

Bungay, H., Clift, S. and Skingley, A. (2010). The Silver Song Club Project: A sense of wellbeing through participatory singing. *Journal of Applied Arts and Health*, **1**(2), 165–78.

Carroll, L.M., Thayer-Stataloff, R.T., Heuer, R.J., Spiegel, J.R., Radionoff, S.L., and Cohn, J.R. (1996). Respiratory and glottal efficiency measures in normal classically trained singers. *Journal of Voice*, **10**(2), 139–45.

Clift, S. (2010). Singing for health: a musical remedy. *British Journal of Wellbeing*, **1**(6), 19–21.

Clift, S.M. and Hancox, G. (2001). The perceived benefits of singing: findings from preliminary surveys of a university college choral society. *Journal of the Royal Society for the Promotion of Health*, **121**(4), 248–56.

Clift, S. and Hancox, G. (2010). The significance of choral singing for sustaining psychological wellbeing: Findings from a survey of choristers in England, Australia and Germany. *Music Performance Research*, **3**(1), 79–96.

Clift, S. and Morrison, I. (2011). Group singing fosters mental health and wellbeing: Findings from the East Kent 'Singing for Health' Network Project. *Mental Health and Social Inclusion*, **15**(2), 88–97.

Clift, S., Hancox, G., Staricoff, R., Whitmore, C., Morrison, I. and Raisbeck, M. (2008a). *Singing and Health: A Systematic Mapping and Review of Non-Clinical Research*. Canterbury: Canterbury Christ Church University.

Clift, S., Hancox, G., Morrison, I., Hess, B., Stewart, D., and Kreutz, G. (2008b). *Choral Singing, Wellbeing and Health: Findings from a Cross-national Survey*. Canterbury: Canterbury Christ Church University.

Clift, S., Hancox, G., Morrison, I., Hess, B., Stewart, D. and Kreutz, G. (2009). What do singers say about the effects of choral singing on physical health? Findings from a survey of choristers in Australia, England and Germany. In: Louhivuori, J., Eerola, T., Saarikallio, S., Himberg, T. and Eerola, P-S. (eds.) *Proceedings of the 7th Triennial Conference of European Society for the Cognitive Sciences of Music (ESCOM 2009)*, Jyväskylä, Finland.

Clift, S., Nicol, J., Raisbeck, M., Whitmore, C., and Morrison, I. (2010a). Group singing and health: A systematic mapping of research. *UNESCO Journal* (Special issue on interdisciplinary research on singing), **2**(1). Available at: http://www.abp.unimelb.edu.au/unesco/ejournal/vol-two-issue-one.html (accessed 15 April 2011).

Clift, S., Hancox, G., Morrison, I., Hess, B., Kreutz, G., and Stewart, D. (2010b). Choral singing and psychological wellbeing: Quantitative and qualitative findings from English choirs in a cross-national survey. *Journal of Applied Arts and Health*, **1**(1), 19–34.

Cohen, G.D., Perlstein, S., Chapline, J., Kelly, J., Firth, K.M., and Simmens, S. (2006). The impact of professionally conducted cultural programs on the physical health, mental health, and social functioning of older adults. *The Gerontologist*, **46**(6), 726–34.

Cohen, G.D., Perlstein, S., Chapline, J., Kelly, J., Firth, K.M., and Simmens, S. (2007). The impact of professionally conducted cultural programs on the physical health, mental health and social functioning of older adults – 2-year results. *Journal of Aging, Humanities and the Arts*, **1**, 5–22.

Cohen, M. (2009). Choral singing and prison inmates: influences of performing in a prison choir. *The Journal of Correctional Education*, **60**(1), 52–65.

Cohen, M.L. (2007). Explorations of inmate and volunteer choral experiences in a prison-based choir. *Australian Journal of Music Education*, **1**, 61–72.

Di Benedetto, P., Cavazzon, M., Mondolo, F., Rugiu, G., Peratoner, A., and Biasutti, E. (2009). Voice and choral singing treatment: A new approach for speech and voice disorders in Parkinson's disease. *European Journal of Physical and Rehabilitation Medicine*, **45**(1), 13–19.

Eley, R. and Gorman, D. (2008). Music therapy to manage asthma. *Aboriginal and Islander Health Worker Journal*, **32**(1), 9–10.

Eley, R. and Gorman, D. (2010). Didgeridoo playing and singing to support asthma management in Aboriginal Australians. *The Journal of Rural Health*, **26**, 100–4.

Engen, R. (2005). The singer's breath: implications for treatment of persons with emphysema. *Journal of Music Therapy*, **42**(1), 20–48.

Giaquinto, S., Cacciato, A., Minasi, S., Sostero, E., and Amanda, S. (2006). Effects of music-based therapy on distress following knee arthroplasty. *British Journal of Nursing*, **15**(1), 576–9.

Gould, W.J. and Okamura, H. (1973). Static lung volumes in singers. *Annals of Otology, Rhinology and Laryngology*, **82**, 89–95.

Grape, C., Sandgren, M., Hansson, L-O., Ericson, M., and Theorell, T. (2003). Does singing promote well-being? An empirical study of professional and amateur singers during a singing lesson. *Integrative Physiological and Behavioral Science*, **38**(1), 65–74.

Heller, S.S., Hicks, W.R., and Root, W.S. (1960). Lung volumes of singers. *Journal of Applied Physiology*, **15**(1), 40–2.

Hulme, C., Wright, J., Crocker, T., Oluboyede, Y., and House, A. (2008). *A Systematic review of Non-drug Treatments for Dementia*. Leeds: Leeds Institute of Health Sciences, Faculty of Medicine and Health, University of Leeds.

Iglesias, C.P., Birks, Y.F., and Torgerson, D.J. (2001). Improving the measurement of quality of life in older people: the York SF-12. *Quarterly Journal of Medicine*, **94**, 695–8.

Jacob, C., Guptill, C., and Sumsion, T. (2009). Motivation for continuing involvement in a leisure-based choir: The lived experiences of university choir members. *Journal of Occupational Science*, **16**(3), 187–93.

Kenny, D.T. and Faunce, G. (2004). The impact of group singing on mood, coping and perceived pain in chronic pain patients attending a multidisciplinary pain clinic. *Journal of Music Therapy*, **41**(3), 241–58.

Kreutz, G., Bongard, S., Rohrmann, S., Grebe, D., Bastian, H.G., and Hodapp, V. (2004). Effects of choir singing or listening on secretory immunoglobulin A, cortisol and emotional state. *Journal of Behavioral Medicine*, **27**(6), 623–35.

Kuhn, D. (2002). The effects of active and passive participation in musical activity on the immune system as measured by salivary immunoglobulin A (SigA). *Journal of Music Therapy*, **39**(1), 30–9.

Lally, E. (2009). 'The power to heal us with a smile and a song': Senior well-being, music-based participatory arts and the value of qualitative evidence. *Journal of Arts and Communities*, **1**(1), 25–44.

Latimer, M.E. (2008). 'Our voices enlighten, inspire, heal and empower.' A mixed methods investigation of demography, sociology, and identity acquisition in a gay men's chorus. *International Journal of Research in Choral Singing*, **3**(1), 23–38.

Levitin, D. (2008). *The World in Six Songs: How the musical brain created human nature*. London: Dutton.

Lord, V.M., Cave, P., Hume, V., Flude, E.J., Evans, A., Kelly, J.L., *et al.* (2010). Singing teaching as a therapy for chronic respiratory disease–randomised controlled trial and qualitative evaluation. *BMC Pulmonary Medicine*, **10**, 41.

Myskja, A. and Nord, P.G. (2008). 'The day the music died': A pilot study on music and depression in a nursing home. *Nordic Journal of Music Therapy*, **17**(1), 30–40.

O'Connor, D.W., Ames, D., Gardner, B., and King, M. (2009a). Psychosocial treatments of behavior symptoms in dementia: a systematic review of reports meeting quality standards. *International Psychogeriatrics*, **21**, 225–40.

O'Connor, D.W., Ames, D., Gardner, B., and King, M. (2009b). Psychosocial treatments for psychological symptoms in dementia: a systematic review of reports meeting quality standards. *International Psychogeriatrics*, **21**, 241–51.

Palmer, R. (2008). Questions arising from the views of some members of four amateur classical music organizations. *International Journal of Community Music*, **1**(2), 203–16.

Pavlakou, M. (2009). Benefits of group singing for people with eating disorders: Preliminary findings from a non-clinical study. *Approaches: Music Therapy and Special Music Education*, 1(1), 30–48.

Pomfret, E. (2009). Credit-crunched? Then lift up your voice and sing. *The Times*, 24 January.

Racette, A., Bard, C., and Peretz, I. (2006). Making non-fluent aphasics speak: sing along! *Brain*, **129**(10), 2571–84.

Rider, M., Mickey, C., Weldin, C., and Hawkinson, R. (1991). The effects of toning, listening and singing on psychophysiological responses. In: C.D.Maranto (ed.) *Applications of Music in Medicine*, pp. 73–84. Washington DC: National Association of Music Therapy.

Sandgren, M. (2009). Evidence of strong immediate well-being effects of choral singing–with more enjoyment for women than for men. In: Louhivuori, J., Eerola, T., Saarikallio, S., Himberg, T. and Eerola, P-S. (eds.) *Proceedings of the 7th Triennial Conference of European Society for the Cognitive Sciences of Music (ESCOM 2009)*, Jyväskylä, Finland.

Schorr-Lesnick, B., Teirstein, A.S., Brown, L.K., and Miller, A. (1985). Pulmonary function in singers and wind-instrument players. *Chest*, **88**(2), 201–5.

Silber, L. (2005). Bars behind bars: the impact of a women's prison choir on social harmony. *Music Education Research*, **7**(2), 251–71.

Skingley, A. and Bungay, H. (2010). The Silver Song Club Project: singing to promote the health of older people. *British Journal of Community Nursing*, **15**(3), 135–40.

Skingley, A. and Vella-Burrows, T. (2010). Therapeutic effects of music and singing for older people. *Nursing Standard*, **24**(19), 35–41.

Southcott, J.E. (2009). 'And as I go, I love to sing': the Happy Wanderers, music and positive aging. *International Journal of Community Music*, **2**(2&3), 143–56.

Svansdottir, H.B. and Snaedal, J. (2006). Music therapy in moderate and severe dementia of Alzheimer's type: a case-control study. *International Psychogeriatrics*, **18**(4), 613–21.

Thomas, T. (2010). The choral cure. *The Independent*, 12 January. Available at: http://www.independent.co.uk/life-style/health-and-families/features/the-choral-cure-1864774.html

Tonneijck, H.I.M., Kinebanian, A., and Josephsson, S. (2008). An exploration of choir singing: Achieving wholeness through challenge. *Journal of Occupational Science*, **15**(3), 173–80.

Unwin, M.M., Kenny, D.T., and Davis, P.J. (2002). The effects of group singing on mood. *Psychology of Music*, **30**, 175–85.

Valentine, E. and Evans, C. (2001). The effects of solo singing, choral singing and swimming on mood and physiological indices. *British Journal of Medical Psychology*, **74**, 115–20.

Wade, L.M. (2002). A comparison of the effects of vocal exercises/singing versus music-assisted relaxation on peak expiratory flow rates of children with asthma. *Music Therapy Perspectives*, **20**(1), 31–7.

Young, L. (2008). The potential health benefits of community based singing groups for adults with cancer. *Canadian Journal of Music Therapy*, **15**(1), 11–27.

Chapter 10

Dance and Health: Exploring Interactions and Implications

Cynthia Quiroga Murcia and Gunter Kreutz

Human movement and dance are activities that often arise from musical stimulation. In some, if not most cultures, music and dance are inextricably linked with each other. For example, music may provide a rhythmic framework to facilitate synchronization between individuals on the basis of regular time intervals, or beats. Dancers may also respond to non-temporal properties of musical sound, such as dynamics or affective characters conveyed through musical meaning. Either when performed alone or, what seems the more common practice, in pairs or groups, dance may be characterized by sequences of bodily movements that give rise to impressions of rhythmic coordination and at least some degrees of entrainment. According to Freeman (2000), the biological basis of musical processing includes the perceptuomotor system. This means that during listening, somatosensory and motor systems in the brain are activated, thus providing a natural foundation for the interconnectedness of dance and music domains. Thus dancing can be characterized as the most visible form of psychophysiological response to as well as aesthetic appreciation of music. Through music, dancers find guidance for the creation and organization of their movements. When observing individual dance movements, it is possible to identify changes of rhythm through changes in body tension and motion speed (e.g. Berrol 1992; Large 2000).

Humans appear to have been attracted to dance both as observers and performers since prehistoric times. Evidence of strong orientations to dance in everyday life can be observed in virtually all societies with great stylistic variations worldwide (McNeill 1995; Nettl 2000). Although the evolutionary origins of dance are far from clear, several hypotheses have been proposed to explain the functions of dancing with the implication of some survival value. For some authors, dance evolved as courtship displays for the biological function of reproduction. Thus, dance might facilitate sexual selection by showing mate quality features such as health, virility, sensitivity, aerobic fitness, coordination, and creativity (e.g. Miller 2000). Other researchers proposed that dance might serve to promote social cohesion. Accordingly, dancing has been fundamental to strengthening community cohesion, encouraging the performance of dull, repetitive tasks, and coordinating group actions (e.g. McNeill 1995). In a different vein, Hagen and Bryant (2003) argued that dance has served as a signalling system for communicating coalition quality, which might have facilitated meaningful cooperative relationships between groups.

One of the most fundamental functions of dancing along human history is its potential to influence people's health. Levy (1988) argued that dance may have served as a cathartic and therapeutic tool in prehistoric times. He believes that in many societies it 'was as essential as eating and sleeping. It provided individuals with means to express themselves, to communicate feelings to others and to commune with nature'. In a similar vein, Arcangeli (2000) reasoned that in pre-modern European societies, dance was regarded as an effective form of exercise. It was particularly recommended when a balanced development of the human body and an alternation of motion and rest were necessary. The author cites medical works from the Middle Ages and Renaissance which document uses of dance as practical parts of health plans. These plans suggest specific beneficial effects on the wellbeing for their practitioners. Notwithstanding the fact that dancing has been associated with healing processes and care-giving since early times, only in recent years has there been a growing and increased interest in the systematic research of its health benefits.

The contributions of dancing to individuals' wellbeing and health can be appreciated from two perspectives. On the one hand, dance can be seen as a recreational activity with potential health promoting benefits, performed by groups of people devoting part of their leisure time to this cultural practice. On the other hand, dance is used in clinical contexts as one supporting therapy across a wide range of physical and mental problems. Thus, the aim of this chapter is to examine the available evidence basis of ascribing specific health benefits to dance. In particular, current approaches that entail clinical as well as non-clinical populations will be reviewed.

Dance as a leisure activity promoting health

Appropriate models of health are needed in order to capture not only the potentially beneficial effects of musical activities such as dancing, but also to examine possible mechanisms that may mediate such effects. For instance, in their seminal paper concerning a related leisure activity that shares many characteristics with dance, namely amateur choral singing, Clift and Hancox (2001) point out the need to understand the contribution of musical activities to wellbeing from a positive perspective of health, which means not just by the mere absence of infirmity, or physical or mental illness.

One approach focusing on the factors that promote health and wellbeing is the salutogenetic model proposed by Antonovsky (1985). This model has contributed to theorizing about the health implications of leisure activities including music (e.g. Ruud 1997). The salutogenetic orientation concentrates on the resources of an individual to maintain health, especially the beliefs that enable a person to cope with difficult situations. Antonovsky's model assumes that each of us is, at a given point in time, somewhere along a healthy/disease continuum. In other words, to the extent that we can exert control over the course of our actions and behaviours, health is a matter of our outlook on life. Antonovsky (1996) proposed that a significant factor here is a person's 'sense of coherence'. Its three main components or rather sets of beliefs entail, again in his terms, comprehensibility, manageability, and meaningfulness. In brief, individual health is subject to making sense of life events, using one's own skills and abilities to take care of oneself, and finally, to find worth and value in one's activities. Therefore, a person with a strong sense of coherence, when facing a stressor will be motivated to cope, will believe that the challenge is understood and that resources are available, or can be obtained.

Questions arise, as to how leisure activities such as dancing may contribute to enhancing the individual sense of coherence and its components. The extend to which dancing may act as a medium for strengthening the sense of coherence has so far not been directly addressed in empirical research. In an explorative study aimed at evaluating the perceived benefits of dancing in amateur dancers, Quiroga et al. (2010) found that dancing is perceived to contribute positively to several aspects of wellbeing. In particular, beneficial effects of dancing were found related to the emotional, physical, social, and spiritual dimensions. Moreover, dance benefits were also associated with the improvement of self-esteem and coping strategies.

If dance contributes to maintaining or improving health and wellbeing, questions arise as to how these influences could be explained. Our model suggests that specific salutary values of dancing emerge from a variety of health-promoting elements. Thus dance is seen here as an integral activity. Its major components include musical stimulation, body movement, and social context. While it is questionable whether direct healing effects can be expected from dance activities, we argue that its therapeutic value lies in potentials such as, for example, the activation of individual psychophysiological resources, the strengthening of sense of control, and the induction of positive mood through these components. A review of the available empirical evidence is presented below.

Musical component

Dancing differs from several other body movement techniques (e.g. yoga, pilates, Feldenkreis, progressive relaxation, etc.), in that music plays an essential active role when dancing. Music is not just an accompanying stimulus, but a crucial component that inspires and drives the intentional rhythmical interpretation of the body movements.

A further fundamental role of music in dancing is its value to integrate and synchronize people's common movement in time and space. Moving to music in a coordinated way within a group is an achievement which promotes social cohesion. Music strengthens the ability to contribute to the community and cope with the environment. McNeill (1995) argues that keeping in time together has been an important means of working in rhythm, strengthening social bonds between individuals and hence an effective way to create and sustain communities.

Besides regulating individuals' body movements to synchronize to the perceived rhythmic structure, music is well-known in inducing and modulating affective states of people. Emotional responses to music are found not only at a subjective level, but also significant effects of music engagement on autonomic responses as well as on neurochemical indicators are well documented (see Kreutz et al., Chapter 30, this volume). Music appears to play a decisive role in modulating the potential benefits of dancing. For example, after asking a group of patients receiving a dance programme which aspects (dance, the music, the art, or the sense of group cohesion) were perceived to have the greatest influence, Bojner Howitz (2004) pointed out that dance was rated as the strongest influence, and music as the second strongest. She argued that music and dance are inseparable, since dancing had the potential to stimulate and activate people's ability to perceive music, and vice versa. Quiroga et al. (2009) found in a study with tango dancers that reductions of the stress hormone cortisol are significantly stronger when dancing to music than without music stimulation. Empirical research addressing the specific influence of music in dancing is imperative for future research.

Finally, a growing body of literature has suggested that music beneficially affects cognitive processes. With recent advances in neuroimaging techniques, contemporary research has shown benefits of music on brain health and cognition. Music appears to increase levels of brain-derived neurotrophic factor, stimulate cortical plasticity, increase capillarization, and decrease oxidative damage (Pantev et al. 2003; Fukui and Toyoshima 2008). It is believed that dance may lead to the improvement of several cognitive processes such as perception, attention, concentration, memory, time and spatial representation, as well as creativity (Berrol et al. 1997; Verghese et al. 2003; Hanna 2008). However, empirical research is needed to determine the neurobiological bases of potential benefits of dancing on brain function and cognition. To date, investigations on both the influence of music as well as of physical activity (e.g. Cotman and Berchtold 2002; Hillman et al. 2008) on cognitive and brain functions have been conducted mainly independently of one another. Research on the interacting effects of moving to music, or rather dancing, on cognitive processes should be more considered in future research (Brown et al. 2006; Jola and Mast 2006).

Body component

Dance is available to almost everyone, since the only instrument needed for this purpose is your own body. The positive impact of body activity on improving health and wellbeing is empirically well documented. In particular, with the increased availability of technology in modern societies, the predisposition to a sedentary lifestyle has been growing considerably. Hence, the promotion of physical activity appears to be an essential issue in the current public health agenda over the recent years (World Health Organization 2010).

The findings of numerous studies have shown that participation in physical activity reduces the risk of physical illnesses (for instance, obesity, cardiovascular diseases, diabetes, respiratory disorders, and osteoporosis) and mental disorders such as depression and anxiety (e.g. Landers 1997; Fox 1999; Warburton et al. 2006). In addition, dance as a form of physical activity has evidenced potential benefits for developing and enhancing fitness indicators such as aerobic capacity, balance, coordination, elasticity, muscle strength and joint mobility, kinesthetic awareness, and body control (Flores 1995; Peidro et al. 2002; Hanna 2006; Verghese et al. 2006; Zhang et al. 2008).

According to Kraus et al. (1991), dance is, however, a unique form of movement; it is more than simple physical movement. Although many of the dance movements skills are similar to those of other forms of physical exercises, the interaction of movement and music, make of dancing an aesthetic way to move, characterized by design, creativity, and self-awareness. Therefore, a powerful motivation for dancing appears to be the need to express oneself through rhythmic play and through exploration of one's bodily powers and physical environment (Lumsdem 2006).

The extent to which dancing, in contrast to other physical activities, may have specific inherent positive benefits, has been addressed in a small number of studies. Lestè and Rust (1990) found reduced anxiety levels in individuals participating in a 3-month modern dancing programme, while no changes were observed in participants attending a physical exercise group. West et al. (2004) reported that after a 90-minute class of African dance and hatha yoga, the levels of perceived stress and negative affect were reduced in both groups, whereas positive affect increased only in the dance group. More research evaluating the specific and unique values that are related to dancing, which may differ from other physical activities, are needed in future research.

Social component

The influence of positive social relationships on health has already been well established (Cohen 2004). Dance as a profoundly social experience provides a supportive setting that gives feelings of identification and togetherness and may serve as a source of interpersonal contact (Quiroga et al. 2010). Kuettel (1982) reported that a group receiving dance sessions show more group cohesion and participation than a group undergoing other activities. According to Houston (2005) dance as a practice that requires cooperation and communication may precipitate creative energy and communal feelings. In addition, since the communication by dancing is non-verbal, it is a way of bringing together a community or people with different cultural backgrounds.

Another important factor in relation to the social dimension of dancing is the existence of physical closeness between the others, especially when dancing with a partner. Dancing represents one of the few contexts in which physical touch between strangers is acceptable. Several studies document that touching and being touched by others elicits a sense of wellbeing. Ditzen et al. (2007), for instance, found that women receiving positive physical contact from their partner evidenced lowered salivary cortisol and heart rate responses to psychosocial stress in laboratory conditions, compared to women receiving only verbal social support or no social interaction.

Central nervous neuroendocrine systems are proposed to mediate in the attenuation of stress response. In particular, oxytocin has shown to be a core component of the processes mediating the health benefits and antistress effects of positive social interactions (Uvnäs-Moberg 1998). Positive sensory stimuli, such as physical contact during social interactions, have shown to elicit oxytocin releases. Oxytocin has been found to mediate reductions in blood pressure, heart rate, and cortisol concentrations in stress situations (e.g. Heinrichs et al. 2003). The specific influence of touching in dancing and the related health advantages attributable to physical contact remains to be explored in detail in future research.

The cited literature suggests that dancing has the potential to support and increase wellbeing in individuals, irrespective of their age, sex, sociodemographic background, or dance skills. However, one obvious question is whether such positive influences are limited to amateur dancing. In fact, professional dancing has been studied predominantly with respect to health risks such as repetitive strain injuries and other, mainly physical disorders that are directly linked with performance demands. Professional dancers must submit themselves to extensive training starting in childhood in order to achieve sufficient expertise to advance individual careers. A growing body of research has begun to identify specific physical and psychosomatic health risks associated with professional dancing, such as injuries, body image problems or eating disorders (e.g. Bowling 1989; Hanna 2006; Rohleder et al. 2007). These reported outcomes from professional dance notwithstanding, it seems an entirely open issue to what extent professional dance might be also associated with health benefits that may outweigh individual problems.

In sum, the health-promoting elements of amateur dancing described above provide a framework, which can serve as a starting point for the acknowledgement of the role that amateur dancing may play as an integral activity that helps to improve people's wellbeing. The recognition that dancing is not only a pleasurable entertainment, but a promoting health activity, may encourage future investigations to contribute to a greater, more in-depth understanding of amateur dancing as a resource for improving health.

Dance as a form of therapy

Dance therapy refers to the therapeutic use of dance as a process that promotes the emotional, cognitive, social and physical integration of the individual (ADTA 2009). Dance therapists assume that the expressive body movements reveal facets of the individual's emotions and personality that are better communicated through non-verbal than verbal means. Because the use of dance therapy is based on the premise that mind and body are intrinsically connected and in constant interaction, therefore a change in a person's movement expression is believed to influence the person's global functioning and promoting health (Levy 1988; Berrol 1992; Hanna 2006).

How effective is dance therapy? Could some disorders be treated, or prevented effectively through dancing? Ritter and Low (1996) pointed out that the efficacy of dance therapy appeared to be promising, but still inconclusive, due to methodological problems, such as lack of control groups, small samples, and inappropriate measures for quantifying changes, in outcome research. Since then, however, empirical well-designed investigations evaluating the effects of dance therapy on health parameters have been increasing. Initial results document the positive impact of dance therapy on a variety of physical and mental conditions such as cognitive disabilities, emotional distress, and chronic diseases. An overview of recent meaningful findings is provided as follows.

Medical contexts

Dancing has been found to be an alternative form to improve functional capacity in patients with cardiac disease. Belardinelli et al. (2008) observed in patients with chronic heart failure that waltz dancing three times a week for 8 weeks improves functional capacity and endothelial dysfunction. Similar results were found in a control group of patients participating in traditional aerobic exercise training. However, in the dance group a more marked improvement in the emotional state and a higher adherence to the programme were observed.

Recent empirical investigations document the benefits of dance therapy on patients with breast cancer. Dibbell-Hope (2000) indicated that dance therapy led to improvements in subjective emotional state, body-image, and self-esteem. Sandel et al. (2005) reported the effects of 12-week dance therapy in a group of woman who underwent breast surgery in the past and compared them with a waiting list control group. A substantial improvement of quality of life was found in the dance therapy group. More recently, data from Mannheim and Weiss (2006) research evidenced a significant improvement in quality of life as well as reductions in depression and anxiety levels and increased self-esteem in a group of women with a tumour diagnosis.

Further, positive evidence of dance therapy has been show in individuals with neurological disorders. In patients diagnosed with Parkinson's disease, Hackney et al. (2007) compared the effects of tango classes with those of a standard exercise classes on functional mobility. Although both groups showed enjoyment and social benefits after their participation in the classes, the authors found improvements in all measures of falls, gait, and balance confidence only in the tango group. Berrol et al. (1997) examined the effects of dance therapy in a population of patients with traumatic brain injury. In comparison to a control group, individuals receiving dance sessions were found to show an improvement of physical (balance), social interaction (participation in group activities, accepting invitations, self-initiating activities), and cognitive function (decision-making, making themselves understood, and short-term memory).

Another example of the positive effects of dance therapy is the outcome study by Bojner Howitz (2004) in female patients diagnosed with fibromyalgia. The author concluded from the data analysis through video interpretation that patients receiving dance therapy, in contrast to a control group, showed significant positive difference in self-perception, mobility, perception of pain when moving, and life energy.

Mental health settings

On the other hand, numerous works in the psychological literature show that dance therapy appears to be a viable and promising form of intervention in mental health contexts. Ravelin et al. (2006) found through a content analysis aimed to identify the benefits of dancing in a mental health nursing context that dance may foster interaction with other people. Given that mental illness may disable one's capability of self-expression and communicating with others, dance may provide a non-verbal way of self-expression. Further, dancing may help patients in exploring and improving body image as well as in releasing emotional and physical pressure. In persons with dementia, for example, Palo-Bengtsson et al. (1998) found that social dancing as an intervention programme improves patients' positive feelings, social contact, and communication with others.

Dance therapy interventions have shown effectiveness in the treatment of patients diagnosed with depression. Koch et al. (2007) assessed the specific effects of a dance programme on psychiatric patients with a main or additional diagnosis of depression, and compared these effects with those of a music intervention and a movement intervention. Whereas positive affect increased in all group conditions, a significant decrease of depression was only found in the in the dance group. Furthermore, significantly more vitality was found in the dance condition than in the music group. In a group of adolescent females with mild depression, Jeong et al. (2005) investigated psychological distress and neurohormonal changes following a 12-week programme of dance therapy. The authors reported that dance therapy led to significant improvements in negative psychological symptoms as well as to a beneficially modulation of neurohormones (increased plasma serotonin concentration and decreased dopamine concentration).

Ritter and Low (1996) concluded in their meta-analysis that dance therapy appears to have a significant positive effect on anxiety levels. Subsequent studies have confirmed the potential benefit of dancing as an effective treatment for anxiety. For example, Erwin-Grabner et al. (1999) found that dance therapy was an effective treatment for reducing the symptoms of test anxiety.

In survivors of traumatic experiences such as torture, dance therapy has shown to be a particularly well-suited psychotherapy, because of its focus on the body and its relationship to psychological processes. Trauma victims often suffer from complex problems as a result from both physical and psychological violence. Since traumatic memories are often non-verbal, rehabilitation must include the body and its expressive voice of movements (Gray 2001; Koch and Weidinger-von der Recke 2009). According to a recent report by Koch and Weidinger-von der Recke (2009), dance therapy can aid traumatized victims of torture to gradually rebuild a positive body experience as well as the ability to experience joy and other pleasurable emotions. Gray (2001) concluded from a case study that dance therapy, following an experience of torture, can be beneficial in rebuilding an individual's sense of wholeness and self and in improving interaction skills.

Further studies have confirmed the positive effects of dance therapy on recovering from traumatic experiences. Harris (2007) reports the benefits of actively participating in a dance therapy programme in a group of former boy combatants in Sierra Leone. A drop in average symptom expression such as anxiety, depression, intrusive recollection, and aggression was evidenced in the ex-fighters, which facilitated the process in overcoming stigma and reconciling to the community after years of brutal war. In a qualitative study, Mills and Daniluk (2002) investigated to what extent dance therapy was perceived to contribute to wellbeing in five women who had been sexually abused as children. The authors found six common themes associated to the women's wellbeing: a sense of spontaneity, permission to play, struggle, sense of freedom, intimate connection and bodily recognition.

Older adults

Research has shown that dancing has the potential to ameliorate aging symptoms (e.g. Verghese 2006; Hachney et al. 2007; Wu et al. 2010). Older adults have to confront several stress aspects related to the aging process such as declining physical capabilities, loneliness, and cognitive deterioration. Since the population of seniors continues to increase dramatically, interest in finding alternative activities for improving physical and mental wellbeing is growing. One of the advantages that dance therapy offer to older people is that it may encourage them to engage in physical activity without the danger that vigorous stressful sports may represent for them. Lima and Vieira (2007) conducted a qualitative study for investigating the meanings of ballroom dancing and its benefits in 60 elderly Brazilians. The authors found that after one year of participation in ballroom dance classes, older people reported rich and varied meanings of dancing such as its perceived benefits on health, its potential to bringing back good reminiscences, its connection to culture, and its usefulness as a vehicle for social integration. In the revision of a 3-year dance project for the inclusion of older people in community dance, Houston (2005) pointed out that dance sessions for older people give them a sense of pride in their work, connectedness, and enjoyment.

Marginalized groups

Finally, dance can be a medium through which participation in society can start to be accomplished (Houston 2005). By dancing, not only inclusion, but also empowerment and active engagement of socially marginal groups in society may be achieved. The author concluded from a case study with male offenders, receiving a programme of dance sessions that dance helped prisoners to feel better about themselves and gave them the confidence to separate their outward persona as a criminal from their life as a responsible person capable of giving and receiving. According to Milliken (2002) dance as a therapeutic approach in prison to the treatment of violence may help to transform violent behaviours, by offering a context in which individuals can rediscover themselves as positive and fully functioning persons. Dancing may thus offer an alternative ways to transform negative ways of coping into adaptive strategies.

Conclusion

Positive influences of dance activities on wellbeing have been recognized since ancient times. However, only in the last decades, empirical research addressing dance within multidimensional frameworks of health is emerging. From these perspectives, empirical research has begun to address issues relating to the health promoting value of dancing as well as its therapeutic benefits.

The literature reviewed here suggests a growing interest of health professionals in investigating how and why dance activities may have beneficial effects on health and wellbeing. Dancing appears to be a multidimensional behaviour that combines several potentially salutary elements in one single activity: music stimulation, body movement, and social interaction. We found initial empirical evidence in support of notions that these components are potential promoting contributors of wellbeing and health in this context.

Given the health potentials of dancing summarized here, it is surprising to see its marginalization especially in Western everyday cultures. One of the challenges of modern societies, which appear to foster individual lifestyles that can be prone to reduced physical movement as well as lack of social engagement, is to promote deeply-rooted human activities such as dance.

Finally, dance as therapy and complementary treatment for patients suffering from different conditions is becoming increasingly accepted among health professionals. Evidence from a variety of empirical studies suggests that dance therapy can be implemented in clinical settings, ranging from physical diseases (cancer, hearth diseases, Parkinson's disease, etc.) to mental disorders (anxiety, depression, etc.). However, more rigorous well-controlled and randomized empirical research is needed. Longitudinal studies could likewise lead to a better understanding of the role of dancing as a healing medium. The investigation of the impact of dance therapy on immune and endocrine variables may contribute to the examination of its validity. Further, benefits in relation to different styles and cultures of dance, as well as their clinical implications remain to be addressed.

Acknowledgements

The first author expresses her gratitude to the DAAD (German Academic Exchange Service) for supporting her research stay in Germany.

References

ADTA (2009). American Dance Therapy Association. http://www.adta.org (accessed 14 April 2011).

Antonowsky, A. (1985). *Health, stress and coping: new perspectives on mental and physical well-being.* San Francisco, CA: Jossey-Bass.

Antonovsky, A. (1996). The salutogenic model as a theory to guide health promotion. *Health Promotion International,* **11**, 1–18.

Arcangeli, A. (2000). Dance and health: the Reinaissance physicians' view. *Dance Research. The Jorurnal of the Society for Dance Research,* **18**, 3–30.

Belardinelli, R., Lacalaprice, F., Ventrella, C., Volpe, L., and Faccenda, E. (2008). Waltz dancing in patients with chronic heart failure: New form of exercise training. *Circulation: Heart Failure*, **1**, 107–14.

Berrol, C. (1992). The neurophysiologic basis of the mind-body connection in dance/movement therapy. *American Journal of Dance Therapy,* **14**, 19–29.

Berrol, C., Lock Ooi, W., and Katz, S.S. (1997). Dance movement/therapy with older adults who have sustained neurological insult: A demostration project. *American Journal of Dance Therapy,* **19**, 135–60.

Bojner Howitz, E. (2004). Dance/movement therapy in fybromalgia patients: aspects and consequeces of verbal, visual and hormonal analysis. Dissertation, University of Uppsala. Availabl at: http://uu.diva-portal.org/smash/record.jsf?searchId=1&pid=diva2:165340 (accessed on 14 April 2011).

Bowling, A. (1989). Injuries to dancers: prevalence, treatment and perceptions of causes. *British Medical Journal,* **298**, 731–4.

Brown, S., Martinez, M.J., and Parsons, L.M. (2006). The neural basis of human dance. *Cerebral Cortex,* **16**, 1157–67.

Clift, S.M. and Hancox, G. (2001). The perceived benefits of singing: Findings from preliminary surveys of a university college choral society. *Journal of the Royal Society for the Promotions of Health,* **121**, 248–56.

Cohen, S. (2004). Social relationships and health. *American Psychologist,* **59**(8), 675–84.

Cotman, C.W. and Berchtold, N.C. (2002). Exercise: A behavioral intervention to enhance brain health and plasticity. *Trends in Neurosciences,* **25**, 295–301.

Dibbell-Hope, S. (2000). The use of dance/movement therapy in psychological adaptation to breast cancer. *The Arts in Psychotherapy,* **27**, 51–68.

Ditzen, B., Neumann, I.D., Bodenmann, G., Von Dwan, B., Turner, R.A., Ehlert, U., *et al.* (2007). Effects of different kinds of couple interaction on cortisol and heart rate responses to stress in women. *Psychoneuroendocrinology,* **32**, 565–74.

Erwin-Grabner, T., Goodill, S.W., Schelly Hill, E., and Von Neida, K. (1999). Effectiveness of dance/movement therapy on reducing test anxiety. *American Journal of Dance Therapy,* **21**, 19–34.

Flores, R. (1995). Dance for Health: Improving fitness in African American and Hispanic adolescents. *Public Health Reports,* **110**, 189–93.

Fox, K.R. (1999). The influence of physical activity on mental well-being. *Public Health Nutrition,* **2**, 411–18.

Freeman, W.J. (2000). A neurobiological role of music in social bonding. In: N. Wallin, B. Merkur, and S. Brown (eds.) *The Origins of music*, pp. 411–24. Cambridge, MA: MIT Press.

Fukui, H. and Toyoshima, K. (2008). Music facilitate the neurogenesis, regeneration and repair of neurons. *Medical Hypotheses,* **71**, 765–9.

Gray, A.E.L. (2001). The body remembers: dance/movement therapy with an adult survivor of torture. *American Journal of Dance Therapy,* **23**, 29–43.

Hackney, M.E., Kantorovich, S., and Earhart, G. (2007). A study on the effects of argentine tango as a form of partnered dance for those with Parkinson disease and the healthy elderly. *American Journal of Dance Therapy,* **29**, 109–27.

Hagen, E.H. and Bryant, G.A. (2003). Music and dance as a coalition signaling system. *Human Nature,* **14**, 21–51.

Harris, D.A. (2007). Dance/movement therapy approaches to fostering resilience and recovery among African adolescent torture survivors. *Torture,* **17**, 134–55.

Hanna, J.L. (2006). *Dancing for Health: Conquering and Preventing Stress*. Lanham, MD: AltaMira Press.

Hanna, J.L. (2008). A nonverbal language for imaging and learning: dance education in k-12 curriculum. *Educational Researcher,* **37**, 491–506.

Heinrichs, M., Baumgartner, T., Kirschbaum, C., and Ehlert, U. (2003). Social support and oxytocin interact to suppress cortisol and subjective responses to psychosocial stress. *Biological Psychiatry,* **54**, 1389–98.

Hillman, C.H., Erikson, K.I., and Kramer, A.F. (2008). Be smart, exercise your heart: exercise effects on brain and cognition. *Nature Reviews Neuroscience,* **9**, 58–65.

Houston, S. (2005). Participation in community dance: A road to empowerment and transformation? *New Theatre Quarterly,* **21**, 166–77.

Jeong, Y.J., Hong, S.C., Soo, L., Park, M.C., Kim, Y.M., and Suh, C.M. (2005). Dance movement Therapy improves emotional responses and modulates neurohormones in adolescents with mild depression. *International Journal of Neuroscience,* **115**, 1711–20.

Jola, C. and Mast, F.W. (2006). Dance images. Mental imagery processes in dance. In: J. Birringer and S. Karoß (eds.) *Tanz im Kopf: Dance and Cognition*, pp. 211–32. Munster: Lit Verlag.

Koch, S.C., Morlinghaus, K., and Fuchs, T. (2007). The joy dance: Specific effects of a single dance intervention on psychiatric patients with depression. *The Arts in Psychotherapy,* **34**, 340–9.

Koch, S.C. and Weidinger-von der Recke, B. (2009). Traumatised refugees: An integrated dance and verbal therapy approach. *The Arts in Psychotherapy,* **36**, 289–96.

Kraus, R., Chapman, S., and Dixon, B. (1991). *History of the Dance in Art and Education*. Englewood Cliffs, NJ: Prentice Hall.

Kuettel, T.J. (1982). Affective change in dance therapy. *American Journal of Dance Therapy,* **5**, 56–64.

Landers, D.M. (1997). The influence of exercise on mental health. *PCPFS Research Digest,* **12**(2).

Large, E.W. (2000). On synchronizing movements to music. *Human Movement Science,* **19**, 527–66.

Lesté, A. and Rust, J. (1990). Effects of dance on anxiety. *American Journal of Dance Therapy,* **12**, 19–26.

Levy, F.J. (1988). *Dance Movement Therapy: A Healing Art*. Reston, VA: American Association for Health, Physical Education, Recreation and Dance.

Lima, M.M.S. and Vieira, A.P. (2007). Ballroom dance as therapy for the elderly in Brazil. *American Journal of Dance Therapy,* **29**, 129–42.

Lumsden, M. (2006). The affective self and affective regulation in dance movement therapy. In: S.C. Koch and I. Bräuninger (Eds.) *Advances in Dance/Movement Therapy*, pp. 29–40. Berlin: Logos Verlag.

Mannheim, E.G. and Weis, J. (2006). Dance/movement therapy with cancer inpatients: evaluation of process and outcome parameters. In S.C. Koch and I. Bräuninger (eds.) *Advances in Dance/Movement Therapy*, pp. 61–72. Berlin: Logos Verlag.

McNeill, W.H. (1995). *Keeping together in time: Dance and drill in human history*. Cambridge, MA: Harvard University Press.

Miller, G.F. (2000). Evolution of human music through sexual selection. In: N.L. Wallin, B. Merker, and S. Brown (eds.) *The origins of music*, pp. 329–60. Cambridge, MA: MIT Press.

Milliken, R. (2002). Dance/movement therapy as a creative arts therapy approach in prison to the treatment of violence. *The Arts in Psychotherapy,* **29**, 203–6.

Mills, L.J. and Daniluk, J.C. (2002). Her body speaks: the experiences of dance therapy for women survivors of child sexual abuse. *Journal of Counseling and Development,* **80**, 77–85.

Nettl, B. (2000). An ethnomusicologist contemplates universals in musical sound and musical culture. In: N.L. Wallin, B. Merker, and S. Brown (eds.) *The Origins of Music*, pp. 463–72. Cambridge, MA: MIT Press.

Palo-Bengtsson, L., Winblad, B., and Ekman, S.L. (1998). Social dancing: a way to support intellectual, emotional and motor fuctions in persons with dementia. *Journal of Psychiatric and Mental Health Nursing,* **5**, 545–54.

Pantev, C., Ross, B., Fujioka, T., Trainor, L.J., Schulte, M., and Schulz, M. (2003). Xx. *Annals of the New York Academy of Science,* **999**, 438–50.

Peidro, R.M., Osses, J., Caneva, J., Brion, G., Angelino, A., Kernage, S., *et al.* (2002). Tango: modificaciones cardiorrespiratorias durante el baile [Tango: cardiorespiratory modifications during the dance]. *Revista Argentina de Cardiologia,* **70**, 358–63.

Quiroga Murcia, C., Bongard, S., and Kreutz, G. (2009). Emotional and neurohumoral responses to dancing tango argentino: The effects of music and partner. *Music and Medicine,* **1**, 14–21.

Quiroga Murcia, C., Kreutz, G., Clift, S., and Bongard, S. (2010). Shall we dance? An exploration of the perceived benefits of dancing on well-being. *Arts & Health: An International Journal for Research, Policy and Practice*, **2**, 149–63.

Ravelin, T., Kylmä, J., and Korhonen, T. (2006). Dance in mental health nursing: a hybrid concept analysis. *Issues in Mental Nursing*, **27**, 307–17.

Ritter, M. and Low, K. (1996). Effects of dance/movement therapy: A meta-analysis. *The Arts in Psychotherapy*, **23**, 249–60.

Rohleder, N., Beulen, S.E., Chen, E., Wolf, J.M., and Kirschbaum, C. (2007). Stress on the dance floor: The cortisol stress response to social-evaluative threat in competitive ballroom dancers. *Personality and Social Psychology Bulletin*, **33**, 69–84.

Ruud, E. (1997). Music and the Quality of life. *Nordic Journal of Music Therapy*, **6**(2), 86–97.

Sandel, S.L., Judge, J.O., Landry, N., Faria, L., Ouellete, R., and Majczak, M. (2005). Dance and movement program improves quality-of-life measures in breast cancer survivors. *Cancer Nursing*, **28**, 301–9.

Uvnäs-Moberg, K. (1998). Oxytocin may mediate the benefits of positive social interaction and emotions. *Psychoneuroendocrinology*, **23**, 819–35.

Verghese, J. (2006). Cognitive and mobility profile of older social dancers. *Journal of the American Geriatrics Society*, **54**, 1241–44.

Verghese, J., Lipton, R.B., Katz, M.J., Hall, C.B., Deby, C.A., Kuslansky, G., *et al.* (2003). Leisure activities and the risk of dementia in the elderly. *New England Journal of Medicine*, **348**, 2508–16.

Warburton, D.E., Nicol, C.W., and Bredin, S. (2006). Health benefits of physical activity: the evidence. *Canadian Medical Association Journal*, **174**, 801–9.

West, J., Otte, C., Geher, K., Johnson, J., and Mohr, D. (2004). Effects of hatha yoga and African dance on perceived stress, affect and salivary cortisol. *Annals of Behavioural Medicine*, **28**, 114–18.

World Health Organization. (2010). *Diet and physical activity: a public health priority.* http://www.who.int/dietphysicalactivity/en/(accessed 14 April 2011).

Wu, W.L., Wei, T.S., Chen, S.K., Chang, J.J., Guo, L.Y., and Lin, H.T. (2010). The effect of Chinese Yuanji-dance on dynamic balance and the associated attentional demands in elderly adults. *Journal of Sport Science and Medicine*, **9**, 119–26.

Zhang, J.G., Ishikawa-Takata, K., Yamazaki, H., Morita, T., and Ohta, T. (2008). Postural stability and physical performance in social dancers. *Gait Posture*, **27**, 697–701.

Chapter 11

Embodied Musical Communication Across Cultures: Singing and Dancing for Quality of Life and Wellbeing Benefit

Jane Davidson and Andrea Emberly

Introduction

The current chapter aims to interrogate the nature and role of the musical arts - singing and dancing - to explore both quality of life and wellbeing impact. Cultural context is a central consideration, with world communities having diverse values, beliefs, and cultural practices. As an example, the Music Council of Australia[1] does not explicitly refer to the embodied experience afforded by musical arts participation, but does note that the music existing in communities provides:

> a vital and dynamic force for opportunities for participation and education... In addition to involving participants in the enjoyment of active music-making and creativity, it provides opportunities to construct personal and communal expressions of artistic, social, political, and cultural concerns. Also it encourages and empowers participants to become agents for extending and developing... and enhanc[ing] the quality of life...

All these quoted concerns are central topics of the current chapter, examining culturally contrasting musical arts practices. Whilst several different cultures are considered in passing, the chapter is focused around two specific cases: the generic Western experience (European heritage of those raised in North America, Europe, and Australasia); and rural South Africa where Venda people engage in cultural musical learning where dancing and singing function as integrated practice in both formal and informal learning contexts across the lifespan.

The chapter is divided into three primary sections, beginning with a discussion of music and its embodied communicative function, with evidence from infancy and early childhood research. A second section considers how musical arts are experienced in Western contexts, especially their contemporary use. The final section introduces the musical culture of the Venda of South Africa, showing how musicality is defined in a culturally-specific manner. Through current research and the historical work of John Blacking, this final section explores how musicality is constructed within and beyond communities. The cross-cultural analysis allows the authors to examine distinct notions of embodied musical communication whilst building on developments that support the idea of musicality and its role in enhancing quality of life and feelings of wellbeing.

---

[1] http://www.mca.org.au/ (accessed 31 January 2010).

Music's embodied communicative function

Ethnomusicologists, music psychologists, sociologists, and educators have identified a plethora of ways in which musical engagement contributes to successful socialization, including when it is used for: mother–infant bonding, developing the capacity to unite people, and providing material from which sharing and learning can take place (see, for example, work by Blacking 1990; Huron 2006; Walker 2007). Ruud (1998, 2002) has argued the value of musical opportunities across the entire lifespan, most specifically contributing to the formation of identity. He gives examples of how children in a Western context make their initial step towards selfhood in their collaborative musical play with parents, peers and siblings, developing from that crucial mother–infant bonding, towards group socialization. At the teenage stage, musical arts facilitate the navigation between a private and public self, whether being used for self-regulation reasons (perhaps changing mood) or the presentation of self to a group (e.g. performance). Musical arts can be used to reflect internal space—listening to music in the bedroom, or relaxing making music (usually pop) with friends. As Tarrant et al. (2002) observe, musical arts can also assist young people to learn to create 'in' and 'out' social groups, that is, those with whom to associate and those to avoid.

The potency of musical arts for both cohesion and social flexibility has been explained by Cross:

> it allows each participant to interpret its significance individually and independently without the integrity of the collective musical behaviour being undermined… Yet, music's capacity to embody, entrain and intentionalise time in both sound and action make it cohesive which helps to establish a sense of group identity'

(Cross 2005, p. 36).

Cross also suggests that music is a metaphorizing medium through which seemingly disparate concepts can be experienced as interlinked. He argues that experiences in infancy may give rise to this metaphorizing, with infants engaging in the same or very similar sorts of (sound and movement) interactions with adults in a wide variety of contexts. Infant behaviour involves exaggerated melodic contours (vocalizations in song-like utterances), rhythmic pulses (including bouncing, patting, tapping and other whole body movements), all of which take place in a social turn-taking framework focused on an interaction with the adult care-giver using both sound and movement. This focus on sound and movement reveals an emerging understanding of music and its embodied nature.

Trevarthen (1999, 2002) observes how infants, when suckling, accompany the process by using both their vocalizations and their hands to conduct (in terms of musical timing and phrasing) the experience with their mother. These behaviours demonstrate sympathy, awareness, and pleasurable sharing with the mother. From these signals (present in all infants, from premature babies to congenitally blind newborns), Trevarthen argues that our adult repertoire of non-verbal gestures and vocal interactions for social discourse emerge. How the voice and body are used in these behaviours, most usually referred to as 'motherese', facilitate communication. Such interaction forms a base from which many other cooperative and collaborative human experiences can develop, all of which bring quality of life experience.

Malloch's (1999) study of motherese demonstrates how mothers typically produced melodic vocalization and rhythms of bodily movements—usually developed in a turn-taking manner with the infant and including a 'balanced' exchange—can cause distress if changed. He observed cases where mothers were experiencing bi-polar disorder in both depressed and hypermanic states. These were compared with the interactions between a control group of mothers and infants. For the ill mothers, the motherese was not 'musically' timed: the depressed mothers were lethargic, barely able to interact with their babies; on the other hand, the hyper manic mothers were extremely excited and agitated, thrusting their bodies into the faces of their infants, bouncing the babies too vigorously, with a lack of awareness of their own actions and the babies' reactions. At either extreme, the infants became distressed: whimpering at the isolation when they were not responded to; and screaming revealing fear when their mothers were overly energetic and aggressive in their sounds and movements.

As babies mature and make the transition to toddlerhood, they continue to demonstrate that reciprocated imitations of vocal and gestural behaviours with adults and peers offer satisfaction and enjoyment to the social sharing being elicited (see Malloch and Trevarthen 2009). In fact, research examining Western pre-schoolers' collaborative play demonstrates that when the peers share vocalized and bodily reactions and experiences (singing and dancing), there is a sympathetic mirroring of types of bodily reactions (Tafuri 2008) and responses which are directly connected to the quality of the experience of emotion: the enharmonic key changes in tonal music are often associated with 'shivers down the spine' or 'goose bumps', reflecting psychological states such as excitement, joy, sadness, etc. (see Sloboda 1991; Sloboda et al. 2001).

These forms of musical interactions, whether listened to or participated in, reveal that musical arts can provide an everyday accompaniment though life, a companionship through the music-making. There is also huge scope for self- and social group identity and expression, especially through peer trends. Identifying with others, leading social and regulated lives leads to sharing, enjoyment and thus, wellbeing. Musical arts are physical activities that can keep the body as well as the mind conditioned.

With these theoretical propositions in mind, it is not difficult to understand the significance of embodied musical communication. But, as the next section reveals, owing to how cultural practice has developed, the integrated musical/movement experiences may become reduced or removed, owing to a prioritizing of different skills. Indeed, in Western formal education there has been a strong trend for literacy and numeracy to be prioritized over expressive and affective artistic experiences. Whilst such a tendency has an understandable base to empower and educate the population, the reduced cultural exposure to the musical arts may not be such a highly recommended long-term cultural practice. Evidence presented in this chapter will reveal that musical arts participation offers important self-identity, group affiliation, and shared emotional experience possibilities: factors crucial to feelings of wellbeing.

Embodied musical companionship: where, when, and how?

A current situation exists in Western cultures where only a minority have been appropriately exposed to the skills acquisition process required to develop musical arts performance competency (McPherson and Davidson 2006). Indeed, musical arts practice is most commonly found in Australia and the USA in specialist arts schools, with expertise in one sub-form being prioritized. For example, our recent fieldwork in Western Australian high schools revealed that students learning musical arts focus on a single form such as classical, jazz, or pop music. In dance, whilst there was a tendency to learn more styles which typically embrace classical ballet, contemporary, modern, jazz, and a range of contemporary dance forms, there would always be a specialism in one specific form, and dancers would not necessarily learn music skills and musicians would not necessarily learn dance skills. The students perceive each form to be highly demanding and so engaged in learning forefronting skills acquisition. In these professionalized learning contexts, though the students often expressed a love of their arts study area, and some recognized the emotional expressive potential engagement in music or dance gave them, they did not consider that wellbeing or social aspects are of equal importance (Davidson et al. submitted).

Unfortunately, performance opportunity is not at the forefront in daily school education, the result being to leave many feeling inhibition and unease around any form of public performance aspects of musical arts such as singing and dancing (Davidson et al. submitted). Yet, as the examples in the opening section attest, it is also known that musical arts are commonly experienced through the more passive form of participation by listening and self-generated private performance—dancing in one's bedroom, or singing in the shower—and have a powerful role in personal and social identification and expression. This sort of performance is typically not culturally valued. In fact, those students in receipt of specialist musical arts training in Western Australia failed to place informal musical experiences as part of the same continuum of experiences as the formal training they were receiving in, say, ballet or a music class.

Of course, the combined embodied musical arts—particularly singing and dancing together—can be found in community arts across the West, and can be seen to occupy social functions associated with cohesion, emotional expression, and a sense of wellbeing: for example, singing and dancing in social rituals such as weddings and festivals. In some cases, however, the musical arts on offer are both presented and received rather more like vestiges from another era than subjects of contemporary relevance; for example, consider how Scottish Country dancing, Maypole dancing, and Morris dancing may be introduced in a village fair. However, even despite a perceived lack of contemporary relevance, Argyle's (1987) psychology of happiness explicitly refers to English traditional musical arts forms such as country dancing as key examples of how cultural practice functions as an opportunity for unity and emotional expression and how this in turn leads to happiness. Though a simple theory, Argyle's idea is indeed consistent with those presented by Cross (2005), that the musical arts can bring about conditions for wellbeing to be experienced.

Much contemporary musical art has emerged through urban nightclub and pub performance culture, for example, indie pop music (Green 2002), with skills being developed collaboratively with peers in domestic contexts, rather than school-rooms. However, such learning practices and results can be achieved in school. Indeed, in cases where contemporary musical arts have overlapped with formal educational opportunity, we have seen that it is possible to sustain considerable interest, develop a range of musical performance skills and promote enjoyment. For example, Bradley Merrick's Music Department at Barker College, Hornsby in New South Wales, Australia, accommodates some 86 bands within its all-male school population (Merrick 2003, 2007). Though not explicitly aiming for wellbeing, the programme has been extremely popular amongst the boys and very many performance opportunities, collaborative and social presentation skills have been facilitated through the musical engagement.

The social and wellbeing value of musical arts embodied participation has been noted in the UK as part of The Music Manifesto which is a £10 million government sponsored programme initiated in 2007. The aim of the programme is to bring individuals and the community together, and 'Sing Up' is a national programme aiming to provide weekly singing engagements for all children across the UK (Welch et al. 2008). The programme has included regular singing activities in school. These activities have been surveyed and outcomes of participation have been assessed and, indicators reveal that those involved in singing have developed enhanced singing skills, improved self-concept, and sense of social inclusions (Welch et al. 2010). The evidence suggests that school is, and should be, an institution which encourages musical arts practice for a range of wellbeing benefits. As an example of the positive effects of daily musical engagement in schools, in Scandinavia, many schools have choirs, owing to a long-existing cultural tradition of group singing. A local pride and support builds for these choirs which filters in two directions from the communities to the schools and from the schools into the broader community. So, as children develop, their choir membership transfers quite naturally from school to community choirs (Durant 2003; Hyyppä and Mäki 2003). Note that in fact one-tenth of the Swedish adult population sing in formal choirs and that singing is a part of social and community life. As such, musical engagement that is germinated in childhood encourages lifelong participation (Durant 2003; Hyyppä and Mäki 2003).

Whilst a transference of cultural practice emerging from school curriculums into the community is found in some communities and cultures across the world, in many cases, transference occurs in the opposite direction, with emergent popular cultural practice influencing schoolyard engagement (Marsh 2008; Campbell 1998/2010). Consider the primary school and the playground games that emerge based on exposure to familial experience and exposure to popular culture (Marsh 2008); also observe how teenagers hanging around in peer groups in the schoolyard 'play out' and shape their own lives in pop music and dance routines found in the mass media (Gaunt 2006). In these regards, musical arts are crucial agents in the development of social self, though the wellbeing potential is not typically fore-fronted in such contexts—physical exercises is associated with hand-clapping and skipping rope games, or the physical intensity of some forms of hip-hop dance, for example.

Some musical arts cultural practices have been developed, however, as hybrid forms for explicit health and wellbeing impact. In the second decade of the twenty-first century, the popular hit is Zumba—a fusion of Latin with international music to choreographed dance for physical fitness outcomes drawing on dances forms as varied as hip-hop, bhangra, tango, cha-cha-cha, and salsa. Functioning as an unpartnered group dance movement, it has been developed to encourage mass participation—anyone can join in without the concern of finding a partner. Indeed, it is estimated that more than 60,000 fitness centres in 105 countries run Zumba programmes, those who participate evidently enjoy the group musical/physical experience over the usual isolated gym workout routine. Despite the solo form of moving, social and community building potential is present within Zumba, owing to the social context of the group dance and the high entrainment necessary to participate in the complex and pulsating rhythms of the music.

In fact, there is a growing body of musical arts practices and related research that brings further useful cases to this discussion. According to Cohen (2005), as people age they begin to realize that arts practices have expressive and communicative values they may never have had opportunities to engage with in their youth. Cohen (2005) describes the desire to seek out engagement with these forms of communication and expression in later life as a Liberation Phase; named so because he observed people overcome inhibitions in a determined effort to be able to enjoy new experiences before their lives are over. Faulkner and Davidson (2005) and Davidson and Faulkner (2010) have seen this attitude in action in adult group singing, including that specifically aimed at those with no former experience. Through their work, they observed: feelings of improved cognitive stimulation; sense of social cohesion; trans-generational understanding where singing groups included people of different generations; a sense of a communion with nature (singing in spaces and places); feelings of spiritual sharing (religious and otherwise); and testing out of identity (singing in competitions).

From the tradition of practice and research exploring music in therapeutic treatment, Aasgaard (1999) has proposed the use of musical arts as an inherent component of an institutional setting. He argues that music enhances the wellbeing of those inhabiting a space. Aasgaard's own working space is a hospital. Using a mobile music station he is able to ask patients, visitors, doctors, nurses, and administrators to contribute towards creating songs in and around the hospital building. His work offers a sense of community and coherence for all, whether long-stay patients, employees, or day visitors. The songs allow for a shared emotion and understanding, as well as an ownership of the space on which the voice is projected.

At a more intimate level, Aldridge (1999) describes how singing with a dying friend heightened understanding where words were potentially awkward, or inadequate. The singing by-passed all formal verbal exchanges and enabled emotional intimacy through the harmonic structure of the music. Similarly, Magee and Davidson (2004a,b) describe the use of singing activities with individuals in the late-stages of multiple sclerosis to permit the use the songs for reminiscence value, and to monitor the level of muscle control and strength of the vocal mechanism. Again, singing enabled expression of emotions around loss and grief which patients had otherwise not been able to express.

Bungay et al. (2010) and Davidson and Fedele (2011) report their work in developing singing groups for older people which are not only becoming increasingly popular, but that have also demonstrated positive social interaction and increased sense of wellbeing for members. In a related manner, Cohen et al. (2006) has shown that older people who engaged in choral participation for the first time, by contrast to a comparison group who did not sing, had fewer visits to doctors and reported a reduction in the number of over-the-counter medications taken. Furthermore, research with Alzheimer's disease patients has shown improved cognitive activity with moments of insight and coherence when engaged in singing activities (Prickett and Moore 1991).

The examples in the paragraph above focus on singing, which is also a topic within this book (see Chapter 10). But, along with singing, there has been a boom in the use of dance (see Chapters 11 and 17) and musical instrument playing for therapeutic benefits. Social tea dances have had a massive revival with older members of society, not having been practiced since the Second World War. Participants clearly engage for reminiscence, as well as companionship and physical benefits, with regional support for such events increasing rapidly with groups like Independent Age (Dublin) and Age Concern (across UK) supporting regular Tea Dances.

Dance movement therapies have become popular in mental health rehabilitation centres, medical and educational settings, nursing homes, day care facilities, and other health promotion programmes. Centring the body, the specialized treatments can aid people to share emotion with the proximity and coordination of group experience, working for therapeutic goals ranging from psychodynamic to practical outcomes, like improved self esteem (see Lewis 1984/1986; Siegel 1984; Chodorow 1991; Meekums 2002; Payne 2006).

In addition to dance therapies, there have been community orchestras established for adult group learning experience, and marching bands revived for people to combine musical experience with exercise. In Queensland, Australia, the community orchestras are listed on the state government's website[2] and indicate that their goals are for the inclusion of beginners through to experienced players. As the Music Council of Australia's initially quoted statement indicates, the 'Community Music' activities have social and educational function. The outcome, from all the evidence cited above, is for wellbeing.

Perhaps the largest growth area for the wellbeing benefits of musical arts have come in cases where the musical arts of other cultures has been adopted as a totally new form of musical arts experience—the earlier example of Zumba as a fusion art form fits this case. There is logic to these practices and their considerable popularity. Firstly, Westerners do not experience anxieties that could stem from impoverished earlier experiences of musical engagement, especially the fear of playing a Western classical instrument which is known to take years of practice to perfect. Secondly, the cultural forms used are often explicitly therapeutic in origin. For example, in Native American culture, the drum—a representation of the mother earth's heartbeat—is used to engender balance and rejuvenation, and this is typically achieved along with singing and dancing. In the Western 'Drum Circle' this original Native American use has been transposed to the new cultural context and the meaning is adapted with the aim of bringing people in touch with spiritual behaviours

---

[2] http://www.slq.qld.gov.au/info/com/music/qco (accessed 31 January 2010).

Browner (2009). Thirdly, these adopted forms offer socio-emotional, physical and even erotic experience not afforded in any of the arts practices of the host culture—e.g. Turkish belly dancing classes in Northern Germany. Indeed, the core characteristics of these cultural traditions are seemingly brought into Western experience and used directly for wellbeing impact.

In addition to the more holistic sense of wellbeing that the activities mentioned in the preceding paragraph seem to elicit, some musical practices have been used to reinforce and rekindle personal and cultural identity. For example, Yoon (2001) wrote about the North American movement where ethnic groups aim to assert their cultural identities through musical arts. The title of her paper title blasts out the message: 'She's really becoming Japanese now!: Taiko drumming and Asian American identifications.' According to Yoon (2001), taiko drums were originally sacred and magical, used to drive off pestilence and call forth rain. In the Asian American context, it seems that engaging Asian Americans in learning these drums has the potential to link this modern culture to the idea of something ancient and romantically meaningful: evoking images of ancient power and strength. Ironically, it is interesting to note that there is a contested history of taiko drumming which surrounds whether or not is was indeed an ancient form. The large group practices currently associated with the form became popular in the 1960s, when a renewed interest in traditional Japanese culture emerged that happened to be coincident with a similar movement in the USA and where it also dovetailed with the birth of Asian American political activism and awareness in the preservation and development of their cultural heritage. Indeed, as Yoon concludes, Asian American identity is not a singular matter, but this musical practice works to enhance at least some Asian Americans searching for a meaningful cultural identity.

From the examples above it is evident that embodied musical experience has core value. However, different cultural frameworks have experiences of musical arts that are profoundly different and these differences both reflect and impact on beliefs, behaviours, and expectations. With this in mind, it is simply not possible to explore embodied musical communication without referring to specific cultural examples.

The case of Venda musical culture in South Africa

Despite having discussed musical arts, it is apparent that in Western practice, one form is typically forefronted above the others in the performance context. For example, we watch a dance recital and even if the dance has music accompanying it, the music is generally in the background. We become passive spectators of classical music concerts. These musical experiences in Western musical settings represent notions of musicality that have been etched into the Western experience. Perhaps a more integrated musical arts experience can be found at rock concerts, where musicians and singers typically engage in a tactile and movement-focused musical experience on stage while scores of youth dance, move and sing along to the music from the audience arena. However, there still remains a distinct divide between performer and listener, an invisible line that distinguishes performer from consumer. This divide, while not omnipresent in all Western musical constructs, does to some extent control the culture of musicality and as such shapes notions of human musicality.

In contrast to this division, African music typically comprises a constellation of arts. Stone (1998, p. 7) notes that: 'African performance is a tightly wrapped bundle of arts that are sometimes difficult to separate, even for analysis'. She argues that this is due in part to the fact that 'honest observers are hard pressed to find a single indigenous group in Africa that has a term congruent with the usual Western notion of "music". . .the isolation of musical sounds from other arts proves a Western abstraction' (Stone 1998, p. 7). Scholars exploring music in sub-Saharan Africa have noted the reintegration of the arts in many African cultures. In a paper describing the integration of the arts in Namibia, Minette Mans discusses the philosophy of *ngoma*, which according to her, encompasses the spirit of music and dance which is linked to the human arts in Bantu language communities in Southern Africa (Mans 1998, pp. 374–375). She notes: 'the holism of arts in many African cultures is relevant to fundamental aspects of life. Music, dance and other arts are functionally interwoven into everyday life' (Mans 1998, p. 375). In addition, an ethnomusicological exploration of music in Africa must take 'into account its historical, social and cultural contexts' (Nketia and DjeDje 1984, p. xi).

Based on current (Emberly 2009; Emberly forthcoming) and historical (Blacking 1973, 1986, 1988) ethnographic research with Venda music in South Africa, we shall discuss how musical arts impact within communities. In many forms of Venda musical learning, music, dance and singing, as well as participant and observer, are integrated forms. Just as language is a tool to becoming an active member of a Venda community, musical arts are integrated tools for immersion into culture from infancy through adulthood. Musical arts in Venda culture are not something separated from culture itself; that is, music is human action within culture. This embeddedness is reflected within the school system where many children learn music in an Arts and Culture curriculum which ties music, dance and culture in one unit for students from primary through secondary schools. Although this marks a distinctive shift in learning, because music was at one time predominantly taught in village settings, it underscores the foundational role of musical culture in Venda and throughout South Africa (Emberly and Davidson, 2011).

This integration of human action and music was readily apparent in an interview in September 2009 with an elderly Venda woman, Denga Mpeiwa, who had lost her vocal range due to illness and said: 'A hu tshe na muthu, a ri tsha kona u imba' (there is no longer a person in me as I can no longer sing). The integration of culture and music is so intrinsically linked that when one can no longer sing one is no longer thought of as a person. The musical voice in Venda culture is fundamentally linked to Venda identity at its core. Music is not an art form for those who choose to perform it, but rather an expected and integrated aspect of culture and being. Thus, in many ways, individual, social and emotional wellbeing are contingent on being able to participate in musical arts.

John Blacking, Venda music, and human musicality

Venda music became the subject of academic study in the 1950s when social anthropologist John Blacking conducted field research on the role of music in Venda culture (specifically Venda children) in the northern area of South Africa. His work led him to conclude that musical skills can develop over a lifespan, and that music is a form of social expression and communication: that music is human action in culture (see Blacking, 1957, 1962, 1964, 1965, 1967, 1971). Throughout his career, Blacking retained focus on the musical culture of Venda people, challenging views that had developed in Western European culture which essentially espoused that musical ability was an endowed gift, attainable only by the elite and exceptionally talented. Blacking's counter-arguments were that all humans are essentially musical and that musical engagement is a natural, life-affirming activity. In his seminal text *How Musical is Man?* (1973), he developed these notions of human musicality, using the music of the Venda as his case for the possibilities that exist in terms of integrated forms of human musicality.

While Blacking might have been rather idealistic in his rendering of Venda culture, he did draw focus to how we understand and determine musicality in a sociocultural context. Blacking's understandings of human musicality and the motivations for engaging with music drew on ideas from works in which he was beginning to explore, namely music psychology, theories of musical ability initiated by Sloboda (1985) and develop subsequently by Sloboda, Davidson, and Howe throughout the 1990s (Sloboda et al. 1994; Howe et al. 1995; Davidson et al. 1996; Sloboda et al. 1996; Davidson et al. 1997; Davidson et al. 1998; Howe et al. 1998a, b) and further developed by Davidson et al. (2009). These theories, which have emerged purely from the study of Western musical learning motivation for engagement, are focused on the individual rather than the communal culture. However, can an individualistic psychological account be applicable to how Venda children engage musically, especially in present times when music-making has shifted from the village to the school?

The central point in this discussion, that musical motivation for learning requires support of home, school, family, and role models, as well as the individual investing large numbers of hours of individual practice time in skills acquisition, argued by Sloboda and colleagues, is culturally specific. Davidson, McPherson, and their colleagues Faulkner and Evans embrace psychological needs fulfilment, having demonstrated crucial pre-requisites of: competency (participants feeling they have both the skills and the potential for engagement); relatedness (that is social connection to others undertaking similar activities and it has relevance to them); and retention of personal autonomy within the whole (McPherson and Davidson 2002, McPherson 2005, 2006). But is there a 'universal needs' fulfilment in terms of musicality, if, as Blacking argued, musicality is a universal human attribute? Based on the current sociocultural status of Venda culture within South Africa, what does Venda children's music at present reveal in terms of musical motivations?

In terms of Venda children's learning and engagement with music, a much larger percentage of the population (and Blacking argued that it would be impossible to find a Venda person who was *not* musical) engage with being what we might title 'musical.' Although Blacking's statement might hold true today, the root of musicality is an inherently cultural one because it challenges our basic notion of what it means to be musical. Unlike most Western musical learning goals, Venda children are motivated to learn music, not only for the musical value but also with the greater goal of self and community knowledge and identity (Emberly 2009; Emberly in press; Emberly and Davidson, 2011).

In Venda culture, the motivations for learning music are integrative, much akin to the arts in general, which refer to music, dance and singing as one form of expression. This is unlike Western contexts where motivation for learning music is context specific, that is:

> learners experience greater psychological needs satisfaction when they are most engaged, and less psychological needs satisfaction at the time they cease musical engagement... in western culture some of the negative beliefs about music could be generated because music performance is often a subject of choice divorced from everyday contexts and even seen as irrelevant to them
>
> (Davidson et al. 2009, p. 1027).

In contrast, Venda children typically embody musical arts in their everyday lives. Musicking is an integral part of Venda culture, not one separated and performed by a chosen few. Although this is constantly changing due to sociocultural, economic, and global factors, unlike Western musical learning that is often motivated by conceptions of ability and individualized effort, in many forms of Venda music are particularly communally driven, requiring great numbers of participants to be successful. In group dances and reed pipe ensembles, a large number of participants are needed to create a successful performance. Participants in Venda music seem less inhibited by ability and effort and instead motivated by pride, expectancy, and embodied musicality.

In Venda children's music, a language of musical arts is imbued from infancy (Emberly 2009). In a construct similar to the one discussed above by Mans and Stone, the musical language of Venda children's music does not draw defined lines between singing, dancing, and musical instrument performance nor between listener and participant. A flexible relationship between these roles allows children to engage as performers and as listeners, as dancers, instrumentalists, and singers.

Comparable to language, musical arts are a cultural phenomenon embedded into cognitive processes of learning. At present, the South African government recognizes the integration of the arts in an African context, as the national curriculum blends music, culture and drama. Therefore, the educational system supports a culturally specific mode of understanding the meaning of musicality, reflecting a national sense of communicated musicality (Emberly 2009; Emberly forthcoming; Emberly and Davidson, 2011).

Building community and wellbeing through Venda music

In the case of Venda musical culture the communal, participatory and integrated nature of music is essential to the perpetuation of Venda culture itself, and as such an individual and collective sense of wellbeing. In this context, musical arts hold great value because it is not simply an artistic object that can be replicated. In interviews with Arts and Culture teachers in 2009 there were unified responses to the question of why it is important to teach Venda musical arts in the classroom: because it promotes health (in terms of exercise); because it teaches young people about Venda culture; because it helps young people to remember the history of their own people.

Although Venda musical arts have now made a shift to the classroom and the institutionalized setting of government sanctioned schools, it does not mean that musical arts are no longer an integrated aspect of Venda culture. Although the functionality of many of these songs has changed, the importance of music within the culture remains central. That is, musical arts still function to teach children about Venda culture, just as it did when Blacking was doing research in the 1950s and how it will likely continue to do. As infants, children are strapped to their mother's backs and engage in music, movement and song. Young children are taught children's songs, some that are no longer functionally relevant, but that nonetheless teach integral aspects of Venda culture. Dancing, movement, drumming, reed pipes, all markers of Venda culture, still dominate the musical landscape.

We can argue, of course, that this experience is not so far removed from Argyle's observation that Scottish Country Dancing results in 'happiness' because it produces engagement through entrainment, social encounter, and provides cultural history. But, the reality is that by comparison with Venda, Westerners are quite far removed from an integrated lifestyle.

Music communicates meaning in Venda culture and it is not just simply that all Venda people can perform music; performance is not the necessitated goal by most people, rather it is the embedded nature of musical arts in Venda culture that Blacking was so interested in and that continues in present day. It is because of the centralized role of music, embedded and rooted deeply in Venda culture, that we can begin to understand how music and wellbeing are intrinsically linked in sociocultural contexts.

Conclusion

Engaging with musical arts practices and their central role in human communication, this chapter has demonstrated that musical arts are an embodied communicative experience for wellbeing. Musical arts practices offer: a personal and cultural identity; social integration, coordination and collaboration; socioemotional regulation; positive physical experiences; and therapeutic benefits. Through diverse notions of musical arts, communities and individuals rely on the embodied nature of practice to create community therefore impacting social, cultural, and individual wellbeing. From mother–infant interactions, to experiences in Western contexts, to musicality embedded within Venda culture, the embodied communicative function of music forms the foundation of human musical interaction. This embodiment, which ranges from the personal to the communal, from the individual to the cultural, directly impacts and regulates what music communicates, why humans use music as a tool of communication and the manner in which people have access to and benefit from any level of musical competency. Functions and roles of musical arts, for both the individual and the community, are a constantly shifting and adapting form to which people both extract and ascribe meaning. It is this meaning, and its cultural-based definition, that identifies the communicative role of music. From this meaning we can determine that the role of community contributes to wellbeing on both individual and communal levels. As such, musicality can be viewed as both an innate and culturally determined function of humanity.

References

Aasgaard, T. (1999). Music therapy as milieu in the hospice and paediatric oncology ward. In: D. Aldridge (ed.) *Music therapy in palliative care: New voices*, pp. 29–42. London: Jessica Kingsley Publications.

Aldridge, D. (1999). Music therapy and the creative act. In: D. Aldridge (ed.) *Music therapy in palliative care: New voices*, pp. 15–28. London: Jessica Kingsley Publishers.

Argyle, M. (1987). *The psychology of happiness*. London: Methuen.

Bungay, H., Clift, S., and Skingley, A. (2010). The Silver Song Club Project: A sense of well-being through participatory singing. *Journal of Applied Arts and Health*, **1**(2), 165–78.

Blacking, J.A. (1957). *The role of music amongst the Venda of the Northern Transvaal, Union of South Africa: A Report*. South Africa: International Library of African Music.

Blacking, J.A. (1962). Musical expeditions of the Venda. *African Music*, **3** (1), 54–72.

Blacking, J.A. (1964). *Black background: The childhood of a South African girl*. London and New York: Abelard Schuman.

Blacking, J.A. (1965). The role of music in the culture of the Venda of the Northern Transvaal. In: M. Kolinski (ed.) *Studies in Ethnomusicology*, pp. 20–52. New York: Oak Publications.

Blacking, J.A. (1967). *Venda children's songs: A study in ethnomusicological analysis*. Johannesburg: Witwatersrand University Press.

Blacking, J.A. (1971). Music in the Historical Process of Vendaland. In: K.P. Wachsmann (ed.) *Essays on Music and History in Africa*, pp. 185–212. Evanston, IL: Northwestern University Press.

Blacking, J.A. (1973). *How musical is man?* Seattle, WA: University of Washington Press.

Blacking, J.A. (1986). Identifying processes of musical change. *The World of Music*, **28**(1), 3–15.

Blacking, J.A. (1988). Dance and music in Venda children's cognitive development. In: G.J. and I.M. Lewis (eds.) *Acquiring Culture: Cross Cultural Studies in Child Development*, pp. 91–112. London: Croom Helm.

Blacking, J.A. (1990). Music in Children's Cognitive and Affective Development. In: F.R. Wilson and F.L. Roehmann (eds.) *The Biology of Music Making: Music and Child Development*, pp. 68–78. St. Louis, MO: MMB Music, Inc.

Browner, T. (2009). *Music of the first nations: tradition and innovation in native North America*. Urbana and Chicago: University of Illinois Press.

Campbell, P. (1998/2010). *Songs in their heads: Music and its meaning in children's lives*. New York: Oxford University Press.

Chodorow, J. (1991). *Dance Therapy and Depth Psychology*. London: Routledge.

Cohen, G.D. (2005). *The Mature Mind*. New York: Basic Books.

Cohen, G.D., Perlstein, S., Chapline. J., Kelly, J., Firthm K.M., and Simmens, S. (2006). The impact of professionally conducted cultural programs on the physical health, mental health, and social functioning of older adults. *Gerontologist*, **46**(6), 726–34.

Cross, I. (2005). Music and meaning, ambiguity and evolution. In: D. Miell, R. MacDonald, and D.J. Hargreaves (eds.) *Musical Communication*, pp. 27–44. Oxford: Oxford University Press.

Davidson, J.W. (2005). Bodily communication in musical performance. In: D. Miell, D.J. Hargreaves, and R. MacDonald (eds.) *Musical Communication*, pp. 215–238. Oxford: Oxford University Press.

Davidson, J.W. and Emberly, A. (submitted). Arts in Education: Learning musical arts in Western Australia.

Davidson, J.W. and Fedele, J. (2011). 'Investigating group singing activity with people with dementia and their caregivers: Problems and positive prospects'. *Musicae Scientiae.* FirstOnline: DOI: 10.1177/1029864911410954.

Davidson, J.W., Howe, M.J.A., Moore, D.M., and Sloboda, J.A. (1996). The role of parental influences in the development of musical ability. *British Journal of Developmental Psychology,* **14**, 399–412.

Davidson, J.W., Howe, M.J.A. and Sloboda, J.A. (1997). Environmental factors in the development of musical performance skill in the first twenty years of life. In: D.J. Hargreaves and A.C. North (eds.) *The Social Psychology of Music,* pp. 188–203. Oxford: Oxford University Press.

Davidson, J.W., Howe, M.J.A., Moore, D.M., and Sloboda, J.A. (1998). The role of teachers in the development of musical ability. *Journal of Research in Music Education,* **46**(1), 141–60.

Davidson, J.W. and Faulkner, R.F. (2010). Meeting in music: the role of singing to harmonise carer and cared for. *Arts and Health,* **2**(2), 164–70.

Davidson, J., Faulkner, R., and McPherson, G.E. (2009). Motivating musical learning. *The Psychologist,* **22**(12), 1026–9.

Durant, C. (2003). *Choral conducting: philosophy and practice.* London: Routledge.

Emberly, A. (2009). Mandela went to China . . . and India too: Musical cultures of childhood in South Africa. PhD dissertation, University of Washington.

Emberly, A. (forthcoming). Venda children's musical cultures in Limpopo, South Africa. In: T. Wiggins and P. Campbell (eds) *Oxford Handbook of Children's Musical Cultures.* Oxford: Oxford University Press.

Emberly, A. and Davidson, J.W. (forthcoming). From the *kraal* to the classroom: Shifting musical arts practices from the community to the school with special reference to learning *tshigombela* in Limpopo, South Africa. *International Journal of Music Education.*

Faulkner, R. and Davidson, J.W. (2005). Men's vocal behaviour and the construction of self. *Musicae Scientiae,* **8**(2), 231–55.

Gaunt, K.D. (2006). *The Games Black Girls Play.* New York: New York University Press.

Green, L. (2002). *How Popular Musicians Learn.* Aldershot: Ashgate.

Howe, M.J.A., Sloboda, J.A., and Davidson, J.W. (1993). What makes a musician? *Upbeat,* **16**, 8–9.

Howe, M.J.A., Davidson, J.W., Moore, D.M., and Sloboda, J.A. (1995). Are there early signs of musical excellence? *Psychology of Music,* **23**, 162–76.

Howe, M.J.A., Davidson, J.W., and Sloboda, J.A. (1998a). Innate gifts and talents: Reality or myth? *Behavioural and Brain Sciences,* **21**(3), 399–407.

Howe, M.J.A., Davidson, J.W., and Sloboda, J.A. (1998b). Natural born talents undiscovered. *Behavioural and Brain Sciences,* **21**(3), 432–42.

Hyyppä, M.T. and Mäki, J. (2003). Social participation and health in a community rich in stock of social capital. *Health Education Research,* **16**(6), 770–9.

Huron, D. (2006). *Sweet Anticipation: Music and the Psychology of Expectation.* Cambridge, MA: MIT Press.

Lewis, P. (1984/1986). *Theoretical Approaches in Dance Movement Therapy* (vols I/II). USA: Kendall/Hunt.

Magee, W.L. and Davidson, J.W. (2004a). Singing In therapy: Monitoring disease process in chronic degenerative illness. *British Journal of Music Therapy,* **18**(2), 65–77.

Magee, W.L., and Davidson, J.W. (2004b). Music therapy in multiple sclerosis: Results of a systematic qualitative analysis. *Music Therapy Perspectives,* **22**(1), 39–51.

Malloch, S. (1999). Mothers and infants and communicative musicality. *Musicae Scientiae,* Special Issue 1999–2000, 29–57.

Malloch, S. and Trevarthen, C. (2009). *Communicative Musicality: Exploring the Basis of Human Companionship.* Oxford: Oxford University Press.

Mans, M. (1998). Using Namibian music/dance traditions as a basis for reforming arts education–theory and practice. In: C. van Niekerk (ed.) *Ubuntu: Music Education for a Humane Society: Conference*

Proceedings of the 23rd World Conference of the International Society for Music Education. Pretoria, South Africa.

Marsh, K. (2008). *The Musical Playground: Global tradition and change in children's songs and games*. Oxford: Oxford University Press.

McPherson, G.E., and Davidson, J.W. (2002). Musical practice: Mother and child interactions during the first year of learning an instrument. *Music Education Research, 4*, 141–56.

McPherson, G.E. (2005). From child to musician: Skill development during the beginning stages of learning an instrument. *Psychology of Music, 33*, 5–35.

McPherson, G.E. (2006). *The child as musician: a handbook of musical development*. Oxford: Oxford University Press.

McPherson, G.E. and Davidson, J.W. (2006). Playing an instrument. In: G.E. McPherson (ed.) *The Child as Musician*, pp. 331–352. Oxford: Oxford University Press.

Meekums, B. (2002). *Dance Movement Therapy: a Creative Psychotherapeutic Approach*. London: Sage.

Merrick, B. (2007). Valuing self-reflection in music performance. An evaluation of purposeful goal setting and strategy development in adolescents. *XXIXth Annual conference of the Australian Association for Research in Music Education*. Perth. AARME, Melbourne.

Merrick, B. (2003). Twenty-first Century Musicians. *Music In Action*, **1**(2). Available at: http://www.musicinaction.org.au/modules.php? op=modload&name=News&file=article&sid=242&mode=thread&order=0&thold=0

Music Council of Australia. Briefing paper: Communities, contexts and constructs. Available at: http://www.mca.org.au/music-in-australia/australian-musical-futures/107–2008-futures-towards-2020/279-restricted-briefing-paper (accessed 31 January 2010).

Nketia, K.J.H. and Djedje, J.C. (eds.) (1984). *Studies in African Music [Selected Reports in Ethnomusicology V]*. Los Angeles, CA: UCLA Department of Music.

Payne, H. (ed.) (2006). *Dance Movement Therapy: Theory, Research and Practice* (2nd edn.) London: Tavistock/Routledge.

Prickett, C.A. and Moore, R.S. (1991). The use of music to aid memory of Alzheimer patients. *Journal of Music Therapy, 28*, 101–10.

Ruud, E. (1998). *Music Therapy: Improvisation, Communication and Culture*. Gilsum, NH: Barcelona Press.

Ruud, E. (2002). *Musikk og identitet*. Oslo: Universitetsforlaget.

Siegel, E. (1984). *Dance Movement Therapy: Mirror of Ourselves: The Psychoanalytic Approach*. New York: Human Science Press.

Sloboda, J.A. (1985). *The musical mind: The cognitive psychology of music*. Oxford: Oxford University Press.

Sloboda, J.A. (1991). Music structure and emotional response: some empirical findings. *Psychology of Music, 19*, 110–20.

Sloboda, J.A., Davidson, J.W. and Howe, M.J.A. (1994). Is everyone musical? *The Psychologist, 7*(7), 349–54.

Sloboda, J.A., Davidson, J.W., Howe, M.J.A., and Moore, D.M. (1996). The role of practice in the development of expert musical performance. *British Journal of Psychology, 87*, 287–309.

Sloboda, J.A., O'Neill, S.A., and Ivaldi, A. (2001). Functions of music in everyday life: An exploratory study using the experience sampling method. *Musicae Scientiae* **5**(1), 9–32.

Stone, R. (1998). African Music in a Constellation of Arts. In: R. Stone (ed.) *The Garland Encyclopedia of World Music*, pp. 2–12. New York: Garland.

Tafuri, J. (2008). *Infant musicality: New research for educators and parents*. Surrey: Ashgate.

Tarrant, M., North, A.C., and Hargreaves, D.J. (2002). Youth, identity and music. In: R. MacDonald, D.J. Hargreaves and D. Miell (eds.) *Musical identities*, pp. 134–50. Oxford: Oxford University Press.

Trevarthan, C. (1999). Musicality and the intrinsic motive pulse: evidence from human psycho- biology and infant communication. *Musicae Scientiae, Special Issue* 1999–2000, 155–215.

Trevarthan, C. (2002). Origins of musical identity: evidence from infancy for musical social awareness. In: R. MacDonald, D. Hargreaves and D. Miell (eds) *Musical Identities*, pp. 21–37. Oxford: Oxford University Press.

Walker, R. (2007). *Music Education: Cultural Values, Social Change and Innovation*. Springfield, IL: Charles C. Thomas Publishers.

Welch. G.E., Himonides, E., Saunders, J., Papageorgi, J., Rinta, T., Stewart, C., *et al.* (2008). *The National singing programme for primary schools in England: An initial baseline study overview*, February. Available at: http://www.imerc.org/research.php (accessed 27 April 2011)

Welch. G.E., Himonides, E., Saunders, J., Papageorgi, J, Rinta, T, Vraka, M., *et al.* (2010). Children's singing development, self-concept and social inclusion. In: S. Demorest, S.L. Morrison, and P. Campbell (eds.) *Proceedings of The Eleventh International conference on Music Perception and Cognition*, Seattle, USA

Yoon, P.J-C. (2001). 'She's really becoming Japanese now!': Taiko drumming and Asian American identifications. *American Music*, **19**(4), 417–38.

Section 3

Music as Therapy and Health Promotion

Chapter 12

Music and Rehabilitation: Neurological Approaches

A. Blythe LaGasse and Michael H. Thaut

Introduction

Music creation and expression has been explored throughout human history for its contribution to the arts, humanity, and community. A beautiful and expressive medium, music is a powerful tool, an art form that is difficult to quantify in terms of how listening to music can create an emotional experience that is both unique to the individual and shared by many. Although some aspects of music perception may be under debate, in-depth efforts using modern brain imaging techniques to understand the neurological processes involving music engagement have flourished since the early 1990s. With advances in technology that can monitor cortical activity during the perception and production of musical stimuli, we have a better understanding of how music engages and changes the brain. Such studies have begun a rapid transformation in how music is used in the therapeutic environment.

Historically, music therapy has been based in models of social science, primarily thought of as a tool to facilitate social learning and emotional wellbeing. Music has been used to alleviate pain, promote emotional expression, and as a method to facilitate social interaction and community. This foundation of modern music therapy, beginning around 1950, arises from helping those with mental illness, disability, or persons injured in war. Early music therapy writings focus on music as an expressive art form, music as redirection from pain, and music as a motivator. Although music continues to be used for these purposes, the scope and reach of music in therapy has changed drastically with scientific studies on music and the brain. Although the social science model is still prevalent in music therapy, current research has contributed to the development of a clinical model of music therapy based in the neuroscience model.

There is some evidence of music therapy within a scientific model in early writings. For example, music therapy pioneer E. Thayre Gaston (1968) wrote of music therapy within the behavioral sciences, but noted that effects of music should be explored scientifically and that the music therapist should have vast multidisciplinary knowledge (p. 27). These ideas begin to allude to the use of music in the neuroscience model, and, in fact, early pioneers wrote about the ability for music to help with speech disorders, hospitalized patients, and in the treatment of older adults (e.g. Gaston 1968). However, with little understanding of the role of music cognition and perception, this model was not popular. The evidence promoting music therapy in the neuroscience model emerged as research studying the relationship between music and brain function began to flourish. Such studies began to integrate fields of neuroscience, music cognition, rehabilitation, and music therapy, which have drastically changed the understanding of the power of music in therapy.

Scientific investigation of music has not diminished the appreciation of music as an aesthetic; rather this paradigm shift has strengthened our appreciation of music as both a powerful stimulus and an art form. As we increase our understanding of how music impacts the brain, the ideas of music theorists can be explored under a new light. For example, in Berlyne's (1971) writing entitled *Aesthetics and Psychobiology,* he explored art in terms of sensory stimulation sought for purposes of achieving a desired state of arousal. In order to maintain homeostasis, we seek out an appropriate level of external stimulation, which can drive motivation to engage in the arts. Furthermore, changes invoked by engagement in musical stimuli can be measured in psychophysiological responses including autonomic responses, motor responses, sensory changes, and central nervous responses. Current studies in music neuroscience have shown that we not only experience emotionally-based cortical activity when engaged with pleasing music (cf. Koelsch 2005), but that prolonged engagement in music promotes changes in the cortex (cf. Särkämö et al. 2008), including rehabilitative gains demonstrated with music therapy treatment (cf. Thaut 2005). Therefore, science has greatly increased our appreciation for this powerful artistic medium.

In this chapter, we will discuss neuroscience and music research and how this research has informed the use of music in therapy for rehabilitation. First, we will begin with evidence of cortical engagement when listening and performing music. Second, we will explore motor synchronization to rhythm. Third, we will present evidence of successful rehabilitation of sensorimotor, cognitive, and communication with populations including Parkinson's, stroke, and multiple sclerosis. Finally, we will present how this research has created and continues to inform the practice of Neurologic Music Therapy (NMT). This evidence, together, will illustrate how the use of music therapy has shifted from a social science model to a neuroscience model and how the use of music in therapy can benefit persons in rehabilitation.

Neuroscience and music

Basic neuroscience studies have provided insights as to how different aspects of music are processed in the brain. In order to study this complex media, controlled studies performed in the laboratory setting using a reductionist method (studying specific/basic elements of music in a confined environment), which allows the researcher to pinpoint brain activity resulting from different musical elements. Although music neuroscience studies have begun to provide some insight as to how we process musical stimuli in the brain, the exact processes are still under debate. In this section we will discuss a few prominent findings have come forth that can be agreed upon by music neuroscientists. First, music processing is cortically distributed and shares non-musical cortical networks. Second, engaging in music changes the brain.

Historically, music processing was thought to occur predominantly in the right hemisphere. This view of music processing has been shown to be oversimplistic with studies indicating distributed processing for the different characteristics of music. Current research has demonstrated that listening to music, performing music, and moving to music engages regions throughout the cortex, subcortex, and cerebellum (cf. Peretz and Zatorre 2005). Furthermore, cortical areas that are engaged in music processing are not unique to music. These areas are also active in non-musical functions, meaning there is a distributed and undedicated network involved in music processing. Should damage occur to a specific cortical area, the distributed nature of music processing allows for the maintenance of musical skill post-injury, despite related loss of nonmusical skill. For example, a person who has an injury to Broca's area of the brain will likely lose speech production ability (a condition known as non-fluent or Broca's aphasia), but will maintain the ability to sing. Neurologically, this occurs because singing activates not only motor speech areas in the dominant hemisphere, but also involves cortical areas that are not typically involved in speech production, including the area in the non-dominant hemisphere that is homologous to Broca's area (Özdemir et al. 2006). The shared cortical network involved in music therefore extends beyond the areas necessary for similar non-musical tasks. This extended cortical network has also been well documented in the processing of rhythm, an extremely important component of music.

Perception of the temporal regularity of an auditory stimulus is essential for the coordination of musical movement, as can be observed in music performance and dance. The ability to perceive the temporal regularity, called the beat or tactus, has only been observed in humans and one species of bird (Patel et al. 2009). The ability to perceive temporal regularity would be essential to coordinating musical movements or movements cued by an external stimulus, a process utilized in rehabilitation. Studies on the neurological processes involved in beat perception have shown that listening to an isochronous rhythmic sequence (i.e. stimuli that occurs in equal time intervals) invokes regions involved in motor control including the dorsal premotor cortex, supplementary motor areas, pre-supplementary motor area, and the lateral cerebellum (Bengtsson et al. 2009). Simple beat-based sequences have been shown to invoke areas the basal ganglia involved in motor control, an activation that is strengthened when internal generation of the beat is required (Grahn 2009). These studies demonstrate that listening to a rhythmic stimulus engages areas beyond the auditory cortex, including several cortical and subcortical areas involved in motor timing and planning (Thaut 2003). Furthermore, when a person engages in music over time, these connections become stronger, resulting in cortical changes.

When compared to non-musicians, adult musicians have differences in the cortex, including sensorimotor areas, auditory areas, and areas involved in multisensory integration (cf. Gaser and Schlaug 2003; Bermudez and Zatorre 2005; Imfeld et al. 2009). More interesting to rehabilitation science are changes due to music engagement in a person with no formal musical training. For example, the child's brain changes after only 15 months of musical training, including differences quantified on magnetic resonance images (MRIs) in motor, auditory, frontal, and occipital regions (Hyde et al. 2009). After 29 months of instrument training, differences have been observed in the anterior corpus callosum of children (Schlaug et al. 2009a). In the adult, research has demonstrated that music can drive plasticity, creating new pathways with music learning. For example, adult non-musicians have shown more connectivity of the hand area of the sensorimotor cortex, after only a few weeks of training on the piano (Pascual-Leone 2001). Furthermore, a short period of musical training can lead to changes in the perception–action mediation, where motor areas of the brain activate in response to a sound (notes played on the piano) that is usually paired with an action (pressing down the keys of the piano).

Cortical areas for motor movement have been shown to activate when listening to rhythmic sequences, even in the absence of movement or impending movement (e.g. Bengtsson et al. 2009). This phenomena, called perception–action mediation or mirror function, has been observed in pianists who hear a piano piece that they have previously played (Haueisen and Knösche 2001; Bangert et al. 2006). In non-musicians, a short period of training on an instrument has been shown to increase motor area activation when listening to the exact melody used in training (Lahav et al. 2007). Listening to practised notes in a different pattern resulted in minor activations, whereas melodies outside of practised notes did not activate the motor areas (Lahav et al. 2007). This research has shown that short periods of practice can drive cortical plasticity, which has excellent implications for rehabilitation with music.

We have, thus far, examined how music is cortically distributed and shares non-musical neurological networks. This logically leads us to questions about the importance of the auditory system for encoding and processing musical stimuli. One hypothesis, called the auditory scaffolding hypothesis, may explain why auditory information is so effective in changing the brain. This hypothesis proposes that everything that deals with temporal processing, timing, and sequencing is assigned to the auditory system (Conway et al. 2009). Since what we hear is temporal in nature, the auditory system is primed for time-based information. The auditory system has been shown to be highly efficient in comparison to other systems, possibly due to the time-ordered nature of the system, and the temporal organization of functional skills (i.e. learning, language, attention, memory, executive function). The auditory scaffolding hypothesis states that due to this complex temporal organization, experiences that are auditory may provide 'scaffolding' for rehabilitating or developing general cognitive abilities (Conway et al. 2009). Music, as a naturally time-ordered and predictable medium, may provide an enhanced auditory 'scaffolding' experience that would help to reach rehabilitative goals more efficiently. One major component of music that has been shown to create immediate changes in cortical activity is the ability to synchronize movement to rhythmic auditory beat patterns.

Rhythmic entrainment

In order to understand the effects of music in the rehabilitation setting, it is important to understand the immediate effect of rhythm on the motor system. The neurological process that occurs in auditory rhythmic motor synchronization is not entirely understood. Research studies have shown that motor synchrony to an external auditory stimulus is quickly achieved and maintained, even with perturbations in the period of the stimulus that are below the level of conscious awareness (Thaut et al. 1998). In changes below the conscious level of perception, the period errors (time difference between auditory stimulus interval and tap interval) are corrected first, followed by a gradual adjustment of synchronization error (time difference between tap and onset of auditory stimuli). When larger perturbations occur (at least 5% change in period), the sensorimotor system responds with a temporary overcorrection, followed by resynchronization (Thaut et al. 1998). Therefore, the auditory system communicates precise and consistent interval-based temporal information to the brain, which directly influences the organization of motor output in relation to time and space.

The motor response to a rhythmic auditory stimulus precedes the actual occurrence of the stimulus (negative asynchrony), indicating that we anticipate the interval between the stimuli. Although responses appear to occur exactly with the stimulus, the actual motor responses have been shown to fluctuate within milliseconds. Despite error in individual responses, the average responses are tightly coupled to the stimulus. The current theory is that the synchronization mechanism is a self-correcting system, with stochastic (or random) noise attributes that create random fluctuations in motor response (Mitra et al. 1997). The human brain, however, has the ability to tightly couple responses with the stimulus period, which is perceived as exact entrainment of response to stimulus. The investigation of sensorimotor synchronization has been furthered by advances in neuroimaging techniques that can begin to observe activation of cortical structures involved in entrainment.

Positron emission tomography (PET) has been used during an isochronous right-handed, finger-tapping task to determine cortical areas involved in entrainment and found that there were no specific 'entrainment' areas in the brain. Rather, there were widespread activations in the cortex, subcortex, and cerebellum, suggesting that temporal auditory information is directly projected into the motor system (Stephan et al. 2002). A later PET study showed that when synchronizing a finger tap to a stimulus (regardless of the degree perturbation) there was more activity in the vermal and hemispheric areas of the anterior lobe of the cerebellum (Thaut et al. 2009b). When there were large perturbations in the period, activations in the posterior lobe of the cerebellum were evident. These cerebellar activation patterns corresponded to activations in areas of the cortex, suggesting that there are distinct coticocerebellar circuits subserving the different aspects of rhythmic synchronization including rhythmic motor control, rhythmic pattern track-ing, and conscious/subconscious response to temporal structure (Thaut et al. 2009b). The cere-bellum has also been shown to be involved in tapping complex rhythms to an auditory pacing cue (i.e. polyrhythm). When musicians tapped 3:2 or 2:3 rhythms, there was activation of the contral-ateral cerebellum and bilateral supplementary motor area (Thaut et al. 2008).

Although it is evident that many areas of the cortex and cerebellum are involved in rhythmic synchronization, the exact neural process responsible for the transformation of auditory-motor information remains unclear. This has been supported in a recent study where repetitive transcra-nial magnetic stimulation (rTMS) was applied separately to the left ventral premotor cortex (vPMC) and the left superior temporal-parietal area (STP), inhibiting the neural impulses from those cortical areas. Results indicated that error in phase synchronization (difference between auditory stimulus and response onset) significantly increased; however, the period error (differ-ence between stimulus and response intervals) was not affected by the rTMS. The phase synchro-nization error results indicated that the vPMC and the STP areas are involved in motor synchronization; however, the ability to maintain absolute period error indicates that there are separate cortical areas involved in period synchronization (Malcolm et al. 2008). This evidence supports the theory that auditory temporal information is directly projected into the motor sys-tem, beginning with the encoding of temporal information in the auditory system (Thaut 2005). However, the pathway from the auditory cortex to the motor system is still unclear, with sugges-tions that information transfers directly to motor areas or that the auditory cortex contributes to entrainment via common thalamic projections shared with cortical motor areas (Thaut 2005).

Additional supporting evidence for different neural pathways for auditory-motor synchroniza-tion comes from studies of persons with interrupted motor processes due to neurological disease or disability. Clinical studies have demonstrated that persons who have damage to the basal gan-glia respond to auditory rhythmic stimulation in treatment of speech and gait. Furthermore, persons with neurological insult to the sensorimotor cortex, due to cerebral vascular accident, have also been shown to improve in measures of gait and volitional movements when involved in treatments utilizing rhythmic motor synchronization. In the next section we will explore relevant clinical evidence showing the positive changes evoked by rhythmic intervention.

Clinical evidence of music in rehabilitation

The previous evidence demonstrates how music is cortically distributed and drives plasticity, which leads to questions about the implications of cortical distribution in rehabilitation medi-cine. The data have shown that entrainment occurs subliminally, with rhythm providing an external temporal cue to finely attune motor movements via direct projection into the motor system from the auditory cortex. In the field of music therapy, the next logical step would be to determine if these attributes of motor synchronization could be used to rehabilitate functions lost due to neurological disability or disease of the cortex. Clinical music therapy studies have, indeed, shown that motor synchronization occurs in persons with neurological disease and disability, and that rhythmic entrainment can be used in rehabilitation of non-musical sensorimotor, cognitive, and communication function.

The largest body of research comes from using rhythm for sensorimotor rehabilitation. Clinical evidence has indicated that the use of external rhythmic auditory cueing can aid in the rehabilita-tion of biologically intrinsic motor movements, such as gait. Using rhythm as an external audi-tory cueing device has been shown to improve gait parameters including step cadence, stride length, velocity, symmetry of stride length, (cf. Thaut et al. 1996; Thaut et al. 1997, 2007; Hausdorff et al. 2007), and centre of mass (Prassas et al. 1997). This technique, termed Rhythmic Auditory

Stimulation, has been successful in improving gait parameters of adults with Parkinson's disease (Miller et al. 1996; Thaut, McIntosh et al. 1996; McIntosh et al. 1997; Prassas et al. 1997; Howe et al. 2003; Arias and Cudeiro 2008; Rochester et al. 2009), traumatic brain injury (Hurt et al. 1998; Kenyon and Thaut 2000), spinal cord injury (De L'Etoile 2008), stroke (Thaut et al. 1997, 2007; Roerdink et al. 2007, 2009; Hayden et al. 2009), and Huntington's disease (Thaut et al. 1999). These studies clearly indicate that engagement of extended networks and auditory-motor entrainment, as discussed previously, has direct and measurable effects in motor rehabilitation that can develop into long-term functional therapeutic outcomes.

In addition to gait, rhythmic auditory cueing can be utilized to organize arm movements into temporally structured patterns, decreasing the motor variability of a volitional movement. Rhythmic cueing has been successful in the treatment of a hemiparetic arm and has resulted in decreased movement variability, increased speed of movement, and a smoothing of the movement trajectory (Thaut et al. 2002). The RAS treatment protocol has also been shown to significantly decrease compensatory trunk movements that often accompany arm movements in persons with stroke, while increasing contribution of the shoulder (Malcolm et al. 2009). These improvements in coordination and execution of volitional movements can be a focus of music therapy treatment with the goal of generalizing learned skills into activities of daily living.

Playing music has also been shown to be beneficial to rehabilitation in persons who have partial paralysis due to cerebral vascular accident. Learning to play the piano or drum set in the therapeutic setting has resulted in improved quality of movements, range of movement, and speed of movements (Schneider et al. 2007; Altenmüller et al. 2009). Although motivational aspects of music making may account for some of the gains, the neurophysiological evidence shows that with musical training, there was an occurrence increased activation of the motor cortex and improved cortical connectivity (Altenmüller et al. 2009). Furthermore, patients who participated in therapeutic instrument playing demonstrated greater generalization of skill to the typical or home environment (Schneider et al. 2007). All of these improvements in sensorimotor functioning, post-neurological disease or disability, would have direct effect on activities of daily living, providing the patient with the greatest amount of functional independence. Similar success can be achieved in the area of speech communication.

Many parallels between speech communication and music have been proposed; however, research using music to rehabilitate speech is in its infancy. Speech communication is a complex skill that is dependent on precisely timed motor sequences that involve not only the oromotor apparatus, but also coordination of laryngeal and bronchial structures. Evidence of shared cortical networks for speech and music are emerging and imaging studies are beginning to show that music activates speech systems differently than non-musical stimuli, which may lead to enhanced rehabilitative outcomes. As previously discussed, persons with non-fluent aphasia may exhibit an unimpaired ability to sing despite loss of speech. A technique called Melodic Intonation Therapy (MIT) has been shown to improve speech production in persons with non-fluent aphasia with some indication that, when successful, MIT improves dominant-side language areas (Belin et al. 1996). Improvements in the non-dominant hemisphere have also been documented. The use of a recent brain imaging technique, called diffusion tensor imaging, has revealed that in patients with chronic non-fluent apahsia, MIT strengthens the white matter pathway called the arcuate fasciculus in the non-dominant hemisphere (Schlaug et al. 2009b). These results demonstrate that music intervention can drive cortical plasticity for speech function, even when the patient is as much as 1-year post-neurological injury. Music intervention has also been shown to improve intelligibility of persons with neurological disorders.

Speech intelligibility is another area often affected in neurologic disease and disorder. Rhythmic cueing can be used to reduce speech rate and increase speech intelligibility in patients with severe dysarthria due to traumatic brain injury (Pilon et al. 1998). Similar results have been found for increasing intelligibility in patients with Parkinson's disease, where patients who exhibited severe speech impairments had the greatest benefit from rhythmic speech cueing (Thaut et al. 2001). Improvements in intelligibility in persons with dysarthria due to traumatic brain injury or stroke have also been documented when patients undergo individualized music therapy treatment including rhythmic cueing, oral motor exercises, vocal intonation therapy, and therapeutic singing (Tamplin 2008). The increase in success with severity of impairment may be due to a multitude of issues in the speech system including auditory speech feedback; however, more research is needed in this area to better understand the impact of rhythm on speech processes. Another rapidly growing area of research is in cognitive rehabilitation.

A growing body of evidence has shown links between cognitive functions and music, demonstrating that the temporal organization of music can be utilized to improve cognitive functions (Thaut 2005). Some studies have indicated that engagement in music during a cognitive task facilitates synchronized firing of neurons, resulting in faster and more efficient learning. Improved neurological timing has been demonstrated with electroencephalogram (EEG) measures of brain-wave activity, where musical stimuli evoked more synchronized firings in alpha and gamma bandwidths (Thaut et al. 2005; Peterson and Thaut 2007). Results of EEG studies have also shown bilateral low-alpha band increases in frontal networks in persons with multiple sclerosis, along with increased learning and memory (Thaut et al. 2005). Furthermore, patients who listen to music in the early stage of recovery following a middle cerebrovascular accident have been shown to improve their verbal memory and focused attention skills (Särkämö et al. 2008), indicating that the presence of musical stimuli can facilitate changes in cognitive functions.

As discussed previously, music involves networks that are not specific to music but are also activated in non-musical tasks. Studies have indicated that music activates shared networks when engaged in a cognitive task and that cortical areas not typically involved in the task are also activated with music. For example, memory function in word list learning with music activates more bilateral frontal cortical areas, whereas spoken words activate only the left hemisphere (Thaut et al. 2005). These activations also utilize networks invoked in a non-musical task, which may help with cognitive re-learning in persons with disease or disability, resulting in a more efficient rehabilitation programme.

Clinical outcome research in music therapy and cognition is relatively new in the field of music therapy; however, preliminary research results show promising effects of music on cognitive rehabilitation. A NMT intervention has been shown to increase executive function skills in persons with traumatic brain injury (Thaut et al. 2009a). Furthermore, the study results indicated that there were improvements in mood, emotional adjustment, and decreased anxiety (Thaut et al. 2009a). Preliminary results indicate that music can be an extremely effective tool for rehabilitation; however, there is a clear need for continued clinical research. Nevertheless, the current research base has led to the formation of specific approaches in music therapy. In the next section we will focus on NMT, one new approach that evolved from the neuroscience of music perception and production.

Neurologic music therapy

The neurobiological and clinical evidence we have presented demonstrates a reciprocal relationship between brain function and musical stimuli. This reaches beyond the scope of traditional music therapy in the social science model, to the neuroscience model, where music is utilized to change brain functioning, resulting in measurable functional outcomes. The vast amount of evidence from rehabilitation science has demonstrated that rhythmic stimuli can help to recover function in persons who have decreased functioning due to stroke, traumatic brain injury, spinal cord injury, Parkinson's disease, and multiple sclerosis. The growing body of evidence has not only improved our understanding of the role of music in the treatment of disease and disorders, but has also propelled a paradigm shift in music therapy from the social sciences to the neurosciences. This logically led to the formation of NMT.

NMT is defined as the therapeutic application of music to cognitive, sensory, and motor dysfunctions due to neurological disease of the human nervous system. This treatment approach is based on neuroscience models of music perception and the influence of music on non-musical behaviour. Clinicians and researchers in NMT use a neuroscience model of music perception and production in order to determine the best course of treatment. This model, called the Rational-Scientific Mediating Model (R-SMM), is utilized to systematically examine the influence of music on changes in non-musical function. The R-SMM guides the development of evidence-based therapeutic interventions that address non-musical needs.

Guided by research, the NMT practitioner is the creator of the therapeutic music interventions (TMI) that are aesthetically pleasing, logical, and are based on client needs. The process of creating TMIs is guided by a five-step model called the Transformational Design Model (TDM). The TDM helps the music therapist determine the best course of treatment based on client diagnosis and client needs. This system helps the therapists to maintain treatment focus while maintaining evidence-based practice. Guided by the TDM, the Neurologic Music Therapist can apply one of several standardized treatment techniques in areas of cognitive rehabilitation, sensorimotor rehabilitation, and speech and language rehabilitation.

The Neurologic Music Therapist maintains a high level of education; not only trained as a music therapist at an accredited university, but also trained in areas specific to rehabilitation including neuroanatomy and physiology, brain pathologies, and medical terminology. Furthermore, the NMT practitioner receives specific training in the implementation of NMT techniques in the sensorimotor, cognitive, and speech and language domains. Periodic peer evaluation is required in NMT in order to promote a further understanding of the use of standardized techniques and to allow the practitioner to receive feedback about further developing his/her skills.

In conclusion, music neuroscience research has brought forth new and fascinating information about how music affects the brain, and how best this complex medium can be used to facilitate rehabilitative changes. Although further research in areas of speech production, cognitive function, and the use of NMT with specific populations is required, the foundation of NMT research has shown that immediate and lasting improvements can be made when music is used in rehabilitation therapy. This is only the beginning for NMT, as this evidence-based model will continue to evolve with future advances in neuroscience.

References

Altenmüller, E., Marco-Pallares, J., Münte, T.F., and Schneider, S. (2009). Neural reorganization underlies improvement in stroke-induced motor dysfunction by music-supported therapy. *Annals of the New York Academy of Sciences*, **1169**, 395–405.

Arias, P. and Cudeiro, J. (2008). Effects of rhythmic sensory stimulation (auditory, visual) on gait in Parkinson's disease patients. *Experimental Brain Research*, **186**(4), 589–601.

Bangert, M., Peschel, T., Schlaug, G., *et al.* (2006). Shared networks for auditory and motor processing in professional pianists: evidence from fMRI conjunction. *NeuroImage*, **30**, 917–26.

Belin, P., Van Eeckhout, P., Zilbovicius, M. *et al.* (1996). Recovery from nonfluent aphasia after Melodic Intonation Therapy. *Neurology*, **47**, 1504–11.

Bengtsson, S.L., Ullén, F., Ehrsson, H.H., *et al.* (2009). Listening to rhythms activates motor and premotor cortices. *Cortex*, **45**(1), 62–71.

Berylne, D.E. (1971). *Aesthetics and Psychobiology*. New York: Appleton, Century & Croft.

Bermudez, P. and Zatorre, R.J. (2005). Differences in gray matter between musicians and nonmusicians. *Annals of the New York Academy of Sciences*, **1060**, 395–9.

Conway, C.M., Pisoni, D.B., and Kronenberger, W.G. (2009). The importance of sound for cognitive sequencing abilities: The auditory scaffolding hypothesis. *Current Directions in Psychological Science*, **18**, 275–9.

De l'Etoile, S.K. (2008). The effect of rhythmic auditory stimulation on the gait parameters of patients with incomplete spinal cord injury: An exploratory pilot study. *International Journal of Rehabilitation Research*, **31**(2), 155.

Gaser, C. and Schlaug, G. (2003). Gray matter differences between musicians and nonmusicians. *Annals of the New York Academy of Sciences*, **999**, 514–17.

Gaston, E.T. (1968). *Music in Therapy*. New York: McMillan.

Grahn, J.A. (2009). The role of the basal ganglia in beat perception: neuroimaging and neuropsychological investigations. *Annals of the New York Academy of Sciences*, **1169**, 35–45.

Haueisen, J. and Knösche, T.R. (2001). Involuntary motoractivity in pianists evoked by music perception. *Journal of Cognitive Neuroscience*, **13**, 786–92.

Hausdorff, J.M., Lowenthal, J., Herman, T., Gruendlinger, L., Peretz, C., and Giladi, N. (2007). Rhythmic auditory stimulation modulates gait variability in Parkinson's disease. *European Journal of Neuroscience*, **26**(8), 2369–75.

Hayden, R., Clair, A.A., Johnson, G., and Otto, D. (2009). The effect of rhythmic auditory stimulation (RAS) on physical therapy outcomes for patients in gait training following stroke: A feasibility study. *International Journal of Neuroscience*, **119**(12), 2183–95.

Howe, T.E., Lovgreen, B., Cody, F.W., Ashton, V.J., and Oldham, J.A. (2003). Auditory cues can modify the gait of persons with early-stage Parkinson's disease: A method for enhancing Parkinsonian walking performance? *Clinical Rehabilitation*, **17**(4), 363–7.

Hurt, C.P., Rice, R.R., McIntosh, G.C., and Thaut, M.H. (1998). Rhythmic auditory stimulation in gait training for patients with traumatic brain injury. *Journal of Music Therapy*, **35**(4), 228–41.

Hyde, K.L., Lerch, J., Norton, A., *et al.* (2009). Musical training shapes structural brain development. *Journal of Neuroscience*, **29**(10), 3019–25.

Imfeld, A., Oechslin, M.S., Meyer, M., Loenneker, T., and Jancke, L. (2009). White matter plasticity in the corticospinal tract of musicians: A diffusion tensor imaging study, *NeuroImage*, **46**(3), 600–7.

Kenyon, G. P. and Thaut, M. H. (2000). A measure of kinematic limb instability modulation by rhythmic auditory stimulation. *Journal of Biomechanics*, **33**, 1319–23.

Koelsch S. (2005). Investigating emotion with music: Neuroscientific approaches. *Annals of the New York Academy of Sciences*, **1060**, 412–18.

Lahav, A., Saltzman, E., and Schlaug, G. (2007). Action representation of sound: Audiomotor recognition network while listening to newly acquired actions. *Journal of Neuroscience*, **27**, 308–14.

Malcolm, M.P., Lavine, A., Kenyon, G., Massie, C., and Thaut, M. (2008). Repetitive transcranial magnetic stimulation interrupts phase synchronization during rhythmic motor entrainment. *Neuroscience Letters*, **435**(3), 240–5.

Malcolm, M.P., Massie, C., and Thaut, M. (2009). Rhythmic auditory-motor entrainment improves hemiparetic arm kinematics during reaching movements: A pilot study. *Topics in Stroke Rehabilitation*, **16**(1), 69–79.

McIntosh, G.C, Brown, S.H., Rice, R.R., and Thaut, M.H. (1997). Rhythmic auditory-motor facilitation of gait patterns in patients with Parkinson's disease. *Journal of Neurology, Neurosurgery and Psychiatry*, **62**, 22–6.

Miller, R.A., Thaut, M.H., McIntosh, G.C., and Rice, R.R. (1996). Components of EMG symmetry and variability in Parkinsonian and healthy elderly gait. *Electroencephalography and Clinical Neurophysiology*, **101**, 1–7.

Mitra, S., Riley, M.A., and Turvey, M. (1997). Chaos in human rhythmic movement. *Journal of Motor Behavior*, **29**, 195–8.

Özdemir, E., Norton, A., and Schlaug, G. (2006). Shared and distinct neural correlates of singing and speaking. *NeuroImage*, **33**, 628–35.

Pascual-Leone, A. (2001). The brain that plays music and is changed by it. *Annals of the New York Academy of Sciences*, **930**, 315–29

Patel, A., Iversen, J., Bregman, M., and Schulz, I. (2009). Experimental evidence for synchronization to a musical beat in a nonhuman animal. *Current Biology*, **19**, 827–30.

Peretz, I. and Zatorre, R.J. (2005). Brain organization for music processing. *Annual Review Psychology*, **56**, 89–114.

Peterson, D.A. and Thaut, M.H. (2007). Music increases frontal EEG coherence during verbal learning. *Neuroscience Letters*, **412**(3), 217–21.

Pilon, M.A., McIntosh, K.W., and Thaut, M.H. (1998). Auditory versus visual speech timing cues as external rate control to enhance verbal intelligibility in mixed spastic-ataxic dysarthric speakers: A pilot study. *Brain Injury*, **12**, 793–803.

Prassas, S.G., Thaut, M.H., McIntosh, G.C., and Rice, R.R. (1997). Effect of auditory rhythmic cuing on gait kinematic parameters in stroke patients. *Gait and Posture*, **6**, 218–23.

Rochester, L., Burn, D.J., Woods, G., Godwin, J., and Nieuwboer, A. (2009). Does auditory rhythmical cueing improve gait in people with Parkinson's disease and cognitive impairment? A feasibility study. *Movement Disorders*, **24**(6), 839–45.

Roerdink, M., Lamoth, C.J.C, Kwakkel, G., van Wieringen, P.C.W., and Beek, P.J. (2007). Gait coordination after stroke: Benefits of acoustically paced treadmill walking. *Physical Therapy*, **87**, 1009–22.

Roerdink, M., Lamoth, C.J.C, van Kordelaar, J., *et al.* (2009). Rhythm perturbations in acoustically paced treadmill walking after stroke. *Neurorehabilitation and Neural Repair*, **23**, 668–78.

Särkämö, T., Tervaniemi, M., Laitinen, S., *et al.* (2008). Music listening enhances cognitive recovery and mood after middle cerebral artery stroke. *Brain*, **131**(3), 866–76.

Schneider, S., Schönle, P.W., Altenmüller, E., and Münte, T.F. (2007). Using musical instruments to improve motor skill recovery following a stroke. *Journal of Neurology*, **254**(10), 1339–46.

Schlaug, G., Forgeard, M., Zhu, L., Norton, A., Norton, A., and Winner, E. (2009a). Training-induced neuroplasticity in young children. *Annals of the New York Academy of Sciences*, **1169**, 205–8.

Schlaug, G., Marchina, S., and Norton, A. (2009b). Evidence for plasticity in white-matter tracts of patients with chronic Broca's aphasia undergoing intense intonation-based speech therapy. *Annals of the New York Academy of Sciences*, **1169**, 385–94.

Stephan, K.M., Thaut, M.H., Wunderlich, G., *et al.* (2002). Conscious and subconscious sensorimotor synchronization: Prefrontal cortex and the influence of awareness. *Neuroimage*, **15**(2), 345–52.

Tamplin, J. (2008). A pilot study into the effect of vocal exercises and singing on dysarthric speech. *NeuroRehabilitation*, **23**(3), 207–16.

Thaut, M.H. (2003). Neural basis of rhythmic timing networks in the human brain. *Proceedings of the New York Academy of Sciences*, **999**, 364–73.

Thaut, M.H. (2005). *Rhythm, music, and the brain*. London, England: Taylor & Francis.

Thaut, M.H., McIntosh, G.C., Rice, R.R., Miller, R.A., Rathbun, J., and Brault, J.M. (1996). Rhythmic auditory stimulation in gait training for Parkinson's disease patients. *Movement Disorders*, **11**(2), 193–200.

Thaut, M.H., McIntosh, G.C., and Rice, R.R. (1997). Rhythmic facilitation of gait training in hemiparetic stroke rehabilitation. *Journal of the Neurological Sciences*, **151**, 207–12.

Thaut, M.H., Miller, R.A., and Schauer, L.M. (1998). Multiple synchronization strategies in rhythmic sensorimotor tasks: Phase versus period adaptation. *Biological Cybernetics*, **79**, 241–50.

Thaut, M.H., Miltner, R., Lange, H.W., Hurt, C.P., and Hoemberg, V. (1999). Velocity modulation and rhythmic synchronization of gait in Huntington's disease. *Movement Disorders*, **14**(5), 808–19.

Thaut, M.H., McIntosh, K.H., McIntosh, G.C., and Hoemberg, V. (2001). Auditory rhythmicity enhances movement and speech motor control in patients with Parkinson's disease. *Functional Neurology*, **16**, 163–72.

Thaut, M.H., Kenyon, G.P., Hurt, C.P., McIntosh, G.C., and Hoemberg, V. (2002). Kinematic optimization of spatiotemporal patterns in paretic arm training with stroke patients. *Neuropsychologia*, **40**(7), 1073–81.

Thaut, M.H., Peterson, D.A., and McIntosh G.C. (2005). Temporal entrainment of cognitive functions: Musical mnemonics induce brain plasticity and oscillatory synchrony in neural networks underlying memory. *Annals of the New York Academy of Sciences*, **1060**, 243–54.

Thaut, M.H., Leins, A.K. Rice, R.R., *et al.* (2007). Rhythmic auditory stimulation improves gait more than NDT/Bobath training in near-ambulatory patients early poststroke: A single-blind, randomized trial. *Neurorehabilitation and Neural Repair*, **21**(5), 455–9.

Thaut, M.H., Demartin, M., and Sanes, J. (2008). Brain networks for integrative rhythmic formation. *PloS One*, **3**(5), e2312.

Thaut, M.H., Gardiner, J.C., Holmberg, D., *et al.* (2009a). Neurologic music therapy improves executive function and emotional adjustment in traumatic brain injury rehabilitation. *Annals of the New York Academy of Sciences*, **1169**, 406–16.

Thaut, M.H., Stephan, K.M., Wunderlich, G., *et al.* (2009b). Distinct cortico-cerebellar activations in rhythmic auditory motor synchronization. *Cortex*, **45**(1), 44–53.

Chapter 13

The Religion of Evidence-Based Practice: Helpful or Harmful to Health and Wellbeing?

Tony Wigram and Christian Gold

Introduction

Preparing a chapter on evidence-based practice (EBP) to underpin the use of music as a therapeutic tool in treatment, in the overall frame of music, health, and wellbeing, presents several challenges. Over the last 20 years, we have seen the growth of EBP into what now at times seems almost a 'religious doctrine', and it has had both helpful and harmful effects on practice in all fields.

The first challenge is the dichotomy of science and scientific fact versus subjective experience and individual preference. Wellbeing, as a concept, lends itself very strongly to an important but frequently unacknowledged aspect of EBP, that of 'patient report'—in other words the effect of a phenomenon or intervention on an individual that enhances or improves his or her own sense of wellbeing that may be unique to that individual and does not rely on scientific veracity for the effect to be accepted.

The second challenge is more to do with the potential extent of such a chapter, and the wide variety of resources that could be documented in a vast range of human conditions relevant to the concepts of health and wellbeing. The fields of music therapy, music in medicine, and music psychology offer an extensive literature where music is shown to be singularly important to the human condition. First, to discuss the concept of evidence, and also the concept of practice will help establish the scope of the potential of music in human life. Perhaps more importantly, the evidence (as will be explained further on) has many styles, qualities, and different degrees of quantification. To present that, it will be useful to select one specific population as an example, and look at how music affects wellbeing and health from the point of view of differing types of evidence. So the challenge of looking at how people experience music for meeting individual needs and personal life situations can be explored by looking through the experiences of individuals, and of the people who work with them and give them musical experiences, and the research that has been amassed to argue the 'effectiveness' of music and why society should value this medium, among others to the extent of music as a provision.

The third and last challenge, perhaps the most important, is to consider the real relevance of EBP in application to a medium such as music when discussing in this text its capacity for providing source of nourishment, emotional comfort, inspiration, and stimulation both physically and mentally. In respect of this, 'evidence' as a 'basis' (foundation) for the multiple applications and usages of music in many forms of 'practice' becomes a term that provokes significant argument. This is no more apparent when considering what medical science regards as a 'gold standard' for evidence, systematic reviews (SRs), meta-analyses and randomized controlled trials (RCTs).

We do not require such rigor in order to gain benefit and comfort from music in everyday life any more than we do for other art forms, sporting activity, or cultural stimulation such as travel, entertainment, or religion. Seeking an 'evidence base' for the 'effectiveness' of religious faith for our souls and bodies is certainly relevant for non-believers, but not for those whose faith is built on belief. This also is relevant when it comes to our personal and collective experience of music as a medium that meets our needs for wellbeing and health. Some people will have a greater propensity to believe in the value of music for health and wellbeing than others. Some will be convinced through an individual, personal experience, whereas others may be more sceptical and require more systematic research evidence. Still others may never believe, regardless of how extensive and convincing the evidence may be.

The terminology of evidence-based practice and evidence-based medicine

In the literature, there is reference to evidence-based practice (EBP) and evidence-based medicine (EBM). As is probably clear from the difference in terms, EBM is more focused and concerned with practitioners of medicine. Its history can be traced back as far as the nineteenth century. More recently the Cochrane Collaboration and the Oxford Centre for Review and Dissemination are two of the leading international organizations for developing EBM. In the USA, a complementary process has been developed by the Agency for Healthcare Research and Quality (AHRQ, formerly AHCPR) who publish clinical guidelines and have established evidence-based practice centres (EPCs) to direct the EBM movement (Else et al. 2007). When considering the many definitions of EBM, one of the most frequently quoted definitions is by Sackett (1996). He stated that EBM is the 'conscientious, explicit, and judicious use of current best evidence in making decisions about care of individual patients'.

EBP is a way of thinking more familiar to music therapists. It is relevant to healthcare in general and can actually be applied widely—to education, social service provision, in fact anywhere where some form of intervention or programme is assessed for its efficacy or effectiveness for a population for which it is supposedly beneficial. As in EBM, the term 'evidence' refers to a synthesis of research findings on specific questions where there may exist multiple and alternative treatment approaches. The two terms EBM and EBP are in fact often used interchangeably, although the latter term carries the wider connotation of including other than medical interventions and purposes (Else and Wheeler 2010). However it is important in our view to take a step back, and consider what really does constitute good, and more importantly, relevant evidence.

Research evidence in applied clinical practice

The assumption in the minds of the general public might be that all clinicians, educators, deliverers of programmes would conscientiously apply the rigorous criteria expected for good practice by both maintaining knowledge of the most recent and relevant research, as well as sustaining skills in applying the methods and techniques reported to have the highest degree of efficacy. To take the field of medicine with its well known adage 'trust me, I'm a doctor', in the USA the late Dr John Eisenberg, former head of Agency for Healthcare Research and Quality, observed that there is 'sufficient evidence to suggest that most clinicians' practices do not reflect the principles of evidence-based medicine but rather are based upon tradition, their most recent experience, what they learned years ago in medical school or what they have heard from their friends' (Eisenberg 2001). One has to assume that not only doctors, but also some practitioners in professions supplementary to medicine, teachers, social services, and many other professions may also be practicing without necessarily incorporating latest research into their work. This is definitely not true of all practitioners. Many read their peer-reviewed journals, listen to their patients and students, as well as building a practice on their own knowledge and experience—all components are important. But we cannot really know to what extent music therapists assess and evaluate the quality and applicability of emerging findings and translate that evidence into practice. Taking the doctoral research at the Graduate School of Music Therapy in Aalborg University as an example, accessibility has become much less of a practical issue than it used to be, with most PhD theses being freely available online.[1] But it is still vital for research findings to demonstrate clinical applicability, and that is an aspect that needs ongoing engagement. When extensive and detailed studies are undertaken over 3–6 years of hard work, it is important to ensure that these findings are taken up by practitioners. We will come back to the issue of the clinical applicability of research findings later. The first step is more concerned with what can be included as evidence, and what is good evidence. There is no doubt that funding bodies and employing authorities (such as purchasers and providers in the UK) increasingly require more robust evidence-based practice protocols as required to support the implementation of therapy or other services for a particular population. Sadly, there have been cuts in some music therapy services due to lack of demonstrated evidence. So perhaps the next step is to consider what is accepted as good enough evidence.

Evidence-based practice: hierarchies for good quality evidence

To start with the most rigorous and demanding criteria we can look at the Oxford Centre for Evidence-based Medicine. Table 13.1 is the current hierarchy for therapeutic interventions and related questions. For prognosis, diagnosis, differential diagnosis, and economic and decision analyses, different hierarchies would apply (the full table can be found on the centre's website[2]). Most practitioners would be mainly concerned with therapy and prognosis. Having worked in a diagnostic assessment unit, the first author of this chapter was more interested in the evidence base for diagnosis and differential diagnosis. But to focus on the therapy column, the gold standard is systematic reviews with homogeneity, leading down in a hierarchy to case series and expert opinion. Qualitative research studies are not considered in this list. The majority of evidence here refers to experimental research in controlled studies.

Some explanations of these categories may be needed. We will develop the hierarchy from the bottom. Where no empirical knowledge exists but a decision is needed, expert opinion (level 5) may be the only source to rely on. Of course the question arises: Which expert should be consulted? It is interesting that all 'bench' research (on the level of cells rather than humans) also falls into this low category, even though this type of research is often seen as the most 'scientific' by the general public. On level 4 (case series) we find a type of research that is common in music therapy. Case series come with many different names, such as 'pre–post study', and have in common that they measure some outcome before and after an intervention but without a control group receiving another or no intervention. Therefore these studies cannot separate between 'normal' development and the effect of an intervention. They are useful only under the rather strong assumption that there would be no change in the absence of treatment. In pharmacological research these studies are commonly used in the early phases of developing a drug. Analogously, their place in music therapy research is best justified when developing a new music therapy approach or applying a known approach to a new clinical area.

The next levels (2–3) contain a number of diverse research designs that have in common that they attempt to compare the outcomes of a treatment group to the outcomes in a group that

---

[1] http://www.mt-doctoralprogramme.aau.dk
[2] http://www.cebm.net

Table 13.1 Oxford Centre for Evidence-based Medicine levels of evidence (March 2009)

Level	Therapy/prevention, aetiology/harm
1a	SR (with homogeneity) of RCTs
1b	Individual RCT (with narrow confidence interval)
1c	All or none
2a	SR (with homogeneity) of cohort studies
2b	Individual cohort study (including low quality RCT; e.g. <80% follow-up)
2c	'Outcomes' research; ecological studies
3a	SR (with homogeneity) of case–control studies
3b	Individual case–control study
4	Case series (and poor quality cohort and case–control studies)
5	Expert opinion without explicit critical appraisal, or based on physiology, bench research or 'first principles'

RCT, randomized controlled trial; SR, systematic review.

Grades:

A = consistent level 1 studies.

B = consistent level 2 or 3 studies or extrapolations from level 1 studies.

C = level 4 studies or extrapolations from level 2 or 3 studies.

D = level 5 evidence or troublingly inconsistent or inconclusive studies of any level.

Produced by Bob Phillips, Chris Ball, Dave Sackett, Doug Badenoch, Sharon Straus, Brian Haynes, Martin Dawes since November 1998. Updated by Jeremy Howick, March 2009. Extracted from http://www.cebm.net (last accessed 12 January 2011).

received no treatment or an alternative treatment, but without using randomization. Groups may for example be matched on some variables (such as age, sex, severity of illness, and so on), typically by a process of selecting similar people based on known characteristics. These designs are more advanced than uncontrolled case series in that they allow a comparison with an alternative treatment or no treatment. However, imbalances between the groups at baseline are difficult to avoid or control for statistically, and this may mean that any such conclusions have to be preliminary. Randomization, the process of assigning participants to treatments in an unpredictable way, is the only procedure that can prevent such imbalances and provide a 'fair' comparison between alternatives. But does it always work? Yes, in principle; no, in practice. Table 13.1 mentions some difficulties that can occur even in RCTs: losses to follow-up (2b) may destroy the balance created by randomization. Confidence intervals (1b), in other words the degree of statistical uncertainty, are only narrow if sample sizes are really large—certainly larger than what is common in music therapy research today. Homogeneity (1a), in other words a high degree of similarity in the results of different RCTs, for example in different countries or clinical settings, can be assessed in a systematic review of RCTs but is rarely if ever achieved. In summary, the hierarchy is logically coherent but sets an ideal standard that will be hard if not impossible to achieve.

This model of defining and categorizing the evidence is regarded as gold standard, and can grade the intervention into an A, B, C, or D level depending on the quality of the scientific reports. Music therapy may sit uncomfortably at level C with a potential to be downgraded to level D in some clinical fields. Music as a resource for healthy living and cultural value that can elevate and maintain wellbeing in the human condition could not claim much more than level D status under this hierarchy.

Other hierarchies have been suggested that are more inclusive and may be seen as more appropriate for music therapy and other allied health professions (see Else and Wheeler 2010, for a critical review). One important distinction to make is between clinical effectiveness and efficacy. Clinical effectiveness is concerned with establishing whether the treatment in question affects outcome in the real world, as compared with efficacy, which intends to show that treatment affects outcomes through a well-controlled, frequently laboratory-style experiment. Efficacy requires high internal validity, but is not aimed at generalizability, while effectiveness requires high external validity but often at the expense of careful controls. Music therapy research is frequently clinically applied research, and is concerned with effectiveness and generalizability, often seeking to find out the extent to which the desired outcome is achieved when an intervention, which is ideally known to be efficacious, is applied to a population. There has always been a strong strand of music therapy research, evident in many articles published in specialized journals such as the *Journal of Music Therapy*, more recently also the *Nordic Journal of Music Therapy*, which documents research supported by inferential statistical analyses evaluating the generalizability of a particular music therapy intervention with a population. Perhaps depending on the clinical area in mind, some alternative hierarchies may also include non-systematic reviews and qualitative studies explicitly (Else and Wheeler 2010). Music therapy research can offer evidence under many of these categories.

Research, clinicians, and people—the balance of evidence

EBP tends to imply that interventions or programmes should be funded and run by guidelines based on research, which usually means RCTs to demonstrate efficacy. This should rightly be a strong part of the evidence accumulated to support interventions. However, is experimental research evidence the only form of evidence that can be accepted? For the purpose of trialling new drugs, this is the most effective and reliable way to test efficacy. In the therapy professions, and in education, the arts, wellbeing in the life of human beings, requiring the highest level of proof of efficacy may deny clients/patients the benefit of potentially valuable and/or cost-effective treatments. The impact of strict-EBM and EBP protocols may have a tendency to undermine healthcare and pull practitioners away from humanistic roots.

The answer to what constitutes evidence varies depending on who one asks. The 'hardline' attitude will only permit RCTs and systematic reviews to be considered. Yet in our modern-day life, there is increasingly a questioning attitude to what the 'experts' or authority figures say. As in religion, there is a greater belief in the knowledge and resources of the individual, and a desire for their opinions and experiences of a healing process to be considered alongside the scientific data. So the definition that best fits EBP, and takes into account scientific research alongside the opinions of patients and healthcare professionals is that it should be informed by an approach to healthcare that promotes the collection, interpretation, and integration of valid, important, and applicable patient-reported, clinician-observed, and research-derived evidence. Evaluation of research literature makes use of defined criteria to assess the level of evidence contained in any particular study; the other components of EBP include practitioner experience and opinion as well as patient/client preferences. It is clear that patient preference is important and influences outcomes. It is important to stress however that complete reliance on any one of these elements may introduce bias, and can result in ineffective and/or unsatisfactory interventions.

The impact on music therapy

Music therapy, to use an old-fashioned term, is a very broad church. In fact, if we add in music psychology, music medicine, and music used remedially in education, we extend that field to an even broader church. Within these diverse fields of theory research and practice, we can find a range of perspectives and philosophies from experimental and behavioural science to music for relaxation and recreation. In reviewing the developments over the last 15 years, the acceptance and understanding of music and music therapy as a vital new force in health and education has changed (Wigram 2002). We are constantly reminded that money to fund interventions and programmes is not unlimited and there is a strong need to prioritize. Music therapists have traditionally worked in some of the less glamorous areas of both the health and social systems in chronic long-term psychiatry, end of life, elderly care, and severe learning disability, and the education system in schools and centres for children with moderate and severe learning disability, and there is already a number of studies and reports supporting its value as a therapeutic intervention that should be considered as relevant evidence (Oldfield and Adams 1990; Schalwijk 1994; Aldridge et al. 1995; Hairston 1990; Wigram et al. 1995, 2002; Hadsell and Coleman 1998; Wigram and De Backer 1999; Gold et al. 2004, 2006, 2007; Oldfield et al. 2003; Elefant and Wigram 2005; Wigram and Lawrence 2005; Jacobsen and Wigram 2007; Hooper et al. 2008a,b; Carr and Wigram 2009). Since the beginning of 2000, there has also been an upsurge of Arts in Health entering hospital and school environments offering arts media delivered by musicians, artists, and actors not trained as therapists, but enhancing the lives of people with arts experiences. Where a therapist was offering a therapeutic intervention, during the development phase of music therapy (and other arts therapies) from 1950–1990, there was enthusiasm for the potential of arts therapies, without a strong demand for rigorous research evidence. In fact, case examples and observed results satisfied most funding and employing authorities that these were valuable and helpful therapeutic interventions, without any harmful side effects. It was also evident during this development phase that arts therapists, and particularly music therapy, had something to offer the more severe cases not considered a priority with other therapeutic interventions such as psychotherapy and speech and language therapy. Music therapists also work in many other fields now, expanding successfully into neurodegenerative disorders, oncology, forensic psychiatry, physical disability, acute care and many other fields. However, the response of the profession as a whole to the challenges of EBP and how that can impact on methods of work, outcomes and particularly on employment and scientific credibility has largely been apathetic, with many almost in a reactive state of denial, rather than a proactive state of belief in the value of music and music therapy. It is clear that the following attitudes were typical:

- Nobody was ready for the events of the last 15 years—when the EBP agenda has become a force of change.
- Nobody working in the field, confident in the relevance and usefulness of music therapy expected the level of challenge that EBP gave us.
- Nobody anticipated that the foundations and research production of our profession internationally, a vast body of knowledge documented in journals, books, and clinical reports would be called into question for quality, rigour, and prioritization for funding as it is now.
- Most music therapists are, after all, employed to treat patients, write reports, and attend meetings closely connected to their clinical caseload, they are certainly not paid to be researchers.

The following section takes the case of autism spectrum disorders (ASD) as an example to illustrate the various effects—whether helpful or harmful—that EBP may have on the practice of music therapy.

Autism spectrum disorders and evidence-based practice

Autism is a disorder that has attracted an increasing amount of attention over the last 20 years in the music therapy literature. The range of studies and clinical reports provide some experimental and a large amount of case study evidence to support the effectiveness and relevance of music therapy to improve communication (Mahlberg 1973; Saperston 1973; Watson 1979; Christie and Wimpory 1986; Edgerton 1994; Ma et al. 2001; Oldfield 2001; Wigram and Elefant 2008), joint attention and social interaction (Pasiali 2004; Kim 2006; Kim et al. 2008, 2009), in diagnostic and general assessment (Wigram 1999, 2000, 2007; Oldfield 2004; Walworth 2007;), to affect emotional response (Heaton et al. 1999), to influence play (Kern and Aldridge 2006), to influence behaviour (Staum and Flowers 1984; Kostka 1993), to impact on comorbid diagnosis (Fuggle et al. 1995), and more widely as a clinical intervention of value for children, adolescents, and adults (Clarkson 1991; Evers 1992; Toigo 1992; Brown 1994, 1999; Wimpory et al. 1995Robarts 1998; Di Franco 1999; Trevarthen 2002; Whipple 2004; Feigh 2006). Alvin (Alvin and Warwick 1992) was reporting the value of music therapy for children with autism more than 40 years ago. Nevertheless, there is controversy and critique as to how music therapy can help children with autism, and the research base to support funding (Accordino et al. 2007). The first author of this chapter sat down to argue this issue with a Deputy Director of Public Health in region in Southern England some 20 years ago. The discussion centred on whether music therapy had enough 'evidence' for the local region in question to consider funding. It rapidly emerged that evidence in this context was only considered to include controlled studies, as is often the case when discussing this issue with a person from a medical background, and case studies or qualitative research had no place in the thinking, let alone expert opinion. The Deputy Director had searched the literature, and attended the meeting with a substantial pile of books and articles. She had clearly done her homework, and was fairly dismissive of the literature she had found as predominately anecdotal and without adequate rigour, validity, and reliability. In many ways she was right, and it was not until 12 years later that systematic reviews and meta-analyses where being undertaken (Wigram 2002; Ball 2004; Whipple 2004; Gold et al. 2006; Wigram and Gold 2006). However the real crux of the argument centred on whether music and music therapy met healthcare needs, as drawn in diagnostic manuals which define presenting pathology.

Communication was put forward as an example of an area of development that music therapy showed consistently good results with ASD, particularly where verbal language was severely disordered or delayed. Communication, in the opinion of the Deputy Director was not a healthcare need. Yet in contradiction to this, she had previously stated that available funds should be used for better researched therapies such as speech and language therapy, which is an intervention primarily aimed at addressing communication disorder, which is also, incidentally, considered in DSM-IV and ICD-10 to be a core impairment of ASD—both in terms of social communication and social interaction. This example is intended to address another issue that relates EBP to intervention. In the cases of illness and disability originating from pathology or psychopathology, good therapeutic practice relies on evidence that demonstrates the intervention will meet needs that are linked to diagnosis and clinical, social or educational needs. People working in the field of music therapy, music and medicine and music for health are not always clear about that connection, thus failing to provide adequate arguments to support funding.

However, there can also be a resistance on the part of funding authorities to want to consider that the use of music in many different ways could influence health and therefore be funded. An example was reported in the field of early intervention in autism by the American Music Therapy Association:

In 1999, the NY State Department of Health, Early Intervention Program published clinical practice guidelines (CPG) on the subject of assessment and intervention for children with autism/PDD aged 0-3 years. . . The autism/PDD guideline technical report includes a disclaimer that the report does not necessarily reflect the policy of the U.S. Department of Education or federal education policy. However, the effect of the recommendations extends beyond the state of New York.

In particular, the recommendation concerning music therapy is that music therapy is 'not a recommended intervention method for young children with autism'. The recommendation was classified as [D1] panel opinion where the information found in the literature did not meet criteria for evidence. The conclusion of the panel is that there lacked a demonstrated efficacy by way of a controlled study. The levels of evidence established by the guideline development panel are as follows:

A: Strong evidence
B: Moderate evidence
C: Limited evidence
D1:   Panel opinion – information did not meet criteria for evidence
D2:   Panel opinion – Literature not systematically reviewed

The conclusion of the panel followed a search of the literature using MEDLINE, PsychINFO, and ERIC from 1980 to present (~1996–1997). Across all topics under review the percentage of articles that met inclusion criteria of the total number of articles screened was 8.6%. The panel identified five articles on music therapy and none passed evidence criteria. Studies had to be controlled trials with random group assignment. Single-subject studies had to report on at least three subjects and use an acceptable research design (i.e. reversal)... Neither AMTA nor any known music therapist was consulted as part of the advisory group (Else et al. 2007).

It should be noted that the grading system used here is again slightly different from those presented above.

Research studies, clinical reports, and opinion for evidence in the field of ASD

As stated above, the gold standards for research evidence are systematic reviews where a review of controlled studies undertaken of an intervention for a particular population is evaluated. There are three relevant systematic reviews of research studies for ASD that offer substantive research evidence or the use of music therapy with individuals with autism (Ball 2004; Whipple 2004; Gold et al. 2006), but they also demonstrate some problems that need to be addressed (Wigram and Gold 2006). The first two were conducted on a wide range of included studies, while the third, a Review for the Cochrane Library, applied more rigorous parameters. The first two reviews showed conflicting results. For example, there was little overlap between the reference lists of the two reviews, and only one study (Brownell 2002) was included in both. The third study was conducted to overcome the shortcomings of these previous reviews. The first review (Whipple 2004) included experimental studies of any design which examined the effects of music (interventions ranged from music therapy to background music) versus no music on outcomes such as challenging behaviour and social interaction. Ten studies were included. Participants were individuals with autism ranging from 2.5–21 years. Sample sizes ranged from 1–20. Results showed a large, significant, and homogeneous overall effect size (d = 0.77), suggesting that conditions involving music were more effective than conditions without music. However, the interventions used in the included studies were so heterogeneous that it is difficult to draw specific conclusions on the effects of music therapy from this review. Furthermore, important design features of the primary studies used, such as randomization and blinding, were not made transparent (Wigram and Gold 2006, p. 539). The second systematic review (Ball 2004) addressed the effects of music therapy versus no treatment on outcomes such as behaviour, communication, and social interaction in children with ASD. RCTs, controlled clinical trials (CCTs), and case series with at least 10 participants were included. Three studies were identified that met these criteria. Their results were summarized in a narrative way without meta-analytic pooling. Although all included studies had found significant effects, the authors concluded that the effects of music therapy were unclear. This shows that systematic reviews are not the end of personal opinion, even though they are often praised as the most objective means to review the effectiveness of an intervention. While it is true that the systematic review method excludes some forms of personal bias, especially in the process of selecting and combining studies (once criteria have been defined), it by no means excludes all. The very definition of the in- and exclusion criteria to be used has a strong influence on the results of a systematic review. Else and Wheeler (2010) have demonstrated this very clearly for two fields of application of music therapy. Likewise, once the results of a review are complete, their interpretation is still subject to personal opinions and agendas and other non-objective influences. Music therapists need to be aware of that when evaluating systematic reviews.

The third, Cochrane review focused on RCTs and CCTs comparing music therapy with standard care, placebo or no treatment. Relevant studies were identified from the two previous reviews and through searching a number of relevant databases using a highly sensitive search strategy (full details in Gold and Wigram 2003). In addition, relevant music therapy journals were searched by hand, and reference lists of identified studies were checked for any further studies. The identified studies were then inspected independently by both authors, and data on design type, population, music therapy, additional treatment, outcome assessment, and results were extracted. From 311 identified records, 50 were identified as potentially relevant. Of these, three were excluded because they concerned other populations (related disorders or relatives of children with ASD). Six studies used other interventions than music therapy (background music, auditory integration training, or melodic intonation therapy). Thirteen further studies were excluded because they concerned an assessment rather than an intervention. Seven unpublished studies could not be obtained to date. Among the remaining studies which addressed music therapy as a treatment for children with ASD, there were eight case studies, 11 case series, and three RCTs with small sample size (Buday 1995; Brownell 2002; Farmer 2003).

Buday (1995) explored the use of music as a therapeutic intervention in promoting better memory of manual signs in 10 children with autism ranging in age from 4.4–9.0 years. The cognitive abilities of the participants also ranged from within the normal range to severe intellectual disability. The design of this study involved learning words and signs in two conditions: music and words; rhythm and words. Each participant received ten trials in each condition in a reversal design (AB/BA repeated measures) where the participants were randomly assigned in equal numbers to the two orders of these conditions. Trials were carried out over 4 days (20 trials a day). The dependent measures were the number of signs correctly imitated during each trial, and the number of words correctly imitated during each trial. Scoring was undertaken by an independent evaluator blind to the nature of the investigation, and interobserver reliability of scoring was established at 98%.

Farmer (2003) examined the effect of music versus no music paired with gestures on spontaneous verbal and nonverbal communication skills of children with autism between the ages 1–5. The sample included 10 children who met the inclusion criteria from the Atlanta region of the USA who were living at home and attending day units and schools. The sessions took place in the participants' homes or day units, where they received five music therapy sessions. These sessions followed a procedural structure, with greeting songs followed by structured movement and simple game activities that involved music in the experimental condition and no music in the control condition. The dependent measures included verbal responses and gestural responses. Figures 13.1 and 13.2 illustrate the significant effect found of music therapy on gestural communicative skills ($p = 0.0006$) and verbal communicative skills ($p = 0.0009$)

The study by Brownell (2002) investigated the effect of a musical presentation of social story information on the behaviour of four male children with autism aged between 6–9 years.

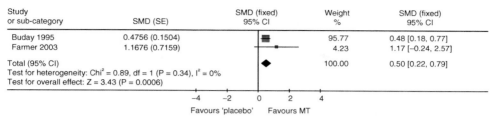

Review: Music therapy for autistic spectrum disorder
Comparison: 01 Music therapy vs. 'placebo' therapy
Outcome: 01 Communicative skills: gestural

Study or sub-category	SMD (SE)	SMD (fixed) 95% CI	Weight %	SMD (fixed) 95% CI
Buday 1995	0.4756 (0.1504)		95.77	0.48 [0.18, 0.77]
Farmer 2003	1.1676 (0.7159)		4.23	1.17 [−0.24, 2.57]
Total (95% CI)			100.00	0.50 [0.22, 0.79]

Test for heterogeneity: Chi² = 0.89, df = 1 (P = 0.34), I² = 0%
Test for overall effect: Z = 3.43 (P = 0.0006)

    −4   −2   0   2   4
Favours 'placebo'   Favours MT

Fig. 13.1 The effect of music therapy on gestural communicative skills. Note: this figure is reproduced from Gold, C., Wigram, T., and Elefant, C. (2006). Music therapy for autistic spectrum disorder. *Cochrane Database of Systematic Reviews*, **2**, CD004381. Cochrane Reviews are regularly updated as new evidence emerges and in response to feedback, so the *Cochrane Database of Systematic Reviews* should be consulted for the most recent version of the Review.

The procedure of this study involved the use of a specially composed story with each participant, with or without original composed music. Participants were randomly assigned to an ABAC/ACAB counterbalanced multiple-treatment conditions. Participants undertook five sessions in each condition over 5 days. Outcome measurement was made on identified target behaviours relevant to each individual child's social and academic development. Data was collected during a baseline phase, and was different for two participants while the other two shared a common target:

Reduction in TV talking behaviour.

Listening to and following directions in class.

Using a quieter voice in class (two participants). Interobserver reliability data was collected for two fifths of the total data.

For the purpose of arguing relevant and valid evidence, the findings from these studies are clearly important in demonstrating the potential of the medium of music therapy for autistic children. However, if the evidence for clinical practice is to depend only on these research findings, the generalizability of these studies is limited. The treatment in all studies was highly structured

Review: Music therapy for autistic spectrum disorder
Comparison: 01 Music therapy vs. 'placebo' therapy
Outcome: 02 Communicative skills: verbal

Study or sub-category	SMD (SE)	SMD (fixed) 95% CI	Weight %	SMD (fixed) 95% CI
Buday 1995	0.3471 (0.1097)		97.42	0.35 [0.13, 0.56]
Farmer 2003	0.8066 (0.6736)		2.58	0.81 [−0.51, 2.13]
Total (95% CI)			100.00	0.36 [0.15, 0.57]

Test for heterogeneity: Chi² = 0.45, df = 1 (P = 0.50), I² = 0%
Test for overall effect: Z = 3.32 (P = 0.0009)

    −4   −2   0   2   4
Favours 'placebo'   Favours MT

Fig. 13.2 The effect of music therapy on verbal communicative skills. Note: this figure is reproduced from Gold, C., Wigram, T., and Elefant, C. (2006). Music therapy for autistic spectrum disorder. *Cochrane Database of Systematic Reviews*, **2**, CD004381. Cochrane Reviews are regularly updated as new evidence emerges and in response to feedback, so the *Cochrane Database of Systematic Reviews* should be consulted for the most recent version of the Review.

and specifically targeted towards one behaviour, and only receptive music therapy techniques were used. The conclusion from this review can only go so far as to state that music therapy may have positive effects on the communication behaviour of children with ASD. In the following we will review a more recent RCT that attempted to improve the clinical applicability of the research in this area, as well as anecdotal reports from a variety of sources suggesting the influence of music therapy on social and communicative interaction in people with ASD.

Since the publication of this Cochrane Review, a randomized clinically controlled study with a small sample but important results was published (Kim 2006; Kim et al. 2008, 2009). This study used a repeated measures, within subjects comparison, in which 10 children aged from 3–6 recruited for the therapy sessions had 12 individual free play sessions with toys as a control condition to compare with twelve individual improvisational music therapy sessions. Each session began with 15 minutes of child led music or play activity, followed by 15 minutes of therapist-led activity. To evaluate joint attention and social behaviour, target behaviours that were clear indicators of joint attention (and social behaviour) included frequency and duration of eye contact, events of joy, turn-taking, emotional synchronicity, musical synchronicity, and frequency of initiation of engagement by the child and by the therapist, and events where the child imitated the therapist. These behaviours were measured by detailed video analysis from sessions 1, 4, 8, and 12. Interobserver reliability was measured by intraclass correlation coefficients, and on all target behaviours except imitation (0.69), correlations were between 0.86–0.98.

The results from both standardized and non-standardized measurements were generally in favour of music therapy over free play, and indicated improvements in joint attention behaviours of children over time. Kim found that the process of music therapy facilitated the simultaneous coordination of 'listening', 'looking at the therapist', and 'responding' and 'engaging', and the results suggested that improvisational music therapy facilitated social learning of children with ASD. Increased motivation was an important outcome, noticeable in the musical interaction whereby improvisational music therapy produced 'joy' and 'emotional synchronicity' events that were more frequent and of a longer duration than free play, which clearly influenced the degree of spontaneous 'initiation of engagement ' behaviours in children (Kim 2006).

The joint attention and social interaction scores in Figure 13.3 show combined scores of initiation of social interaction and responsiveness to social interaction bid behaviours over time. In

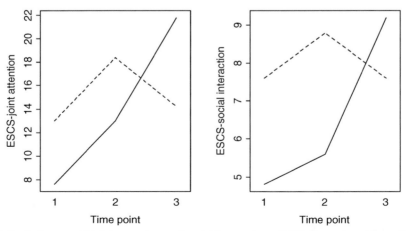

Fig. 13.3 Pooled scores of joint attention and social interaction—ESCS. Reproduced from Kim, J. (2006). Joint attention in improvisational music therapy with autistic children. PhD thesis. Denmark, Aalborg University.

both graphs, group 1 (dotted line) who had music therapy first and free play second, improved after music therapy, and then got worse after free play. Group 2 (solid line) who had free play therapy first and music therapy second, improved slightly after free play, and to a larger degree after music therapy. However, the improvement was more pronounced in joint attention behaviours than social interaction behaviours. The graph suggests that there was improvement over time in both groups and the improvement appears to be greater after music therapy than after free play.

The results of video analysis of both eye contact and turn-taking behaviour in the sample were also significant. In Figures 13.4 and 13.5 the boxplots show more spontaneous eye contact frequency and duration respectively in the music therapy condition than the free play condition where the median value of eye contact was zero in both analyses. Significant effects (p <0.0001) were found for both frequency and duration when comparing the music therapy condition with free play

Figure 13.6 illustrates the results of an analysis of turn-taking frequency with a boxplot, which found a significant difference between the music therapy and the free play condition (p <0.0001). Interobserver reliability was measured at 0.94.

Figure 13.7 indicated that music therapy was more effective at facilitating a longer turn-taking duration than the free play condition. In contrast with other variables measured such as initiation of engagement, joy, or emotional synchronicity, there were longer durations of turn-taking activity in the second (therapist led) half of the sessions in both music therapy and the free play condition than in the first (child led) half. This is perhaps understandable as the protocol for this study required the therapists to initiate turn-taking.

Case material evidence

As long ago as 1969, Stevens and Clark (1969) reported a study on the effect of music therapy in promoting social behaviour. Five male participants aged 5–7, diagnosed autistic were included, and three independent evaluators rated behaviour in the 1st, 10th, and 18th sessions of music therapy. Observer reliability was established, and a Friedman two-way Anova found significant

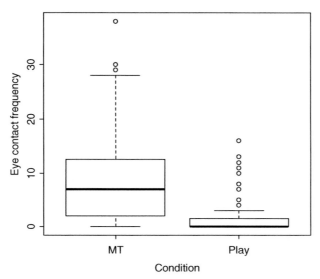

Fig. 13.4 Eye contact frequency comparing music therapy with free play. Reproduced from Kim, J. (2006). Joint attention in improvisational music therapy with autistic children. PhD thesis. Denmark, Aalborg University.

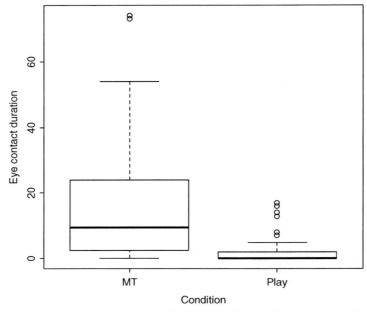

Fig. 13.5 Eye contact duration comparing music therapy with free play. Reproduced from Kim, J. (2006). Joint attention in improvisational music therapy with autistic children. PhD thesis. Denmark, Aalborg University.

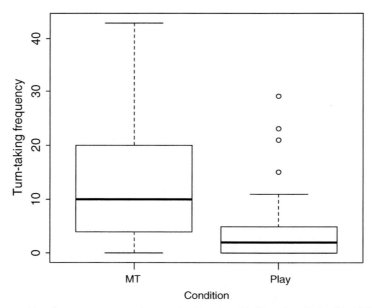

Fig. 13.6 Turn-taking frequency comparing music therapy with free play. Reproduced from Kim, J. (2006). Joint attention in improvisational music therapy with autistic children. PhD thesis. Denmark, Aalborg University.

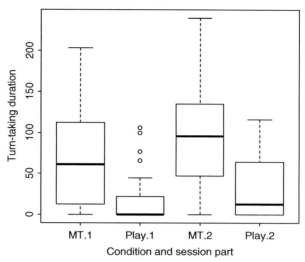

Fig. 13.7 Turn-taking duration comparing music therapy with free play. Reproduced from Kim, J. (2006). Joint attention in improvisational music therapy with autistic children. PhD thesis. Denmark, Aalborg University.

improvement in scores over 18 sessions (p <0.039). Instrumental, singing activities, and action songs were used in therapy, and four of the participants demonstrated improvement in their social behaviour as a result of weekly music therapy over 18 sessions, measured by the Autism Scale (Ruttenberg et al. 1966). Three were able to progress to regular kindergarten. Five years previously, Goldstein (1964) wrote up a single case study of an autistic child with violent tantrums, isolated behaviour, self-directed aggression, and emotional and mental retardation, including intolerance to sound. Results over time showed increased tolerance and attention, progress in interpersonal relationships, reduction of rigidity and aggressive, and a tested increase in developed intelligence over the 6 months of therapy that was measured as a 10-month improvement in mental age (Stanford-Binet Intelligence Scale). Kostka (1993) reported a within subject case study comparing the presence of autistic and non-autistic behaviours in two different conditions—normal music group and a social educational lesson. Results showed a significant decrease in autistic flapping and rocking, with increase in appropriate participation during the music session. Edgerton (1994) researched the effect of individual improvisational music therapy on 11 autistic children aged 6–9 years. They received 10 individual music therapy sessions. A reversal design was used, and results strongly suggest the efficacy of improvisational music therapy in increasing autistic children's communicative behaviour. A very large effect size was found on a measure of communicative acts when comparing the first and last sessions of therapy (d = 4.56, 95% confidence interval: 3.11 to 6.01, p <0.01; calculated in Gold et al. 2004) Substantial decreases in scores were found in reversal.

A survey by Evers (1992) was undertaken related to the theoretical research on the use of Music Therapy in the treatment of autism. In a postal survey, data from Paediatricians and paediatric institutions showed that music therapy is already accepted as a treatment. Results from 191 child psychiatrists and 127 paediatric institutions revealed that music therapy is recommended as a treatment by 14.5% of paediatricians and 56% of psychiatrists. It is used in 11.1% of general paediatric clinics and 28.6% of child psychiatry institutions.

Expert opinion from a person diagnosed with ASD

Toigo (1992) reported the views of a well published author and person diagnosed with ASD. Dr Temple Grandin is supportive of music therapy and recommends it in her writings. In this paper, her views about the experience of autism, the causes of autism and treatment of autism are summarized. Grandin's recommendations that music therapy can help by the following methods are discussed: rhythmic activities with musical instruments; the pleasure of music for children; the development of communication skills; the development of potential of musical giftedness in autistic people. Relating to clinical practice and using current research, the author defines the importance of music therapy for integrating auditory, proprioceptive, tactile, and vestibular stimulation; learning to control and predict the timing of sounds; calming the hyper-responsive central nervous system; acceptance and understanding for people who are at the lower end of the spectrum; toleration of sound, reduction of hypersensitivity and hyperacousis; combining language melody and rhythm to develop communication skills.

Lest we forget the third valuable source of evidence, the clients themselves have a voice in reporting what they find helpful. Hibben (1999) edited an extensive text with 33 contributions from clients or proxies. A majority of people with ASD are unable to speak up themselves. However, parents are the watchful guardians and dedicated suppliers of their needs, and frequently see more of what may be beneficial than clinicians, researchers, or funding authorities. Jones and Oldfield (1999) provide an insightful perspective to the music therapy intervention provided by Oldfield to Jones' young son John, a 3-year-old boy with ASD. From an early age, Jones described the value music had as a calming influence for her frequently upset and crying son. She reported her intense emotional reaction to the first time her son calls her 'Muma' on the way home from a music therapy session (Jones and Oldfield 1999, pp. 168–169). The process of therapy described by both authors involves understanding John's need for 'time off', which gradually recedes as he gains trust in the situation and delighted excitement in musical games. Allgood (2005) reported the parents' perceptions of group music therapy, where again, as in the Jones and Oldfield study, they relied on the main carer speaking on behalf of the child. Two mothers found out that their own approaches needed to be adapted to include more structure. One of the mothers said 'My drawbacks are that I want to say 'that's not working, let's change it'. . . but I found out that I probably need more structure than (my daughter) does'. Another mother said 'I have a tendency to do something a couple of times and if (my son) doesn't come around then I try something else. . . if I just give him a chance to keep going at it, which is what his therapists do all of the time, he'll probably get it' (Allgood, 2005, pp. 97–98). This author draws attention to the effectiveness of a therapy approach by asking the parents how they see things working.

While we rely on research and the clinician's expertise, the reaction of people to therapeutic interventions should not be lost in the quest for the scientific answer. Whatever labels we attach to define any type of problem, and whatever scientific evidence there is for the effect of therapies on those populations, people are individuals, and are differentially responsive to treatment.

Conclusion

If we look back on the last 60 years of the development of music therapy as a recognized and relevant intervention, there is no doubt that the honeymoon period is over, and EBPis here to stay. While we know of some examples where there is attrition in music therapy practice as health, education and social services tighten their belts and the demand on their resources grows, there is an increasing interest in the value of music for health and wellbeing, despite even less 'hard' evidence that it is effective against illness and disability. Many years ago, a doctor once told the first author that he saw music (and music therapy) as a tool to prevent illness, and that by the time people had become ill, Western medicine in the form of surgery and pharmacological interventions takes over. However for a disorder such as autism, there is no surgery and few pharmacological treatments that can help, other than manage symptoms. However, in looking at what can help people with autism, the highest 'success' rate for any intervention is only about 50%. No single therapy helps everyone, no single therapy helps everything, and it is hard to know who will benefit from what. What the research does show us is that early intervention, intense intervention, structure, and predictability, increasing 'attention' to others, and building up motivation are most likely to be successful. Although there is not enough research looking at the value of music therapy if it is applied as an 'intense intervention' music therapy ticks the boxes on all of these other criteria.

The evidence for music therapy as an intervention for autism was considered in a recent evaluation by autism researchers at the University of London for the website of ResearchAutism, and was rated as an intervention with strong positive evidence of effectiveness.[3] In the submitted evidence, no studies in music therapy as an intervention for autism reported negative results. It is an intervention with apparently no harmful side effects, what cannot be said of some pharmacological interventions, such as risperidone. EBP can be a force for good and ensure the delivery of up-to-date, effective interventions. This should be supported not only by rigorous research, but by clinical knowledge, wisdom, and personal experience.

Contributions of authors

Tony Wigram wrote the original draft. Christian Gold helped to critically revise it in response to reviewer comments. Both authors have approved the final version.

References

Accordino, R., Comera, R., and Hellera, W.B. (2007). Searching for music's potential: A critical examination of research on music therapy with individuals with autism. *Research in Autism Spectrum Disorders*, **1**(1), 101–15.

Agency for Healthcare Research and Quality (AHRQ). http://www.ahrq.gov/clinic/epcix.htm

Allgood, N. (2005). Parents'perceptions of family-based group music therapy for children with Autism Spectrum Disorders. *Music Therapy Perspectives*, **2**, 92–9.

Aldridge, D., Gustorff, D., and Neugebauer, L. (1995). A preliminary study of creative music therapy in the treatment of children with developmental delay. *The Arts in Psychotherapy*, **21**(3), 189–205.

Alvin, J. and Warwick, A. (1992). *Music therapy for the autistic child* (2nd edn.). Oxford: Oxford University Press.

Brown, S.M. (1994). Autism and music therapy–is change possible, and why music? *Journal of British Music Therapy*, **8**, 15–25.

Brown, S. (1999). The music, the meaning, and the therapist's dilemma. In: T. Wigram and J. De Backer (eds.) *Clinical Applications of Music Therapy in Developmental Disability, Pediatrics and Neurology*, pp. 183–200. London: Jessica Kingsley Publishers.

Brownell, M.D. (2002). Musically adapted social stories to modify behaviors in students with autism: four case studies. *Journal of Music Therapy*, **39**(2), 117–44.

---

[3] http://www.researchautism.net (last updated 7 October, 2010, accessed 12 January, 2011).

Buday, E.M. (1995). The effects of signed and spoken words taught with music on sign and speech imitation by children with autism. *Journal of Music Therapy*, **32**(3), 189–202.

Carr, C. and Wigram, T. (2009). Music therapy with children and adolescents in mainstream schools: A systematic review. *British Journal of Music Therapy*, **23**(1), 3–18.

Christie, P. and Wimpory, D. (1986). Recent research into the development of communicative competence and its implications for the teaching of autistic children. *Communication. 20*(1), 4–7.

Clarkson, G. (1991). Music therapy for a non-verbal autistic adult. In: K. Bruscia (ed.) *Case Studies in Music Therapy*, pp. 374–82. Gilsum, NH: Barcelona Publishers.

Di Franco, G. (1999). Music and autism. Vocal improvisation as containment of stereotypes. In: T. Wigram., and J. De Backer (eds.) *Music Therapy Applications in Developmental Disability, Pediatrics and Neurology*, pp. 99–113. London: Jessica Kingsley Publishers.

Edgerton, C.L. (1994). The effect of improvisational music therapy on the communicative behaviors of autistic children. *Journal of Music Therapy*, **31**(1), 31–62.

Eisenberg, J.M. (2001). What does evidence mean? Can the law and medicine be reconciled? *Journal of Health Politics, Policy and Law*, **26**(2), 369–82.

Elefant, C. and Wigram, T. (2005). Learning ability in children with Rett syndrome. *Brain and Development* 27, S97–S101.

Else, B. and Wheeler, B. (2010). Music therapy practice: relative perspectives in evidence-based reviews. *Nordic Journal of Music Therapy*, **19**(1), 29–50.

Else, B.A., Simpson, J., and Farbman, A. (2007). AMTA research priority: executive summary. Personal Communication.

Evers, S. (1992). Music Therapy in the treatment of autistic children: Medico-Sociological data from the Federal Republic of Germany. *Acta Paedipsychiatrica International*, **55**(3), 157–8.

Feigh, M. (2006). Music to our ears: the positive effects of music therapy on adults with autism. *Autism Advocate*, **42**(2), 48–50.

Fuggle, K., Fixter, A., and Brown, S.W. (1995). Music therapy in the treatment of a child with epilepsy and autism. *Epilepsia*, **36**(3).

Gold, C., Voracek, M., and Wigram, T. (2004). Effects of music therapy for children and adolescents with psychopathology: A meta-analysis. *Journal of Child Psychology and Psychiatry and Allied Disciplines*, **45**, 1054–63

Gold, C., Wigram, T., and Elefant, C. (2006). *Music therapy for autistic spectrum disorder (Cochrane Review), The Cochrane Library, 2, 2006*. Chichester: John Wiley & Sons, Ltd.

Gold, C., Wigram, T., and Voracek, M. (2007). Effectiveness of music therapy for children and adolescents with psychopathology: A quasi-experimental design. *Psychotherapy Research* **17**(3): 292–300

Goldstein, C. (1964). Music and creative arts therapy for an autistic child. *Journal of Music Therapy*, **1**(4), 135–8.

Heaton, P., Hermelin, B., and Pring, L. (1999). Can children with autistic spectrum disorders perceive affect in music? An experimental investigation. *Psychological Medicine*, **29**(6), 1405–10.

Hadsell, N.A. and Coleman, K.A. (1998). Rett syndrome: A challenge for music therapists. *Music Therapy Perspectives*, **5**(2), 52–6.

Hairston, M.P. (1990). Analyses of responses of mentally retarded autistic and mentally retarded nonautistic children to art therapy and music therapy. *Journal of Music Therapy*, **27**(3), 137–50.

Hibben, J. (1999). *Inside Music Therapy: Client Experiences*. Gilsum, NH: Barcelona Publishers.

Hooper, J., Wigram, T., Carson, D., and Lindsay, B. (2008a). A review of the music and Intellectual disability literature (1943–2006) Part one – descriptive and philosophical writing. *Music Therapy Perspectives*, **26**(2), 66–79.

Hooper, J., Wigram, T., Carson, D., and Lindsay, B. (2008b). A review of the music and intellectual disability literature (1943–2006) Part two – descriptive and philosophical writing. *Music Therapy Perspectives*, **26**(2), 80–96.

Jacobsen, S. and Wigram, T. (2007). Music therapy for the assessment of parental competencies for children in need of care. *Nordic Journal of Music Therapy*, **16**(2), 129–43.

Jones, A. and Oldfield, A. (1999). Sharing sessions with John. In: J. Hibben (ed.) *Inside Music Therapy: Client Experiences*, pp. 165–71. Gilsum, NH: Barcelona Publishers.

Kern, P. and Aldridge, D. (2006). Using embedded music therapy interventions to support outdoor play of young children with autism in an inclusive community-based child care program. *Journal of Music Therapy*, **43**(4), 270–94.

Kim, J. (2006). Joint attention in improvisational music therapy with autistic children. PhD thesis. Denmark, Aalborg University.

Kim, J., Wigram, T., and Gold, C. (2008). The effects of improvisational music therapy on joint attention behaviors in autistic children: A randomized controlled study. *Journal of Autism and Developmental Disorder*, **38**(9), 1758–66.

Kim, J., Wigram, T., and Gold, C. (2009). Emotional, motivational and interpersonal responsiveness of children with autism in improvisational music therapy. *Autism: The International Journal of Research and Practice*, **13**(4), 389–409.

Kostka, M.J. (1993). A comparison of selected behaviours of a student with autism in special education and regular music classes. *Music Therapy Perspectives*, **11**(2), 57–60.

Ma, Y.C., Nagler, J., Lee, M.H., and Cabrera, I.N. (2001). Impact of music therapy on the communication skills of toddlers with pervasive developmental disorder. *Annals of the New York Academy of Sciences*, **930**, 445–7.

Mahlberg, M. (1973). Music therapy in the treatment of an autistic child. *Journal of Music Therapy*, **10**(4), 189–93.

Oldfield, A. (2001). Music therapy with young children with autism and their parents: Developing communications through playful musical interactions specific to each child. In: D. Aldridge, G. Di Franco, E. Ruud, and T. Wigram (eds.) *Music Therapy in Europe*, pp. 47–62. Ismez: Rome.

Oldfield, A. (2004). A comparison of Music Therapy Diagnostic Assessment (MTDA) and the Autistic Diagnostic Observation Schedules (ADOS). Unpublished PhD Dissertation. Cambridge: Anglia Polytechnic University.

Oldfield, A. and Adams, M. (1990). The effects of music therapy on a group of profoundly handicapped adults. *Journal of Mental Deficiency Research*, **34**, 107–25.

Oldfield, A., Bunce, L., and Adams, M. (2003). An investigation into short-term music therapy with mothers and young children. *British Journal of Music Therapy*, **17**, 26–45.

Pasiali, V. (2004). The use of prescriptive songs in a home-based environment to promote social skills acquisition by children with autism: Three case studies. *Music Therapy Perspectives*, **22**(1), 11–20.

Robarts, J. (1998). Music therapy for children with autism. In: C. Trevarthen, K. Aitkin, D. Papoudi, and J. Robarts (eds.) *Children with autism: Diagnosis and interventions to meet their needs*, pp. 172–202. London: Jessica Kingsley Publishers.

Ruttenberg, B.A., Dratman, M.L., Fraknoi, J., and Wenar, C. (1966). An instrument for evaluating autistic children. *Journal of the American Academy of Child Psychiatry*, **5**(3), 453–78.

Sackett, D.L., Rosenberg, W.M., Gray, J.A., Haynes, R.B., and Richardson, W.S. (1996). Evidence based medicine: what it is and what it isn't. *British Medical Journal*, **312**, 71–2.

Saperston, B. (1973). The use of music in establishing communication with an autistic mentally retarded child. *Journal of Music Therapy*, **10**(4), 184–8.

Schalwijk, F.W. (1994). *Music and people with developmental disabilities: music therapy, remedial music making and musical activities*. London: Jessica Kingsley Publishers.

Staum, M.J. and Flowers, P.J. (1984). The use of simulated training and music lessons in teaching appropriate shopping skills to an autistic child. *Music Therapy Perspectives*, **1**(3), 14–17.

Stevens, E. and Clark, F. (1969). Music therapy in the treatment of autistic children. *Journal of Music Therapy*, **6**(4), 98–104.

Toigo, D. (1992). Autism: Integrating a personal perspective with music therapy practice. *Music Therapy Perspectives*, **10**, 13–20.

Trevarthen, C. (2002). Autism, sympathy of motives and music therapy. *Enfance*, **1**, 86–99.

Walworth, D.D. (2007). The use of music therapy within the SCERTS model for children with autism spectrum disorder. *Journal of Music Therapy*, **44**(1), 2–22.

Watson, D. (1979). Music as reinforcement in increasing spontaneous speech among autistic children. *Missouri Journal of Research in Music Education*, **4**(3), 8–20.

Whipple, J. (2004). Music in intervention for children and adolescents with autism: A meta-analysis. *Journal of Music Therapy* **41**(2), 90–106.

Wigram, T. (1999). Assessment methods in music therapy: a humanistic or natural science framework? *Nordic Journal of Music Therapy*, **8**(1), 7–25.

Wigram, T. (2000). A method of music therapy assessment for the diagnosis of autistic and communication disordered children. *Music Therapy Perspectives*, **18**, 13–22.

Wigram T. (2002). Indications in music therapy: Evidence from assessment that can identify the expectations of music therapy as a treatment for autistic spectrum disorder (ASD). Meeting the challenge of evidence based practice. *British Journal of Music Therapy*, **16**(1), 5–28.

Wigram, T. (2007). Music therapy assessement. psychological assessment without words. *Psyche & Logos*, **28**(1), 333–57.

Wigram, T. and de Backer, J. (1999). *Clinical Applications of Music Therapy in Developmental Disability, Paediatrics and Neurology*. London: Jessica Kingsley Publishers: London.

Wigram, T. and Lawrence, M.(2005). Music therapy as a tool for assessing hand use and communicativeness in children with Rett syndrome. *Brain and Development* **27**, S95–6.

Wigram, T. and Gold, C. (2006). Research evidence and clinical applicability of music therapy for autism spectrum disorder. *Child Care: Health and development* **32**(5), 535–42.

Wigram, T. and Elefant, C (2008). Therapeutic dialogues in music: Nurturing musicality of communication in children with autistic spectrum disorder and Rett syndrome. In Malloch, S. and Trevarthen, C. (eds.) *Communicative Musicality*. Oxford: Oxford University Press.

Wigram, T., Saperston, B., and West, R. (1995). *The Art and Science of Music Therapy: A Handbook*. London: Harwood Academic Publications.

Wigram, T., Nygaard Pedersen, I., and Bonde, L.O. (2002). *A comprehensive guide to music therapY. Theory, clinical practice, research and training*. London: Jessica Kingsley Publications.

Wimpory, D., Chadwick, P., and Nash, S. (1995). Brief report: Musical interaction therapy for children with autism: An evaluative case study with two-year follow-up. *Journal of Autism and Developmental Disorders*, **25**(5), 541–52.

Chapter 14

Health Musicking: A Perspective on Music and Health as Action and Performance

Brynjulf Stige

A gamut of practices and perspectives

Interest in relationships between music, health, and wellbeing has been thriving in several fields of practice and study for a number of years. A review of the literature (Bonde 2008) reveals a range of interests and foci, from muscle management for musicians (Andrews 2005) to the effects of music listening as a nursing intervention (Biley 2000), or from noise as a health risk (Borchgrevink 2003) to the perceived benefits of singing in a university college choral society (Clift and Hancox 2001). Music, health, and wellbeing is certainly not a unified field. Educators, nurses, doctors, psychologists, music therapists, and musicians take interest in the relationships involved in ways that are much more diverse than what could be embraced by any one theory or approach.

Given the gamut of practices and contexts as well as the range of research paradigms that inform the literature, a lack of cohesion could only be expected and there is little reason to believe that any one general theory or paradigm could be established. This should not cause too much worry, since the diversity could be thought of as a resource representing supplementing perspectives on music, health, and wellbeing. It is perhaps more worrying that there has been limited dialogue and discussion between some of the academic disciplines that take interest in this area. For instance, Gregory Barz (2006) studied HIV/AIDS and music in Uganda and discussed medical ethnomusicology with no reference to music therapy as a field of study and practice. The example is not unique. Much more substantial interdisciplinary work seems to be required for a solid understanding of relationships between music and health (Stige 2008).

Currently there is a growing interdisciplinary awareness and interest and the present volume could be said to address this situation. In this chapter I will try to contribute with an integrative perspective developed within the discipline of music therapy. I argue that music therapy has a special responsibility in relation to the challenge of developing an interdisciplinary discourse, since it is an established discipline with bridging of the subjects music and health as its main focus, while health is only one of many topics of study for other disciplines of music (and music only one of many topics of study for the various disciplines of health). The present chapter could partly be read as a response, then, to a challenge put forward by anthropologist John Janzen (2000), who suggests that music therapy could define itself as a field of study where integrative perspectives on health-related music practices could be developed.

The discipline of music therapy could be defined as the study and learning of relationships between music and health (Stige 2002, p. 198). This definition suggests that music therapy research could be conceptualized broadly to comprise various health related music practices, including studies of music and health in people's everyday life. By defining the agenda of the discipline this broadly, music therapy will be able to contribute to an interdisciplinary discourse, which in the next round could be important for the development of new perspectives on professional music therapy practice also. For example, a better understanding of people's everyday use of music is essential for music therapy practices that focus upon contextual perspectives and the client's active contribution in the change processes.

To define the discipline of music therapy as the study and learning of relationships between music and health should not be read as a territorial claim. Other disciplines naturally also take interest in investigating such relationships. Territorial claims are perhaps more legitimate when focusing upon the level of professional practice. At this level it makes sense to define music therapy as a practice that requires the authorized professional competency of a trained music therapist (Bruscia 1998). This does not suggest, however, that music therapists have monopoly on working with music, health, and wellbeing. Many different music activities could be experienced as therapeutic and could promote health in various ways. There are some shared territories, then, and possibilities for developing shared frameworks across practices and disciplines should be explored.

The focus of this chapter is the notion of health musicking. It is a concept I originally developed in a discussion of music therapy theory, where I focused upon a contextual understanding of music and health (Stige 2002). In this perspective, musical artefacts and activities offer certain possibilities. The health effects are not given but created through use by the involved participants of a situation. The term use does not have a restricted functional sense here but is related to Wittgenstein's (1953/1967) discussion of meaning, where he argues that words do not have stable meanings that mirror reality; they achieve their meanings through use in particular contexts. In music sociology, Tia DeNora (2000, 2007) has developed a related perspective, when she argues that certain musical pieces or activities can afford certain things but that the effects depend upon people's appropriation of these possibilities in given settings. These perspectives draw our attention to music as human action and as performance of relationships, which could be communicated by use of the term musicking (Small 1998).

Through combining Wittgenstein's perspective on meaning, DeNora's discussion of affordance and appropriation, and Small's concept of music, I generated the notion of health musicking to communicate the idea that relationships between music and health could be understood as processes where various agents collaborate and negotiate in relation to the agendas, artefacts, and activities of any given arena (Stige 2002, p. 211). In articulating the notion of health musicking, I also took inspiration from Kenneth Burke's (1949/1969) narrative theory on human action.

What music could afford in relation to health and wellbeing, then, grows out of the relationships established in each case. In this chapter I will elaborate upon this idea and put it forward as a possible interdisciplinary framework for exploring relationships between music, health, and wellbeing.

Conceptualizing health in dramaturgical terms

Several authors on relationships between music and health have discussed health as performance, which implies a focus upon individual and collaborative action in context. Influential examples include the work of Even Ruud (1979, 1998), David Aldridge (1996, 2004), and Tia DeNora (2000, 2007). DeNora elaborates upon the idea of health as performance in the following way:

> ... health is performed in social settings and in relation to performance conventions and materials. For example, in some countries today, when we visit a health professional – for a medical check-up, let us say – we submit ourselves to a battery of tests (blood pressure, heart rate, cholesterol, and so on). We then receive an assessment (like a report card) of how 'healthy' we are in relation to established

measures. Our 'bad' cholesterol is low, our blood pressure 'perfect', our short-time memory is failing, we are experiencing 'mild depression'. When we repeatedly 'pass' or 'fail' the tests designed to ascertain these things, we are deemed, by medical practitioners, to be healthy or ill. Health, in other words, is indicated by the passing of some tests or trials that accord with cultural conceptions of what it means to be healthy. When we have received a good 'report card' time and time again, we accumulate an identity – we are 'healthy'

(DeNora 2007, p. 272).

There are several theoretical routes that lead to a focus upon health as performance. We could think of health as an exemplar illuminating the broader theme of how relationships between organism and environment develop. The culture-historical perspective pioneered by Vygotsky and other Russian scholars of the early twentieth century represents one such tradition which highlights how agents, activities, and artefacts constitute each other reciprocally over time. Artefacts are obviously produced through activity but equally we could explore how artefacts make activity possible. Similarly, who we are as persons depends upon what we do with which tools (Cole 1996; Cole et al. 1997; Engeström et al. 1999).

Links between music and health are therefore implied in investigations of music and identity (MacDonald et al. 2002) and music and communication (Miell et al. 2005). These links become pertinent in a new way in light of cultural developments of late modernity. Modernization typically leads to less reliance upon the norms and identities defined by traditional communities; one's identity is not a given but becomes a personal project. Currently, very many people seem to define health as an important part of this project. Health, then, is viewed not just as freedom from serious injury and disease but becomes a central element in the individual's search for meaning. A logical corollary is that the 'monopoly' of medical expertise is challenged. The sociologist David Chaney describes the process in this way:

> … it will not be surprising to reflect that a greater concern with health, and the deployment of increasingly elaborate technologies of health interventions, has been bracketed with a more pervasive discrediting of conventional medical expertise. It is as though the very search for meaning in a healthy life and privileging bodily concerns more generally cannot be contained in the scientism of orthodox medicine
>
> (Chaney 2002, p. 91).

As the notion of health is expanded from 'not being sick' to include personal and social wellbeing, it is obvious that the health sector is only a small (though important) factor defining our health. Our education and work situation, the social relationships we are part of, and the cultural activities we take part in are all seminal influences. We do not exactly choose these things freely, as our lives are subject to financial, social, and cultural constraints, but we can seek for possibilities of making a difference in our own lives. It is perhaps not surprising, then, that the discourse on music as treatment has been supplemented and challenged lately by a discourse on music as empowerment (Procter 2002; Rolvsjord 2004, 2010). The implication is hardly that conventional medical and psychological knowledge has been made irrelevant, but the dominance of the professional expert is challenged and there is a request for more relational, collaborative, and contextual approaches to health work.

Conceptualizing health in dramaturgical terms does not imply a one-sided focus upon human action with neglect of the organism's reactions to music. It does suggest, however, that action is a primary focus. Health is related to biology and music affects our bodies, but the effects and meanings depend upon discursive fields and situations of use. There is, for instance, evidence to suggest that the organism's reactions to music in clinical or quasi-clinical settings are linked to the individual's musical actions in everyday life (Mitchell et al. 2008).

Investigations of relationships between music and health could not be reduced to the study of the direct effect of musical parameters but must also include investigations of the use of musical and paramusical features of a situation. The term 'paramusical' is used here as an alternative to 'extramusical,' to avoid the misleading impression that things are either 'totally' musical or not musical (Stige et al. 2010, p. 298). We need to understand the relationships between those phenomena that we perceive as specifically musical and those actions and activities that go with these, and as Korsyn (2003) reminds us, what we consider musical is not given but continuously constructed musically and discursively. When we listen to music, for instance, we do not just hear sounds and silences. Sometimes we can hear the arena of the music, such as when we hear the acoustics of a church as an element of choral singing or a noisy audience as part of the sound of a live recording. Perhaps we can hear aspects of the agenda also, as when someone sings to praise or please, to challenge or tease.

I have outlined some theoretical contributions that could inform our understanding of health as performance. Burke considered literature as 'equipment for living' and he discussed social interaction and communication in terms of the 'dramatistic pentad' of act, scene, agent, agency, and purpose.

Musical and paramusical resources for health musicking

Health musicking could be defined as the appraisal and appropriation of the health affordances of the arena, agenda, agents, activities, and artefacts of a music practice (Stige 2002, p. 211). In the following section I will outline some possible characteristics of these components and I will try to show how each term could give us a template for reflecting upon similarities and differences between various music practices. In the description of each component I will include examples illuminating use of music in nursing homes, as the nursing home is a meeting place for a variety of music practices, such as the residents' own use of music, the nurses' 'care-singing,' music therapy practices, and concerts by volunteers and professional musicians. The concrete articulation of the examples at times refers to specifics of the Norwegian situation (Hauge et al. in prep.), but there are many similarities between countries concerning this context of music use.

Arena

Musicking is situated activity; it is always linked to a site and a situation. One implication is that there are several levels of analysis to take into consideration, such as body, person, dyad, group, organization, and locality. These are all sites of interaction, and there is interaction between them. An arena is also a field, as defined by Bourdieu (see, e.g. Fornäs 1995); it is a site of struggle between various interests and values. The resources of an arena can be manifold, as it represents the physical, social, and cultural foundation for the activities agents engage with. There is a reciprocal shaping involved, as with the other components to be described here: An arena allows certain agendas to be negotiated, affords certain activities, and so on, while the activities use and produce agendas and artefacts that contribute to a continuous (re)construction of the arena.

The nursing home illuminates this point. It is an institution with diverse objectives. It is a site for delivery of complex medical and health-related services but it is also a residence where people should be allowed to live personal lives, a point that in Norway has been stressed clearly in national guidelines on quality in services. At the same time, there is an institutional logic involved, produced by the history of the organization (Goffman 1961/1991). In the nursing home, then, music activities are situated in tensions between the logic of everyday life, a medical logic, and an institutional logic. While the guidelines highlight the residents' rights to a personal and private life, these rights are under pressure from the institutional logic and at times also from the medical logic. Any health worker using music as part of the health care of the institution needs to reflect upon how the activities relate to the residents' right to take part in decisions in their own lives. Any musician coming in to perform needs to take into consideration that the nursing home is not a concert arena, it is a home and a medical institution. Space for concert performance must be actively and respectfully created and maintained.

Agenda

The term agenda refers to evolving issues, goals, and themes as conceived consciously and unconsciously by the participants of a situation. Agendas can have intrapersonal elements and implications, but they are negotiated interpersonally and they relate to community and culture in various ways. In relation to health musicking, it is not only important to consider what an agenda can afford in itself, by focusing upon issues of value for the participants. The process of developing an agenda can also be valuable, by affording communication and collaboration, for instance.

Given the diverse logics that characterize the nursing home as an arena, music could be defined in relation to various agendas, with focus upon issues such as management, treatment, and entitlement. Music as management focuses upon music as an instrument in the running of the institution. Music as treatment focuses upon music as a tool in the development of better therapies. Music as entitlement focuses upon music as a human and cultural right. In each of these agendas, music could be empowering or disempowering for the residents. Evaluation of the legitimacy of various agendas requires explication and negotiation of values.

Agents

The term agents, as used here, refers to the human actors involved. Agents can form alliances and they can experience agency to a higher or lower degree. When alliances are formed, a dyad, group, or community can also be considered an agent in a change process.

In the nursing home, agents include the residents and their families, nurses, and music therapists and other professional health workers, musicians, and visiting volunteers. These agents have different qualifications for health musicking. The residents contribute with their musicality, musical preferences, and reminiscence. Nurses provide care and assessment of needs 24 hours a day, in contrast to music therapists who are usually much less available for the residents. When available, the music therapists could contribute with specialized skills in bridging musical and health-related needs. The visiting musicians could connect the life of the nursing home to the broader community and often contribute with music of high artistic quality.

Activities

The term activity is often used at two levels, partly referring to the interaction between organism and environment (as discussed theoretically earlier in this chapter) and partly referring to various forms of engagement with music (as in this section). Music practice involves various types of activities, such as listening, playing, creating, performing, interpreting, and reflecting (Stige 1995). The act of listening can also be considered a basic attitude common to all other music activities. To a somewhat lesser degree the same could be said about playing (understood as engagement involving joy and pleasure). The act of creating could be systematic and spontaneous, in various combinations, as when composing and improvising. The act of performing often takes an existing piece of music as point of departure and typically involves an audience. The act of interpretation, as used here, involves the translation of the sounds of music through use of another modality, such as movement, art, or poetry. The act of reflection puts the other activities in perspective, usually through verbal processing but also through use of other modalities. For instance, the combined use of movement, sound, and visual effects in a ritual can provide occasions for a community to view itself critically, as Victor Turner (1967) demonstrated. The affordances of each type of activity could not be described comprehensively but must be assessed in each specific situation.

Typical activities in the nursing home include the residents' listening to the radio, the nurses' singing in situations of care, the music therapists' initiation of improvisation and community singing, and the musicians' concerts and performances. These activities are perhaps initiated in relation to needs such as relaxation, reminiscence, stimulation, connectivity, and pleasure. Affordances must be understood in relation to situations of use. For instance, research has demonstrated that established structures of power could make seemingly positive or harmless activities, such as listening to the radio, problematic. In many nursing homes the radios or TVs represent noisy elements of the environment and there is little residence influence on the activity (Hauge 2004, 2008; Jacobsen 2005).

Artefacts

Musicking involves use of several types of artefacts, such as instruments, songs, and lyrics. According to the culture-historical theory tradition, a person's sense of self and agency is constituted through internalization and creative use of cultural artefacts in social contexts. Instruments can invite playing and participation, lyrics can invite reflection and recreation, and so on. How and what each artefact affords is again relative to person and situation.

In the nursing home it is often quite important to consider carefully how cultural artefacts are perceived as carriers of meaning and how use of them can involve serious identity issues. For instance, in nursing homes in Norway instruments associated with folk music—such as the accordion or the violin—could be highly controversial. Some residents find them especially stimulating. The sound of the instruments evokes warm memories of dancing and can make them forget their feeble feet. Others would for religious reasons consider the same instruments and their sounds and uses as inappropriate. Similarly, in activities such as community singing, there is always the question of cultural fit between the chosen music and the involved participants. Artefacts quickly become part of the negotiations on agenda and they help constitute the arena as well as the activities that the agents engage with.

Rituals for mobilization of resources

The five components discussed above—arena, agenda, agents, activities, and artefacts—all link in various ways and could form complex webs of relationships. It is important to note that all the components are ambivalent resources. Any arena, agenda, or activity, for instance, represents possibilities as well as constraints concerning participation. One example is provided by Twani (2007) in a book chapter on 'music behind bars,' where he argues that music can be used by participants as a 'technology of self' with empowering functions but that it also can be used by authorities as an instrument to control and discipline inmates.

We need to understand, then, how the resources described above are appropriated and put into circulation. The definition of health musicking as appraisal and appropriation of health affordances of arena, agenda, agents, activities, and artefacts could be perceived as (over)stressing the cognitive aspects of the process. When we music, whether through listening or playing, we usually do not sit down and think about what this or that could afford but engage in a 'forgetful' pleasurable activity without too much of a controlling focus upon over-conscious goals. It is tempting to say that 'it is just music.' Nevertheless, scholars such as DeNora (2000), Ruud (2002), and Batt-Rawden (2007) have been able to demonstrate that music as a resource in everyday life depends upon ways and contexts of use.

One way of overcoming what initially could be viewed as a bias overstressing conscious goals and cognitive choices, is to consider the social nature of music, which could help us see how action, emotion, and cognition intertwine in musical activity. Recent research indicates quite clearly that there is a psychobiological foundation for musical participation (see, e.g. Wallin et al. 2000; Cross 2003; Cross and Morley 2009). This foundation could be understood as part of a social-musical motivational system (see, e.g. Dissanayake 2000a,b, 2001; Trevarthen 2000; Trevarthen and Malloch 2000; Malloch and Trevarthen 2009). This view suggests that the evolution of the human species has provided us with a basic protomusicality that could be understood as a psychobiological capacity for relating to sounds, rhythms, and movements. Malloch and Trevarthen (2009) call this communicative musicality. This capacity comes to use very early in a baby's life, as it constitutes the possibility of building intimate relationships. The baby seems to be 'programmed' biologically to be directed to other humans. Communicative musicality, then, enables the child to enter in affiliate interaction and start on a trajectory of cultural learning. Dissanayake (2000b) therefore argues that participation in music is a human need related to the experience of meaning. Out of the early affiliate interactions of sounds and gestures, musicking and musicianship develop.

If the account of the previous paragraph is defendable, then we should take special interest in music as a social phenomenon as this throws light on the idea that musical and paramusical elements interact. Some would argue that the social and the musical are separable only in an abstract analytical exercise, so that it makes sense to think in terms of social-musical process (see, e.g. Stige et al. 2010). Pavlicevic and Ansdell (2009) have developed an interesting discussion of this theme, through introduction of the term collaborative music(k)ing.

Some of the implications of the idea of social-musical process become clearer if we take into consideration theories that explore emotion and cognition as social process also. Specific examples include Lave and Wenger's (1991) theory of situated learning and Rosenwein's (2006) concept of emotional communities. Broader traditions exploring emotion and cognition as social process include the culture-historical perspectives referred to previously in this chapter and developmental theories stressing contextual perspectives (see, e.g. Lerner 2001).

The integration of the social and the musical could be developed in light of theory on interaction rituals, and I will argue that this perspective could help us grasp how the resources of arena, agenda, agents, activities and artefacts could be mobilized in the service of health and wellbeing. Collins's (2004) has elaborated upon a sociological tradition of ritual studies pioneered by Durkheim and Goffman, and he has developed a comprehensive theory of interaction rituals. In this tradition of scholarship, formal procedure and stereotyped actions are not what constitute rituals. Mutual focus of attention and emotional entrainment is much more central. 'Scripts' can function as scaffolding, as a container for actions and emotions so to say, but interaction rituals could also be spontaneous and improvised. What is vital to these rituals, according to Collins, is that joint action characterized by a mutual focus of attention leads to shared mood, increased emotional energy, and the construction of a sense of community.

In a previous case study I have used the theory of interaction rituals as a tool for analysing and interpreting social-musical interactions in a group of participants with intellectual disabilities (Stige 2010a). In the analysis, I used a simple greeting song (a partially scripted ritual) as an example. In the song, bodily co-presence was established at two levels. First, the group was seated in a semicircle, visibly present for each other in a very clear way. Second, the structure of the song was arranged so that each person was given attention in a separate verse where the therapist intensified the dimensions of bodily co-presence by approaching the person in question. This ensured that each person got involved and engaged in the activity and that the group's attention was drawn to the person in question. Mutual foci of attention were established. This observation relates to another point in Collins's (2004) list of interaction ritual ingredients; the establishment of shared mood. Collins describes interaction rituals as 'emotion transformers' and many of the participants in the music group I observed did their best to live up to this description. The logic of the song was 'each verse a new person' and this was at times transformed to 'each verse a new mood'. In some verses the social-musical interaction introduced delicacy or hesitation, while other verses were characterized by energetic performances of passion.

The above description illuminates how musicking can be carefully tailored in order to meet the specific needs of a group of participants. The psychobiological foundation of human musicality as well as the wide range of musical norms available makes music an extremely versatile tool for maintaining human interaction even when the resources of each participant are limited. The benefits, such as increased emotional energy and the construction of a sense of community, could be considered therapeutic or health-promoting (Stige 2010a). Other musical activities, much less specifically tailored than the one described here, could also be interpreted as types of interaction ritual. In a different case study, I explored the activities and experiences of the members of a Senior Choir (Stige 2010b). The singers, coming together once a week, had no need for the specific arrangements described in the previous paragraph. Their musicking was seemingly much more conventional; they would stand or sit together in a typical choir arrangement and sing traditional songs arranged for two or three voices. The integration of the social and the musical was a central theme in this case also, however. When the participants reflected upon the experience of singing in a choir, their descriptions illuminated collaborative efforts that contributed to a sense of co-presence with corresponding changes in mood and an experience of community. In fact, many of the participants claimed that singing was their only possibility for survival as a group, since differences in values and assumptions among them created many conflicts (often linked to agenda and arena, namely what to sing for whom, where and why).

Appraisal and appropriation of affordances is an integrated aspect of the act of musicking. If an interaction ritual such as a choir rehearsal works successfully, we enjoy the music and want to come back for the next rehearsal. Mutual foci of attention, joint musical action, shared moods, and a sense of community develop in ways that build positive emotional energy. The effect of an interaction ritual that does not work well is a very different story. We should also remember that a ritual that works for some participants can be an energy drainer for others. There is, for instance, a potential problem of stratification of emotional energy in such rituals. Some individuals could be able to put themselves where the action is in ways that build energy for themselves but work less positively for participants who find themselves forced into more subordinate roles. The dynamics of interaction rituals can be complex and there is a need to examine how spacious each ritual is in relation to the challenge of creating experiences of unity with recognition of diversity.

Rituals of everyday life

Collins (2004) explains that the emotional energy and sense of community produced by interaction rituals lasts for some time, and then gradually vanishes. The creation of symbols is required for the group members to become conscious of themselves as individuals and as group, and symbols and emblems contribute to the perpetuation of that consciousness also. Nevertheless, interaction rituals need to be repeated in order to have a maintained effect. Perhaps, Collins suggests, this explains why religious ceremonies often are repeated regularly, for instance on weekly basis. Following this line of thinking, we could ask if this also partly explains why choirs and other musical ensembles come together on a regular basis. Of course, there is a skill component involved; you need to meet recurrently in order to develop the required competence according to certain norms of performance. But for many musical ensembles, this is hardly the whole explanation. After a few days, it is time to make music again, in order to renew the emotional bonds that musicking can create.

In relation to our everyday lives, this clearly suggests how limiting it would be to primarily think of health musicking as a mechanism for individual health-related change, even though that could be part of the picture. The logic of the health sector should not be exported to health musicking in everyday life. The singers of the Senior Choir referred to above come to the choir for social-musical reasons; they want to sing and they enjoy the experience of community. Perhaps they also keep going to the choir because it keeps them going in some way. When talking about the choir some of them even claim that it is therapeutic, for instance if they experience that the warming up exercises and the singing are good for their asthmatic breathing (Stige 2010b). But apart from such concrete aspects, we are not talking about a defined intervention where it would be sensible to explore dose-effect relationships in relation to specific symptoms in each individual. We are talking about a multifaceted everyday resource which when mobilized seems to be good at mobilizing other resources (what we above have described as the dynamics between musical and paramusical elements). These are resources many people choose to use and reproduce on a regular basis, in contrast to the typical logic of a therapeutic intervention, where there is usually a limited and focused period of time.

Even Ruud (2002) has collected and analysed narratives about the use of music as a technology of health in everyday life, with focus upon continuous use for prevention and health promotion. More recently, Saarikallio (2007), Skånland (2007), and others have explored how individuals use music in order to regulate thoughts and emotions in relation to everyday challenges. With the development of portable personal stereos, such as mp3-players of various sorts, an affordable technology now enables many people to select a sound track for almost any activity and situation (Bull 2000, 2007). The research on this area of music use reveals how people make music choices as an integrated element of the efforts of managing everyday life.

It is pertinent to consider these forms of music use at this point as they supplement the interaction rituals described above. We could perhaps think of them as 'individualized rituals.' This label is adequate for two reasons. First, the work of DeNora (2000) and others indicate that these forms of music use are not free-floating or arbitrary; they seem to be characterized by some type of procedure. Second, if the term individualized ritual is seen in relation to the interaction rituals discussed above, relationships between personal and social use as well as between internal and external processes are suggested. The issue of how the internal and personal relates to external and social processes is important in the activity theory of the culture-historical tradition of scholarship, where human emotion and cognition is acknowledged as activities that are nurtured by an intersubjective space of joint activity and dialogue (Cole 1996; Engeström et al. 1999). These examples imply that we should be careful not to polarize interaction rituals and individualized rituals, as extensive experience with the first type probably is of immense value in the development of the second.

Conclusion

The notion of health musicking was originally developed in a discussion of music therapy theory, but is offered here as a possible framework for a broader interdisciplinary area of music, health, and wellbeing. The notion draws our attention to human action and performance of relationships. I have conceptualized health in dramaturgical terms, which does not imply that biological processes are unimportant but that these processes are experienced and interpreted within socio-cultural contexts. Investigations of relationships between music and health could not be reduced to the study of the direct effect of musical parameters but must also focus upon people's use of the musical and paramusical features of a situation. Taking this interplay between musical and para-musical elements into consideration, I have described health musicking as the appraisal and appropriation of the health affordances of arena, agenda, agents, activities, and artefacts of a music practice.

Interaction rituals represent one possibility for mobilization of health resources through musicking. They are typical of many music practices, such as the choirs and ensembles of amateur music life and the groups found in community music projects, music education, and music therapy. These rituals exemplify social-musical possibilities and remind us about the social nature of music, which probably can be linked to its evolutionary origins. In a late modern society, with individualization and the availability of advanced technology as typical characteristics, musicking can take many forms. The individualized rituals of listening through use of portable personal stereos have been met with increasing interest among researchers lately, who explore what such rituals afford in relation to the management of the challenges of people's everyday lives.

In discussing the term health musicking, I have focused upon some possible sources of available resources, such as arena, agenda, agents, activities, and artefacts, as well as some possible proc-esses for mobilization of these resources, such as interaction rituals and various individualized rituals. Every discipline and tradition of practice taking interest in music and health will explore both of these dimensions. In community music, for instance, there is a long tradition for explor-ing how various activities (such as singing) and artefacts (such as specific songs) afford in relation to the experience of musical community. In music therapy, there is a tradition of exploring the affordances of the interpersonal relationships that the involved agents develop through music. The evolving community music therapy movement has initiated a debate about the affordances of various arenas and agendas, within and without the clinic. In music education, there is a con-tinuous debate about relationships between locally negotiated agendas and the agendas implied by national or regional curricula. Many more examples could be given, and each of these disci-plines and practice traditions will take interest in the concrete ways resources are mobilized in situations of use.

The focus of this chapter has not been upon medical and paramedical aspects of music and health but upon the mobilization of musical and paramusical resources in the service of health and wellbeing. I have stressed music in everyday life, not because the clinic is never relevant but because the majority of factors influencing our health are found in other sectors of society. A perspective on music and health as action and performance in everyday contexts could inform our professional practice as well (Stige 2002). Health musicking should not be thought of in terms of professional specialization only, then, but particularly in terms of participation.

As scholars and practitioners, how could we promote participation? Understanding participa-tion is a beginning. Perspectives on musical participation exist within a variety of fields (see, for instance, Elliott 1995; Everitt 1997; Veblen 2004; Pitts 2005; Stige 2006). Future research on music, health, and wellbeing hopefully will help us arrive at a better understanding of the many different rituals of musicking developed for mobilization of health resources. I have proposed that interaction rituals and individualized rituals represent two major categories, but there is much more work to do in the exploration of this. One pertinent issue to explore is how rituals are not isolated events but elements in broader ecologies. Interaction rituals, for instance, could be repeated to build interaction ritual chains (Collins 2004), which for the individual could establish trajectories of participation (Lave and Wenger 1991) and for the group represent possibilities for building emotional communities (Rosenwein 2006) and communities of practice (Wenger 1998).

In addition to these 'outward movements,' interaction also is internalized and forms a basis for human emotion and cognition (Leiman 1999). The claims of this final paragraph are sweeping and integrate notions developed in several different traditions of research. They are not taken out the blue, however, as they synthesize some of the insights developed within the current literature. Future research could qualify them.

References

Aldridge, D. (1996). *Music Therapy Research and Practice in Medicine. From Out of the Silence*. London: Jessica Kingsley Publishers.

Aldridge, D. (2004). *Health, the Individual and Integrated Medicine*. London: Jessica Kingsley Publishers.

Andrews, E. (2005). *Muscle Management for Musicians*. Lanham, MD: Scarecrow Press.

Barz, G. (2006). *Singing for Life. HIV/AIDS and Music in Uganda*. New York: Routledge.

Batt-Rawden, K. (2007). Music and health promotion: The role and significance of music and musicking in everyday life of the long term ill. Unpublished doctoral thesis, University of Exeter.

Biley, F. (2000). The effects on patient well-being of music listening as a nursing intervention: a review of the literature. *Journal of Clinical Nursing*, 9(5), 668–77.

Bonde, L. O. (2008). *Music and Health. An Annotated Bibliography*. Retrieved 29 November, 2009, from: http://www.nmh.no/Senter_for_musikk_og_helse/Litteratur/66817

Borchgrevink, H.M. (2003). Does health promotion work in relation to noise? *Noise and Health*, 5(18), 25–30.

Bruscia, K. (1998). *Defining Music Therapy* (2nd edn.). Gilsum, NH: Barcelona Publishers.

Bull, M. (2000). *Sounding Out the City: Personal Stereos and the Management of Everyday Life*. New York: Berg Publishers.

Bull, M. (2007). *Sound Moves: iPod Culture and Urban Experience*. London: Routledge.

Burke, K. (1945/1969). *A Grammar of Motives*. Los Angeles, CA: California University Press.

Chaney, D. (2002). *Cultural Change and Everyday Life*. New York: Palgrave.

Clift, S. M. and Hancox, G. (2001). The perceived benefits of singing. Findings from preliminary surveys of a university college choral society. *The Journal of the Royal Society for the Promotion of Health*, 121(4), 248–56.

Cole, M. (1996). *Cultural Psychology. A Once and Future Discipline*. Cambridge, MA: The Belknap Press of Harvard University Press.

Cole, M., Engeström, Y., and Vasquez, O. (eds.) (1997). *Mind, Culture, and Activity. Seminal Papers from the Laboratory of Comparative Human Cognition*. Cambridge, MA: Cambridge University Press.

Collins, R. (2004). *Interaction Ritual Chains*. Princeton, NJ: Princeton University Press.

Cross I. (2003). Music and biocultural evolution. In: Clayton, M., Herbert, T., and Middleton, R. (eds.) *The Cultural Study of Music. A Critical Introduction*, pp. 19–30. London: Routledge.

Cross, I. and Morley, I. (2009). The evolution of music: Theories, definitions and the nature of the evidence. In: Malloch, S. and Trevarthen, C. (eds.) *Communicative Musicality*, pp. 61–81. Oxford: Oxford University Press.

DeNora, T. (2000). *Music in Everyday Life*. Cambridge: Cambridge University Press.

DeNora, T. (2007). Health and music in everyday life–A theory of practice. *Psyke & Logos*, 28(1), 271–87.

Dissanayake, E. (2000a). Antecedents of the temporal arts in early mother-infant interaction. In: Wallin, N.L., Merker, B., and Brown, S. (eds.) *The Origins of Music*, pp. 389–410. Cambridge, MA: The MIT Press.

Dissanayake, E. (2000b). *Art and Intimacy: How the Arts Began*. Seattle, WA: University of Washington Press.

Dissanayake, E. (2001). An ethological view of music and its relevance to music therapy. *Nordic Journal of Music Therapy*, 10(2), pp. 159–75.

Elliott, D.J. (1995). *Music Matters. A New Philosophy of Music Education.* New York: Oxford University Press.

Engeström, Y., Miettinen, R., and Punamäki, R.L. (eds.) (1999). *Perspectives on Activity Theory.* New York: Cambridge University Press.

Everitt, A. (1997). *Joining In: An Investigation into Participatory Music.* London: Calouste Gulbenkian Foundation.

Fornäs, J. (1995). *Cultural Theory & Late Modernity.* London: Sage Publications.

Goffman, E. (1961/1991). *Asylums. Essays on the Social Situations of Mental Patients and Other Inmates.* London: Penguin Books.

Hauge, S. (2004). Jo mere vi er sammen, jo gladere vi blir?: Ein feltmetodisk studie av sjukeheimen som heim [The more we are together, the merrier we get?: A field study of the nursing home as a home]. Unpublished doctoral dissertation. Oslo: The University of Oslo.

Hauge, S. (2008). Identitet og kvardagsliv i sjukeheim [Identity and everyday life in the nursing home]. In: Hauge, S. and Jacobsen, F.F. (eds.) *Hjem. Hjemlighet i eldre år [The home and the logic of heart and home]*, pp. 121–33. Oslo: Cappelen Academic Publishing.

Hauge, S., Jacobsen, F. and Stige, B. (in preparation). In between mute residents and noisy environments— music as therapy and everyday life in the nursing home.

Jacobsen, F.F. (2005). *Cultural Discontinuity as an Organizational Resource: Nursing in a Norwegian Nursing Home.* Bergen: NLA-Forlaget.

Janzen, J.M. (2000). Theories of music in African ngoma healing. In: Gouk, P. (ed.) *Musical Healing in Cultural Contexts*, pp. 46–66. Aldershot: Ashgate.

Korsyn, K. (2003). *Decentering Music. A Critique of Contemporary Musical Research.* New York: Oxford University Press.

Lave, J. and Wenger, E. (1991). *Situated Learning. Legitimate Peripheral Participation.* Cambridge: Cambridge University Press.

Leiman, M. (1999). The concept of the sign in the work of Vygotsky, Winnicott, and Bakhtin: Further integration of object relation theory and activity theory. In: Engeström, Y., Miettinen, R., and Punamäki, R.L. (eds.) *Perspectives on Activity Theory*, pp. 419–34. New York: Cambridge University Press.

Lerner, R.M. (2001). *Concepts and Theories of Human Development* (3rd edn). Mahwah, NJ: Lawrence Erlbaum Associates.

Malloch, S. and Trevarthen, C. (eds.) (2009). *Communicative Musicality.* Oxford: Oxford University Press.

MacDonald, R.R., Hargreaves, D., and Miell, D. (eds.) (2002). *Musical Identities.* New York: Oxford University Press.

Miell, D., MacDonald, R.R., and Hargreaves, D. (eds.). (2005). *Musical Communication.* New York: Oxford University Press.

Mitchell, L.A., MacDonald, R.R., and Knussen, C. (2008). An investigation of the effects of music and art on pain perception. *Psychology of Aesthetics, Creativity, and the Arts*, **2**(3), 162–70.

Pavlicevic, M. and Ansdell, G. (2009). Collaborative musicing. In: Malloch, S. N. and Trevarthen, C. (eds). *Communicative Musicality*, pp. 357–76. Oxford: Oxford University Press.

Pitts, S. (2005). *Valuing Musical Participation.* Aldershot: Ashgate Publishing.

Procter, S. (2002). Empowering and enabling: Improvisational music therapy in non-medical mental health provision. In: Kenny, C. and Stige, B. (eds.) *Contemporary Voices in Music Therapy: Communication, Culture, and Community*, pp. 95–107. Oslo: Unipub.

Rolvsjord, R. (2004). Therapy as empowerment: Clinical and political implications of empowerment philosophy in mental health practices of music therapy. *Nordic Journal of Music Therapy*, **13**(2), 99–111.

Rolvsjord, R. (2010). *Resource-oriented Music Therapy in Mental Health Care.* Gilsum, NH: Barcelona Publishers.

Rosenwein, B.H. (2006). *Emotional Communities in the Early Middle Ages*. Ithaca, NY: Cornell University Press.

Ruud, E. (1979). Musikkterapi [Music Therapy]. *Musikk i Skolen*, **4**, 34–35.

Ruud, E. (1998). *Music Therapy: Improvisation, Communication and Culture*. Gilsum, NH: Barcelona.

Ruud, E. (2002). Music as a cultural immunogen–Three narratives on the use of music as a technology of health. In: Hanken, I. M., Nilsen, S.G., and Nerland, M. (red.), *Research in and for Higher Music Education. Festschrift for Harald Jørgensen*, pp. 109–20. Oslo: NMH-Publications 2002–2.

Saarikallio, S. (2007). *Music as mood regulation in adolescence. Academic dissertation. The Faculty of Humanities*. Jyväskylä: University of Jyväskylä.

Skånland, M. (2007). Soundescape: En studie av hvordan musikk blir integrert i hverdagen til brukere av mp3-spillere [Soundescape: A Study of How Music is an Integrated Part of the everyday Life of Users of mp3-players]. Master thesis, University of Oslo.

Small, C. (1998). *Musicking. The Meanings of Performing and Listening*. Hanover, NH: Wesleyan University Press.

Stige, B. (1995). *Samspel og relasjon. Perspektiv på ein inkluderande musikkpedagogikk [Interaction and relationship. Perspectives on inclusive music education]*. Oslo: Samlaget.

Stige, B. (2002). *Culture-Centered Music Therapy*. Gilsum, NH: Barcelona Publishers.

Stige, B. (2006). Toward a notion of participation in music therapy. *Nordic Journal of Music Therapy*, **15**(2), 121–38.

Stige, B. (2008). Dancing the drama and singing for life: On ethnomusicology and music therapy. *Nordic Journal of Music Therapy*, **16**(1), 155–71.

Stige, B. (2010a). Musical participation, social space, and everyday ritual. In: Stige, B., Ansdell, G., Elefant, C, and Pavlicevic, M. *Where Music Helps. Community Music Therapy in Action and Reflection*, pp. 125–47. Farnham: Ashgate.

Stige, B. (2010b). Practicing music as mutual care. In: Stige, B., Ansdell, G., Elefant, C., and Pavlicevic, M. *Where Music Helps. Community Music Therapy in Action and Reflection*, pp. 253–75. Farnham: Ashgate.

Stige, B., Ansdell, G., Elefant, C., and Pavlicevic, M. (2010). Conclusion: When things take shape in relation to music: Towards an ecological perspective on music's help. In: Stige, B., Ansdell, G., Elefant, C, and Pavlicevic, M. *Where Music Helps. Community Music Therapy in Action and Reflection*, pp. 277–308. Farnham: Ashgate.

Trevarthen, C. (2000). Musicality and the intrinsic motive pulse: Evidence from human psychobiology and infant communication. *Musicae Scientiae* (Special Issue 1999–2000), 155–215.

Trevarthen, C. and Malloch, S. (2000). The dance of wellbeing: Defining the musical therapeutic effect. *Nordic Journal of Music Therapy*, **9**(2), 3–17.

Turner, V.W. (1967). *The Forest of Symbols: Aspects of Ndembu Ritual*. Ithaca, NY: Cornell University Press.

Twani, Z. (2007). The musicians behind bars: Can music help renew identities? In: Akrofi, E. Smit, M. and Thorsén, S.-M. (eds.) *Music and Identity. Transformation and Negotiation*, pp. 297–310. Stellenbosch, South Africa: Sun Press.

Veblen, K.K. (2004). The many ways of community music. *International Journal of Community Music*, **A**(1).

Wallin, N.L., Merker, B., and Brown, S. (eds.) (2000). *The Origins of Music*. Cambridge, MA: The MIT Press.

Wenger, E. (1998). *Communities of Practice: Learning, Meaning and Identity*. New York: Cambridge University Press.

Wittgenstein, L. (1953/1967). *Philosophical Investigations*. Oxford: Blackwell.

Chapter 15

Between Beats: Group Music Therapy Transforming People and Places

Mercédès Pavlicevic

Overture

Group music therapy happens in a range of health, education, care, and community settings, offering possibilities for addressing the personal and collective disruptions of illness and disability, and for transforming the social context within which such disruptions are situated. Although such work involves a range of activities before, during, after, as well as within and around 'the sessions' (logistics and liaising with staff, getting to know people in the setting, preparing musical material and instruments, and more), here group music therapy is delineated to signify participatory, inclusive musical action enacted and crafted collaboratively by all who attend the group music therapy 'session': be they music therapist, clients/patients, carers, families, staff—or whoever.

Despite music therapy participants generally acknowledging the 'magic' of group music therapy work, describing such events is complex. Music therapists who attempt to talk about music in music therapy, experience what Ansdell (1996) identified as the 'music therapist's dilemma'—drawing from ethnomusicologist Charles Seeger's observation that music does not readily translate into words. Another complication is how and where to situate accounts of the music therapy event—both in terms of close-up description of the practice, and as a theoretical discipline. Increasingly, music therapists' writings that emphasize 'the therapeutic relationship' within a social vacuum (i.e. as though the people, places, economics, and politics around such events did not need too much attention) have been challenged by texts both within and around the discipline. Thus, sociologically informed perspectives call for a thorough understanding of the 'complex social processes' (Daykin 2007) that form part of any such event, and consider how music and 'everyday life' constitute one another (Elliot 1995; Cook 1998; DeNora 2003, 2006). From within the music therapy discipline, Community Music Therapy texts consider the complex cultural, social-musical worlds within which music therapy is situated; not just as a psychological-therapeutic practice, but more broadly as socially engaged and participative musicking events; happenings that impact on people's lives, connect people with one another and create possibilities for social participation. How musicking happens is understood here as part of—rather than separate from—a fluid, dynamic environment. Thus, within the special needs school, hospital clinic, community centre, or care home, how people engage with one another, their ongoing relationships with music, the ambience of the place at any time, become part of the musicking events in that place on that day. Conversely, musicking contributes to people's ongoing musical experiences, their sense of themselves and of one another in that time and place, contributes to the ambience, and so on. (Hence, also, the notion of music therapist's musical mapping of people and places, later in this text.) (Ansdell 2002; DeNora 2003; Stige 2003; Pavlicevic and Ansdell 2004).

Such a broadening descriptive and conceptual palette enriches and complicates the portrayal of explicitly and delineated music-making at the heart of group music therapy: in a word, do we risk losing the musicking heart of the matter in the interests of a broadening narrative? Conversely, does emphasizing this musicking heart signal a return to ignoring the 'complex social processes' that are part of the therapeutic musicking narrative?

The intention here is to explore how close descriptions of the 'musicking heart' of group music therapy might convey the value of such practices for enhancing people's social networks and resources. It would seem that, especially for funders of health practices, who (hopefully) seek to be convinced that such work 'makes a difference' to people's lives, accounts need to convey how group music therapy and its situated social contexts mutually energize and animate one another. This chapter emphasizes musicking events in group music therapy work, on the understanding that while complex layers of social structures and processes make possible—and indeed are part of—such events, therapeutic musicking is a distinctive phenomenon. Music therapists use music's communicative, aesthetic and therapeutic qualities to transform people's experiences of themselves and of one another; offering an experience of coherence and connection whose impact continues beyond the time, the people and the place of the session. The question becomes: how does participatory group musicking transform people and places?

The descriptive focus here is on Magic Moments in sessions, that—despite lasting no more than seconds—appear to signal participants' experiences of shared meaning, pleasure, dignity and collective belonging in 'the present moment' (Stern 2004). This paper suggests that 'Magic Moments' are key to music's transformative work. The term emerged as a result of a 4-year international study of Community Music Therapy practices funded by the Norwegian Research Council. Repeated participant-observations of a range of South African group music therapy events revealed electrifying moments recognisable by practitioner and researcher peers. The children and young people often described watching themselves on film as 'magic', hence the term used here, rather than the more usual 'optimal' or 'peak' moments. These became the focus points for microanalysis of group musicking, helped by the emergent heuristic frame of 'Collaborative Musicking' (Ansdell and Pavlicevic 2005; Pavlicevic and Ansdell 2009; Stige et al. 2010). 'Magic Moments' describe optimal moments in group musical flow and coherence. In microanalysis and peer debriefings, magic moments were characterized as qualitatively distinctive phenomena, in which live spontaneous singing, playing, and dancing and the collection of individual participants propelled and shaped one another towards unified musicking-time-space organism. The musicians constantly ebbed and flowed towards and away from Magic Moments. Discussions of such moments revealed that identities to do with being 'ill', 'marginalized', or 'expert musician' are dissolved (or shared) in the interests of being people together in music in this place and in this time. Magic moments may well signal the transformative nature of participatory therapeutic musicking (Pavlicevic 2010). However, bearing in mind a broadening and more socially attuned music therapy discourse, an attempt is made to explore these *as part of* a social, musical, temporal, and spatial map that, rather like a musical phrase, spans various connecting events before, during, and after, as well as in and around these moments.

This exploration of the musicking heart of group music therapy is inspired and informed by direct participation–observation of such work and from project-planning discussions and interviews with music therapy participants. The first section ('Mapping life musically'), presents a musical mapping of people and places, followed by a group music therapy vignette situated within a social care residential setting that caters for people with dementia, and identifies three transformative Magic Moments within a group musicking event. The second section ('Considering magic moments') describes and characterizes these Magic Moments with help from theories of Communicative Musicality (Malloch and Trevarthen 2009) and Collaborative Musicking

(Ansdell and Pavlicevic 2005; Pavlicevic and Ansdell 2009), and recent Community Music Therapy texts (Ansdell 2003; Pavlicevic and Ansdell 2004; Stige et al. 2010). The final section ('Valuing, evaluating, and building bridges') touches on how to consider and give value to such moments—and to such music-based practices—while not ignoring the social-cultural structures and processes that facilitate such practices—and may well be transformed by them.

Mapping life musically

A 'musical' take on human communication, relating, and of illness and health helps to frame how music therapists approach and engage with people and places, through therapeutic musicking.

Whereas biomedicine might map wellness/illness within a person's neuromotor-biological functioning, a musical mapping considers the quality of their ongoing experiential 'flow', i.e., the dynamic vitality of people's intra- and interpersonal actions, attentiveness, motivation, intention, as they participate and act in social life. Forms of vitality (Stern 2010), characterized by temporal contour, space, force, directionality and intentionality, are experienced internally (in the mind) and externally (as a result of ongoing and direct physical, emotional and mental experiences) as well as between people. Vitality flows provide human beings with a continuous, coherent experience of life and meaning-making over time. The notion of optimal states of dynamic flow (using Stern's discourse) corresponds in part to Csikszentmihalyi's (1997) being 'in the zone' or optimal experiences; although Csikszentmihalyi's notion tends to emphasize a mental/cognitive experience, in contrast to the correspondence—indeed the duality—of physical and mental, outer as well as inner experience.

The fluidity and agility of people's responsive and expressive acts as they participate in everyday life, whether in speech, gestures, movement, breathing or being still can be portrayed through music improvisation; using elements of pitch, melodic contour, harmonic texture, rhythm, and tempo to represent human vital flow (Trevarthen and Malloch 2000). Equally, entire groups and systems can be characterized as flowing (or not), as people and places and 'things' happen continuously in an ongoing choreography and shaping of time and events. Such improvisations—with their vast range of regulation, adaptation, disruptions, repair, recovery, modulations—might be said to musically characterize optimal social wellbeing.

A musical map of illness then, would consider the subjective and collective disruptions of such flow: within and between people and also between people and places at certain times. Thus, a disruption as a result of a stroke impacts on the person's capacity to 'flow' within themselves and, correspondingly, with others. The stroke sufferer experiences their 'timing' as out of synchrony—as in Condon and Ogston's (1966) notion of 'interactional asynchrony'. The loss of capacity for optimal flow is evident in their speech, thoughts, gaze, vocal sounds, their gait and gestures. A stroke destabilizes the person's ongoing experience of themselves, of meaning, of relationships and engagements and—critically—is distressing also to their friends/family members. Indeed most of us have experienced the discomfort (and embarrassment perhaps) of not quite managing to understand, or to attune to someone who has had a paralysing stroke: we're unsure, for example, of whether to wait for them to complete phrases, or to complete phrases on their behalf. We become self-conscious that we may be talking and walking too quickly, uncertain whether or not to reach out when they seem to be losing their balance: having a stroke not only affects the stroke sufferer. The person's loss of confidence and motivation to participate in social life, as well as the loss of self-worth and accompanying depression, are well known. Musically, the person's social networks and networking can be characterized as disrupted, with unstable temporal flows of social participation. Moreover, the result of unexpected demands on their immediate social circle's time, energy, skills, and economic resources, means that this person's social network, itself embedded in socio-economic and political structures, can correspondingly be considered disrupted and 'vulnerable' (Daykin 2007; Edwards 2007; White 2009).

The 'musical framing' of 'life' (for want of a better expression) has been presented in some detail to help clarify how music therapists work to transform people and places. To sum up: by attuning to the 'flow' between people and events and places as a musical phenomenon—irrespective of whether this flow is manifested in everyday life or in conventional musicking enactments (i.e. singing, dancing)—music therapists can consider how best to: (1) characterize the flow, (2) become part of it through musicking, and (3) 'mend' such disruptions within and between people. Whilst musicking with others, music therapists remain acutely attentive to micropossibilities in musicking, in order to address discontinuities of separate and collective flow (Aldridge 1996; Malloch and Trevarthen 2000; Batt-Rawden et al. 2007; Pavlicevic and Ansdell 2009).

We now step into a fictitious dementia care setting, in an affluent corner of the UK's South-East. This fictitious and hypothetical vignette is assembled from four pre-study planning visits to dementia care settings where we participated in group music therapy sessions and talked with a range of participants including music therapists, clients, staff members, and visitors. The four music therapy events happened in broadly similar settings (dementia care homes) and organizational structures, and in each of the sites there was a dedicated music therapy group session time with staff members and people in various stages of dementia. The common approach by the therapists—all of whom were Nordoff–Robbins trained—was evident in their engagements throughout the time of the visits, their musical descriptions of the place and people, and was further reflected in the fluid and spontaneous musical engagements with participants both during and around the sessions. For this composite vignette, the four visits are collapsed into one account, with essential observational fragments imported in order to present an essential, composite account (Campbell and McNamara 2007). This streamlining technique further helps protect anonymity of people, through ensuring that work sites or organizations cannot be identified. While the dementia care sector is singled out here for describing group music therapy, similar work happens in a range of education, social care, community, and health sector-defined social spaces. The vignette weaves together a description of the event (in italics), and my reflections and thinking (drawn from participant observation notes). Three 'Magic Moments' are identified in the texts, and considered subsequently.

Between Beats—a social-musicking happening

Diana, the music therapist, walks around the 'Memory Lane' part of the care home for elderly people, greeting folk along the way. She's employed on a two day a week, sessional basis. The ambience today is both quiet and active; there is an early morning somnambulance as people sleep or look dazed, accompanied by a quiet purposeful activity that signals industry and 'things to do'—care staff chivvy old folk along. (As a musician I am instantly reminded of a two voice fugue, one still voice and another busier one, progressing in parallel motion, at times in counterpoint to one another, criss-crossing, and at times going separate ways. As a music therapist I know how I would start musicking here, now.)

Diana enquires of a nurse after someone's health, checks that the living room space is ready and available, chats about the weather, the local football club's dire weekend performance... Her walk and talk are constantly modulated: her pace, length of sentences, her volume and intonation shift constantly in response to whoever she meets. (I note that Diana is already in full 'music therapist' mode, drawing from her repertoire of finely honed communicative musicality strategies,[1] using micro shifts in her movement, gestures, voice to receive communicative signals that inform her of 'where and how

---

[1] See Malloch and Trevarthen (2009).

folk are today', whilst also conveying her attentiveness to those she meets. A delicately negotiated social dance is well under way.)

All this time, care staff accompany elderly folk towards the spacious living room, with large bay windows overlooking woodland, and a grand piano towards one corner. People begin to arrive and settle into the living room where chairs and settees have been set up in a large circle. There is a sense of people gathering towards this time and place, even while energy levels feel rather low and flat. Diana is now inside the circle, playing softly on her piano accordion as she greets various people. As they speak, utter sounds, move, and settle themselves, she modulates her volume, tempo, harmonic timbre and phrasing. There is a sense of 'preparing' for something, and folk seem to attend to her and to one another sporadically, in a way that seems in tune with the quiet open ended music. There are some 20 people gathered, five of whom are easily identifiable as care staff. (As yet her open-ended chords aren't recognizable as a structured piece of music, but hints of musical possibilities appear and disappear—I wonder whether this is like a Mozart opera overture, offering snippets that are recognized retrospectively.)

Imperceptibly, people's gestures, movements and sounds guide and lead her playing, which in turn seems to be gathering and shepherding folk towards what emerges as a 'good morning' song. The idiomatic transition from a loose collection of musical fragments to a recognizable 'song' with coherent musical direction is seamless—and yet, everyone is ready when 'the song' begins. (Here is 'Magic Moment no. 1': we have all arrived here together…. And I realize that this 'arriving' began this morning, with Diana walking through the care home. The image I now have is of a thread ready to emerge from a tapestry that has been woven all morning, with the help of everyone in this home today. Her role seems to include the tapping into, and shaping of, the day's ambience to optimize the impact of group musicking).

During the song, some tap their feet, sing along, everyone seems to constantly adapt their tempo and volume—there are many musicians in this room! The song has melodic coherence, despite the disparate assembly of people's communicative musicalities, each apparently locked within their own time-space and orbit of energy. Someone shouts 'Oh no! Not you again!' and Diana reflects the tightening intensity and tempo of this contribution in her playing, while singing 'Oh No! Oh Yes! It's me and you! It's us again!' Oh No No No! It's me again!' which draws amusement, and this in turn raises the collective musical-social energy and level of alertness in the room. Two of the care staff, perched in different parts of the circle, begin to clap with some animation, followed by some of the old folk. (Magic Moment no. 2: it is the care staff who now offer a direction for the ensemble.)

Moments later, in the midst of a growing crescendo of energy, I notice Diana attending closely to a gentleman apparently dozing in the corner, playing chords in another key as she listens to him and to everyone concurrently. Soon we are singing 'My Bonnie Lies over the ocean' (Magic Moment no. 3), with the singing and foot tapping accumulating intensity along the way, while Diana walks around, nodding, singing, smiling. (Again the transition from one musical genre to another is imperceptible; as are changes in energy, intensity and ambience. It seems to be the perfect song for here, now, with these folk—how did this song 'arrive'? The work is musically and socially subtle.)

Some time later, three people are on their feet together with care staff: they dance, while others clap, chat to their neighbours, smile—and others sleep. As the session continues, the musical energy of the group fluctuates constantly, as do the connections between people: constantly re-clustering between some who are physically engaged, some semi-engaged, others not at all. (It appears that any contribution from anyone in this group event—no matter how apparently irrelevant or unconnected—is received by everyone else as having musical 'threads'. It is not only Diana who responds to gestures, vocalizing, movements through musical action, but all participants in the group—staff as well as residents—seem to respond to, and engage with one another as musicians, regulating their own movements, gestures, vocalizing in response to one another. Diana weaves these threads through delicately weaving everyone's timing, intensity, intonational contours, rhythm, phrasing in a way that attends to, reflects and 'drives' micro shifts from, towards, and between people. This event parallels a phenomenon I became aware of when studying group musicking with lively youngsters in Cape Town who danced and jived as they made music: as the music gathered they moved closer together, and vice versa when the music loosened in intensity. As in Cape Town, the musical and spatial choreography in this dementia care home are one.)

At the end of 90 minutes (with tea and cakes in between), there is a marked change of atmosphere in this place. Care staff are animated and smile, there is more chat between people, greeting one another as they begin to dissemble and return to their rooms. The care home feels light and lyrical, and as I walk around helping folk to return to their living areas, this lighter ambience seems to spread through the home, with cleaners and admin staff responding to waves, smiles and greetings from the 'musicians'. It seems that group musicking has indeed transformed this space-time, and its people.

After this group music therapy session, Diana and I meet with the manager of the home. She's humming the last song as we enter her office, and greets us enthusiastically: 'I am so pleased you did this song today, we can hear it up here in the office—it is one of my favourite songs! Always puts me in a good mood...'

Coda: some time after this visit, as part of a local council evaluation, the group music therapy session is scored using Dementia Care Mapping before, during and after a group music therapy session. The scores ceiling is reached almost immediately during the session: it seems that this instrument cannot capture *the power of shared musicking's transformative effects.*

This group musicking vignette can be characterized as an ongoing stream of musicking that is constantly negotiated by all group music therapy participants. This doesn't necessarily mean that everyone's actions are musical, in the conventional sense. Rather, the music therapist maps everyone's presence and acts as part of a composite, musical flowing (or not) vitality, and engages with the individuals and the group through musicking that expertly matches this flow. This, in turn, makes it possible for various people to enter into musicking in their own way and at their own pace—which perfectly (and at times miraculously) fits the musicking flow that is prepared and constantly microregulated by the therapist. As hinted at in the vignette, therapeutic group musicking is explicitly inclusive and collaborative, so that all participants' acts are an acknowledged part of the emergent and ongoing musicking process—whether a staff member clapping, a gentleman beginning a 'new' song in the middle of something else, or someone exclaiming 'No No No!'. Any of these offer new avenues for the musical collaboration. This inclusive stance creates possibilities for spontaneous and idiosyncratic mutual influencing and negotiating. While studying group music therapy, Ansdell and Pavlicevic developed the notion of Collaborative Musicking (Pavlicevic and Ansdell 2009; Pavlicevic 2010) to help understand the nature of the musicking organism's susceptibility to the microfluctuating nature of multiple engagements. At times, group musicking flows smoothly; at times this stalls, dissembles, re-assembles; at times musicking peters out into silence or chat; at other times silence comes crashing in, interrupts, and so on. People's participation constantly fluctuates from being 'absent', apparently inattentive, to attending alongside, engaging without overt movement, to 'going through the motions', to being engaged, being distracted and so on. At the same time, their roles shift all the time: joining in or exiting (mentally or physically), following the rest, joining in with parallel but not quite congruent acts, imposing their enactments on the rest, seizing the initiative, supporting one another and more. Coupled with this is a complex ongoing movement between polarities of isolation and optimal collaboration, where the musicking organism becomes one musicking community.

Magic Moments signal easily missed moments of musicking community; moments where a collection of participants become one organism characterized by unifying and unified experience of people, time and space. This is a qualitatively distinctive phenomenon from 'a group playing music together'. Magic Moments help to crystallize cumulative past musicking actions and energize subsequent ones, signalling a threshold into a change in the musicking enactment, or a threshold into 'something new'. Arguably, their occurrences signal the difference between good-enough group musicking experiences and powerfully transforming ones.

The following section now focuses on the characteristics of the three Magic Moments presented in the vignette, using microlevel analysis to clarify.

Considering magic moments

The music therapist's musical mapping of everyday life clarifies that, for Diana, the entire day at the care setting is a continuous musical happening of people-time-place. Within this ongoing musical flow, the group music therapy session can be seen as a delineated time and space for therapeutic musicking. The temporal phrase that began in the morning, through (at times fleeting) engagements with people, continues through and then beyond the session, expanding outwards from Diana and the session, into the life of the residential care home. Diana's therapeutic task is to engage with, and transform this phrasing during session time. There are clues in the vignette that the flow has indeed been altered. Not only during, but also after the magic moments, changes in people's demeanour, in greeting, waves, speech sounds, and movements after group music therapy; the manager hums bits of the song, and the general 'feel' of the care home has shifted from quiet and purposeful activity to 'lyrical'. These, it would seem, signal the transformative impact of unifying experiences in group music therapy: the quality of interactions and engagements within the place—indeed the entire system—is transformed. The musical mapping of life (which is a modern version of medieval physicians' understandings of music as part of the body, and healing as a musical art) helps to explain both how entire time–space–people networks are rendered vulnerable by illness, injury, or disability, through destabilizing flow, and how shared musicking helps to repair and re-stabilize this (Stern 2004; Bradley 2005; Ehrenreich 2007; Hoffman 2009).

Magic Moment no. 1 is perhaps the most complex. If we start with its consequences, we see that the entire group is ready to tip into the good-morning song together. This seems a far cry from music sessions where an 'animateur' works desperately hard to chivvy a sluggish group of old people or silent teenagers towards a musical 'start', or an orchestra tuning-up before the 'proper' rehearsal or concert begins. How does this magic moment happen? How do the people—who are in disparate and separate intrasubjective orbits, some with reduced and fractured capacities for 'being social'—gather into one shared musical moment that parallels a rehearsed start by an ensemble that's 'warmed-up'?

Here it may be useful to recall studies of performing musicians who have described their finally honed multi-attentiveness and adjustments (Davidson and Good 2002; Sawyer 2003; Davidson 2005; Davidson and Malloch 2005). In response to co-musicians and audiences, the musicians constantly modulate and co-modulate their gestures, facial expressions and musical utterances (sung or instrumental), whilst also paying attention to the demands of the idiomatic conventions of the piece of music and to the social conventions of the 'event'. This 'multi' attentiveness and responsiveness to people, places and music resonates with the music therapist's stance before and during the group music therapy session—and here, moreover, it seems that all music therapy participants do this, including (so-called) 'vulnerable' people.

How does this multi-attentiveness happen? Who is paying attention to what? From the moment of entering the care setting, Diana has been kinaesthetically and socially attentive and responsive to the way people move, talk, and gesture, 'reading' their communicative musicality and absorbing the separate and shared qualities of flows of vitality in the environment. She is continually attentive to the home's qualitative ambience and soundscape at this time, and has accumulated what we might call a social, temporal, sensory 'imprint' of these qualities. This continuous attentiveness forms part of group music therapy work: it is part of gathering sonic–temporal–spatial information, which will inform (and continue to flow through) the group music therapy session, and beyond it.

Thus, as residents and care staff begin gathering in the day room for group music therapy, Diana has already accumulated a morning's reservoir of impressions and experiences, while also continuing to attend closely (and at times indirectly) to what's happening around her as the music therapy session is about to begin. She can draw from all and any of these direct experiences and sensations, portraying their qualities through the way she plays (rather than through *what* she plays). Concurrently, Diana attends to the ongoing clustering and re-clustering of various musicking solos, duets, trios, that may emerge unexpectedly, fleetingly, concurrently; each with (at times) distinctive musical characteristics, as part of a constantly shifting participatory choreography. While multiply alert—akin to the performers mentioned earlier—Diana adapts, discards, and extends the musical 'narrative' spontaneously in response to the needs of the present moment. This multi-musical, multi-modal, multi-temporal alertness forms part of music therapy improvisation strategies, crafted towards building inclusive musical-communicative experiences, however disparate and uneven participants' musical and social experiences and capacities (Pavlicevic 1997, 2000, 2007; Wigram 2004).

It seems from this moment, all participants, including the people with dementia, have the capacity to be attentive and responsive to multiple cues, be these musical, visual, gestural, or verbal—and also to initiate these. This accounts for the extraordinarily precise timing and elegance of various people's participation in the session. Hence, perhaps, the Dementia Care Mapping score going off the radar. How might such multi-attentiveness be enabled with people with a disrupted sense of themselves? The magic, it seems, is in the detail.

Improvisational music therapists sustain microattentiveness to possibilities for shared musicking. This includes any person's sounds, movements, gestures, and breathing—no matter how nuanced or idiosyncratic. Music therapists are trained to reflect, refract or contrast in their own playing, using deliberate strategies of 'sympathetic' musicking such as exaggerating, repeating, extending, waiting, anticipating, amplifying, slowing, and so on—in the interests of inviting a shared flow. Critically, though, some of these musical responses may be counter-intuitive in terms of local or current musical cultural norms and genres. In contrast to jazz improvisation/ riffs that are embedded within temporal, idiomatic conventions, music therapy improvisation at times may need to transgress idiomatic norms, or navigate between several in the interests of shared, microcommunicative enactments whilst also attending to disrupted, interrupted, suddenly surging or disappearing flows of engagements (Ansdell 1995; Pavlicevic 2000; Wigram 2004; Nordoff and Robbins 2007; Elefant and Wigram 2009). This helps to explain Diana's open-ended accordion music—at times this sounds closer to Schoenberg and Webern, with incomplete and interrupted snippets that continue to weave a sounded thread that reflects this moment with these people in this place. In conventional terms this is not music that (to this generation and demographic at any rate) would generally be considered aesthetically alluring—and yet it 'fits' *these* people in *this* time and in *this* place. We might call this 'reflective' musicking, or 'socially attentive' musicking: musicking that attends to people and places; it is playing music *with*, rather than *to*, people.

The transformative power of Magic Moment no. 1 is its social elegance, its economy of energy, its effortlessness and inclusiveness. It seems the most natural and simple thing in the world for people living with a debilitating condition, who live in separate and often distressed states with little access to other people, to begin singing a song at the same time, together with those who are (apparently) cognitively and physically able, together with some who have no musical skills and others who are highly trained. All are part of this beginning: there is no excluding or marginalizing from this moment.

Magic Moment no. 2 happens when two care staff members begin clapping, with perfect synchrony of timing, catching the wave of the group's rising energy. This act, by the care staff, suggests that they too are invested in co-generating and sustaining group musicking. Critically, in some settings where care staff are from foreign countries, it is they who can feel marginalized in group musicking, through lack of familiarity with language, or musical idioms and conventions. Music therapists generally remain alert to such possibilities. My understanding, as participant—observer, is that the two staff members who clap are energized by the shared participatory musicking stream, responding to the physically and mentally co-energizing and co-motivating properties of musicking. This experience offers them a role rather different to that of their daily identity as 'care worker'—with its well-known difficulties and demands. While Diane's movements, singing, and playing need to represent everyone's participation as well as the improvised music's cultural conventional demands, equally, the two staff participants enact the gathering stream of collectively propelled sound. They could be said to enact this on behalf of less able others in the group.

We might say that the care staff's clapping enacts 'shared' vitality affects (Stern 1985, 2004) which seem to be both subjective and collective, individual and supra-individual. All seem to know (more or less) where and how the song works, and everyone is up for some detours. Nobody complains or mutters when something unexpected happens or someone else is out of tune or out of time. There is no absolute tune or time in collaborative musicking. The music therapist's strategy is to enable precisely this kind of collaborative crafting of musicking space and time. Confirmation that the clapping is temporally, socially and qualitatively appropriate is retrospective: it is taken up by others. Were it inappropriate, it would fade (with some embarrassment by the two who initiated it).

Magic Moment no. 2 can be characterized as one where the distinctive roles of being a staff member, an elderly person with dementia, or music therapist are replaced by the shared roles of musicians. The collaborative social and musical norm of the work invites anyone to 'lead' or 'conduct' at any time. The social-musical congruence of the 'temporary leader's' acts is determined retrospectively, i.e. whether their initiative is taken up by the rest of the group or not. This democratic and collaborative social musicking event is enabled by the therapist's inclusive alertness to all persons' participatory potential. This magic moment signals spontaneous, permissive shared musicking. Its transformative power is that people who are marginalized as a result of illness or social status can be the very ones who re-energize and propel a collective socially bonding event.

Magic Moment no. 3—using 'everyday' music. Songs that are in the public social arena, such as 'My Bonnie Lies Over the Ocean' provide 'everyday' idiomatic form and content, familiar to people within a shared demographic range. Most British and Irish people over 50 would know this song. Rolvsjord's Resource Oriented approach to music therapy would identify it as a cultural resource, familiar and available to most people in the group. The song's familiarity provides the potential to empower participants to display their musicking skills and experiences collectively (Rolvsjord 2004). Part of the music therapist's toolkit is preparatory exploration of the songs' idiosyncratic possibilities: knowing how to play the song in several different keys, with variations of tempo, metre, and possibly structure and timbre, during the same performance of the song by the group. The therapist also needs to make sudden musical detours and deviations, popping into sudden switches of idiomatic renderings of the same song (a bluesy or rock-and-roll version of 'My Bonnie'), and return to its more usual rendering. Such idiosyncrasies can then be enacted in response to the separate and collective personal and musical demands of the moment. That said, the song's shared idiomatic conventions afford a common temporal musicking 'frame of reference' for all participants, even those less familiar with it. Their experiential knowledge of such music and body memory helps people to coordinate their bodies in time (and in tune) with others: the symmetrical verse and chorus structure present opportunities for humming, singing along, even if sporadically; tapping, clapping and gesturing. Folk know how this song—and others with similar genres—works in terms of melodic and rhythmic structures, repetitions of phrases and words, the chorus and verse structure, and so on, which provides a conduit for shared participation.

However, where illness disrupts people's motor capacities to coordinate fluently, the music therapist's task is to help bring people into flow with themselves and with one another. Given that many people with dementia have severely reduced access to experiences of sharing, mutuality and reciprocity that most of us take for granted, the songs' everyday conventions (which operate on the basis of neurologically intact capacities to sing), need interweaving with idiosyncratic strategies of timing, pauses, sudden detours into alterations of tempo, rhythm, even sudden changes of tonality, idiom, and, at times, of verbal content. These detours enable people's idiosyncratic, un-flowing, disruptive utterances to become part of the singing at any given moment. Such (at times) curious detours are in the interests of musicking that belongs with these participants in *this* time and space. In the vignette, the music therapist's improvisatory stance is conveyed to all participants: the music therapist, the residents and the care staff seem alert to unexpected musical offerings that might lock into moments of shared singing. Thus, after listening attentively to the elderly apparently dozing gentleman, while simultaneously attending to the entire group, everyone tips effortlessly into 'My Bonnie'.

Finally, this magic moment can be described as everyone in the room collaboratively knowing and enacting the 'right' music for the 'right' moment in the right way.

This chapter closes by considering how this and other group musicking events in healthcare contexts are assigned value—by whom and for what purpose. The consideration here is that all too often it seems that something of the magic of such work becomes 'lost in (scholarly and economic) translation'.

Valuing, evaluating, and building bridges

In accounting for the transformational possibilities of group music therapy through evaluations and research, ideological, disciplinary (and economic) intricacies present themselves. While some may be political or at least competitive (e.g. which and whose framework dominates representations of such happenings), there are more nuanced complexities to do with whose (and which) values are presented and represented, for what purpose accounts are generated, and how they help or hinder people and places being helped by music. Since some of these are addressed in various texts in some detail (Ansdell 2006, DeNora 2006; Wigram 2006; Pavlicevic et al. 2009), some brief questions suffice. How do people's immediate, emergent and shifting musicking experiences during sessions intersect with research and evaluation exercises, which are by their very nature, temporally fixed? How accessible are practice-grown discourses—often arisen from direct music therapy experiences—to those alongside or outside these events? At this time of demand for user-led evidence, how do clients'/participants' experiences translate into rigorous and economically useful accounts? How much restrain is needed by practitioner-researchers and evaluators to ensure minimal interference with, and optimal translation of, clients' idiosyncratic narratives? How closely representative of practices and experiences do practitioners' discourses become, when situated in financial, bio-medical, educational or cognitive behavioural psychology contexts? Conversely, how does any one of these contexts impact on practitioners, participants, care home staff, and others in assigning value and accounting for practices? These and other questions invite ongoing revision as to how best to translate group music therapy experience and values into scholarly and politically apt values; and how these, in turn, translate into evaluative/research methods and accounts that build bridges between practices such as music therapy and its neighbourly practices and professions. All too often such complexities—and there are innumerable—get in the way of what all societies know: that musicking connects people to places and to one other, gives a special hue to life events, and creates powerful continuity to collective experience and memory (Gouk 2000).

A quick characterization of a range of accounts soon brings into focus some of the problems of valuing, representing and justifying the musicking heart of music's transformative work. The accounts selected here are not intended to make a case for music's transformative work—but are based on the premise that this is a given. Moreover, while acknowledged by health-funding establishments as the 'gold standard' in health research, Quantitative/Cochrane type accounts are intentionally side-stepped here; their methodological systems may appeal to funders and medical scientists, but these very systems often themselves prevent conclusive findings about musicking's efficacy (see Vink et al 2009). Their tacit and powerful message is that methodological flaws suggest a flawed practice (DeNora 2006). However, when considered in concert with additional portrayals—such as presented below—then far richer, more complex and idiosyncratic scenarios emerge, which together suggest that no single approach is suffice. Some portrayals, however, seem more helpful in conveying the musicking heart of group musicking practices.

Four approaches (portrayed through a range of exemplars) are considered with the caveat that rather than covering the entire range, these help consider how values and practices intersect. The first is explicitly music-centred and practitioner friendly—and risks being exclusive to the music therapy profession. The second broadens the discursive territory by inviting clients to voice their experiences of music therapy. In the third—an evaluative questionnaire—pre-set values restrict spontaneity and idiosyncratic speech while enabling substantial numbers of participants to contribute to findings. Finally we have the 'external' stance—the observer's narrative from alongside the musicking event—with a distributed interest in how the musicking event transforms people and places while this is going on.

In the first approach, the music-therapeutic focus of assessment scales ensures that practitioner-specific values are privileged over criteria that may have to do with clients' lives beyond the sessions: other persons in the client's life rarely feature in such approaches.

From the start of their collaboration in the 1950s, Nordoff and Robbins developed a system of 'indexing' their session recordings. Their system (pioneering for the 1950s) ensured detailed descriptions of moment-by-moment musicking shifts, identified alongside a real-time continuum of the session. In today's methodological alertness their meticulous attentiveness to the musical flow within and between therapist and client would be described as microanalysis and thick description. Accumulated documenting of their sessions helped them to develop the Nordoff–Robbins Assessment Scales (1977). Emerging from practice, this evaluative framework provided music therapists with embedded values and criteria—as well as with a language to understand, describe, and plot clients' developments from session to session, with the use of quantifiable pegging of different levels of engagement and communication. The practice of indexing continues: practitioners combine the 'close-up' documenting of musical events (using musical notation in sketch form to document pertinent musical events) with their reflections and recalled experiences. This multi-format reflective account, informed by music therapy praxis, is explicitly (and exclusively) by (and generally but not always for) practitioners, and is restricted to what happens during music therapy time. Indexing provides a solid basis for microanalytic techniques, helping to describe ongoing musicking, and helping to underpin case study accounts (Aldridge 2004; Ansdell et al 2010; Wosch and Wigram 2007). Indexing attends closely to the musicking heart of sessions.

Other music therapy assessment scales (e.g.Bruscia 2001; Wigram 2002; Baxter et al. 2007; Pavlicevic 2007) equally ensure and convey that practitioners evaluate their work as part of 'good practice'. While focused on the musicking heart of music therapy, this is evaluated as an isolated, temporally delineated act. Arguably their function is restricted to criteria based on values that matter to practitioners: for example, 'musical communication' or 'evoked response' is not necessarily a helpful value to the teacher of children on the autistic spectrum in a busy inner city school, or to the care worker helping an isolated man with mental health problems in his supported accommodation. Also, while they make sense to music therapy practitioners, the client participant voice is absent. As stand-alone accounts these fall short of the values and demands of workplaces, and of convincing funders and co-health professionals that changes during sessions filter beyond their temporal, social and geographical delineations.

A second approach considers clients'/participants' voices through semi-structured/open-ended conversations—and inevitably whose values are represented depends on who 'tells the story'. Three examples portray a broadening narrative.

During one of the visits to a dementia residential care setting alluded to earlier, a care staff member who participated in the group music therapy session volunteers spontaneously: 'it feels like dementia gets left at the door and we get to see the real person'. Here is an astute commentary on the impact of music therapy: evidence that illness recedes and wellbeing is kindled. From her perspective, it's not the intricacies of the musicking heart that matter, but that music works and affirms her values as a care worker. 'Patients' become 'persons'—and tacitly perhaps, the care staff member experiences a parallel concurrent shift in her own self-perception and role. (A scholarly commentary could elaborate on music transforming illness identities to health identities.)

In group discussions with South African children from under-resourced areas who sing in a community choir, the children voice their values. Singing in the choir is cool, special, it's fun, it's magic, it means they make friends. The music therapists, they say, look after them, are like their parents, help them when they are down; the children learn new things in the choir, including how to behave properly. Without music, they would be lonely and sad (Pavlicevic 2010). Here are values that link music with social and cultural capital: values to do with belonging, agency, social status, and participation. Music makes a difference. No music therapy assessment scale seems as imaginative as these children's contextualized statements. Such values are accessible to scholars from a range of disciplines; from local authorities through to funders seeking to address crime and gang warfare. It is, after all, more economically viable to run a choir than to fund the judiciary, youth courts, rehabilitation centres, and prisons.

In a rather different setting, loosely structured interviews with adults with mental health problems, who attended at least 10 music therapy sessions (Ansdell and Meehan 2010), result in clients' spontaneous connections between their musicking experiences and their everyday life. They report that when playing music they develop rapport with others; playing takes their mind of their illness, shifts their mood, gives them a sense of achievement, and a feeling of their heart and whole body being creative. The clients convey their awareness of the kind of difference that musicking makes during and afterwards, not only in their bodies and minds, but also to their self-perception and sense of agency in the world. The authors frame this transformative account as 'music-health-illness narratives' situating the frame at some distance from more medical hospital-based discourses—with values that suggest a redressing of social 'flow' that illness disrupts and destabilizes.

This second approach is more collaborative, and hints at a closer fit between spontaneous musicking experiences and verbal accounts, even if, inevitably, the practitioner-authors' conveying and portraying of participants' voices on their behalf raises complexities of values and representations. One advantage of music therapists engaging in such conversations—as in all three examples—is that their skills are finely attuned to enabling optimally reciprocal, mutually created conversations. Music therapists would, on the whole, not only attend closely to the words that people use to express themselves, but be equally alert to the prosodic nuances, the expressive dimensions, and the delicate synchronies of meaning needed for as authentic and representative an account as possible. This second approach offers additional possibilities for addressing the complexities presented earlier. Any of the three examples could be positioned alongside a randomized control trial with the same set of clients, (e.g. using pre- and post-test measures for the effects of music therapy sessions), and enrich and enliven the rather distancing reporting of such studies.

The third approach is characterized by pre-structuring the values of practice through a tighter documenting format. In one study, participants respond to questionnaires, which enable large numbers of responses, helpful for 'harder' economic evaluative tasks. Here, choir members report that belonging to a choir makes a difference to their lives, makes them feel valued and cared for, as well as caring for others; membership gives them a sense of belonging, fellowship, increase in confidence and self-esteem (Clift et al. 2010). This format enables convincing testing of values not dissimilar to those voiced spontaneously by the South African school children. While the cost of this more distant representation of group musicking is the loss of spontaneity and idiosyncratic descriptions, the gains are that quantifiably powerful statements signal how people's lives are changed through musicking. Economists and policy makers are likely to take note, while practitioners and participants are likely to be encouraged by strong outcomes.

Finally we have the 'external' account—that of the observer positioned alongside or outside (if watching recordings) the musicking event. What possibilities here for conveying the social-musical topographical flow, from its musical source to and from the people in that place at that time? In a sociologically informed study of music provision in a hospital ward (Batt-Rawden et al. 2007), a panorama of social-musicking is conveyed through the mind of the note-taker. Here are details of how people participate and are brought together towards a collective social musicking experience. Rather like the vignette in this chapter, the moment-by-moment description conveys what happens to the people and place during this unfolding event. However, were its purpose to clarify how music as a distinctive phenomenon works with and between people, then the musicking heart, and participants' voices, would feel thinly represented.

These four approaches return us to one of the opening considerations of this chapter: how can the musicking heart remain the focus of any music therapy account (whether the format is evaluative, theory-building, anecdotal; whether its purpose is economic, political, or scholarly) while not neglecting participants' voices, and while also attending to the interests of scientific, economic or professional values. Is this an unending dilemma? If we return to the Vignette, we can imagine all approaches complementing one another: a music therapy assessment scale used together with Dementia Care Mapping exercise hopes to make a case for music therapy addressing the needs of people with dementia. In addition, the music therapist's practice-specific indexing and documenting together signal good practice—and portray the practice's musicking heart. Representational ballast could be added by interview/questionnaires targeting care home residents, care staff, managers, and family members. Together, these formats could be underpinned by clear considerations and delineations regarding what values need representing, for whom, by whom and for what purpose.

This chapter concludes with considering one ambitious and rather costly endeavour by a group of music therapy practitioner-researchers who together studied Community Music Therapy practices in four countries, and called their final product, simply, 'Where Music Helps'. This title acknowledges that, as practitioners, they know that music does help, and that it helps in situated contexts when values embedded in the sociocultural practice milieus are respected and acknowledged (Stige et al. 2010). The agreed methods for documenting and representing this work emerged after extensive deliberations and negotiations between the researchers, on-site practitioners and participants concerning 'what matters to whom, where, why and when'. A crucial aspect of this long-term study was the need for trust: that the portrayals of the practices would resonate with participants' experiences.

The researchers' participation included being musicians, interviewers, observers, listeners, thinkers, and music therapists. They were positioned inside, alongside and outside the musicking events, as well as before, during and after, through ongoing engagement with people and places over a period of some 4 years. Unsurprisingly, these multiple research roles and tasks were immensely complicated to draw together into a coherent narrative, especially since the group's stance was to resist imposing methodological or theoretical frames onto the events studied, but instead to allow for such 'framings' to emerge from the direct experiencing and documenting of practices. The product of this intricate endeavour is a narrative with multiple descriptive viewpoints and voices, with a range of group music therapy practices portrayed through accounts that draw from musical, psychological, sociological, philosophical, and anthropological discourses and knowledge worlds. The deliberately open-ended narrative ranges from the micro-close-up moment by moment descriptions of group musicking, to people talking about their direct experiences, to people outside the events commenting on the impact of these events on places and people. The intended audience for this account includes readers alongside as well as those fairly distant from music therapy practices and values. What such a narrative does not set out to do is to convince *that* musicking works. Rather it conveys *how* musicking works, with whom, in which places. And who's doing the talking.

To conclude, group music therapy work invites ongoing, fluid, spontaneous, musicking actions from all, enabling a redressing, repairing, adjusting, and enhancing of shared vital flowing between and within persons. Music's structure offers purposeful direction and momentum—even if people are unable to move or remember songs or know who they are. Shared participative musicking reconfigures illness-defined identity (of therapist, patient, care-worker); transforming these into musician, leader, soloist, listener, accompanist, dancer, singer, drummer, or conductor. Moreover, shared participative musicking is fun! Magic Moments signal that music is doing its powerful transformative work, and for the magic of such work to be understood, a complementary range of accounts are needed. While the musicking heart of group music therapy work needs to beat strongly in some accounts, the idiosyncratic voices of those it serves need preserving, alongside the more economically powerful methods that transform musicking experiences into disembodied data mass. There is no single set of values that best presents music's impact on people's lives. Rather, the intricacies of musical representations and of people's experiences need to be respected: all are part of the vast representational mosaic that helps us to understand how music transforms lives.

References

Aldridge, D. (1996). *Music Therapy Research and Practice in Medicine*. London: Jessica Kingsley Publishers.

Aldridge, D. (ed). (2004). *Case Study Design in Music Therapy*. London: Jessica Kingsley Publishers.

Ansdell, G. (1995). *Music for Life: Aspects of Creative Music Therapy with Adult Clients*. London: Jessica Kingsley Publishers.

Ansdell, G. (1996). Talking about music therapy: A dilemma and a qualitative experiment. *British Journal of Music Therapy*, **10**, 4–16.

Ansdell, G. (2002). Community music therapy and the winds of change. In: C. Kenny and B. Stige (ed.) *Contemporary Voices in Music Therapy: Communication, Culture and Community*, pp. 109–43. Oslo: Unipub Forlag.

Ansdell, G. (2003). Community music therapy: 'Big British balloon' or future international trend? In: *Community, Relationship and Spirit: Continuing the Dialogue and debate, BSMT and AMPT Annual Conference*, February 2003. London: British Society of Music Therapy Publications.

Ansdell, G. and Pavlicevic, M. (2005). Musical companionship, musical community. Music therapy and the process and value of musical communication. In: D. Miell, R.A.R. MacDonald, and D. J. Hargreaves (ed.) *Musical Communication*, pp. 193–213. New York: Oxford University Press.

Ansdell, G. (2006). Response to Tia DeNora 'Evidence and effectiveness in music therapy'. *British Journal of Music Therapy*, **20**(2), 96–9.

Ansdell, G. and Meehan, J. (2010). 'Some Light at the End of the Tunnel' Exploring Users' Evidence for the Effectiveness of Music Therapy in Adult Mental Health Settings. *Music and Medicine*, **2**(1): 29–40.

Batt-Rawden, K., Trythall, S., and DeNora, T. (2007). Health Musicking as Cultural Inclusion. In: J. Edwards (ed.) *Music: Promoting Health and Creating Community in Healthcare Contexts*, pp. 64–82. Newcastle: Cambridge Scholars.

Baxter, H.T., Berghofer, J.A., Macewan, L., Nelson, J., Peters, K., and Roberts, P. (2007). The Individualized Music Therapy Assessment Profile, *IMTAP*. London: Jessica Kingsley Publishers.

Bradley, B. (2005). *Psychology and Experience*. Cambridge: Cambridge University Press.

Bruscia, K. (2001). A qualitative approach to analyzing client improvisations. *Music Therapy Perspectives*, **19**(1), 7–21.

Bunt, L. (1994). *Music Therapy: An Art Beyond Words*. London: Routledge.

Campbell, A., and McNamara, O. (2007). Ways of Telling. The use of practitioners' stories. In: A. Campbell and S. Groundwater-Smith (eds.) *An Ethical Approach to Practitioner Research*, pp. 99–112. London and New York: Routledge.

Clift, S., Hancox, G., Morrison, I., Hess, B., Kreutz, G., and Stewart, D. (2010). Choral singing and psychological wellbeing: Quantitative and qualitative findings from English choirs in a cross-national survey. *Journal of Applied Arts and Health*, **1**(1) 19–34.

Condon, W.S. and Ogston, W.D. (1966). Sound film analysis of normal and pathological behaviour patterns, *Journal of Nervous and Mental Diseases*, **143**(4), 338–47.

Cook, N. (1998). *Music: A Very Short Introduction*. Oxford: Oxford University Press.

Czikszentmihalyi, M. (1997). *Living Well: The Psychology of Everyday Life*. London: Phoenix.

Darnley-Smith, R. and. Patey, H.M (2003). *Music Therapy* London: Sage.

Davidson, J.W. (2005). Bodily communication in musical performance. In: D. Miell, R.A.R. MacDonald, and D.J. Hargreave (eds.) *Musical Communication*, pp. 215–38. Oxford: University Press.

Davidson, J., and Malloch, S. (2009). Musical communication: The body movements of performance. In: S. Malloch and C. Trevarthen (eds.) *Communicative musicality – Exploring the basis of human companionship*, pp. 565–83. Oxford: Oxford University Press.

Davidson, J.W. and Good, J.M.M. (2002). Social and musical co-ordination between members of a sting quartet: An exploratory study. *Psychology of Music*, **30**, 186–201.

Daykin, N. (2007). Context, culture and risk: Towards an understanding of the impact of music in health care settings. In: J. Edwards (ed.) *Music: Promoting Health and Creating Community in Healthcare Contexts*, pp. 83–104. Newcastle: Cambridge Scholars.

DeNora, T. (2003). *After Adorno. Rethinking Music Sociology*. Cambridge: Cambridge University Press.

DeNora, T. (2006). Evidence and effectiveness in music therapy. *British Journal of Music Therapy*, **20** (2), 81–93.

Dissanayake, E. (2001). An ethological view of music and its relevance to music therapy. *Nordic Journal of Music Therapy*, **10**(2), 159–75.

Dissanayake, E. (2009). Root, leaf, blossom, or bole: Concerning the origin and adaptive function of music. In: S.N. Malloch, and C. Trevarthen (eds.) *Communicative Musicality*, pp. 17–30. Oxford: Oxford University Press.

Edwards, J. and Hadley, S. (2007). Expanding music therapy practice: incorporating the feminist frame. *The Arts in Psychotherapy*, **34**(3), 199–207.

Elliot, D. (1995). *Music Matters: A New Philosophy of Music Education*. Oxford: Oxford University Press.

Ehrenreich, B. (2007). *Dancing in the Streets. A History of Collective Joy*. London: Granta Books.

Gouk, P. (ed.) (2000). *Musical Healing in Cultural Contexts*. Aldershot: Ashgate.

Malloch, S. N. (2000). Mothers and infants and communicative musicality. *Musicae Scientiae* (Special Issue 1999–2000), 29–58.

Malloch, S.N. and Trevarthen, C. (eds.) (2009). *Communicative Musicality*. Oxford: Oxford University Press.

Nordoff, P. and Robbins, C. (2007). *Creative Music Therapy: A Guide to Fostering Clinical Musicianship* (2nd edn.). Gilsum NH: Barcelona Publishers.

Pavlicevic, M. (1991). Music in Communication: Improvisation in Music Therapy. Unpublished PhD. Edinburgh: University of Edinburgh.

Pavlicevic, M. (1997). *Music Therapy in Context*. London: Jessica Kingsley Publishers.

Pavlicevic, M. (1999). *Music Therapy Intimate Notes*. London: Jessica Kingsley Publishers.

Pavlicevic, M. (2000), Improvisation in Music Therapy: Human Communication in Sound. *Journal of Music Therapy*, **XXXVII**(4), 269–85.

Pavlicevic, M. (2007). The Music Interaction Rating Scale (Schizophrenia) (MIR(S)): microanalysis of co-improvisation in music therapy with adults suffering from chronic schizophrenia. In: T. Wosch and T. Wigram (eds.) *Microanalysis in Music Therapy*, pp. 174–85, London: Jessica Kingsley Publishers.

Pavlicevic, M. (2010). Reflection: Let the music work: Optimal moments of collaborative musicking. In: B. Stige, G. Ansdell, C. Elefant and M. Pavlicevic. *Where Music Helps: Community Music Therapy in Action and Reflection*, pp. 99–112. Aldershot, Ashgate.

Pavlicevic, M. and Ansdell, G. (2004). *Community Music Therapy*. London: Jessica Kingsley Publishers.

Pavlicevic, M. and Ansdell, G. (2009). Between communicative musicality and collaborative musicking; A perspective from community music therapy. In: S.N. Malloch and C. Trevarthen (eds.) *Communicative Musicality*. pp. 357–76. Oxford: Oxford University Press.

Pavlicevic, M., Ansdell, G., Procter, S. and Hickey, S. (2009). *Presenting the Evidence: A Guide for Music Therapists Responding to the Demands of Clinical Effectiveness and Evidence-Based Practice*. London: Nordoff Robbins.

Rolvsjord, R. (2004). Therapy as empowerment: clinical and political implications of empowerment philosophy in mental health practices of music therapy, *Nordic Journal of Music Therapy*, **13**(2), 99–111.

Sawyer, R.K (2003). *Group Creativity: Music, Theater, Collaboration*. London: New Erlbaum.

Sawyer, R.K. (2005). Music and conversation. In: D. Miell, R.A.R. MacDonald and D.J. Hargreaves (eds.) *Musical Communication*, pp. 45–60. Oxford: Oxford University Press.

Stern, D. (1985). *The Interpersonal World of the Infant*. New York: Basic Books.

Stern, D. (2004). *The Present Moment in Psychotherapy and Everyday Life*. New York: Norton.

Stern, D.N. (2010). *Forms of Vitality: Exploring Dynamic Experience in Psychology, the Arts, Psychotherapy, and Development*. Oxford: Oxford University Press.

Stige, B. (2002). *Culture-Centred Music Therapy*. Gilsum, NH: Barcelona Publishing.

Stige, B. (2003). *Elaborations towards a Notion of Community Music Therapy, Dr. Art*. Oslo: University of Oslo.

Stige, B., Ansdell, G., Elefant, C. and Pavlicevic, M. (2010). *Where Music Helps: Community Music Therapy in Action and Reflection*. Aldershot: Ashgate.

Trevarthen, C. and Malloch, S.N. (2000). The dance of wellbeing: Defining the musical therapeutic effect. *Nordic Journal of Music Therapy*, **9**(2), 3–17.

White, M. (2009). *Arts Development in Community Health – A Social Tonic*. Oxford: Radcliffe Publishing.

Vink, A., Birks, J., Bruinsma, M., and Scholten, R.J.P.M. (2009). Music therapy for people with dementia (Review). *The Cochrane Library*, **1**, 1–22.

Wigram, T. (2002). Indications in music therapy: evidence from assessment that can identify the expectations of music therapy as a treatment for autistic spectrum disorder (ASD); meeting the challenge of evidence based practice. *British Journal of Music Therapy*, **16**(1), 11–28.

Wigram, T. (2004). *Improvisation: Methods and Techniques for Music Therapy Clinicians, Educators and Students*. London: Jessica Kingsley Publishers.

Wigram, T. (2006), Response to Tia DeNora 'Evidence and effectiveness in music therapy'. *British Journal of Music Therapy*, **20**(2), 93–6.

Wigram, T., and Elefant, C. (2009). Therapeutic dialogues in music: Nurturing musicality of communication in children with autistic spectrum disorder and Rett syndrome. In: S. Malloch and C. Trevarthen (eds.) *Communicative musicality: Exploring the basis of human companionship*, pp. 423–45. Oxford: Oxford University Press.

Chapter 16

Aspects of Theory and Practice in Dance Movement Psychotherapy in the UK: Similarities and Differences from Music Therapy

Vicky Karkou

Introduction

Dance Movement Psychotherapy (DMP)[1] is the youngest of the arts therapies[2] with practitioners coming together to form the first professional association in the discipline in the UK in 1982, less than 30 years ago (Karkou and Sanderson 2006). This first group became the Association for Dance Movement Therapy (currently the Association for Dance Movement Psychotherapy UK—ADMP UK) with Helen Payne being the first chair. In comparison, music therapy (MT) for example, was first organized as a professional group as early as 1958 by Juliette Alvin; almost 25 years before DMP. DMP is therefore a relatively new profession which is currently used in clinical and non-clinical settings with a wide range of client groups (e.g. people with mental health problems, learning disabilities, and medical and/or complex conditions). Although research evidence regarding its effectiveness is growing (Karkou 2009, 2010; Meekums 2009; Rohrich 2009; see also Quiroga Murcia and Kreutz, Chapter 10, this volume), there is still limited public awareness about what and who DMP is for, what DMP practitioners do and why.

Within the arts therapies field, practitioners agree that DMP has a lot in common with the other arts therapies. According to Waller (Waller 1997, cited in ADMT UK 1997, p. 15) for example, all arts therapies share enough between them to be joined together 'as a single professional body for regulatory purposes'. This position has led to the registration of arts therapists in the same part of the register of the Health Professions Council (HPC), the regulatory body of health professions that is responsible for setting standards of practice and protecting the public.[3] However, until recently clarifying the particular areas that are shared amongst arts therapists has received very little attention; similarly what is distinctive and unique remains unclear.

In this chapter I will, therefore, aim to highlight some similarities and differences between DMP and the other arts therapies. I will pay attention to DMP and MT as two particularly affiliated disciplines, and draw, in the first instance, upon existing definitions of the two disciplines.

---

[1] In the UK, the discipline is also known as dance movement therapy. Different names are used in different parts of the world. For example, in the USA the term dance/movement therapy is preferred, while in certain parts of Europe the discipline is referred to as dance therapy.

[2] The other three are music, drama, and art therapy.

[3] At the time of writing this paper, the Association for Dance Movement Psychotherapy UK (ADMP UK) has been in the process of completing its registration with HPC as the fourth arts therapy joining the same location of the register that use the umbrella term: 'arts therapies'.

I will also discuss historical influences, key concepts, and principles of theory and practice that I regard as pertinent to both disciplines. Findings from a survey of arts therapists (drama, dance movement, music, and art therapists) registered with their professional associations in the UK (Karkou 1998; Karkou and Sanderson 2006) will offer some empirical support to this discussion. It is worth noting that findings from the particular study have already informed the development of benchmark statements for arts therapies (QAA/NHS 2004). As such this chapter will make interesting links with UK policy and expected best practice. Given this all-inclusive-arts therapies starting point, even if my focus will remain primarily upon DMP and MT, other arts therapies will also be mentioned where appropriate.

Definitions

DMP is defined by the UK professional association as:

> ... the psychotherapeutic use of movement and dance through which a person can engage creatively in a process to further their emotional, cognitive, physical and social integration
>
> (ADMK UK 2010, p. 1).

Central to this definition is the role of 'movement and dance'. However, as the definition suggests, DMP is not merely about a creative engagement with the medium. Movement and dance are used in a 'psychotherapeutic' manner having a wide, albeit clear, therapeutic direction. This definition implies that DMP is different from dance as an art form, different from community dance and/or dance education. It also highlights links with psychotherapy. These links are not tenuous. Both this definition as well as the recent change of the name of the discipline from Dance Movement Therapy to Dance Movement Psychotherapy[4] suggests that a large number of practitioners define their practice as a form of psychotherapy.

It is interesting that in the description of MT offered by the Association of Professional Music Therapists (APMT), a similar value is placed on ideas and principles stemming from psychotherapy. For example, there is an acknowledgement that there are a number of different approaches to MT but: 'Fundamental to all approaches . . . is the development of a relationship between the client and therapist' (APMT 2010, p. 1) with music-making being the medium through which this relationship is formed. Although within the British MT literature the term Music Psychotherapy is not that widely used, dance movement psychotherapists and music therapists, along with the other arts therapists, are currently considered as psychotherapists for banding and salary purposes within the National Health Service (NHS 2010).

The similarity between the two definitions offers a first indication that both DMP and MT share some common ground. References to aspects of the history of the two disciplines will bring to the foreground further similarities and highlight differences as we will see in the following section.

Historical influences

I find that a number of factors enabled the emergence of DMP and MT as modern professions. A first strong influence comes from movements within the arts. Such movements for example, have

---

[4] The change of the name from the Association for Dance Movement Therapy UK (ADMT UK) to the Association for Dance Movement Psychotherapy UK (ADMP UK) has taken place in June 2008. This change corresponds to a respective change of the name of the discipline from a number of DMP practitioners. Still however, the old name (i.e. dance movement therapy) persists and can be found in publications, websites and some practitioners' professional titles.

advocated a shift away from the creation of highly stylized artistic products of the classical era. Halprin (2003) argues that modernism did exactly this, shifted the attention of the artist to natural expressions. She uses a number of examples to illustrate this point. From dance she draws upon Isadora Duncan, the mother of modern dance, who introduced natural movements as a way of abandoning the highly technical ballet vocabulary, while in music she refers to John Cage, who introduced experimentation in silence and sound. Halprin (2003) continues that postmodernism has shifted the process even further away from classical and stylized expressions to questioning them as 'grand narratives'[5] and as such valuing the small, the personal, and mundane.

Furthermore, within shifts away from the supremacy of the artist and towards exploring 'natural' and/or 'personal' artistic expressions, permission has been given to both artists and non-artists alike to engage with arts-making processes. This, in turn, has supported artists working in the community and in hospitals and has given rise to movements such as 'the arts for all' and 'the arts for health' (Waller 1991; Bunt, 1994). These movements have highlighted social action, active engagement for all and have had a strong impact on the democratization of the arts (Landy 2001). Karkou and Sanderson (2006) argue that such movements have also offered a significant leverage to the emergence of arts therapies.

Other important starting points for the arts therapies have come from:

- Occupational therapists and the rehabilitation movement for veterans after the Second World War.
- Psychiatrists and psychotherapists valuing the power of the arts as alternative means of communication with patients who were difficult to engage in verbal or other type of therapy, and
- Arts educators finding that child-centred education was largely about children's emotional and social being and as such very closely linked to therapy.

(Karkou and Sanderson 2006.)

Over the years, attempts have been made to bring the different arts therapies together. For example a movement for the study of all four arts therapies was initiated in 1977 by Anthony Storr (1920–2001) and was connected with the Sesame Institute (Jones 1996). However, these movements were not fruitful. Separate developments remained the norm and continue to be so, despite the fact that, as I mentioned before, arts therapists are currently registered under the same professional umbrella within HPC. In order to achieve their registration, they are also expected to have been educated in validated and accredited 2-year Masters programmes that are often located at a university and/or receive validation from a higher education institution.

Next to these common starting points, in the case of DMP and MT it is also interesting to highlight a few key differences, as I see them.

The role dance as an art form has played in the UK has been very different from music. The former has traditionally held a less prominent place than the latter. This has impacted upon the development of DMP and MT respectively with the former, for example, being delayed in reaching the point of professionalization (see earlier comments regarding 25 years of difference between founding the professional association in DMP compared to MT). Karkou and Sanderson (2006) trace negative connotations associated with dance and the use of the body from ideas originated

---

[5] This is a term first introduced by Lyotard (1979) in his seminal book *The Postmodern Condition*, and referred to cohesive explanations of historical events but also of knowledge as a whole. A meta narrative or grand narrative is often associated with modernity, while postmodern positioning often implies questioning such cohesive and all encompassing explanations of the world as leading to exclusion of difference. Instead, 'micronarratives' are valued in ways in which different perspectives and thus different 'truths' can coexist.

by Plato. In the Middle Ages the same ideas were adopted by Christianity and further highlighted in the Renaissance era by Descartes' dualism. Looking at recent times, Sanderson (1996, 2001) and Meekums (2000) argue that negative connotations of dance can also be linked with the perception of dance as a primarily female and thus frivolous activity. It is possible that the growth of feminism and feminist studies, input from social and humanistic psychology (e.g. in Gestalt, see Perls et al. 1969), body psychotherapy (e.g. Reich 1960), as well as recent challenges of the Cartesian dualism by neuroscience (Rizzolatti et al. 1996; Damasio 2000, 2005; Gazzola et al. 2006) have offered new ways of looking at and perceiving the body, movement, and dance. This, in turn, has direct implications for the value placed not only on dance as an art form but also on applied uses of dance and movement as is the case with therapy.

Still, the change of the name of the discipline from Dance Movement Therapy to Dance Movement Psychotherapy in 2008 (ADMT UK 2007a,b) indicated a further need for value and recognition. Arguments put forward for the change of the name of the discipline from 'therapy' to 'psychotherapy' included the idea that as a form of psychotherapy it can be taken seriously. It is interesting that lengthy discussions preceded this change with arguments put forward to remove the word 'dance' from the title of the discipline altogether. Although this change was finally outvoted, the discussion itself can be seen as an indication that negative connotations associated with dance still persist.

In contrast, I find that music has had a very different reception. Within the twentieth century, for example, physicians have seen music as an agent for benign and potentially therapeutic outcomes. Both Bunt (1994) and Tyler (2000) testify how this has led to extensive experimental work on the 'sedative' effects of music, while encouraging the use of music as a recreational activity within hospital environments. Although similar uses of dance in hospitals have been reported (Meier 2008), it is possible that they have not received as much attention as music-related activities. Moreover, to date, I have found that hospital-based work remains a less accessible place for dance movement psychotherapists (Karkou 1998). Rather, there are strong influences upon the field from educational dance and Laban (Payne 1992). It is possible that within mainstream and special schools dance movement psychotherapists found more receptive colleagues who understood the need to address the child as a whole and attempt to support his/her emotional and social needs through movement and dance (Karkou and Sanderson 2000, 2001).

Key features of current practice

A study of professional definitions and relevant literature in the arts therapies has revealed that there are some key features of current practice shared across disciplines (Karkou and Sanderson 2006). These features seem to be common for all arts therapies and include:

+ The role of the arts within sessions.
+ The role of creativity.
+ Imagery, symbolism, and metaphor.
+ Non-verbal communication.

Although the list is not exhausted, I find these ideas to be particularly important for both DMP and MT practice.[6]

---

[6] Note that all arts therapies also rely heavily on the development of a therapeutic relationship, a clear therapeutic contract with a more or less explicit aim/s and an ongoing evaluation of the therapeutic process and outcomes. Some of these ideas are embedded in the therapeutic frameworks adopted by practitioners and discussed in the following section.

The role of the arts

Within both DMP and MT, movement/dance and music are seen as key agents for therapeutic change and are defined in a very wide manner. Music-making may refer to a piece of music with a clearly organized form, but more often it refers to the client striking a drum or making noise in what can be seen as a random way (Pavlicevic 1997). Similarly, in DMP dance can be associated with people potentially engaging in both clearly defined and highly choreographed pieces as well as in looking at the meaning of gestures, postures or simple movement (Payne 1992). As mentioned earlier, this way of defining music and dance fits within modern and even more within postmodern practices in the arts as:

1) It allows for both the skilful and unskilled to be present.

2) It leads to inclusive (both . . .. and. . .) rather than exclusive (either . . . or . . .) practices.
   Other important aspects of the role of the arts within arts therapies as I see them are:

♦ Practitioners seem to pay attention to the arts-making process as opposite to attending to the artistic outcome (Bunt 1994; Landy 2001; Shreeves 2006).

♦ There is an underlying belief that engagement in the arts stems from an early pre-verbal place and as such constitutes a deeply felt form of knowing (Payne 1992; Pavlicevic 1997). These ideas echo views in child psychology (Trevarthen and Aitken 2001), in body psychotherapy (Reich 1960) and in recent findings from neuroscience (Rizzolatti et al. 1996; Damasio 2000, 2005; Gazzola et al. 2006).

♦ There is an assumption that the arts involve the person as a whole (Bruscia 1988; Dosamantes-Beaudry 1997).

♦ The arts can be powerful; as such they can lead to transformative or even potentially damaging results, especially in the case of vulnerable clients (Karkou and Glasman 2004). The need for appropriate arts therapies training is therefore often highlighted (Payne 1992; Bunt 1994; Karkou and Sanderson 2006).

Creativity

Creativity is so central to the field that arts therapies are also known as 'creative arts therapies'. I have defined creativity elsewhere (Karkou and Sanderson 2006, p. 53) as 'the capacity to find new and unexpected connections, new relationships and therefore new meanings' (adapted from Stanton-Jones 1992 and Smitskamp 1995). Based on this definition, creativity does not require originality and/or something entirely new but relies on what is already in place. In arts therapies creativity is therefore, seen as a capacity that can be cultivated in all and can be therapeutic in itself. Winnicott (1971) for example values the therapeutic potential of creativity so much that regards it as an indicator of mental health. Finding ways in which to support clients to engage with artistic media 'creatively' is an important part of the therapeutic process in all arts therapies including DMP and MT. For example, offering a safe and non-judgemental environment is important for creativity to emerge. As Malchiodi (1998) argues, creating such an environment is an essential part of the role of the arts therapist.

Closely linked with creativity are some other important features of arts therapies, that is, imagery, symbolism, and metaphor.

Imagery

First of all, imagery refers to inner representations of objects and events that are created at will (Walrond-Skinner 1986). I find that imagery is often used in connection with imagination.

As Gordon (1987) puts it, the two terms have a similar relationship as still pictures have with moving pictures, i.e. a film. Imagery provides the still pictures, while imagination stands for the whole of the film. And similar with watching a film, through imagination, people can experience and enjoy an 'inner film', while at the same time be able to critically evaluate it.

Within DMP, imagination is supported in a number of ways. Dosamantes-Alperson (1981) suggests some essential steps to activate kinetic imagination that involve:

♦ Becoming receptive through relaxation.

♦ Paying attention to subtle physical sensations.

♦ Allowing the imagination to unfold in movement, and

♦ Eventually finding words to discuss these experiences.

Similar steps towards engaging clients' imagination can also be seen in Bonny's (1994) approach to MT known as Guided Imagery and Music (GIM). However, unlike the active engagement of the client in the movement-making process in DMP, in GIM the therapist plays recorded music to the client. Still, clients' own response to the music and their imaginative process is placed in the centre of the process as a transformative experience.

Symbolism

While imagination is often associated with internal and intrapersonal processes, I see symbolism as referring more readily to relational/interpersonal processes. Walrond-Skinner (1986, p. 338) defines it as: '. . . the representation of an . . . idea or wish . . . by something else that either possesses analogous qualities or comes to stand for this idea or wish due to consistent associations.'

Understanding the meaning of symbols is important within the therapeutic process (Pavlicevic 1997) and can be explored in a number of different ways. For example, through:

1) Social and/or cultural conventions; for example through using Freudian or Jungian theory, or

2) What Jones (1996) calls a 'local dictionary', that is the phenomenological experience of the client in the particular time and place.

While the first type of meaning is often associated with a search for 'universal' truths, the second tends to value to specific, the personal and the 'unique truth' of the client's experience there and then.

Metaphor

Metaphor is also an important concept for arts therapists to such an extent that Meekums (2002) for example, places it at the heart of DMP practice as a central tool. According to Walrond-Skinner (1986) metaphor is defined as follows:

> Metaphor is an indirect method of communication by which two discrete elements are juxtaposed, the comparison between the two serving to create new meanings… Within symbolism, the symbol represents something else; with a metaphor it is said to be something else
>
> (Walrond-Skinner 1986, p. 213).

I find symbolism and metaphor as relevant to both DMP and MT practice because:

♦ They allow for 'as if' situations to emerge which are less threatening than dealing with the actual problem.

♦ They allow for unearthing deeply rooted issues and/or problems.

- They encourage people to engage with abstract thinking and elusiveness which can be useful for people who operate with concrete thinking only.
- They allow for multiple meaning to emerge as they lend themselves for several readings of the same thing.
- They are closely linked with creativity and thus can enable creative solutions to emerge.

Non-verbal communication

Focusing on body postures and gestures as well as the moving body is central to DMP because of its potential to communicate without using words. Similarly, the use of music, sound, or vocalizations can be the main emphasis of the music therapist as a means for non-verbal communication. This has already been explored in other chapters in this book (e.g. Quiroga Murcia and Kreutz, Chapter 10). I find that in both DMP and MT as well as the other arts therapies, non-verbal communication can take place in three levels:

- The internal, which deals with emotions and intrapersonal processes within the person and it is closely linked with imagery and imagination.
- The dyadic, which deals with two people interacting and thus the interpersonal; in the case of arts therapies this interaction often relies on symbols, metaphors, and other creative/artistic media.
- The group, which refers to social processes, may have a regulatory or preservation function and a sense of direction; in arts therapies group non-verbal communication also relies heavily on artistic, creative, symbolic and/or metaphoric communication.

In all cases particular attention is paid not only on what the content of this communication is but also how this communication takes place. Dance movement psychotherapists for example, often refer to Laban's term 'effort' which stands for the quality of one's movement and refers to the emotional intention associated with this movement (Koch and Brauninger 2006; Koch and Bender 2007). Effort is about how something is carried out rather than what is done. Similar attention to the quality of the musical interaction can take place within MT; this interaction can lead to a musical dialogue and form the basis for a client–therapist relationship. The way the artistic interaction unfolds, the relationship is understood and the therapeutic process is guided and safeguarded relies heavily on adopting therapeutically sound frameworks.

Therapeutic frameworks

Looking at the different therapeutic frameworks available in the arts therapies literature, it is clear that there is an enormous amount of diversity. In an attempt to identify common patterns of practice as they emerged from the field and discover important differences, a survey of practitioners in the UK has been completed (Karkou 1998; Karkou and Sanderson 2006). The survey used a questionnaire that was developed based on interviews with 12 'key informants', that is, experts from the four disciplines of arts therapies. Statements collected from these interviews referred to theory, clinical methodology and assessment/evaluation and comprised a large part of the questionnaire. The questionnaire was subsequently disseminated to all registered arts therapists in the UK (N=580, a response rate of 39% of the total population).

Six therapeutic trends were revealed as relevant to all arts therapists:

- Humanistic
- Eclectic/integrative

- Psychoanalytic/psychodynamic
- Developmental
- Artistic/creative
- Active/directive.

These trends were the result of statistical analysis of 580 responses of practising arts therapists to more than 100 statements rated on a scale of 1–5 (5=strongly agree to 1=strongly disagree); factor analysis was performed on these items that related to theory, clinical methodology, and assessment/evaluation. Although all six factors that emerged from the factor analysis received high scores, the factors I named humanistic, eclectic/integrative, and psychoanalytic/psychodynamic were particular relevant to both DMP respondents (7.1% of the total sample) and MT respondents (21%). Certain characteristics of all of these groups of statements (factors) and their corresponding therapeutic trends are presented in the following sections.

Humanistic

Examples of the statements included in the humanistic factor are:

- 'What I am working towards is a sense of self-responsibility.'
- 'The purpose of the therapy has to do with the 'wholeness.'
- 'One of my fundamental hypotheses is that there is a strong body-mind relationship.'
- 'I am trying to respond with my whole self.'

(Karkou and Sanderson 2006, p. 77.)

These statements appeared to be closely connected with the humanistic school of thought and received strong agreement amongst both DMP and MT respondents. This was in accordance with DMP literature that makes regular references to child-centred education and ideas that value wholeness and the body–mind relationship (Karkou and Sanderson 2006). 'Humanistic-oriented therapists' (dance movement or verbal psychotherapists alike) often talk about the need to follow the lead of the client and create an 'I-You' or 'real' relationship (Clarkson 1994, p. 37), that is a relationship between the client and therapists that has an equal power dynamic and is guided by mutual respect. Clear links between this 'humanistic' trend and DMP practice can be found in the approach developed by Marion Chace (Chaiklin and Schmais 1986) who, at the time when DMP was emerging as a separate discipline in the USA, was strongly influenced by Sullivan, the founder of interpersonal psychotherapy. Her work was closely connected with patients faced with long-term mental health problems such as schizophrenia and lengthy institutionalization. Given the influence of humanistic thinking upon Chace's work, dance was perceived as expressing an innate need to communicate and thus the aim of therapy was to enable such communication to take place.

In MT literature, references to humanistic therapeutic frameworks can also be found. Bunt (1994) for example, acknowledges that his approach is closely linked with humanistic thinking. He also argues that humanistic/existential ideas are particularly relevant to working with people with terminal illnesses, cancer and so on.

Psychoanalytic/psychodynamic

Next to humanistic thinking, psychoanalytic/psychodynamic ideas are also strongly influential upon DMP and MT practice. For example, some of the statements that fell under the psychoanalytic/psychodynamic factor are:

- 'I do analyse in a psychoanalytic way.'

- ◆ 'I am trying to link the client's past with their present lives.'
- ◆ 'I am looking at the transference between client and therapist.'
- ◆ 'Psychoanalytic theory provides me with an explanation of what is going on in the session.'

(Karkou and Sanderson 2006, p. 79.)

For dance movement psychotherapists, acknowledging unconscious processes and encouraging the client to work with their inner self has been introduced by Mary Whitehouse (1979), originally a dance teacher and Jungian analyst who adopted and adapted key Jungian ideas for movement experiences. Mary Whitehouse (1979) encouraged kinaesthetic awareness, worked with polarities, supported active imagination and authentic movement and highlighted the therapeutic relationship and intuition. The links of this work with Jung are very clear.

Since Whitehouse's time there are further and diverse influences from the psychoanalytic/psychodynamic school of thought upon DMP practice. There are approaches that combine movement analysis and psychoanalytic thinking (Kestenberg 1975), movement patterns and object relations theory (Siegel 1984), in group work (Sandel and Johnson 1983) or in individual therapy (Penfield 1992). In all cases, the 'transferential' relationship is valued as one that enables clients to relive and rework older ways of relating to significant others in the safety of therapy (Clarkson 1994, p. 32).

Very similar to the input made by Mary Whitehouse in DMP has been the input of Mary Priestley in MT. Priestley (1975, 1995) was amongst the first music therapists to seek conceptual understanding of her work through a psychoanalytic perspective. Although her approach, known as analytical MT, became more popular in the USA, in the UK it triggered a number of different developments that have clear references to psychoanalytic/psychodynamic thinking (e.g. Levinge 1993; Odell-Miller 2000, 2002).

Developmental

In the survey of practitioners referred to here, a broad developmental therapeutic framework also emerged as relevant to the work of arts therapists. For example, statements like the following emerged:

- ◆ 'I hold developmental stage in mind most of the time.'
- ◆ 'The objectives are linked to the developmental stage the client is at.'

(Karkou and Sanderson 2006, p. 83.)

The developmental framework seems to be in accordance to relevant literature in DMP which highlights strong influences from Laban and Laban-based models of movement development (Laban 1975; Sherborne 1990). Developmental models can also be found extensively within MT; the focus in this case is often on musical development, drawing from existing models in music education or music psychology (e.g. Hargreaves 1982; Swanwick and Tillman 1986).

Both dance movement psychotherapists and music therapist also appeared to draw upon early psychoanalytic/psychodynamic models of development as a way of understanding their work with their clients. For example, Kestenberg (1975) looks at Laban's movement framework and connects it with Freudian psychosexual development; Siegel (1984) draws upon object relations theory and Klein in particular for her developmental DMP approach; while Levinge (1993) relies on Winnicott for her understanding of the MT process with her work with children. In these cases, either offering 'reparation' or a 'developmentally-appropriate' relationship becomes the aim of the therapeutic process (Clarkson 1994, p. 34).

Artistic/creative

Artistic/creative ideas seemed to also remain strongly embedded within arts therapies practice with statements like the following emerging:

- 'The therapeutic process is always about encouraging clients to do something.'
- 'I try to enable clients to really engage with the art process as fully as possible.'

(Karkou and Sanderson 2006, p. 89.)

Furthermore, the literature suggests that there are particular artistic/creative models in the field that draw extensively upon the arts as art forms, value creativity as a therapeutic model that can guide and support the process and ultimately encourage clients to become artists. Within DMP for example, Meekums (2000, 2002) describes a creative approach to therapy in which the therapeutic process closely resembles the creative process. Creative approaches to MT are often connected with the Nordorff-Robbins school of thought (Nordorff and Robbins 1971, 1977), where music and music-making appears to play a central role in the therapeutic process.

Active/directive

A factor called active/directive was also revealed through the factor analysis which included the following statements:

- 'Sometimes I will actively do artwork myself during the session.'
- 'I may concentrate my work on physical aspects.'
- 'I do direct more than just for basic safety.'
- 'I do have certain techniques that I bring out when it is appropriate.'

(Karkou and Sanderson 2006. p. 91.)

This group of statement seems to refer to a number of different ways of approaching therapeutic work:

1) The therapist may be actively involved in the session as a way of guiding the artistic work.

2) S/he might be 'directive' in terms of introducing particular techniques as seen appropriate.

3) S/he might hold specific aims and objectives that can be fairly narrow. The discussion about the degree to which there is more or less direction within the sessions and more or less structure is pertinent as revealed in relevant arts therapies literature (McNeilly 1983; Liebmann 1986; Bruscia 1988; Oldfield 1995).

The needs of the clients, the duration of the intervention, and the theoretical orientation of the therapists seem to play a key role in the decision of how much structure and direction should be offered. For example links with short-term therapy and behaviourism can often be made when active/directive approaches are introduced. Examples of working within behavioural thinking can be found in MT in the USA (Madsen 1981; Thaut 1985; Standley 1991) and less often in the UK (Wigram 1996; Wigram and Dileo 1997). However, such models do not appear to have become popular amongst neither DMP nor MT practitioners. Therefore, it is not surprising that this set of statements had the lowest score indicating that respondents to the survey showed the weakest agreement with these ideas.

As pressure to engage with such models is becoming increasingly relevant within a competitive job market that values short term interventions and behavioural approaches (e.g. CBT), DMP and MT practitioners are often forced to engage with such approaches. It is possible that further consideration is needed on how best to respond to such pressures.

Eclectic/integrative

Finally, and unlike the active/directive group of statements that received the least agreement amongst arts therapists, the eclectic/integrative set of statements scored fairly high amongst DMP and MT respondents. Some of the statements included in this set were:

+ 'I use a number of different approaches for each client.'
+ 'It depends which population I am working with, what sort of theoretical approach I am adopting.'
+ 'I do not think that I have one model that I follow.'

(Karkou and Sanderson 2006, p. 96.)

The above statements suggest the presence of flexible work that adapts to the needs of client groups and clients. Although, eclectic/integrative approaches have been criticized as potentially being atheoretical and bearing the danger of lumping together ideas that may clash (Thorne 1967; Abram 1992; Valente and Fontana 1993), their relevance to DMP and MT remains pertinent. Within DMP for example, Payne (1994) argues for the value of eclectic/integrative approaches. In MT the interactive (or free improvisational) MT approach that began with Juliette Alvin and the Guildhall training programme draws heavily upon a number of different psychotherapeutic schools of thoughts. According to Wigram et al. (2002), Alvin's approach is closely linked with an eclectic approach to MT as it incorporates medical, recreational, educational, psychological, and musical perspectives.

Eclectic/integrative approaches retain memories of the range of the original influences and bodies of knowledge that have come together to form arts therapies as modern professions (Karkou and Sanderson 2006). They also allow for contemporary ideas to be incorporated within current practice such as postmodern ideas stemming from sociology and the arts (Lyotard 1979; Gergen 1985, 1991; Grentz 1996). Within DMP these ideas have been further developed by Best (2000), Best and Parker (2001) and Allegranti (2009), and have close affiliation with social contructionism in particular. In MT, Pavlicevic (1997) makes references to postmodernism, while similar discussion can be found in the wider arts therapies literature (e.g. Byrne 1995; Karkou and Sanderson 2006; Karkou et al. in press). Within a postmodern framework, being flexible and in flux is an expected state. Both the definition of the self, the social context within which one is located and the usefulness of therapeutic interventions are seen as having such fluidity and needing to be constantly defined and redefined.

According to Byrne (1995), the postmodern self is faced with the danger of fragmentation (Byrne 1995). Similarly, a postmodern view to DMP and MT might bear similar danger because:

+ As a reactionist approach to existing theories, is limited in terms of its ability to suggest something new.
+ It remains poor in terms of full conceptualizations of a therapeutic model; postmodernism has derived from sociology and the arts, not therapy.
+ Can allow for far too much diversity to the extent that 'everything might go'.

Within a constant state of flux, knowledge of existing practices, and clear definitions of guiding principles are vital for the development of coherent, yet flexible, professional identities that accounts for core practices and their variations.

Some variations of practice

The survey of practitioners (Karkou 1998; Karkou and Sanderson, 2006) revealed that statistically significant differences existed between responses from DMP and the other arts therapies in that dance movement psychotherapists showed stronger agreement with the humanistic group of statements (accepted at a 0.05 level of significance). This was probably the result of historical links of DMP with child-centred education and the contribution of Laban and creative educational dance, as well as the value placed on the body by humanistic and body psychotherapies referred to before.

The same study also showed that there were statistically significant differences between MT and the other arts therapies regarding the humanistic, the eclectic/integrative and the psychoanalytic/ psychodynamic trends (accepted at a 0.01 level of significance) with the former showing weaker agreement with these trends than the latter. It appeared that the music therapists who partici- pated in the study were more sceptical about these therapeutic frameworks than other arts thera- pists. This might be the result of music therapists attempting to define their work from within and thus without borrowing therapeutic frameworks and/or making external references to psycho- therapy, psychology, sociology and/or the arts as argued by Ansdell (1995) in the UK and Aigen (2005) in the USA.

Finally, some additional variations of practice can be found in relation to working environ- ments and client groups. For example arts therapists including DMP and MT practitioners work- ing in the health service often drew more heavily upon psychoanalytic/psychodynamic frameworks than when they were located in other settings (Karkou 1998; Karkou and Sanderson 2006). It is possible that within hospitals, psychoanalytic/psychodynamic thinking can be more readily understood than, let's say humanistic or artistic/creative ideas. Furthermore, with clients who are psychologically unwell and thus need to be inpatients, psychodynamic thinking can offer a solid theoretical framework for the therapist to make sense of the needs of the clients and the therapeutic process.

Regarding client groups, when arts therapists were working with adults with mental health problems, they preferred psychoanalytic/psychodynamic ideas as most relevant to their practice (Karkou 1998; Karkou and Sanderson 2006). Working with clients with learning difficulties, developmental, artistic/creative and active/directive therapeutic ideas were particularly relevant, albeit there was only weak statistical support for this. Finally with clients with no apparent diffi- culties, humanistic and artistic/creative perspectives were particularly relevant. It appears that the needs of the clients are taken seriously on board and as such diverse needs lead therapists to ascribe value and usefulness for their practice to equally diverse therapeutic frameworks.

Conclusions

In this chapter I have argued that DMP is a growing field with clear links with MT; also with clear and distinct differences.

First of all, they both belong to the same family of arts therapies and in many ways I see practi- tioners defining their work in similar ways, while sharing similar standards for training and agreed requirements for professional practice and registration. I have also argued that different views of the value of music over dance, stemming primarily from a Cartesian dualism and the association of dance with the low status of women, have delayed the development of DMP as an organized profession.

Furthermore, I find that both DMP and MT, along with other arts therapies, share some com- mon features of practice such as the way they view and use the arts, the central role of creativity, imagery, symbolism and metaphor, the significant place of non-verbal communication in the development of the client-therapist relationship and in the transformative aspects of the thera- peutic process. As these are concepts primarily emerging from a review of relevant definitions and the literature, it is not clear how much they are indeed used by DMP and MT practitioners. Further empirical work is needed to ascertain these and any other key elements shared across these two disciplines.

Finally, and unlike the previous theoretical ideas, empirical findings from a survey of practitioners in the UK, revealed that arts therapists including dance movement psychotherapists and music therapists, are in overall agreement with the use of certain therapeutic frameworks, that is humanistic, psychoanalytic/psychodynamic, developmental, artistic/creative, active/directive and eclectic integrative. Variations of practice exist based on client groups and settings, but also based on the type of arts therapies considered. For example, DMP practitioners appear to be in stronger agreement with humanistic ideas, while MT practitioners seem more sceptical with adopting therapeutic frameworks borrowed from outside the MT discipline itself.

Further work is needed in terms of:

Professional identity: It appears that there is a need for the development of stronger professional identities that remain fluid and flexible. A shift away from relying heavily on therapeutic frameworks that have not emerged from within arts therapies practice might also be needed as this shift can question the prevalence of 'grant narratives' found in modern psychotherapy. Calls for valuing the development of theoretical justifications of arts therapies practice from within the discipline have already been made in DMP (Meekums 2002) and other arts therapies (Jones 1996).Ways in which professional identities might be strengthened include clear mapping of what is already there and identifying needs and gaps. Calls to expand mapping of the field of arts therapies across disciplines with particular client groups have already being made. One such example comes from Burns (2009) who identified patterns of practice across arts therapies in dementia care and developed useful 'thick' descriptions of current practice. Such comparisons can also take place across countries. For example, arts therapists in Russia, and Latvia have taken this challenge on (Martinsone et al. 2009; Karkou et al. 2010) aiming to identify 'cultural borrowing' and learn from each others' differences. Looking at the way different arts therapists work could enable practitioners to learn from each other and ultimately offer better care.

Development of evidence-based practices: Although research evidence from both DMP and MT is growing (see relevant chapters in this book such as Quiroga Murcia and Kreutz, Chapter 10, and Wigram and Gold, Chapter 13), practice that is clearly informed by existing research evidence is not widely available. Furthermore, practitioners often engage with unique and innovative ways of working which are potentially useful for clients, but miss out from thoroughly evaluating their work through engaging clients in the process, considering active improvement of practice and disseminating any benefits to a wider audience. Engagement in evidence-based practice and practice-based evidence are key areas for further development in the area within the current postmodern climate of flux and instability.

Collaborative work: Collaborative work is needed regarding resources, training, and practice between DMP, MT, and the other arts therapies. Examples from collaborative projects involving arts therapists from different disciplines can be found in Karkou et al. (2010) and Meekums et al. (2010). These however, remain the exception rather than the norm. Such collaborations can expand beyond the field of arts therapies and create connections with artists and caring professions in ways that build bridges between professions. Ultimately collaboration will place clients in the centre of their own recovery and enable the development of agreed care pathways that offer cohesive and potentially transformative experiences.

References

Abram, J. (1992). *Individual Psychotherapy Trainings: A Guide*. London: Free Association Books.

Aigen, K. (2005). *Music-Centered Music Therapy*. Gilsum, NH: Barcelona Publishers.

Allegranti, B. (2009). Embodied performances of sexuality and gender: A feminist approach to dance movement psychotherapy and performance practice. *Body, Movement and Dance in Psychotherapy*, **4**(1), 17–31.

Ansdell, G. (1995). *Music for Life: Aspects of Creative Music Therapy with Adult Clients*. London: Jessica Kingsley.

Association for Dance Movement Therapy UK (ADMT UK 1997). 1997 UK news: Council for Professions Supplementary to Medicine (CPSM): about the setting up of the Arts Therapies Board. *e-motion. ADMT UK Quarterly*, **IX**(2), 15.

Association for Dance Movement Therapy UK (ADMT UK 2007a). News from ADMT UK Council, *e-motion, Spring*, **XIV**(19), 3–4.

Association for Dance Movement Therapy UK (2007b). News from ADMT UK Council, *e-motion, Autumn*, **XIV**(21), 3.

Association of Professional Music Therapists (APMT) (2010). *What is Music Therapy?* Available at: http://www.apmt.org/Info/MusicTherapy/tabid/69/Default.aspx (accessed 1 October 2010)

Best, P. (2000). Theoretical diversity and clinical collaboration: Reflections by a dance/movement therapist. *The Arts in Psychotherapy*, **27**(3), 197–211.

Best, P. and Parker, G. (2001). Moving reflections: the social creation on identities in communication. In: Kossolapow. L., Scoble, S., and Waller, D. (eds.) *Arts–Therapies–Communication: On the Way to a Communicative European Arts Therapy*, vol. 1, pp. 142–148. Munster: Lit Verlag.

Bonny, H. (1994). Twenty-one years later: a GIM update. *Music Therapy Perspectives*, **12**(2), 70–4.

Bruscia, K.E. (1988). A survey of treatment procedures in improvisational music therapy. *Psychology of Music*, **16**, 10–24.

Bunt, L. (1994). *Music Therapy: An Art Beyond Words*. London and New York: Routledge.

Burns, J. (2009). An Interpretive Description of the Patterns of Practice of Arts Therapists working with Older People who have Dementia in the UK. Unpublished PhD Thesis, Queen Margaret University. Department of Occupational Therapy and Arts Therapies, Edinburgh, UK.

Byrne, P. (1995). From the depths to the surface: Art therapy as a discursive practice in the post-modern era. *The Arts in Psychotherapy*, **22**(3), 234–9.

Chaiklin, S. and Schmais, D. (1986). The Chace approach to dance therapy. In: P. Lewis (ed.) *Theoretical approaches in dance/movement therapy, Vol 1*. Dubuque, IO: Kendall/Hunt.

Clarkson, P. (1994). The Nature and Range of Psychotherapy. In: P. Clarkson and M. Pokorny (eds.) *The Handbook of Psychotherapy*, pp. 3–27. London and New York: Routledge.

Damasio, A. (2000). *The Feeling of What Happens: Body and Emotion in the Making of Consciousness*. London: Harvest Books.

Damasio, A. (2005). *Descartes' Error: Emotion, Reason, and the Human Brain*. London: Penguin Books.

Dosamantes-Alperson, E. (1981). Experiencing in movement therapy. *American Journal of Dance Therapy*, **4**(2), 33–44.

Dosamantes- Beaudry, I. (1997). Reconfiguring identity. *The Arts in Psychotherapy*, **24**(1), 51–7.

Gazzola, V., Aziz-Zadeh, L., and Keysers, C. (2006) Empathy and the somatotopic auditory mirror system in humans. *Current Biology*, **16**, 1824–29.

Gergen, K.J. (1985). The social constructionist movement in modern psychology. *American Psychologist*, **40**, 3, 266–75.

Gergen, K.J. (1991) *The Saturated Self*. New York: Basic Books.

Gordon, R. (1987). Playing on many stages: Dramatherapy and the individual. In: S. Jennings (ed.) *Dramatherapy: theory and practice 1*, pp. 119–45. London: Routledge.

Grentz, S. (1996). *A Primer on Postmodernism*. Grand Rapids, MI: William B. Eermans.

Halprin, D. (2003). *The expressive body in life, art and therapy: working with movement, metaphor and meaning*. London: Jessica Kingsley.

Hargreaves, D.J. (1982). The development of aesthetic reactions to music. *Psychology of Music*, special Issue, 51–4.

Jones, P (1996). *Drama as Therapy: Theatre as Living*. London: Routledge.

Karkou, V. (1998). A Descriptive Evaluation fo the Practice of Arts Therapies in the UK. Unpublished PhD Thesis, University of Manchester, School of Education.

Karkou V. (2009). Evidence based practice and practice based evidence. In: Arts Therapies, keynote speech at the 7th international arts therapies conference *Contemporary Arts Therapies–Theory and Practice*, 17–19 July 2009, Riga Stradins University, Cesis, Latvia.

Karkou V. (2010). Research in Arts Therapies: On the Way towards Evidence-Based Practice and Practice-Based Evidence. In: 1st Moscow International Arts Therapies Conference *Building the Present - Looking into Future: Arts Therapies in the Modern World*, Moscow.

Karkou, V. and Glasman, J. (2004). Arts, education and society: The role of the arts in promoting the emotional well-being and social inclusion of young people, *Support for Learning*, **19**(2), 56–64.

Karkou, V. and Sanderson, P. (2000). Dance movement therapy in UK Education. *Research in Dance Education*, **1**(1), 69–85.

Karkou, V. and Sanderson, P. (2001). Dance movement therapy in the UK: Current orientations of a field emerging from dance education. *European P.E. Review*, **7**(2), 137–55.

Karkou, V. and Sanderson, P. (2006). *Arts Therapies: A Research-Based Map of the Field*. Edinburgh: Elsevier.

Karkou, V., Fullarton, A., and Scarth, S. (2010). Finding a way out of the labyrinth through dance movement psychotherapy: Collaborative work in a mental health promotion programme for secondary schools. In: V. Karkou (ed.) *Arts Therapies in Schools: Research and Practice*, pp. 59–84. London: Jessica Kingsley.

Karkou, V., Martinsone, K., and Nazarova, N. (in press). Art Therapy in the Postmodern World: Findings from a Comparative Study across the UK, Russia, and Latvia. *The Arts in Psychotherapy*.

Kestenberg, J. (1975). *Children & Parents: Psychoanalytic Studies in Development*. New York: Jason Aronson.

Koch, S.C. and Brauninger, I. (2006). *Advances in Dance/Movement Therapy: Theoretical and Empirical Findings*. Berlin: Logos.

Koch, S.C. and Bender, S. (2007). *Movement Analysis: The Legacy of Laban, Bartenieff, Lamb and Kestenberg*. Berlin: Logos.

Laban, R. (1975). *Modern Educational Dance*. London: MacDonald and Evans.

Landy, R. (2001). Establishing a model of communication between an arts-based discipline and its applied creative art therapy. In: Kossolapow, L. Scoble, S. and Waller, D. (eds.) *Arts–Therapies–Communication: On a way to a communicative European Arts Therapy*, vol. 1, pp. 305–10. Munster: Lit Verlag.

Levinge, A. (1993). Permission to play: the search for self through music therapy; Research with children presenting with communication difficulties. In: H. Payne (ed.) *Handbook of inquiry in the Arts Therapies: One River, Many Currents*, pp. 218–28. London: Jessica Kingsley.

Levy, F. (1988). *Dance Movement Therapy: A Healing Art*. Reston, VA: American Alliance for Health, Physical Education, Recreation and Dance.

Lyotard, J.F. (1979, trans. 1984). *The Postmodern Condition*. Manchester: Manchester University Press.

Madsen, C.K. (1981). *Music Therapy: A Behavioral Guide for the Mentally Retarded*. Washington DC: National Association for Music Therapy.

Malchiodi, C. (1998). *The art therapy sourcebook*. Los Angeles, CA: Lowell House.

Martinsone, K., Karkou, V., and Nazarova, N. (2009). Art Therapy Practice in Latvia, in the UK and in Russia: A Comparison of different Environments of Work. In: *Collection of Scientific Papers 2009*. Riga: Riga Stradins University.

McNeilly, G. (1983). Directive and non-directive approaches in art therapy. *The Arts in Psychotherapy*, **10**(4), 211–19.

Meekums, B. (2000). *Creative Group Therapy for Women Survivors of Child Sexual Abuse*. London: Jessica Kingsley.

Meekums, B. (2002). *Dance Movement Therapy: A Creative Psychotherapeutic Approach*. London: Sage.

Meekums, B. (2009). Moving towards evidence for dance movement therapy: Robin Hood in dialogue with the King. *The Arts in Psychotherapy*, **37**(1), 35–41.

Meekums B., Karkou V. Elefant, C. Nundy-Mala, A., and Nelson, A. (2010). *Dance Movement Therapy for Depression*. Cochrane Review title. Approved 1 July 2010. Available at: http://www2.cochrane.org/reviews/en/title_15557680582621679857100701134014.html

Meier, W. (2008). Dance movement therapy: My story. *e-motion*, **XVIII**(2), 11–12.

National Health Service (NHS) (2010). *Agenda for Change*. Available at: http://www.nhsemployers.org/PayAndContracts/AgendaForChange/Pages/Afc-Homepage.aspx (accessed 20 April 2011)

Nordoff, P. and Robbins, C. (1971). *Therapy in music for handicapped children*. Plymouth: Northcote House.

Nordoff, P. and Robbins, C. (1977). *Creative Music Therapy*. New York: Harper & Row Publishers.

Odell-Miller, H. (2000). Music Therapy and its Relationship to Psychoanalysis. In: Y. Searle and I. Sterng (eds.) *Where Analysis Meets the Arts*, pp. 127–52.London: Karnac.

Odell-Miller, H. (2002). One man's journey and the importance of time in music therapy. In: A Davies and E Richards (eds.) *Music therapy and Group Work: Sound Company*, pp. 63–76. London: Jessica Kingsley.p

Oldfield, A. (1995). Communicating through music: The balance between following and initiating. In: T. Wigram, B. Saperston, and R. West (eds.) *The Art and Science of Music Therapy: A Handbook*, pp. 226–37. Switzerland: Harwood Academic Publications.

Pavlicevic, M. (1997). *Music Therapy in Context: Music, Meaning and Relationship*. London: Jessica Kingsley.

Payne, H. (1992). Introduction. In: H. Payne (ed.) *Dance Movement Therapy: Theory and Practice*, pp. 1–17. London: Routledge.

Payne, H. (1994). Dance movement therapy. In: D. Jones (ed.) *Innovative Therapy*. Milton Keynes: Open University.

Penfield, K. (1992). Individual movement psychotherapy: Dance movement therapy in private practice. In: H. Payne (ed.) *Dance Movement Therapy: Theory and Practice*, pp. 163–82. London and New York: Tavistock/Routledge.

Perls F., Hefferline R., Goodman P. (1969). *Gestalt Therapy: Excitement and Growth in the Human Personality*. New York: Julian Press.

Priestley, M. (1995). Linking sound and symbol. In: T. Wigram, B. Saperston, and R. West (eds.) *The Art and Science of Music Therapy: A Handbook*, pp. 129–38. Switzerland: Harwood Academic Publishers.

Priestley, M. (1975). *Music Therapy in Action*. London: Constable and Company Ltd.

Quality Assurance Agency (QAA) and National Health Service (NHS) (2004). *Subject benchmark statement: healthcare programmes, phase 2: Arts Therapy, QAA 05909/04*. Available at: http://www.qaa.ac.uk/academicinfrastructure/benchmark/health/artsTherapy.asp#nature (accessed 1 October 2010).

Reich, W. (1960). *An Introduction to Orgonomy: Selected Writings*. New York: Noonday.

Rizzolatti, G., Fadiga, L., Gallese, V., and Fogassi, L. (1996). Premotor cortex and the recognition of motor actions. *Cognitive Brain Research*, **3**, 131–41.

Rohricht, F. (2009). Body oriented psychotherapy. The state of the art in empirical research and evidence-based practice: A clinical perspective. *Body, Movement and Dance in Psychotherapy*, **4**(2), 135–56.

Sandel, S. and Johnson, D. (1983). Structure and process of the nascent group: dance movement therapy with chronic patients. *The Arts in Psychotherapy*, **10**, 131–40.

Sanderson, P. (1996). Dance within the National Physical Education Curriculum of England and Wales. *The European Physical Education Review*, **2**(1), 54–63.

Sanderson, P. (2001). Age and gender issues in adolescent attitudes to dance. *European Physical Education Review*, **7**(2), 137–55.

Sherborne, V. (1990). *Developmental movement for children*. Cambridge: Cambridge University Press.

Shreeves, R. (2006). Full circle: From choreography to dance movement therapy and back. In: H. Payne (ed.) *Dance Movement Therapy: Theory, Research and Practice*, pp. 232–44. London: Routledge.

Siegel, E. V. (1984). *Dance movement therapy: Mirrors of ourselves. The psychoanalytic approach*. New York: Human Sciences Press.

Smitskamp, H. (1995). The problem of professional diagnosis in the arts therapies. *The Arts in Psychotherapy*, **22**(3), 181–7.

Standley, J.M. (1991). The role of music in pacification/stimulation of premature students with low birth weights. *Music Therapy Perspectives*, **9**, 19–25.

Stanton-Jones, K. (1992). *An introduction to dance movement therapy in psychiatry*. London: Tavistock/Routledge.

Swanwick, K. and Tillman, J. (1986). The sequence of musical development: a study of children's composition. *British Journal of Music Education* 3(3), 305–39.

Thaut, M.H. (1985). The use of auditory rhythm and rhythmic speech to aid temporal muscular control in children with gross motor dysfunction. *Journal of Music Therapy*, 22(3) 129–45.

Thorne, F.C. (1967). *Integrative Psychology*. Brandon, VT: Clinical Publishing.

Trevarthen, C. and Aitken, K.J. (2001). Infant intersubjectivity: Research, theory and clinical application. *Journal of Psychology and Psychiatry*, **42**(1), 3–48.

Tyler, H. (2000). The music therapy profession in modern Britain. In: P. Horden (ed.) *Music as Medicine: The history of music therapy since antiquity*, pp. 375–93. Aldershot: Ashgate.

Valente, L. and Fontana, D. (1993). *Research into Dramatherapy: Theory and practice: Some Implications for Training*. London: Jessica Kingsley.

Waller, D. (1991). *Becoming a profession: the history of art therapy in Britain 1940–1982*. London and New York: Tavistock/Routledge.

Walrond-Skinner, S. (1986). *Dictionary of Psychotherapy*. London: Routledge and Kegan Paul.

Whitehouse, M.C.G. (1979). Jung and dance-therapy: two major principles. In: P.L. Bernstein (ed.) *Eight theoretical approaches in dance/movement therapy, Vol. I*. Iowa: Kendall/Hunt.

Wigram, T. (1996). The effect of vibroacoustic therapy on clinical and non-clinical populations. Unpublished PhD Psychological research thesis. St George's Medical School, University of London.

Wigram, T. and Dileo, C. (eds.) (1997). *Music, vibration and health*. New Jersey: Jeffrey Books.

Wigram, T., Pedersen, I.N., and Bonde, L.O. (2002). *A Comprehensive Guide to Music Therapy: Theory, Clinical Practice, Research and Training*. London: Jessica Kingsley.

Winnicott, D.W. (1971). *Playing and reality*. London: Routledge.

Chapter 17

Music and Pain: Evidence from Experimental Perspectives

Laura Mitchell and Raymond MacDonald

Challenge of pain

The last decade has seen greater acknowledgement of pain as one of the most significant challenges to health and wellbeing, with the potential to impact considerably upon many elements of quality of life (Breivik et al. 2006). The extent of the consequences for both the individual and society has been increasingly recognized by international research; most often focusing on 'chronic' pain lasting longer than 3 months. Despite unprecedented medical advances during this time, the UK Chief Medical Officer's report of 2008 acknowledges chronic pain to be a more commonly reported problem today than 40 years ago (Donaldson 2008), and it remains the primary reason for most healthcare consultations (Turk and Dworkin 2004).

While exact figures are difficult to obtain due to variation in methodologies, most studies report prevalence close to the overall World Health Organization primary care survey figure of 22% (Gureje et al. 1998). In Europe, a 2006 survey by Breivik et al. of 46,000 people reported 19% to have moderate to severe pain for at least 6 months. When averaging across slight discrepancies between countries, a third of this group reported not receiving treatment at all for their condition, and 40% to find their treatment inadequate. The impact on psychological wellbeing was notable, with 21% of sufferers having been diagnosed with depressive illnesses relating to their pain. Anxiety, social isolation, concentration, mood, and sleep disturbance all contribute to a decrease in quality of life (Ashburn and Staats 1999), which unsurprisingly is frequently found to be lowest in those with higher levels of pain (Gerdle et al. 1994).

These personal consequences of pain and related societal and economic repercussions have led to substantial research interest in pain management intervention, with an aim to empower sufferers with self-management strategies to optimize physical function and psychological wellbeing; improving overall health, mobility, emotional wellbeing, and work/social interaction (Philips et al. 2008). One such strategy has been music listening on pain; its potential benefits having been investigated in a range of contexts and using varied methodologies (Pothoulaki et al. in press). As a pain intervention, music has been proposed specifically as a low-cost, widely available treatment useful both in conjunction with basic treatment and at times when medication is less effective, not desired, or not allowed sufficient time (Whipple and Glynn 1992; Hargreaves et al. 2012).

Early experimental work

Much of the early work on auditory stimuli as a pain management intervention published in the 1960s focused on pain during dental procedures, often using white noise rather than musical stimuli for its perceived distracting properties. Following a study by Gardner et al. (1960) that proposed music and noise suppressed pain in 65% of a dental surgery sample and sufficiently in

25% to relieve need for anaesthetic, a series of studies began using experimental pain to test effects.

In addition to the study of clinical populations, a substantial empirical literature on pain derives findings from such techniques of experimental pain induction in healthy volunteers. Techniques used most frequently include thermal (e.g. cold water, laser), mechanical (e.g. pressure, Von Frey hairs), ischaemic (e.g. blood pressure cuff), and chemical methods (e.g. topical or muscular capsaicin). As standardized protocols have been developed, benefits afforded of such procedures are the controlled, constant levels of stimulus intensity and duration, and ability to quantify and compare physiological and psychological responses (Petersen-Felix and Arendt-Nielsen 2002). Repeated measures design further allows minimization of interindividual variability.

The limitations of such procedures are, however, also clear and accepted within the pain literature. The pathophysiology of clinical pain, involving deep structures and inflammatory response, obviously cannot be replicated (Petersen-Felix and Arendt-Nielsen 2002), and emotional/motivational aspects may differ since it is within the participant's control to stop the pain at any point, making the fundamental meaning of the pain different (Gracely 1991). Yet the important contribution of pain induction is uncontested, with authors such as Edwards et al. (2005) citing the agreement between clinical and experimental pain measurement of group differences, such as by sex and age, in addition to clear evidence of application to classification of chronic disorders.

In the context of audioanalgesia, Melzack et al. (1963) reported auditory stimulation combined with suggestion of a positive effect increased tolerance of cold pressor pain, yet neither alone was effective. The issue of participant control over volume was investigated by Morosko and Simmons (1966) using electrical pain and a manipulation of explicit and implicit suggestion. Suggestion in this study was not found to have an effect but the auditory stimulus again increased tolerance and threshold of pain.

With the subsequent publication of the multidimensional 'gate control' theory of pain (Melzack and Wall 1965), however, a rapid development of the role of Psychology in pain research and treatment took place which, in acknowledging the importance of cognitive and emotional processes in pain modulation, provided the beginning of a theoretical framework for the use of stimuli such as music. Studies reported over the following two decades were carried out in diverse clinical populations, and in the 1980s began to introduce a substantially wider range of psychological and physiological dependent variables, aiming to increase evidence for the full range of musical effects and to move towards greater understanding of the mechanisms of action. In 1986, Standley published a meta-analysis of the effects of music in medical and dental contexts on a comprehensive range of dependent variables including pain. This analysis suggested an increased effect of music when lower levels of pain are experienced, and increased efficacy when used in conjunction with anaesthesia.

At this point, however, the evidence remained piecemeal, with no clear integration of findings published independently in the fields of medicine, nursing, psychology, and music therapy. Furthermore, an audioanalgesia literature review by Good (1996) highlighted the importance of repeated measures design, randomization, and pre-test measurements when examining pain responses due to the substantial interindividual variation. Indirect and unreliable pain measurement and heavy reliance upon the anecdotal comments of participants were further issues noted by Michel and Chesky (1995), in addition to incomplete information as to means of presentation of music, listening volume and length of pieces which impeded replication of methodologies. The increasing use of experimental pain methodologies in the following decade therefore reflected the recognized need for a systematic approach, with controlled trials using standardized methodology and measurement leading to properly grounded future clinical application.

Self-selection of music

In keeping with a developing literature on the influence of perception of control over pain, this potential benefit of music listening was highlighted in a study of a small sample of cancer patients by Beck (1991). 'Perceived control' over an experience has been defined as the belief in an ability to respond in a way which will decrease the aversiveness of an event (Skevington 1995), influencing whether a specific stressful encounter is viewed as a threat or a challenge, determining how able the individual is to cope with and perhaps altering the outcome of the experience (Lazarus and Folkman 1984). Although a complex psychophysiological mechanism, research findings have, in general, linked perception of control to wide ranging aspects of adjustment and quality of life in chronic pain patients such as lower rates of disability and disruption of activity (Haythornthwaite et al. 1998).

While a percentage change in pain levels of approaching statistical significance was found when a relaxing music group was compared to control, Beck proposed that the scheduled nature of the intervention (i.e. participants were unable to listen to music at the times when they most desired) may have reduced beneficial feeling of control over pain. This important theoretical development began to be investigated primarily, however, through greater participant choice of musical stimuli in clinical studies (e.g. Updike 1990; Menegazzi et al. 1991).

Two studies had investigated the efficacy of preferred music listening for relieving experimentally induced pain. Pain induced by hand immersion in cold water (cold pressor pain), firstly, was used in a between-subjects study of preferred choice from four instrumental musical selections, a randomly allocated choice from the non-preferred pieces, no music with experimenter present, and no music while alone (Hekmat and Hertel 1993). When compared to baseline measures, only preferred music was found to significantly increase tolerance. No effect was found, however, on rating of pain intensity.

Perlini and Viita (1996) asked participants to rate six musical selections in order of preference. While undergoing finger pressure pain trials, participants then listened to either their favourite choice, least favourite choice, or no music. Greater control over the experience, greater expectations of pain reduction, and greater actual pain reduction were found in those listening to their preferred music.

Yet musical stimuli in these studies remained a choice from an experimenter-chosen selection rather than participants' free selection; limiting the ecological validity of the musical stimuli. To test the hypothesis that completely self-selected music will be most effective, while minimizing any confounding factors, we have carried out a series of studies to investigate the role of preference in audioanalgesia. The first two studies showed that preferred music could be an effective aid to reducing anxiety for patients in hospital contexts (MacDonald et al. 2003). However the results from these studies showed no effects of music listening on pain perception and so we then undertook a series of laboratory studies utilizing the cold pressor technique (Mitchell et al. 2004).

Considering underpinning mechanisms to support increased efficacy through self-selection, distraction of attention had been most frequently proposed in the literature as a mechanism of pain relief through music; possibly since distraction may be the most intuitive, 'common sense' strategy when in pain (deGood 2000). Certainly features of music such as flow through melodic contour and rhythmic patterns, as recognized since the work of Meyer (1956), do appear to make it particularly fitting in capturing, holding, and distracting our attention from other stimuli.

It appeared, however, that two salient and interacting factors must also be considered regarding our present-day relationship with music. The first is the highly individualized, constant, and controlled listening habits made possible by technological advances, noted to make us more 'sophisticated' listeners than ever before and allowing music to be more pervasive within an individual's lifestyle, attitudes, beliefs, and behaviours (North and Hargreaves 2007). Concurrently, our increasing understanding within the field of psychology of music of the personal and emotional factors beyond the music itself began to highlight the 'associative' context of listening as highly personal meanings and memories connected with the music (Sloboda and Juslin 2001; MacDonald et al. 2002; Miell et al. 2005). The relevance of familiarity and past associations to listening choices would therefore call into question the level of emotional involvement with a piece of music chosen by someone else. As mentioned earlier, self-selection appears also to relate to feelings of control over pain, where familiar music can be brought easily into an unfamiliar environment to promote a sense of controllability (Brown et al. 1989).

In the first of our studies (Mitchell and MacDonald 2006), 54 participants brought their own choice of music to the lab, where it was compared in a within-subjects design to white noise and a relaxing music choice selected from a pilot study. These auditory stimuli were presented in counterbalanced order to avoid possible order effects in testing. In this study, participants tolerated the painful stimulus significantly longer and reported feeling significantly more control when listening to their preferred choice compared to both other conditions. Interestingly, relaxing music did not significantly increase tolerance compared to control. With regards to pain intensity rated between 'no pain' and 'worst possible pain' on visual analogue scale, only female participants rated the intensity as significantly lower in the preferred music condition.

Our following study (Mitchell et al. 2006) then compared preferred music to two stimuli investigated previously in the pain literature—mental arithmetic and humour. In line with 'limited capacity' models of attention (Shiffrin 1988) that propose an outside task will leave limited mental resources for pain perception, much of the work on pain had focused on mental tasks of varying degrees of difficulty. When the expected relationship between task level and pain perception did not emerge (e.g. Brucato 1978; Beers and Karoly 1979), authors suggested that arithmetical tasks may influence pain only in part, potentially reducing sensation but not the accompanying emotional aspects (Hodes et al. 1990). The interaction between emotion and attention therefore became a main focus of research, applying the hypothesis that emotional stimuli will capture attention more strongly. As theoretically this should mean negative emotions also to be effective (Leventhal 1992), studies compared various pleasant and unpleasant stimuli in order to unpick effects and propose a comprehensive mechanism of action.

Two such studies found efficacy to relate to positive emotions in particular; Weisenberg et al. (1998) finding humorous films to increase pain tolerance and reduce intensity following a 30-minute waiting period when compared to neutral and unpleasant film, and DeWied and Verbaten (2001) reporting pleasant pictures to increase tolerance of pain while unpleasant pictures, particularly those containing pain-related information, to reduce tolerance. These authors propose their findings to support an appraisal mechanism, where positive affect alters the meaning of a painful stimulus and renders it less threatening; yet the role of attention suggested by the effect of pain-related information remained unclear. Using odours as a rapidly effective inducer of mood, however, Villemure et al. (2003) began to clarify the effects through a manipulation of both pleasantness of odour and direction of attention towards either odour or pain. They found differing effects for attention and mood, with attention influencing perceived pain intensity and to a lesser extent unpleasantness, while pleasantness of odour altered pain unpleasantness, mood and anxiety. Their proposal of differing neural networks of attention and emotion has since been confirmed by a later functional magnetic resonance imaging (fMRI) study also using odour (Villemure and Bushnell 2009).

In our study, 44 participants underwent three cold pressor trials in counterbalanced order; the mental arithmetic trial using the paced auditory serial addition task (PASAT; Gronwall 1977) and the humour trial a choice from three recordings of standup comedy. In this study, preferred music listening resulted in significantly longer tolerance of painful stimulation than the PASAT task, but did not significantly differ from humour on this measure. Ratings of perceived control, however, were significantly greater during the preferred music condition than the humour condition, but did not differ from the PASAT condition. Ratings of pain intensity in this study did not significantly differ between the stimuli.

Following this study, we made an experimental comparison of visual and auditory stimuli (Mitchell et al. 2008a), drawing upon the work proposing the viewing of positive emotional pictures as a method of pain relief (DeWied and Verbaten 2001; Rhudy et al. 2006). Our study compared effects of self-chosen music to a selection from 15 well-known paintings, and to silence control in 80 participants (44 females). Additionally, a measure of state anxiety was taken following each condition and a detailed music listening behaviour questionnaire introduced to look in more detail at how everyday listening habits, perceived uses of music in everyday life and relationship with the selected piece may influence efficacy of the intervention.

Findings of this study largely replicated our earlier results; preferred music listening leading to significantly longer tolerance and greater perceived control than both silence control and chosen art. Anxiety, measured by a short-form state anxiety questionnaire (Spielberger 1983) was significantly lower during music listening compared to both other conditions. Pain intensity ratings were however inconsistent, as in our previous two studies. Visual analogue ratings were significantly lower in the music condition when compared to control, but ratings on the McGill Pain Questionnaire (Melzack 1975) did not differ between conditions. Together, these studies have suggested perceived intensity of pain not to be significantly reduced, or if so, potentially only in females.

The musical behaviour questionnaire in this study gave interesting findings, our aim being to map individual differences in musical habits and the extent to which these may explain differences in efficacy and help pinpoint who may benefit most from the intervention. When participants rated how frequently they listened to their chosen piece, for example, a significant negative correlation was found with anxiety rating in the music condition. This suggests that familiarity may indeed be important in this therapeutic context, potentially combining anticipation and tension release from the musical flow and structure itself with the emotionally engaging associations held with it. A significant correlation was further found between knowledge of lyrics of the chosen song and tolerance during the music condition, again supporting importance of familiarity in engagement.

The underpinning question of the role of specific musical structures remains important and our current work is addressing the interplay between musical structure and preference. Across our studies, the musical choices of participants cover a broad range within a general 'popular' genre, including chart pop, rock, punk, hip-hop, and dance. These very different styles of music, with many different structural features, appeared to produce similar effects of increased tolerance and perceived control; leading us to the conclusion that personal preference can render varied types of music 'functionally equivalent'. That is, the participants chose music with contrasting structural features to produce the same effect, namely, reducing pain and anxiety perceptions. That participants had selected the music themselves, we suggest, supports the importance of extra-musical factors in engagement with music and its subsequent pain-relieving qualities. Recent neuropsychological investigation of autobiographical memory also supports the salience of associative factors in engagement, finding contrasting neural response between musical excerpts that are solely familiar to those that are personally relevant (Janata et al. 2007).

Regarding underpinning mechanisms, we therefore proposed that listening to self-chosen music during painful stimulation may evoke heightened emotional response and distract attention more effectively. Concurrently, the act of selecting and listening to one's chosen music may facilitate a sense of heightened control in unfamiliar or threatening situations. Certainly though, our conclusion of a distraction of attention mechanism is, due to the complexity of making direct measurement of attention, an extrapolation from the tolerance-increasing effect. Bushnell et al. (2004), however, recognize that although attentional tasks have been employed in pain studies such as ours, attention is not usually the only variable to change. Although their conclusion on the effect of attention is that studies do overwhelmingly show participants to report less pain when distracted; mood, arousal and anxiety correspondingly change. Distraction may therefore be, as proposed by Roy et al. (2008, p. 141), the 'most parsimonious explanation'.

Emotional and arousal mechanisms have therefore been the focus of recent investigations employing manipulation of musical variables. Two pieces selected to be pleasant and unpleasant but matched on arousal level were firstly compared to silence control using heat pain (Roy et al. 2008). In this study only pleasant music reduced intensity rating of pain, and rating of pain unpleasantness compared to control. Participants also felt less anxiety after the pleasant selection. Zhao and Chen (2009) in a related study examined the interaction between mood and valence through two melodies from within the same piece; both pleasant but of happy and sad mood. This study found that both selections lowered pain ratings when compared to baseline or neutral lecture, yet the happy melody significantly lowered pain distress when compared to lecture. The authors concluded, like Roy et al., that pleasant valence rather than specific mood is a mediator of pain relief. Yet interestingly in both of these studies, perceived pleasantness correlated with pain ratings; pain decreasing as pleasantness increased in Roy et al. (2008), and distress decreasing as pleasantness increased in Zhao and Chen (2009).

Most recently, Garza et al. (under review) have compared effects of music to auditory stimuli with similar emotional characteristics on acute heat pain, using lesser-known Mozart compositions to control for familiarity and pleasant environmental sounds of rain and water. Interestingly here when rated similarly for valence, liking, and arousal, sounds and music equally reduced pain perception compared to control. The authors suggest perceived emotional content of a stimulus plays a greater role than the particular structural features of the stimulus. As all musical stimuli in the above-mentioned studies were experimenter selected, we would maintain that music individually self-selected from the widest choice, for pleasantness or any similar desired personal effect, is most effective.

To address the assertion that the cognitive and emotional relationship listeners have with favourite music may override the effects of specific musical structure, our recent work has performed detailed structural and content analysis of a selection of tracks found to be effective in our previous studies (Knox et al. 2011). Utilizing technology allowing for detailed analysis of the digital musical file, we were able to investigate relationships between the structural content of preferred music chosen for pain relief and its specific effects in our experiments. Our ongoing work in this area is focused upon developing methods of automatic classification of emotions expressed by music with the aim of examining whether emotions expressed by music influence efficacy for pain relief.

From three of our previous studies (Mitchell et al. 2008a,b; Mitchell 2009), 76 tracks were selected as having the greatest overall effect on pain perception and response, as indicated by measurements of tolerance, intensity, perceived control, and anxiety as compared to silence control condition. Analysis was performed on 30-second clips of each track, corresponding to the section of the piece heard during painful stimulation, and a comparison of these experimental tracks to a corpus of a broad range of music was also possible using 160 clips from a selection of genres matching those selected by participants. Comparison of the preferred music with this training corpus revealed the experimental music to be significantly brighter, indicating that these clips were more likely to be of major mode. Mood classification likewise showed the participant selections to fall significantly within the 'content' mood cluster of the circumplex model (Thayer 1989); that with a tendency towards low arousal and positive valence. These analyses, albeit from a limited sample size, therefore suggested that music content and structure do play a role in the choices made by participants, with acoustical content and emotion expressed interacting with personal meanings and associations to make preferred choices particularly effective.

In summary, this chapter highlights the experimental evidence supporting the efficacy of music for pain relief and for cognitive and emotional mechanisms underpinning it. Although it is clear that induced pain is a different physiological and psychological experience to that which occurs through injury or illness, this experimental work is, in unison with clinical studies, providing valuable evidence that can be applied effectively in healthcare. Several interesting areas are highlighted for further investigation, such as the addition of tasks to test effects on attention directly, and the role of arousal, which has been implicated in the findings of various studies but seldom measured systematically. While these laboratory-based studies are important, there is an urgent research imperative to develop more ecologically valid methods of investigating the effects of music upon pain in a real world context since this is where pain is experienced (Pothoulaki et al. 2008). Also, various studies have compared the effects of music on pain to other distracting or emotionally-engaging stimuli and found these to be effective for certain aspects too (e.g. Garza et al. under review). The question therefore remains if music is unique in its ability to mitigate pain. However, the evidence suggests, that when utilized knowledgeably, music can be valuable intervention as part of treatment for pain and for enhancing wellbeing in those suffering from it.

References

Ashburn, M.A. and Staats, P.S. (1999). Management of chronic pain. *Lancet*, **353**, 1865–9.

Beck, S.L. (1991). The therapeutic use of music for cancer related pain. *Oncology Nursing Forum*, **18**, 1327–37.

Beecher, H.K. (1956). Relationship of significance of wound to the pain experienced. *Journal of the American Medical Association*, **161**, 1609–13.

Beers, T.M. and Karoly, P. (1979). Cognitive strategies, expectancy and coping style in the control of pain. *Journal of Consulting Clinical Psychology*, **47**, 179–80.

Breivik, H., Collett, B., Ventafridda, V., Cohen, R., and Gallacher, D. (2006). Survey of chronic pain in Europe; prevalence, impact on daily life, and treatment. *European Journal of Pain*, **10**, 287–333.

Brown, C.J., Chen, A.C.N., and Dworkin, S.F. (1989). Music in the control of human pain. *Music Therapy*, **8**, 47–60.

Bushnell, M.C., Villemure, C., and Duncan, G.H. (2004). Psychophysical and neurophysiological studies of pain modulation by attention. In: D.D. Price and M.C. Bushnell (eds.) *Psychological Methods of Pain Control: Basic Science and Clinical Perspectives, Progress in Pain Research and Management 29*, pp. 99–167. Seattle, WA: IASP Press.

Brucato, D.B. (1978). The psychological control of pain–the role of attentional focusing and capacity for experience of pain. *Dissertation Abstracts International*, **39**, 2488b.

deGood, D.E. (2000). Relationship of pain coping strategies to adjustment and functioning. In: R.J. Gatchel and J.N. Weisberg (eds.) *Personality Characteristics of Patients with Pain*, pp. 129–64, Washington, DC: American Pain Society.

deWied, M. and Verbaten, M. (2001). Affective pictures processing, attention and pain tolerance. *Pain*, **90**, 163–72.

Donaldson, L.J. (2008). *Chief medical officer's report on the state of public health*. London: HMSO.

Edwards, R., Sarlani, E., Wesselmann, U., and Fillingim, R. (2005). Quantitative assessment of pain perception: Multiple arenas of clinical relevance. *Pain*, **114**, 315–19.

Gardner, W.J., Licklider, J.C.R., and Weisz, A.Z. (1960). Suppression of pain by sound. *Science*, **132**, 32–3.

Garza-Villareal, E.A., Brattico, E., Vase, L., Østergaard, L., and Vuust, P. (under review). Superior analgesic effect of an active distraction versus pleasant unfamiliar sounds and music: the influence of emotion and cognitive style.

Gerdle, B., Bjork, J., Henriksson, C., and Bengtsson, A. (1994). Prevalence of current pain and their influences upon work and healthcare seeking: A population study. *Journal of Rheumatology*, **31**, 1399–406.

Good, M. (1996). Effects of relaxation and music on postoperative pain: A review. *Journal of Advanced Nursing*, **24**, 905–14.

Gracely, R.H. (1991). Experimental pain models. In: M.M.R. Portenoy and E. Laska (eds.) *Advances in Pain Research and Therapy vol. 18*, pp. 33–53. New York: Raven Press Ltd.

Gronwall, D.M.A. (1977). Paced auditory serial addition task: A measure of recovery from concussion. *Perceptual and Motor Skills*, **44**, 367–73.

Gureje, O., Von Korff, M., Simon, G.E., and Gater, R. (1998). Persistent pain and well-being: A World Health Organization Study in Primary Care. *JAMA*, **280**, 147–51.

Hargreaves D.J., MacDonald R.A.R., and Miell, D. (eds.) (2012). *Musical Imaginations*. Oxford: Oxford University Press.

Haythornthwaite, J.A., Menefee, L.A., Heinberg, L.J., and Clark, M.R. (1998). Pain coping strategies predict perceived control over pain. *Pain*, **77**, 33–9.

Hekmat, H. and Hertel, J.B. (1993). Pain attenuating effects of preferred versus non-preferred music interventions. *Psychology of Music*, **21**, 163–73.

Hodes, R.L., Howland, E.W., Lightfoot, N., and Cleeland, C.S. (1990). The effect of distraction on responses to cold pressor pain. *Pain*, **41**, 109–14.

Janata, P., Tomic, S.T., and Rakowski, S.K. (2007). Characterization of music-evoked autobiographical memories. *Memory*, **15**, 845–60.

Knox, D., Beveridge, S., Mitchell, L.A., and MacDonald, R.A.R. (2012). Acoustic analysis and mood classification of pain-relieving music. *JASA*, **130**, 1–10.

Lazarus, R.S. and Folkman, S. (1984). *Stress, Appraisal and Coping*. New York: Springer.

Leventhal, H. (1992). I know distraction works even though it doesn't. *Health Psychology*, **11**, 208–9.

MacDonald R.A.R., Miell D., and Hargreaves D.J. (eds.) (2002). *Musical Identities*. Oxford: Oxford University Press.

MacDonald R.A.R., Mitchell, L., Dillon, T., Serpell, M.G., Davies, J.B., and Ashley, E.A. (2003). An empirical investigation of the anxiolytic and pain reducing effects of music. *Psychology of Music* **31**(2), 187–203.

Melzack, R. (1975). The McGill Pain Questionnaire: Major properties and scoring methods. *Pain*, **1**, 277–99.

Melzack, R. and Wall, P.D. (1965). Pain mechanisms: A new theory. *Science*, **150**, 971–9.

Melzack, R., Weisz, A.Z., and Sprague, L.T. (1963). Stratagems for controlling pain: Contributions of auditory stimulation and suggestion. *Experimental Neurology*, **8**, 239–47.

Menegazzi, J.J., Paris, P.M., Kersteen, C.H., Flynn, B., and Trautman, D.E. (1991). A randomised controlled trial of the use of music during laceration repair. *Annals of Emergency Medicine*, **20**(4), 348–50.

Meyer, L.B. (1956). *Emotion and meaning in music*. Chicago, IL: Chicago University Press.

Michel, D.E. and Chesky, K.S. (1995). A survey of music therapists using music for pain relief. *Arts in Psychotherapy*, **22**, 49–51.

Miell, D., MacDonald, R.A.R. and Hargreaves, D.J. (eds.) (2005). *Musical Communication*. Oxford: Oxford University Press.

Mitchell, L.A. (2009). Can music overcome hypervigilance and fear of pain? Paper presented at the 7th Triennial Conference of the European Society for the Cognitive Sciences of Music, Jyväskylä, Finland.

Mitchell, L.A. and MacDonald, R.A.R. (2006). An experimental investigation of the effects of preferred and relaxing music on pain perception. *Journal of Music Therapy*, **63**, 295–316.

Mitchell, L.A., MacDonald, R.A.R., and Brodie, E.E. (2006). A comparison of the effects of preferred music, arithmetic, and humour on cold pressor pain. *European Journal of Pain*, **10**, 343–51.

Mitchell, L.A., MacDonald, R.A.R., and Knussen, C. (2008a). An investigation of the effects of music and art on pain perception. *Psychology of Aesthetics, Creativity and the Arts*, **2**(3), 162–70.

Mitchell, L.A., McDowall, J.W., and MacDonald, R.A.R. (2008b). The influence of cognitive style on pain relief using preferred music. Paper presented at the 10th International Conference on Music Perception and Cognition (ICMPC10), Sapporo, Japan.

Morosko, T.E. and Simmons, F.F. (1966) The effect of audio-analgesia on pain threshold and pain tolerance. *Journal of Dental Research*, **45**, 1608–17.

North, A.C. and Hargreaves, D.J. (2007). Lifestyle correlates of musical preference: 1. Relationships, living arrangements, beliefs and crime. *Psychology of Music*, **35**, 58–87.

Perlini, A.H. and Viita, K.A. (1996). Audioanalgesia in the control of experimental pain. *Canadian Journal of Behavioural Science*, **28**(4) 292–301.

Petersen-Felix, S. and Arendt-Nielsen, L. (2002). From pain research to pain treatment; the role of human experimental pain models. *Best Practice and Research Clinical Anaethesiology*, **16**(4), 667–80.

Phillips, C., Main, C., Buck, R., Aylward, M., Wynne-Jones, G., and Farr, A. (2008). Prioritising pain in policy making: The need for a whole systems perspective. *Health Policy*, **88**, 166–75.

Pothoulaki, M., MacDonald, R.A.R., and Flowers, P. (2008). An investigation of the effects of music on anxiety and pain perception in patients undergoing haemodialysis treatment. *Journal of Health Psychology*, **13**(7), 912–20.

Pothoulaki, M., MacDonald, R.A.R & Flowers, P. (in press). A qualitative study of psychological processes in music therapy session with cancer patients. *Journal of Music Therapy*.

Rhudy, J.L., Williams, A.E., McCabe, K.M., Rambo, P.L., and Russell, J.L. (2006). Emotional modulation of spinal nociception and pain: The impact of predictable noxious stimulation. *Pain*, **126**(1), 221–33.

Roy, M., Peretz, I., and Rainville, P. (2008). Emotional valence contributes to music-induced analgesia. *Pain*, **134**, 140–7.

Shiffrin, R.M. (1988). Attention. In: R.C. Atkinson, R.J. Herrnstein, G. Lindzey, and R.D. Luce (eds.) *Stevens' Handbook of Experimental Psychology*, pp. 739–811. New York: Wiley.

Skevington, S.M. (1995). *Psychology of Pain*. Chichester: Wiley.

Sloboda, J.A. and Juslin, P.N. (2001). Psychological perspectives on music and emotion. In: P.N. Jusling and J.A. Sloboda (eds.) *Music and Emotion*, pp. 71–104. Oxford: Oxford University Press.

Spielberger, C.D. (1983). *State-Trait Anxiety Inventory*. Palo Alto, CA: Consulting Psychologists Press.

Standley, J.M. (1986). Music research in medical/dental treatment: Meta analysis and clinical applications. *Journal of Music Therapy*, **23**, 56–122.

Thayer, R.E. (1989). *The Biopsychology of Mood and Arousal*. Oxford: Oxford University Press.

Turk, D.C. and Dworkin, R.H. (2004). What should be the core outcomes in chronic pain clinical trials? *Arthritis Research and Therapy*, **6**, 151–54.

Updike, P (1990). Music therapy results for ICU patients. *Dimensions of Critical Care Nursing*, **9**(1), 39–45.

Villemure, C. and Bushnell, M.C. (2009). Mood influences supraspinal pain processing separately from attention. *Journal of Neuroscience*, **29**(3), 705–15.

Villemure, C., Slotnick, B.M., and Bushnell, M.C. (2003). Effects of odors on pain perception: deciphering the roles of emotion and attention. *Pain*, **106**, 101–8.

Weisenberg, M., Raz, T., and Hener, T. (1998). The influence of film-induced mood on pain perception. *Pain*, **76**, 365–75.

Whipple, B. and Glynn, H.J. (1992). Quantification of the effects of listening to music as a non-invasive method of pain control. *Scholarly Inquiry for Nursing Practice*, **6**, 43–62.

Zhao, H. and Chen, A.C.N. (2009). Both happy and sad melodies modulate tonic human heat pain. *Journal of Pain*, **10**, 953–60.

Chapter 18

The Use of Music in Chronic Illness: Evidence and Arguments

Maria Pothoulaki, Raymond MacDonald, and Paul Flowers

According to the World Health Organization (WHO), cardiovascular disease and cancer are two of the main causes of death worldwide, being responsible for 30% and 13% respectively, of the total deaths in 2005 (WHO 2005). The impact of cancer and chronic illness is likely to grow over the next century, particularly in the developed world where the morbidity and mortality associated with acute and infectious disease is still decreasing (National Center for Health Statistics 2006). Chronic diseases are varied, including cancer and neoplasms, cardiovascular diseases, respiratory diseases, autoimmune diseases, renal failure, diabetes, hepatitis, arthritis, osteoporosis, psychiatric disorders, mental health disorders, chronic fatigue syndrome, and chronic pain. Music interventions have been applied to many of these health conditions, addressing the needs of individuals with cancer (Pothoulaki et al. 2005; Joske et al. 2006), mental illness (Gold et al. 2009; Silverman 2009), renal failure (Schuster 1985; Pothoulaki et al. 2008) multiple sclerosis (Aldridge et al. 2005), traumatic brain injury (Guetin et al. 2009), chronic pain (McCaffrey 2008; Siedliecki 2009), cardiac disease (Barnason et al. 2006; Bruscia et al. 2009), and those in rehabilitation suffering from diverse muscular and neurological diseases (Batt-Rawden 2006). In a meta-analysis by Dileo (2006), 12 different clinical settings were identified examining the effects of music and/or music therapy, with five of them referring to chronic illness; cardiology intensive care units, HIV, rehabilitation-neurological diseases and chronic pain, Alzheimer's disease, and cancer. This chapter presents a current review of the literature addressing the therapeutic use of music among those affected by: (1) chronic illness, (2) cancer, and (3) cardiac disease. The chapter includes a systematic analysis of each of these areas, highlighting music listening (both music therapy and other types of music listening) as the most prevalent type of music activity reported. Results suggest beneficial effects of music listening upon a range of physiological (e.g. blood pressure, heart rate, enzyme production, respiration) and psychological variables (e.g. anxiety, mood, relaxation, pain). Theoretical integration and synthesis is then explored, with three mechanisms presented as possible explanations for the positive effects of music listening: (1) musical communication as a form of social support; (2) emotional engagement with music; (3) increased levels of perceived control.

Systematic literature review

Taking into consideration the diverse clinical settings that have utilized music interventions, the following section presents a systematic literature review conducted in three stages, focusing on chronic illness, cancer, and cardiac disease. Searches were conducted using four electronic databases: PSYCHINFO, WEB OF SCIENCE, SCIENCEDIRECT, and EBSCO (including AMED,

CINAHL, Health Source and MEDLINE databases). Selection criteria involved research reports of journal articles from empirical quantitative and/or qualitative studies published within the period 2006–2009 and written in English; building on earlier reviews by Pothoulaki et al. (2005, 2006). Information on the applied systematic process for all three thematic stages can be found in Table 18.1.

Music and chronic illness

The first stage of the search involved the terms 'music' and 'chronic illness' that initially revealed 821 papers. The term 'music' was utilized in order to include all types of music activity, both listening and participation. The 821 papers represent the total number of papers initially identified from all databases regardless of keywords included in papers. After the initial identification, all papers were examined in terms of keywords and title relevance. So, for instance, papers that involved the above keywords were included in the search as well as papers that did not involve the above keywords but their title was relevant to the search topic. Further to this stage, papers were then examined in order to identify empirical research reports, quantitative and/or qualitative, published in scientific journals. All the above stages took place for each of the thematic sections presented below. In terms of 'music and chronic illness', the above stages revealed 10 papers examining music interventions in relation to chronic illness. The search also revealed one literature review and one meta-analysis of extant research. Table 18.2 provides a summary of the 10 identified studies, in terms of location, sample type, research design, and dependent variables when applicable.

Findings indicate that seven out of the 10 reported studies were randomized controlled trials (RCTs); experimental protocols viewed as the most scientifically robust way of investigating the efficacy of interventions within healthcare contexts (Schulz et al. 2010). In addition, six studies were conducted in the USA, one in Germany, one in Norway, one in China, and one in Taiwan. The underlying health conditions that were addressed in relation to music were: mental disorders (Silverman 2009), cancer and cardiac disease (Bruscia et al. 2009), chronic pain (Siedliecki and Good 2006; Siedliecki 2009), paediatric patients with sleep apnoea (Smith et al. 2009), migraine (Oelkers-Ax et al. 2007), and cerebral palsy (Yu et al. 2009), rehabilitation patients with different types of diseases, such as muscular diseases, chronic fatigue, neurological diseases, etc. (Batt-Rawden 2006), and lastly, dementia patients (Sung et al. 2006; Yu et al. 2009). In addition, with reference to sample characteristics (when available), female participants outnumbered male participants. This is in keeping with previous literature reviews (Pothoulaki et al. 2005). The above

Table 18.1 Information on the applied systematic process

Literature reviews	Databases	Time period	Keywords used	Selection criteria
Music and chronic illness	PSYCHINFO, WEB OF SCIENCE, SCIENCEDIRECT and EBSCO (including AMED, CINAHL, Health Source and MEDLINE databases)	2006–2009	Music and Chronic Illness	Research reports of journal articles from empirical quantitative and/or qualitative studies written in English
Music and cancer			Music and Cancer	
Music and cardiac disease			a) Music and cardiac disease	
			b) Music and heart disease	

Table 18.2 Summary of relevant identified studies 'music and chronic illness'

Study	Sample details	Research design	Dependent variables
Silverman (2009) USA	n=105 (psychiatric patients)	RCT	Satisfaction with life Knowledge of illness Treatment perceptions Response type and frequency
Bruscia et al. (2009) USA	n=182 (f=57%, m=43%) (cancer patients=55) (cardiac patients=127) b) mean age=59.8	Survey	
***Siedliecki (2009) USA**	n=60 (f=46, m=14) (African American and Caucasian patients with chronic pain) b) 21–65 years	RCT—secondary analysis of data	Racial variation in response to music Racial variation in post-treatment pain scoring
Smith et al. (2009) USA	n=97 (f=44, m=53) (sleep apnoea patients)	RCT	Adherence to CPAP Physical health Mental health Depression Patient satisfaction
Park (2009) USA	n=15 (f=11, m=4) (dementia patients) b) 60–100 years	Quasi-experimental design—pilot study (within-subjects/ repeated measures design)	Pain
Yu et al. (2009) China	n=60 (children patients with cerebral palsy undergoing acupuncture)	RCT	Anxiety Blood pressure Heart rate
Oelkers-Ax et al. (2008) Germany	n=58 (paediatric migraine patients) 8–12 years	RCT	Headache frequency Depression Stress Behavioural and emotional problems
Batt-Rawden (2006) Norway	n=22 (f=13, m=9) (rehabilitation patients) 34–65 years	Qualitative study (ethnography and grounded theory)	
***Siedliecki and Goood (2006) USA**	n=60 (f=46, m=14) (African American and Caucasian patients with chronic pain) b) 21–65 years	RCT	Pain depression disability power

(continued)

Table 18.2 (Continued) Summary of relevant identified studies 'music and chronic illness'

Study	Sample details	Research design	Dependent variables
Sung et al. (2006) Taiwan	n=36 (f=10, m=26) (institutionalized elders with dementia) 76–79 years	RCT	Agitation

F, female; m, male, RCT, randomized controlled trial.

finding could have epidemiological foundations, relating to specific disease prevalence and gender. Alternatively females are perhaps more inclined to engage with in complementary therapies than men.

Music utilized in these studies involved predominantly music listening interventions that did not include a music therapist, with the exception of the studies by Silverman (2009) and Oelkers-Ax et al. (2008). Listening interventions were varied, e.g. Siedliecki and Good (2006) utilized both self-selected music and pre-selected music whereas Yu et al. (2009) and Park (2009) employed preferred music listening. Other studies applied alternative types of music listening, such as music-based audiotape with instructions for continuous positive airway pressure (CPAP) and instructions for muscle relaxation (Smith et al. 2009), group music with movement interventions (Sung et al. 2006), and CD listening in combination with patients' narratives (Batt-Rawden 2006). Studies mainly examined psychological variables such as anxiety, pain, agitation, perception of power, mood, depression, disability, and other parameters related to health and quality of life, in addition to physiological variables, such as sleep, headaches, blood pressure, and heart rate. These variables are concurrent with the 40 outcome variables presented in the meta-analysis of Dileo (2006) focusing on the effects of music and music therapy in medical patients.

Findings of the above studies revealed that the use of music and music therapy significantly influenced many of the outcome measures and positively enhanced standard care. More specifically, in the study by Siedliecki and Good (2006) with patients suffering from chronic non-malignant pain, researchers reported that participants in both music groups experienced and perceived significantly more power, less pain, less depression and disability than the control group. In addition, Yu et al. (2009) reported that preferred music listening significantly reduced anxiety for children undergoing acupuncture, with supporting physiological measures showing reduced blood pressure and heart rate. Park (2009) reported a significant post-test (after music listening) pain decrease and Smith et al. (2009) reported a significant increase of patients adhering to CPAP procedures at the end of the first month. Sung et al. (2006) reported a significant reduction in the occurrence of agitated behaviour in older adults with dementia over time. A qualitative study by Batt-Rawden (2006) reported an increase in self-awareness, consciousness, and quality of life and a motivation for social interaction with direct implications for recovery and healing. With reference to the studies that applied music therapy as an intervention, Oelkers-Ax et al. (2008) reported a significant reduction of headache frequency during treatment period. Finally Silverman (2009) suggested that music therapy can be successfully used in psychoeducational contexts with psychiatric patients.

Music and cancer

Before presenting the current literature review it is worth outlining our previous review (Pothoulaki et al. 2005), which reviewed 24 papers published between 1985–2002 investigating music and cancer. Key positive effects reported were the reduction in side effects of chemotherapy (Frank 1985; Standley 1992) such as reduction in patients' perceived degree of vomiting, reported nausea, and reported anxiety (Frank 1985; Palakanis et al. 1994; Sabo and Michael 1996) as well as reductions in state anxiety and psychological effects such as emotional changes, improvement in wellbeing and quality of life (Pfaff et al. 1989; Bunt and Marston-Wyld 1995; Weber et al. 1997; Burns et al. 2001; O'Callaghan 2001; Barrera et al. 2002); physiological effects (Bartlett et al. 1993; Burns et al. 2001; Kuhn 2002) with particular reference to the enforcement of the immune system; behavioural improvements (Pfaff et al. 1989; Robb 2000; Burns 2001; Waldon 2001; Barrera et al. 2002) and communication and expression improvements (Bunt and Marston-Wyld 1995; O'Callaghan 1996; Weber et al. 1997; Tobia et al. 1999; Gallagher and Steele 2001).

Critical design and methodology issues were also identified, including the questionable reliability and validity of assessment tools used as well as the method of administration, limited description of the actual process of the music intervention, and limited follow-up data (Pothoulaki et al. 2006). These are important hurdles to overcome if the results of studies are to be viewed as reliable in term of developing evidence based music interventions.

The present literature review initially revealed 1612 papers. Following a thorough analysis by applying the previously mentioned search criteria (please see Table 18.1), a total of 26 distinct research reports were identified as directly relevant to the topic of music and cancer. Table 18.3 provides methodological details of the studies in terms of location, sample type, research design, and dependent variables when applicable.

Table 18.3 Summary of relevant identified studies 'music and cancer'

Study	Sample details	Research design	Dependent variables
Bulfone et al. (2009) Italy	a) n=60 (female breast cancer patients during adjuvant post-surgical chemotherapy treatment)	RCT	Anxiety
Nakayama et al. (2009) Japan	a) n=10 (Hospice residents)	Quantitative study (within-subjects design)	Mood stress
Burns et al. (2009) USA	a) n=12 (f=5, m=7) (adolescents and young adults hospitalized receiving stem cell transplantation) b) 13–24 years	RCT	Anxiety Pain Mood Defensive and courageous Coping Derived meaning Resilience Quality of life
O'Callaghan et al. (2009) Australia	a) n=27 (f=20, m=7) (cancer patients/parents)	Qualitative study	
Wan et al. (2009) China	a) n=136 (cancer patients)	RCT	Anxiety depression pain
Horne-Thompson and Grocke (2008) Australia	a) n=25 (hospice residents)	RCT	Anxiety Symptoms (pain, tiredness, drowsiness)

(continued)

Table 18.3 (Continued) Summary of relevant identified studies 'music and cancer'

Study	Sample details	Research design	Dependent variables
Magill and Berenson (2008) USA	—	Qualitative study—case study reports	
Magill et al. (2008) USA	a) n=39 (critically ill cancer patients)	Mixed-methods	Cancer distress
Lu et al. (2008) China	a) n=38 (cancer patients)	Quantitative study (within-subjects design)	Quality of life
O'Callaghan (2008) Australia	—	Qualitative analysis— grounded theory	
Robb et al. (2008) USA	a) n=83 (paediatric oncology patients) b) 4–7 years	RCT	Coping related behaviours (positive facial affect, active engagement, initiation)
Burns et al. (2008) USA	a) n=49 (f=30, m=19) (patients receiving intensive myelosuppressive chemotherapy) b) mean age=55.5	RCT	Positive and negative affect Fatigue Anxiety
Cooper and Foster (2008) UK	a) n=250 (patients waiting to undergo chemotherapy or radiotherapy)	Quantitative study	Anxiety
Wlodarczyk (2007) USA	a) n=10 (f=8, m=2) (hospice residents) b) 26–75 years	Within-subjects design	Spiritual wellbeing
Oneschuk et al. (2007) Canada	a) 136 (Canadian palliative care settings)	Online survey	
O'Callaghan et al. (2007) Australia	a) n=102 (paediatric radiotherapy patients=39, family members and friends= 63) b) ≥14 years	Qualitative study—Case study reports	
O'Callaghan and Dermott (2007) Australia	a) n=257 (patients who experienced MT=128, patients who overheard=27, hospital visitors=41, staff=61)	Qualitative study— discourse analysis	
Daykin et al. (2007) UK	a) n=23 (cancer patients in a CAM centre)	Qualitative study— grounded theory	
Windich-Biermeier et al. (2007) USA	a) n=50 (children and adolescents cancer patients)	Intervention-comparison group design (between-subjects design)	Pain fear distress

Table 18.3 (Continued) Summary of relevant identified studies 'music and cancer'

Study	Sample details	Research design	Dependent variables
Gallagher et al. (2006) USA	a) n=200 (f=59%, m=41%) (patients with chronic and advanced illnesses) b) 24–87 years	Quantitative study (within-subjects design)	Mood Anxiety Depression Pain Shortness of breath
Daykin et al. (2006) UK	a) 80 UK cancer care organizations (hospices, hospitals, and cancer help centres)	Survey	
Nelson (2006) USA	a) n=15 (f=8, m=7) (hospice residents) b) 26–83 years	Qualitative study—ethnography	
Hanser et al. (2006) USA	a) n= 70 (female patients with metastatic breast cancer) 26–77 years	RCT (longitudinal)	Psychological functioning Quality of life Physiological stress arousal
Shaban et al. (2006) Iran	a) n=100 (cancer patients)	Quantitative study (between-subjects design)	Pain relief
Clark et al. (2006) USA	a) n=63 (patients undergoing radiation therapy)	RCT	Emotional distress (anxiety, depression and treatment related distress) Symptoms (fatigue, pain)
Bozcuk et al. (2006) Turkey	a) – (breast cancer patients during chemotherapy)	Within-subjects design	Quality of life and parameters (insomnia, appetite)

F, female; m, male, RCT, randomized controlled trial.

In terms of location, most studies were conducted in the USA (n=11), five studies in Australia, five in Asia and Middle East (including countries such as Japan, China, Iran, and Turkey), four studies in Europe, and one in Canada. Location of studies provides a geographical 'mapping' of relevant research; for instance, the USA and Australia have increased research activity in music therapy, and an active music therapy 'corpus'. In addition, studies conducted in Asia mainly derive from the medical field.

A total of 1619 patients participated in the above identified studies. Most studies involved cancer patients, with various types and stages of cancer, although there were studies that involved also other types of patients such as HIV patients and those with pain disorders, Gardner's syndrome, sickle cell diseases and other chronic and advanced illnesses (Gallagher et al. 2006; Wlodarczyk 2007). Furthermore, four studies involved paediatric cancer patients such as children and adolescents and in some cases young adults (O'Callaghan et al. 2007; Windich-Biermeier et al. 2007; Robb et al. 2008; Burns et al. 2009).

With reference to study design, 18 studies were quantitative, out of which the majority described their design as an RCT. The remaining quantitative studies involved five studies using within-subjects design, three studies using between-subjects design, and two surveys. Seven studies were qualitative in nature. Three of the studies involved case study reports, two involved grounded theory analysis, one involved discourse analysis, and one ethnography. Finally, only one study applied a mixed-methods approach by using both quantitative and qualitative methods.

Although most studies (n=15) reported using music therapy as an intervention, they did not specify the types of music therapy utilized. Two studies applied preferred music listening, four studies applied pre-selected music listening, and two studies involved music with other techniques and/or interventions with the involvement of a music therapist.

Most quantitative studies applied measures for anxiety or distress either as a distinct outcome variable or these were combined with other psychological outcome variables such as depression, pain, mood and fatigue (Clark et al. 2006; Gallagher et al. 2006; Hanser et al. 2006; Horne-Thompson and Grocke 2008; Magill et al. 2008; Bulfone et al. 2009; Burns et al. 2009; Nakayama et al. 2009; Wan et al. 2009). Other studies measured quality of life as a single outcome variable or in addition to other dependent variables (Bozcuk et al. 2006; Lu et al. 2008; Burns et al. 2009; Hanser et al. 2006). Two studies also applied physiological measures in addition to psychological, namely cortisol levels (Nakayama et al. 2009) and heart rate measurements (Hanser et al. 2006).

Music and cardiac disease

Cardiac disease is a major area under the broader spectrum of chronic illness, and as such it is the third topic of investigation of this literature review. In terms of providing an overview of the extant research, previous research literature on music and cardiac disease published within 1985–2004 focused primarily on music's physiological effects in relation to cardiac disease. It is of interest that all relevant studies identified within this period were quantitative in nature. Suggested evidence supported the effectiveness of music in a variety of psychosocial outcome measures: anxiety reduction (Robichaud-Ekstrand 1999; Knight and Rickard 2001; Tsai 2004); mood changes (MacNay 1995; Mockel et al. 1995; Cadigan et al. 2001); relaxation increase (Robichaud-Ekstrand 1999; Tsai 2004); psychological parameters such as reduction in 'fear' and 'worries', reported sleep improvement and perceived exertion (MacNay 1995; Vollert et al. 2003; Metzger 2004; Tsai 2004); and physiological parameters such as blood pressure, heart rate, and hormones in patients and healthy individuals (Guzzetta 1989; Mockel et al. 1995; Escher and Evequoz 1999; Robichaud-Ekstrand 1999; Cadigan et al. 2001; Knight and Rickard 2001; Schein et al. 2001; Vollert et al. 2002; Vollert et al. 2003; Chafin et al. 2004).

Across this corpus of work there were noticeable methodological limitations, such as issues related to study design and uncontrollable factors/confounding variables, issues related to the rationale for the selection of music interventions, reliability, validity and appropriate administration of assessment tools and limited follow-up data. Unfortunately this raises questions regarding the credibility of the evidence and implies the need for a more thorough approach, with particular reference to research design and the appropriate use of psychometric instruments.

The present search provides additional evidence on the body of literature reviewed above. Keywords used for this search involve: 'music' and 'cardiac disease' and in cases where there were no results, 'cardiac disease' was replaced by the words 'heart disease' (see Table 18.1). The search initially revealed 558 papers. Following a thorough analysis of the identified papers involving the previously mentioned stages 551 papers were excluded and a total of seven journal articles were deemed relevant to this chapter. These studies are presented in Table 18.4.

Table 18.4 Summary of relevant identified studies 'music and cardiac disease'

Study	Sample details	Research design	Dependent variables
Twiss et al. (2009) USA	a) n=60 (patients admitted for surgery) b) <65 years	RCT	Postoperative anxiety Intubation time
Nilsson (2009) Sweden	a) n=58 (patients who had undergone open coronary artery bypass grafting or aortic valve replacement surgery) b) mean age=66.5	RCT	Stress physiological response Pain Anxiety
Tang et al. (2009) USA	a) n=41 (f=35, m=6) (older adults with hypertension) b) mean age=85	RCT	Blood pressure (systolic, diastolic)
Okada et al. (2009) Japan	a) n=87 (patients with CVD)	Between-subjects design	Cardiac autonomic activity (heart rate) Plasma cytokine Catecholamine levels
Buffum et al. (2006) USA	a) n=170 (f=4, m=166) (patients waiting to undergo vascular angiography) b) mean age=66.8	Quasi-experimental design—RCT	Anxiety
Sendelbach et al. (2006) USA	a) n=86 (f=30.2%, m=69.8%) (patients undergoing cardiac surgery) b) mean age=63.3	RCT	Pain intensity Anxiety Physiological parameters (systolic and diastolic blood pressure, heart rate) Opioid consumption
Hatem et al. (2006) Brazil	a) n=84 (children in paediatric cardiac intensive care unit) b) day 1–16 years	RCT	Heart rate Blood pressure and mean blood pressure Respiratory rate Temperature Oxygen saturation Pain

F, female; m, male, RCT, randomized controlled trial.

Studies identified were conducted in the USA (n=4), Japan (n=1), Sweden (n=1), and Brazil (n=1). Participants in these studies involved individuals with some type of cardiovascular problems (e.g. hypertension), individuals who had undergone cardiovascular surgery, and one study involved paediatric cardiac patients. With the exception of a pediatric patients study, all participants were older adults of a similar age range.

Most of the studies applied an RCT design and examined the effects of music in both physiological and psychological parameters. In particular, in terms of music interventions, most studies used music listening, with one study using preferred music (Buffum et al. 2006) and two (Sendelbach et al. 2006; Okada et al. 2009) utilizing music therapy.

Outcome measures were both physiological and psychological. However, greater emphasis tended to be placed upon physiological variables, possibly due to the fact that the majority of researchers/authors were coming from medical disciplines. Physiological measures involved heart rate, parameters of heart rate variability (e.g. rMSSD and pNN50), plasma cytokine and catecholamine levels, respiratory rate, mean arterial pressure, systolic blood pressure, diastolic blood pressure, arterial oxygen pressure, arterial oxygen saturation, and opioid consumption. Psychological variables examined were anxiety and pain. Two studies indicated that the use of music was beneficial for a number of physiological parameters (Hatem et al. 2006; Okada et al. 2009) while others did not find any significant differences between groups with reference to physiological variables (Sendelbach et al. 2006).

Towards a synthesis

To summarize, studies focused upon cancer patients tend to utilize music therapy as a music intervention. However, studies focusing on cardiac patients and other types of chronic illnesses tended to use mostly music listening interventions without the input of a music therapist. Although methodological shortcomings can be identified in a number of studies across conditions, such as the assertion of using of a RCT design with a convenience sample and/or small sample of participants and the incorrect administration of psychometrics, the methodological quality of the above studies is considerably improved compared to methodological issues raised in preceding studies identified in previous literature review (Pothoulaki et al. 2006). In the present selection of studies the increased use of RCT designs should be highlighted as a major improvement within the reported literature compared to previous years, where RCT designs were rarely used. In addition, qualitative studies reported theoretical frameworks such as ethnography, discourse analysis, and grounded theory whereas earlier qualitative studies existing in the literature tended not to report theoretical approaches and analysis details.

With reference to the above issues, the examination of both physiological and psychological outcome variables related only to short-term aspects of wellbeing. The outcome measures indicate an increased interest in short-term effects, due to the nature of illness, the related symptoms and the notion and sense of 'future'. More specifically, in life-threatening illnesses such as cancer, the 'future' perspective and consequently long-term outcomes may not be as critical as short-term outcomes and references to the 'present' (Pothoulaki et al. under review). Still, the reported research context, regardless of the adopted methodology and outcome differences, does share with previously identified studies in the literature (Pothoulaki et al. 2005) the research interest in the 'musical presence and process' in clinical settings. As such, differing evidence, settings and methodologies can be linked by an underlined theoretical framework. Studies supporting the effects of music interventions and music therapy rely upon different psychological outcome variables and suggest fragmentary explanations for their findings. In the section that follows we synthesize and integrate these diverse findings and draw upon three distinct theoretical perspectives which together illuminate the emerging consensus regarding the relevancy and effectiveness of music interventions in chronic illness.

Implications for theory

Music may have no direct effect in terms of the underlying physiological causes of chronic disease; however, this chapter provides evidence that music can affect components that are related to perceived quality of life as well as psychological wellbeing. Three main theoretical arguments can be provided in order to contextualize the above findings and support the role of music interventions in the course of chronic illness. These arguments refer to: musical communication and support, emotional engagement, and, locus of control (perceived control).

Musical communication as social support

Many authors have suggested that musical communication and musical interaction can provide social support and positive social interaction (Neugebauer and Aldridge 1998; Trevarthen and Malloch 2000; MacDonald and Miell 2002; Ansdell and Pavlicevic 2005; Miell et al. 2005). More specifically, the concept of 'communication' and 'connectivity' is an underlying premise in most studies. With reference to this issue, primary importance can be placed not only on the musical communication but also on the group interaction and the desire for communication through the musical expression. As a result, musical communication, as a creative means of self-expression, serves to establish and develop a 'connective' bond between patients/participants, relatives and healthcare staff. The group context or the 'musical companionship', as described by Ansdell and Pavlicevic (2005), is of essential importance when looking at group music therapy processes. Cancer is an illness with serious physical symptoms that change the everyday life of patients and often creates feelings of isolation. Therefore, the formation of a group, offers participants the opportunity to constructively interact, establish strong social bonds and receive social support in an atypical, but nevertheless, fundamental and 'holistic' context. Furthermore, when relating these concepts to health and social support, a number of studies have outlined in the past the importance of social support in perceiving and coping with illness (Heitzmann and Kaplan 1984; Peterson and Seligman 1984; Groarke et al. 2004; Pattenden et al. 2002). Consequently, it can be argued that if musical communication and musical interaction is a form of social support and 'companionship', then the application of music interventions is of direct relevance to the clinical and healthcare services.

Emotional engagement with music

Emotional engagement with music is the second theoretical argument that supports the relevance of music interventions in healthcare settings. For instance, researchers relating the musical experience with emotional responses have suggested that emotional responses to music can be shaped by 'iconic relationships. . . between a musical structure and some event or agent carrying emotional tone' (Sloboda and Juslin 2001, p. 93). 'Iconic relationships' (Sloboda and Juslin 2001) are also related to associative theories of musical communication (Davies 1978; Hargreaves et al. 2005). Associative theories refer to the relationship of experienced musical stimuli and non-musical events that are attributed emotional meaning. For example, a particular piece of music maybe reminiscent of a family holiday or a past relationship. While this approach suggests that feelings and emotional responses to music are individual and distinctive, there are examples of cultural influences leading to collective emotional responses (Sloboda and Juslin 2001), such as lyrical themes in Christian religious ceremonies.

This theoretical argument provides a basis for studies that have utilized participants' preferred music as an intervention (Clark et al. 2006; Buffum et al. 2006; Bulfone et al. 2009; Mitchell et al. 2007; Park 2009; Yu et al. 2009), in that the reported effects can be related to participants' musical choices and the emotional meaning that they attributed to the particular musical stimuli that they chose. Based on this argument, particular interest would lie on the investigation of the effects of preferred versus pre-selected music to patients (Mitchell et al. 2008; Pothoulaki et al. 2008). Related to the emotionally engaging aspects of music listening is the possibility that music provides a means for listeners to be distracted from other stimuli that may have negative effects (MacDonald et al. 2003; Mitchell et al. 2007).

Music and perceived control

Locus of control and perceived control is a major issue for patients suffering from chronic illnesses. Models of illness representations have outlined the importance of perceived control and locus of control in relation to patients' illness representations (Wallston et al. 1976; Bandura 1980; Leventhal et al. 1984; Turnquist et al. 1988). Most patients suffering from diverse types of chronic illnesses experience lack of control due to physical and psychological symptoms that restrict their activities and their lifestyle. As a result, patients can feel a reduced sense of control over their illness and over their life in general which means that interventions that help to regain a sense of control have considerable utility within a healthcare context.

Studies which involved preferred music and focused on pain, have indicated that music interventions can be effective in modifying the perception of pain and increasing participants' coping abilities (Brown et al. 1989; Mitchell et al. 2008). With reference to the findings of qualitative studies outlined in this literature review, the issue of control constitutes a strong theoretical basis for explaining these results. More specifically, Magill et al. (2008) reported that preferred music is important in terms of sense of control and emotional coping. Furthermore, the issue of control can also be traced in themes that are related to identity, self-expression and self-awareness (Daykin et al. 2007; O'Callaghan and McDermott 2007; O'Callaghan et al. 2007). Such findings are in line with Aldridge (1991) suggesting that interventions involving creative forms of expression are applicable to individuals with chronic illness because they can help them regain a sense of control and autonomy.

In light of this argument, it should also be noted that most hospitalized patients suffering from chronic illnesses experience a reality based on 'loss of control'. They do not have control of their treatment and of their everyday activities and more importantly sometimes, they do not have control of their physical activities due to the side effects of medication and illness symptoms.

In conclusion, this chapter has presented an overview of research investigating the efficacy of music interventions for individuals with chronic illness with a particular focus on cancer and cardiac disease. A number of positive outcomes were highlighted relating to psychological and physiological measures. Musical interaction in all its manifestations elicits human reactions that address wider and topical research questions in healthcare. Further research can continue these advances to highlight how music interventions can complement the biomedical management of the healing process within chronic illness. For example, the evidence presented here does not suggest that all music listening will produce beneficial effects and further studies investigating under what conditions music may be beneficial are required. Also, there is much work to be done on the nature of both the music and the social context within the musical activities take place. The extent to which structural features such as tempo and melodic contour interact with psychological features such as preference and familiarity needs to be understood in more detail. In addition, within the context of music and health, 'iconic relationships' should be further examined with reference to musical events and health 'moments/memories'. If a musical stimulus has emotional connotations and can be associated to an experienced life moment/memory, then is it possible that 'preferred' musical stimuli may be associated to individual health moments/memories in life? And if so, what effect do these reminiscences have on chronically ill patients and to what extend is this related to wellbeing within the context of chronic illness? Future research could shed light on the recollection and emotional revival of health memories. Other questions to be investigated include to what extent music is a unique intervention and can other interventions produce similar effects. It may be that the capacity of music listening to distract and engage the listener both cognitively and emotionally and to produce these effects with relatively little effort from the listener does indeed make it a unique stimulus. However, what is clear is that theories of musical communication, emotional engagement with music, and perceived control provide a framework to contextualize and explain why music can produce beneficial effects in the contexts presented. These explanations bind musical experiences to wider psychological principles of healing. This also highlights the inextricable link that exists between music listening and psychological and social variables related to health and wellbeing. These factors make investigating the relationship between music, health and wellbeing both timely and urgent.

References

Aldridge, D. (1991). Physiological change, communication, and the playing of improvised music: some proposals for research. *The Arts in Psychotherapy, 18*, 59–64.

Aldridge, D., Schmid, W., Kaeder, M., Schmidt, C., and Ostermann, T. (2005). Functionality or aesthetics? A pilot study of music therapy in the treatment of multiple sclerosis patients. *Complementary Therapies in Medicine, 13*(1), 25–33.

Ansdell, G. and Pavlicevic, M. (2005). Musical companionship, musical community. Music therapy and the process and value of musical communication. In: D. Miell, R. MacDonald, and D.J. Hargreaves (eds.) *Musical Communication*, pp. 193–213. Oxford: Oxford University Press.

Bandura, A. (1980). *Social learning theory*. Englewood Cliffs, NJ: Prentice Hall.

Barnason, S., Zimmerman, L., and Nieveen, J. (2006). The effects of music interventions on anxiety in the patient after coronary artery bypass grafting. *Heart & Lung: the Journal of Acute and Critical Care, 24*(2), 124–32.

Barrera, M.E., Rykov, M.H., and Doyle, S.L. (2002). The effects of interactive music therapy on hospitalized children with cancer: A pilot study. *Psycho-Oncology, 11*(5), 379–88.

Bartlett, D., Kaufman, D., and Smeltekop, R. (1993). The effects of music listening and perceived sensory experiences on the immune system as measured by interleukin–1 and cortisol. *Journal of Music Therapy, 30*(4), 194–209.

Batt-Rawden, K.B. (2006). Music: a strategy to promote health in rehabilitation? An evaluation of participation in a 'music and health promotion project'. *International Journal of Rehabilitation Research, 29*, 171–3.

Bozcuk, H., Artac, M., Kara, A., Ozdogan, M., Sualp, Y., Topcu, Z., *et al.* (2006). Does music exposure during chemotherapy improve quality of life in early breast cancer patients? A pilot study. *International Medical Journal of Experimental and Clinical Research, 12*(5), 200–5.

Brown, C.J., Chen, A.C.N., and Dworkin, S.F. (1989). Music in the control of human pain. *Music Therapy, 8*, 47–60.

Bruscia, K., Dileo, C., Shultis, C., and Dennery, K. (2009). Expectations of hospitalized cancer and cardiac patients regarding the medical and psychotherapeutic benefits of music therapy. *The Arts in Psychotherapy, 36*, 239–44.

Buffum, M.D., Sasso, C., Sands, L.P., Lanier, E., Yellen, M., and Hayes, A. (2006). A music intervention to reduce anxiety before vascular angiography procedures. *Journal of Vascular Nursing, 24*(3), 68–73.

Bulfone, T., Quattrin, R., Zanotti, R., Regattin, L., and Brusaferro, S. (2009). Effectiveness of music therapy for anxiety reduction in women with breast cancer in chemotherapy treatment. *Holistic Nursing Practice, 2*(4), 238–42.

Bunt, L. and Marston-Wyld, J. (1995). Where words fail music takes over: A collaborative study by a music therapist and a counselor in the context of cancer care. *Music Therapy Perspectives, 13*(1), 46–50.

Burns, D.S. (2001). The effect of the Bonny method of guided imagery and music on the mood and life quality of cancer patients. *Journal of Music Therapy, 38*(1), 51–65.

Burns, S.J.I., Harbuz, M.S., Hucklebridge, F., and Bunt, L. (2001). A pilot study into the therapeutic effects of music therapy at a cancer help center. *Alternative Therapies in Health and Medicine, 7*(1), 48–56.

Burns, D.S., Azzouz, F., Sledge, R., Rutledge, C., Hincher, K., Monahan, P.O., *et al.* (2008). Music imagery for adults with acute leukaemia in protective environments: a feasibility study. *Supportive Care in Cancer, 16*(5), 507–13.

Burns, D.S., Robb, S., and Haase. J. E. (2009). Exploring the feasibility of a therapeutic music video intervention in adolescents and young adults during stem-cell transplantation. *Cancer Nursing*, **32**(5), E9–E16.

Cadigan, M.E., Caruso, N.A., Haldeman, S.M., McNamara, M.E., Noyes, D.A., Spadafora, M.A. *et al.* (2001). The effects of music on cardiac patients on bed rest. *Progress in Cardiovascular Nursing*, **16**(1), 5–13.

Chafin, S., Roy, M., Gerin, W., and Christenfeld, N. (2004). Music can facilitate blood pressure recovery from stress. *British Journal of Health Psychology*, **9**, 393–403.

Clark, M., Isaacks-Downton, G., Wells, N., Redlin-Frazier, S., Eck, C., Hepworth, J.T., et al. (2006). Use of preferred music to reduce emotional distress and symptom activity during radiation therapy. *Journal of Music Therapy*, **43**(3), 247–65.

Cooper, L. and Foster, I. (2008). The use of music to aid patients' relaxation in a radiotherapy waiting room. *Radiography*, **14**, 184–8.

Davies, J.B. (1978). *The Psychology of Music*. London: Hutchinson.

Daykin, N., Bunt, L., and McClean, S. (2006). Music and healing in cancer care: A survey of supportive care providers. *The Arts in Psychotherapy*, **33**(5), 402–13.

Daykin, N., McClean, S., and Bunt, L. (2007). Creativity, identity and healing: participants' accounts of music therapy in cancer care. Health: *An Interdisciplinary Journal for the Social Study of Health, Illness and Medicine*, **11**(3), 349–70.

Dileo, C. (2006). Effects of music and music therapy on medical patients: a meta-analysis of the research and implications for the future. *Journal of the Society for Integrative Oncology*, **4**(2), 67–70.

Escher, J. and Evequoz, D. (1999). Music and heart rate variability. Study of the effect of music on heart rate variability in healthy adolescents. *Schweizerische Rundschau fur Medizin Praxis*, **88**(21), 951–52.

Frank, J.M. (1985). The effects of music therapy and guided visual imagery on chemotherapy induced nausea and vomiting. *Oncology Nursing Forum*, **12**(5), 47–52.

Gallagher, L.M. and Steele, A.L. (2001). Developing and using a computerized database for music therapy in palliative medicine. *Journal of Palliative Care*, **17**(3), 147–54.

Gallagher, L.M., Lagman, R., Walsh, D., Davis, M.P., and LeGrand, S.B. (2006). The clinical effects of music therapy in palliative medicine. *Supportive Care in Cancer*, **14**(8), 859–66.

Gold, C., Solli, H.P., Kruger, V., and Lie, S.A. (2009). Dose-response relationship in music therapy for people with serious mental disorders: Systematic review and meta-analysis. *Clinical Psychology Review*, **29**, 193–207.

Groarke, A., Curtis, R., Coughlan, R., and Gsel, A. (2004). The role of perceived and actual disease status in adjustment to rheumatoid arthritis. *Rheumatology*, **43**(9), 1142–9.

Guetin, S., Soua, B., Voiriot, G., Picot, M-C., and Herisson, C. (2009). The effect of music therapy on mood and anxiety–depression: An observational study in institutionalised patients with traumatic brain injury. *Annals of Physical and Rehabilitation Medicine*, **52**(1), 30–40.

Guzzetta, C.E. (1989). Effects of relaxation and music therapy on patients in a coronary care unit with presumptive acute myocardial infarction. *Heart and Lung: The Journal of Critical Care*, **18**(6), 606–16.

Haetzman, M., Elliott, A.M, Smith, B.H., Hannaford, P., and Chambers, W.A. (2003). Chronic pain and the use of conventional and alternative therapy. *Family Practice*, **20**(2), 147–54.

Hanser, S.B., Bauer-Wu, S., Kubicek, L., Healey, M., Manola, J., Hernandez, M., *et al.* (2006). Effects of a music therapy intervention on quality of life and distress in women with Metastatic breast cancer. *Journal of the Society for Integrative Oncology*, **4**(3), 116–24.

Hargreaves, D.J., MacDonald, R.A.R., and Miell, D. (2005). How do people communicate using music? In D. Miell, R.A.R. MacDonald, and D.J. Hargreaves (eds.) *Musical Communication*, pp. 1–26. Oxford: Oxford University Press.

Hatem, T.P., Lira, P.I, and Mattos, S.S. (2006). The therapeutic effects of music in children following cardiac surgery. *Jornal de Pediatria*, **82**(3), 186–92.

Heitzmann, C.A. and Kaplan, R.M. (1984). Interaction between sex and social support in the control of type II diabetes mellitus. *Journal of Consulting and Clinical Psychology*, **52**, 1087–9.

Horne-Thompson, A., and Grocke, D. (2008). The effect of music therapy on anxiety in patients who are terminally ill. *Journal of Palliative Medicine*, **11**(4), 582–90.

Joske, D.J.L., Rao, A., and Kristjanson, L. (2006). Critical review of complementary therapies in haemato-oncology. *Internal Medicine Journal*, **36**, 579–86.

Knight W.E. and Rickard, N.S. (2001). Relaxing music prevents stress-induced increases in subjective anxiety, systolic blood pressure and heart rate in healthy males and females. *Journal of Music Therapy*, **XXXVIII** (4), 254–72.

Kuhn, D. (2002). The effects of active and passive participation in musical activity on the immune system as measured by salivary immunoglobulin A (SigA). *Journal of Music Therapy*, **39**(1), 30–9.

Leventhal, H., Zimmerman, R., and Gutmann, M. (1984). Compliance: a self-regulation perspective. In: D. Gentry (ed.) *Handbook of behavioural medicine*, pp. 369–434. New York: Pergammon Press.

Lu, X., Lu, Y., and Liao, X. (2008). Study on influence of music therapy on quality of life of cancer patients. *Chinese Nursing Research*, **22**(1B), 106–8.

MacDonald, R.A.R. and Miell, D. (2002). Music for individuals with special needs: A catalyst for developments in identity, communication and musical ability. In: R.A.R. MacDonald, D. Miell, and D.J. Hargreaves (eds.) *Musical Identities*, pp. 163–79. Oxford: Oxford University Press.

MacDonald, R.A.R., Mitchell, L.A., Dillon, T., Serpell, M.G., Davies, J.B., and Ashley, E.A. (2003). An empirical investigation of the anxiolytic and pain reducing effects of music. *Psychology of Music*, **31**(2), 187–203.

MacNay, S.K. (1995). The influence of the preferred music on the perceived exertion, mood and time estimation scores of patients participating in a cardiac rehabilitation exercise program. *Music Therapy Perspectives*, **13**(2), 91–6.

Magill, L. and Berenson, S. (2008). The conjoint use of music therapy and reflexology with hospitalized advanced stage cancer patients and their families. *Palliative and Supportive Care*, **6**, 289–96.

Magill, L., Levin, T., and Spodek, L. (2008). One-session music therapy and CBT for critically ill cancer patients. *Psychiatric Services*, **59**(10), 1216.

McCaffery, M. (1990). Nursing approaches to non-pharmacological pain control. *International Journal of Nursing Studies*, **27**(1), 1–5.

McCaffrey, R. (2008). Using music to interrupt the cycle of chronic pain. *Journal of Pain Management*, **1**(3), 215–21.

Metzger, L.K. (2004). Assessment of use of music by patients participating in cardiac rehabilitation. *Journal of Music Therapy*, **41**(4), 55–69.

Miell, D., MacDonald R.A.R, and Hargreaves D.J. (eds.) (2005). *Musical Communication*. Oxford: Oxford University Press.

Mitchell, L.A., MacDonald, R.A.R., Serpell, M.G., and Knussen, C. (2007). A survey investigation of the effects of music listening on chronic pain. *Psychology of Music*, **35**(1), 39–59.

Mitchell, L.A., MacDonald, R., and Knussen, C. (2008). An investigation of the effects of music and art on pain perception. *Psychology of Aesthetics, Creativity and the Arts*, **2**(3), 162–70.

Mockel, M., Stork, T., Vollert, J., Rocker, L., Danne, O., Hochrein, H., *et al.* (1995). Stress reduction through listening to music-Effects on stress hormones, hemodynamics and psychological state in patients with arterial hypertension and in healthy subjects. *Deutsche Medizinische Wochenschrift*, **120**(21), 745–52.

Nakayama, H., Kikuta, F., and Takeda, H. (2009). A pilot study on effectiveness of music therapy in hospice in Japan. *Journal of Music Therapy*, **46**(2), 160–72.

National Center for Health Statistics. (2006). *National vital statistics reports*. Hyattsville, MD: Author.

Nelson, J.P. (2006). Being in tune with life. complementary therapy use and well-being in residential hospice residents. *Journal of Holistic Nursing*, **24**(3), 152–61.

Neugebauer, L. and Aldridge, D. (1998). Communication, heart rate and the musical dialogue. *British Journal of Music Therapy*, **12**(2), 46–53.

Nilsson, U. (2009). The effect of music intervention in stress response to cardiac surgery in a randomized clinical trial. *Heart & Lung: The Journal of Acute and Critical Care,* **38**(3), 201–7.

O'Callaghan, C. (1996). Lyrical themes in songs written by palliative care patients. *Journal of Music Therapy,* **33**(2), 74–92.

O'Callaghan, C. (2001). Bringing music to life: A study of music therapy and palliative care experiences in a cancer hospital. *Journal of Palliative Care,* **17**(3), 155–60.

O'Callaghan, C., Sexton, M., and Wheeler, G. (2007). Music therapy as a non-pharmacological anxiolytic for paediatric radiotherapy patients. *Australasian Radiology,* **51**(2), 159–62.

O'Callaghan, C. and McDermott, F. (2007). Discourse analysis reframes oncologic music therapy research findings. *The Arts in Psychotherapy,* **24**, 398–408.

O'Callaghan, C. (2008). Lullament: Lullaby and lament therapeutic qualities actualized through music therapy. *American Journal of Hospice & Palliative Medicine,* **25**(2), 93–9.

O'Callaghan, C., O'Brien, E., Magill, L., and Ballinger, E. (2009). Resounding attachment: cancer inpatients' song lyrics for their children in music therapy. *Support Cancer Care,* **17**, 1149–57.

Oelkers-Ax, R., Leins, A., Parzer, P., Hillecke, T., Bollay, H.V., Fischer, J., *et al.* (2008). Butterbur root extract and music therapy in the prevention of childhood migraine: An explorative study. *European Journal of Pain,* **12**, 301–13.

Oneschuk, D., Balneaves, L. Verhoef, M., Boon, H., Demmer, C., and Chiu, L. (2007). The status of complementary therapy services in palliative care settings. *Support Care in Cancer,* **15**(8), 939–47.

Okada, K., Kurita, A., Takase, B., Otsuka, T., Kodani, E., Kusama, Y., *et al.* (2009). Effects of music therapy on autonomic nervous system activity, incidence of heart failure events and plasma cytokine and catecholamine levels in elderly patients with cerebrovascular disease and dementia. *International Heart Journal,* **50**(1), 95–110.

Palakanis, K.C., Denobile, J.W., Sweeney, W.B., and Blankenship, C.L. (1994). Effect of music therapy on state anxiety in patients undergoing flexible sigmoidoscopy. *Diseases of the colon and rectum,* **37** (5), 478–81.

Park, H. (2009). Effect of music on pain for home-dwelling persons with dementia. *Pain Management Nursing,* 11, 1–7.

Pattenden, J. Watt, I., Lewin, R.J.P., and Standford, N. (2002). Decision making processes in people with symptoms of acute myocardial infarction: qualitative study. *British Medical Journal,* **324**, 1006–11.

Peterson, C. and Seligman, M.E.P. (1984). Causal explanations as a risk factor for depression: theory and evidence. *Psychology Review,* **91**, 347–74.

Pfaff, V.K., Smith, K.E., and Gowan, D. (1989). The effects of music assisted relaxation on the distress of pediatric cancer patients undergoing bone marrow aspirations. *Children's Health Care,* **18**(4), 232–36.

Pothoulaki, M., MacDonald, R.A.R., and Flowers, P. (2005). Music Interventions in Oncology Settings: A Systematic Literature Review. *British Journal of Music Therapy,* **19**(2), 75–83

Pothoulaki, M., MacDonald, R.A.R., and Flowers, P. (2006). Methodological issues in music interventions in oncology settings: A systematic literature review. *The Arts in Psychotherapy,* **33**, 446–55.

Pothoulaki, M., MacDonald, R.A.R., Flowers, P., Stamataki, E., Filopoulos, V., Stamatiadis, D., *et al.* (2008). An investigation of the effects of music on anxiety and pain perception in patients undergoing haemodialysis treatment. *Journal of Health Psychology,* **13**(7), 904–12.

Pothoulaki, M., MacDonald, R., and Flowers, P. (under review). A qualitative study of the psychological processes involved in music therapy sessions with cancer patients. *Journal of Music Therapy.*

Robb, S.L. (2000). The effect of therapeutic music interventions on the behaviour of hospitalized children in isolation: Developing a contextual support model of music therapy. *Journal of Music Therapy,* **37**(2), 118–46.

Robb, S.L., Clair, A.A., Watanabe, M., Monahan, P.O., Azzouz, F., Stouffer, A.E., *et al.* (2008). Randomized controlled trial of the active music engagement (AME) intervention on children with cancer. *Psycho-Oncology,* **17**, 699–708.

Robichaud-Ekstrand, S. (1999). The influence of music in coronary heart disease (CHD) patients waiting for hemodynamic tests. *Circulation,* **100**(18), 3889.

Sabo, C.E. and Michael, S. (1996). The influence of personal message with music on anxiety and side effects associated with chemotherapy. *Cancer Nursing,* **19**(4), 283–9.

Schein, M.H., Gavish, B., Herz, M., Rosner-Kahana, D., Naveh, P., Knoshkowy, B., *et al.* (2001). Treating hypertension with a device that slows and regularises breathing: a randomised, double-blind controlled study. *Journal of Human Hypertension,* **15**(4), 271–8.

Schulz, K.F., Altman, D.G., and Moher D. (2010). CONSORT 2010 Statement: updated guidelines for reporting parallel group randomised trials. *British Medical Journal,* **340**, c332.

Schuster, B.L. (1985). The effect of music listening on blood pressure fluctuations in adult hemodialysis patients. *Journal of Music Therapy,* **22**(3), 146–53.

Sendelbach, S.E., Halm, M.A., Doran, K. A., Miller, E.H., and Gaillard, P. (2006). Effects of music therapy on physiological and psychological outcomes for patients undergoing cardiac surgery. *Journal of Cardiovascular Nursing,* **21**(3), 194–200.

Shaban, M., Rasoolzadeh, N., Mehran, A., and Moradalizadeh, F. (2006). Study of two non-pharmacological methods, progressive muscle relaxation and music on pain relief of cancerous patients. *HAYAT,* **12**(3), 87.

Siedliecki, S. and Good, M. (2006). Effect of music on power, pain, depression and disability. *Journal of Advanced Nursing,* **54**(5), 553–62.

Siedliecki, S. (2009). Racial variation in response to music in a sample of African-American and Caucasian Chronic Pain Patients. *Pain Management Nursing,* **10**(1), 14–21.

Silverman, M.J. (2009). The effect of single-session psychoeducational music therapy on verbalisations and perceptions in psychiatric patients. *Journal of Music Therapy,* **46**(2), 105–31.

Sloboda, J.A. and O'Neill, S.A. (2001) Psychological perspectives on music and emotion. In: P.N. Juslin and J.A. Sloboda (eds.) *Music and Emotion: Theory and Research,* pp. 415–29. New York: Oxford University Press.

Sloboda, J.A. and Juslin, P.N. (2001). Psychological perspectives on music and emotion. In: P.N. Juslin and J.A. Sloboda (eds.) *Music and Emotion: Theory and Research,* pp. 71–104. New York: Oxford University Press.

Smith, C.E. Dauz, E. Clements, F. Werkowitch, M., and Whitman, R. (2009). Patient education combined in a music and habit-forming intervention for adherence to continuous positive airway (CPAP) prescribed for sleep apnea. *Patient Education and Counselling,* **74**, 184–90.

Standley, J.M. (1992). Clinical applications of music and chemotherapy: The effects on nausea and emesis. *Music Therapy Perspectives,* **10**(1), 27–35.

Strauss, A.L., Corbin, J., Fagerhaugh, S., Glaser, B.G., Maines, D., Suczek, B., *et al.* (1984). *Chronic illness and the Quality of Life.* St. Louis, MO: Mosby.

Sung, H., Chang, S., Lee, W., and Lee, M. (2006). The effects of group music with movement intervention on agitated behaviours of institutionalized elders with dementia in Taiwan. *Complementary Therapies in Medicine,* **14**, 113–19.

Tang, H., Harms, V., Speck, S.M., Vezeau, T., and Jesurum, J.T. (2009). *European Journal of Cardiovascular Nursing,* **8**(5), 329–36.

Tobia, D.M., Shamos, E.F., Harper, D.M, Walch, S.E., and Currie, J.L. (1999). The benefits of group music at the 1996 music weekend for women with cancer. *Journal of Cancer Education,* **14**(2), 115–19.

Trevarthen, C. and Malloch, S. (2000). The dance of well-being: Defining the musical therapeutic effect. *Nordic Journal of Music Therapy,* **9**(2), 3–17.

Tsai, S. (2004). Audio-visual relaxation training for anxiety, sleep and relaxation among chinese adults with cardiac disease. *Reasearch in Nursing & Health,* **27**, 458–68.

Turnquist, D.C., Harvey, J.H., and Anderson, B.L. (1988). Attributions and adjustment to life-threatening disease. *British Journal of Clinical Psychology,* **27**, 55–65.

Twiss, E., Seaver, J., and McCaffrey, R. (2006). The effect of music listening on older adults undergoing cardiovascular surgery. *Nursing in Critical Care,* **11**(5), 224–31.

Vollert, J.O., Stork, T., Rose, M., Rocker, L., Klapp, B.F., Heller, G., *et al.* (2002). Reception of music in patients with systemic arterial hypertension and coronary artery disease: Endocrine changes, hemodynamics and actual mood. *Perfusion,* **15**(4), 142–9.

Vollert, J.O., Stork, T., Rose, M., and Mockel, M. (2003). Music accompanying treatment of coronary heart disease: therapeutic music lowers anxiety, stress and beta-endorphin concentration in patients of a coronary sport unit. *Deutsche Medizinische Wochenschrift,* **128**(51–52), 2712–16.

Waldon, E.G. (2001). The effects of group music therapy on mood states and cohesiveness in adult oncology patients. *Journal of Music Therapy,* **38**(3), 212–38.

Wallston, B.S., Wallston, K.A., Kaplan, G.D., and Maides, S.A. (1976). Development and validation of the health locus of control (HLC) scales. *Journal of Consulting and Clinical Psychology,* **44**, 580–5.

Wan, Y., Mao, Z. and Qiu, Y. (2009). Influence of music therapy on anxiety, depression and pain of cancer patients. *Chinese Nursing Research,* **23**(5A), 1172–5.

Weber, S., Nuessler, V., and Wilmanns, W. (1997). A pilot study on the influence of receptive music listening on cancer patients during chemotherapy. *International Journal of Arts Medicine,* **5**(2), 27–35.

Wellard, S. (1998) Constructions of chronic illness. *International Journal of Nursing Studies,* **35**, 49–55.

World Health Organization. *Chronic diseases and their common risk factors.* Available at: http://www.who.int/chp/chronic_disease_report (accessed 1 March 2010).

Windich-Biermeier, A. Sjoberg, I.Dale, J.C., Eshelman, D., and Guzzetta, C.E. (2007). Effects of distraction on pain, fear and distress during venous port access and venipuncture in children and adolescents with cancer. *Journal of Pediatric Oncology Nursing,* **24**(1), 8–19.

Wlodarczyk, N. (2007). The effect of music therapy on the spirituality of persons in an in-patient hospice unit as measured by self-report. *Journal of Music Therapy,* **44**(2), 113–22.

Yu, H., Liu, Y. Li, S., and Ma, X. (2009). Effects of music on anxiety and pain in children with cerebral palsy receiving acupuncture: A randomized controlled trial. *International Journal of Nursing Studies,* **46**, 1423–30.

Chapter 19

Music as Non-Pharmacological Pain Management in Clinics*

Günther Bernatzky, Simon Strickner, Michaela Presch, Franz Wendtner, and Werner Kullich

Introduction

The capacity for music to stimulate social-emotional processes and to affect our moods in every-day life is now well evidenced (Panksepp and Bernatzky 2002; Hesse 2003; Koelsch 2005; Dileo 2008).

As such, this powerful stimulus works on social-emotional processes and affects our moods in everyday life and can have various beneficial health effects. Chapters throughout this volume suggest increasing empirical evidence that music may be effective as a non-pharmacological intervention in clinical as well as non-clinical contexts. Specifically, music can alleviate pain, stress, and feelings of depression in individuals suffering from acute and chronic pain (e.g. Mitchell et al., Chapter 17, this volume). Music stimulation may also relieve negative cognitions such as feelings of helplessness and hopelessness and undesired stresses that many patients experience especially in clinics (e.g. Spintge, Chapter 20, this volume).

The specific aim of this chapter is to evaluate the effects of music on acute and chronic pain in inpatients with and without surgery. There are two goals; first to present an overview of research, and second to address issues surrounding the implementation of music in pain therapy for inpatients.

Pain is still a major healthcare problem. Postoperative pain remains a great challenge despite sufficient treatment concepts, including systemic and regional analgesia techniques (Pschowski and Motsch 2008). Appropriate pain management is still unavailable to the majority of patients (Breivik et al. 2006). Whereas the efficacy of systemic and regional analgesia techniques is well evidenced, only a few references show the efficacy of non-pharmacological management of pain (Nadler 2004). Music as one of such non-pharmacological interventions has not been thoroughly established. Music has been found to affect and stimulate many different parts of the brain and body. It has a remarkable power to stimulate many social-emotional processes and to influence emotions in everyday life. This emotional power is used as a non-pharmacological intervention in some clinical pain patients.

Music can be seen as a very old therapeutic 'drug'. Apparently, all human cultures, including indigenous and ancient ones, have used music for therapeutic purposes (Gouk 2000; Horden 2001). Music, often in association with ritual chants and dances, was considered as a healing

* We dedicate this chapter to Prof. Gerhard Harrer (Salzburg, Austria) who has died shortly some weeks before his 95th birthday. Prof. Harrer's ground-breaking studies include investigation of the heart-rate of the conductor Herbert von Karajan, during conducting as well as during flying his airplane.

resource. For example, ancient Egyptian frescoes from the fourth millennium BC depict music therapeutic interventions. Although there seems to be no way to reconstruct the sound of such interventions, Egyptian priests presumably used incantations to influence fertility in women. The oldest written documents mentioning the use of music in the context of mystic or religious healing ceremonies are Assyrian cuneiform tablets dating from the second millennium BC. The Greeks (Pythagoras) and Romans also used music and rhythm to heal sickness and injuries. Hebrews and Greeks treated physical and mental illness by playing music. The healing effects of music were recognized even in Grecian times, where it was employed as a mainstream psychiatric treatment. The Greek 'physicians' Zenocrates, Sarpander, and Arien were the first to use music therapy as a regular practice. They employed harp music to reduce seizures in cases of mental illness (Shapiro 1969). In the Middle Ages, music was used therapeutically in medicine (Spintge and Droh 1992). In the twentieth century, scientifically-oriented research into the therapeutic effectiveness of music has drawn commensurate attention (Cunningham et al. 1997). Nickel et al. (2005) documented selected articles to give music therapy a scientific reputation based on empirical evidence. The results of their investigations have shown that music therapy is an effective intervention for patients with chronic pain, children with migraine, and patients with chronic tinnitus. In future trials, an emphasis should be put on a comparison of music therapy with standard treatments.

Music has a strong influence on emotion (Blood et al. 1999; Panksepp and Bernatzky 2002; Altenmüller et al. 2007), stress (Winter et al. 1994; Lee 2003; Salamon et al. 2003a,b; Esch et al. 2004; Pelletier 2004), relaxation (Gauthier and Dallaire 1993; Duffy and Fuller 2000; Kemper and Danhauer 2005), sleep disturbances, and pain (Panksepp and Bernatzky 2002; Kullich et al. 2003; Hesse 2003).

In recent years, a mounting number of studies follow principles of evidence-based medicine. These studies have shown the effectiveness of defined interventions and suggest music as a powerful resource for the treatment of various illnesses (Hillecke et al. 2005; Bernatzky and Strickner 2008) and that engagement in musical activities has strong effects on the human brain. It exerts effects on subcortical brain centres and has a strong influence on the psychological and physiological state of the organism (Panksepp and Bernatzky 2002; Hesse 2003).

Limbic and paralimbic systems show strong changes caused by listening to music in following regions: the ventral striatum, amygdala, anterior cingulate, and auditory cortices in relation to processing musical emotions (Blood et al. 1999; Blood and Zatorre 2001). At the same time other structures which are associated with the endocrine system are also influenced by music (Quiroga et al. 2011; Kreutz et al., Chapter 30, this volume).

Music in medicine for therapeutic benefits

Perioperative music stimulation has evolved as an increasingly common therapeutic strategy in surgeries (see Spintge, Chapter 20, this volume). But when talking of music in medicine, it is important to take the problem of terminology into consideration. We have to distinguish first between music stimulation and music therapy.[1] Music stimulation has various possibilities that include habitual or designed listening to the radio at home as well as the involuntary hearing of music in waiting rooms or in the supermarket. Many people are not pleased about this involuntary aspect, but music can be applied in a controlled manner as a therapy with curative effects.

---

[1] Definition of music therapy. Available at: http://en.citizendium.org/wiki/Music_therapy (accessed 28 January 2010).

Listening to music has its power in the arousal of emotions. These emotions, whether elicited by sounds, or as a result of associations in patients' memories, can become topical in therapeutic conversations to enhance self-experience and coping strategies. In active music therapy, the therapist sings and plays instruments together with the patients and encourages them to improvise.

Music and its power as a non-pharmacological treatment

It is well documented that music affects heart rate (HR) and its variability (HRV) (Trappe 2009). Musical accents and rhythmic phrases appear to resonate well with physiological variables. Reactions to music are considered subjective, but studies suggest that cardiorespiratory variables are influenced under different circumstances (Bradt and Dileo 2009). It has been shown that relaxing music significantly decreases the level of anxiety in a preoperative setting to a greater extent than orally-administered midazolam (Bringman et al. 2009). Higher effectiveness and absence of apparent adverse effects make preoperative relaxing music a useful alternative to pharmacological substances like the sedativum midazolam for premedication. However, carefully selected music that includes a patient's own preferences may offer an effective method to reduce anxiety and to improve quality of life. Anecdotal evidence suggests that classical and meditation music are often perceived as beneficial whereas heavy metal music or techno-sounds could be ineffective or even induce physiological stress.

Music (listening) can help to reduce pain and anxiety in patients undergoing haemodialysis (Pothoulaki et al. 2008). Patients were assigned to a music group, where they listened to their preferred music and to a control group without music intervention. Changes of anxiety and pain were included in the measurements. At the end of the study the control group had significantly higher state anxiety scores and significantly higher pain intensity.

Many studies have shown that inpatients gain an advantage by listening to music. Music played to premature babies may help to reduce their pain and encourage better oral feeding (Schwartz et al. 2004; Cignacco et al. 2007). There are also trials, which provide preliminary evidence for therapeutic benefits of music for specific indications. As well as pain reduction, benefits most often reported were to physiological parameters such as heart rate, respiratory rate, and oxygen saturation. Other studies (51 studies including 3663 subjects), synthesised in a Cochrane report, (Cepeda et al. 2006) have shown that listening to music reduces pain intensity levels by more than 50% and reduced opioid requirements. Participants exposed to music had a 70% greater probability of having at least 50% pain relief than unexposed participants. This is equivalent to the so-called number needed to treat of 5 (NNT=5; this means that 5 people out of 100 are necessary to get a relief of pain of 50%). These studies included people with pain during a diagnostic or therapeutic procedure such as colonoscopy, lithotripsy, with postoperative pain as well as chronic non-cancer pain, cancer pain, labour pain, or experimental pain. Nevertheless the magnitude of these benefits is small and therefore the clinical importance is still unclear (Cepeda et al. 2006). In a systematic review on online-databases from 1998–2007, Engwall and Duppils have found influences of music on postoperative pain (Engwall and Duppils 2009). Different types of music and different kinds of surgery were performed in the 18 studies considered in this report. A significant positive effect on postoperative pain was found in 15 studies and the use of analgesics was lower in the music groups in four studies. The conclusion was that music can be used as a low-priced adjuvant for the relief of postoperative pain.

Kullich et al. (2003) reported that listening to certain music during both acute and chronic pain leads to a significant pain relief and further improves sleep quality and quality of life. Sixty-five patients suffering from low back pain were randomly divided into two therapy groups: one with standardized physical therapy accompanied by music and instructions for relaxation, the other group without music. A specially-produced music for application with pain was listened to once daily over a period of 3 weeks by CD and headphones. The global pain (visual analogue scale, VAS) as well as the pain on pressure improved significantly. The Roland–Morris Disability Questionnaire for low back pain revealed that the subjective disability in the group with music therapy improved more distinctly than in the control group. Music therapy showed a positive influence on sleep disturbances due to chronic low back pain as measured by the Pittsburgh Sleep Quality Index (PSQI).

Cancer patients can benefit from music interventions according to a recent review (Richardson et al. 2008). Music therapy (in conjunction with conventional cancer treatment) helped patients to manage stress better, to learn how to communicate their sadness and fear, and to alleviate discomfort and physical pain, leading to a better quality of life.

Pain, anxiety and the efficacy of music therapy in children during clinical procedures were of interest in a systematic review (Klassen et al. 2008). Three hundred and ninety-three studies were included, whereas only 19 studies met the inclusion criteria (e.g. randomized controlled trial, children aged 1 month to 18 years). Although the methodological quality of the studies was generally poor, it was shown that music therapy significantly reduced pain and anxiety in children undergoing medical procedures. These authors concluded that music can be considered as an adjunctive therapy in clinical situations that produce pain or anxiety.

Music (therapy) also has powerful effects on carers of advanced cancer patients (Magill 2009). Prior to the death of close relatives who had received music therapy, seven carers completed open-ended interviews. They said that the music affected them directly, but also the joy they felt was based on remembering seeing the patient happy during the music therapy. The sessions helped them to bring back happy memories, to connect with themselves, with others and the time 'beyond' and so alleviate the 'psychological' pain. All in all, music can help to find a meaning through transcendence and can give strength to the carers through memories of joy and empowerment.

Cancer patients often suffer from fatigue, pain, and sleep disturbance. To examine the influence of different interventions, including music (therapy), a literature search was conducted (Kwekkeboom et al. 2009). A categorization based on the type of intervention was made: relaxation, imagery/hypnosis, cognitive-behavioural therapy/coping skills training [CBT/CST], meditation, music and virtual reality. Fatigue, sleep disturbances and experienced pain improved through imagery/hypnosis and CBT/CST interventions. Pain and sleep disturbances ameliorated with relaxation techniques and meditation had positive effects on fatigue and sleep disturbances. Music interventions have demonstrated efficacy for pain and fatigue.

Next to increased relaxation, music has been used to reduce anxiety and distress. One example is the use for patients with coronary heart disease (CHD), who often have a higher risk of complications due to severe distress (Bradt and Dileo 2009). The conclusion of a review indicated that anxiety in patients with CHD decreased but the results were inconsistent across the 23 studies. Also, a reduction of respiratory rate, rather, and blood pressure was found, as well as a small and consistent pain-reducing effect.

Zhao and Chen (2009) provide evidence that the valence of music (pleasant vs. unpleasant) is more crucial than mood (happy vs. sad) in affective modulation of pain. They describe tonic heat pain to be significantly reduced through both happy and sad melodies and that the valence of music appears to be the mediator of the hypoalgesic effect of the different music.

The effect of low volume, classical background music in doctors' surgeries was evaluated in another study (Zalewsky et al. 1998). One hundred and eighteen people completed the questionnaire: 95% did not feel disturbed by the background music, 89% found to feel better, and 80%

thought the music enhances the doctors' efforts and therefore leads to a better patient–doctor interaction.

Pyati and Gan (2007) discussed a reduction of analgesic use such as opioids like tramadol, NSAIDs (non-steroidal anti-inflammatory drugs) like paracetamol, and other non-opioid analgesics and their combinations. Furthermore, the usage of non-pharmacological therapies such as acupuncture, relaxation, music therapy, hypnosis, and transcutaneous nerve stimulation as a substitute for conventional analgesic therapy needs to be discussed to achieve an effective and successful perioperative pain management.

Music as an analgesic tool in surgery

Anxiety, stress, and sleep disorders can often be found in postoperative pain. These components also exist before surgery. As pain is a subjective feeling it is experienced differently by everyone. Mainly the mental toughness and the physiological component play an important role. Psychological factors such as anxiety, depression, etc. increase the effect of pain which affects as a physiological stressor and thus the feeling of pain and pain intensity. In addition, the emotional factor is a crucial component of how pain is perceived (Bernatzky et al. 2007).

Mok et al. (2003) showed that patients, who were allowed to choose music for themselves, had significantly less stress, a reduced HR and blood pressure compared to patients, who did not listen to music. These patients underwent minor surgical procedures with local anaesthesia.

The influence of music before surgery

Before surgery, psychophysiological stress is particularly strong. Therefore, music stimulation is used in some surgeries to minimize anxiety and to reduce pain (Heitz et al. 1992; Cunningham et al. 1997; Spintge 2000). Music also provides a compensation for ambient noise. A relaxation-promoting music stimulation in combination with spoken relaxation instructions influences affective, cognitive, and sensory processes and therefore has reducing effects on pain and stress. In addition, there is the emotional aspect, such as attention and social support in the care of patients.

A standardized perioperative therapy with a music programme, including guidance for relaxation, contributes to health promotion in an effective and competitive way. The objective of one study was the evaluation of such a standardized music programme before and after surgery (Miller et al. 2002). Patients were divided into a music programme (A) and a comparison group (B). Both patient groups had comparable body mass indices (BMIs), sleeping indices (PSQI), and wellbeing indices before surgery. Postoperatively, the PSQI improved significantly in Group A and the consumption of analgesics decreased. Also the patients of this group needed no hypnotics or sedatives, whereas in Group B three of 10 patients needed hypnotics after surgery. Regarding the VAS for pain, Group A reported less pain. Concerning the postoperative need of the nursing service, no difference was reported. There was also no difference in the duration of the hospital stay after surgery. In respect of the scale of wellbeing Group A outmatched Group B. In this study, the number of evaluated patients was too small to calculate a statistical significance and further research is needed.

The influence of music during surgery

As children can experience pain during blood sampling, a comparison of the pain-reducing effects of local anaesthetic cream (EMLA®), Indian classical instrumental music and placebo was undertaken (Balan et al. 2009). VAS scores were significantly higher in the placebo group than in the other two groups (noted by all the categories of observers). The authors conclude that the pain experienced during venipuncture can be significantly reduced by using a local anaesthetic cream (EMLA[R]) or Indian classical instrumental music.

After total knee arthroplasty, massive pain often affects the recovery (Simcock et al. 2008). In this study, patients in a music group had the chance to select their preferred music, while a control group did not listen to music. The postoperative pain scores were measured by VAS. At 3 and 24 hours after the surgery, the music group experienced less pain than the non-music group. The conclusion of the authors is that intraoperative music provides an inexpensive, non-pharmacological option to reduce postoperative pain.

In a systematic review of 42 randomized controlled trials (perioperative settings), music interventions had positive effects in approximately half of the reviewed studies (Nilsson 2008). Music also has some influence during (and after) cardiovascular surgery. Measurable effects, however, are not only on physical pain; music can also have relaxing effects (Nilsson 2009). To measure relaxation, plasma oxytocin, heart rate, mean arterial blood pressure, PaO_2 and SaO_2 were determined in a music group with bed rest and in a control group with bed rest only. Levels of oxytocin, arterial oxygen (PaO_2) and subjective relaxation levels increased significantly in the music group compared to the control group. There were no differences in HR, mean arterial blood pressure, and oxygen saturation (SaO_2) between the groups. These results suggest music as an effective aspect in contexts of multimodal treatment.

Nilsson et al. (2005) conducted a study on intra- and postoperative effects of music therapy on stress and immune responses during and after anaesthesia. Seventy-five hernia patients were examined. Stress responses were measured by plasma cortisol and blood glucose, and immune responses by determining the IgA levels. In this study, it was found that a significant decrease of cortisol levels was achieved by postoperative music intervention. Patients in the music group had less stress, less pain, and required less morphine. However, no changes in IgA levels, blood glucose, blood pressure, HR, and oxygen saturation were noted. The authors suggest that intraoperative music therapy can facilitate a decrease in postoperative pain, and that postoperative music therapy produces a reduction of anxiety, pain, and morphine consumption.

In a further study the authors reported a pain reduction of 16–40% in patients after intestinal surgery with the help of music therapy (Good et al. 2005). In this study, three non-pharmacological intervention groups (relaxation, music selected, and the combination) were compared with a control group. In addition, the authors also highlight that these interventions are recommended in combination with analgesia to gain a greater postoperative relief without side effects.

The influence of music after surgery

The influence of non-pharmacological strategies to reduce pain and anxiety in patients after a total hip or knee arthroplasty was investigated in a study by Pellino et al. (2005). Patients were divided into a group that received usual care and a group that received usual care plus non-pharmacological treatments. On the first and second postoperative day the non-pharmacological group needed less opioid and experienced less anxiety compared to patients who did not use the kit. Significant correlations were found for postoperative pain intensity, opioid use and anxiety. MacDonald et al. (2003), however, reported no differences in pain and consumption of analgesics in people after minor surgery of the foot and those undergoing total abdominal hysterectomy when listening postoperatively to self-selected music. All patients in the music groups in the foot surgery condition reported significantly less anxiety than the control group.

After orthopaedic surgery, wound care is often painful for the patients. One article describes the experience of a nurse who used music therapy to reduce the acute physical pain during wound care (Hsiao and Hsieh 2009). It was possible to reduce pain by an individual music therapy. Additionally, negative feelings decreased and the patients increased their own spiritual strength.

Eighty children aged from 7–16 years were split up into a music group and a control group, the music group listened to music after the day of surgery (Nilsson et al. 2009). A possible reduction of morphine, distress, anxiety, and pain before and after surgery was measured. The instruments were the Coloured Analogue Scale (CAS), the Facial Affective Scale (FAS), and the Short State-Trait Anxiety Inventory (STAI). Children in the music group needed less morphine and their distress was reduced, but no other differences could be seen. Listening to music was 'calming and relaxing' for the children.

Music can help to improve the early contact of mothers with their babies after Caesarean section (Ebneshahidi and Mohseni 2008). The sedative and emetic effects of routinely administered analgesics (opioids and benzodiazepines) may impair the immediate close contact of mother and neonate. In this study, the music was selected by the patients. Anxiety, HR, blood pressure, opioid requirement, and postoperative pain were measured. One group listened to music after surgery for 30 minutes, whereas the other group listened to silence. In the music group, there was significantly less opioid consumption and reduction of pain scores compared to the silence group, while there were no differences in terms of anxiety score, blood pressure, or HR.

Good and Ahn (2008) investigated influences of Korean and American music on subjective pain after gynaecological surgery. Women were classified in a music group, with the option to choose between American piano music and Korean ballads (both plus analgesics), and a control group with bed rest only (plus analgesics). The patients listened to music four times postoperatively. There was significantly less postoperative pain in the music group compared to the control group. Two-thirds in the music group (n=21; 62%) chose Korean music and one-third (n=13; 38%) chose American. Both music styles were equally effective.

Table 19.1 shows an overview of some references that cover the topic 'music and surgery' and emphasizes the importance to discuss and define a standardized music stimulation as a non-pharmacological intervention in pain. Most of the studies conclude that music improves quality of life and sleep and has different effects on the heart rate. It reduces physiological and psychological pain and anxiety before, during and after clinical surgeries. It also reduces stress and depression and leads to relaxation.

Table 19.1 summarizes the cited research studies above of various surgeries with music stimulation or music therapy. The onset of music stimulation and the measured parameters including the results are shown.

Table 19.1 A systematic overview of the effects of music therapy in clinics with or without surgery

Reference	Samples and design	Intervention	music	Point of MI pre/inter/post	Measured parameters and results
Chlan (1998)	n=54 alert, non-sedated pat. receiving mechanical ventilation; two-group, pre-post-test; exp. design with repeated measures; subjects rand. to either a 30-min music condition or a rest period	Artificial respiration	KI, CW, NA, EL		Anxiety, HR, RR ↓

(continued)

Table 19.1 (Continued) A systematic overview of the effects of music therapy in clinics with or without surgery

Reference	Samples and design	Intervention	music	Point of MI pre/inter/post			Measured parameters and results
Zalewsky et al. (1998)	n=118 people completed a questionnaire		Classical background music, low volume				95% did not feel disturbed; 89% felt better ↑ 80% better patient–doctor interaction ↑
Good et al. (2001)	n=468; repeated measures design; rand. assigned to one of four groups: relaxation, music, combination, and control	abdominal s.	NA, H, PO, J			X	Pain ↓
Lepage et al. (2001)	n=50 unpremedicated patients; rand. assigned to listen to music of their choice via headset during the perioperative period (Group I) or to have no music (Group II)	Spinal anesthesia	Pop, J, Kl, NA	X	X	X	Sedativa ↓
Nilsson et al. (2001)	n=110 women; rand. allocated to receive either music or no music	Hysterectomy; varicose vein s.	Calm instrumental music		X	X	Pain intensity, morphine ↓; anxiety, nausea, ibuprofen and paracetamol— fatigue ↓
Good et al. (2002)	n=311, ages 18–70; relaxation, music, and the combination of relaxation and music on pain	Gynecologic s.	Calming music			X	pain, pulse, respiration ↓
Miller et al. (2002)	18 out of planned 40 patients: Group A (music programme): n=8, Group B (as usual): n= 10	S. for morbid obesity	Music programme including guidance for relaxation	X		X	sleep ↑; pain ↓; no hypnotics and sedatives in A

Table 19.1 (Continued) A systematic overview of the effects of music therapy in clinics with or without surgery

Reference	Samples and design	Intervention	music	Point of MI pre/inter/post	Measured parameters and results
Wang et al. (2002)	People choosing self-selected music (30 min self-selected music) and a control group		30 min self-selected music	X	Electrodermal activity, blood pressure, HR, Cortisol and catecholamin—
Kullich et al. (2003)	n=65; rand. allocated to two therapy groups: one with standardized physical therapy accompanied by music and instructions for relaxation, the other group without additional music application: Once daily for 3 weeks	Low back pain	Relaxation music with a spoken relaxation text (imagery journey)		Global pain, pain on pressure ↓\n\nRoland–Morris Disability Questionnaire ↑\n\nPSQI sleep disturbances ↓\n\nimprovement of impatient rehabilitation success ↑
MacDonald et al. (2003)	Exp.1: n=40; two groups: music of their own choice and no music; Anxiolytic and pain reducing effect of music\n\nExp.2: n=58 fem., two groups: music/no music	Minor surgery on the foot;\n\ntotal abdominal hysterectomy	Self-selected music	X	Anxiety in music gr. ↓:\n\nno difference in pain and consumption of analgetica
Mok et al. (2003)		Minor surgical procedures with local anaesthesia	Self-selected music	X	Stress, anxiety, HR, BP ↓
Nilsson et al. (2003, 2005)	n=75; examined by measuring plasma cortisol and blood glucose, immune responses by determining the IgA levels	Hernia inguinalis s.	Calm instrumental music	X X	Pain, morphine ↓;\n\nanxiety, nausea, fatigue ↓ ibuprofen/ paracetamol —\n\nIgA levels, blood glucose, blood pressure, HR, oxyg. Saturation —

(continued)

Table 19.1 (Continued) A systematic overview of the effects of music therapy in clinics with or without surgery

Reference	Samples and design	Intervention	music	Point of MI pre/inter/post			Measured parameters and results
Chikamori et al. (2004)	n=50; Two groups: using a simple key-lighting keyboard system in n=37 elderly patients compared with n=13 patients who were not applied MT	Digestive tract		X	X	X	Bliss ↑
Ikonomidou et al. (2004)	n=60; Music group (peaceful pan flute) and no music	Gynecological laparoscopy		X		X	Nausea ↓; wellbeing ↑; vital signs ↑
Voss et al. (2004)	n=61; three groups: randomly assigned to receive 30 min of sedative music (n=19), scheduled rest (n=21), or treatment as usual (n=21) during chair rest	Open-heart s.	NA, H, P, O, J, F	X			Anxiety, distress, pain sensation ↓
Good et al. (2005)	n=167; three groups: RCT: relaxation, chosen music, and their combination	Intestinal s.				X	Post-test pain ↓ (16–40%)
Lee et al. (2005)	n=64; rand. assigned to undergo either 30 min. of music intervention or a rest period	Artificial respiration	CC, RM, KW, LB				HR, RR, DBP, SBP ↓; C-STAI —
Pellino et al. (2005)	n=65; two groups: one received usual care and one usual care plus a kit of non-pharmalogical strategies.	Knee arthroplasty					Less opioid and experienced less anxiety ↓
Harikumar et al. (2006)	n=78; randomized to either not listen to music (n=40) or listen to music of their choice (n=38)	Elective colonoscopy	FS, FL, B, SI, CI, RL	X			DosEs of sedative meds, discomfort ↓

Table 19.1 (Continued) A systematic overview of the effects of music therapy in clinics with or without surgery

Reference	Samples and design	Intervention	music	Point of MI pre/inter/post	Measured parameters and results
Ovayolu et al. (2006)	n=60; randomized into either listening to music (n=30) or not listening to music (n=30)	Elective colonoscopy	Turkish, classical music		Anxiety, pain ↓; wellbeing ↑
Twiss et al. (2006)	n=60 adults older than 65 years; rand. assigned to the control and exp. groups. The exp. group listened to music during and after surgery, while the control group received standard postoperative care	Cardiovasculary s.		X X	Anxiety, shorter postoperative time of intubation ↓
Jaber et al. (2007)	n=30; intubated group n=15, non-intubated group n=15); rand. assigned to receive either 20 min of uninterrupted rest or then 20 min of MT or the MT first and then the uninterrupted rest period. Patients selected a relaxing track	Intubation	Music of their choice from a selection including different types of music		SBP, HR, RR, BIS score, NRS, RASS ↓
Pyati et al. (2007)	Test of analgesic use such as opioids like tramadol and NSAIDs like paracetamol, and other non-opioid analgetics and their combinations				Pain, opioid consumption ↓
Ebneshahidi and Mohseni (2008)	Test of early contact of mothers with their babies	Cesarean section s.	30 min self-selected music compared to silence	X	Opioid consumption, pain ↓; anxiety, blood pressure, HR—

(continued)

Table 19.1 (Continued) A systematic overview of the effects of music therapy in clinics with or without surgery

Reference	Samples and design	Intervention	music	Point of MI pre/inter/post	Measured parameters and results
Good and Ahn (2008)	Two groups: women were classified in a music group; selection between American piano music and Korean ballads (both plus analgetics) and a control group with bed rest only (plus analgetics)	Gynecological s.	American piano music; Korean ballads	X	Post-test pain ↓; no difference in experienced pain between the two music groups
Klassen et al. (2008)	Systematic review of 393 studies on the efficacy of music therapy in children (e.g. RCT, children aged 1 month to 18 years)	Clinical procedures		X	Pain ↓; anxiety ↓
Nilsson (2008)	Systematic review of 42 RCTs				Music has positive effects in approximately half of the reviewed studies, pain ↓; anxiety ↓
Pothoulaki et al. (2008)	n=60; diagnosed with end-stage renal failure; preferred music listening was applied as an intervention	Haemodialysis	Their own preferred music		Pre-post-test: anxiety, pain ↓
Richardson et al. (2008)	Review on the effects of music therapy in cancer patients	Cancer patients	Music therapy (combined with conventional cancer treatment)		Stress management ↑; discomfort ↓ ; physical pain ↓

Table 19.1 (Continued) A systematic overview of the effects of music therapy in clinics with or without surgery

Reference	Samples and design	Intervention	music	Point of MI pre/inter/post	Measured parameters and results
Balan et al. (2009)	n=50 children; a comparison of the pain reducing effect of local anaesthetic cream (EMLA®), music, and placebo was carried out	Venepuncture	Indian classical instrumental music	X	Pain ↓
Hsiao and Hsieh (2009)	Experience of a nurse using music therapy to reduce the acute pain	Wound care *after* orthopaedic s.	Individual-tailored music therapy	X	Pain, negative feelings ↓; own spiritual strength ↑
Kwekkeboom et al. (2009)	Investigation of different interventions on fatigue, pain, sleep disturbances in cancer patients	Cancer patients	Relaxation, imagery/ hypnosis, cognitive-behavioural therapy/ coping skills training, meditation, music and virtual reality		Fatigue, sleep disturbances, pain ↑ (imagery/ hypnosis); pain, sleep disturbances ↑ (relaxation techniques); fatigue, sleep disturbances ↑ (meditation)
Nilsson (2009)	n=40; RCT; two groups: either music listening during bed rest (n=20) or bed rest only (n = 20).	Open coronary artery bypass grafting and/or aortic valve replacement s.	Soothing music	X X	Oxytocin, PaO$_2$, subj. relaxat. levels ↑; HR, mean arterial blood pressure, and SaO2 —
Nilsson et al. (2009)	n=80 children aged 7–16 years were split up into a music- and a control group; music group listened to music after day surgery	Day surgery in children		X	Distress, morphine ↓

(continued)

Table 19.1 (Continued) A systematic overview of the effects of music therapy in clinics with or without surgery

Reference	Samples and design	Intervention	music	Point of MI pre/inter/post	Measured parameters and results
Zhao and Chen (2009)	n=24; female; pre-posttest; exp. test about happy and sad music	Tonic heat pain	Happy and sad melodies		Pain ↓

Key:

rand.=randomized; RCT=randomized controlled clinical trial; min=minutes; MT=Music Therapy; MI=Music Intervention;

↑ improvement; ↓ reduction; — no changes; B, Bioacoustic; BIS score, Bispectral Index; BP, blood pressure; chir., chirurgical; CC, Chinese Classic; CI, calm instrumental music; CI, classic music

C-STAI, Chinese State Trait Anxiety Invento ry; CW, Country-Western; DBP, diastolic blood pressure; EL, easy listening; F, American Indian Flute; FL, famous movie songs; gyn., gynaecological; H, harp; HR, heart rate; J, slow modern jazz; KW, classic from Western regions; LB, music with slow beat; NA, New Age; NRS, Numerical-Rating-Scale; O, orchestra; P, piano; PO, piano orchestra; PSQI, Pittsburgh Sleep Quality Index; RASS, Richmond-Agitation-Sedation-Scale; RL, religious songs; RM, religious music; RR, respiratory rate; s., surgery; SBP, systolic blood pressure; FS, folk songs.

Conclusion

With all the different forms of application, music should be used as a concomitant, non-pharmacological form of therapy in the multimodal setting of pain therapy.

Music as this ideal adjuvant therapy has following pros and cons:

Pros: central effect (limbic system, PAG), reduction of medication, configuration of conviction of self competence, no or few side effects, a combination therapy with other pain medications is possible, reduction of anxiety, partially cost-saving due to reduction of drugs, preventive efficient, stimulation of self-repair mechanisms.

Cons: high expectation, (often) long-term effects are not proved, lack of guidelines, sometimes no evidence for effectiveness, need of more randomized controlled studies, poor compliance.

As stressors, pain and anxiety are able to interact. In addition to an increased vegetative agitation, pain causes an elevation of emotional and affective agitation. Especially with surgical patients, it leads to a limited cognition on pain-relevant aspects. This behaviour is regulated by individual locus of control (Rotter 1966) and modulated by expectance of self-efficacy (Bandura 1977). Therefore, it is very important for individual patients to develop effective coping strategies in the presence of pain, stress, and anxiety. Together with a hypothalamic changeover it is possible that music causes distraction and relaxation, which leads to a disruption of the pain–stress–pain feedback-loop. This leads to an alteration of the sensing of pain. Individually chosen music is able to activate inhibitory pain reducing endogenous mechanisms, improve quality of life, and reduce consumption of analgesics. These effects can be reinforced by combination of music and a relaxation guide (Bernatzky et al. 2007, Miller et al. 2002). With continuous application of music this reaction is reproducible and the processes of conditioning lead to a development of competence and to a reduction of helplessness. Adequate music has no side effects and can be combined with the usual medication.

Unfortunately, there is a lack of strict pharmacological or medical applications that correspond to the criteria of quality of natural scientific research. Further studies on long-time effects and contra-indications with a prospective, double-blind randomized and placebo-controlled design are clearly needed. For future studies, it would be useful to know how long the mood effect of music sustains and how specific mood changes are conveyed to the specific emotions by music (Panksepp and Bernatzky 2002).

Evidence shows the effectiveness of music therapy for the treatment of certain diseases. But the question for the source of the therapeutic effects remains largely unanswered (Hillecke et al. 2005). This group has focused on a heuristic model, consisting of five music therapy working factors: attention, emotion modulation, cognition modulation, behaviour modulation, and communication modulation.

In some cases the goal of treatment is not the complete elimination of pain but to manage it and restore functionality (Nadler, 2004).

Summary

Surgery causes stress and anxiety. The implementation of a multimodal pain therapy including non-pharmacological interventions after surgery is still lacking in many hospitals but music can enhance therapy efficacy and should be used as a non-pharmacological intervention in combination with conventional treatment forms. It is also important to evaluate indications and contraindications for music stimulation/music therapy.

Most studies suggest the importance of providing the patients with control over which music to select, when music is selected, at which loudness levels, and the amount of time during which music is played. Although non-preferred music also has its benefits, preferred music has the power to awaken happy memories that can raise spirit and acuity level. For this reason it is important that the patients choose music that makes them happy, not sad.

Acknowledgements

We thank Sokrates-Stiftung (Schweiz), Stiftungs- und Förderungsgesellschaft der Paris-Lodron Universität Salzburg, Paracelsus-University Salzburg, and the Austrian Pain Society for financial support. For checking the English version we thank Mr Keith Ryan (Plymouth, UK).

References

Altenmüller, E., Grewe, O., Nagel, F., and Kopiez, R. (2007). Der Gänsehaut-Faktor. *Gehirn und Geist*, **1–2**, 58–63.

Balan, R., Bavdekar, S.B., and Jadhav, S. (2009). Can Indian classical instrumental music reduce pain felt during venepuncture? *Indian Journal of Pediatrics*, **76** (5), 469–73.

Bandura, A. (1977). Self-efficacy: Toward a unifying theory of behavior change. *Psychological Review*, **84**, 191–215.

Bernatzky, G., Kullich, W., Wendtner, F., Hesse, H.P., and Likar, R. (2007). Musik mit Entspannungsanleitung bei Patienten mit Schmerzen. In: G. Bernatzky, R. Likar, F. Wendtner, G. Wenzel, M. Ausserwinkler, and R. Sittl (eds.) *Nichtmedikamentöse Schmerztherapie*, pp. 157–169. New York: Springer.

Bernatzky, G. and Strickner, S. (2008). Was kann und was leistet die musiktherapie im lichte der evidence based medicine? *Denisia*, **23**, 61–4.

Blood, A.J. and Zatorre, R.J. (2001). Intensely pleasurable responses to music correlate with activity in brain regions implicated with reward and emotion. *Proceedings of the Natural Academy of Sciences*, **98**, 11818–23.

Blood, A.J., Zatorre, R.J., Bermudez, P., and Evans, A.C. (1999). Emotional responses to pleasant and unpleasant music correlate with activity in paralimbic brain regions. *Nature Neuroscience*, **2**(4), 382–7.

Bradt, J. and Dileo, C. (2009). Music for stress and anxiety reduction in coronary heart disease patients. *Cochrane Database of Systematic Reviews*, **15**(2), CD006577.

Breivik, H., Collett, B., Ventafridda, V., Cohen, R., and Gallacher, D. (2006). Survey of chronic pain in Europe: Prevalence, impact on daily life, and treatment. *European Journal of Pain*, **10**, 287–333.

Bringman, H., Giesecke, K., Thörne, A., and Bringman, S. (2009). Relaxing music as pre-medication before surgery: a randomised controlled trial. *Acta Anaesthesiologica Scandinavica*, **53**, 759–64.

Cepeda, M.S., Carr, D.B., Lau, J., and Alvarez, H. (20060). Music for pain relief. *Cochrane Database Systematic Reviews*, **19**(2), CD004843.

Chikamori, F., Kuniyoshi, N., Shibuya, S., and Takase, Y. (2004). Perioperative music therapy with a key-lighting keyboard system in elderly patients undergoing digestive tract surgery. *Hepatogastroenterology*, **51**(59), 1384–6.

Chlan, L. (1998). Effectiveness of a music therapy intervention on relaxation and anxiety for patients receiving ventilatory assistance. *Heart and Lung*, **27**(3), 169–76.

Cignacco, E., Hamers, J., Stoffel, L., and van Lingen, R. (2007). The efficacy of non-pharmacological interventions in the management of procedural pain in preterm and term neonates. A systematic literature review. *European Journal of Pain*, **11**(2), 139–52.

Cunningham, M.F., Monson, B., and Bookbinder, M. (1997). Introducing a music program in the perioperative area. *Journal of the Association of periOperative Registered Nurses*, **66**(4), 674–82.

Dileo, C., Bradt, J., Grocke, D., and Magill, L. (2008). Music interventions for improving psychological and physical outcomes in cancer patients. *Cochrane Database of Systematic Reviews*, **1**, CD006911.

Duffy, B. and Fuller, R. (2000). Role of music therapy in social skills, development in children with moderate intellectual disability. *Journal of Applied Research in Intellectual Disabilities*, **13**, 77–89.

Ebneshahidi, A. and Mohseni, M. (2008). The effect of patient-selected music on early postoperative pain, anxiety, and hemodynamic profile in cesarean section surgery. *Journal of Alternative and Complementary Medicine*, **14**(7), 827–31.

Engwall, M. and Duppils, G.S. (2009). Music as a nursing intervention for postoperative pain: a systematic review. *Journal of Perianesthesia Nursing*, **24**(6), 370–83.

Esch, T., Guarna, M., Bianchi, E., Zhu, W., and Stefano, G.B. (2004). Commonalities in the central nervous system's involvement with complementary medical therapies: limbic morphinergic processes. *Medical Science Monitoring*, **10**(6), MS6–17.

Gauthier, P.A. and Dallaire, C. (1993). Music therapy. *Canadian Nurse*, **89**(2), 48.

Good, M. and Ahn, S. (2008). Korean and American music reduces pain in Korean women after gynecologic surgery. *Pain Management and Nursing*, **9**(3), 96–103.

Good, M., Stanton-Hicks, M., Grass, J.A., Anderson, G.C., Lai, H.L., Roykulcharoen, V., *et al.* (2001). Relaxation and music to reduce postsurgical pain. *Journal of Advanced Nursing*, **33**(2), 208–215.

Good, M., Anderson, G.C., Stanton-Hicks, M., Grass, J.A., and Makii, M. (2002). Relaxation and music reduce pain after gynecologic surgery. *Pain Management and Nursing*, **3**(2), 61–70.

Good, M., Anderson, G.C., Ahn, S., Cong, X., and Stanton-Hicks, M. (2005). Relaxation and music reduce pain following intestinal surgery. *Research in Nursing and Health*, **28**(3), 240–51.

Gouk, P. (2000). *Musical Healing in Cultural Contexts*. Aldershot: Ashgate.

Harikumar, R., Mehroof, R., Antony P., Sunil Kumar, K., Sandesh, K., Syed, A., *et al.* (2006). Listening to music decreases need for sedative medication during colonoscopy: a randomized, controlled trial. *Indian Journal of Gastroenterololology*, **25**(1), 3–5.

Heitz, L., Symreng, T., and Scamman, F.L. (1992). Effect of music therapy in the postoperative care unit: a nursing intervention. *Journal of Post Anesthesia Nursing*, **7**(1), 22–31.

Hesse, H.-P. (2003). *Musik und Emotion–wissenschaftliche Grundlagen des Musik-Erlebens*. New York: Springer.

Hillecke, T., Nicke, A., and Bolay, H.V. (2005). Scientific perspectives on music therapy. *Annals of the New York Academy of Sciences*, **1060**, 271–82.

Horden, P. (2001). *Music as Medicine. The History of Music Therapy since Antiquity*. Aldershot: Ashgate.

Hsiao, T.Y. and Hsieh, H.F. (2009). Nurse's experience of using music therapy to relieve acute pain in a post-orthopedic surgery patient. *The Journal of Nursing*, **56**(4), 105–10.

Ikonomidou, E, Rehnström, and A, Naesh, O. (2004). Effect of music on vital signs and postoperative pain. *Journal of the Association of periOperative Registered Nurses*, **80**(2), 269–74, 77–78.

Jaber, S., Bahloul, H., Guétin, S., Chanques, G., Sebbane, M., and Eledjam, J.J. (2007). Effects of music therapy in intensive care unit without sedation in weaning patients versus non-ventilated patients. *Annales françaises d'anesthèsie et de rèanimation*, **26**(1), 30–8.

Kemper, K.J. and Danhauer, S.C. (2005). Music as therapy. *Southern Medical Journal*, **98**(3), 282–8.

Klassen, J.A., Liang, Y., Tjosvold, L., Klassen, T.P., and Hartling, L. (2008). Music for pain and anxiety in children undergoing medical procedures: a systematic review of randomized controlled trials. *Ambulatory Pediatrics*, **8**(2), 117–28.

Koelsch, S. (2005). Investigating emotion with music: neuroscientific approaches. *Annals of the New York Academy of Sciences*, **1060**, 1–7.

Kullich, W., Bernatzky, G., Hesse, H.-P., Wendtner, F., Likar, R., and Klein, G. (2003). Musiktherapie–Wirkung auf Schmerz, Schlaf und Lebensqualität bei Low back pain. *Wiener Medizinische Wochenschrift*, **153**, 217–21.

Kwekkeboom, K.L., Cherwin, C.H., Lee, J.W., and Wanta, B. (2009). Mind-body treatments for the pain-fatigue-sleep disturbance symptom cluster in persons with cancer. *Journal of Pain and Symptom Management*, **39**, 126–38.

Lee, H.R. (2003). Effects of relaxing music on stress response of patients with acute myocardial infarction. *Taehan Kanho Hakhoe Chi*, **33**(6), 693–704.

Lee, O.K., Chung, Y.F., Chan, M.F., and Chan, W.M. (2005). Music and its effect on the physiological responses and anxiety levels of patients receiving mechanical ventilation: a pilot study. *Journal of Clinical Nursing*, **14**(5), 609–20.

Lepage, C., Drolet, P., Girard, M., Grenier, Y., and DeGagné, R. (2001). Music decreases sedative requirements during spinal anesthesia. *Anesthesia and Analgesia*, **93**(4), 912–16.

MacDonald, R.A.R., Mitchell, L.A., Dillon, T., Serpell, M.G., Davies, J.B., and Ashley, E.A. (2003). An empirical investigation of the anxiolytic and pain reducing effects of music. *Psychology of Music*, **31**(2), 187–203.

Magill, L. (2009). The spiritual meaning of pre-loss music therapy to bereaved caregivers of advanced cancer patients. *Palliative & Supportive Care*, **7**(1), 97–108.

Miller, K., Bernatzky, G., and Wendtner, F. (2002). The purpose of music and relaxation for health promotion after surgical procedures–results of a prospective, randomised study. Presented at the 10th World Congress on Pain (IASP), San Diego, 17–22 August 2002.

Mok, E. and Wong, K.Y. (2003), Effects of music on patient anxiety. *Journal of the Association of periOperative Registered Nurses*, **77**(2), 396–97, 401–6, 409–10.

Nadler, S.F. (2004). Nonpharmacologic management of pain. *Journal of the American Osteopathic Association* (Supplement 8), **104**, S6–S12.

Nickel, A.K., Hillecke, T., Argstatter, H., and Bolay, H.V. (2005). Outcome research in music therapy: a step on the long road to an evidence-based treatment. *Annals of the New York Academy of Sciences*, **1060**, 283–93.

Nilsson, U. (2008). The anxiety- and pain-reducing effects of music interventions: a systematic review. *Journal of the Association of periOperative Registered Nurses*, **87**(4), 780–807.

Nilsson, U. (2009). Soothing music can increase oxytocin levels during bed rest after open heart surgery: a randomised control trial. *Journal of Clinical Nursing*, **18**(15), 2153–61.

Nilsson, U., Rawal, N., Uneståhl, L.E., Zetterberg, C., and Unosson, M. (2001). Improved recovery after music and therapeutic suggestions during general anaesthesia: a double-blind randomised controlled trial. *Acta Anaesthesiologica Scandinavica*, **45**(7), 812–17.

Nilsson, U., Rawal, N., and Unosson, M. (2003). A comparison of intra-operative or postoperative exposure to music - a controlled trial of the effects on postoperative pain. *Anaesthesia*, **58**(7), 699–703.

Nilsson, U., Unosson, M., and Rawal, N. (2005). Stress reduction and analgesia in patients exposed to calming music postoperatively: a randomized controlled trial. *European Journal of Anaesthesiology*, **22**(2), 96–102.

Nilsson, S., Kokinsky, E., Nilsson, U., Sidenvall, B., and Enskär, K. (2009), School-aged children's experiences of postoperative music medicine on pain, distress, and anxiety. *Paediatric Anaesthesia*, **19**(12), 1184–90.

Ovayolu, N., Ucan, O., Pehlivan, S., Pehlivan, Y., Buyukhatipoglu, H., Savas, M.C., *et al.* (2006). Listening to Turkish classical music decreases patients' anxiety, pain, dissatisfaction and the dose of sedative and analgesic drugs during colonoscopy: a prospective randomized controlled trial. *World Journal of Gastroenterology*, **12**(46), 7532–36.

Panksepp, J. and Bernatzky, G. (2002). Emotional sounds and the brain: the neuro-effective foundations of musical appreciation. *Behavioural Processes*, **60**, 133–55.

Pellino, T.A., Gordon, D.B., Engelke, Z.K., Busse, K.L., Collins, M.A., Silver, C.E., *et al.* (2005). Use of nonpharmacologic interventions for pain and anxiety after total hip and total knee arthroplasty. *Orthopaedic Nursing*, **24** (3), 182–90, quiz 91–2.

Pelletier, C.L. (2004). The effect of music on decreasing arousal due to stress: a meta-analysis. *Journal of Music Therapy*, **41**(3), 192–214.

Pothoulaki, M., Macdonald, R.A., Flowers, P., Stamataki, E., Filiopoulos, V., Stamatiadis, D., et al. (2008). An investigation of the effects of music on anxiety and pain perception in patients undergoing haemodialysis treatment. *Journal of Health Psychology*, **13**(7), 912–20.

Pschowski, R. and Motsch, J. (2008). Die postoperative Schmerztherapie. *Wiener Medizinische Wochenschrift*, **158**(21), 603–9.

Pyati, S. and Gan, T.J. (2007). Perioperative pain management. *CNS Drugs*, **21**(3) 185–211.

Quiroga Murcia, C., Kreutz, G., and Bongard, S. (2011). Endokrine und immunologische Wirkungen von Musik. In: C.Schubert (ed.) *Psychoneuroimmunologie und Psychotherapie*, pp. 248–262. Stuttgart: Schattauer.

Richardson, M.M., Babiak-Vazquez, A.E., and Frenke, M.A. (2008). Music therapy in a comprehensive cancer center. *Journal of the Society for Integrative Oncology*, **6**(2), 76–81.

Rotter, J.B. (1966). Generalized expectancies for internal versus external control reinforcement. *Psychological Monographs*, **80**, 1–28.

Salamon, E., Kim, M., Beaulieu, J., and Stefano, G.B. (2003a). Sound therapy induced relaxation: down regulating stress processes and pathologies. *Medical Science Monitoring*, **9**(5), RA116–121.

Salamon, E., Bernstein, S.R., Kim, S.A., Kim, M., and Stefano, G.B. (2003b). The effects of auditory perception and musical preference on anxiety in naive human subjects. *Medical Science Monitoring*, **9**(9), CR396–9.

Schwartz, F.J. and Ruthann, R. (2004). Music listening in neonatal intensive care units. Available at: http://www.transitionsmusic.com/final_version_Dileo.html (accessed 18 May 2004).

Shapiro, A. (1969). A pilot program in music therapy with residents of a home for the aged. *The Gerontologist*, **9**, 128–33.

Simcock, X.C., Yoon, R.S., Chalmers, P., Geller, J.A., Kiernan, H.A., and Macaulay, W. (2008). Intraoperative music reduces perceived pain after total knee arthroplasty: a blinded, prospective, randomized, placebo-controlled clinical trial. *Journal of Knee Surgery*, **21**(4), 275–78.

Spintge, R. (2000). Music and anaesthesia in pain therapy. *Anaesthesiologie, Intensivmedizin, Notfallmedizin und Schmerztherapie*, **35** (4), 254–61.

Spintge, R. and Droh, R. (1992). *Musik-Medizin, Physiologische Grundlagen und praktische Anwendungen*. Stuttgart: Fischer.

Trappe, H.J. (2009). Music and health—what kind of music is helpful for whom? What music not? *Deutsche Medizinische Wochenschrift*, **134**(51–52), 2601–6.

Twiss, E., Seaver, J., and McCaffrey, R. (2006). The effect of music listening on older adults undergoing cardiovascular surgery. *Nursing and Critical Care*, **11**(5), 224–31.

Voss, J.A., Good, M., Yates, B., Baun, M.M., Thompson, A., and Hertzog, M. (2004). Sedative music reduces anxiety and pain during chair rest after open-heart surgery. *Pain*, **12**(1–2), 197–203.

Wang, S.M., Kulkarni, L., Dolev, J., and Kain, Z.N. (2002). Music and preoperative anxiety: a randomized, controlled study. *Anesthesia & Analgesia*, **94**(6), 1489–94.

Winter, M.J., Paskin, S., and Baker, T. (1994). Music reduces stress and anxiety of patients in the surgical holding area. *Journal of Post Anesthesia Nursing*, **9**(6), 340–3.

Zalewsky, S., Vinker, S., Fiada, I., Livon, D., and Kitai, E. (1998). Background music in the family physician's surgery: patient reactions. *Harefuah*, **135**(3–4), 96–7, 168, 167.

Zhao, H. and Chen, A.C. (2009). Both happy and sad melodies modulate tonic human heat pain. *Journal of Pain*, **10**(9), 953–60.

Chapter 20

Clinical Use of Music in Operating Theatres

Ralph Spintge

Many if not most patients undergoing medical treatment in hospital operating theatres suffer from complex sets of conditions including pain, anxiety, and distress, and even aggressive non-compliance (Spintge 1983; Badner et al. 1990; Evans 1995; Kain et al. 1995; Wang et al. 2002). The term operating theatre, as it is used here, entails a wide range of settings where invasive and emotionally aversive medical interventions are carried out. Music is increasingly used in operating theatres for specific purposes of alleviating patients' physical and emotional condition before, during, and after surgeries. The aim of this chapter is to address available empirical evidence to support the use of music in operating theatres and to assess underlying mechanisms explaining how and why music may be suitable for use in these specific settings (Spintge 1981, 2000).

Clinical setting and patients' perioperative stress

Waiting for a medical procedure is not always easy. The general psychophysical state of the patient waiting for invasive treatment may be characterized by negative emotions and perceptions including distress, anxiety, and pain (Tolksdorf 1985; Kain et al. 1995). Patients often anticipate even more stress and pain while being asked to stay silent and calm by anonymous staff and fellow patients. Moreover, reduced mobility, control over the situation and uncertainty can lead to high levels of arousal and (more negative than positive) excitement. Perhaps not surprisingly, responses to these challenges may affect the medical treatment negatively; manifesting in potential aversive behaviours and non-compliance.

The vicious circle of stress and pain described above may keep the patient in a state of anxiety, fear of pain and death, combined with impaired conscious perception, reduced self-esteem, anger, feeling of helplessness and disappointment (Spintge and Droh 1981). Psychophysiological consequences include disturbances in central nervous (neurovegetative) regulation of cardiovascular and cardiorespiratory systems with increased energy demand and oxygen consumption, inadequate endocrinological control of metabolism, vegetative disturbances such as nausea and vomiting, and motor dysfunction like tremor (Gellhorn 1964; Spintge and Droh 1991; Keller 1995). Symptoms of such disturbances as observed by clinical physicians include, but are not restricted to:

- Increased plasma levels of catecholamines, steroid hormones, endogenous opioids.
- Cardiac arrhythmias, angina pectoris, hypertension, hyperventilation, asthma.
- Increased muscle tonus, cramps, trembling with excitement.
- Lowered pain tolerance, general hyperaesthesia, ephaptic spreading of pain.
- Inadequate defence reactions, panic reactions, reduced compliance.

♦ Increased demand for sedatives, anaesthetics and analgetics perioperatively.

♦ Prolonged postoperative rehabilitation phase.

From such anecdotal observations, important implications and questions emerge. It appears that over the entire time-span from informing patients that they will undergo surgery until release from hospital (and beyond), each patient's emotions and perceptions need to be addressed in the interest of the success of medical interventions as a whole. What factors are involved in mediating aversive responses with all its consequences to surgical treatment? How can these emotions and perceptions be addressed within the routine treatment plans? What are the mechanisms that will allow us to break the vicious circle of patients' anxiety and pain in operating theatres?

Empirical work so far has identified cognitive and emotional factors, namely: (1) lack of information and perceived control as well as (2) insufficient emotional support (Spintge 1983; Tolksdorf 1985). These are believed to significantly influence perioperative stress in patients undergoing surgery and anaesthesia. Medical administrations such as, for example, the British General Medical Council, have responded to part of these findings by establishing specific guidelines for ethical, evidence-based patient information. However, patients' emotional needs are still neglected (General Medical Council 1999, 2008; Trevena et al. 2006).

It is worth noting that environmental conditions may pose problems in hospital wards in general, and in operating theatres in particular. Typical noise levels in intensive care units and operating rooms may well exceed 85dBA, noise pollution arising from machines (running sound, alarm signal), as well as human interaction (door slamming, conversation, handling of equipment) (Kain et al. 1995; Thompson et al. 1995). Such levels are subject to regulatory action in the European Union, yet odour of detergents for disinfection and of other materials, as well as cold air streams from air conditioning, may also contribute. Research has also found strange and frightening looking rooms and equipment combined with staff behaviour such as hectic speech to be perceived as aversive stimuli (Spintge and Droh 1981; Tolksdorf 1985; Tolksdorf 1997; Stirling 2006). The factors listed above may generally enhance negative associations with operating theatres, resulting in a common 'state of negative emotional emergency' (Spintge 1983; Nolan 1992; Nijkamp et al. 2004; Salimpoor et al. 2009).

A number of clinical studies have investigated the above listed undesired perioperative responses, applying advanced multimodal monitoring to measure psychological, physiological, behavioural and clinical parameters (McGlinn 1931; Spintge and Droh 1981; Tolksdorf 1985; Norman and Fink 1997; Tolksdorf 1997; Munafo 1998; Grossi 1999; Caumo and Ferreira 2003; Buyukkocak et al. 2006; Shigeki et al. 2006; Stirling 2006; Schön et al. 2007). The following section outlines measures that can be introduced to combat these issues, analysing the evidence for music in particular.

Measures designed to alleviate perioperative stress and pain

Pharmacological interventions such as analgesics and sedatives are often insufficient in alleviating stress response and resolving anxiety perioperatively (Badner et al. 1990; Arts et al. 1994; Caumo et al. 2003; Buyukkocak et al. 2006). They may also have undesired side effects, and can even reduce the patient's ability to cooperate (Fishman and Greenberg 1996; Cunningham et al. 1997; Sullivan et al. 2009). Obviously, there is an urgent need to satisfy need for patient information and alleviate psychological suffering with its pathophysiological sequela. With these aims in mind, we developed a new technique called Perioperative Patient Ergonomics (PPE, Spintge 1991). The rationale of this synaesthetic approach addresses the entire sensory input from the perioperative environment on our patients including acoustic, visual, tactile, and caloric sensory modalities as well as the staff–patient communication and relationship. In this chapter we focus on the acoustic environment through specific musical interventions called Medicofunctional Music, or, more specifically, Anxioalgolytic Music (AAM).

The role of the music

Underpinning our consideration of music-based interventions is the importance of robust research standards and guidelines, necessary to initiate informed discussions about evidence-based use of music in medicine in general (Spintge and Droh 1992; Robb 2009). Clinical applications of Medicofunctional Music follow guidelines and standards of music medicine, defined as 'the scientifically based, medico-functional application of music in order to complement usual medical procedures in prevention, therapy and rehabilitation' (Spintge and Droh 1989; Spintge 1996). Within this, we propose the reason why music can be used perioperatively with high efficacy is due mainly to the fact that groups of different individuals do react to similar musical stimuli in a predictive way more easily, if the setting creates an identical, and reproducible emotional state.

The concept of AAM (Spintge 1983) was developed over the last decades specifically to reduce perioperative stress and pain. The concept has been refined using pre- and post-test patient questionnaires, and empirically evaluated in many clinical settings using state-of-the-art research protocols for mainstream medical trials (Spintge 1992); our observation period now spans around 30 years and 160,000 patients. This includes a multimodal research protocol, incorporating psychological and physiological measurements such as self-reports (open questionnaires, Thematic Apperception Test, e.g. Westen 1991), observable behaviour and facial action coding systems (Ekman 2003), plasma levels of stress-hormones, electroencephalogram, positron emission tomography, neurovegetative and cardiovascular responses, drug consumption, length of hospital stay, and other economic outcome variables. (Hatano et al. 1983a,b; Spintge 1992). To date, AAM is widely applied in surgery and anaesthesia, dental care, pain medicine, palliative care, intensive care, obstetrics, paediatrics, geriatrics, ophthalmology and neurology (Hatano et al. 1983a,b; Spintge 1983; Fowler and Lander 1987; Spintge and Droh 1987; Maranto 1991; Steinke 1991; Spintge and Droh 1992; Arts et al. 1994; Pratt and Spintge 1996; Spintge 2000; Bradt 2001; Nijkamp et al. 2004; Arnon et al. 2006; Leins 2006; Brice 2007). Table 20.1 shows the evidence for AAM in reducing psychological and pathophysiological symptoms and behaviours associated with perioperative stress outlined earlier.

Overall, patients undergoing anaesthesia show and report significant effects as displayed in table one in 95% of all cases. Scientific evaluation of AAM in general surgery, orthopaedic surgery, traumatology, obstetrics, dentistry and neonatal intensive care was undertaken through a series of controlled studies. Today there are a significant number of studies showing similar results for a variety of perioperative settings. Table 20.2 gives a selection, however not complete, of recent clinical, randomized controlled trials comparing standard care during respective operative procedures to music alone, or, in addition to several other stimuli such as silence, environmental sound, etc.

Technical considerations

While the basic standards in methodology, technique, and music design apply to all perioperative situations in all surgical specialties such as obstetrics, gynaecology, traumatology, and so forth, it should be kept in mind that the methods and techniques have to be adapted to the individual clinical situation. Using the example of AAM in the surgical operating theatre, consideration

Table 20.1 Clinical benefits of anxioalgolytic music (AAM)

Physiological and other variables related to medical interventions	Response to AAM
Cardiorespiratory system	Decrease of heart rate and arterial blood pressure
	Harmonizing rhythmic action/increase of heart rate variability
	Decrease of respiratory minute-volume and oxygen-consumption
	Synchronization/harmonization of rhythm
Endocrinum and metabolism	Reduced plasma levels of catecholamines, adrenocorticotropic hormone (ACTH), cortisol, prolactin, β-endorphin
	Decrease in basal metabolic rate
	Sleep induction
Vegetative system	Reduced nausea, sweating and vertigo
Immune system	Psychoneuronal modulation of neuroendocrine receptors for Catecholamines, endorphins, substance P, dopamine, Interleukin-6 leading to:
	Increase in IgA-saliva-levels, T-cell counts and killer cells activity
Secretion and excretion	Reduced perspiration
Self-perception	Increase in pain threshold pain tolerance
	Relief of inflammatory pain
Cognitive function and compliance	Decrease in postoperative confusion
	Enhanced compliance
	Improved perioperative mental functioning
Motor control	Reduced restlessness and muscle tonus/spasms
Drug consumption	Premedication 50–100% reduced
	Postoperative analgesics reduced during first hours
Hospital treatment period	3 days less in premature infants on intensive care
	1 day less in cataract surgery for high risk elderly patients
	Improved staff efficiency

must be made of some basic preconditions. Any electronic device brought into the theatre as such is subject to safety as well as hygienic measures (surface disinfection of equipment). Operating devices require staff education and quality management by using standardized regimes, checklists and quality control questionnaires. Above all, it is crucially important for the successful implementation of a musical intervention program that members of staff are able to incorporate it into their working routines.

For practical and hygienic reasons, individual earphones should be supplied in the ward before transfer to surgery department. As discussed below, music should then be offered according to the patient's choice fixed in her/his record upon entering the operating area. Patients are

Table 20.2 Selection of randomized controlled clinical studies showing improved treatment outcome as outlined in table1 comparing music added to perioperative standard care to standard alone, or, in addition to other interfering variables in the specialties listed

Specialty	Clinical setting	Reference
Obstetrics	Caesarean section under regional anaesthesia	Laopaiboon et al, 2009
Cardiothoracic Surgery	Coronary angiography	Nilsson et al, 2009
	Coronary artery bypass graft surgery	Schwartz 2009
Pain medicine	Chronic non-malignant pain	Siedlecki 2009
	Postanaesthesia care unit	Fredriksson et al, 2009
	General anaesthesia for cholecystectomy	Oyama et al, 1987
Paediatric anaesthesia	Outpatient surgery	Kain et al, (2001, 2004), Wang et al, (2002)
Orthopaedic surgery	Postoperative rehab after hip or knee surgery in elderly	McCaffrey 2009
Gynaecological surgery	Laparoscopic surgery	Ikonomidou and Rehnstrom (2004)
	Mastectomy	Binns-Turner (2008)
Paediatrics	Neonate Intensive Care Unit (NICU) for preterm infants	Collins and Kuck (1991), Standley and Moore (1995), Coleman (1997), Schwartz et al, (1998), Loewy (2000), Standley (2003), Loewy et al, (2005), Golianu et al, (2007), Lubetzky et al, (2009), Stewart (2009)
Ophthalmic surgery	Ambulatory ophthalmic surgery	Allen et al, (2001), Fernell (2002)
	Inpatient cataract surgery	Reilley (1999)
Palliative care	Hospice	Krout (2001)
Surgery	Day surgery	Nilsson et al, (2005), Leard (2007)
	Cancer surgery	Cunningham et al. (1997)
Gastroenterology	Endoscopy	Ovayola (2006)
	Digestive tract surgery	Chikamori et al. (2004)
Intensive Care	Intensive Care Unit (ICU)	Conrad et al, (2007), Nelson et al, (2008)
Dentistry	Caries cavity treatment	Hatano et al, (1983a,b)

encouraged to keep earphones on and listen to their music during all following procedures to gain partial acoustic isolation plus desired medicofunctional effects. Music can be applied during regional anaesthesia and general anaesthesia, however, the question of whether there are direct beneficial effects during general anaesthesia is still open (Gross 2003; Nilsson et al. 2003; Nilsson et al. 2005; Kölsch et al. 2006).

The application of music itself involves various salient considerations. Patients in most settings listen to the music of their choice through earphones and are able to adjust the volume. Maximum loudness should be set to 70dB(A). If earphones must be replaced by loudspeakers (which brings the potential for acoustic pollution for staff), loudness should be set to plus 10dB(A) above usual acoustic environment, but still lower than 80dBA.High fidelity quality is mandatory and the musical selections should last continuously over a period of several hours, comprising of single pieces of 5–8 minutes each, in line with attention limits. The music library should be updated about every 3 months.

We may only speculate which musical parameters might contribute to the pain and anxiety relieving effects of music listening as suggested from empirical evidence. From our clinical experience and with consideration to some neurophysiological studies, one particularly effective parameter may be musical rhythm (Rider 1985; Koepchen et al. 1992; Thaut 2003; Avancini et al. 2005; Bernardi et al. 2009) as well as timbre qualities in the music (Cook 2007; Cook and Hayashi 2009). Influences of rhythm may arise through the physiological phenomenon of entrainment, in which exogenous rhythms interact with bodily rhythms such as heart rate variability or cardiorespiratory variables. Yet, further neurophysiological studies are necessary to identify the missing link between musical structure and biological function (Koepchen et al. 1992; Spintge 1999).

Aspects of evaluation

Guidelines for medicofunctional music such as AAM must adhere to general medical standards, enabling validation and reproduction. Accurate record keeping of the procedure is therefore essential, including: full details of the chosen musical composition, the 'dosage' (i.e. volume, duration), current aims of the musical intervention (desired clinical effects, whether that be anxiolytic, sleep-inducing, performance enhancement, etc.), undesired side effects (overly distracting, negative memories), contraindications (psychotic state, borderline, addiction, epileptic seizures), and the technical administration (earphone/loudspeaker, stereo/mono, 2-dimensional (D)/3-D, analogue/digital, wire/wireless, foreground/background, subliminal).

Conclusions

Music is now widely applied in perioperative settings (Thompson 1995), and meta-analyses underline the effectiveness of music in acute stress, anxiety and pain (Standley 1986; Maranto 1991; Pratt and Spintge 1996; Standley 2002; Dileo 2003; Pelletier 2004; Hilliard 2005; Cepeda et al. 2006; Bradt and Dileo 2007). It remains to be seen, to what extent rhythmic aspects of music may be major determinants of physiological responses to music in this specific context (Gomez and Danuser 2007; Koepchen et al. 1992).

Initial evidence clearly suggests that music may have beneficial and significant impact on clinical outcome in perioperative medical settings such as in operating theatres. Current research focuses address clinical outcomes as well as economic benefits (Walworth 2005; Romo et al. 2007; Goodman and Sims 2009). In particular, music offers the potential for cost containment with respect to medication, duration of hospital stay, effectiveness of staff utilization, and procedural times (Spintge 1981; Coleman et al. 1997; Schwartz et al. 1998; Reilly 1999; DeLoach 2005; Nilsson et al. 2005). Not surprisingly, increasing numbers of practitioners and clinicians express their interest in incorporating medicofunctional music into their health care practice, especially to alleviate pain, stress and anxiety perioperatively (Pölkki et al. 2001; Mathur et al. 2008). Therefore, there is a need for further research that should address the neurobiological bases to further stimulate clinical practice.

References

Allen, K., Golden, L.H., Izzo, J.L., Ching, M.I., Forrest, A., Niles, C.R., *et al.* (2001). Normalization of hypertensive responses during ambulatory surgical stress by perioperative music. *Psychosomatic Medicine*, **63**, 487–92.

Arnon, S., Shapsa, A., Forman, L., Regev, R., Bauer, S., and Litmanovitz, I. (2006). Live music is beneficial to preterm infants in neonatal intensive care unit environment. *Birth*, **32**(2), 131–6.

Arts, S.E., Abu-Saad, H.H., Champion, G.D., Crawford, M.R., Fisher, R.J., Juniper, K.H. et al. (1994). Age-related response to lidocaine-prilocaine (EMLA) emulsion and effect of music distraction on the pain of intravenous cannulation. *Pediatrics*, **93**, 797–801.

Avanzini, G., Lopez, L., Koelsch, S. and Majno, M. (eds.) (2005). The neurosciences and music vol 2. From perception to performance. *Annals of the New York Academy of Sciences*, **1060**.

Badner, N., Nielson, W., and Munk, S. (1990). Preoperative anxiety: detection and contributing factors. *Canadian Journal of Anesthesia*, **37**, 444–7.

Bernardi, L., Porta, C., Balsamo, R. Bernardi, N.F., and Sleight, P. (2009). Dynamic interactions between musical, cardiovascular, and cerebral rhythms in humans. *Circulation*, **119**, 3171–80.

Binns-Turner, P.G., Boyd, G.L., Pryor, E.R., Prickett, C., and Harrison, L. (2008). Effects of perioperative music on anxiety, hemodynamics, and pain in women undergoing mastectomy. *Anesthesiology*, **109**, A1351.

Bradt, J. (2001). The effect of Music Entrainment on postoperative pain perception in pediatric patients. Dissertation submitted to the Temple University Graduate Board.

Bradt, J. and Dileo, Ch. (2007). Music for people with coronary heart disease. *Cochrane Database of Systematic Reviews*, **3**, CD006577.

Brice, J. and Barclay, J. (2007). Music eases anxiety of children in cast room. *Journal of Pediatric Orthopedics*, **27**, 831–3.

Buyukkocak, U., Caglayan, O., Daphan, C., Aydinuraz, K., Saygun, O., Kaya, T., et al. (2006). Similar effects of general and spinal anaesthesia on perioperative stress responses in patients undergoing haemorrhoidectomy. *Mediators of Inflamation*, **2006**(1), 97257

Caumo, W. and Ferreira, M.B.C. (2003). Perioperative anxiety: psychobiology and effects in postoperative recovery. *The Pain Clinic*, **15**(2), 87–101.

Cepeda, M.S., Carr, D.B., Lau, J., and Alvarez, H. (2006). Music for pain relief. *The Cochrane Database Systematic Reviews*, **19**(2), CD004843.

Chikamori, F., Kuniyoshi, N., Shibuya, S., and Takase, Y. (2004). Perioperative music therapy with key-lighting keyboard system in elderly patients undergoing digestive tract surgery. *Hepato-gastroenterology*, **51**(59), 1384–6.

Coleman, J.M., Pratt, R.R., Stoddard, R.A., Gerstman, D.R., and Abel, H.H. (1997). The Effects of the male and female singing and speaking voice on selected physiological and behavioral measures of premature infants in the intensive care unit. *International Journal of Arts Medicine*, **5**(2), 4–11.

Collins, S. and Kuck, K. (1991). Music Therapy in the neonatal intensive care unit. *Neonatal Network*, **9**(6), 23–6.

Conrad, C., Niess, H., Jauch, K.W., Bruns, C.J., Hartl, W., and Welker, L. (2007). Overture for growth hormone: requiem for interleukin-6. *Critical Care Medicine*, **35**(12), 2709–13.

Cook, N.D. (2007). The sound symbolism of major and minor harmonies. *Music Perception*, **24**(3), 315–19

Cook, N.D. and Hayashi, T. (2009). Die biologie des wohlklangs [The biology of harmonics]. *Spektrum der Wissenschaft*, **3**, 64–70.

Cunningham, M.F., Monson, B., and Bookbinder, M. (1997). Introducing a music in the perioperative area. *Journal of the Association of periOperative Registered Nurses*, **10**, 67–9.

DeLoach, D. (2005). Procedural-support music therapy in the healthcare setting: A cost-effectiveness analysis. *Journal of Pediatric Nursing*. **20**(4), 276–84.

Dileo, C. (2003). A meta-analysis of the literature in medical music therapy and MusicMedicine with an agenda for future research. *Volume of Abstracts VIII. International Symposium for Music in Medicine of the International Society of Music in Medicine (ISMM)*, pp. 100–1. Hamburg: ISMM.

Ekman, P. (2003). Facial expression of emotion. In: R.J. Davidson, K.R. Scherer, and H.H. Goldsmith (eds.) *Handbook of Affective Sciences*, pp. 415–131. New York: Oxford University Press.

Fishman, S.M. and Greenberg, D.B. (1996). Psychological Issues in the Treatment of Pain. In: D. Borsook, A.A. LeBel, and B.C. McPeck (ed.) *The Massachusetts General Hospital Handbook of Pain Management*, pp. 40–6. Boston, MA: Little Brown.

Fernell, J. (2002). Listening to music during ambulatory ophthalmic surgery reduced blood pressure, heart rate, and perceived stress. *Evidence Based Nursing*, **1**(5), 16–26.

Fowler-Kerry, S. and Lander, J.R. (1987). Management of injection pain in children. *Pain*, **30**, 169–75.

Fredriksson, A.C., Hellström, L., and Nilsson, U. (2009). Patient's perception of music versus ordinary sound in a postanaesthesia care unit: a randomised crossover trial. *Intensive and Critical Care Nursing*, **25**(4), 208–13.

General Medical Council (1999). *Protecting patients, guiding doctors. Seeking patients' consent: the ethical considerations.* London: GMC.

General Medical Council (2008). *Consent: patients and doctors making decisions together. Ethical guidance.* London: GMC.

Gellhorn, E. (1964). Motion and emotion. *Psychological Review*, **71**, 457–72.

Goodman, O. and Sims, E. (2009). State of the Field Report: Arts in Healthcare. *State of the Field Committee*. Washington, DC: Society for the Arts in Healthcare.

Golianu, B., Krane, E., Seybold, J., Almgren, C., and Anand, K.J.S. (2007). Non-pharmacological techniques for pain management in neonates on ICU: music clearly effective. *Seminars in Perinatology*, **31**(5), 318–22.

Gomez, P. and Danuser, B. (2007). Relationships between musical structure and psychophysiological measures of emotion. *Emotion*, **7**(2), 377–87.

Gross, M.A.F., Nager, W., Schalk, F., Piepenbrock, S.A., Münte, T.F., and Münte, S. (2003). Unbewußte wahrnehmung bei patienten im operationssaal unter allgemeinanaesthesie. *Anaesthesiologie, Intensivmedizin, Notfallmedizin und Schmerztherapie*, **11**(43), 755.

Grossi, E.A., Zakow, P.K., Ribakove, G., Kallenbach, K., Ursomanno, P., Gradek, C.E., *et al.* (1999). Comparison of post-operative pain, stress response, and quality of life in port access vs. standard sternotomy coronary bypass patients. *European Journal of Cardio-Thoracic Surgery*, **16**(2), 39–42.

Hatano, K., Oyama, T., Kogure, T., Ohkura, I., and Spintge, R. (1983a). Anxiolytic effect of music on dental treatment. Part 1: Subjective and objective evaluation. *Journal of the Japanese Society for Dental Anesthesiology*, **11**(3), 332–7.

Hatano, K., Oyama, T., Tsukamoto, A., Sakaki, T., and Spintge, R. (1983b). Anxiolytic effect of music on dental treatment. Part 2: endocrine evaluation. *Journal of the Japanese Society for Dental Anesthesiology*, **11**(3), 338–45.

Hilliard, R.E. (2005). Music therapy in hospice and palliative care: A review of the empirical data. *Evidence-Based Complementary and Alternative Medicine*, **2**, 173–8.

Ikonomidou, E., Rehnstrom, A., Naesh, N. (2004). Effect of music on vital signs and postoperative pain. *Journal of the Association of periOperative Registered Nurses*, **80**, 269–78.

Kain, Z.N., Mayes, L., and Cicchetti, D. (1995). Measurement tool for pre-operative anxiety in children: the Yale Preoperative Anxiety Scale. *Child Neuropsychology* **1**, 203–10.

Kain, Z.N., Wang, S.M., Mayes, L.C., Krivutza, D.M., and Teague, B.A. (2001). Sensory stimuli and anxiety in children undergoing surgery: a randomized, controlled trial. *Anesthesia and Analgesia*, **92**(4), 897–903.

Kain, Z.N., Caldwell-Andrews, A.A., Krivutza, D.M., Weinberg, M.E., Gaal, D., Wang, S.-M., *et al.* (2004). Interactive music therapy as a treatment for preoperative anxiety in children: a randomized controlled trial. *Anesthesia and Analgesia*, **98**, 1260–6.

Keller, V. (1995). Management of nausea and vomiting in children. *Journal of Pediatric Nursing*, **24**(1), 280–6.

Kölsch, S., Heinke, W., Sammler, D., and Olthoff, D. (2006). Auditory processing during deep propofol sedation and recovery from unconsciousness. *Clinical Neurophysiology*, **117**(8), 1746–59.

Koepchen, H.P., Droh, R., Spintge, R. Abel, H.H., Kluessendorf, D., and Koralewski, E. (1992). Physiological rhythmicity and music in medicine. In: R. Spintge, and R. Droh (eds.) *MusicMedicine vol 1*, pp. 39–70. Saint Louis, MO: MMB.

Krout, R.E. (2001). The effects of single-session music therapy interventions on the observed and self-reported levels of pain control, physical comfort, and relaxation of hospice patients. *American Journal of Hospice and Palliative Medicine*, **18**(6), 383–90

Laopaiboon, M., Lumbiganon, P., Martis, R., Vatanasapt, P., and Somjaivong, B. (2009). Music during caesarean section under regional anaesthesia for improving maternal and infant outcomes. *Cochrane Database Systemic Review*, **15**, (2), CD006914.

Leard, R. (2007). Randomized clinical trial examining the effect of music therapy in stress response to day surgery. *British Journal of Surgery*, **94** (8), 943–47

Leins A.K. (2006). *Heidelberger Musiktherapiemanual: Migräne bei Kindern* [Heidelberg Music Therapy Manual: Migraine in Children]. Bochum: uni-edition.

Loewy, J.V. (2000). Music therapy in the neonatal intensive care unit. New York: BIMC by Satchnote Press.

Loewy, J., Hallan, C., Friedman, E., and Martinez, C. (2005). Sleep/sedation in children undergoing EEG testing: A comparison of chloral hydrate and music therapy. *Journal of PeriAnesthesia Nursing*, **20**(5), 323–32.

Lubetzky, R., Mimouni, F.B., Dollberg, S., Reifen, R., Ashbel, G., and Mandel, D. (2009). Effect of Mozart on energy expenditure in growing preterm infants. *Pediatrics*, **125**(1), e24–8.

MacDonald, R.A.R., Ashley, E.A., Davies, M.G., Serpell, M.G., Murray, J.L., Rogers, K., et al. (1999). The anxiolytic and pain reducing effects of music on post-operative analgesia. In: Pratt, R.R. and Grocke, D. (eds.). *MusicMedicine 3*, pp. 12–18. Melbourne: University of Melbourne Press.

Maranto, Ch. (1991). *Applications of Music in Medicine*. Washington D.C.: NAMT.

Mathur, A., Duda, L., and Kamat, D.M. (2008). Knowledge and use of music therapy among pediatric practitioners in Michigan. *Clinical Pediatrics*, **4**(2), 15–159.

McCaffrey, R.G. (2009). The effect of music on cognition of older adults undergoing hip and knee surgery. *Music and Medicine*, **1**(1), 22–8.

McGlinn, J.A. (1931). Music in the operating theatre. *British Medical Journal*, **1**(3654), 108.

Micci, N. (1984). The use of music therapy with pediatric patients undergoing cardiac catheterization. *The Arts in Psychotherapy*, **11**, 261–6.

Munafo, M.R. (1998). Perioperative anxiety and postoperative pain. *Psychology, Health and Medicine*, **3**(4), 429–33.

Nijkamp, M.D., Kenens, C.A., Dijker, A.J.M., Ruiter, R.A.C., Hiddema, F., and Nuijts, R.M.A. (2004). Determinants of surgery related anxiety in cataract patients. *British Journal of Ophthalmology*, **88**, 1310–14.

Nelson, A., Hartl, W., Jauch, K.W., Fricchione, G.L., Benson, H., Warsha A.L., et al. (2008). The impact of music on hypermetabolism in critical illness. *Current Opinion Clinical Nutrition Metabolic Care*, **11**(6), 790–94

Nilsson, U., Rawal, N., and Unosson, M. (2003). A comparison of intraoperative or postoperative exposure to music–a controlled trial of the effects on postoperative pain. *Anaesthesia*, **58**(7), 699–703.

Nilsson, U. Unosson, M., and Rawal, N. (2005). Stress reduction and analgesia in patients exposed to calming music postoperatively: a randomized controlled trial. *European Journal of Anaesthesiology*, **22**(2), 96–102.

Nilsson, U., Lindell, L., Eriksson, A., and Kellerth, T. (2009). The effect of music intervention in relation to gender during coronary angiographic procedures: a randomized clinical trial. *European Journal of Cardiovascular Nursing*, **1**, 29.

Nolan, P. (1992). Music therapy with bone marrow transplant patients: Reaching beyond the symptoms. In Spintge, R., and Droh, R. (eds.) *MusicMedicine*, pp. 209–12. St. Louis, MO: MMB Music.

Norman, J.G. and Fink, G.W. (1997). The effect of epidural anesthesia on the neuroendocrine response to major surgical stress: a randomized prospective trial. *American Journal of Surgery*, **63**(1), 75–80.

Oyama, T., Sato, Y., Kudo, T., Spintge, R., Droh, R. (1987) Effect of anxiolytic music on endocrine function in surgical patients. In: R. Spintge, and R. Droh (ed.) *Music in Medicine*, pp. 169–74. Heidelberg/Berlin: Springer.

Ovayola, N., Ucan, O., Pehlivan, S., Pehlivan, Y, Buyukhatipoglu, H., Savas, C., et al (2006). Listening to Turkish Classical music during colonoscopy decreases patient´s anxiety, pain, dissatisfaction and the dose of sedative (Midazolam) and analgesic (Meperidine) drugs: A prospective and randomized controlled trial. *World Journal of Gastroenterology, 14*(46), 7532–6.

Pelletier, C. (2004). The effect of music on decreasing arousal due to stress: A meta-analysis. *Journal of Music Therapy, 41*, 192–214.

Pölkki, T., Vehviläinen-Julkunen, K., Pietilä, A.M. (2001). Nonpharmacological methods in relieving children´s postoperative pain: A survey on hospital nurses in Finland. *Journal of Advanced Nursing, 34*(4), 483–92.

Pratt, R.R., and Spintge, R. (1996). *MusicMedicine (vol. 2)*. Saint Louis, MO: MMB.

Reilly, M.P. (1999). Music, a cognitive behavioural intervention for anxiety and acute pain control in the elderly cataract patient. Dissertation Faculty of the University of Texas Graduate School of Biomedical Sciences. San Antonio

Rider, M.S. (1985). Entrainment mechanisms are involved in pain reduction, muscle relaxation, and music-mediated imagery. *Journal of Music Therapy, 22*, 183–92.

Robb, S.L. (2009). A review of music-based intervention reporting in pediatrics. *Journal of Health Psychology, 14* (4), 490–501.

Romo, R. and Gifford, L. (2007). A cost–benefit analysis of music therapy in a home hospice. *Nursing Economics, 25*(6), 353–58.

Salimpoor, V.N., Benovoy, M., Longo, G., Cooperstock, J.R., and Zatorre, R.J. (2009). The rewarding aspects of music listening are related to degree of emotional arousal. *PloS One, 4*(19), e7487.

Siedlecki, S.L. (2009). Racial variation in response to music in a sample of african-american and caucasian chronic pain patients. *Journal of Pain Management in Nursing, 10*(1), 14–21.

Schön, J., Gerlach, K., and Hüppe, M. (2007). Einfluss negativer Stressverarbeitung auf postoperatives Schmerzerleben und–verhalten. *Der Schmerz 21*(2), 146–53.

Schwartz, F. Ritchie, R., Sacks, L.L., and Phillips, C.E. (1998). Music, stress reduction and medical cost savings in the neonatal care unit. In: R.R. Pratt, and D.E. Grocke (eds.) *MusicMedicine vol. 3*, pp. 120–30. Melbourne: University of Melbourne Press.

Schwartz, F. (2009). A pilot study of patients in postoperative cardiac surgery. *Music and Medicine, 1*(1), 70–4.

Shigeki, M., Genyuki, Y., and Morio, T. (2006). Postoperative pain and stress-related hormone responses to surgery in jaw deformities. *Japanese Journal of Oral and Maxillofacial Surgery, 52*(3), 162–6.

Spintge, R. (1983). Psychophysiologische Operations-Fitness mit und ohne anxiolytische Musik [Psychophysiological fitness for surgery with and without anxiolytic music]. In R. Droh, and R. Spintge (ed.) *Angst, Schmerz, Musik in der Anaesthesie [Anxiety, pain, music in anesthesia]*, pp. 77–88. Grenzach: Editiones Roche.

Spintge, R. (1992) Toward a research standard in musicmedicine/music therapy: A proposal for a multimodal approach. In R. Spintge, and R. Droh (eds.). *MusicMedicine*, pp 345–47. Saint Louis, MO: MMB.

Spintge, R. (1999). MusicMedicine: applications, standards, and definitions. In R. Pratt, and D. Grocke (eds.) *MusicMedicine Vol. 3*, pp. 3–11. Melbourne: University of Melbourne Press.

Spintge, R. (2000). Musik in anaesthesie und schmerztherapie. [Music in anaesthesia and pain therapy]. *Anaesthesie Intensivtherapie Notfallmedizin Schmerztherapie, 35*, 254–61.

Spintge, R. and Droh, R. (1981). Die präoperative Angst [Preoperative Anxiety]. *Intensivmedizinische Praxis, 4*, 29–33.

Spintge, R. and Droh, R. (1987). *Music in Medicine*. Heidelberg-New York: Springer.

Spintge, R. and Droh, R. (1989). *The International Society for Music in Medicine ISMM–MusicMedicine, Music Therapy, Musicmedicine. Book of Abstracts*, Rancho Mirage, CA: ISMM.

Spintge, R. and Droh, R. (1991). Ergonomic approach to treatment of patient's perioperative stress. *Canadian Anesthetist Society Journal, 35* (3), 104–6.

Spintge, R., and Droh, R. (1992). *MusicMedicine*. Saint Louis, MO: MMB.

Standley, J.M. (1986). Music research in medical/dental treatment: meta-analysis and clinical applications. *Journal of Music Therapy*, **23**, 56–122.

Standley, J.M. (2002). A meta-analysis of the efficacy of music therapy for premature infants. *Journal of Pediatric Nursing*, **17**, 107–13.

Standley, J.M. (2003). Music therapy with premature infants: Research and developmental interventions. Silver Spring, MD: American Music Therapy Association.

Standley, J.M. and Moore, R. (1995). Therapeutic effects of music and mother's voice on premature infants. *Pediatric Nursing*, **21** (6), 509–74.

Steinke, W. (1991). The use of music, relaxation and imagery in the management of postsurgical pain for scoliosis. In: C. Maranto (ed.) *Applications of Music in Medicine*, pp. 141–62. Washington, DC: National Association for Music Therapy.

Stewart, K. (2009). PATTERNS–A model for evaluating trauma in NICU music therapy: Part 2–treatment parameters. *Music and Medicine*, **1**(2), 123–8.

Stirling, L. (2006). Reduction and management of perioperative anxiety. *British Journal of Nursing*, **15**(7), 359–61.

Sullivan, M., Tanzer, M., Stanish, W., Fallaha, M., Keefe, F.J., Simmonds, M., et al. (2009). Psychological determinants of problematic outcomes following Total Knee Arthroplasty. *Pain*, **143**, 23–129.

Thompson, J.F. and Kam, P.C. (1995). Music in the operating theatre. *British Journal of Surgery*, **82**, 1586–7.

Thaut, M.H. (2003). Neural basis of rhythmic timing networks in the human brain. *Annals of the New York Academy of Sciences*, **1999**, 364.

Thaut, M.H. (2005). *Rhythm, music, and the brain*. New York: Routledge.

Thaut, M.H., Kenyon, G.P., Schauer, M.L., and McIntosh, G.C. (1999). The connection between rhythmicity and brain function. *IEEE Engineering in Medicine and Biology*, **18**, 101–8.

Tolksdorf, W. (1985). *Der präoperative stress [Preoperative stress]*. Heidelberg–New York: Springer.

Tolksdorf, W. (1997). Preoperative stress. Research approach and methods of treatment. *Anaesthesiologie, Intensivmedizin, Notfallmedizin, Schmerztherapie*, **32**(3), 318–24.

Trevena, L.J., Davey, H.M., Barratt, A., Butow, P., Caldwell, P. (2006). A systematic review on communicating with patients about evidence. *Journal for Evaluation of Clinical Practice*, **12**, 13–23.

Walworth, D. (2005). Procedural-support music therapy in the healthcare setting: A cost-effectiveness analysis. *Journal of Pediatric Nursing*, **20** (4), 276–84.

Wang, S.M., Kulkarni, L., Dolev, J., Kain, Z.N (2002). Music and preoperative anxiety: a randomized, controlled study. *Anesthesia and Analgesia*, **94**, 1489–94.

Westen, D. (1991). Clinical assessment of object relations using the TAT. *Journal of Personality Assessment*, **56**(1), 56–74.

Section 4

Educational Contexts

Songs Without Words: Exploring How Music Can Serve as a Proxy Language in Social Interaction with Autistic Children

Adam Ockelford

Introduction

> It was then a short step in the lesson that followed to leave Derek where he was on the piano stool, and to engage in the 'play-copy' dialogue with no physical intervention on my part at all. In due course, I started to imitate what *he* was doing too, enabling us to have a genuine musical 'conversation'. And it wasn't just a matter of a musical ball bouncing between us like echoes in an alleyway. Whatever you lobbed at Derek would invariably come hurtling back with interest, and it was challenging to keep up with his musical repartee, which combined wit and ingenuity with an incredible speed of thought.
>
> With no words to get in the way, a whole world of sophisticated social intercourse was now opened up to him. It was the second 'eureka' moment of his life: having first discovered that he was able to play what he could hear, he now came to realise that he could communicate *through* music. Indeed, for Derek, music came to function as a proxy language, and it was through music that his wider development was increasingly channelled.
>
> (Ockelford 2008b, p. 106).

So runs my account of a turning point early in the relationship between the young Derek Paravicini and me, having recently become his music teacher. Derek was just 5 years old and, despite being blind, having severe learning difficulties and autism spectrum disorder, he had already taught himself to play the piano fluently, if idiosyncratically. Yet his grasp of many everyday concepts was tenuous; his capacity for verbal communication very limited. Unsurprisingly, then, he had no idea of what it meant to be taught or even informally guided to learn. And little wonder that those around him found his behaviour unpredictable, since life appeared to pass *him* by as a series of surprises: he was rarely able to anticipate what was going to happen next, and had little control over the nature of his moment-to-moment experiences. It seemed to me that Derek's inability to assert his wishes or views was a significant source of frustration, and my concern was that his restricted capacity for communication might come to jeopardize his emotional wellbeing more and more as the growing urge to exert his will was increasingly thwarted.

Yet, in a few short improvisatory exchanges on the piano, everything changed—or at least started to change. Derek came to grasp, quite intuitively, that the musical sounds that suffused his environment, which he had learnt to imitate and subsequently pressed into service as his own, private playthings, could be used to relate to other people and, above all, to *influence* them—to control situations without resorting to the physical means that invariably ended in confrontation and distress. And although Derek's subsequent social and emotional development was by no means straightforward, there seems little doubt that it was the many thousands of hours of live musical interaction in which he gladly engaged that underpinned a large part of his evolving sense of personal identity and wellbeing; for music was the one domain where his cognitive capacities and his ability to communicate were wholly in kilter.

While Derek was exceptional, his use of music as a primary means of communication was, I discovered, far from unique among children on the autism spectrum—particularly for those who were non-verbal or whose language development was delayed. Over the years, I developed a range of intuitive strategies that were more or less successful in facilitating individuals to communicate through musical improvisation and enabling them to act as equal partners in their interactions with me. My hope was that, through the advancement of their musical skills, the children would develop socially and emotionally too, and that their sense of wellbeing would be enhanced. But how could I gauge the impact that these musical collaborations were having?

To this end, three questions needed to be addressed. First: how, and to what extent, did pupils influence the course of our improvised musical dialogues? Second: what (if anything) could be done to promote this capacity? And third: was there a demonstrable link between the evolution of the children's interactive improvisatory musical skills and experiences, and their wider social and emotional development and self-esteem?

To make the research manageable, I decided initially to focus on question one. In terms of a potential methodology, I turned first to music therapy literatures, since relating to clients through improvisation is core to many therapeutic approaches (see, for example, Bunt and Hoskyns 2002; Wigram 2004; Markou 2010). However, while it became evident that efforts had been made to develop ways of evaluating this area of work—for instance, Kenneth Bruscia's 'Improvisation Assessment Profiles' (1987, p. 403ff) and recent developments of these (set out, for example, in Abrams 2007; Wigram 2007; Wosch 2007), as well as other contemporary tools including Mercédès Pavlicevic's 'Music Interaction Rating Scale . . . of Co-Improvisation' (2007) and Julie Sutton's 'Analysis of . . . Free Musical Improvisation as Conversation' (2007)—none offered an approach that would enable me to measure the extent of pupils' musical influence in improvisation precisely.

However, another way forward presented itself in the form of my 'zygonic' theory (see, for example, Ockelford 1991, 1999, 2005a,b, 2009b), which had been devised to explain how pieces make sense to listeners of varying interests, experience, and expertise. The central hypothesis of zygonic theory is that musical structure is created or cognized when one element is deemed (consciously or non-consciously) to exist in imitation of another. It seemed reasonable to extend this principle to interpret the interactions that occur in improvisations involving two performers or more, and this was borne out by my first efforts in this direction: the analysis of a song extemporized by a 4-year-old girl who was blind with septo-optic dysplasia ('Kay') and me, who provided a repeating harmonic and rhythmic framework on the piano (Ockelford, 2006, 2007, 2008a, and see below). This research showed that a zygonic approach could provide an intuitively persuasive metric for the fluctuating patterns of musical influence as they unfolded, event by event. And the effect of the moment-to-moment forces of imitation could be averaged over the improvisation as a whole, yielding the somewhat discomforting finding (for one who considered himself a child-centred practitioner) that, over the 90 seconds of the song, I exerted around twice the musical influence on Kay than she did on me (see Figure 21.20 later in this chapter).

But could the analytical principles developed in the context of a conventionally structured piece survive the more fluid interactions that occurred with my autistic pupils? Preliminary investigations into two quite different interactions between a music-communication specialist and her client with autism, and an autistic piano pupil and me, suggested that they could (Ockelford and Matawa 2009; and see below).

This chapter seeks to formalize the theory that underpinned these analyses, uses it to examine different musical interactions involving children with autism in the early stages of language development, and informally considers their potential impact on wellbeing. The link between the former and the latter is an issue that requires a good deal of further research, although as Edward Deci and Richard Ryan and their co-workers have persuasively shown in a range of other contexts, a powerful connection can exist between autonomy, competence, and relatedness on the one hand and a sense of well-being on the other (see, for example, Deci and Ryan 1985, 2000; Kasser and Ryan 1999; Ryan et al. 2006, 2010). It is hoped that the thinking set out here will offer a platform for systematic work in this area in relation to children with autism, ultimately enabling practitioners to gauge the impact of musical interaction on their socioemotional development and the advancement of their wellbeing.

A zygonic model of musical influence in improvisation involving two people or more.

This model will be introduced through two examples: a short verbal interaction and a brief musical one.

Scenario 1

I have come to pick up my 7-year-old son, Tom, from school. It is raining hard, and as I get out the car to greet him, I say:

'Hello, soggy superman!'

Quick as a flash he retorts:

'Hi, dry diplodocus-brain!'

Scenario 2

I am waiting in a music room to give an 8-year-old girl, Romy, her weekly piano lesson. Romy is on the autism spectrum, and does not speak (though she understands some everyday language). The door opens, and as she runs over to the piano, I play (Figure 21.1):

Fig. 21.1 The author's opening gambit in a music session with Romy.

Pushing me out of the way, she gleefully responds with (Figure 21.2):

Fig. 21.2 Romy's counter.

In addition to the obvious differences, there are surprising parallels in the way that these two interactions work.

Let us turn first to Scenario 1, which will be analysed by combining the thinking of T.S. Eliot, Gilles Fauconnier, and Mark Turner. According to Eliot (1920/1997; 1933) words speak to us in three ways: through the ideas that are represented, which Eliot calls the *objective correlative* (for instance, a set of objects, a situation or a chain of events); through the *manner of representation* (including, for example, the use of metaphor); and through the *sound qualities and structure* of the language itself. More recently, Fauconnier and Turner (2002) posited the notion of 'conceptual integration networks', which explain how meaning can arise from the blends of concepts that inhabit mental space. Here, in a development of Eliot's ideas, the 'blend' is taken to be the composite meaning that arises from the objective correlative, the way it is represented, and the nature of the language that is used; that is, from the fusion of the semantic, syntactic, and sonic elements of verbal communication.

Stage 1 in the interaction, before I spoke to my son, but as I was thinking of greeting him, can be modelled as shown in Figure 21.3.

As this illustration shows, even in so simple a situation, the initial thinking is multi-levelled: the desire to greet Tom and the observation that he is rain-soaked resulting in a wish to cheer him up by reminding him of one of his superheroes in a humorous way. The language that crystallizes as these thoughts are formulated both reflects the complexity of this thinking and enriches it (see Figure 21.4): the notion of physical wetness is bound to the 'superman' analogy through alliteration, which draws the idea of 'sogginess' into the metaphor and imbues it with a sense of friendly derision, implying a mushy and ineffectual personality (rather than steely and potent one).

Tom recognizes the different dimensions of meaning captured in my three-word utterance almost immediately (Figure 21.5), and he wrests control of the dialogue with a witty retort, that uses the same syntax, and matches the metaphor and alliteration of the original (Figure 21.6).

And so a new conversation is born—a shared verbal string whose changing loci of influence depend upon the nature of the connections between the ideas that are conveyed, although in this case supplementary links play a part as syntactic and sonic structures are repeated, in effect usurping them, and reinforcing the sense that ownership of ideas is transferred from leader to follower (Figure 21.7).

How does this compare with the interaction that occurs in Scenario 2? Stage 1 can be modelled as shown in Figure 21.8.

These hasty cogitations result in my playing the first phrase of 'Twinkle, Twinkle, Little Star', in C major, with an embellishment on the penultimate note (Figure 21.9).

Like Tom, Romy recognizes the import of my greeting straightaway, including its twist at the end (Figure 21.10), and she reciprocates with the second phrase of 'Twinkle, Twinkle', but realized

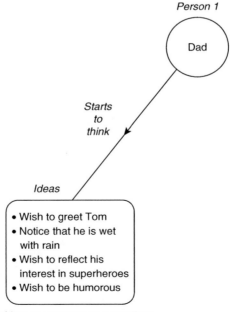

Fig. 21.3 Model of my thinking as I prepare to greet Tom.

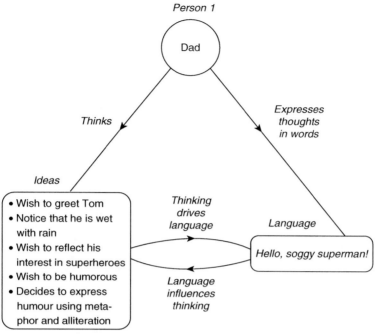

Fig. 21.4 Interaction between thought and language.

in a different key (A major), and with my embellishment adorning every pair of notes. Hence in four or five seconds of abstract sound, she manages to acknowledge my presence, yet, through her own wit and imagination, trumps what I have done and assumes control (Figure 21.11).

Hence a new musical dialogue kicks off—a shared string of sounds. But here there is no objective correlative (unlike the words of greeting that Tom and I used, the notes do not refer to anything concrete in the outside world). So how does one participant influence the other? Returning again to Eliot's conceptualization of language and meaning, there are two elements that apply to communication through music—its *sound qualities* and *structure* (see Figure 21.12). How do these function to produce the impression of control between sequences of abstract sounds? One answer is suggested by zygonic theory.

Zygonic theory holds that one sound or group of sounds may be deemed to *derive* from another when one salient feature or more of the second event is thought to exist in imitation of the first. The imitation may be exact or approximate, and may involve any aspect of the perceived sound or sounds concerned (pitch, interval, harmony, tonality, duration, inter-onset interval, metre, timbre, loudness, and so on). Hence the perceived derivation may be of differing strengths and types (Ockelford 2009a).

The easiest place to hear the notion of musical derivation in action is in musical 'canons', which are explicitly structured through repetition—one line consciously being made to copy another (cf. Ockelford 2008a, p. 64). Take, for example, 'Et in unum Dominum' from the B Minor Mass, where Bach uses the derivation of the alto part from the soprano to symbolize his Christian belief that the Father begat the Son. Irrespective of the listener's stance on the underlying dogma, the opening four notes in the alto voice intuitively do sound as though they derive from the series of preceding, identical events sung by the soprano. Zygonic theory asserts that, to the listener,

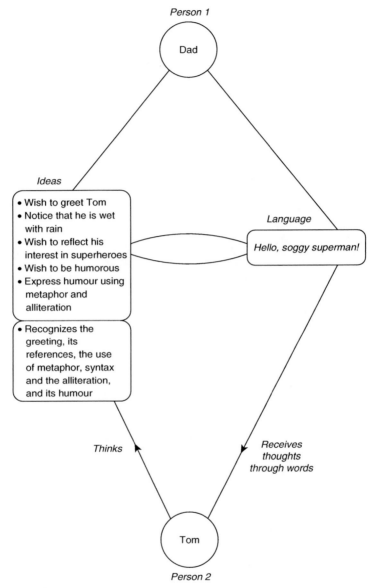

Person 1

Dad

Ideas

- Wish to greet Tom
- Notice that he is wet with rain
- Wish to reflect his interest in superheroes
- Wish to be humorous
- Express humour using metaphor and alliteration

Language

Hello, soggy superman!

- Recognizes the greeting, its references, the use of metaphor, syntax and the alliteration, and its humour

Thinks

Receives thoughts through words

Tom

Person 2

Fig. 21.5 Tom gets the message . . .

the groups of sounds appear to be connected via a mental bridge, spanning the two vocal parts. Each of these is termed a 'zygonic relationship' or 'zygon' (after the Greek word for 'yoke', meaning the union of two similar things). In order to facilitate analysis and understanding, these cognitive connections can be presented visually—at its simplest, by using an arrow with a superimposed 'Z', as shown in Figure 21.13. Observe that the initial canon at the unison is followed by imitation a perfect fourth below, and this connection too is represented graphically in zygonic terms

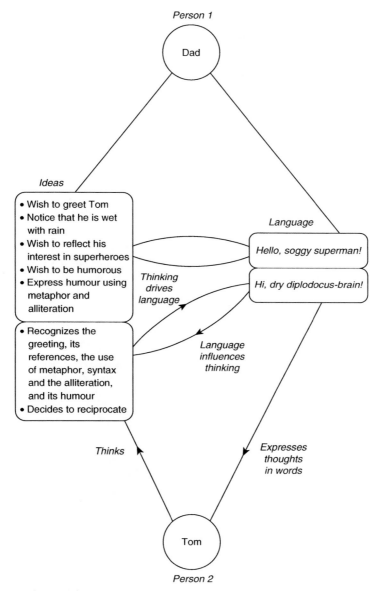

Fig. 21.6 . . . and responds.

The notion of derivation applies in the context of *improvised* musical interactions as well, but here, if one performer ('A') introduces material A(♪) into a musical dialogue and the second ('B') imitates it B(♪), then there may be a transfer of thinking over and above the purely auditory information that is conveyed: A may be heard to exert an effect on B—to be perceived as *influencing* B. In phenomenological terms (cf. Husserl, 1905–10/1964) this influence will be felt as the second contribution is made. Further, if A influences B, then A can be said, to a greater or lesser degree, to *control* the musical dialogue at the point when the imitation occurs. The nature and perceived

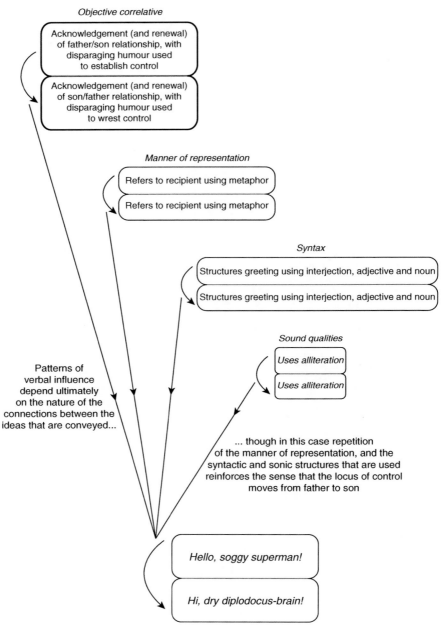

Objective correlative

Acknowledgement (and renewal) of father/son relationship, with disparaging humour used to establish control

Acknowledgement (and renewal) of son/father relationship, with disparaging humour used to wrest control

Manner of representation

Refers to recipient using metaphor

Refers to recipient using metaphor

Syntax

Structures greeting using interjection, adjective and noun

Structures greeting using interjection, adjective and noun

Sound qualities

Uses alliteration

Uses alliteration

Patterns of verbal influence depend ultimately on the nature of the connections between the ideas that are conveyed...

... though in this case repetition of the manner of representation, and the syntactic and sonic structures that are used reinforces the sense that the locus of control moves from father to son

Hello, soggy superman!

Hi, dry diplodocus-brain!

Fig. 21.7 Analysis of the dialogue in terms of objective correlative, manner of representation, syntax and sound qualities.

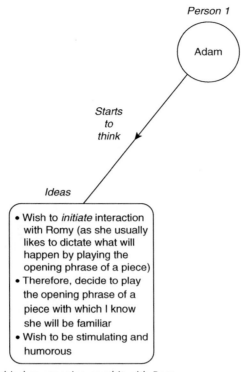

Fig. 21.8 The thinking behind my opening gambit with Romy.

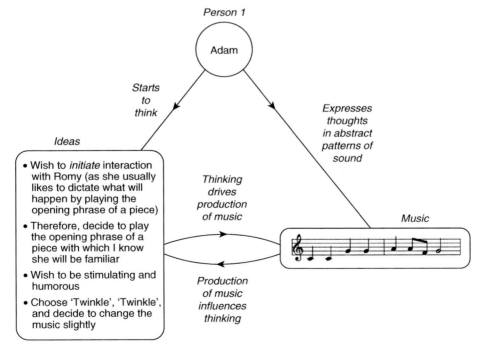

Fig. 21.9 Interaction between thought and improvisation.

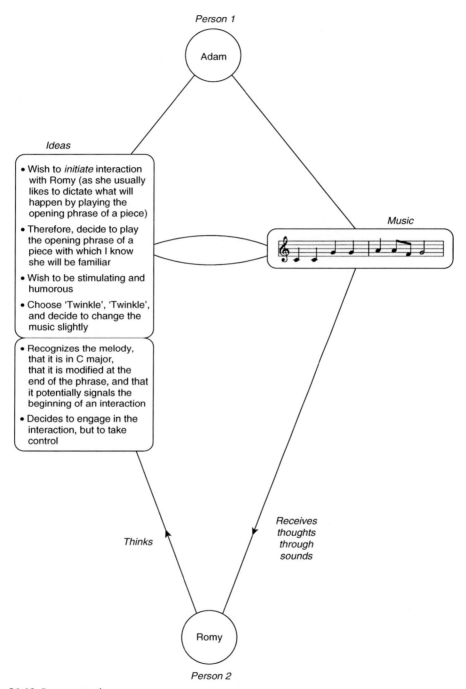

Fig. 21.10 Romy gets the message . . .

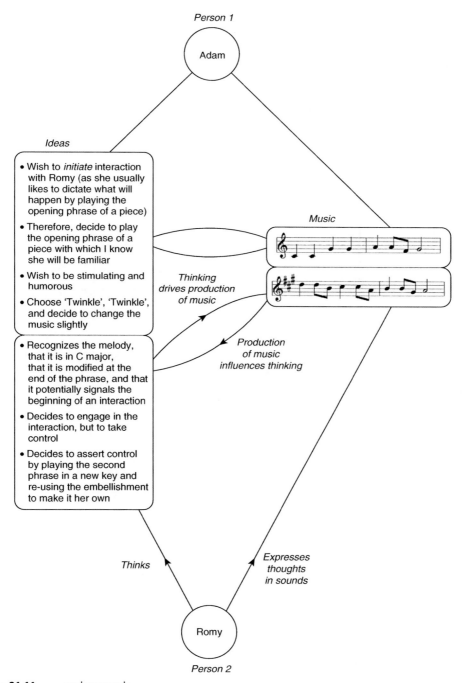

Fig. 21.11 . . . and responds.

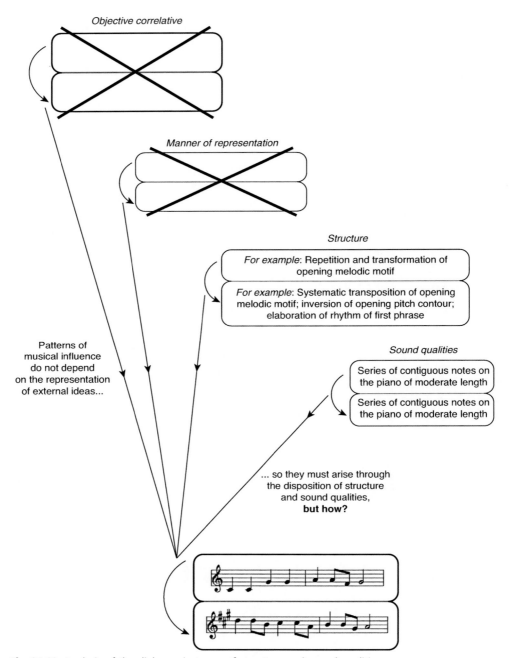

Fig. 21.12 Analysis of the dialogue in terms of structure and sound qualities.

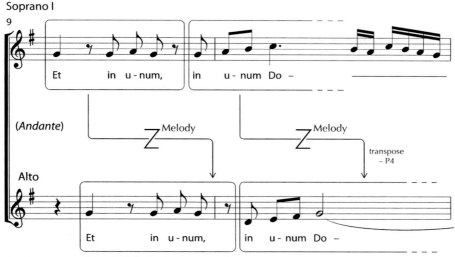

Fig. 21.13 A sense of musical derivation operates in canonic writing.

strength of such control will depend on the relationship between the way in which A influences B, and B derives material *other than* from A (Figure 21.14). It is suggested that the extent to which B produces musical ideas that do *not* stem from A's contribution is a measure of his or her dialogic *autonomy*.

It is further hypothesized that the ratio between B's control and autonomy is proportional to the ratio between B's derivation of material from A and from 'not A' (A'). In formal terms:

$$B \text{ (control : autonomy)} \propto A(\text{♪})—Z{\rightarrow}B(\text{♪}) : A'(\text{♪})—Z{\rightarrow}B(\text{♪})$$

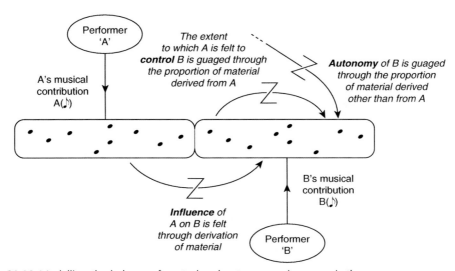

Fig. 21.14 Modelling the balance of control and autonomy using zygonic theory.

As this formula suggests, although control and autonomy are functionally opposite, and while complete control would necessarily imply zero autonomy and vice versa, due to the multidimensional nature of music, the two can coexist in a virtually limitless variety of ways, as the following examples illustrate.

Theory in action: examples of musical interactions with children on the autism spectrum, and their impact on wellbeing

First, here are two instances of *complete* control, which occur when the material produced by one participant is derived entirely from that provided by another. The context was one of a weekly series of two-piano sessions I had with 'Rosa', a 5-year-old who was blind through retinopathy of prematurity. At the outset, Rosa displayed a high degree of introversion, and did not communicate expressively at all in our first eight meetings (Ockelford and Matawa 2009). Nonetheless, she appeared to be listening intently to the pieces I played for her and, as I later discovered, absorbed a good deal of what she heard (assisted, no doubt, by her sense of absolute pitch). My goal, after 2 months of chronic inhibition, was simply to entice Rosa to interact at all. To this end I adopted a number of strategies, including playing pieces up to the last cadence, but stopping short of the final tonic chord, and leaving a silence for Rosa to fill. Eventually, the musical desire for closure proved irresistible, and, from tentative beginnings, Rosa increasingly participated in our sessions. Initially she interacted almost exclusively through the medium of music, though gradually musical terminology came to figure in the equation too. In a way that I could never have anticipated, within only a few more weeks, Rosa's was the dominant force in proceedings.

The passage transcribed in Figure 21.15, around 40 seconds in length, occurred 6 months into our sessions together. The material derives from 'Lord of the Dance'—a favourite source of musical ideas for Rosa, with which we would produce extended improvisations together. Often, these took the form of musical 'conversations', with rapid give and take of musical fragments, supplemented with words that described or dictated the action. Within the rich tapestry of music threads shown in Figure 21.15, there are two examples of complete control: initially, when Rosa plays the opening phrase of 'Lord of the Dance' in A minor and I copy her exactly, as I know she intends me too (although, for the avoidance of doubt, she says 'Play it on this one'); and subsequently when she precisely imitates my rendition of the same motif on B diminished. Observe that the forces of influence operating within an improvised musical dialogue can switch rapidly with no sense of incongruity.

The sessions with Rosa took place some years ago, and no attempt was made at the time to gauge their impact on her wider learning, development, or evolving sense of self. In any event, it would have been very difficult, in the context of a single case study involving interventions that lasted for just half an hour a week, to ascertain credible links between the musical interactions that occurred and Rosa's cognitive abilities, social skills and her general state of mind. There were simply too many variables within and beyond the sessions to have enabled causal connections to be identified. However, informal evidence suggests Rosa's evolving control in music sessions may have had a positive effect on her sense of wellbeing: her family's account of the increasing eagerness with which she anticipated sessions as her ability to influence their content developed, for example; and her growing confidence in and enjoyment of music lessons, shown through her more assertive body language and frequent smiling. Rosa's ability and willingness to engage socially with another person became evident in other contexts too—though, of course, one could not say for sure whether music-making was a catalyst for this change (or vice versa). At the very least, though, it seems reasonable to assert that the personal development that was facilitated through Rosa's interactive music sessions made a positive contribution to a more general process of social and emotional maturation.

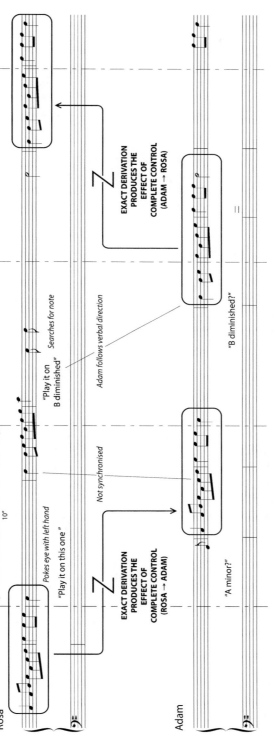

Fig. 21.15 Rosa and I improvising on 'Lord of the Dance' on two pianos.

Complete *autonomy*, where A is felt to have no influence on B,

$$A(\flat)—\cancel{Z}\rightarrow B(\flat)$$

⇨   B (control) = 0, and B (autonomy) = 1

is, as one would expect, a wholly different matter: since, in these circumstances, A($\flat$) and B($\flat$) are not logically connected, the dialogue is necessarily musically incoherent at the point where the autonomy is expressed. However, this very disjunction may be what was intended. To hear an example of this in action, let us return to my session with Romy (whose opening gambits were sketched out above).

In Figure 21.16, we are about 45 minutes into the session, with no indication that Romy is yet running out of steam. I am playing what I know to be one of her favourite pieces, Beethoven's 'Für Elise', whose opening section was programmed into the first keyboard she owned. She listens intently, her face almost at keyboard level, looking along the length of the keys from the left hand edge of the piano. I decide to continue playing into the middle part of the piece, to see how Romy reacts, since her father made me aware that her *new* keyboard included this additional material, and that Romy found it disconcerting—habitually turning the machine off when this point was reached. What would she do in the context of a human performer?

The answer becomes clear after only a few seconds. Romy introduces a 'rocking' motif that she typically uses to end a musical conversation. The patterns she utilizes are generally distinct from what has just occurred or is occurring, tonally and rhythmically. With no sense of derivation from their contexts, such motifs are completely autonomous; the thread of the musical conversation is lost, and matters grind to a halt.

However, on this occasion, Romy misjudges things, since the A and the C of her alternating figure can be heard as deriving from elements of 'Für Elise'—that is, resulting from 'unintentional' zygonic relationships—and the effect is not as musically destructive as usual. She also struggles to make the pulse of her repeated motif distinct from the regular beat of the Beethoven, and is drawn towards it before changing tempo in an apparently conscious effort to avoid conformance. The final straw comes when 'Für Elise' moves back to A minor, at which point Romy's two notes become fully compatible with my contribution to the musical dialogue, and her strategy of dialogic dissonance runs onto the rocks of concord. She is not to be deterred, however, and takes direct action, pushing my right hand off the keyboard with her right elbow, while, through a considerable contortion, playing a series of chromatic chords, including D♯ minor (which, tonally, is as far removed from A minor as it is possible to get) with her right hand. Hence all logical connections with preceding material are terminated at this point, the musical thread is lost, and the interchange comes to an abrupt halt. Romy squeals with delight, then sets off once more with her familiar rocking motif—this time on C and E. As discreetly as possible, I play a C major chord above in an attempt to inveigle myself back into our musical interchange by imitating her (and thus demonstrating I have ceded control), but evidently this was not on Romy's agenda: my olive branch is spurned, she stops playing and moves away from the piano.

So much for Romy's capacity to control an improvised musical discourse, but what is the significance of the way in which she interacts with me? And to what extent does the zygonic analysis or her musical engagement offer insights into her thinking and state of mind?

It takes only a few moments of observing Romy in everyday life to realize the challenges that her lack of expressive language poses. Her strong feelings and wishes cannot be communicated through words, and so she resorts to gesture, physical manipulation and loud vocalizations to try to get her message across. Despite the remarkable empathy of her family in interpreting her signals, inevitably, Romy erupts from time to time in bouts of distress, anger and, above all, frustration. One senses that, more than anything else, Romy would love to be able to take control in

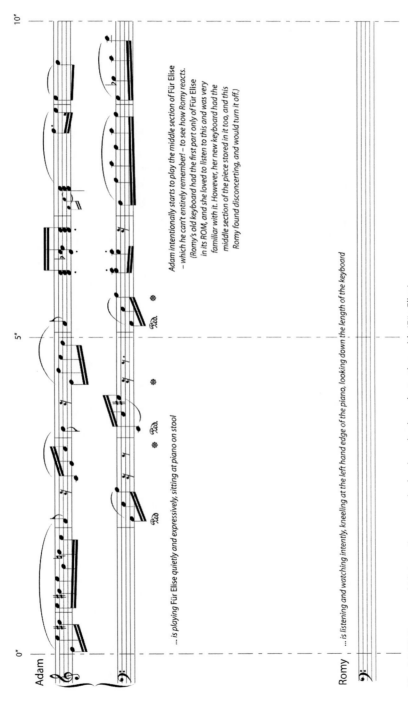

... *is playing Für Elise quietly and expressively, sitting at piano on stool*

Adam intentionally starts to play the middle section of Für Elise – which he can't entirely remember! – to see how Romy reacts. (Romy's old keyboard had the first part only of Für Elise in its ROM, and she loved to listen to this and was very familiar with it. However, her new keyboard had the middle section of the piece stored in it too, and this Romy found disconcerting, and would turn it off.)

... *is listening and watching intently, kneeling at the left hand edge of the piano, looking down the length of the keyboard*

Fig. 21.16 Romy and I interacting on a single piano keyboard, starting with 'Für Elise'.

Fig. 21.16 (Continued)

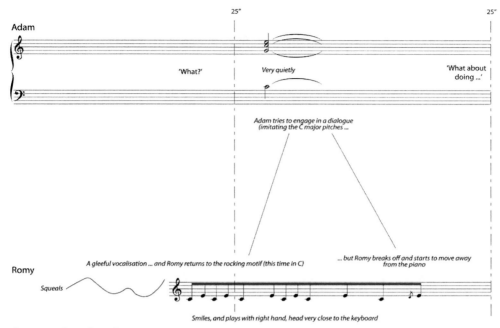

Fig. 21.16 (Continued)

social situations, and this is where her advanced musical abilities, including absolute pitch and the ability to play by ear on the keyboard, come in: they provide her with a unique medium through which to assert her will—provided that her musical partner of the moment can keep up! Indeed, Romy apparently tests the musical adequacy of all new visitors to her house by leading them over to the piano, and playing the first phrase of a piece in a key of her choice (in my case it was 'If You're Happy and you Know it' in F♯ major) and then prompting them with a nudge, a look or a vocalization to continue. Romy's judgement is quick and irrevocable!

However, once a musical relationship has been established, the effects can be dramatic and rewarding. As Romy's parents observe, during music lessons her eyes sparkle and she fizzes with musical energy and fun. Again and again, she seeks to control the dialogue—as though making up for all the verbal conversations whose thread she has never been able to dictate. Most importantly of all, though, looking back over the 12 sessions we have had to date, one can trace how Romy's capacity to interact through music is advancing. The type of exchange illustrated in Figure 21.16 above, where her control comes about largely through the destruction of any musical ideas that are offered, are increasingly being complemented with patterns of influence that are rather more subtle, involving some degree of mutuality. Inevitably, such scenarios are more complex to analyse and understand, since they entail separate strands of imitation operating simultaneously. But the zygonic approach can shed light on what is happening. By way of example, we will pick up the session where Figure 21.16 left off, when Romy, having reasserted her authority, seems temporarily to lose interest in the exchange of musical ideas (Figure 21.17).

In an attempt to regain her attention, I introduce another musical idea that I imagine may appeal to Romy's sense of tonal structure: a B♭ major scale, ascending an octave and then starting to descend, realized within a repetitive rhythmic framework. Romy's interest is indeed aroused, and she vocalizes briefly with the submediant (G) on the way up and then again on the way down, at which point she takes over entirely from me, next singing the dominant (F), and subsequently

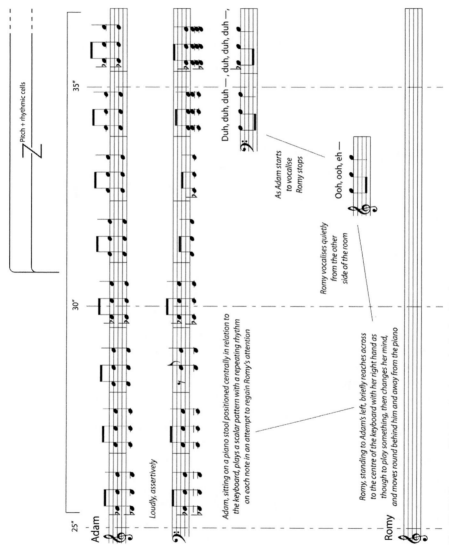

Fig. 21.17 Romy and I interact using a rhythmized scale.

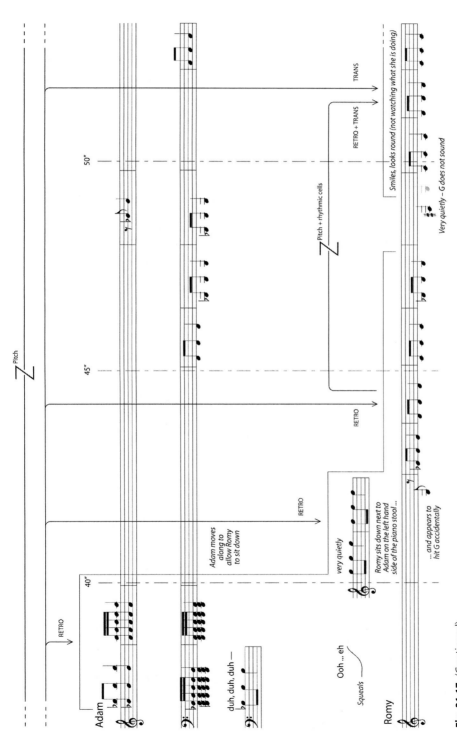

Fig. 21.17 (Continued)

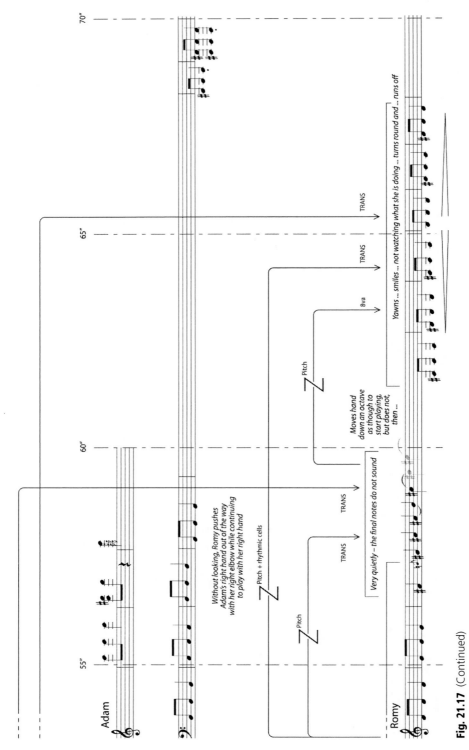

Fig. 21.17 (Continued)

playing the four remaining pitches of the scale (E♭, D, C and B♭), in each case employing the same three-note rhythm. Here, then, is an example of a more intricate form of influence between performers, as Romy completes the retrograde version of the scale that was one of the continuations implied in the material that I originally produced.

After this, the interaction rapidly grows in complexity: my efforts to join in the dialogue by adding a simple bass line to the last two notes of the descending scale (C and B♭) and then heading upwards once more are swept aside by Romy who, typically for her, seizes the ideas that are hanging in the air and makes them her own. The resulting material appears to be derived in part from what she just played and partly from my ascending figure—with the added twist of being transposed to G major. So there are shades of both autonomy and the acceptance of control in what she does.

Again, I seek to complement Romy's input with a cadential figure (played both above and below her melodic line), but, once more, she will have none of it, asserting her independence more strongly this time, interrupting my contribution with a fleeting F♯ major ascent, which she somehow manages to overlap with the end of her G major scale. My repeated rhythm has evaporated, and she presses some of the notes so gently that they do not sound at all—indeed, she just touches the last (E♯). At this point, one has the sense that autonomy has gained the upper hand over her willingness to cede control, though the latter is not entirely eradicated and there is enough sense of logical connection with what has gone before for the musical dialogue to continue. After a slight hesitation, Romy does precisely this: she repeats the F♯ major scale (two octaves lower)—this time using my opening rhythmic motif on each note—and the corresponding forces of autonomy and control change again to reflect the new blend of musical influences that are at work. Once more, I attempt to join in with a perfect cadence as the scale rises from leading note to tonic, but Romy stops as she sees me starting to play, and runs off, omitting her final two notes: she knows that she can dominate proceedings without having to dot the final 'i', and I am left alone to cross the last 't' according to the musical implications established in what she had played.

These 45 seconds of music show just how complex even a short musical exchange between two people can be in terms of seeking to establish patterns of influence that can wax and wane with astonishing volatility. However, for a teacher or therapist seeking to gauge a child's capacity to engage in and influence the course of a musical interaction, it is important to know how the nature and extent of the ebb and flow of autonomy and control. But this raises a number of questions. For example, how can one be sure that a pupil's intentions have been interpreted accurately? Where there are potentially multiple sources of derivation, how is one to assess their relative import? How far back in a dialogue should one go in tracing potential sources of material? What units of analysis should one choose? Of course, problems like these are familiar to music analysts seeking to understand a composer's intentions, who feel comfortable being led by their ears. Zygonic theory seeks to capture and formalize the outcomes of these musical intuitions (though not to replace them; see Ockelford 2009b), and initial work suggests that it offers an effective tool for quantifying patterns of influence in improvisation involving two people or more.

For example, a zygonic approach was used to analyse how autonomy and control function in the song extemporized by my pupil 'Kay' and me, mentioned above (see Figure 21.18). This was done by assessing each note in relation to its probable musical sources, which could be found either in

> Adam's vocal introduction (bars 1–4, with notes labelled AV1, AV2, etc.),
> Adam's piano melody (the uppermost notes in the right-hand part, identified as AM1, AM2, and so on),
> Adam's bass ostinato (AB1, AB2, and so forth), or
> Kay's vocal line (K1, K2, . . .).

For every note, up to ten zygonic relationships were considered in relation to pitch, melodic interval, harmonic context and rhythm. These were weighted as follows:

- *Pitch* scored **2** for exact repetition, and **1** for the transfer of pitch-class to a different octave.
- *Melodic interval* scored **2** for identity, **1.5** for approximate imitation, **1** for inversion or retrogression, and **0.5** for approximate transformations of this type.
- *Harmonic context* scored **2** for exact repetition, **1.5** for variation, **1** for transposition and **0.5** for transposed variation; and
- *Rhythm* scored **4** for identity, **3** for approximate derivation (including a change of relative location within the relevant metrical level), **2** for repetition of duration or interonset interval only, and **1** where the sole connection was the variation of duration or interonset interval.

Since each aspect of every note could be considered to be derived from up to ten others, a further system of weighting was necessary, whereby each 'raw' derivation-strength score was multiplied by a factor based on the theorized salience of the zygonic relationship concerned, such that the sum of the factors pertaining to the given feature of a particular note was invariably 1. For example, Kay's seventh pitch (labelled K7 in Figure 21.18) could be considered to derive from K6, K5, K4, AM13, K3, K2, AV12, AM11, AV11, and AM10—the order determined by their temporal adjacency to K7. The pragmatic decision was made to separate each of the factors that were used to moderate the raw scores pertaining to a series such as this by a common difference (implying a linear decrease in the strength of their zygonic influence). In this case, with ten factors required, the values used to modify the raw derivation scores were 0.182, 0.164, 0.145, 0.127, 0.109, 0.091, 0.073, 0.055, 0.036, and 0.018 respectively. The result of applying these proportions to the raw scores was a series of 'derivation indices'. The indices for each feature were summed separately in relation to the material improvised by Kay and me ('A'). The total potential derivation index for each note ranged between 0 and 10 from either of the two sources, Kay or Adam. With regard to K7, the subtotals pertaining to Adam- and Kay-derived material are show in Figure 21.19: pitch has a derivation index of 0.618 from Adam and 1.382 from Kay; melodic interval, 0.334 from Adam and 1.666 from Kay; harmonic context, 1.335 from Adam and 0.666 from Kay; and rhythm, 1.620 from Adam and 2.136 from Kay. This yields a total derivation index of 3.907 from Adam's material, equivalent to 39%—a measure of the *control* I exert at this point. The derivation index from Kay's own material is 5.850. Given the maximum total derivation index of 10, the sum of these two figures (9.757) leaves a residue of 0.243, reflecting aspects of K7 that cannot be accounted for through derivation from other material in the song. Hence Kay's musical *autonomy* in producing the event in question (K7) is judged to be 61% (since 5.850 + 0.243 = 6.093).

The usefulness of these figures in interpreting the relationship between Kay's and my contributions lies principally in the ratios between them, taken either as averages over a given period or in terms of event-by-event patterns of variation. For example, the derivation indices for the piece as a whole are as follows (see Figure 21.20), giving rise to the conclusion that 83% of my production was autonomous (being generated from other of my material in the piece or elsewhere), with only 17% controlled by Kay. In contrast, 65% of Kay's melody is autonomous, with approximately 35% controlled by me: a somewhat sobering statistic for a music educator who at the time felt that he was providing a responsive foil for Kay's efforts, when, in fact, zygonic analysis indicates that the flow of musical ideas was greater from teacher to pupil than *vice versa*.

The derivation indices also enable us to track how the influence of one performer on another varied over time. For example, the mean scores, phrase by phrase, are shown in Figure 21.21. They show Kay drawing significantly on my material in her first phrase, less so in the second, and more again in the third and the fourth. Subsequently, there is a gradual decrease in my impact over phrases five to nine—the central part of Kay's improvisation with the descending sequence

Fig. 21.18 Kay improvises a song over the harmonic and rhythmic framework I provide.

Fig. 21.18 (Continued)

Fig. 21.18 (Continued)

Pitch									
Derived from A					**Derived from K**				
Event number	Relative position	Raw score	Weight factor	Derivation index	Event number	Relative position	Raw score	Weight factor	Derivation index
AM13	4	2	0.127	0.254	K6	1	2	0.182	0.364
AV12	7	2	0.073	0.146	K5	2	2	0.164	0.328
AM11	8	2	0.055	0.110	K4	3	2	0.145	0.290
AV11	9	2	0.036	0.072	K3	5	2	0.109	0.218
AM10	10	2	0.018	0.036	K2	6	2	0.091	0.182
Totals	5	10	0.309	0.618	Totals	5	10	0.691	1.382

Interval									
Derived from A					**Derived from K**				
Event number	Relative position	Raw score	Weight factor	Derivation index	Event number	Relative position	Raw score	Weight factor	Derivation index
AM12	6	2	0.083	0.166	K6	1	2	0.222	0.444
AV12	7	2	0.056	0.112	K5	2	2	0.194	0.388
AM11	8	2	0.028	0.056	K4	3	2	0.167	0.334
					K3	4	2	0.139	0.278
					K1	5	2	0.111	0.222
Totals	3	6	0.167	0.334	Totals	5	10	0.833	1.666

Harmonic context									
Derived from A					**Derived from K**				
Event number	Relative position	Raw score	Weight factor	Derivation index	Event number	Relative position	Raw score	Weight factor	Derivation index
AM9	2	2	0.267	0.534	K6	1	2	0.333	0.666
AV10	3	2	0.200	0.400					
AM2	4	2	0.133	0.267					
AV4	5	2	0.067	0.134					
Totals	4	8	0.667	1.335	Totals	1	2	0.333	0.666

Rhythm									
Derived from A					**Derived from K**				
Event number	Relative position	Raw score	Weight factor	Derivation index	Event number	Relative position	Raw score	Weight factor	Derivation index
AM12	4	3	0.133	0.399	K5	4	1	0.200	0.800
AM11	5	3	0.111	0.333	K3	4	2	0.178	0.712
AV8	6	4	0.089	0.356	K1	4	3	0.156	0.624
AM7	7	4	0.067	0.268					
AV6	8	4	0.044	0.176					
AM5	9	4	0.022	0.088					
Totals	6	22	0.466	1.620	Totals	12	3	0.534	2.136

Totals	
Autonomy	**Control**
5.850 + 0.243 = **6.093**	**3.907**

Fig. 21.19 The derivation of note K7.

	A			K		
	Material generated from			Material generated from		
	A	Original	K	K	Original	A
Sum: Derivation indices	1827.04	453.36	329.60	522.77	147.63	369.59
Number of events	261			104		
Average derivation index	7.00	1.26	1.74	1.42	5.03	3.55
	Autonomy		**Control by K**	**Autonomy**		**Control by A**
	83%		**17%**	**65%**		**35%**

Fig. 21.20 Average derivation indices for 'I Have a Dog'.

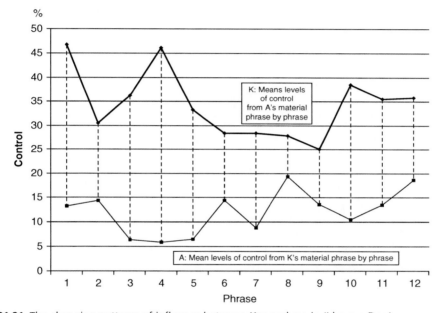

Fig. 21.21 The changing patterns of influence between Kay and me in 'I have a Dog'.

at its heart—during which Kay's efforts become ever more self-sufficient. In contrast, my influence is felt more strongly in Kay's tenth phrase, whose lack of verbal coherence suggests that Kay may be flagging. Indeed, after rallying briefly in the eleventh phrase, Kay's creative flow almost completely dries up at the beginning of the twelfth, and she draws heavily on material in the accompaniment to sustain her vocal line (although in the concluding notes she finally wrests back the initiative). Kay's global pattern of derivation from me, invariably lower than my derivation from Kay, is inversely related to it with a striking consistency (82%). That is to say, during the improvisation, as Kay chose to rely less on me for material, I tended to rely more on Kay, and vice versa—perhaps through an intuitive desire on the part of one performer or both to ensure coherence by balancing autonomy and control in the improvised texture as a whole.

Analysis such as this potentially presents practitioners with a precise and powerful tool for gauging how patterns of influence, control, and autonomy function in their musical interactions with children—and, even more importantly, perhaps, may enable them to plan future music activities with distinct types and levels of interchange in mind. So, for example, if it were felt that a child's wellbeing would be enhanced through her exerting more control in one-to-one improvisation sessions, then different strategies could be tested using music-analytical techniques of the kind set out above (probably in simplified form), to ascertain which were most effective in enabling the pupil concerned to influence the course of the musical dialogues.

Finally, we return to my exchange with Romy (see Figure 21.12) to illustrate a scenario that is ubiquitous within child–adult musical interactions: influence (and therefore control) occurring through a shared knowledge of given material. Here, there may well be no imitation of sounds that are made, so how does the process work? Consider again the situation. I decided to initiate proceedings by playing the beginning of a piece with which I knew Romy was familiar: 'Twinkle, Twinkle'. We can assume that my decision to play the piece stimulated in me a cognitive representation of the requisite melodic and inter-onset intervals, which I realized starting on fourth octave C and at a tempo of $♪ = 96$. We can further suppose that hearing these notes activated a comparable mental model in Romy, and that it was from this that she derived the information necessary to play the second phrase (although, as we know, she consciously opted to use a different tonal centre: A major). Hence the main route of influence was not via sounds heard directly, but through patterns encoded in long-term memory (though, in addition, I improvised an embellishment on the penultimate note of the first phrase, which Romy used to ornament the second of each repeated pair of notes in her contribution; see Figure 21.22).

This form of oblique influence can be used to control musical interactions just as effectively as the direct imitation of sounds. Striking examples are to be found in the 'music and communication' sessions that Sally Zimmermann, Music Advisor at the Royal National Institute for Blind People, London, undertook with Shivan, who is blind, has cerebral palsy and a diagnosis of autism, when he was at primary school. Shivan spoke very little, sometimes talking quietly to himself using unrecognisable words and sounds. When conversing with others, although his articulation was louder and clearer, the single words that he used usually repeated what he had just heard (so-called 'echolalia'), rather than conveying meaning in the semantic sense.

In his music sessions with Sally, however, things were very different. She observed (Ockelford and Matawa 2009, p. 63):

> Shivan will continue and sometimes complete lines from familiar songs that are stopped mid-phrase, using both the correct words and notes. He will also fill in the silences at the ends of phrases by repeating the last word or words that have just been sung. Occasionally, he will sing phrases at the same time as someone else. However, he does not sing entire songs from beginning to end unprompted. If he wants a song to be repeated, he sings or hums the starting note. Often, he is happy to hear a song many times over. Shivan's contributions are usually quiet and reserved; occasional periods of higher energy and excitement appear to have more to do with a self-awareness of his participation in a musical dialogue than as a result of recognising or responding to particular features of the music.

Figure 21.23 is a transcription of 60 seconds of a session that occurred when Shivan was 9 years old, which powerfully illustrates Sally's observations in action. The effect is the auditory equivalent of looking at a familiar image through distorted glass: the general shape of 'London's Burning' is maintained, but its surface is fragmented. The pieces are distributed unequally between participants: Sally's efforts account for 71% of the notes that are sung, and Shivan's, 29%. As one would expect, therefore, her control is greater: 60% as opposed to Shivan's 40%. However, these figures suggest that, thanks to Sally's responsiveness to a relatively small input from Shivan (only around one note in four), he nonetheless manages to exert an almost equal influence in the musical dialogue.

Music sessions such as these provided Shivan with a medium through which to pursue social discourse with a level of sophistication that was simply not available to him in any other way. And his pleasure in the give and take of musical conversations with Sally was physically evident in his

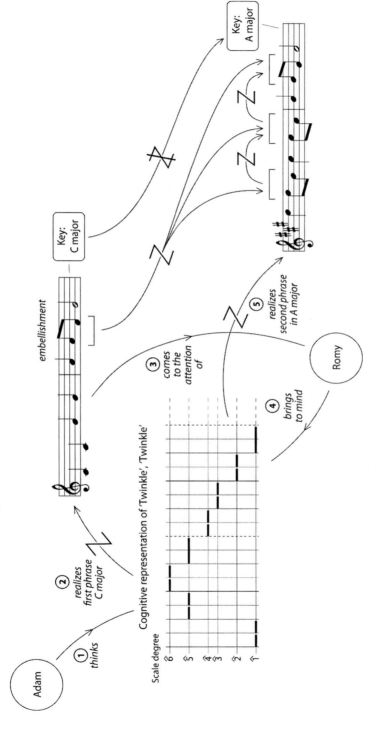

Fig. 21.22 Model of interaction using shared knowledge of a piece.

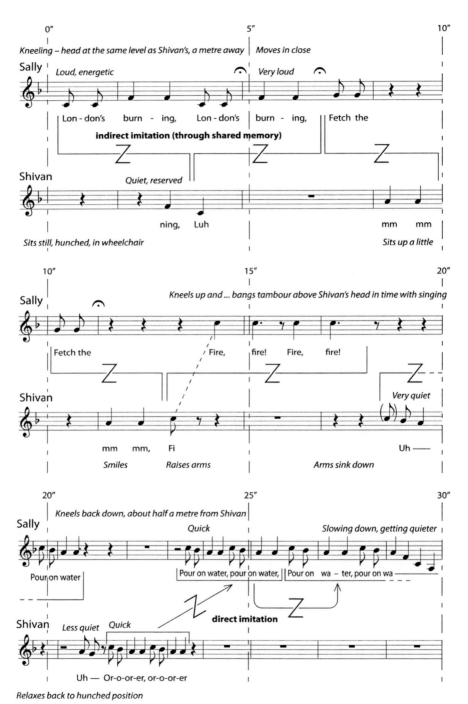

Fig. 21.23 Shivan and Sally improvising vocally on 'London's Burning'.

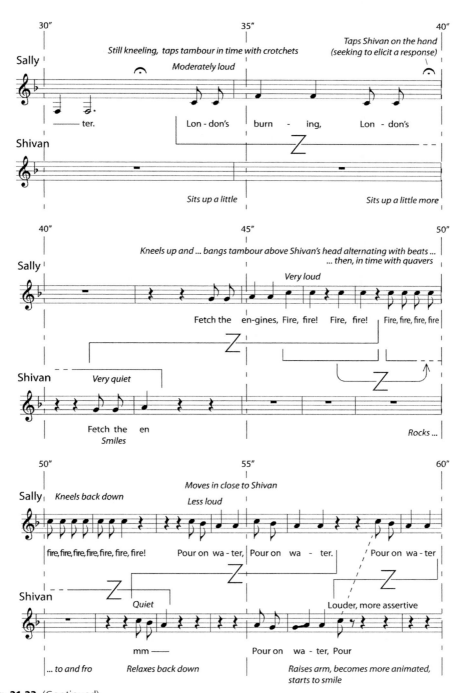

Fig. 21.23 (Continued)

body language, often smiling and rocking with excitement. As Shivan's mother says (Ockelford and Matawa, 2009, p. 60), 'music is the only way for him . . . to relate to the world'—it is fundamental to his sense of self and his wellbeing.

Conclusion

Some children and young people on the autism spectrum who use few or no words have the capacity to co-opt music as a proxy language—as a fully-fledged medium of social interaction—and will do so given an empathetic and musically competent partner with whom to engage. According to zygonic theory, imitation lies at the heart of musical structure, and it is through repeating, transforming or even consciously avoiding the material that is offered in dialogues that patterns of influence, control and autonomy between participants can be established, maintained or changed. As the examples in this chapter have shown, such interactions may be relatively simple or highly sophisticated, and analysis using a zygonic approach permits teachers and therapists to gauge with some precision the impact that one participant has on another. Finally, although the necessary empirical work still needs to be undertaken, there is mounting anecdotal evidence that enabling those children who find it difficult to convey their wishes in social situations through language, to exert an appropriate level of control through music, is likely to enhance their sense of wellbeing and self-esteem. This accords with the work on self-determination in other contexts carried out by Deci and Ryan and their colleagues, and represents an exciting and potentially highly fruitful area of future research in the areas of music-therapeutic and music-educational engagement with children on the autism spectrum.

Acknowledgements

I would like to thank the children and their families whose stories are reported in this chapter for their support, and for the telling insights they have offered.

References

Abrams, B. (2007). The use of improvisation assessment profiles (IAPs) and RepGrid in microanalysis of clinical music improvisation. In: T. Wosch and T. Wigram (eds.) *Microanalysis in Music Therapy: Methods, Techniques and Applications for Clinicians, Researchers, Educators and Students*, pp. 92–103. London: Jessica Kingsley.

Bruscia, K. (1987). *Improvisational Models of Music Therapy*. Springfield, IL: Charles C. Thomas.

Bunt, L. and Hoskyns, S. (eds.) (2002). *The Handbook of Music Therapy*. East Sussex: Brunner-Routledge.

Deci, E. and Ryan, R. (1985). *Intrinsic Motivation and Self-Determination in Human Behavior*. New York: Plenum.

Deci, E. and Ryan, R. (2000). The 'what' and 'why' of goal pursuits: human needs and the self-determination of behavior'. *Psychological Enquiry*, **11**(4), 227–68.

Eliot, T.S. (1920/1997). *The Sacred Wood: Essays on Poetry and Criticism*. London: Faber and Faber.

Eliot, T.S. (1933). *The Use of Poetry and the Use of Criticism*. London: Faber and Faber.

Fauconnier, G. and Turner, M. (2002). *The Way We Think: Conceptual Blending and the Mind's Hidden Complexities*. New York: Basic Books.

Husserl, E. (1905–10/1964). *The Phenomenology of Internal Time-Consciousness*. The Hague: Martinus Nijhoff.

Kasser, V. and Ryan, R. (1999). The relation of psychological needs for autonomy and relatedness to vitality, well-being, and mortality in a nursing home. *Journal of Applied Social Psychology*, **29**(5), 935–54.

Markou, K. (2010). The relationship between music therapy and music education in special school settings: the practitioners' views. Unpublished PhD thesis, Roehampton University.

Ockelford, A. (1991). The role of repetition in perceived musical structures. In: P. Howell, R. West, and I. Cross (eds.) *Representing Musical Structure*, pp. 129–60. London: Academic Press.

Ockelford, A. (1999). *The Cognition of Order in Music: A Metacognitive Study*. London: Roehampton Institute.

Ockelford, A. (2005a). *Repetition in Music: Theoretical and Metatheoretical Perspectives*. London: Ashgate.

Ockelford, A. (2005b). Musical structure, content and aesthetic response: Beethoven's Op. 110. *Journal of the Royal Musical Association*, **129**(2), 112–55.

Ockelford, A. (2006). Using a music-theoretical approach to interrogate musical development and social interaction. In: N. Lerner and J. Straus (eds.) *Sounding Off: Theorizing Disability in Music*, pp. 137–55. New York: Routledge.

Ockelford, A. (2007). Exploring musical interaction between a teacher and pupil, and her evolving musicality, using a music-theoretical approach. *Research Studies in Music Education*, **28**, 3–23.

Ockelford, A. (2008a). *Music for Children and Young People with Complex Needs*. Oxford: Oxford University Press.

Ockelford, A. (2008b). *In the Key of Genius: The Extraordinary Life of Derek Paravicini*. London: Arrow Books.

Ockelford, A. (2009a). Similarity relations between groups of notes: music-theoretical and music-psychology perspectives. *Musicae Scientiae*, Discussion Forum **4B**, 47–93.

Ockelford, A. (2009b). Zygonic theory: Introduction, scope, prospects. *Zeitschrift der Gesellschaft für Musiktheorie*, **6**(2), 91–172.

Ockelford, A. and Matawa, C. (2009). *Focus on Music 2: Exploring the Musical Interests and Abilities of Blind and Partially-Sighted Children with Retinopathy of Prematurity*. London: Institute of Education.

Pavlicevic, M. (2007). The musical interaction rating scale (schizophrenia) (MIR(S)) microanalysis of co-improvisations in music therapy with adults suffering from chronic schizophrenia. In: T. Wosch and T. Wigram (eds.) *Microanalysis in Music Therapy: Methods, Techniques and Applications for Clinicians, Researchers, Educators and Students*, pp. 174–85. London: Jessica Kingsley.

Ryan, R., Deci, E., Grolnick, W. and LaGuardia, J. (2006). The significance of autonomy and autonomy support in psychological development and psychopathology. In: D. Cicchetti and D. Cohen (eds.) *Developmental Psychopathology, Volume 1, Theory and Methods (2nd edn.)*, pp. 295–849. New York: John Wiley and Sons.

Ryan, R., Bernstein, J. and Brown, K. (2010). Weekends, work, and well-being: psychological need satisfactions and day of the week effects on mood, vitality, and physical symptoms. *Journal of Social and Clinical and Social Psychology*, **29**(1), 95–122.

Sutton, J. (2007). The use of micro-musical anlaysis and conversation analysis of improvisation: 'the invisible handshake' – free musical improvisations as conversation. In: T. Wosch and T. Wigram (eds.) *Microanalysis in Music Therapy: Methods, Techniques and Applications for Clinicians, Researchers, Educators and Students*, pp. 186–97. London: Jessica Kingsley.

Wigram, T. (2004). *Improvisation: Methods and Techniques for Music Therapy Clinicians, Educators and Students*. London: Jessica Kingsley.

Wigram, T. (2007). Event-based analysis of improvisations using the improvisation assessment profile (IAP). In: T. Wosch and T. Wigram (eds.) *Microanalysis in Music Therapy: Methods, Techniques and Applications for Clinicians, Researchers, Educators and Students*, pp. 211–26. London: Jessica Kingsley.

Wosch, T. (2007). Microanalysis of processes of interactions in clinical improvisation with IAP-autonomy. In: T. Wosch and T. Wigram (eds.) *Microanalysis in Music Therapy: Methods, Techniques and Applications for Clinicians, Researchers, Educators and Students*, pp. 241–54. London: Jessica Kingsley.

Chapter 22

Cognitive Performance After Listening to Music: A Review of the Mozart Effect

E. Glenn Schellenberg

Introduction

The goal of the present chapter is to review studies that examined effects of music listening on cognitive performance. My focus is on performance *after* listening to music, in contrast to Hallam (Chapter 32, this volume) who focuses on *background* music, or listening to music while doing something else. Despite the difference in focus our conclusions are similar. Music influences how a listener feels, and feelings influence a wide range of behaviours including *cognitive performance* (i.e. thinking, reasoning, problem solving, creativity, and mental flexibility). It is also important to clarify that the present focus is on music *listening* rather than music *lessons*, a topic reviewed by Costa-Giomi (Chapter 23, this volume). Although both types of experience involve exposure to music, music listening is ubiquitous and typically a *passive* activity, with obvious exceptions such as dancing. By contrast, only a small proportion of people take music lessons for significant durations of time, and lessons involve *active* participation for years on end in order for skilled levels of performance to emerge. As I and others have argued (Schellenberg 2001, 2003, 2005, 2006; Rauscher and Hinton 2006), there is no reason to believe that non-musical byproducts of music listening would be similar to those that might be accrued from years of intensive music training.

Research on associations between music listening and cognitive performance occurred within a social and cultural context. Indeed, social and contextual factors played a role in the design of the studies that were conducted, the way the results were reported and interpreted, and the public's and the media's response and interest in the topic. Because others (Campbell 2000; Bangerter and Heath 2004; Dowd 2008) have provided insightful commentaries on these sorts of issues, the present chapter focuses solely on the history of the relevant research rather than the social-cultural context in which this literature developed. My review also excludes studies of rodents (Rauscher et al. 1998; Aoun et al. 2005; Chikahisa et al. 2006; Amagdei et al. 2010) and studies of brain-activation patterns in humans (e.g. Sarnthein et al. 1997; Bodner et al. 2001 ; Jaušovec and Habe 2003; Jaušovec et al. 2006; Suda et al. 2008) simply because these areas are beyond my realm of expertise.

If music listening does indeed have benefits that generalize across a wide range of tests of cognitive performance, the ramifications for health and wellbeing would be profound. In principle, music listening could serve as a means of reducing cognitive deficits in many different groups of people, including the elderly, patients with Alzheimer's disease or dementia, and atypically developing populations such as individuals with autism, Down syndrome, or Williams syndrome. Music listening could also be used as a tool to enhance academic achievement in particular, as well as the acquisition of knowledge more generally. By contrast, if links between music listening and cognition prove to be limited to some specific aspects of cognitive functioning such as spatial abilities, the ramifications would be similarly specific. For example, music listening could be incorporated into occupations that rely heavily on spatial reasoning, such as architecture or navigation, and music-listening therapies could be tailored for groups with noted deficits in spatial abilities (e.g. Williams syndrome). In short, documenting the links between music listening and subsequent cognitive performance is important for health and wellbeing broadly construed. But what is the evidence for such links, and if they exist, might the associations be mediated by other variables that are known to influence cognitive performance?

The origin

The publication of a brief (one-page) article in *Nature* almost 20 years ago (Rauscher et al. 1993) was the impetus for widespread interest in the possibility that simply listening to music has cognitive benefits. The participants in the original study were undergraduates at the University of California—Irvine who completed one of three spatial tasks after 10 minutes of: (1) listening to a Mozart sonata (K. 448), (2) listening to relaxation instructions, or (3) sitting in silence. Each participant was tested three times in a single visit to the laboratory: once in each of the three listening conditions and once with each of the three spatial tasks. Because performance was better on the spatial tasks after listening to Mozart than in the other two conditions, this result became known as the *Mozart effect*.

The brevity of the article precluded inclusion of several important methodological details that were required to judge its merit and interpret the findings. For example, the reader needed to assume that the six possible orders of the three listening conditions were counterbalanced with the six possible orders of the three spatial tests. Because the authors had a sample of 36 undergraduates, this would mean that there was a single participant in each cell. Without this assumption, testing order would have been confounded with the different listening conditions (or spatial tests), and the results would be meaningless. Rather, performance could have improved over time due to practice effects or to increased comfort in the testing environment. Conversely, performance may have declined due to fatigue or boredom. To complicate matters further, the main statistical result was reported incorrectly in the article (i.e. the degrees of freedom do not correspond to the analysis the authors said they conducted).

The article stated clearly, however, that participants who scored high (or low) on one of the spatial tests also tended to score high (or low) on the other two tests, which provided evidence that the three tests were measuring a single construct (i.e. spatial ability or general intelligence). Indeed, the authors considered the three tasks to be identical in order to analyse differences between listening conditions with a repeated-measure analysis. Each participant had a single spatial score in each listening condition, but each score came from a different task. Thus, examination of differences among listening conditions made no sense unless the authors assumed that the three different tests were measuring the same thing.

In a second paper from the same research team (Rauscher et al. 1995), the authors replicated and extended the original effect. In contrast to the first study, which involved repeated testing in a single test session, participants were tested daily for 5 consecutive days. On the first day, they completed a test of spatial abilities. Performance on this test was used to divide the sample into three groups with equivalent abilities. On the second day, participants completed the same spatial test (with different items) after 10 minutes of listening to a Mozart sonata (K. 448), sitting in silence, or listening to a minimalist piece of music composed by Philip Glass. Performance for the Mozart group was significantly better than it was for the other two groups. Subsequent days were similar except that participants who heard the minimalist piece on the second day heard something unique each day (e.g. a narrated story or a piece of dance music). Group differences were no longer evident on these days, probably because performance on the spatial task reached a plateau after repeated testing.

On the fifth day of testing, the researchers compared performance on a test of short-term memory after participants listened to the Mozart sonata or sat in silence. The two groups did not differ. Because the Mozart effect did *not* extend to short-term memory, the null finding was used to justify claims of a special link between listening to Mozart and spatial abilities. It is also possible, however, that participants simply became bored or frustrated after 5 days of repeated testing, which masked group differences that may have been evident on the first day. Group dynamics may also have changed over time as participants became acquainted with other members of their group.

The theory

Gordon Shaw (2000, p. 163), a physicist and the second author of both reports, discussed briefly the review process at *Nature* after the authors submitted the original article. He noted that they were required to remove any mention of the theory that motivated their experiment in order to make their manuscript acceptable for publication. This comment was particularly revealing because the theory—called the *trion model* (Leng and Shaw 1991)—set the stage for subsequent research and scholarly debates about how the Mozart effect could be explained and whether it was even replicable. The trion model posited that neuronal activation patterns in the cortex are similar when listening to Mozart (or other complex music, with 'complexity' poorly defined) as when doing a task that requires spatial abilities. Rauscher et al. (1995) also speculated that Mozart's precociousness as a composer was a consequence of relatively well-developed activation patterns early in life, which allowed him to compose complex music. In psychological terms, however, the model was without empirical support (e.g. Waterhouse 2006) because it described similar brain-activation patterns arising from different activities that have nothing in common (i.e. passive listening to music, performing tasks that require spatial skills). Thus, although the basic finding that listening to music enhances cognitive performance was provocative and newsworthy, it is not surprising that *Nature* refused to publish unsubstantiated and dubious speculation about the source of the effect.

The three spatial tasks used by Rauscher et al. (1993) in the original study were subtests from *The Stanford-Binet Scale of Intelligence* (Thorndike et al. 1986), a widely used measure of intelligence. One was the *Paper-Folding-and-Cutting* (PF&C) test; the others were *Matrices* and *Pattern Analysis*. Because the PF&C test has been used widely in subsequent research, and because differences among tasks became an important issue in the literature, an example of a test item is provided in Figure 22.1. Each item on the test visually depicts a rectangular piece of paper being folded one or more times in a series of folding manipulations. One or more sections are cut out of the final folded piece. The participant's task is to determine how the paper will look when it is unfolded by choosing one of several options (usually from five alternatives).

The issue of the specific task is closely related to the authors' description of the proposed link between listening to music composed by Mozart and cognitive abilities, and the way this hypothesized link changed over time. In the original paper (Rauscher et al. 1993), the link was said to be between listening to 'complex music' and 'abstract reasoning,' with spatial abilities being just one aspect of abstract reasoning. All three tests they administered were measures of spatial abilities and abstract reasoning, and, as noted, the three tests were correlated and appeared to measure the same construct. In the second paper (Rauscher et al. 1995), the link was narrowed considerably, involving listening to Mozart and 'spatial-temporal' abilities. Even though the authors still claimed that all three tests from the original study were spatial-temporal tasks, they also noted

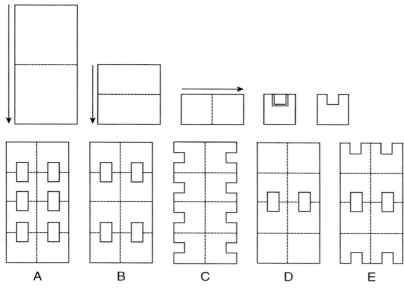

Fig. 22.1 An example of an item from the Paper-Folding-and-Cutting test. In the upper row, a rectangular piece paper is folded three times: in half going downward, in half again going downward, and in half from left to right. A section is then cut out of the folded paper, and the final folded and cut piece of paper is illustrated on the right. In the lower row, five alternatives are provided. The task is to choose the one that represents what the folded and cut piece of paper will look like when it is unfolded. The correct answer is B.

that the one of the three tasks—PF&C—'best fit our concept of spatial-temporal pattern development' (Rauscher et al. 1995, p. 45).

A few years later (Rauscher and Shaw 1998; Rauscher 1999), the same authors claimed that *only* the PF&C task was a measure of spatial-temporal ability; the other two tests from the original study were now considered to measure other (undefined) types of spatial abilities. Narrowing the nature of the association and the appropriate task helped the authors to explain why other researchers could not replicate the effect: They had used the wrong task. To support this notion, Rauscher and Shaw (1998) re-analysed the data from the original study and claimed that the Mozart effect was evident only for the PF&C task. As before, when they compared performance across listening conditions, they found a Mozart effect. When they compared performance across tasks, they found a task effect (i.e. better performance on PF&C than on the other two tasks). Both of these results may have been consistent with the actual data, but once again, the statistical analyses were reported incorrectly (see also Fudin and Lembessis 2004), which does not instill much confidence in the reader. Specifically, the authors reported results from an analysis (i.e. a 3×3 repeated-measures ANOVA) that was impossible to conduct with their data set, and the degrees of freedom they reported did not correspond to any legitimate analysis that could have been conducted.

Moreover, the claim of a Mozart effect for one task but not for others was a claim of an interaction between listening condition and task. A test of the interaction could not have been conducted with the original data because of the experimental design. Rather, such a test would require: (1) all participants to be tested nine times (three tasks for each of the three conditions; both variables manipulated within-participants); (2) each participant to be tested three times in the same listening condition (a between-groups variable), once with each task (a within-participants variable); or (3) each participant to be tested with the same task (a between-groups variable) in each of the three conditions (a within-participants variable). Even then, testing order would need to be counter-balanced so that response patterns could be attributed unequivocally to the different listening conditions, the different tasks, and/or an interaction between listening condition and task. Another possibility would be to test each participant a single time in one of nine different groups, with both listening condition and task manipulated as between-group variables. Because of substantial pre-existing individual differences in cognitive abilities, this last option would likely require a very large sample size in order for significant effects to emerge.

For the scientific community at large, the unusual details of the Mozart effect as described by these articles (Rauscher et al. 1993, 1995; Rauscher and Shaw 1998) presented a paradox. On the one hand, the initial report was published in a prestigious, high-impact journal, it received widespread media coverage and public interest, and the main result was provocative yet intuitively appealing to many scientists and lay people. On the other hand, the original report's brevity left many important questions unanswered, the experimental designs and statistical analyses were less than optimal, and the underlying theory was unsubstantiated and shifted from paper to paper. Moreover, the third paper in the series (Rauscher and Shaw 1998) as well as the original description of the trion model (Leng and Shaw 1991) were published in journals with very poor reputations (*Perceptual and Motor Skills*, *Concepts in Neuroscience*, respectively).[1] This particular combination of factors led to a response from the scholarly community that varied from initial disinterest, to dismay and confusion, and, eventually, to hostility and personal animosity between some researchers in the field (e.g. Rauscher 1999; Steele 2000, 2001, 2003, 2006). More generally, the psychological dubiousness of the underlying theory led many to believe that: (1) the effect must be a consequence of psychological mechanisms less mystical than those posited by the trion model, or (2) the effect simply did not exist.

To highlight this paradox further, I calculated the number of papers that have been published on the topic, the year of publication, and the quality of the average publication. First, to document the history of research and media interest in the effect, I conducted an Internet search for published articles using the keyword 'Mozart effect'. This search uncovered journal articles, magazine articles, unpublished dissertations, editorials, and so on. The results, shown in Figure 22.2, illustrate that interest has been relatively high and consistent for several years (see also Bangerter and Heath 2004), with the number of published articles reaching a notable peak in 1999. In 2009, however, only two articles were published, which suggests that interest may finally have waned. Accordingly, now is likely to be as good a time as any to review what was discovered about music listening and cognitive performance between 1993 and the present day.

A second analysis examined articles from the previous sample that appeared in journals with documented impact factors, which served as an approximate measure of differences in journal quality. Whenever available, I recorded the impact factor averaged over 5 years (2004–2008) of each journal that published one or more articles about the Mozart effect. Figure 22.3 illustrates the association between impact factor and the number of articles published. The association is unambiguously negative. On the one hand, then, the first analysis demonstrated long-term,

---

[1] Impact factor is an index of how many times, on average, articles in a journal are cited in a particular year. In 2008, *Perceptual and Motor Skills* and its sister journal, *Psychological Reports* (same publisher, website, policies, and so on) had impact factors of 0.402 and 0.309, respectively. For the same year, *Nature* had an impact factor of 31.434, *Psychological Science* had an impact factor of 4.812, and *Neuroscience Letters* had an impact factor of 2.200. As far as I can tell, *Concepts in Neuroscience* does not have a documented impact factor, it published only five volumes, it has no website, and Gordon Shaw was co-editor.

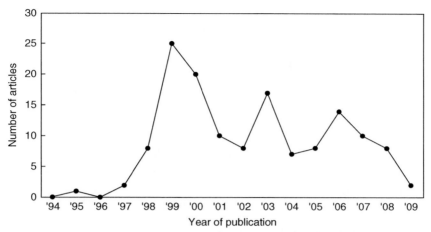

Fig. 22.2 The results from a literature search on the keyword 'Mozart effect'. The search was conducted in February 2010. The figure illustrates the number of articles published in each year from 1994–2009.

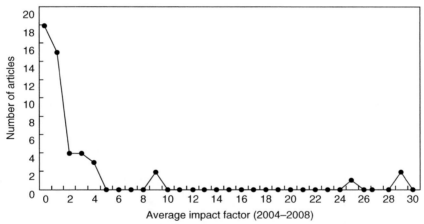

Fig. 22.3 The results from a subset of articles from Figure 22.1 (i.e. those that appeared in journals with available impact factors). The figure illustrates the number of articles published as a function of impact factor (0–1, 1–2, 2–3, and so on).

relatively high and consistent scholarly and media interest in the effect because it was so topical. On the other hand, the second analysis indicated that, with some notable exceptions, relatively few articles were published in good- or medium-quality journals (i.e. with impact factors higher than 1). Indeed, the vast bulk of the research appeared in low-quality scientific journals, presumably because it was conducted without sound theoretical motivation and/or the findings were not particularly edifying.

Arousal and mood

An alternative explanation of the Mozart effect (Thompson et al. 2001; see also Steele et al. 2000) proposes that it is mediated by the listener's emotional state, specifically arousal levels and moods, which can be modified by music listening. For example, when undergraduates are tested on a computer game while listening to music, they perform better when listening to the music they prefer (Mozart K. 448 or the Red Hot Chili Peppers; Cassity et al. 2007). Even low-level measures of attention reveal better performance while listening to a pleasant stimulus (Mozart K. 448) compared to an unfamiliar-sounding stimulus (the Mozart sonata played backward) or silence, an effect that appears to be a consequence of differences in arousal and mood (Ho et al. 2007).

In other words, music can change how listeners feel (Jones et al. 2006), and their feelings, in turn, influence their cognitive performance (Jones and Estell 2007; Jones et al. 2006). In stark contrast to the trion model, both parts of the hypothesized association are well documented in the literature. For example, in an extensive review article, Juslin and Västfjäll (2008) concluded that 'people use music to change emotions, to release emotions, to match their current emotion, to enjoy or comfort themselves, and to relieve stress' (p. 559; see also Sloboda 1992; Laukka 2007). In other words, there is no doubt about the link between music listening and its ability to influence listeners' emotional state.

The link between emotional state and cognitive performance is similarly unequivocal. For example, in another review article, Isen and Labroo (2003) concluded that 'positive affect promotes cognitive flexibility and thus facilitates problem solving and decision making in many situations' (p. 365). Conversely, negative emotional states such as anxiety (Cassady 2004) and boredom (O'Hanlon, 1981) often have detrimental influences on cognitive performance. Positive and negative moods, respectively, appear to facilitate and inhibit the formation of associations between stimuli and pre-existing mental representations (Storbeck and Clore 2005), whereas negative moods increase the amount of subjective effort required for a task (Gendolla et al. 2001). Positive and negative moods are also associated with reliable differences in physiological responses such as blood pressure (Gendolla and Krüsken 2001; Gendolla et al. 2001).

In a series of studies that I conducted with my colleagues (Nantais and Schellenberg 1999; Thompson et al. 2001; Husain et al. 2002; Schellenberg and Hallam 2005; Schellenberg et al. 2007), our goals were to replicate the Mozart effect and to determine the boundary conditions under which it would be evident. As we will see, all of the evidence proved to be consistent with the arousal and mood hypothesis. The initial study (Nantais and Schellenberg 1999) involved two experiments. In the first one, undergraduates came to the laboratory individually on two different days. On both visits, they completed one of two versions of the PF&C task that were equally difficult. The PF&C test was preceded by 10 minutes of listening to music or sitting in silence. Both experiences involved wearing headphones while sitting in a sound-attenuating booth facing a computer monitor. The order of the two listening conditions and the order of the two versions of the PF&C task were counterbalanced. Performance was better after listening to music than after sitting in silence, regardless of whether the music was composed by Mozart or Schubert. In other words, we replicated the Mozart effect but we also found a *Schubert effect* that was equivalent in magnitude.

In the second experiment, we contrasted PF&C performance after listening to Mozart or a narrated story written by Stephen King. Listening to a story represented a better control condition than sitting in silence because, like the music, the story was an auditory stimulus that changed over time, and it was presented at the same amplitude as the music. Moreover, the story was deemed to be approximately as interesting and pleasant for undergraduates as listening to Mozart would be. As expected, we found no difference in PF&C performance between the two listening conditions. When we asked these participants which listening experience they preferred, approximately half preferred Mozart whereas the other half preferred the story. We then analysed the data as a function of preference and listening condition. A significant interaction between preference and condition revealed that performance was higher among the preferred conditions (i.e. the Mozart condition for those who preferred Mozart, the story condition for those who preferred the story) compared to the non-preferred conditions. In other words, participants who preferred Mozart showed a Mozart effect whereas listeners who preferred the story showed a *Stephen King effect*. Although we had no direct measures of arousal or mood, it seems fairly safe to assume that arousal levels and moods would be better after the preferred compared to the non-preferred listening experience.

The second study (Thompson et al. 2001) had the same basic design but it tested specifically the arousal and mood hypothesis. Each participant was tested individually on the PF&C task on two different days, once after listening to music and once after sitting in silence. The music was Mozart (K. 448) for half of the participants and Albinoni's Adagio for the other half, with order of the two PF&C tasks and the two listening conditions counterbalanced. We also measured arousal and mood before and after the listening experience. In contrast to the Mozart sonata, which was relatively fast and in a major key, the Albinoni Adagio was slow and minor. It is well established that fast-tempo and major-mode music tends to make listeners feel happy, whereas slow-tempo and minor-mode music makes listeners feel sad (e.g. Hunter and Schellenberg 2010). Our prediction was that we would once again find evidence of a Mozart effect but *not* of an Albinoni effect, and that this difference between groups would be a consequence of differential changes in arousal and mood. The data were consistent with this prediction. For the Mozart group, arousal levels and mood improved after listening to music but not after sitting in silence. For the Albinoni group, there were no differences between the music and silence conditions. Moreover, compared to sitting in silence, performance on the PF&C task was enhanced after listening to Mozart but not to Albinoni. Finally, the observed Mozart effect disappeared when changes in either arousal or mood were held constant in the statistical analyses.

The null finding for the Albinoni piece could be a consequence of specific associations between the piece and personal experiences, such as a recent death in the family (the Albinoni piece is played commonly at funerals) or previously learned associations between this particular piece and sadness. To address this concern, in the next experiment (Husain et al. 2002), the stimuli consisted of different versions of the *same* music (Mozart K. 448) recorded as a MIDI file. The file was manipulated to create four versions that varied only in tempo and mode (fast–major, fast–minor, slow–major, slow–minor). As noted, these two musical characteristics have clear associations with emotion. Each participant was tested individually on the PF&C task only once (a between-subjects design) after listening to one of the four versions, and arousal and mood were measured before and after the test session. PF&C performance was better after listening to the fast compared to the slow-tempo versions of the sonata, and after the major compared to the minor versions. Tempo influenced arousal levels (faster = higher arousal), whereas mode influenced mood (major = more positive). Again, individual differences in arousal and mood accounted for the bulk of the variance in performance on the PF&C task.

In the next study (Schellenberg et al. 2007), we tested non-spatial abilities. Participants were tested twice on different days after listening to Mozart (K. 448) or to Albinoni's Adagio. After both listening experiences they completed one of two tests: a measure of processing speed or a test of working memory. Order of the two tests and the two musical pieces was counterbalanced. We also measured arousal and mood before and after the test session. At the first test session, we found that mood improved after listening to Mozart but not to Albinoni, whereas arousal levels *decreased* for both groups. Because the arousal and mood measures were inconsistent, we were not surprised to discover that there were no group differences on either cognitive test. At the second session, however, arousal levels *and* mood both improved after listening to Mozart but became worse after listening to Albinoni. In line with the arousal and mood hypothesis, performance on one of the cognitive tests (processing speed) was enhanced after listening to Mozart compared to Albinoni. In other words, we replicated the Mozart effect with a non-spatial task. There was no difference on the test of working memory, however, which implies that tests of some cognitive abilities may be relatively impervious to effects of arousal and mood. Some previous evidence also suggests that performance on tests of working memory may be relatively immune to the Mozart effect (Rauscher et al. 1995; Steele et al. 1997).

If the arousal and mood perspective on the Mozart effect is correct, then the most appropriate music to influence how listeners feel, and how they perform subsequently on a cognitive task, should depend critically on the particular sample of listeners. In line with this view, rock musicians show specific brain activation patterns (i.e. lower P3 amplitudes) when listening to rock music, whereas classical musicians show the same patterns when listening to classical music (Caldwell and Riby 2007). The next experiment (Schellenberg and Hallam 2005) tested directly whether the specific music that leads to better cognitive performance depends on the particular sample. It was conducted in collaboration with the BBC, which issued a call to schools in the UK to participate in a study on the Mozart effect. Approximately 200 schools responded and over 8000 10- and 11-year-olds participated. Each school divided students into three groups at random. Each group was assigned to a different room at the school. At precisely the same time, students listened to music by Mozart (not K. 448) on BBC Radio 3 in one room, popular songs (including 'Country House' by the UK band Blur) on BBC Radio 1 in another room, or to a discussion about the experiment on BBC Radio 5 in a third room. Afterwards, they completed two tests of spatial abilities. We expected that emotional states would be enhanced for these children after listening to pop music compared to music by Mozart or a scientific discussion, and, consequently, that cognitive performance would show a similar pattern. Spatial-task performance was consistent with this prediction for one of the two tasks, the one that proved to be more difficult. In short, the results revealed a *Blur effect* for school-age children. They also suggested that effects of emotional state on cognitive performance might be more likely as the difficulty of the task increases.

The final experiment in this series tested the creative abilities of Japanese 5-year-olds (Schellenberg et al. 2007). Each child was initially given a piece of paper and 18 crayons and asked to draw whatever they wanted (i.e. a *baseline* drawing). They made a second *music* drawing on a different day after one of four musical experiences to which they were assigned randomly. The experiences involved hearing Mozart (K. 448), Albinoni's Adagio, or Japanese children's songs for one hour during lunch, or singing children's songs for 20 minutes after lunch. The dependent measures involved comparisons between baseline and music drawings (one pair for each child) in terms of: (1) time spent drawing, and (2) adults' ratings of the drawings' creativity, energy, and technical proficiency. (The adults did not know which drawing was the baseline or music drawing.) Our prediction was that all outcome measures would differ between the two classical music conditions (Mozart and Albinoni) and the two children's music conditions (listening or singing), with the results favouring creativity in the latter case. In line with these predictions, drawing times increased more from the baseline to the music condition for children who heard or sang familiar children's songs, and their music drawings were judged to be more creative, energetic, and technically proficient. In short, we found a *children's playsong effect* for creativity among 5-year-olds.

Successful and unsuccessful attempts to replicate

Many researchers have attempted simply to replicate the Mozart effect. When the dependent variable was a measure of spatial abilities, some studies succeeded (e.g. Rideout and Laubach 1996; Rideout and Taylor 1997; Wilson and Brown 1997; Rideout et al. 1998; Twomey and Eastgate 2002; Ivanov and Geake 2003; Cacciafesta et al. 2010) but others did not (e.g. Carstens et al. 1995; Steele et al. 1999a,b,c; McCutcheon 2000; McKelvie and Low 2002; Jackson and Tlauka

2004; Črnček et al. 2006b; Hui, 2006) Similarly, when the dependent variable was a measure of performance on a test of some other kind of cognitive ability, some studies reported an effect (e.g. Roth and Smith 2008) but others did not (e.g. Stough et al. 1994; Newman et al. 1995; Steele et al. 1997; Bridgett and Cuevas 2000; Twomey and Eastgate 2002; Gray and Della Sala 2007). In some instances, the effect was evident for some participants (non-musicians: Aheadi et al. 2010; women: Gilleta et al. 2003) but not for others (musicians or men). In addition to the *Schubert, Stephen King, Blur,* and *children's playsong effects* described above, others have provided evidence of *Bach* (Ivanov and Geake 2003), and *Yanni* (Rideout et al. 1998) *effects.*

A meta-analysis of the Mozart effect from 1999 concluded that the effect was weak or non-existent (Chabris 1999), whereas a second meta-analysis published the very next year concluded that the effect was robust but limited to spatial tasks similar to PF&C (Hetland 2000). One review article concluded that there was 'no strong evidence of a Mozart effect in children' (Črnček et al, 2006a, p. 581), which is not surprising because children are unlikely to find Mozart's music particularly pleasant. A more recent meta-analysis (Pietschnig et al. 2010) found a small but significant effect on spatial abilities when they examined studies that compared listening to Mozart with a non-musical stimulus (usually silence). When they examined studies that used music other than Mozart, the effect size was similar in magnitude. As in the present chapter, the authors attributed the observed effects to differences in arousal.

In any event, simple attempts to replicate the Mozart effect are not informative whether they succeed or not. If the replication is successful without informing us about the underlying mechanisms that are the source of the effect, then we have not learned much. Failures to replicate are even less instructive. First of all, the null hypothesis can never be proven. Secondly, when researchers from independent laboratories have replicated the effect, what does a failure to do so indicate? That all previous findings of a Mozart effect were due to experimenter bias or Type I error? Both of these interpretations are implausible. My own view is that failures to replicate indicate that the researchers did not try hard enough, typically because they relied on the convenience of group testing (e.g. Carstens et al. 1995; Steele et al. 1999a,b,c; McCutcheon 2000; McKelvie and Low 2002; Lints and Gadbois 2003; Črnček et al. 2006b; Hui 2006). In normal circumstances, listeners often talk to one another when pre-recorded music is heard in group situations (e.g. in bars, at parties), yet these studies required participants *not* to talk, thereby creating an artificial listening context with little or no ecological validity. Requiring a group of people to sit in silence is even more artificial. One can only imagine the smiles, smirks, and rolling eyes as groups of participants were required to sit together in silence doing absolutely nothing. Failures to replicate also have no ramification for the arousal and mood hypothesis, which was formulated to explain *successful* replications of links between exposure to music and cognitive performance. The hypothesis does *not* predict that exposure to music (composed by Mozart or anyone else) at any time in any context will lead to cognitive improvements, or that whenever differences in arousal or mood are observed, differences in cognitive performance will also be evident.

Conclusion

The arousal and mood hypothesis offers an explanation of the Mozart effect that has nothing to do with Mozart or with spatial abilities. Rather, it proposes that Mozart's music is simply one example of a stimulus that can change how people feel, which, in turn, influences how they perform on tests of cognitive abilities. In other words, the hypothesis offers a simple and sensible explanation of the effect when it is evident. As described in the above review, many factors appear to influence whether effects of music listening on cognition will be observed in an experimental setting, including the match between the sample of listeners and the music, whether listeners are tested in groups or individually, the particular test, and the difficulty of the test. Participants' performance also depends on whether they are aware of the experimental hypothesis (Lints and Gadbois 2003; Verpaelst and Standing 2007; Standing et al. 2008).

The arousal and mood hypothesis was designed to be very general, extending beyond Mozart and music to any stimulus that affects how the perceiver feels, and beyond spatial abilities to cognitive performance broadly construed. In retrospect, however, the hypothesis was not general enough. Applied research reveals that listening to music has positive effects that extend well beyond cognition. For example, self-selected music can reduce pain perception (Mitchell et al. 2006), particularly when the music is very familiar (Mitchell et al. 2008). In these instances, music's positive effect on emotional state appears to act jointly with its ability to distract the listener's attention away from a negative stimulus. Music (typically lullabies) also promotes weight gain for pre-term infants and decreases length-of-stay in hospital (Standley 2002), perhaps by slowing energy expenditure (i.e. metabolic rate; Lubetsky et al. 2010). After suffering from a stroke, daily listening to music improves mood in addition to facilitating recovery of memory and attention (Särkämö et al. 2008), whereas patient-selected music can reduce the amount of anaesthesia required during surgery (Ayoub et al. 2005). Finally, music listening in older age improves quality of life by helping the elderly cope with pain and confusion (McCaffrey 2008).

In sum, conclusions that can be drawn about the impact of music listening on health and wellbeing are both disappointing as well as promising. On the one hand, there does not appear to be a specific link between music listening and cognitive abilities, and certainly not between listening to Mozart and spatial abilities. Hence, direct benefits of music listening on cognition are more of a fantasy than a reality. On the other hand, it is clear that music can change listeners' emotional state, which, in turn, may impact their cognitive performance, and the fact that the link is mediated by arousal and mood does not make it less meaningful. Moreover, unlike other stimuli that influence how we feel (e.g. candy, cigarettes, drugs, exercise), portable devices with hundreds of digital recordings can accompany listeners almost anywhere, and if the music is played at a reasonable volume, there are no adverse effects. In this sense, music is special because it is an easily transportable but non-toxic stimulus that influences how we feel, and because how we feel affects virtually all aspects of human experience.

Acknowledgement

Supported by the Natural Sciences and Engineering Research Council of Canada. I thank Jeff Millar for his assistance in the analyses of the Mozart effect publications.

References

Aheadi, A., Dixon, P., and Glover, S. (2010). A limiting feature of the Mozart effect: Listening enhances mental rotation abilities in non-musicians but not musicians. *Psychology of Music,* **38**, 107–17.

Amagdei, A., Baltes, F.R., Avram, J., and Miu, A.C. (2010). Perinatal exposure to music protects spatial memory against callosal lesions. *International Journal of Developmental Neuroscience,* **28**, 105–9.

Aoun, P., Jones, T., Shaw, G.L., and Bodner, M. (2005). Long-term enhancement of maze learning in mice via a generalized Mozart effect. *Neurological Research,* **25**, 791–6.

Ayoub, C.M., Rizk, L.B., Yaacoub, C.I., Gaal, D., and Kain, Z.N. (2005). Music and ambient operating room noise in patients undergoing spinal anesthesia. *Anesthesia and Analgesia,* **100**, 1316–19.

Bangerter. A. and Heath, C. (2004). The Mozart effect: Tracking the evolution of a scientific legend. *British Journal of Social Psychology,* **43**, 605–23.

Bodner, M., Muftaler, L.T., Nalcioglu, O., and Shaw, G.L. (2001). fMRI study relevant to the Mozart effect: Brain areas involved in spatial-temporal reasoning. *Neurological Research,* **23**, 683–90.

Bridgett, D.J. and Cuevas, J. (2000). Effects of listening to Mozart and Bach on the performance of a mathematical test. *Perceptual and Motor Skills,* **90**, 1171–5.

Cacciafesta, M., Ettorre, E., Amici, A., Cicconetti, P., Martinelli, V., Linguanti, A., *et al.* (2010). New frontiers of cognitive rehabilitation in geriatric age: the Mozart Effect (ME). *Archives of Gerontology and Geriatrics,* **51**(3), e79–e82.

Caldwell, G.N. and Riby, L.M. (2007). The effects of music exposure and own genre preference on conscious and unconscious cognitive processes: A pilot ERP study. *Consciousness and Cognition,* **16**, 992–6.

Campbell, G.J. (2000). Mozart went down to Georgia. *Southern Cultures,* Spring 2000, 94–101.

Carstens, C.B., Huskins, E., and Hounshell, G.W. (1995). Listening to Mozart may not enhance performance on the Revised Minnesota Paper Form Board Test. *Psychological Reports,* **77**, 111–14.

Cassady, J.C. (2004). The influence of cognitive test anxiety across the learning-testing cycle. *Learning and Instruction,* **14**, 569–92.

Cassity, H.D., Henley, T.B., and Markley, R.P. (2007). The Mozart effect: Musical phenomenon or musical preference? A more ecologically valid reconsideration. *Journal of Instructional Psychology,* **34**, 13–17.

Chabris, C.F. (1999). Prelude or requiem for the 'Mozart effect'? *Nature,* **400**, 826–7.

Chikahisa, S., Sei, H., Morishima, M., Sano, A., Kitaoka, K., Nakaya, Y., *et al.* (2006). Exposure to music in the perinatal period enhances learning performance and alters BDNF/TrkB signaling in mice as adults. *Behavioral Brain Research,* **169**, 312–19.

Črnčec, R., Wilson, S.J., and Prior, M. (2006a). The cognitive and academic benefits of music to children: Facts and fiction. *Educational Psychology,* **26**, 579–94.

Črnčec, R., Wilson, S.J., and Prior, M. (2006b). No evidence for the Mozart effect in children. *Music Perception,* **23**, 305–317.

Dowd, W. (2008). The myth of the Mozart effect. *Skeptic,* **13**(4), 21–3.

Fudin, R. and Lembessis, E. (2004). The Mozart effect: Questions about the seminal findings of Rauscher, Shaw, and colleagues. *Perceptual and Motor Skills,* **98**, 389–405.

Gendolla, G.H.E. and Krüsken, J. (2001). Mood state and cardiovascular response in active coping with an affect-regulative challenge. *International Journal of Psychophysiology,* **41**, 169–80.

Gendolla, GH.E., Abele, A.E., and Krüsken, J. (2001). The informational impact of mood on effort mobilization: A study of cardiovascular and electrodermal responses. *Emotion,* **1**, 12–24.

Gilleta, K.S., Vrbancic, M.I., Elias, L.J., and Saucier, D.M. (2003). A Mozart effect for women on a mental rotations task. *Perceptual and Motor Skills,* **96**, 1086–92.

Gray, C. and Della Sala, S. (2007). The Mozart effect: It's time to face the music! In S. Dalla Sala (ed.) *Tall tales about the mind and brain: Separating fact from fiction,* pp. 148–57. Oxford: Oxford University Press.

Hetland, L. (2000). Listening to music enhances spatial-temporal reasoning: Evidence for the 'Mozart Effect'. *Journal of Aesthetic Education,* **34**, 105–48.

Ho, C., Mason, O., and Spence, C. (2007). An investigation into the temporal dimension of the Mozart effect: Evidence from the attentional blink task. *Acta Psychologica,* **125**, 117–28.

Hui, K. (2006). Mozart effect in preschool children? *Early Child Development and Care,* **176**, 411–19.

Hunter, P.G., and Schellenberg, E.G. (2010). Music and emotion. In: M.R. Jones, A.N. Popper, and R.R. Fay, and A.N. Popper (ed.), *Music perception,* pp. 129–64. New York: Springer.

Husain, G., Thompson, W.F., and Schellenberg, E.G. (2002). Effects of musical tempo and mode on arousal, mood, and spatial abilities. *Music Perception,* **20**, 151–71.

Isen, A.M. and Labroo, A.A. (2003). Some ways in which positive affect facilitates decision making and judgment. In: S. Schneider, and J. Shanteau (eds.) *Emerging perspectives on judgment and decision research,* pp. 365–93. New York: Cambridge University Press.

Ivanov, V.K., and Geake, J.G. (2003). The Mozart effect and primary school children. *Psychology of Music,* **31**, 405–41.

Jackson, C.S. and Tlauka, M. (2004). Route-learning and the Mozart effect. *Psychology of Music,* **32**, 213–20.

Jaušovec, N. and Habe, K. (2003). The influence of Mozart's sonata K. 448 on brain activity during the performance of spatial rotation and numerical tasks. *Brain Topography,* **17**, 207–18.

Jaušovec, N., Jaušovec, K., and Gerli , I. (2006). The influence of Mozart's music on brain activity in the process of learning. *Clinical Neurophysiology,* **117**, 2703–14.

Jones, M.H., and Estell, D.B. (2007). Exploring the Mozart effect among high school students. *Psychology of Aesthetics, Creativity, and the Arts,* 1, 219–24.

Jones, M.H., West, S.D., and Estell, D.B. (2006). The Mozart effect: Arousal, preference, and spatial performance. *Psychology of Aesthetics, Creativity, and the Arts,* S, 26–32.

Juslin, P.N. and Västfjäll, D. (2008). Emotional responses to music: The need to consider underlying mechanisms. *Behavioral and Brain Sciences,* 31, 559–621.

Laukka, P. (2007). Uses of music and psychological well-being among the elderly. *Journal of Happiness Studies,* **8**, 215–41.

Leng, X. and Shaw, G.L. (1991). Toward a neural theory of higher brain function using music as a window. *Concepts in Neuroscience,* **2**, 229–58.

Lints, A. and Gadbois, S. (2003). Is listening to Mozart the only way to enhance spatial reasoning? *Perceptual and Motor Skills,* **97**, 1163–74.

Lubetzky, R., Mimouni, F.B., Dollberg, S., Reifen, R., Ashbel, G., and Mandel, D. (2010). Effect of music by Mozart on energy expenditure in growing preterm infants. *Pediatrics,* **125**, e24–28.

McCaffrey, R. (2008). Music listening: Its effects in creating a healing environment. *Journal of Psychosocial Nursing,* **46**, 39–44.

McCutcheon, L.E. (2000). Another failure to generalize the Mozart effect. *Psychological Reports,* **87**, 325–30.

McKelvie, P. and Low, J. (2002). Listening to Mozart does not improve children's spatial ability: Final curtains for the Mozart effect. *British Journal of Developmental Psychology,* **20**, 241–58.

Mitchell, L.A., MacDonald, R.A.R., and Brodie, E.E. (2006). A comparison of the effects of preferred music, arithmetic and humour on cold pressor pain. *European Journal of Pain,* **10**, 343–51.

Mitchell, L.A., MacDonald, R.A.R., and Knussen, C. (2008). An investigation of the effects of music and art on pain perception. *Psychology of Aesthetics, Creativity, and the Arts,* 3, 162–70.

Nantais, K.M. and Schellenberg, E.G. (1999). The Mozart effect: An artifact of preference. *Psychological Science,* **10**, 370–37.

Newman, J., Rosenbach, J.H., Burns, K.L., Latimer, B.C., Matocha, H.B., and Rosenthal Vogt, E. (1995). An experimental test of 'the Mozart effect': Does listening to his music improve spatial ability? *Perceptual and Motor Skills,* **81**, 1379–87.

O'Hanlon, J.F. (1981). Boredom: Practical consequences and a theory. *Acta Psychologica,* **49**, 53–82.

Pietschnig, J., Voracek, M., and Formann, A.K. (2010). Mozart effect—Shmozart effect: A meta-analysis. *Intelligence,* **38**, 314–23.

Rauscher, F.H. (1999). Prelude or requiem for the 'Mozart effect'? Reply. *Nature,* **400**, 827–28.

Rauscher, F.H. (2006). The Mozart effect in rats: Response to Steele. *Music Perception,* **23**, 447–53.

Rauscher, F.H. and Hinton, S.C. (2006). The Mozart effect: Music listening is not music instruction. *Educational Psychologist,* **41**, 233–38.

Rauscher, F.H. and Shaw, G.L. (1998). Key components of the Mozart effect. *Perceptual and Motor Skills,* **86**, 835–41.

Rauscher, F.H., Shaw, G.L., and Ky, K.N. (1993). Music and spatial task performance. *Nature,* **365**, 611.

Rauscher, F.H., Shaw, G.L., and Ky, K.N. (1995). Listening to Mozart enhances spatial-temporal reasoning: Towards a neurophysiological basis. *Neuroscience Letters,* **185**, 44–47.

Rauscher, F.H., Robinson, K.D., and Jens, J.J. (1998). Improved maze learning through early music exposure in rats. *Neurological Research,* **20**, 427–32.

Rideout, B.E. and Laubach, C.M. (1996). EEG correlates of enhanced spatial performance following exposure to music. *Perceptual and Motor Skills,* **82**, 427–32.

Rideout, B.E. and Taylor, J. (1997). Enhanced spatial performance following 10 minutes of exposure to music: A replication. *Perceptual and Motor Skills,* **85,** 112–114.

Rideout, B.E., Dougherty, S., and Wernert, L. (1998). Effect of music on spatial performance: A test of generality. *Perceptual and Motor Skills,* **86,** 512–514.

Roth, E.A. and Smith, K.H. (2008). The Mozart effect: Evidence for the arousal hypothesis. *Perceptual and Motor Skills,* **107,** 396–402.

Särkämö, T., Tervaniemi, M., Laitinen, S., Forsblom, A., Soinila, S., Mikkonen, M., *et al.* (2008). Music listening enhances cognitive recovery and mood after middle cerebral artery stroke. *Brain,* **131,** 866–76.

Sarnthein, J., vonStein, A., Rappelsberger, P., Petsche, H., Rauscher, F.H., and Shaw, G.L. (1997). Persistent patterns of brain activity: An EEG coherence study of the positive effect of music on spatial-temporal reasoning. *Neurological Research,* **19,** 107–116.

Schellenberg, E.G. (2001). Music and nonmusical abilities. *Annals of the New York Academy of Sciences,* **930,** 355–71.

Schellenberg, E.G. (2003). Does exposure to music have beneficial side effects? In: I. Peretz, and R.J. Zatorre (eds.) *The cognitive neuroscience of music,* pp. 430–48. Oxford: Oxford University Press.

Schellenberg, E.G. (2005). Music and cognitive abilities. *Current Directions in Psychological Science,* **14,** 322–25.

Schellenberg, E.G. (2006). Exposure to music: The truth about the consequences. In G. E. McPherson (ed.) *The child as musician: A handbook of musical development,* pp. 111–34. Oxford: Oxford University Press.

Schellenberg, E.G. and Hallam, S. (2005). Music listening and cognitive abilities in 10- and 11-year-olds: The Blur effect. *Annals of the New York Academy of Sciences,* **1060,** 202–209.

Schellenberg, E.G., Nakata, T., Hunter, P.G., and Tamoto, S. (2007). Exposure to music and cognitive performance: Tests of children and adults. *Psychology of Music,* **35,** 5–19.

Shaw, G.L. (2000). *Keeping Mozart in mind.* San Diego, CA: Elsevier Academic Press.

Sloboda, J.A. (1992). Empirical studies of emotional response to music. In: M.R. Jones, and S. Holleran (eds.) *Cognitive bases of musical communication,* pp. 33–46. Washington, DC: American Psychological Association.

Standing, L.G., Verpaelst, C.C., and Ulmer, B.K. (2008). A demonstration of nonlinear demand characteristics in the 'Mozart effect' experimental paradigm. *North American Journal of Psychology,* **10,** 553–66.

Standley, J.M. (2002). A meta-analysis of the efficacy of music therapy for premature infants. *Journal of Pediatric Nursing,* **17,** 107–13.

Steele, K.M. (2000). Arousal and mood factors in the 'Mozart effect'. *Perceptual and Motor Skills,* **91,** 188–90.

Steele, K.M. (2001). The 'Mozart effect': An example of the scientific method in operation. *Psychology Teacher Network,* November-December 2001, 2–5.

Steele, K.M. (2003). Do rats show a Mozart effect? *Music Perception,* **21,** 251–65.

Steele, K.M. (2006). Unconvincing evidence that rats show a Mozart effect. *Music Perception,* **23,** 455–58.

Steele, K.M., Ball, T.N., and Runk, R. (1997). Listening to Mozart does not enhance backwards digit span performance. *Perceptual and Motor Skills,* **84,** 1179–84.

Steele, K.M., Bass, K.E., and Crook, M.D. (1999a). The mystery of the Mozart effect: Failure to replicate. *Psychological Science,* **10,** 366–69.

Steele, K.M., Brown, J.D., and Stoecker, J.A. (1999b). Failure to confirm the Rauscher and Shaw description of recovery of the Mozart effect. *Perceptual and Motor Skills,* **88,** 843–48.

Steele, K.M., Dalla Bella, S., Peretz, I., Dunlop, T., Dawe, L.A., Humphrey, G.K., *et al.* (1999c). Prelude or requiem for the 'Mozart effect'? *Nature,* **400,** 827.

Storbeck, J., and Clore, G.L. (2005). With sadness comes accuracy; With happiness, false memory. *Psychological Science,* **16,** 785–91.

Stough, C., Kerkin, B., Bates, T., and Mangan, G. (1994). Music and spatial IQ. *Personality and Individual Differences,* **17**, 695.

Suda, M., Morimoto, K., Obata, A., Koizumi, H., and Maki, A. (2008). Cortical responses to Mozart's sonata enhance spatial-reasoning ability. *Neurological Research,* **30**, 885–8.

Thompson, W.F., Schellenberg, E.G., and Husain, G. (2001). Arousal, mood, and the Mozart effect. *Psychological Science,* **12**, 248–51.

Thorndike, R.L., Hagen, E.P., and Sattler, J.M. (1986). *The Stanford-Binet scale of intelligence.* Chicago: Riverside.

Twomey, A. and Eastgate, A. (2002). The Mozart effect may only be demonstrable in nonmusicians. *Perceptual and Motor Skills,* **95**, 1013–26.

Verpaelst, C.C. and Standing, L.G. (2007). Demand characteristics of music affect performance on the Wonderlic Personnel Test of intelligence. *Perceptual and Motor Skills,* **104**, 153–4.

Waterhouse, L. (2006). Multiple intelligences, the Mozart effect, and emotional intelligence: A critical review. *Educational Psychologist,* **41**, 207–25.

Wilson, T.L., and Brown, T.L. (1997). Reexamination of the effect of Mozart's music on spatial-task performance. *Journal of Psychology,* **131**, 365–70.

Chapter 23

Music Instruction and Children's Intellectual Development: The Educational Context of Music Participation

Eugenia Costa-Giomi

In the early 1990s, a powerful media campaign about the intellectual benefits of music generated much interest among researchers, educators, parents, politicians, and the general public. Almost overnight, the effects of music instruction on cognitive development became a popular topic of discussion in talk shows, magazines, and newspapers. These discussions centred around the belief that music lessons and music listening increase intelligence and improves children's cognitive development. What triggered such media interest was the dissemination of new research on the intellectual benefits of music. The idea that music listening and music instruction affect cognitive performance in adults and children was viewed as original at the time, despite decades of research on the non-musical benefits of learning music.

In this chapter, I will provide a historical overview of research on the intellectual benefits of music and the most popular interpretations of the research findings. After questioning such interpretations and providing alternative explanations, I will describe selected experimental studies that focused on the causal relationship between music instruction and intellectual prowess.

Research showing that learning music may increase intelligence and enhance certain cognitive abilities has broad implications for health and wellbeing. Making people smarter in such a simple way as providing them with music lessons seems like a dream come true. Everybody likes music and many would benefit from improvements in general intelligence quotient (IQ) or specific cognitive abilities: from adults in search of a better job requiring specialized skills to those with cognitive deficiencies; from children in impoverished educational environments that fail to develop their cognitive potential to students who have difficulty in mastering academic tasks; or from parents anxious to provide their children with the best possible education to young children with cognitive disabilities. Unfortunately, the dream may be too good to be true. In this chapter, I will describe the educational context in which music lessons are usually provided and explore the limitations of the claim that music makes children smarter. My goal is to set realistic expectations regarding the intellectual benefits of music instruction.

Historical overview

The beginnings: the study of relationships

Research on the relationship between music and intelligence emerged at the beginning of the twentieth century when the first standardized measures of musical ability and intelligence were published. For example, in 1911, Smith proposed that those who succeed in pitch tasks may be better and brighter learners than those who don't on the basis of the high correlations he found between pitch discrimination and intelligence in boys and girls. But Seashore (1919), the author of the first comprehensive measure of musical ability, dismissed this hypothesis arguing that 'the most sensitive and responsive musicians find but little interest in intellectual pursuits' and 'some intellects are notoriously devoid of musical ear.' More solid evidence for Seashore's assertion that pitch discrimination as well as musical ability are not strongly related to intelligence was provided by studies completed with school children and college students (Hollingworth 1926; Fracker and Howard 1928). These studies used tests such as the Seashore's 1919 version of the Measures of Musical Talent, the 1916 Stanford-Binet intelligence scales, and the Army Alpha intelligence test which had been standardized during the same time period. Although the contradictory findings of these early investigations did not allow for clear conclusions regarding the relationship between musical ability and intelligence, finding predictors of musical talent continued to attract the attention of researchers even outside the field of music. For example, Beckham (1942), a school psychologist, conducted a study with children a couple of decades later and concluded that intelligence did not affect musical aptitude scores. What is interesting about the investigations completed during the first half of the century is that they focused on the effects of IQ on music scores and not music scores on IQ. The researchers described the results regarding the relationship between these two parameters in such a way as to make it clear that their intent was to understand the development of musical ability or musical talent rather than the development of intelligence.

Later, the focus of research shifted from the relationship between musical ability and intelligence to the association between music study and intelligence (Ross 1936; Bienstock 1942). The idea that music students are superior in terms of intellectual ability than those in other disciplines was commonplace at the time (Wheeler and Wheeler 1951). For example, Antrim (1945) showed that students attending a music high school in New York had higher IQ scores than those of other public schools in the city. He believed that the study of music improves concentration which in turn improves performance in cognitive tasks. But Farnsworth (1946) proposed a more parsimonious explanation for the association between IQ and music participation: the study of music may simply be more attractive to brighter students. In fact, prior to Farnsworth's study, Ross (1936) had found that students who *choose* to study music in high school are slightly superior in terms of intelligence than those who don't. Additionally, he found that the most musically talented students score higher in scholastic achievement tests than do other students.

The study of causality

Ross' findings support the idea that music instruction attracts more intelligent students and question the casual nature of the relationship between music training and IQ. However, it was not until 1975 that an experimental study specifically addressed the question of whether the relationship between music participation and cognitive skills is of a causal nature. Hurwitz et al. (1975) studied the effects of music instruction on first graders' sequencing skills, spatial abilities, and academic achievement. In this landmark study, a group of children attending a public school was matched to other groups of children on many demographic characteristics. One of the groups received 7 months of daily music instruction based on the Kodaly method and the other ones didn't. The authors believed that the spatial-temporal processes involved in learning music following the Kodaly method would benefit specific cognitive functions in children. Indeed, the results showed that the music group outperformed the non-music group in most spatial and sequencing tasks. Additionally, children in the music group obtained significantly higher scores in the reading achievement test than did control children. It is important to mention that there were no differences in reading achievement between the groups before the start of Kodaly instruction. Further comparisons completed after a second year of instruction reiterated the superiority of the music group in terms of reading achievement. Although the results of this longitudinal investigation provided convincing evidence that music instruction benefits children's cognitive development, the authors were careful in interpreting the findings. They exerted much caution in generalizing the conclusions and making applications to educational or therapeutic settings. They stressed the need to first understand the mechanism by which the positive effects of music instruction take place and emphasized the importance of exploring the limits of such effects. Although recent research has addressed Hurwitz et al.'s first concern, not much effort has been invested in addressing the latter.

Other studies on the relationship between music and specific cognitive abilities were published in the second half of the twentieth century (e.g. Berel et al. 1971; Wolff 1978; Karma 1979; Hassler et al. 1985; Mason 1986). But it was only in 1994 that this type of research became a popular topic of discussion outside the music and psychological milieu. That year, Rauscher et al. presented the results of an experimental study at the meeting of the American Psychological Association showing significant improvements in specific spatial skills in young children who received weekly music lessons for 8 months. Children from a different daycare who had not received music lessons didn't show such improvement in one of the multiple subtests of an intelligence measure. The headline in the front page of a national newspaper about the study read: 'Music may open mind to math and science' (Elias, M. 1994, p. D1). This headline was not based on the results of the study but on Rauscher's comments to journalists at the time the piece was published. Her belief that the power of music lessons assures 'that every child reaches his or her potential in math and science' became the centre of attention of the media campaign. As there was no evidence that performance in a specific subtest predicts success in math or sciences later in life, the assertion that music contributes to intellectual development in these disciplines was arguable. Furthermore, children's performance in other subtests of the intelligence measures did not show significant improvements after 8 months of music instruction questioning the broadly disseminated idea that music makes children smarter.

The attention generated by the media triggered many interesting applications of this research for the education and wellbeing of children. The main educational application consisted in exposing young children to Mozart's compositions or classical music in general. For example, in 1998, the governor of Georgia distributed free classical music CDs to mothers of newborns and daycare centres in Florida were required to play classical music daily (Science Daily 2010). That not a single research study has yet shown that exposing young children to classical music improves their IQ makes these purported research applications look absurd. It is now clear that there was no research justification for implementing such applications and most of them are no longer in practice. Even profitable enterprises such as Baby Einstein or Baby Mozart have recently become under serious public scrutiny. The Campaign for a Commercial-Free Childhood argued that advertising Baby Einstein's videos and DVDs as educational materials is misleading and that the extensive use of such materials may actually be detrimental to the wellbeing of children. In response to these complaints, the Walt Disney Company, responsible for the distribution of such materials, offered parents refunds for Baby Einstein products purchased between 2004 and 2009 (Klein 2009).

The perfect storm: educational policy, research, and media

The powerful 1990s campaign about the intellectual benefits of music produced not only an array of educational and commercial applications but also a renewed research interest on the relationship between music instruction and performance in cognitive tasks. A wide variety of studies completed with children and adults showed a significant association between learning music and memory, spatial abilities, IQ, reading, and maths achievement (e.g. Philbrick and Mallory 1996;

Rauscher et al. 1997; Chan and Cheung 1998; Gromko and Poorman 1998; Costa-Giomi 1999; Taetle 1999: Bilhartz et al. 2000; Rauscher et al. 2000; Thompson et al. 2004; Zafranas 2004). By the year 2000, there was enough research to allow for integrated analyses of these findings. A series of meta-analyses concluded the following: music learning enhances the spatial-temporal performance of children during and up to 2 years following instruction (Hetland 2000); music instruction improves mathematical achievement in children (Vaughn 2000); and music students score higher in reading achievement tests (Butzlaff 2000). These conclusions were welcomed by music education advocates because they provided an attractive justification for supporting music programmes in schools. In fact, these conclusions couldn't have been disseminated at a more critical time for arts education in the United States. The passing of the No Child Left Behind Act of 2001 (i.e. NCLB 2001) by congress under President George W. Bush imposed unprecedented pressure on schools to achieve specific achievement goals. These goals have required that *all* students attending public schools meet the academic standards set by the state and measured by standardized assessments. The failure of schools to show progress towards this goal has resulted in reduced funding and eventually the closing of schools. To achieve such goals, schools have often increased the resources allocated to programmes that are subjected to the mandated assessments (e.g. language arts, maths, and sciences) and have reduced resources to programmes that are not (e.g. the arts). This may explain why music educators and the music industry capitalized on the research findings regarding the positive effects of music on children's cognitive abilities and academic achievement to promote music in the education of children.

As required by NCLB, schools started disclosing the average academic performance of their student population in state exams publicly. The analysis of these data shows that student enrolment in art courses is related to student drop-out rate, academic performance, and school attendance. For example, in Texas, schools rated as academically exemplary or recognized on the basis of student performance in the mandated state exams have more than 50% of students enrolled in art classes as opposed to 44% in schools classified as academically low performing (Academic Performance 2007). Similarly, student school attendance is higher at schools with a higher proportion of students registered in arts electives and lower at schools with a lower student participation in the arts. Not surprisingly, high school drop-out rate is lowest for schools with the highest art enrolment. Although these findings provide further evidence of the association between participation in school music and academic achievement, they do not necessarily indicate that music instruction produces academic gains, or increases student school attendance, or reduces drop-out behaviour. Alternative explanations for these findings will be discussed extensively in the next section of this chapter.

Other possible indications that music instruction benefits students intellectually can be found in the results of national assessments of students' achievement in language and maths. In the USA, thousands of college-bound high school students take standardized verbal and maths achievement tests as part of their college admission process (e.g. Scholastic Aptitude Test or SAT). Comparisons of the performance in these tests of students who had or had not participated in music courses during high school show very consistent results. Every year, the results highlight the academic superiority of those who had participated in music courses while in high school as compared to those who had not (e.g. Catterall 1998; College Board 2010). Additionally, it was found that the number of years of music engagement during secondary school is correlated to performance in these tests: The more semesters students choose music as an elective, the higher their scores in the SAT (College Board 2010). These findings have often been used in music education advocacy campaigns and are widely disseminated in the educational field as evidence of the intellectual benefits of music education. However, the data may be also interpreted in other ways that will be discussed later in the chapter.

There is further support for the existence of a strong relationship between students' performance in national academic achievement tests and engagement in music. A number of music education organizations have started disclosing the average tests' scores of the best music students in various states of the USA. These students are identified when they become members of All-State Ensembles through a rigorous statewide audition process completed annually. Being selected to be part of one of the All-State Ensembles is considered an honour and an indication of the high level of musicianship of the student. It was found that All-State students' scores in the SAT are higher than state averages (DeCarbo et al. 1990; Tobin 2005; Academic Performance 2007; Henry and Braucht 2007). For example, the Texas Music Educators Association's records for the year 2010 show that the average SAT score of students in the All-State String Orchestra is strikingly higher than the national and state averages (i.e. 2077, 1509, and 1467 respectively; TMEA 2010). Not surprisingly, most of these accomplished students report their intent in attending university upon high school graduation showing a distinct interest in academic pursuits. The Texas records for previous years and those of music educators associations in other states show the same trend. In summary, the statewide findings are in agreement with the national reports discussed earlier: music students, particularly those who excel in their music studies, score higher in standardized tests of academic achievement.

Summary of historical overview

The review of the extensive research conducted during the last hundred years on the relationship between music and intelligence or music and academic achievement shows a clear change in the purpose of the studies. Whereas early studies attempted to understand musical talent by determining the predictive value of intelligence on musical ability and music achievement, research completed during the last decades examined the relationship in the opposite direction by determining the predictive value of music instruction on intelligence and achievement. The shift to a more utilitarian view of the value of music that occurred throughout the twentieth century was not only reflected in the purpose of research studies but also in the reasons for providing students with music experiences. During times in which music programmes were at risk of being reduced or eliminated from schools, evidence regarding the intellectual benefits of music education became particularly valuable. Research on the contribution of music instruction to children's cognitive development has had clear impact on education and thus the wellbeing of children.

Who benefits from music instruction?

The results of studies showing an association between music instruction and cognitive abilities have often been taken as evidence that music lessons improve intelligence. Similarly, positive correlations between years of school arts instruction and scores in the SAT or between success in music studies and academic achievement have been interpreted as reflective of the intellectual benefits of music instruction. However, there are alternative explanations for these associations. It is possible that other personal or environmental factors mediate the relationship between music participation and intellectual abilities. Likely factors are those that characterize students who choose to study music, persevere for years, and are successful in learning an instrument. For example, in general, students who elect to participate in music activities are more academically capable than those who don't (Young 1971; Frakes 1985; Klinedinst 1991; Fitzpatrick 2006; McCrary and Ruffin 2006; Kinney, 2008, 2010). They are also different in other characteristics known to be related to superior academic performance such as socioeconomic status, parental education, and participation in extracurricular activities (Wolfe 1969; McCarthy 1980; Bowman and VanderArk 1982; Klinedinst 1991; Stewart 1991; Brandstrom and Wiklund 1996;

McNeal 1998; Phillips 2003; Albert 2006; Feldman and Matjasko 2007; National Endowment for the Arts 2009; Elpus and Abril 2011; Kinney 2010). Furthermore, those who persist in learning music for years are different from those who drop-out of lessons (Pruitt 1966; Mawbey 1973; McCarthy 1980; Klinedinst 1991; Cutietta and McAllister 1997; Coremblum and Marshall 1998; Costa-Giomi 2004, 2006; Costa-Giomi et al. 2005). And those who are more successful in learning an instrument are different from those who are less successful (Young 1971; Stancarone 1992; Davidson et al. 1996; Costa-Giomi and Sasaki 2003). In other words, the superior intellectual performance of students who choose, persist, and succeed in learning music may be the result of other educational opportunities in which they participate, or the characteristics of their parents and home environment, or certain personality traits that contribute to their intellectual development.

Characteristics of music students: academic achievement

In order to determine that participation in music instruction is the cause of the superiority of music students in cognitive and achievement tests it is first necessary to discard the possibility that such superiority preceded instruction. The lack of differences in academic achievement between music and non-music students *before* the onset of lessons and significant differences between them *after* a period of music instruction would support the idea that music learning contributes to children's intellectual development. But the results of studies that compared the academic achievement of students who did and did not take music courses failed to conform to this outcome. For example, data from students enrolled in middle school music electives at a large public school district in Ohio showed the expected trend regarding the academic advantage of the music students over others (Fitzpatrick 2006; Kinney 2008, 2010). However, this advantage was already evident in elementary school and thus, was prior to students' enrolment in middle school music electives. That the academic achievement in math, language, and science of students who later chose to study music were significantly higher than those who chose not to participate and that this academic difference between the two groups of students remained evident (and statistically significant) throughout the middle school years suggest that music programmes attract high academic achievers and not that music programmes improve student academic achievement.

Furthermore, not only does academic achievement play a significant role in predicting initial enrolment in instrumental programmes but it also becomes increasingly salient in predicting students' participation over time. Kinney (2010) studied theoretical models of prediction of students' decisions to enrol and persist in urban USA middle school band programmes. He focused on independent variables such as academic achievement, SES, family structure, mobility, ethnicity, and gender. One model predicted initial enrolment (i.e. sixth grade) and the other predicted retention (i.e. eighth grade enrolment). He found that academic achievement and family structure were the only significant predictors of initial enrolment decisions and that these two factors, in addition to SES, also predicted band retention. In other words, higher academically achieving students and those from two-parent or two-guardian homes were more likely to begin band instruction and continue participation during middle school and moreover, those from higher SES were more likely to remain in band for three years. The idea that participation in music lessons produces gains in academic achievement is not supported by the study. In fact the results show that academic achievement is a predictor of participation in music instruction and also of persistence in studying music.

Socioeconomic status

The studies completed in Ohio were based on the analysis of student music enrolment and academic achievement in public schools. This is important because it indicates that students did not have to pay to receive music instruction. However, even in this setting, there were significant differences in socioeconomic status between the students who elected and did not elect to study music and between those who persisted in learning an instrument and discontinued instruction (Fitzpatrick 2006; Kinney 2008, 2010). Those enrolled in the music programmes came from families with higher socioeconomic status (i.e. SES.). This conclusion does not apply only to Ohio or to the public school system but to many other educational settings as well. Investigations completed in public schools in other states (Pruitt 1966; Young 1971; Mawbey 1973; Klinedinst 1991; Nabb 1995; Corenblum and Marshall 1998; Rickels and Stauffer 2010;) or countries (Branstrom and Wilklund 1996), and in the private sector (Duke et al. 1997) have arrived to the same conclusion: Music programmes attract higher SES students. Data from a nationwide longitudinal study in the United States provide additional evidence supporting this conclusion. Music enrolment information from over 13,000 high school students in both public and private schools in the USA over a period of 6 years clearly shows that SES is significantly associated with music participation (Elpus and Abril 2011). Furthermore, adolescents from a higher SES are more likely to study music as an extracurricular activity than those from a lower SES (Feldman and Matjasko 2007). In summary, SES is related to participation in music instruction regardless of whether instruction is imparted in public or private schools or as a curricular or extracurricular activity.

It may come as no surprise then that schools serving students with higher SES have a higher enrolment in their music programmes than do lower SES schools (Costa-Giomi 2007, 2008; Costa-Giomi and Chapell 2007; Rickels and Stauffer 2010). The SES gap in music participation is greater for instrumental programmes than choral programmes and, within the instrumental programmes, it is more dramatic for orchestra than band courses (Nabb 1995; Braza and Porter 2001). Furthermore, the SES enrolment gap is greater for music than other arts (Nabb 1995). These findings and the ones presented earlier stress the pervasive association between music instruction and SES. High SES schools have higher music enrolments than low SES schools, and schools that serve a similar proportion of higher and lower SES students have music programmes with more of the former than the latter. These differences exist even in settings in which music instruction is provided as part of the public school curriculum rather than as a paid extracurricular activity. Given the known relationship between SES and achievement (e.g. Fitzpatrick 2006; Kinney 2008), and the now well-documented SES advantage of music students, one may speculate that the superior academic achievement of music participants is due to SES rather than music instruction. In fact, a recent study based on longitudinal data gathered from two large cohorts of children and adolescents concluded that music is not a predictor of achievement but rather a mediator of family background and student status and that music involvement varies systematically as a function of social class (Southgate and Roscigno 2009).

Family

There are other demographic characteristics besides socioeconomic status that differentiate children who participate and do not participate in music instruction. Students' race, sex, parental education, and family structure have also been found to be associated with music engagement. For example, a nationwide study of piano students in the USA showed that most children who take piano lessons are white Caucasian (80%), female (70%), have family incomes exceeding $40,000 per year (83%), live in two-parent households (84%), and have parents with college degrees (80%) (Duke et al. 1997). In other words, the profile of a typical private piano student is representative of a small and selective group of North-American children. The conclusion that children who participate in music come from a rather privileged environment is also supported by data gathered in American schools. Elpus and Abril (2011) analysed the demographic characteristics of 13,200 high school students participating in a longitudinal study. The 21% of students who chose to take music courses in school had a profile similar to the one described by Duke et al. (1993). Most of these students lived in two-parent families (79%), had family incomes above $40,000 (87%), and were predominantly female (61%) and white Caucasian (66%). Additionally, the authors found that parent's educational attainment was significantly associated with student enrolment in music ensembles. Children of parents with less than 2 years of post-secondary education were under-represented in music classes while those with parents who had earned a college degree were almost twice as likely to enrol in music ensembles than were other students. In summary, there are clear differences in the family environment of children who participate and do not participate in music instruction. That these differences are apparent not only in situations in which students are required to seek and pay for music lessons but also in situations in which music instruction is offered in public schools further supports the idea that music programmes attract children from a privileged population.

Characteristics of students who drop out

The selectivity of the children who are engaged in music lessons seems to get magnified over time because of a process of attrition that occurs throughout the years of instruction. Learning to play a musical instrument requires a long-term commitment. Regrettably, it is common for children to drop out of music instruction soon after starting lessons. For example, in Texas, there were approximately 225,000 students enrolled in middle school band in 2002 but only 90,000 in high school band. In other words, more than 75% of the students who started to learn to play a band instrument discontinued the lessons within 3 years. This drop-out rate is not exclusive of band instrument and can be observed in enrolment data in orchestra and choir programmes (Southwestern Musician 2004). Who drops out of lessons? Are the students who continue taking lessons different from those who discontinue them? Is there a process of selection that occurs systematically over time by which certain students discontinue participation in lessons? The answers to these questions are relevant to the discussion about the long-term effects of music instruction. If there is indeed a process of selection affecting who starts and persists in learning music, claims about the causal relationship between music instruction and intellectual abilities may then be questioned.

Indeed, research has identified many differences between students who persist and drop out of lessons. For example, initial music achievement differentiates children who persevere in taking piano lessons for three years from those who drop out of the lessons during the first 2 years of study (Costa-Giomi 2004) and SES and academic achievement are significant predictors of perseverance in music participation in school settings (Kinney 2010). Costa-Giomi (2004) also found behavioural differences between the children who dropped out or continued taking piano lessons for 3 years. The former missed more lessons, completed their piano homework to a lesser degree, and practised piano less time per week and throughout the years than did the latter. Other researchers have also concluded that motivation to learn an instrument, practice behaviours, and music achievement differentiates students who persevere and do not persevere in taking lessons (Pitts et al. 2000; McPherson and Davidson 2002). It is possible that the differences in practice routines and music achievement of children who persist in learning an instrument or discontinue music instruction are related to certain personality traits of the students. Costa-Giomi (2006) studied this hypothesis by observing children for 3 years as they started, continued, and discontinued piano lessons. They found that those who completed 3 years of lessons were significantly more disciplined than those who dropped out and that they tended to be more responsible and able to concentrate than the latter. These personality traits characterized the students even before they started learning an instrument and did not change as a result of participating in music instruction. In other words, the traits remained stable throughout the 3 years of lessons. It seems likely that the discipline, responsibility, and concentration of students who persevere in learning an instrument may explain their effective music practice behaviours and thus their superior music achievement. More important, these traits may also explain their superior performance in tests of intellectual ability and academic achievement.

Who benefits from music instruction? Summary

In summary, the findings regarding the characteristics of students who continue and discontinue music instruction indicate that there is in fact a process of selection that occurs over the years by which students with higher SES, motivation, discipline, responsibility, concentration, and music achievement persist in learning music while those with lower levels of motivation and SES and who are less disciplined and responsible drop-out of music lessons. The findings that there are demographic, personality, and behavioural characteristics that differentiate children who persevere in studying music and those who discontinue instruction are associated with superior academic performance is important to the present discussion because the purported effects of music instruction on academic achievement may be attributed simply to the fact that those who are less likely to excel in academics discontinue music studies. It is important to note that this process of selection occurs in addition to the one described earlier by which students from less privileged environments choose not to participate in music instruction. In other words, those who choose to study music come from a more privileged environment than those who don't. Furthermore, those who remain engaged in music have a more privileged environment than those who discontinue instruction. Such privileged environment may explain the intellectual superiority of children who take lessons.

Are the cognitive benefits of music instruction long lasting?

Longitudinal investigations that follow-up students who become engaged in music programmes as well as those who don't participate in formal instruction provide compelling evidence about the benefits of music participation. Such studies allow for critical comparisons in IQ or academic achievement scores between the groups prior to the start of lessons and after a number of months or years of music instruction. Most longitudinal studies conducted to date have been based on music interventions shorter than one year (Kokas 1969; Hurwitz 1975; Zuluaf 1993, 1994; Philbrick and Mallory 1996; Rauscher et al. 1997; Gromko and Poorman 1998; Taetle 1999; Graziano et al. 1999; Bilhartz et al. 2000; Hetland 2000; Persellin 2000; Rauscher and Zupan 2000; Rauscher et al. 2003; Schellenberg 2004; Thompson et al. 2004; Zafranas 2004). Their results showed that children participating in music instruction outperform those not involved in music in certain tests of cognitive abilities after weeks or months of music lessons. None of these studies continued observing children after the completion of the relatively short music intervention. Are the cognitive improvements attributed to music instruction long lasting? Are they permanent? Do the cognitive advantages outlast the treatment? Do the cognitive differences between music participants and non-participants increase throughout years of lessons? The answers to these questions are critical when discussing the contribution of music education to children's cognitive development and wellbeing. Regrettably, there is little conclusive evidence supporting the widespread belief that the intellectual benefits associated with music instruction are long lasting.

Neurological evidence

The belief that the intellectual benefits are long lasting may have been triggered by the results of neurological studies showing distinct structural and functional brain differences between musicians and non-musicians (Elbert et al 1995; Schlaug et al. 1995; Zatorre 1998; Pascual Leone 2001;

Pantev et al. 2001, 2003; Schlaug 2001; Gaser and Schlaug 2003; Hutchison et al. 2003; Bermudez and Zatorre 2005; Zatorre et al. 2007). The results of these studies suggest that music practice and learning produce structural and functional changes in the brain. These changes are often associated with improvements in the perception of sound but not with improvements in the processing of analytical or spatial information typically included in intelligence or academic achievement tests. In other words, the findings of neurological investigations simply explain the superiority of musicians (e.g. Pantev et al. 2001) and children engaged in music learning (e.g. Hyde et al. 2009) in tests of sound perception. Furthermore, a number of neurological studies that observed children over 6–8 months of music instruction failed to reveal other neurological changes or IQ improvements associated with the lessons (Schlaug et al. 2005; Hyde et al. 2009; Moreno et al. 2009) questioning the claim that music instruction makes children smarter.

Overall, neurological studies have shown that learning music early in life does produce structural changes in the brain (Elbert et al. 1995; Schlaug et al. 1995; Pantev et al. 2001, 2003; Pascual Leone et al. 2001; Hutchison et al. 2003) and that these changes are associated with performance in sound-related tasks (Schlaug et al. 2005; Hyde et al. 2009; Moreno et al. 2009). In other words, there is evidence that music instruction improves children's performance in sound-related tasks and that such improvements are reflected in structural changes in the brain. However, neurological studies have provided no evidence that music instruction increases children's IQ or produces structural brain changes that may be interpreted as conducive to improved performance in intelligence tests.

Behavioural evidence

On the other hand, longitudinal studies have shown clear cognitive benefits associated with music lessons during childhood (Kokas 1969; Hurwitz 1975; Zuluaf 1993, 1994; Mallory and Philbrick 1996; Rauscher et al. 1997; Gromko and Poorman 1998; Costa-Giomi 1999, 2004; Graziano 1999; Taetle 1999; Bilhartz, et al. 2000; Hetland 2000; Persellin 2000; Rauscher and Zupan 2000; Rauscher et al. 2003; Schellenberg 2004; Schlaug et al. 2005; Thompson et al. 2004; Zaffranas 2004; Johnson and Memmoth 2006; Forgeard et al. 2008). Children participating in a variety of music education programmes such as Orff instruction, singing lessons, Kindermusik, piano lessons, and Kodaly instruction outperformed those who do not in cognitive tests. As mentioned earlier, such improvements are observable after up to 1 year of music instruction. There have been very few attempts to determine whether such improvements last longer than 1 year. Those studies that did follow-up children longer than 1 year concluded that the cognitive improvements are only temporary (Costa-Giomi 1999; Costa-Giomi and Ryan 2007).

Costa-Giomi (1999, 2004; Costa-Giomi and Ryan 2007) completed a longitudinal study on the effects of piano instruction on children's cognitive abilities, self-esteem, and academic achievement. This study was different from similar longitudinal investigations because of the characteristics of the sample and the duration of the intervention. Whereas most studies focused on the cognitive benefits of participating in music instruction for less than a year, Costa-Giomi studied the effects of 3 years of music lessons. The selection of the sample was done is such a way as to address many of the concerns described earlier in the chapter, namely the selectivity of those who usually choose to study music and persevere in the study of an instrument. Many of the children lived with a single parent, had unemployed parents, and had parents with no postsecondary education. Boys and girls were randomly assigned to an experimental group and a control group at each of nine schools and seven schools were randomly assigned to either the experimental or control condition. Each child in the experimental group received, at no cost to the families, three years of individual piano instruction plus an acoustic piano. Children in the control group did not participate in individual music instruction for the duration of the project. The two groups of children were comparable in terms of musical ability, cognitive abilities, academic achievement in math and language, motor skills, and self-esteem according to the results of standardized tests administered prior to the start of the piano lessons (see Costa-Giomi 1999 or 2004).

The results of the study showed that the piano lessons improved children's general cognitive abilities and spatial abilities but that these improvements were only temporary (Costa-Giomi 1999). After 2 years of piano instruction, children in the experimental group obtained significantly higher total scores in the cognitive abilities test than did the children in the control group. The spatial scores of the experimental group were also significantly higher than those of the control group after 1 and 2 years of individual piano lessons. However, no differences in cognitive abilities were found between the groups after 3 years of instruction thus questioning the long-term effects of the lessons. Other findings of the study that point to the limitations of the cognitive benefits of music instruction were those regarding the magnitude of the effects: the temporary improvements in cognitive abilities attributed to the lessons were statistically significant but small. Additionally, no differences in the quantitative and verbal cognitive abilities of the two groups were found throughout the 3 years of the study.

A follow-up study conducted 7 years after the completion of the lessons corroborated the results regarding the limited and temporary benefits of music instruction on cognitive abilities. A sample of young men and women who had participated in the original study as part of the control or experimental groups completed a series of standardized tests of intelligence and immediate and delayed memory. The adults who had and had not taken lessons in childhood were comparable in critical variables such as musical ability, cognitive abilities, academic achievement, and motor skills as well as parental income and education according to data gathered when they were children and prior to the start of the lessons. The analyses of the 10-year follow-up data showed no differences in IQ or memory between the two groups of adults (Costa-Giomi and Ryan 2007). Of particular interest to the present discussion is the fact that the *temporary* improvements in cognitive abilities found in the original study were also found in this follow-up investigation. The analysis of the childhood data of the adults showed the lack of difference in cognitive abilities between the groups before the lessons, the cognitive advantages of the piano group after 1 year of instruction, and the lack of differences between the groups after 3 years of piano lessons. In other words, the findings of the original study completed with a large sample for 3 years were the same as those of the follow-up study completed with a reduced sample for 10 years: the initial cognitive gains attributed to music instruction become negligible over time.

Overall, the results of Costa-Giomi's study are in agreement with the findings of related research as they show that studying music for a short time (e.g. 1 year) does in fact improve performance in cognitive abilities tasks. But the results also indicate that these improvements are small and only temporary. In neither of the studies did the group receiving the lessons showed a permanent cognitive or achievement advantage over the group not receiving the lessons which suggests that participating in music instruction for longer periods of time (e.g. 3 years) does not necessarily result in longer-lasting or more pronounced cognitive benefits. What seems to be more consequential in terms of long-lasting improvements in IQ is the level of engagement in learning music. Costa-Giomi (1999) found that the improvement in cognitive abilities was dependent upon children's efforts in learning to play the instrument. In her study, piano teachers completed weekly reports about each student' practice routines and progress in the lessons. She found that after 3 years of lessons, 22% of the variance in cognitive improvements of the children receiving piano instruction was explained by their attendance at the lessons and time spent practising. This suggests that children who participated more actively in the process of learning the piano benefited to a greater extent than those who were less likely to attend the lessons and practice. While providing children with music lessons may produce a temporary boost in their cognitive development, it is the long-term and dedicated commitment to learning an instrument that may provide them with more lasting cognitive benefits.

Conclusions

In this chapter, I presented an overview of research on the intellectual benefits of music instruction and its implication to the education and, ultimately, the wellbeing of children. I discussed the evidence showing the selectivity of those who choose to learn music, persevere in their efforts, and are successful in performing an instrument. The multiple demographic and personal characteristics that differentiate those who remain engaged in music education and those who don't makes the study of the long-term cognitive benefits of music lessons very difficult. The difficulty lies in the need to randomize the sample into experimental and control groups to control for such differences, as well as in following up the complete sample for years. Not surprisingly, there are very few studies that have attempted to do so. The results of these few studies showed that the improvements in cognitive abilities test attributed to music lessons are only temporary and last no longer than 2 years.

On the other hand, the results of the many studies that observed children for a short period of time (i.e. up to 1 year), have shown convincing evidence that there are temporary cognitive benefits associated with music instruction. Such benefits include improvements in general IQ, spatial skills, and verbal tasks. Additionally, learning music produces structural and functional changes in the brain. Such changes are associated with improvements in sound processing, motor skill, and melodic and rhythmic discrimination. However, neurological investigations do not support the claim that music makes children smarted as the results have failed to show any neurological changes associated with improvements in IQ.

The finding that the intellectual benefits of music instruction are only temporary has important implications for the education of children. Providing children with music lessons gives them an intellectual advantage that is short-lived. Such advantage, however, may be valuable in certain therapeutic or educational settings that require observable short-term improvements. On the other hand, hoping for long-term cognitive benefits for all children involved in music lessons is an unrealistic expectation. Similarly, justifying the existence of music programmes on the basis of such intellectual advantage seems to be a misleading and ultimately ineffectual campaign. Doing so on the basis that good schools have music programmes seems a more reasonable and well-founded campaign.

It is important to note that the multiple studies conducted to date have shown no negative effects, short-term or long-term, on children's cognitive development or intellectual performance. This is important when one considers the effort and time that music students spend practising and attending lessons and rehearsals. It is clear that the time invested in learning music does not seem to decrease music students' dedication to academic pursuits and does not affect their academic achievement or performance in standardized tests or at school. Additionally, as is the case with every activity that requires long-term commitment, success in learning to play an instrument is dependent upon the level of personal motivation. The finding that the relationship between long-term cognitive benefits of music instruction and motivation becomes significant after 2 years of lessons suggests that in the long-term, music instruction may be intellectually beneficial to those truly committed to practising and learning an instrument. In other words, simply providing music lessons to children may have very limited effects on their intellectual development. Supporting children's interests and efforts in learning music may have more substantial and long lasting effects.

Acknowledgements

Supported by the National Piano Foundation and the University of Texas–Austin.

References

Academic Performance, Drop-Out Rates, and Attendance Rates in Texas Public Schools Correlated to Fine Arts Course Enrollment. (2007). An analysis of 2005–2007 data reported by Texas public school campuses completed by the Texas Music Educators Association and the Texas Coalition for Quality Arts Education (unpublished report).

Albert, D.J. (2006). Socioeconomic status and instrumental music: What does the research say about the relationship and its implications? *Update: Applications of Research in Music Education* (Online), **25**(1).

Antrim, D.K. (1945). Do musical talents have higher intelligence? *Etude*, **63**, 127–8.

Beckham, A.S. (1942). *A study of social background and music ability of superior Negro children. Journal of Applied Psychology*, **26**(2), 210–17.

Berel, M., Diller, L., and Orgel, M. (1971). Music as facilitator for visual motor sequencing tasks in children with cerebral palsy. *Developmental Medicine & Child Neurology*, **13**, 335–42.

Bermudez, P. and Zatorre, R.J. (2005). Differences in gray matter between musicians and nonmusicians. *Annals of the New York Academy of Sciences*, **1060**, 395–9.

Bienstock, S.F. (1942). A predictive study of musical achievement. *The Pedagogical Seminary and Journal of Genetic Psychology*, **61**, 135–45.

Bilhartz, T., Bruhn, R., and Olson, J. (2000). The effects of early music training on child cognitive development. *Journal of Applied Developmental Psychology*, **20**, 615–36.

Bowman, B. and VanderArk, S. (1982). The relationships of music aptitude, music background, self-esteem, and social status of the attitudes of elementary students towards music. In: P. Sink (ed.) *Research symposium on the psychology and acoustics of music*, pp. 56–62. Lawrence, KA: University of Kansas.

Brandstrom, S. and Wiklund, C. (1996). The social use of music and music education. *Canadian Music Educator*, **37**(3), 33–6.

Braza, M. and Porter, K. (2001). High school music program participation: Evidence from the Grammy Foundation Signature School Award applications and a review of literature. Available at: http://hems. aed.org/case_studies/grammy/index.html.

Butzlaff, R. (2000). Can music be used to teach reading? *Journal of Aesthetic Education*, **34**(3–4), 167–78.

Catterall, J.S. (1998). Involvement in the arts and success in secondary school [Monograph]. *American for the Arts*, **9**.

Chan, A. and Cheung, M. (1998). Music training improves verbal memory. *Nature*, **396**, 128.

College Board (2010). http://professionals.collegeboard.com/data-reports-research/sat/cb-seniors-2010 (accessed 8 August 2010).

Corenblum, B. and Marshall, E. (1998). The band played on: Predicting students' intentions to continue studying music. *Journal of Research in Music Education*, **46**, 128–40.

Costa-Giomi, E. (1999). The effects of three years of piano instruction on children's cognitive development. *Journal of Research in Music Education*, **47**, 198–212.

Costa-Giomi, E. (2004). 'I do not want to study piano!' Early predictors of student dropout behavior. *Bulletin of the Council for Research in Music Education*, **161/162**, 57–64.

Costa-Giomi, E. (2006). The personality of children who study piano, drop out of piano lessons, or never play a note: a longitudinal study. Paper presented at the meeting of the Texas Music Educators Association, February, San Antonio, TX.

Costa-Giomi, E. (2007). Music education programs in Texas: Sources of inequalities. *Southwestern musician*, 54–7.

Costa-Giomi, E. (2008). Characteristics of elementary music programs in urban schools: What money can buy. *Bulletin of the Council for Research in Music Education*, **177**, 19–28.

Costa-Giomi, E. and Chappell, E. (2007). Characteristics of band programs in a large urban school district: Diversity or inequality? *Journal of Band Research*, **42** (2), 1–18.

Costa-Giomi, E. and Ryan, C. (2007). The benefits of music instruction: What remains years later. Paper presented at the Symposium for Research in Music Behavior, March, Baton Rouge, LO.

Costa-Giomi, E. and Sasaki, W. (2003). What differentiates high and low achievement piano students? Teacher and student behaviors during three years of lessons. Paper presented at the International Symposium for Research in Music Behavior, April, Chicago, IL.

Costa-Giomi, E., Flowers, P.J., and Sasaki, W. (2005). Piano lessons of beginning students who persist or drop out. *Journal of Research in Music Education*, **53**(3), 234–47.

Cramer, K.M., Million, E., and Perreault, L.A. (2002). Perceptions of musicians: Gender stereotypes and social role theory. *Psychology of Music*, **30**(2), 164–74.

Cutietta, R.A. and McAllister, P.A. (1997). Student personality and instrumental participation, continuation and choice. *Journal of Research in Music Education*, **45**(2), 282–94.

Davidson, J.W., Howe, M.J.A., Moore, D.G., and Sloboda, J. A. (1996). xx. *British Journal of Developmental Psychology*, **14**(4), 399–412.

DeCarbo, N., Fiese, R., and Boyle, D. (1990). A profile of all-state instrumentalists. *Research Perspectives in Music Education*, **1**, 32–40.

Duke, R.A., Flowers, P., and Wolfe, D. (1997). The National Piano Project: Teachers', Parents' and Students' Perceptions of the Role of Piano Instruction in Students' Lives. *Bulletin of the Council for Research in Music Education*, **132**, 51–85.

Gromko, J.E. and Poorman, A.S. (1998). The effect of music training on preschoolers' spatial-temporal task performance. *Journal of Research in Music Education*, **46**(2), 173–81.

Elbert, T., Pantev, C., Wienbruch, C., Rockstroh, B., and Taub, E. (1995). Increased cortical representation of the fingers of the left hand in string players. *Science*, **270**, 305–7.

Elias, M. (1994, August 15). Music lessons may open mind to math, science. *USA TODAY*, D1.

Elpus, K., and Abril, C.R. (2011). High school music students in the United States: A demographic profile. *Journal of Research in Music Education*, **59**(2), 128–145.

Farnsworth, P.R. (1946). Chapter IV: School instruction in Music. *Review of Educational Research*, **16**, 182–90.

Feldman, A.F., and Matjasko, J.L. (2007). Profiles and portfolios of adolescent school-based extracurricular activity participation. *Journal of Adolescence*, **30**(2), 313–32.

Fitzpatrick, K.R. (2006). The effect of instrumental music participation and socioeconomic status on Ohio fourth-, sixth-, and ninth-grade proficiency test performance. *Journal of Research in Music Education*, **54**, 73–84.

Fracker, G.C. and Howard, V.M. (1928). Correlation between intelligence and musical talent among university students. *Psychological Monographs*, **39**, 157–61.

Frakes, L. (1985). Differences in music achievement, academic achievement, and attitude among participants, dropouts, and nonparticipants in secondary school music. *Dissertation Abstracts International*, **46**(2A), 370. (University Microfilms No. AAC8507938.)

Gaser, C. and Schlaug, G. (2003). Brain structures differ between musicians and non-musicians. *Journal of Neuroscience*, **23**, 9240–5.

Graziano, A.B., Peterson, M., and Shaw, G.L. (1999). Enhanced learning of proportional math through music training and spatial temporal reasoning. *Neurological Research*, **21**, 139–52.

Graves, S.L. (2009). Albert Sidney Beckham: The First African American School Psychologist. *School Psychology International*, **30**(1), 5–23.

Hassler, M. (1992). Creative musical behavior and sex hormones: Musical talent and spatial abilities in the two sexes. *Psychoneuroendocrinology*, **17**, 55–70.

Hassler, M., Birbaumer, N., and Feil, A. (1985). Musical talent and visual-spatial abilities: A longitudinal study. *Psychology of Music*, **13**, 99–113.

Henry, M. and Braucht, M. (2007). Are all-state musicians our future music educators? *Southwestern Musician*, November, 36–7.

Hetland, L. (2000). Learning to make music enhances spatial reasoning. *Journal of Aesthetic Education*, **34**, 179–238.

Hollingworth, L. (1926). Musical sensitivity of children who test above 135 IQ (Standford-Binet). *Journal of Educational Psychology*, **17**, 95–109.

Hurwitz, I., Wolff, P., Bortnick, B., and Kokas, K. (1975). Nonmusical effects of the Kodaly music curriculum in primary grade children. *Journal of Learning Disabilities*, **8**(3), 45–52.

Hutchison, S., Lee, L.H., Gaab, N., and Schlaug, G. (2003). Cerebellar volume of musicians. *Cerebral Cortex*, **13**, 943–49.

Hyde, K.L., Lerch, J., Norton, A., Forgeard, M., Winner, E., Evans, A.C., *et al.* (2009). Musical training shapes structural brain development. *The Journal of Neuroscience*, **29**(10), 3019–25.

Johnson, C.M. and Memmott, J.E. (2006). Examination of relationships between participation in school music programs of differing quality and standardized test results. *Journal of Research in Music Education*, **54**, 293–307.

Karma, K. (1979). Musical, spatial and verbal abilities. *Bulletin of the Council for Research in Music Education*, **59**(13), 50–53.

Kinney, D.W. (2008). Selected demographic variables, school music participation and achievement test scores of urban middle school students. *Journal of Research in Music Education*, **56**, 145–61.

Kinney, D. (2010). Selected nonmusic predictors of urban students' decisions to enroll and persist in middle school band programs. *Journal of Research in Music Education*, **57**, 334–50.

Klein, K. (2009). Disney's ingenious refund for Baby Einstein. *Los Angeles Times, Opinion*, 28 October. http://opinion.latimes.com/opinionla/ (accessed 10 February 2010).

Klinedinst, R. (1991). Predicting performance achievement and retention of fifth-grade instrumental students. *Journal of Research in Music Education*, **39**, 225–38.

Kokas, K. (1969). Psychological testing in Hungarian music education. *Journal of Research in Music Education*, **17**, 125–34.

Mawbey, W.E. (1973). Wastage from instrumental classes in schools. *Psychology of Music*, **1**, 33–43.

Mason, S. (1986). Relationship among mathematical, musical, and spatial abilities. Unpublished doctoral dissertation, University of Georgia, Athens, GA.

McCarthy, J. (1980). Individualized instruction, student achievement, and dropout in an urban elementary instrumental music program. *Journal of Research in Music Education*, **28**, 59–69.

McCrary, J. and Ruffin, M. (2006). Seventh-grade music ensemble participants' and non-ensemble participants' academic achievement and school attendance. Paper presented at MENC's 60th National Biennial In-Service Conference, April, Salt Lake City, UT.

McNeal, R. (1998). High school extracurricular activities: Closed structures and stratifying patterns of participation. *Journal of Educational Research*, **91**(3), 183–91.

McPherson, G.E. and Davidson, J.W. (2002). Musical practice: mother and child interactions during the first year of learning an instrument. *Music Education Research*, **4**(1), 141–56.

Moreno, S., Marques, C., Santos, A., Santos, M., Castro, S. L., and Besson, M. (2009). Musical training influences linguistic abilities in 8-year-old children: More evidence for brain plasticity. *Cerebral Cortex*, **19**(3), 712–23.

Nabb, D.B. (1995). Music performance program enrollment and course availability for educationally disadvantaged versus non-educationally disadvantaged high school students in Texas. *Dissertation Abstracts International Section A: Humanities & Social Sciences*, **56**, 1701.

National Center for Educational Statistics. (1998). *The NAEP 1997 arts report card (NCES 1999–486)*. Washington, DC: U.S. Department of Education, Office of Educational Research and Improvement.

National Endowment for the Arts. (2009). *Arts participation 2008: Highlights from a national survey.* Washington, DC: National Endowment for the Arts.

Norton, A., Winner, E., Cronin, K., Overy, K., Lee, D. J., and Schlaug, G. (2005). Are there pre-existing previous neural, cognitive, or motoric markers for musical ability? *Brain and Cognition*, **59**, 124–34.

Pantev, C., Engelien, A., Candia, V., and Elbert, T. (2001). Representational cortex in musicians. Plastic alterations in response to musical practice. *Annals of the New York academy of sciences*, **930**, 300–14.

Pantev, C., Ross, B., Fujioka, T., Trainor, L. J., Schulte, M., and Schulz, M. (2003). Music and learning-induced cortical plasticity. *Annals of The New York Academy Of Sciences*, **999**, 438–50.

Pascual-Leone, A. (2001). The brain that plays *music* and is changed by it. *Annals of the New York academy of sciences*, **930**, 315–29.

Persellin, D.C. (2000). The effect of activity-based music instruction on spatial-temporal task performance of young children. *Early Childhood Connections*, **6**, 21–29.

Philbrick, K. and Mallory, M. (1996). Music and the hemispheres: stimulating brain development through music education. Paper presented at the meeting of the Music Educators National Conference, April, Kansas City.

Phillips, S. (2003). Contributing factors to music attitude in sixth-, seventh-, and eighth-grade students. Unpublished doctoral dissertation, University of Iowa, Iowa City, IO.

Pitts, S., Davidson, J., and McPherson, G. (2000). Models of success and failure in instrumental learning: case studies of young players in the first 20 months of learning. *Bulletin of the Council of Research in Music Education*, **146**, 51–69.

Pruitt, J.S. (1966). A study of withdrawals from beginning instrumental music programs in selected schools of the school district of Greenville County, South Carolina. *Dissertation Abstracts International*, **27**(4A), 1075.

Rauscher, F. and Zupan, M.A. (2000). Classroom keyboard instruction improves kindergarten children's spatial-temporal performance: A field experiment. *Early Childhood Research Quarterly*, **15**, 215–28.

Rauscher, F., Shaw, G., and Ky, N. (1993). Music and spatial task performance. *Nature*, **365**, 611.

Rauscher, F., Shaw, G., Levine, L.J. and Ky, K.N. (1994). Music and Spatial Task Performance: A Causal Relationship. Paper presented at the American Psychological Association 102nd Annual Convention, August, Los Angeles: CA.

Rauscher, F., Shaw, G., Levine, L., Wright, E., Dennis, W. and Newcomb, R. (1997). Music training cause long-term enhancement of preschool children's spatial-temporal reasoning. *Neurological Research*, **19**, 2.

Rickels, D.A. and Stauffer, S.L. (2010). Access, equity, and effectiveness: Challenging the music education paradigm. Paper presented at the 23rd International Seminar on Research in Music Education, July, Changchun/Beijing, China.

Ross, V.R. (1936). Relationship between intelligence, scholastic achievement, and musical talent. *Journal of Juvenile Research*, **20**, 47–64.

Seashore, C.E. (1919). *The Psychology of Musical Talent.* New York: Silver Burdett Co.

Seashore, C.E. and Mount, G.H. (1918). Correlation of factors in musical talent and training. *University of Iowa Studies in Psychology*, **7**, 47–92.

Schellenberg, E.G. (2004). Music lessons enhance IQ. *Psychological Science*, **15**, 511–14.

Schellenberg, E.G. (2006). Long-term positive associations between music lessons and IQ. *Journal of Education Psychology*, **98**, 457–68.

Schlaug G. (2001). The brain of musicians. A model for functional and structural adaptation. *Annals of the New York Academy of Science*, **930**, 281–99.

Schlaug, G., Jancke, L., Huang, Y. and Steinmetz, H. (1995). In vivo evidence of structural brain asymmetry in musicians. *Science*, **267**, 699.

Schlaug, G., Norton, A., Overy, K. and Winner, E. (2005). Effects of music training on the child's brain and cognitive development. *Annals of the New York Academy of Science*, **1060**, 219–30.

Science Daily (2010). Mozart's Music Does Not Make You Smarter, Study Finds, 10 May. http://www.sciencedaily.com/releases/2010/05/100510075415.htm (accessed 10 May, 2010).

Smith, C. (1997). Access to string instruction in American public schools. *Journal of Research in Music Education*, **45**, 650–62.

Southgate, D.E. and Roscigno, V. J. (2009). The impact of music on childhood and adolescent achievement. *Social Science Quarterly*, **90**(1), 4–21.

Stancarone, M. (1992). The role of music aptitude, fine motor skills, coding, ability, behavioral and academic achievement in predicting achievement in instrumental music. *Dissertation Abstracts International*, **53**(3-B), 1596.

Stewart, C. (1991). Who takes music? Investigating access to high school music as a function of social and school factors. *Dissertation Abstracts International*, **52**(10), 3554A.

Taetle, L.D. (1999). The effects of music instruction on the spatial ability of kindergarten children. Unpublished doctoral dissertation. University of Arizona.

Thompson, W., Schellenberg, E.G., and Husain, G. (2004). Perceiving prosody in speech: Do music lessons help? *Emotion*, **4**, 46–64.

TMEA (2010). http://www.tmea.org/programs/all-state/average-sat (accessed 8 August 2010).

Tobin, R.N. (2005). A study of the music, academic, leadership, and extracurricular achievements of Massachusetts all-state participants. *Research and Issues in Music Education*, **3**. On-line journal, availabl at: http://www.stthomas.edu/rimeonline/vol3/index.htm

Vaughn, K. (2000). Music and mathematics: modest support for the oft-claimed relationship. *Journal of Aesthetic Education*, **34**(3–4), 149–66.

Waggoner, T. (2004). New default high school graduation plan: How could this affect your classroom? *Southwestern Musician*, **73**(2), 52–54.

Wheeler, L.R. and Wheeler, V.D. (1951). xxx. *The intelligence of music students*, **42**, 223–30.

Wolfe, E.E. (1969). Relationships between selected factors and participation and non-participation in instrumental music in the Cincinnati Public Schools. *Dissertation Abstracts International*, **30**, 2565A–6A.

Wolff, K. (1978). The nonmusical outcomes of music education: A review of the literature. *Bulletin of the Council for Research in Music Education*, **55**, 1–27.

Young, W. (1971). The role of musical aptitude, intelligence, and academic achievement in predicting the musical attainment of elementary instrumental music students. *Journal of Research in Music Education*, **19**, 385–98.

Zafranas, N. (2004). Piano keyboard training and the spatial-temporal development of young children attending kindergarten classes in Greece. *Early Child Development and Care*, **17**, 199–211.

Zatorre, R.J. (1998). Functional specialization of human auditory cortex for musical processing. *Brain*, **121**, 1817–18.

Zatorre, R.J., Chen, J. L., and Penhune, V. B. (2007). When the brain plays music: auditory-motor interactions in music perception and production. *Nature Review of Neuroscience*, **8**, 547–58.

Zuluaf, M. (1993/1994). Three-year experiment in extended music teaching in Switzerland: The different effects observed in a group of French-speaking pupils. *Bulletin of the Council for Research in Music Education*, **119**, 11–121.

Chapter 24

Health Promotion in Higher Music Education

Jane Ginsborg, Claudia Spahn, and Aaron Williamon

As we have seen throughout this book, there is considerable evidence that both listening to music and making music can have significant positive effects upon wellbeing and health. In this chapter we consider the potentially deleterious effects on performers of making music. These have been shown to include occupational stress, musculoskeletal disorders, and non-musculoskeletal disorders including performance anxiety. Such problems seem to be attributable, in part, to performers' lifestyles when they were students, according to the findings of research exploring music performance students' attitudes to health, health-promoting lifestyles, self-reported experiences of ill health, and levels of fitness. While many music colleges and university music departments recognize that it is important for health promotion to be prioritized within the curriculum, we conclude this chapter by arguing that the changes in training for musicians should be made from the earliest stages, so that they learn not only to prevent injury and avoid other disorders, but also to enhance their health and wellbeing.

It is worth noting that health was defined by the World Health Organization (WHO) in 1948 as 'a state of complete physical, mental and social wellbeing and not merely the absence of disease or infirmity' (WHO, 2006). This suggests that health includes wellbeing, although the distinction is often made between physical or physiological health and psychological wellbeing (see MacDonald et al., Chapter 1, present volume), and indeed researchers have become increasingly interested over the past decade in the factors underlying wellbeing and happiness (e.g. Seligman and Csikszentmihalyi 2000; Diener 2000; Diener and Seligman 2002), including mood (Robinson 2000), and the relation of these factors to health (Fredrickson 2000).

There is a great deal of evidence that music is important to wellbeing. Background music, for example, can have positive effects on the health and wellbeing of those who do not identify themselves as musicians (see Hallam, Chapter 32, present volume), and so can listening to music in everyday situations (see Västfjäll et al., Chapter 27, present volume) as well as more formal contexts. It can induce emotional states (Juslin and Laukka 2004), from 'peak experiences' (Panzarella 1980) involving strong emotions (Gabrielsson 2002) to mood (Västfjäll 2002), particularly when self-selected (Haake 2006; Laukka 2007). Furthermore, it decreases stress-related arousal (Davis and Thaut 1989), promotes relaxation (Pelletier 2004) and can reduce blood pressure (Chaffin et al. 2004). Making music, too, has benefits for health and wellbeing, as reported in the research outlined by Stige (Chapter 14, this volume) perhaps to an even greater extent than listening (Kreutz et al. Chapter 30, this volume).

Deleterious effects of music-making on professional musicians' health and wellbeing

Professional music-making places extremely high demands on the performer, which—as we shall see—constitutes a potential risk to health. Such risks are particularly threatening to the development and/or maintenance of musicians' careers; for this reason the prevention of health problems is a key theme of the present chapter. There is a vast literature on the topic of disorders associated with music performance.[1] In this section, we highlight studies using large sample sizes and representative studies investigating the prevalence of different music-related disorders. Further information on the epidemiology of such disorders can be found in the relevant literature on music and medicine (Sataloff et al. 2010; Spahn et al. 2011).

Occupational health studies show that 50–75% of all professional musicians suffer from a medical condition related to their activity as performers (Fishbein et al. 1988; Blum 1995; Zaza 1998; Roset-Llobet et al. 2000). About half of these suffer from chronic pain, which may or may not be psychosomatic. The first comprehensive survey drawing attention to the problems of professional musicians was carried out in 1987 in the USA, during the International Conference of Symphony Orchestras. Of the 2212 orchestral players questioned, 47% reported pain in the back and cervical spine, around 25% reported pain in the shoulder, arm, or hand, and 39% reported psychological problems including performance anxiety, depression, sleep disturbance, and fear (Fishbein et al. 1988).

The strain on musicians' health that can be attributed to playing varies with instrument and repertoire. According to the literature, violinists and viola players endure the greatest amount of stress (Fishbein et al. 1988; Manchester 1988; Middlestadt and Fishbein 1988; Manchester and Flieder 1991; Larsson et al. 1993; Zaza and Farewell 1997; Pak and Chesky 2001; Davies and Mangion 2002). While it may be that the literature is biased—there are more violinists and viola players in orchestras than any other group of instrumentalists, so they are investigated more often—it is also the case that, aside from pianists and other keyboard players, they practise more than any other group of musicians (Jørgensen 1997) and are therefore at high risk of problems arising from overuse.

This research identifies a number of protective factors that suggest potential mechanisms for preventing or at least reducing risks to performers' health. Those that are under the control of the musician include knowledge of responsible health behaviour, self-awareness in relation to physical condition and fitness, positive coping mechanisms for dealing with stress, and a healthy attitude towards the musical profession so that the individual does not risk his or her health in attempting to meet unreasonable demands. All instrumentalists, however, have to face the challenges posed by the interaction between their own body, taking into account the length and proportions of their upper extremities, for example, and the characteristics of their instrument; they should find an optimal playing position, making use of ergonomic aids where available (e.g. straps, chin-rests, etc.) so as to reduce physical risks (Cayea and Manchester 1998; Zetterberg et al. 1998; Barton and Feinberg 2008).

It is difficult, however, to avoid risk factors beyond the individual musician's control, such as inadequate conditions in the workplace and the psychosocial stress that may arise from working for long hours in close proximity to colleagues. This is particularly the case for female orchestral musicians who can find it difficult to gain acceptance by their colleagues in the predominantly male world of the professional orchestra (Allmendinger and Hackman 1996); also, they often take on the responsibility of combining work with family life to a greater extent than their male colleagues. Such risk factors may only be reduced by efforts to improve performers' working environments made at the institutional level via trades unions, for example, and musicians' professional bodies.

The musician's own constitution, physical and psychological, is also to a certain extent beyond the individual's control. Brandfonbrener (1990), for instance, found that musicians with

---

[1] See, for example, http://www.musicianshealth.co.uk/links.html (accessed 23 November 2010).

hyperflexibility are more at risk of developing symptoms arising from overuse of their locomotor system. It is vital for musicians to have effective strategies and techniques for staying healthy from the beginning of their professional lives, since ageing affects everyone. Many older musicians, after 20 years or more in the profession, experience physical symptoms affecting their ability to perform, or psychological symptoms such as reduced attention span. Those who take effective measures early in their careers to prevent such deterioration later on are at an advantage compared with those who do not take such measures (Zander and Spahn 2006).

According to Dawson (2003), musicians' most common complaints relate to the locomotor system, often diagnosed as tendonitis or muscular strain syndrome of the upper extremity (Schuppert and Wagner 1996). The causes lie mainly in the overuse that the body or certain body parts (especially soft tissue) have to endure, but also in the psychological stress generated by the high pressure of competition and by the high standards performers have both to live up to and expect from themselves. Internal, psychological conflicts are often manifested in the form of physical symptoms; this is known as somatization (Spahn et al. 2001a). Neurological disorders comprise mainly nerve compression syndromes and focal dystonia, a condition that is specifically related to the movements made while playing the instrument (Altenmüller and Jabusch 2006).

Another common complaint (Dawson 2003) is emotional strain (Marchant-Haycox and Wilson, 1992), typically manifesting as stage fright or (music) performance anxiety (Robson et al. 1995; Spahn 2006). Whether musicians simply learn to cope with it (Brodsky 1996), or seek treatment, depends to a large extent on the severity of their symptoms and the extent to which they affect performance. It is very important, however, that young musicians are prepared, in the course of their higher music education, for successful careers. This preparation should include learning about, preventing and mitigating the effects of performance anxiety, since problems can occur without warning at any time and continue throughout professional life (Fishbein et al. 1988).

While it is possible in principle to use behavioural methods to reduce symptoms, it is necessary in practice to address underlying cause(s) as well as symptoms. Music performance anxiety has been attributed variously to social phobia (Cox and Kenardy 1993), trait anxiety, and perfectionism (Kenny et al. 2003), although all of these are likely to produce maladaptive cognitions which, in turn, play an important role in the development of performance anxiety (Steptoe and Fidler 1987; Möller and Castringius 2005). Even though some studies have revealed no significant correlation between musicians' reported experiences of anxiety and their physical symptoms (Craske and Craig 1984; Abel and Larkin 1990; Fredrikson and Gunnarsson 1992; Spahn et al. 2010), we would argue that cognitions and physical symptoms can interact in such a way that they reinforce each other, and that altering cognitions appropriately can reduce symptoms. Given the variety of causes and their interactions with each other, however, and the nature of their effects on music-making (Kenny, 2011), we recommend that a range of therapeutic approaches be made available to students—including behavioural, psychoanalytic, biodynamic and above all the use of cognitive strategies—and indeed that they should be combined and integrated where possible and appropriate, since this has been shown empirically to be most effective (Spahn et al. 2011).

In addition, orchestral musicians are subject to partial hearing loss and tinnitus, due to enormously high sound levels both in their individual practice and in the orchestra (Backus et al. 2007; Richter et al. 2007; Backus and Williamon 2009). Finally, orchestral musicians aged 35–49 years were found to be more likely than their younger colleagues to reveal attitudes towards their profession associated with a high risk of burn-out (Voltmer et al. 2008).

Music performance students' experiences of ill health

The success with which professional musicians tackle the challenges of their chosen occupation is likely to depend on the extent to which they take responsibility for their health and wellbeing, and on the habits formed early in the course of their training. Several studies undertaken by the authors of this chapter have explored music performance students' experiences of ill health in the context of students' psychological characteristics and self-reported health-promoting lifestyles (Spahn et al. 2001a,b, 2002, 2004; Kreutz et al. 2008, 2009; Ginsborg et al. 2009). We begin by summarizing the evidence relating to music performance students' experiences of ill health.

Guptill et al. (2000) and Spahn et al. (2002) suggest that 68–88% of music performance students had suffered from health-related problems during their pre-tertiary music training, and 25% start their tertiary studies with health-related problems (Spahn et al. 2004). Furthermore, 43% of music performance students experience problems affecting their ability to perform during their degree courses (Zaza 1992). For this reason, 45% of 257 music performance students at a German music university surveyed by Spahn et al. (2002) reported seeking professional help during their studies.

In two subsequent studies Spahn et al. (2004) showed that 32% of music performance students reporting locomotor problems suffered from back pain, 26% from pain in the shoulders and neck, 17% in the arms, and 11% in the hands and fingers. Twelve per cent had taken painkillers (Spahn 2006). In the latter study, Spahn used the AVEM questionnaire (Schaarschmidt and Fischer 2003) to assess risk profiles for burnout and other difficulties preventing students from continuing with their studies. In a third of cases, strong identification with the act of performing music, combined with great ambition and insufficient capacity for self-detachment, was associated with a risk pattern characterized by excessively heightened stress and unstable performance levels ('risk pattern A'). Such a pattern may be linked to the experience of performance anxiety, a topic of great concern for educators since it is a recurring psychological problem for music performance students.

Kreutz et al. (2008) also carried out a survey of 273 music performance students in the UK. More than half of the respondents reported musculoskeletal and non-musculoskeletal symptoms severe enough to interfere with the quality of practice and performance, as perceived by the students themselves. Generally, the strongest predictors of impaired practice and performance were pain in the elbow and upper part of the arms, and pain in the left hand and right lower arm and hand. Other factors included pain along the spine, fatigue, and the orofacial musculature.

Health-conscious behaviours

Evidence of music performance students' attitudes to health and health-conscious behaviours, on the basis of their responses to the Health Promoting Lifestyle Inventory (HPLP II: Walker et al. 1987), suggests that they were more likely to attend to their psychosocial and nutritional needs and less likely to take responsibility for their own health, manage stress effectively and participate in recreational physical activity. Nevertheless, they reported greater self-efficacy (Schwarzer and Jerusalem, 1995) and self-regulation (Schwarzer et al. 1999) than the general population. Correlational analyses suggested that students with high levels of self-efficacy were more likely to have a healthy lifestyle (Kreutz et al. 2009).

These findings add to those of Spahn et al. (2002) who found that half of the music performance students in their German study reported taking measures to prevent ill health. A total of 38% regularly practised some kind of sport, 16% employed relaxation techniques, and 9% used the Alexander Technique or the Feldenkrais method. Psychological measures were rarely mentioned by the students. Yet these activities cannot be defined unambiguously as preventive, since only 6% of the students interviewed reported no health problems.

What factors underlie health-conscious behaviour? Mullen and Suls (1982) suggest that self-attention permits faster and more accurate assessment of one's own condition and therefore the taking of appropriate measures where necessary. Accordingly, Spahn and Zschocke (2002) investigated the role of attention to the self in health-conscious behaviour by asking 197 music performance students to complete the Dispositional Self Consciousness Questionnaire (Filipp and Freudenberg 1989). Higher-scoring respondents were more strongly motivated to take preventive measures. At the same time, however, they were also more likely to report suffering from psychological problems. Spahn et al. (2005) followed-up this study by assessing 326 music performance students' attitudes towards illness and health by means of the Locus of Control (LOC) Inventory for Illness and Health (Lohaus and Schmitt 1989), and comparing them with those of medical students and other young people of the same age. Music performance students' scores were highest for 'internal' LOC (and higher than those of their peers), intermediate for 'powerful others' and lowest for 'chance' LOC. Thus they were less likely to be fatalistic, and more likely to take responsibility for their own health, either independently or by following someone else's example. This study concluded that previous playing-related problems, high 'powerful others' combined with low 'chance' LOC, and the fact of being a string player or a singer, all predicted behaviour in relation to health promotion and the prevention of ill health.

Several studies involving the comparison of music performance and non-music performance students have been undertaken. Miller et al. (2002) found that string players and pianists at a UK conservatoire were five times as likely to experience upper limb pain as non-music performance students, and that this was associated with years of experience of playing, daily practice time, and previous injury. Spahn et al. (2004) showed that music performance students are more likely than students of medicine and sport to begin their studies with physical problems. They are also more likely to report psychological issues such as heightened anxiety. Similarly, when their risk profiles were compared to those of students of medicine, sport and psychology, using the AVEM questionnaire to assess likelihood of burnout and other difficulties, a larger proportion of music performance students showed risk pattern A (see above: Spahn 2006).

In a study following-up those of Kreutz et al. (2008, 2009), findings for music performance students were compared with those for non-music performance students at two UK universities (Ginsborg et al. 2009). At one institution the respondents were studying biomedical sciences, and at the other they were studying nursing and midwifery ('health'). The overall scores of the music performance students on the HPLP II were significantly lower than those of the health students overall, as were their scores on health responsibility, physical activity and spiritual growth. They also scored significantly lower for self-regulation and self-efficacy. Music performance students gave lower ratings for their present state of health than the health students, and reported musculoskeletal symptoms experienced during the previous week at more sites on the body (it should be noted that the music performance students were asked to report those that were severe enough to interfere with the quality of practice and performance, while the health students reported those that interfered with the quality of academic study and clinical practice). In addition, music performance students gave higher ratings for the severity of these symptoms than the health students, overall and, specifically, in relation to pain in the spine, lower right arm and hand, and upper and lower left shoulder, arm and hand—all, as we have seen, related to if not actually arising from instrumental practice.

Training for young musicians to enhance health and wellbeing

Given the findings to emerge from recent studies on health-conscious behaviours (or lack thereof) among music students, the argument in favour of implementing active health promotion programmes in educational contexts could not be clearer. One such programme is based on an injury prevention model developed by Spahn (2001b, 2006) taking into account the different student profiles identified in the latter study. Similar programmes are offered in European and North

American music departments and conservatoires (see Manchester 2007, for a review). Since the Spahn programme is, as yet, one of the few that has been thoroughly evaluated (Zander et al. 2010), we now describe it—and the evaluation—in some detail. It was first implemented as a compulsory course at the University of Music, Freiburg (Germany) in 2000, and is delivered in two hour-long sessions each week over two semesters during the second year of study.

The aim of the first part of the programme is to raise students' consciousness of their own health by providing them with a basic theoretical knowledge of the physiological processes that underlie music performance including movement and breathing, and the neurological basis of learning. They are also introduced to some selected aspects of applied psychology, learning, for example, how relaxation procedures and psychotherapy can be used for coping with stress.

In the second part of the programme, students are encouraged to behave in ways that not only improve their playing or singing but also contribute to optimum physical and psychological health. They share their experiences with each other, thereby increasing their communication skills, breaking the performer's traditional taboo against revealing weaknesses or fears, and developing solidarity. They learn about professional musicians who have experienced and coped successfully with similar problems, thus finding out more about what is likely to be involved in a career as a performer. They learn and are encouraged to use a repertoire of exercises (see below) as part of their daily routine as a musician, and to find out which are likely to be most helpful to them. They create their own individual timetables for effective and healthy practice, so as to establish a good 'practice-life balance'. A large proportion of their work in this part of the programme concerns their attitude to their own playing; it is often crucial for them to learn that perfection is not absolute, but relative.

The third part of the programme is essentially practical: students are taught how to enhance their proprioceptive (body awareness) skills and use of the body via a range of methods. They learn the importance of warming-up and cooling-down and are given instrument-specific exercises to practise; they are taught relaxation techniques and strategies for coping with stress when they perform.

In the fourth part of the programme the students are expected to apply the knowledge and skills they have acquired. At this stage they are asked to report how they are doing this in relation to their daily practice and the performances they give; they must show evidence of how they have attempted to improve their working conditions (such as where and how they sit, and the amount of light they have in orchestral rehearsals, for example), and their own assessment of the extent to which they are successful in meeting their own and others' expectations of them. The evidence can be in the form of diary entries and/or the analysis of audio- and video-recordings.

Once students have completed the whole programme, they are encouraged to maintain the behaviours they have learned so as to avoid ill health, injury and other disorders, improve their performance and enhance their wellbeing. To this end it is possible for them to attend refresher courses throughout the remainder of their time at the university. While these reflect the four stages of the programme described above, each course is tailored to the students' individual requirements. Typically, students attend shortly before their examinations and when preparing for their transition into professional life.

Zander et al. (2010) carried out a 3-year longitudinal comparison of two groups of students: the intervention group, who engaged in the programme (n = 144) and a comparison group who did not (n = 103). Their health-conscious behaviours were observed, and psychometric tests were used to measure their physical and psychological status at the beginning, during and at the end of the study.

When the students were first tested, as a single group (N = 247), they were in worse health, physically and psychologically, than non-musicians of the same age. By the end of the second year, the programme had had a positive effect on the students' psychological health: while those in the intervention group demonstrated stable powers of concentration and the ability to perform, those of the comparison group deteriorated. There was no clear evidence of a similar effect on physical health. Within the intervention group, however, more advanced students were more likely than their younger colleagues to take courses on effective use of the body, relaxation and mental skills, all of which are useful for preventing injuries and other disorders.

These results support the use of a health promotion and injury-prevention curriculum for young musicians. It clearly raises students' consciousness and improves their knowledge of the factors underlying health, and can have a positive impact on their attitudes to health and therefore their health-conscious behaviours, with beneficial effects on performance. It would be unrealistic to expect that such a curriculum could cure existing problems; indeed Zander et al. (2010) argue that when students experience physical symptoms related to their musical activities, they should be treated in an appropriate therapeutic setting rather than the educational institution. No doubt, each institution will need to adapt the model presented here to the needs of and the demands placed on its own students.

Conclusions

At least two striking paradoxes emerge from the above review. We have seen throughout this book that music can bring improved health and happiness to people's lives. Individually and in groups, people use music to regulate their moods, to distract themselves from daily stresses and anxieties, and to sharpen their physical and mental condition. Given the evidence that playing a musical instrument can help prevent degenerative diseases of the brain (Verghese et al. 2003), it would not be surprising if professional musicians were found to benefit from their occupation. Although this topic would be well worth investigating, we are not aware of research to support this conclusion. Instead, it has focused on studies showing rather that for those who perform professionally, music-making can bring pain, discomfort, and distress alongside pleasure. For a group of people who bring such relief to the masses, they seem to suffer disproportionately.

Secondly, given the current evidence of ill health within the profession and the clear need for acute health surveillance and active health promotion by musicians themselves, many seem surprisingly unable—or perhaps unwilling—to prioritize and advance their own physical and psychological wellbeing. For individuals who engage daily in physically and mentally demanding jobs, a high proportion do not do regular physical activity, take responsibility for their health, or manage their stress effectively (Kreutz et al. 2008, 2009; Ginsborg et al. 2009; Williamon et al. 2009). Overall, the situation seems worse among students than professionals (Zaza 1992; Guptill et al. 2000), suggesting somewhat discouragingly that the survival of such challenges is a key selection criterion for those who make it into the profession and those who succeed thereafter.

While further scientific investigation of the above paradoxes and their implications is needed, the published literature, as it stands now, presents a challenge to those who train, educate, employ, and manage aspiring professional musicians. The time for education, application, and research into musicians' health promotion is now.

References

Abel, J.L. and Larkin, K.T. (1990). Anticipation of performance among musicians: Physiological arousal, confidence and state anxiety. *Psychology of Music*, **18**, 171–82.

Allmendinger, J., Hackman, J. R., and Lehman, E. V. (1996). Life and work in symphony orchestras. *The Musical Quarterly*, **80**, 194–219.

Altenmüller, E. and Jabusch, H.C. (2006). Neurologische Erkrankungen bei Musikern. *Medizinische Welt*, **57**(12), 569–75.

Backus B. and Williamon A. (2009). Evidence of noise-induced hearing loss among orchestral musicians. In: A. Williamon, S. Pretty, and R. Buck (eds.) *Proceedings of the International Symposium on Performance Science 2009*, pp. 225–30. Utrecht: European Association of Conservatoires (AEC).

Backus B., Clark T., and Williamon A. (2007). Noise exposure and hearing thresholds among orchestral musicians. In: A. Williamon and D. Coimbra (eds.) *Proceedings of the International Symposium on Performance Science 2007*, pp. 23–8. Utrecht: European Association of Conservatoires (AEC).

Barton, R. and Feinberg, J.R. (2008). Effectiveness of an educational program in health promotion and injury prevention for freshman music majors. *Medical Problems of Performing Artists*, **23**(2), 47–53.

Blum, J. (1995). Das Orchester als Ort körperlicher und seelischer Harmonie? Eine Erhebung unter bundesdeutschen Streichern. *Orchester*, **4**, 23–9.

Brandfonbrener, A.G. (1990). Joint laxity in instrumental musicians. *Medical Problems of Performing Artists*, **5**(3), 117–19.

Brodsky, W. (1996). Music performance anxiety reconceptualized: A critique of current research practices and findings. *Medical Problems of Performing Artists*, **11**(3), 88–98.

Cayea, D. and Manchester, R.A. (1998). Instrument-specific rates of upper-extremity injuries in music students. *Medical Problems of Performing Artists*, **13**(1), 19–25.

Chafin, S., Roy, M., Gerin, W., and Christenfield, N. (2004). Music can facilitate blood pressure recovery from stress. *British Journal of Health Psychology*, **9**, 393–403.

Cox, W. and Kenardy, J. (1993). Performance anxiety, social phobia, and setting effects in instrumental music students. *Journal of Anxiety Disorders*, **7**(1), 49–60.

Craske, M.G. and Craig, K.D. (1984). Musical performance anxiety: The three-systems model and self-efficacy theory. *Behaviour Research and Therapy*, **22**, 267–80.

Davies, J. and Mangion, S. (2002). Predictors of pain and other musculoskeletal symptoms among professional instrumental musicians: Elucidating specific effects. *Medical Problems of Performing Artists*, **17**, 155–68.

Davis, W.B. and Thaut, M.H. (1989). The influence of preferred relaxing music on measures of state anxiety, relaxation, and physiological responses. *Journal of Music Therapy*, **26**(4), 168–87.

Dawson, W.J. (2003). The bibliography of performing arts medicine. *Medical Problems of Performing Artists*, **18**, 27–32.

Diener, E. (2000). Subjective well-being: The science of happiness and a proposal for a national index. *American Psychologist*, **55**, 34–43.

Diener, E. and Seligman, M.E.P. (2002). Very happy people. *Psychological Science*, **13**(1), 80–3.

Filipp, S.-H. and Freudenberg, E. (1989). *Der Fragebogen zur Erfassung dispositionaler Selbstaufmerksamkeit SAM (A scale for assessing dispositional self-consciousness)*. Göttingen, Germany: Hogrefe.

Fishbein, M., Middlestadt, S., Ottati, V., Straus, S., Ellis, A. (1988). Medical problems among ICSOM musicians: Overview of a national survey. *Medical Problems of Performing Artists*, **3**, 1–8.

Fredrickson, B. (2000). Cultivating positive emotions to optimize health and well-being. *Prevention and Treatment*, **3**(1), Article 0001a, posted March 7, 2000 (accessed 4 November 2009).

Fredrikson, M. and Gunnarsson, R. (1992). Psychobiology of stage fright. The effect of public performance on neuroendocrine, cardiovascular and subjective reactions. *Biological Psychology*, **33**, 51–61.

Gabrielsson, A. (2002). Perceived emotion and felt emotion: Same or different? *Musicae Scientiae, Special Issue 2001–2002*, 123–47.

Ginsborg, J., Kreutz, G., Thomas, M., and Williamon, A. (2009). Healthy behaviours in music performance and non-music performance students. *Health Education*, **109**(3), 242–58.

Green, R.G. and Green, M.L. (1987). Relaxation increases salivary immunoglobulin A. *Psychological Reports*, **61**, 623–9.

Guptill, C., Zaza, C., and Paul, S. (2000). An occupational study of physical playing-related injuries in college music students. *Medical Problems of Performing Artists*, **15**, 86–90.

Haake, A.B. (2006). Music listening practices in workplace settings in the UK: An exploratory survey of office-based settings. Paper presented at the 9th International Conference on Music Perception and Cognition, Bologna, 22–26 August, 2006.

Houston, D.M., McKee, K.J., Carroll, L., and Marsh, H. (1998). Using humour to promote psychological well-being in residential homes for older people. *Aging and Mental Health*, 2(4), 328–32.

Jørgensen, H. (1997). Time for practising? Higher level music students' use of time for instrumental practising. In: H. Jørgensen and A.C. Lehmann (eds.) *Does practice make perfect? Current theory and research on instrumental music practice*, pp. 123–39. Oslo: Norwegian Academy of Music.

Juslin, P.N. and Laukka, P. (2004). Expression, perception and induction of musical emotions: A review and a questionnaire study of everyday listening. *Journal of New Music Research*, **33**, 217–38.

Kenny, D.T. (2005). A systematic review of treatments for music performance anxiety. *Anxiety, Stress & Coping*, **18**, 183–208.

Kenny, D. (2011). *The Psychology of Music Performance Anxiety*. Oxford: Oxford University Press.

Kenny, D., Davis, P., and Oates, J. (2003). Music performance anxiety and occupational stress amongst opera chorus artists and their relationship with state and trait anxiety and perfectionism. *Journal of Anxiety Disorders*, **18**(6), 757–77.

Kreutz, G., Bongard, S., Rohrmann, S., Hodapp, V., and Grebe, D. (2004). Effects of choir singing or listening on secretary immunoglobulin A, cortisol, and emotional state. *Journal of Behavioral Medicine*, **27**, 623–35.

Kreutz, G., Ginsborg, J., and Williamon, A. (2008). Music students' health problems and health-promoting behaviours. *Medical Problems of Performing Artists*, **23**(1), 3–11.

Kreutz, G., Ginsborg, J., and Williamon, A. (2009). Health-promoting behaviours in conservatoire students. *Psychology of Music*, **37**(1), 47–60.

Larsson, G., Baum, J., Mudholkar, G., and Kollia, G. (1993). Nature and impact of musculoskeletal problems in a population of musicians. *Medical Problems of Performing Artists*, **8**, 73–6.

Laukka, P. (2007). Uses of music and psychological well-being among the elderly. *Journal of Happiness Studies*, **8**, 215–41.

Lohaus, A. and Schmitt, G.M. (1989). *Fragebogen zur Erhebung von Kontrollüberzeugungen zu Krankheit und Gesundheit (KKG)*. Göttingen: Hogrefe.

MacDonald, R., Hargreaves. D. and Miell, D. (eds.) (2005). *Musical Communication*. Oxford: Oxford University Press.

Manchester, R.A. (1988). The incidence of hand problems in music students. *Medical Problems of Performing Artists*, **3**, 15–18.

Manchester, R.A. (2007). Health promotion courses for music students: Part 1. *Medical Problems of Performing Artists*, **22**(1), 26–9.

Manchester, R. and Flieder, D. (1991). Further observations on the epidemiology of hand injuries in music students. *Medical Problems of Performing Artists*, **6**, 11–14.

Marchant-Haycox, S.E. and Wilson, G.D. (1992). Personality and stress in performing artists. *Personality and Individual Differences*, **13**, 161–8.

Middlestadt, S.E. and Fishbein, M. (1988). Health and occupational correlates of perceived occupational stress in symphony orchestra musicians. *Journal of Occupational Medicine*, **30**(9), 687–92.

Miller, G., Peck. F., and Watson, J. S. (2002). Pain disorders and variations in upper limb morphology in music students. *Medical Problems of Performing Artists*, **17**(4), 169–72.

Möller, H. and Castringius, S. (2005). Aufführungsangst–ein gesundheitliches Risiko bei Musikern–Ursachen, Therapie und Prävention. *Musikphysiol Musikermed*, **12**, 139–54.

Mullen, B. and Suls, J. (1982). "Know thyself": Stressful life changes and the ameliorative effect of private self-consciousness. *Journal of Experimental Social Psychology*, **1**, 43–55.

Pak, C.H. and Chesky, K. (2001). Prevalence of hand, finger, and wrist musculoskeletal problems in keyboard instrumentalists: The University of North Texas Musician Health Survey. *Medical Problems of Performing Artists*, **16**, 17–23.

Panzarella, R. (1980). The phenomenology of aesthetic peak experiences. *Journal of Humanistic Psychology*, **20**, 69–85.

Pelletier, C.L. (2004). The effect of music on decreasing arousal due to stress: A meta-analysis. *Journal of Music Therapy*, **41**, 192–214.

Richter, B., Zander, M., and Spahn, C. (2007). Gehörschutz im Orchester. In: C. Spahn (ed.) *Schriftenreihe des Freiburger Instituts für Musikermedizin, Freiburger Beiträge zur Musikermedizin'Bd. 4*. Freiburg, Bochum: Projektverlag.

Robinson, M.D. (2000). The reactive and prospective functions of mood: Its role in linking daily experiences and cognitive well-being. *Cognition and Emotion*, **14**(2), 145–76.

Robson, B., Davidson, J., and Snell, E. (1995). "But I'm not ready, yet": Overcoming audition anxiety in the young musician. *Medical Problems of Performing Artists*, **10**, 125–30.

Roset-Llobet, J., Cubells, D.R., and Orfila, J.M. (2000). Identification of risk factors for musicians in Catalonia (Spain). *Medical Problems of Performing Artists*, **15**, 167–74.

Sataloff, R.T., Brandfonbrener, A.G., and Lederman, R.J. (ed.) (2010). *Performing Arts Medicine, 3rd edition. Medical Problems of Performing Artists*. Narbeth, PA: Science and Medicine.

Schaarschmidt, U. and Fischer, A. (2003). *AVEM–Arbeitsbezogenes Verhaltens- und Erlebensmuster*. Frankfurt/M: Swets & Zeitlinger.

Schuppert, M. and Wagner, C. (1996). Wrist symptoms in instrumental musicians: Due to biomechanical restrictions? *Medical Problems of Performing Artists*, **11**, 37–42.

Schwarzer, R. and Jerusalem, M. (1995). Generalized self-efficacy scale. In: J. Weinman, S. Wright, and M. Johnston (eds.) *Measures in Health Psychology: A User's Portfolio. Causal and Control Beliefs*, pp. 35–7. Windsor: NFER-Nelson.

Schwarzer, R., Diehl, M., and Schmitz, G.S. (1999). *The Self-regulation Scale*. Berlin: Freie Universität.

Seligman, M.E.P. and Csikszentmihalyi, M. (2000). Positive psychology: An introduction. *American Psychologist*, **55**, 5–14.

Spahn, C. (2006). Gesundheit für Musiker–Entwicklung des Freiburger Präventionsmodells. In: C. Spahn (ed.) *Schriftenreihe des Freiburger Instituts für Musikermedizin. Freiburger Beiträge zur Musikermedizin Bd. 1*. Freiburg, Bochum: Projektverlag.

Spahn, C. and Zschocke, I. (2002). Selbstaufmerksamkeit als Persönlichkeitsmerkmal von Musikern. In: K.-E., Behne, G.Kleinen, H. de la Motte-Haber (eds.) *Wirkungen und kognitive Verarbeitung in der Musik. Jahrbuch der deutschen Gesellschaft für Musikpsychologie Bd.16*, pp. 30–44. Göttingen: Hogrefe-Verlag.

Spahn, C., Ell, N., and Seidenglanz, K. (2001a). Psychosomatic findings in musician patients at a department of hand surgery. *Medical Problems of Performing Artists*, **16**, 144–51.

Spahn, C., Hildebrandt, H., and Seidenglanz, K. (2001b). Effectiveness of a prophylactic course to prevent playing-related health problems of music students. *Medical Problems of Performing Artists*, **16**, 24–31.

Spahn, C., Richter, B., and Zschocke, I. (2002). Health attitudes, preventive behavior, and playing-related health problems among music students. *Medical Problems of Performing Artists*, **17**, 22–8.

Spahn, C., Strukely, S., and Lehmann, A. (2004). Health conditions, attitudes toward study, and attitudes toward health at the beginning of university study: Music students in comparison with other student populations. *Medical Problems of Performing Artists*, **19**, 26–33.

Spahn, C., Burger, T., Hildebrandt, H., and Seidenglanz, K. (2005). Health locus of control and preventive behaviour among students of music. *Psychology of Music*, **33**(3), 257–69.

Spahn, C., Richter, B., and Altenmüller A. (2011). *MusikerMedizin. Diagnostik, Therapie und Prävention von musikerspezifischen Erkrankungen*. Stuttgart: Schattauer-Verlag.

Spahn, C., Echternach, M., Zander M.F., Voltmer, E., and Richter, B. (2010). Music performance anxiety in opera singers. *Logopedics, phoniatrics, vocology*, **35**(4), 175–82.

Steptoe, R. and Fidler, H. (1987). Stage fright in orchestral musicians: A study of cognitive and behavioural strategies in performance anxiety. *British Journal of Psychology*, **78**, 241–9.

Västfjäll, D. (2002). A review of the musical mood induction procedure. *Musicae Scientiae, Special Issue 2001–2002*, 173–211.

Verghese, J., Lipton, R., Katz, M., Hall, C., Derby, C., Kuslansky, G., *et al.* (2003). Leisure activities and the risk of dementia in the elderly. *New England Journal of Medicine*, **348**, 2508–16.

Voltmer, E., Schauer, I., Schröder, H., and Spahn, C. (2008). Musicians and physicians–A comparison of psychosocial strain patterns and resources. *Medical Problems of Performing Artists*, **23**, 164–8.

Walker, S., Sechrist, K., and Pender, N. (1987). The health-promoting lifestyle profile: Development and psychometric characteristics. *Nursing Research*, **36** (2), 76–81.

WHO (2006). *Constitution of the World Health Organization*. Available at: www.who.int/governance/eb/who_constitution_en.pdf (accessed on 14 April 2011).

Williamon, A., Wasley, D., Burt-Perkins, R., Ginsborg, J., and Hildebrandt, W. (2009). Profiling musicians' health, well-being, and performance. In: A. Williamon, S. Pretty, and R. Buck (eds.) *Proceedings of the International Symposium on Performance Science 2009*, pp. 85–90. Utrecht: European Association of Conservatoires (AEC).

Zander M.F. and Spahn, C. (2006). Epidemiologie von Musikererkrankungen–Risiko- und Protektivfaktoren. *Medizinische Welt*, **57**, 545–9.

Zander, M.F., Voltmer, E., and Spahn, C. (2010). Health promotion and prevention in higher music education–results of a longitudinal study. *Medical Problems of Performing Artists*, **25**, 54–65.

Zaza, C. (1992). Playing-related health problems at a Canadian music school. *Medical Problems of Performing Artists*, **7**(2), 48–51.

Zaza, C. (1998). Playing-related musculoskeletal disorders in musicians: a systematic review of incidence and prevalence. *Canadian Medical Association Journal*, **158**(8), 1019–25.

Zaza, C. and Farewell, V. T. (1997). Musicians' playing-related musculoskeletal disorders: an examination of risk factors. *American Journal of Industrial Medicine*, **32**(2), 292–300.

Zetterberg, C., Backlund, H., Karlsson, J., Werner, H., and Olsson, L. (1998). Musculoskeletal problems among male and female music students. *Medical Problems of Performing Artists*, **13** (4), 160–6.

Chapter 25

Music-Making as a Lifelong Development and Resource for Health

Heiner Gembris

Introduction

This chapter has two main topics: Firstly, music-making (in terms of singing and playing instruments) is described as an activity that has to be seen in the context of the general human (musical) development and that is subject to specific changes during the course of life. Secondly, the connection between music-making and health is portrayed as an interaction in which music affects health and vice versa, music-making exerts an influence on health. The effects and the extent of this interaction depend largely on the kind and context of music-making.

Musical development can be understood as a lifelong process, which comprises time-related changes in musical abilities, motivations, functions, and musical activities. This process is influenced by individual, social, and cultural factors. Biographical literature on composers and musicians usually regards the entire human lifespan as the period of musical development and productivity. For developmental psychology, the study of the entire lifespan is still a relatively young topic (e.g. Gembris 2006); the Austrian psychologist Charlotte Bühler (1933) being possibly the first to empirically investigate relationships between life and work of eminent musicians such as the composers Franz Liszt and Giuseppe Verdi or the opera singer Benjamino Gigli. Later authors such as Lehman and Ingerham (1939), Dennis (1966), Sosniak (1985), and Simonton (e.g. 1977, 1991, 2000) have expanded this research on lifespan creativity within the domain of classical music (for a review, see Gembris 2008a). Recently, Kopiez et al. (2009) used Clara Schumann's concert playbills to investigate relationships between life events and artistic activity over her entire career (in this instance playbill refers to a concert programme that would normally be expected to outline the pieces performed, the performers, the composers, etc.).

General principles of lifespan psychology in music

A fundamental proposition of lifespan psychology states that ontogenetic development 'is a lifelong process that is co-constructed by biology and culture. No age period holds supremacy in regulating the nature of development.' (Baltes et al. 2006, p. 581) The general framework and principles of lifespan developmental psychology (for an overview see Baltes et al. 2006) also apply to musical development (e.g. Gembris 2006). Musical learning and changes in musical abilities, music experience, interests and activities can potentially take place at any stage in life. There is now evidence that musical development begins prenatally (Parncutt 2006), and continues throughout the entire lifespan.

Dynamic of stability, gains, and losses

Development from the perspective of lifespan psychology is a constantly evolving dynamic of changes in terms of psychological gains, deterioration, and stability (e.g. Baltes et al. 2006). The relationship between stability, gains, and losses changes over time. At a young age, the gains are typically far greater than the losses. This ratio gradually changes in the course of life and is reversed in old age. Development in this sense includes also the loss of capacity and skills.

Multidirectionality

Developmental changes can take place simultaneously in different musical fields and at different levels. Gains in one area (e.g. through practice, specialization) can occur at the same time as losses in other areas (e.g. caused by lack of performance or age related impairments). An example is the different course of development of crystalline and fluid intelligence: while information processing speed, memory or problem solving (fluid intelligence) starts to decrease in the third decade of life, knowledge, experience, wisdom, and social skills tend to increase with time (e.g. Baltes 1987). Dixon (2000) suggests that age-related losses 'occurring late, less uniformly, or less universally than expected' may be also viewed as a gain (Dixon 2000, p. 33). This means, for example, that being in good physical and mental health at the age of 80–90 years can be viewed as a gain (or piece of luck), because at this age diseases are to be expected.

Plasticity and reserve capacity

Lifespan psychology underlines the plasticity and modifiability of psychological development and of cognitive functioning. Younger and older adults both possess a considerable amount of cognitive and other potential which is not used and which can be activated by training (reserve capacity; e.g. Baltes 1987; Baltes et al. 2006). Analogous to the cognitive reserve capacity, it is assumed that most people possess a musical reserve capacity, i.e. a more or less extensive musical potential which is underutilized, but which can be activated by musical learning and practice (Gembris 2009a). It is necessary to differentiate between the musical reserve capacities of amateur musicians (i.e. people without an education as professional musician and who do not earn their livings with music) and professional musicians (i.e. persons who have had an education as professional musician and/or whose primary income depends on making music). The latter will only have little or no residual of musical reserve capacity as compared to the former as it is their profession to exhaust their musical capacities completely, they usually keep developing their potential continuously. By contrast, amateur musicians presumably hold a larger share of musical potential which is unused and which can be activated through learning and practice. This enables virtually every adult (except professional musicians) to develop new and unexpected musical abilities and to enhance existing musical skills.

Cultural embeddedness and generation-specific socialization

Individual musical development is related to the surrounding musical culture and situated in a historical context. It is shaped by socialization within a specific sociocultural environment. Generation-specific as well as historical factors may influence musical development. They may affect an individual's musical biography, preferences, interests, and activities strongly and permanently (Eckhardt et al. 2006; Mende and Neuwöhner 2006; Gembris 2009a, pp. 209ff).

For example, the emergence of rock and pop music in the 1950s and 1960s in Western countries has shaped musical biographies and identities of the generation whose formative years were during this period in unique ways. Later generations have also grown up with this kind of music, but they also experienced rapid changes in media technology which influenced listening habits and the use of music in everyday life (North and Hargreaves 2008). Today, certainly for the first time in cultural history, adults over the age of 60 may be fans of pop and rock music. However, the individual is not only shaped by the sociocultural environment, but is able to contribute and to influence music culture by his or her own musical activity as a musician, composer, and music consumer.

Differentiation and individual differences

Individual differences tend to increase throughout life. Within the same age group, there may be greater differences in physical and mental performance, perceptual abilities, health status, etc. than between different age groups (e.g. Kliegel and Jäger 2008). Therefore, individual differentiation should also apply to investigating musical development. In fact, individual differences, which already exist during childhood and adolescence, enlarge in early adulthood and keep continuously increasing in the course of life. This becomes obvious when professional musicians are compared to amateurs and people untrained in music. For example, the differences in the amount of time spent on practice and the related differences in performance and musical experiences accumulate over the decades (Krampe 1994). While professional musicians need to maintain high levels of performance and practice, musical achievements of amateurs and people untrained in music normally degenerate as a consequence of a lack of practice, because they have different professions and pursue other interests, motivations and activities. This means that the developmental processes of professional musicians and amateurs move in opposite directions. Health implications of these divergent musical activities of amateurs and professionals are explored in various chapters throughout this volume.

Developmental phases, transitions, and health of professional musicians

Maria Manturzewka conducted presumably the largest study on the professional development of musicians during the 1960s and 1970s (e.g. Manturzewska 1990, 2006). She investigated the career of more than 165 Polish musicians using biographical questionnaires, interviews, and other materials. Based on these data, she suggested a theoretical model describing the lifelong development of professional musicians in six different phases. Every developmental phase is characterized by typical activities, roles, and developmental tasks. The transitions between these phases have large overlaps. The transitions are critical periods which are characterized by increased occurrences of emotional crises. For example, such a critical period is the time between the ages of 45–55. As Manturzewska describes, a distinct drop in efficiency and ability to learn new musical pieces can be observed: 'This drop in energy, learning capacity and artistic efficiency is usually accompanied by vacillating self-esteem, depression and various psychosomatic symptoms. The musician begins to visit physicians and therapists, to seek deliverances in parapsychology and alcohol.' (Manturzewska 2006, p. 44).

In their analysis of the lifespan development of the career of Clara Schumann, Kopiez et al. (2009) identified four phases, which were clearly influenced by critical life events (e.g. birth or death of children) and health problems. At the end of a very successful period between the ages of about 37–56 years (phase 3), in which she performed most of the concerts she ever played, Clara Schumann began to suffer from rheumatism in arms and hands (54–56 years). Health problems characterize the transition from phase 3 to 4 and she was unable to continue performing because of these problems. In the fourth and last phase (56–77 years) hearing problems increased, and at the same time the number of concerts decreased. Kopiez et al. (2009, p. 58) suggest that these problems were reason enough 'to search for an alternative source of income which would not be affected by the instability of her health'. Fortunately, she had the opportunity to commence a teaching position as professor of piano.

This example of Clara Schumann demonstrates the strong influence of health aspects on a career as a soloist. The career trajectories of other musicians will be different, but they also are influenced, shaped, interrupted or stopped by health issues. For instance, the playing and the career of the pianist Vladimir Horowitz (1903–1989) was significantly affected by health and mental instability over some decades. He interrupted his public concerts for 12 years between the ages of 50–62 years as a result of depression: 'From 1975 to 1985 he was under heavy sedation from drugs prescribed by his psychiatrist. His playing suffered; it was often incoherent, with memory lapses and wrong notes. But he finally managed to regain his health and mental stability, and he played with serenity and joy during the last five years of his life.' (Schonberg 2010). These examples appear to conform to the developmental model of Manturzewska (1990, 2006) which indicates that a critical period seems to be reached by the age of 45–55, where first signs of physical and psychological exhaustion and a decrease of efficiency can occur.

Another critical period is the transition from employment to retirement. Violinists and opera singers often give their last concerts around the age of 60, while pianists and members of orchestras may retire later (Manturzewska 1990, 2006). Among orchestra musicians, differences between instruments are most likely. In a study with retired members of a great American symphony orchestra, Smith (1988) observed that wind and brass players retired in their 60s, while some string players continued to play into their 70s. Health problems were mentioned by these musicians, but they did not seem to make playing on a high level impossible. One has to keep in mind that this study contained only those musicians who were healthy enough to play up to their 60s or 70s, and not those leaving the orchestra earlier because of health problems or other reasons (Smith 1988).

In other domains such as sports the connection between high performance and health risks is well known. The connection between health hazards and peak performance also exists in the domain of music, especially in the long trajectory of a musical career.

In his in-depth study with British symphony orchestra musicians, Brodsky (2006) explores the 'gains', 'risks', and 'costs' connected with a career as professional musician. Quite often, considerable discrepancies between the musician's career expectations and the reality of orchestral work become apparent, e.g. the subordination of solo assertiveness and personality, the disruption of a 'normal life-style' and its consequences for social and family life, etc., which often lead to disappointment. As Brodsky (2006, p. 674) states: 'it often comes as a shock to the musicians themselves that achievement of their career goal is at the expense of their own personal health.'

Brodsky explains:

> That is, players quickly learn that there is a connection between music performance and physical/psychological wellbeing. While most people (including naïve and amateur musicians) view music-making as having many benefits including relaxation and the development of leisure-time activity, music performing expertise on the professional level involves autonomic and proprioceptive systems, which require an exceptionally high (almost superhuman) degree of training and skill, as well as the blending of emotion-intelligence, response-control, and empathy-command (Dunsby 2002). Furthermore, concerting makes painstaking demands on mental/cognitive abilities (involving attention, concentration and memory) as well as on emotional requirements. It is unfortunate that players entering an orchestral career have not always been prepared for the costs of their chosen occupation
>
> (Brodsky 2006, p. 674).

Unlike athletes, musicians are expected to provide high performance over a long period of 30, 40, years or more. In these decades the interrelation between musical performance and health becomes increasingly important, because the effects of work-related health problems and age-related restrictions on musical performance sum up. This can lead to earlier retirement of musicians. As a consequence, only those musicians, who do not have serious health problems, remain in the orchestra until old age (Fishbein et al. 1988; Smith 1989).

Further details about the interrelations between specific health aspects, aging and making music on a professional level can be found in Chapter 7, this volume, and in the studies by Manchester (2009), Rohwer (2008), Črnivec (2004); Johansson and Theorell (2003); Schuele and Ledermann (2003); Warrington et al. (2002); Henoch and Chesky (1999); Lederman (1999), Hoppmann and Ekman (1999), Smith (1992) and Fry (1988).

Only a very few studies have explored health- and aging problems of musicians in other domains than classical music (Brodsky 1995; Barton 2004). However, it is evident that in domains like rock, pop, or jazz music health aspects influence musical careers to a large extent, but research has neglected this topic.

All these studies lead to the conclusion that health is a main resource and a prerequisite for performing music on a high professional level (see Chapter 7, this volume). At the same time, health is endangered by performing music on a high level over a long time. Health and health-problems are main factors influencing the duration and course of professional musicians' careers. On the other hand, making music may be also a resource for health for professional musicians in a broader sense: making music creates the artistic, emotional, and social world in which the musician needs to live in and which musicians need for their psychological equilibrium (see Brodsky 2006, p. 687). Therefore, it is a main and permanent developmental task for professional musicians to create a balance between health as a resource for making music and making music as resource for health. With increasing age, the time spent on healthcare and maintaining bodily functions presumably also will increase (see Krampe 2006, p. 99).

Developmental processes and health of amateur musicians

While professional musicians increase their musical activities and achievements after the second decade of life, we generally find a decrease in musical activities and achievements for amateur musicians in the following decades.

In a study with senior amateur musicians (Gembris 2008b), more than 90% of the participants had interrupted their musical activities between the ages of 20–60 years. The mean interruption time amounted to nearly 20 years. Job, family, and education of children were the most frequent reasons for long interruptions. Around the time of retirement, sometimes even in the fifth decade of life, when children have grown up and left home, more time is available which allows an expansion of musical activities, opportunities to practise and improve musical skills. Among other things the respondents in this study assessed the quality of their instrumental performance. The personal best performance on an instrument is by no means located only in younger years (see Figure 25.1). Instead, it is identified within the first three decades of life as well as between the ages of 60–69. This contradicts the widespread opinion that with increasing age, the performance will inevitably decline. It is also remarkable that almost 30% of the interviewed senior musicians (average age 71 years) reported that they currently reached 90–100% of their former best instrumental performance (see Figure 25.2).

Biological aspects

Age-related changes in cognitive, sensory, and physiological functioning constitute an important aspect of lifespan development, since they also affect musical activities (Figure 25.3).

Their influence is smaller with younger adults and increases at an older age (cf. Baltes et al. 2006.; general overview, e.g. Birren and Schaie 1996; Park 2000; Park and Gutchess 2000; Kliegel

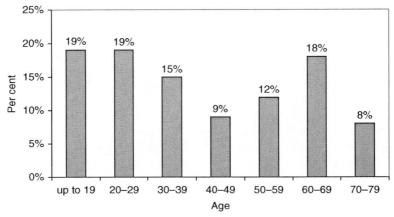

Fig. 25.1 Age at the time of best performance rated by senior musicians (Gembris 2008b).

and Jäger 2008, p. 71). Starting at the age of 30, human physiological functions statistically lose about 1% of efficiency every year. However, the body has great capacities of compensation so that a slow process of reduction can remain without any symptoms for a long time. These changes in physiological processes start to become a problem once a critical limit is exceeded (Maier et al. 1994, p. 167). The decrease of sensorimotor speed and dexterity, reduction of the sense of touch, and other micromotor limitations which occur with increasing age, can lead to more or less restrictions in instrumental playing. In addition, the speed of cognitive processing and the discrimination of stimuli already start to decrease in early adulthood (e.g. Park 2000; Baltes et al. 2006). The slowing down of cognitive and physiological speed may result in a tendency to slow down the tempo of musical performances (Jennen and Gembris 2000). Another effect of getting older is the continuous decline of hearing, which is primarily affecting high frequencies (e.g. Kline and Scialfa 1996).

A severe problem for singers evolves from the vocal changes at an older age. These are not directly related to chronological age, but rather to biological age (i.e. biological fitness, state of health;

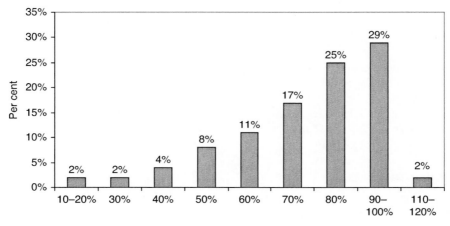

Fig. 25.2 Estimated percentage of the former best performance, rated by senior orchestra musicians (Gembris 2008b).

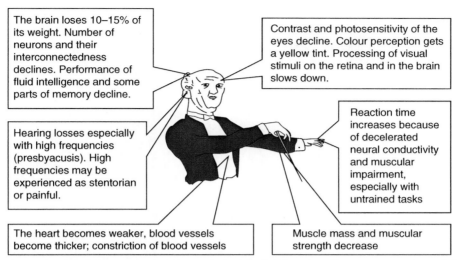

Fig. 25.3 Age-related changes in cognitive and physiological functions (from Jennen and Gembris 2000, p. 32).

Habermann 1986, p. 149). Changes of the voice's function can be accompanied by effects like loss of the chest voice, fast change of pitch and timbre of the voice, loss of intensity, less resonance, less ability to control the voice and its intonation, detonation and tremolo, reduction of the voice's ambitus. However, all of these changes do not appear at the same time (Habermann 1986, p. 148 cf; Moore et al. 1992; Sataloff 1992; Seidner and Wendler 1997, p. 180; Spahn and Richter 2006).

The beginning of age-related changes in function is subject to individual differences and cannot be attributed to a specific age. In addition, the amount of age-related changes and their significance for musical activities differs widely and also depends on, for instance, the level of musical training. Professional piano players, for example, are less affected by age-related restrictions of manual abilities than untrained amateurs (s. Krampe 1994). The problem of age-related constraints and their compensation concerns soloists and professional orchestra musicians as well as amateur musicians. In the case of professional musicians this problem seems to be a kind of taboo. This problem clearly exists in practice (e.g. Schmitt-Ott 2008), but has been discussed infrequently among professional musicians.

Adaptation to age-related restrictions

Baltes and colleagues (for an overview: Baltes et al. 2006, p. 591ff) suggested a general model describing adaptation strategies to cope with age-related constraints. This model is based on the principles of selection, optimization, and compensation (SOC). Because of its generality, this model can be applied to many situations, but needs domain-specific refinement.

Baltes and Baltes (1990) illustrated the SOC model with some statements of the pianist Arthur Rubinstein, who said that he played less pieces (selection), which he practised more (optimization). Before fast passages he inserted a ritardando, which makes the following passage appear faster (compensation). These strategies seem very convincing at first glance, but in musical practice they are not always valid, because a professional orchestra musician can choose neither the pieces to play nor the tempo of their performance. The only strategy a professional musician can apply in a relatively self-governed way is optimization by more practising. In fact, practising seems to be an effective means to maintain a high level of performance in advanced age.

In a study with young (mean age = 24 years) and older amateur and expert pianists (mean age = 60 years), Krampe (1994) found that the older pianists showed the typical age-related general decline in mental speed and cognitive mechanics. But in expertise-related measures like tapping tasks, finger sequencing, and coordination tasks this was not the case:

> Older concert pianists had largely maintained their performances at the same levels as young pianists did; however, the critical factor for successful maintenance was the practice they had invested during the last 10 years (i.e. the 5th and 6th decades of life). Obviously, high-level skills require active mainte-nance on the part of the individual, and this is even more important at advancing ages
>
> (Krampe 2006, p. 96f).

Compared to the younger expert pianists, the older pianist had less leisure time. Krampe (2006, p. 99) suggests:

> that older experts compensate for the increased resource (time and energy) requirements from age-related changes in bodily functions and professional requirements (teaching, organization) by reduc-ing their leisure time. At this level, freeing time for maintenance practice can be viewed as another process of selective optimization that has compensatory consequences.

Kopiez et al. (2009, p. 69) observed in their study on the career of Clara Schumann that she 'reduced the number of newly studied works and instead relied on existing ones (selection) and performed a larger number of pieces with reduced demands on the piano part (compensation)'.

It is evident that pianists are able to perform music on a high professional level longer than any other group of instrumentalists (except conductors). With violinists, players of wind instruments or especially singers there are presumably greater limitations brought about by decreases of bio-logical functions, which cannot be compensated by more practice (e.g. decrease in vital capacity, lung function and respiratory control, changes in the voice). Additionally, hearing losses, increas-ing stress and stage fright may preclude high performance in advanced age.

The situation may be different for amateur musicians, because an amateur orchestra does not exert the pressure to perform typical for a professional orchestra which works under very com-petitive conditions. Furthermore, there are more possibilities to select suitable pieces of music and to accommodate to different constraints.

In the aforementioned study on members of senior orchestras (Gembris 2008b), 52% of respondents reported that they felt age-related constraints on their musical performance. These constraints increase with age (see figure 25.4).

The most agreed-on kind of constraints (approximately 40%) were physical problems (e.g. problems with gross and fine motor skills, problems with neck, shoulders, back, leg; pains; restricted mobility of fingers, hands, arms; respiratory problems and problems with embouchure, lips, tongue). Furthermore, slowing down of several functions plays an important role for 30% of the respondents. It becomes particularly noticeable with the motor system, finger mobility, reaction time, and score reading as well as with the tempo of learning. In the cognitive sector, respondents reported primarily lack of concentration and memory problems. Constraints on the sensory organs referred mainly to a decrease in audition and vision.

The senior orchestra musicians in this study employed different kinds of coping strategies to accommodate to their individual situation:

- Physical strategies (e.g. training of muscles, joints, and back; physiotherapy, gymnastics; relaxa-tion exercises; gymnastics of hands and fingers and/or respiratory exercises).

- Mental coping strategies (e.g. acceptance of constraints, adjusting to them, tolerance, patience, humour).

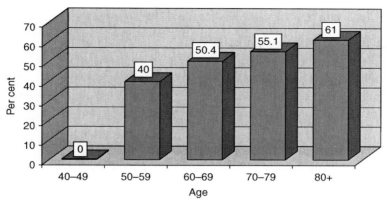

Fig. 25.4 Emergence of age-related constraints of instrumental activities, reported by amateur senior musicians (Gembris 2008b).

◆ Musical strategies (e.g. practising more often, more efficient practising techniques, shorter practice sessions, practising difficult parts more often [optimization]; reducing the number of musical pieces [selection]; leaving difficult parts to others; playing more slowly; skipping fast passages and single tones; simplifying difficult parts and notes [compensation]; reducing musical demands; giving up solo performing).

Making music as a resource of health for amateur musicians

Usually, we do not pursue music for health reasons as is the case with sports and gymnastics, but for its own sake. Still, quite unintentionally, singing and instrumental playing can have positive effects on health, if they are not practised under the permanent pressure to bring about musical excellence and not under the compulsion of earning a living. There are a number of empirical studies which suggest that singing in a choir has positive effects on subjective physical, mental, and social wellbeing as well as on perceived health and on other important aspects of singing people's life (see Chapter 9, this volume)

Several qualitative as well as quantitative studies have investigated the importance and benefits of active music-making for older people and have pointed out that music-making can improve the quality of life in many respects (e.g. Cooper 2001; Coffman 2002; Cohen et al. 2002; Hartogh 2005).

Hays and Minichiello (2005) carried out 52 in-depth interviews with seniors between 60–98 years of age. The analysis of the interviews provides a detailed insight into the multifaceted functions and benefits of music. An essential function of music after retirement was the stabilization of identity and a redefinition of identity through greater involvement with music. Music was used as a communication medium that makes the participants feel connected to themselves and others in many ways: to their own emotions and their own life experiences as well as to other persons, too. Music was a medium to make contacts with other people, creating social networks and interactions. If the language-based communication to spouses, friends, or others was restricted due to Parkinson's disease, dementia, stroke, and other diseases, music as a medium of communication was particularly important. 'Many participants felt music was the key to feeling a sense of wellbeing and good health, regardless of their particular personal medical condition' (Hays and Minichiello 2005, p. 443). Music as an accompaniment to daily activities conveyed a sense of satisfaction and security. With music, the respondents felt happier, more satisfied, hopeful, relaxed, and peaceful. Among other findings, the experience of spirituality conveyed through music appears to play a more important role in old age than in earlier decades of life.

A questionnaire study with members of senior amateur orchestras (mean age 71 years, standard deviation = 7.9) yielded similar findings (Gembris 2008b). The functions and benefits of music-making are listed in Figure 25.5.

The individual benefits of music-making in younger adult amateurs may differ slightly from that in elderly persons. Jutras (2006) studied the benefits of making music in adult piano students aged between 24–94 years (N = 711). The average age of these amateur musicians from different parts of the United States was 51 years, 20 years younger than in the survey on senior orchestras mentioned earlier (Gembris 2008b). The analysis of the questionnaire data revealed three broad categories of benefits: personal benefits, social/cultural benefits, and skill-based benefits. Skill-based benefits (e.g. skill improvement, musical knowledge, musicianship) were the most agreed benefits. The degree of agreement ranged from 91–99% (mean percentage: 96.04%). The personal benefits were also rated relatively high. The most agreed benefits in this category were accomplishment, play/fun, escape from routine and personal growth (between 90.2–97.3%). The least agreed benefits were spirituality (55.7%) and aesthetic appreciation (66.0%). The mean percentage of agreement for personal benefits was 78.56%. The least agreed upon category of benefits were social/cultural benefits (mean percentage of agreement: 53.96%). The most agreed benefits in this category were cultural understanding (82.1%), performance for others (75.1%), and meeting new friends (70.8%). The least agreed items were social status (22.4%) and community (28.7%). The relatively low agreements to social/cultural benefits in this study seem to contrast with the results of other studies. There are several possible explanations. Jutras (2006, p. 107) suggests that the piano is an instrument that is typically practised and played by oneself.

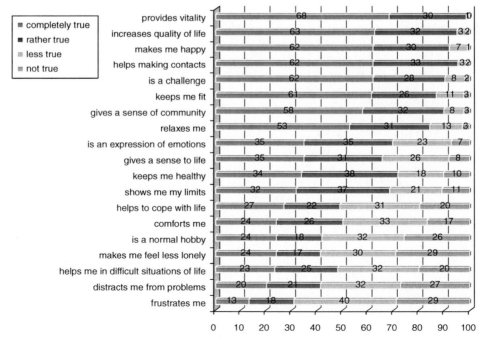

Fig. 25.5 Making music… Functions and benefits of making music rated by senior amateur musicians. Agreement in per cent (N = 308), multiple answers possible (data from Gembris 2008b).

Compared to strings or wind instruments, the piano is less reliant on other instruments. Perhaps the adult music students of this study did not possess sufficient skills to perform in social/public settings. Furthermore, with an average age of 51 years, most of the participants of this study may have been employed, many may have had families. Therefore, they presumably did not need additional social contacts.

Benefits from music-making like vitality, happiness, and connectedness to other people are among the most important goals in human life. Musical activities (not only) in old age appear to be a very good means to make and keep contacts. Therefore, musical activities can make a significant contribution to the quality of life, regardless of musical genre or skills. This conclusion is also confirmed by a study by Moser (2003). He examined 120 musically active individuals from four different US states regarding their cognitive and psychomotor skills and the satisfaction with their lifestyle. The results were compared with average demographic data. He found that those persons who were musically active showed improved cognitive and psychomotor performance and a higher level of life satisfaction. As the author notes, the data suggest a clear link between musical activity and healthy cognitive aging.

A highly essential aspect for health (not only) in old age is exercise and bodily movement. To make music and to play in an ensemble necessarily involves movement in many respects, not only in a strictly musical sense, but also in a very mundane and physical way. It means having to leave the house to go to rehearsals and performance locations, to carry and to service instruments, to plan and to organize gigs, to negotiate with other people, etc. These secondary or tertiary activities may be bothersome in other phases of life, but in old age they may contribute to maintaining physically mobility (Gembris 2009b).

In this context it is notable that the cognitive demands associated with the music, may have protective effects against dementia. In a longitudinal study Verghese et al. (2003) discovered that people who regularly played a musical instrument in their leisure time showed a 7% reduced risk of developing dementia at older age. Similar effects were found for dancing and playing board games. Even with professional musicians, musical activity seems to have positive effects on the brain. Sluming et al. (2007) found among the male members of a professional symphony orchestra a higher density of grey matter in the frontal lobe (Broca's area) in comparison to nonmusicians. They conclude that their findings provide 'additional objective evidence to support the suggestion that the development and maintenance of musical performance abilities confers benefit to nonmusical cognitive domains' (Sluming et al. 2007, p. 3804). Jäncke (2008, pp. 391ff) points out that musical activity seems to counteract the age-related reductions of grey matter in those areas that are involved in musical activities.

Bugos and colleagues (Bugos et al. 2007) found in an experimental study that individualized piano instructions over a time span of 6 months improved cognitive performance in older adults (ages 60–85). The experimental group showed significant advancements in attention, concentration, and planning compared with controls. These results indicate that individualized piano instructions had transfer effects on general cognitive measures which had not been specifically trained. The authors hypothesize 'that as the performer actively allocates attentional resources to musical passages or music theory exercises, the integration of multiple networks by repeated practice (bimanual coordination) is reinforced and transferred to multiple cognitive domains' (p. 470). To maintain the positive effects on cognitive functions, it is necessary to continue regular practice and teaching, since some of the cognitive benefits in this study disappeared when teaching and practice were interrupted.

These results do not mean, however, that making music immunizes against decline in cognitive functioning or dementia. For instance, the violinist Helmut Zacharias (1920–2002), one of the most successful violinists of his generation, was forced to abandon his career because he suffered from Alzheimer's disease (Zacharias 2000). One could speculate about whether the outbreak of his disease would have happened earlier if he had not extensively played the violin. To answer these and similar questions, epidemiological studies are needed to compare the health status of musically active and musically inactive persons on the basis of cohort studies and longitudinal data.

Benefits of music listening

Music listening is clearly the most common musical activity. In a questionnaire study with 280 seniors (aged 65–75 years), Laukka (2007) investigated the associations between music listening behaviours (listening situations, motives for listening etc.), psychological wellbeing, and several background variables (e.g. education level, health status, activity level, personality characteristics). Two-thirds of the participants listened to music once or several times per day. The importance of music, for those aged 65 years and older, was rated significantly higher than in earlier decades of life, even more important than in their teenage years and the period between 20–30 years of age. This result corresponds with similar findings of Gembris (2008b). Among the great variety of motives for listening (listening strategies), aesthetic reasons (because music 'is beautiful'), hedonic reasons ('it gives me pleasure') and entertainment purposes were the most important aspects (Laukka 2007, p. 225). A factor analysis revealed four basic dimensions of listening strategies: 'Identity and agency', 'Mood regulation', 'Relaxation and company', and 'Enjoyment'. The most important predictors of wellbeing were health status and emotional stability (and other personality aspects). Concerning music listening strategies, '"Agency and identity" and "Mood regulation" were the most important predictors of well-being' (Laukka 2007, p. 228). Admittedly, the correlations between wellbeing variables and listening strategies were highly significant, but rather low (between $r = 0.13$ and $r = 0.32$). Nevertheless, they may be important because of their practical implications. Laukka argues (as suggested in the related literature on wellbeing) 'that a person's happiness level is determined by three major factors: a genetically determined set-point for happiness, happiness-relevant circumstantial factors, and happiness-relevant activities and practices' (Laukka 2007, p. 231). Genetic and circumstantial factors contribute most to a person's level of happiness, but 'the practical implications of happiness-relevant activities are great, because they are often the only factors that can be changed' (p. 232). In this respect, music listening generally can be a resource to improve wellbeing. Particularly with regard to older adults, 'the cumulative challenges and losses may easily tap the limits of the adaptive self-regulation processes responsible for maintaining the level of well-being'. Therefore, Laukka (2007, p. 233f) concludes, 'every effort that may support well-being in late adulthood should be taken into consideration'.

Concluding remarks

Research on lifespan development in music is still in its infancy. With respect to the plurality of developmental pathways in different domains and genres of music, one of the basic tasks for future research is the building of a fundamental phenomenology and typology of developmental trajectories in music and of the factors influencing them.

One of the most important assumptions with respect to lifelong musical music education is the concept of an unused musical reserve capacity or plasticity. As stated earlier in the chapter, the musical reserve capacity is the unused part of the fundamental musicality and general musical ability, which all humans possess to a more or less extent. It can be activated and developed by practice and learning. It builds a basic resource for musical activities and, in a second line, for positive health effects of making music, too. However, musical reserve capacity remains largely unexplored. Therefore, to explore the nature, possibilities and limitations of musical reserve capacity is a very important challenge for future research.

The relationship between music-making, lifelong development, and health is a Janus-faced one. On the one hand, good health is a prerequisite for professional instrumentalists and singers to perform music on a high level. Doing this under the conditions of a competitive music market over many years clearly can cause serious impairment of physical and mental health. Therefore, it is an important task for professional musicians to take care for their health in order to be able to master the high-quality demands and to maintain a successful career (Johansson and Theorell 2003).

On the other hand, both individual experiences and results of research indicate that making music as an amateur instrumentalist or choral singer may have positive effects on health, as it contributes to self-actualization, wellbeing, social connectedness, etc.

So for both music amateurs and professional musicians, musical development, and health aspects are interrelated, but in very different ways. A major task of future research in musicians' medicine will be the field of prevention, which is very important even at early stages of professional development. One of the main questions of research concerning health and amateur musicians will be the nature and mechanisms of health effects of music-making in comparison to other activities. In particular, epidemiological studies are required. Last but not least: research has almost exclusively focused on health and development in classical music and it is now necessary to include popular music and other genres.

References

Baltes, P.B. (1987). Theoretical propositions of life-span developmental psychology: On the dynamics between growth and decline. *Developmental Psychology,* **23**(5), 611–26.

Baltes, P.B. Baltes, M.M. (Eds.) (1990). *Successful aging: Perspectives from the behavioral sciences* (New York: Cambridge University Press).

Baltes, P.B., Lindenberger, U., and Staudinger, U.M. (2006). Life-span theory in developmental psychology, in R.M. Lerner and W. Damon (ed.) *Handbook of Child Psychology. Sixth Edition, Volume One: Theoretical Models of Human Development*, pp. 569–664 (Hoboken, NJ: Wiley).

Barton, R. (2004). The aging musician. *Work: Journal of Prevention, Assessment and Rehabilitation,* **22**(2), 131–8.

Birren, J.E., and Schaie, K.W. (eds.) (1996). *Handbook of the psychology of aging. Fourth edition* (San Diego, CA: Academic Press).

Brodsky, M. (1995). Blues musicians' access to health care. *Medical Problems of Performing Artists*, March, 18–23.

Brodsky, W. (2006). In the wings of British orchestras: A multi-episode interview study among symphony players. *Journal of Occupational and Organisational Psychology,* **79**, 673–90.

Bugos, J.A., Perlstein, W.M., McCrae, S.C., Brophy, T.S., and Bedenbaugh, P.H. (2007). Individualized Piano Instruction enhances executive functioning and working memory in older adults. *Aging and Mental Health,* **11**(4), 464–71.

Bühler, C. (1933). *Der menschliche Lebenslauf als psychologisches Problem* (Leipzig: Hirzel).

Coffman, D.D. (2002). Music and quality of life in older adults. *Psychomusicology,* **18**, 76–88.

Cohen, A., Bailey, B., and Nilsson, T. (2002). The importance of music to seniors. *Psychomusicology,* **18**, 89–102.

Cooper, T.L. (2001). Adult's perceptions of piano study: Achievements and experiences. *Journal of Research in Music Education,* **49**(2), 156–68.

Črnivec, R. (2004). Assessment of health risks in musicians of the Slovene Philharmonic Orchestra, Ljubljana, Slovenia. *Medical Problems of Performing Artists*, September, 140–5.

Dennis, W. (1966). Creative productivity between the ages of 20 and 80 years. *Journal of Gerontology,* **21**, 1–8.

Dixon, R.A. (2000). Concepts and mechanisms of gains in cognitive aging, in D.C. Park and N. Schwarz (ed.) *Cognitive aging. A primer*, pp. 23–41 (Philadelphia, PA: Psychology Press).

Dunsby, J. (2002). Performers on performance, in J. Rink (ed.). *Musical Performance. A Guide to Understanding*, pp. 225–36 (Oxford: Oxford University Press).

Eckhardt, J., Pawlitza, E., and Windgasse, T. (2006). Besucherpotential von Opernaufführungen und Konzerten der klassischen Musik. Ergebnisse der ARD-Musikstudie 2005. *Media Perspektiven* (5), 273–82.

Fishbein, M., Middlestadt, S.E., Ottati, V., Straus, S., and Ellis, A. (1988). Medical problems among ICSOM musicians: Overview of a national survey. *Medical Problems of Performing Artists* **3**, 1–8.

Fry, H.J.H. (1988). Patterns of over-use seen in 658 affected musicians. *International Journal of Music Education*, **11**, 3–16.

Gembris, H. (2006). Research on musical development in a lifespan perspective – An introduction, in: H. Gembris (ed.) *Musical Development from a Lifespan Perspective*, pp. 11–20 (Frankfurt: Peter Lang).

Gembris, H. (ed.) (2008a). *Musik im Alter: Soziokulturelle Rahmenbedingungen und individuelle Möglichkeiten* (Frankfurt: Peter Lang).

Gembris, H. (2008b). Musical activities in the third age: An empirical study with amateur musicians, in: A. Daubney, E. Longhi, A. Lamont, and D.J. Hargreaves (eds.), *Musical Development and Learning. Conference Proceedings, 2nd European Conference on Developmental Psychology of Music*, pp. 103–8 (Hull: GK Publishing).

Gembris, H. (2009a). *Grundlagen musikalischer Begabung und Entwicklung* (3rd edn., Augsburg: Wißner).

Gembris, H. (2009b). Musik ist Bewegung und vermittelt Orientierung. Perspektiven für das Alter. In: Landesstiftung Baden-Württemberg (ed.) *Training bei Demenz. Dokumentation der Ergebnisse zum Kongress 'Training bei Demenz' Dezember 2008*, pp. 73–88. Stuttgart: Schriftenreihe der Landesstiftung Baden-Württemberg. Available at: http://www.bwstiftung.de/uploads/tx_ffbwspub/training_bei_demenz.pdf (accessed 25 September 2010)

Habermann, G. (1986). *Stimme und Sprache. Eine Einführung in ihre Physiologie und Hygiene* (2nd, revised ed., Stuttgart: Thieme).

Hartogh, T. (2005). *Musikgeragogik - Ein bildungstheoretischer Entwurf. Musikalische Altenbildung im Schnittfeld von Musikpädagogik und Geragogik* (Augsburg: Wißner).

Hays, T. and Minichiello, V. (2005). The meaning of music in the lives of older people: a qualitative study. *Psychology of Music,* **33**(4), 437–51.

Henoch, M. and Chesky, K. (1999). Hearing loss and aging: Implications for the professional musician. *Medical Problems of Performing Artists*, June, 76–9.

Hoppmann, R. and Ekman, E.F. (1999). Arthritis in the aging musician. *Medical Problems of Performing Artists*, June, 80–4.

Jäncke, L. (2008). *Macht Musik schlau? Neue Erkenntnisse aus den Neurowissenschaften und der kognitiven Psychologie* (Bern: Huber).

Jennen, M. and Gembris, H. (2000). Veränderungen des musikalischen Tempos bei Dirigenten. Eine empirische Untersuchung anhand von Schallplattenaufnahmen von Mozarts 'Don Giovanni' und 'Die Zauberflöte', in: K.-E. Behne, G. Kleinen, and H. de la Motte-Haber (eds.), *Jahrbuch Musikpsychologie. Die Musikerpersönlichkeit*, pp. 29–46 (Göttingen: Hogrefe).

Johansson, Y.L. and Theorell, T. (2003). Satisfaction with work task quality correlates with employee health. A study of 12 professional orchestras. *Medical Problems of Performing Artists*, 141–9.

Jutras, P.J. (2006). The benefits of adult piano study as self-reported by selected adult piano students. *Journal of Research in Music Education*, **54**(2), 97–110.

Kliegel, M. and Jäger, R.S. (2008). Die kognitive Leistungsfähigkeit im mittleren und höheren Erwachsenenalter aus Sicht der Entwicklungspsychologie, in: H. Gembris (ed.) *Musik im Alter. Soziokulturelle Rahmenbedingungen und individuelle Möglichkeiten*, pp. 69–91 (Frankfurt: Peter Lang).

Kline, D.W. and Sicalfa, Ch. T. (1996). Visual and auditory aging, in: J.E. Birren and K.W. Schaie (ed.) *Handbook of the Psychology of Aging (Fourth edn.)*, pp. 181–203 (San Diego, CA: Academic Press).

Kopiez, R., Lehmann, A.C., and Klassen, J. (2009). Clara Schumann's collection of program leaflets: A historiometric analysis of life-span development, mobility, and repertoire canonization. *Poetics*, **37**(1), 50–73.

Krampe, R.Th. (1994). *Maintaining Excellence: Cognitive-Motor Performance in Pianists Differing in Age and Skill level*. Berlin: Max-Planck-Institut für Bildungsforschung.

Krampe, R. Th. (2006). Musical expertise from a lifespan perspective, in: H. Gembris (ed.) *Musical Development from a Lifespan Perspective*, pp. 91–106 (Frankfurt: Peter Lang).

Laukka, P. (2007). Uses of music and psychological well-being among the elderly. *Journal of Happiness Studies*, **8**(2), 215–41.

Lederman, R.J. (1999). Aging and the instrumental musician. *Medical Problems of Performing Artists*, June, 67–75.

Lehman, H.C. and Ingerham, D.W. (1939). Man's creative years in music. *The Scientific Monthly*, **48**, 431–43.

Maier, K., Ambühl-Caesar, G., and Schandry R. (1994). *Entwicklungspsychophysiologie.Körperliche Indikatoren psychischer Entwicklung* (München: Psychologie Verlags Union).

Manchester, R.A. (2009). Looking at musicians' health through the 'ages'. *Medical Problems of Perfoming Artists*, June, 55–57.

Manturzewska, M. (1990). A biographical study of the life-span development of professional musicians. *Psychology of Music*, **18**(2), 112–39.

Manturzewska, M. (2006). A biographical study of the lifespan development of professional musicians, in: H. Gembris (ed.) *Musical development from a lifespan perspective*, pp. 21–53 (Frankfurt: Peter Lang).

Mende, A. and Neuwöhner, U. (2006). Wer hört heute klassische Musik? ARD-E-Musikstudie 2005: Musiksozialisation, E-Musiknutzung und E-Musikkompetenz. *Media Perspektiven*, **5**, 246–58.

Moore, R.S., Staum, M.J., and Brotons, M. (1992). Music preferences of the elderly: Repertoire, vocal ranges, tempos, and accompaniments for singing. *Journal of Music Therapy*, **29**(4), 236–52.

Moser, S.R. (2003). Beyond the Mozart effect: Age-related cognitive functioning in instrumental music participants. *Dissertation Abstracts International Section A: Humanities and Social Sciences*, 64 (3-A), 760.

North, A.C. and Hargreaves, D.J. (2008). *The Social and Applied Psychology of Music* (Oxford: Oxford University Press).

Park, D.C. (2000). The basic mechanisms accounting for age-related decline in cognitive function, in: D.C. Park and N. Schwarz (eds.) *Cognitive Aging. A Primer*, pp. 3–22 (Philadelphia, PA: Psychology Press).

Park, D.C. and Gutchess, A.H. (2000). Cognitive aging and every day life, in: G. McPherson (ed.) *The Child As Musician. A Handbook of Musical Development*, pp. 1–31 (Oxford: Oxford University Press).

Parncutt, R. (2006). Prenatal development, in: G. McPherson (ed.) *The Child As Musician. A Handbook of Musical Development*, pp. 1–31 (Oxford: Oxford University Press).

Rohwer, D. (2008). Health and wellness issues for adult band musicians. *Medical Problems of Performing Artists*, June, 54–8.

Sataloff, R.T. (1992). Vocal aging: medical considerations in professional voice users. *Medical Problems of Performing Artists*, **7**(1), 17–21.

Schmidt-Ott, T. (2008). Altern im Orchester: Altersbezogene Leistungseinbußen und der Umgang damit, in: H. Gembris (ed.), *Musik im Alter. Soziokulturelle Rahmenbedingungen und individuelle Möglichkeiten*, pp. 173–93 (Frankfurt: Peter Lang).

Schonberg, H.C. (2010). Horowitz, Vladimir. In: *Grove Music Online. Oxford Music Online*. Available at: http://www.oxfordmusiconline.com/subscriber/article/grove/music/13372 (accessed 24 February, 2010).

Schuele, S. and Lederman, R.J. (2003). Focal dystonia in woodwind instrumentalists: Long-term outcome. *Medical Problems of Performing Artists*, March, 15–20.

Seidner, W. and Wendler, J. (1997). *Die Sängerstimme. Phoniatrische Grundlagen der Gesangsausbildung* (3rd, revised edn, Berlin: Henschel).

Simonton, D.K. (1977). Creative productivity, age, and stress: A biographical time-series analysis of 10 classical composers. *Journal of Personality and Social Psychology*, **35**(11), 791–804.

Simonton, D.K. (1991). Emergence and realization of genius: The lives and works of 120 classical composers. *Journal of Personality and Social Psychology*, **61**(5), 829–40.

Simonton, D.K. (2000). Creative development as acquired expertise: Theoretical issues and an empirical test. *Developmental Review, 20*(2), 283–318.

Sluming, V., Brooks, J., Howard, M., Downes, J.J., and Roberts, N. (2007). Broca's area supports enhanced visuospatial cognition in orchestral musicians. *Journal of Neuroscience, 27*(14), 3799–806. Available at: http://www.jneurosci.org/cgi/content/abstract/27/14/3799 (accessed 25 September 2010).

Smith, D.W.E. (1988). The great symphony orchestra – A relatively good place to grow old. *International Journal of Aging and Human Development, 27*, 233–47.

Smith, D.W.E. (1989). Aging and the careers of symphony orchestra musicians. *Medical Problems of Performing Artists, 4*(2), 81–5.

Smith, D.W.E. (1992). Medical problems of orchestral musicians according to age and stage of career. *Medical Problems of Performing Artists* (December), 132–4.

Sosniak, L.A. (1985). Learning to be a concert pianist, in: B.S. Bloom (ed.) *Developing Talent in Young People,* pp. 19–67 (New York: Ballantine).

Spahn, C. and Richter, B. (2006). The development of the singing voice across the lifespan, in: H. Gembris (ed.) *Musical Development from a Lifespan Perspective,* pp. 119–30 (Frankfurt: Peter Lang).

Verghese, J., Lipton, R.B., Katz, M.J., Hall, C., Derby, C.A., Kuslansky, G., *et al.* (2003). Leisure activities and the risk of dementia in the elderly. *New England Journal of Medicine, 25*, 2508–16.

Warrington, J., Winspur, I., and Steinwede, D. (2002). Upper-extremity problems in musicians related to age. *Medical Problems of Performing Artists*, September, 131–4.

Zacharias, S. (2000). *Diagnose Alzheimer: Helmut Zacharias.* Köln: Hirnliga. Available at: http://www.hirnliga.de/Fordern_Spenden/sylvia_zacharias.htm (accessed 25 September 2010).

Chapter 26

Music Education and Therapy for Children and Young People with Cognitive Impairments: Reporting on a Decade of Research

Adam Ockelford and Kyproulla Markou

Introduction

A little over a decade ago, the first author set out a position paper that considered the place of music in the education of children and young people with severe or profound cognitive impairments (Ockelford 2000). A number of issues were identified, including a dearth of knowledge as to the music provision that was made for these pupils and students. There was a perception, nonetheless, that music-pedagogical thinking and practice had largely neglected learners with such levels of disability, and a belief that music therapy had evolved to fill the void—often *substituting* for music education rather than *complementing* it. As a consequence, there was a lack of conceptual clarity as to what should reasonably constitute music *education* for those with severe or profound levels of learning disability as opposed to what could appropriately be regarded as falling within the remit of music *therapy*, and no clear idea of how education and therapy were related in this context.

The scant evidence that was available—a few references in the literature and informal observation of practice in schools—suggested that the content of music lessons and therapy sessions were likely to be similar in content, and that the difference between them probably lay in the teacher's or therapist's approach. It seemed that music therapy tended to promote the notion of wellbeing among clients more strongly through adopting a more child-centred approach, whereas music education laid a greater emphasis on fostering the development of skills, knowledge and understanding, through a combination of internally and externally determined goals. (It was suggested that a third category, 'training', was driven entirely by extrinsic factors.)

Research was proposed that would:

- Investigate what music provision was made for pupils and students with learning difficulties in the England.
- Map the musical development of children and young people with severe or profound learning difficulties.
- Elucidate the relationship between education and therapy for this group, with a particular focus on issues such as the locus of control and wellbeing.

Provision

The *PROMISE* research project was set up to investigate what music provision was being made for children and young people with learning difficulties in special schools in England (Welch et al. 2001; Ockelford et al. 2002). Although the work was to be undertaken in England, the research team believed that the findings would have wider relevance, since there was no research evidence, or indications in policy or curricular documentation, to suggest that provision was significantly more advanced elsewhere. In total, data from 52 special schools were obtained.

Curriculum

The research shows that, at the turn of the twenty-first century, there appears to have been no common music curriculum in place for pupils with severe or profound cognitive impairments, references to the framework theoretically offered by the English National Curriculum notwithstanding. Indeed, it seems that music education provision for young people with complex needs in England was characterized by diversity and idiosyncrasy. In some cases, approaches that were developed in the context of the early years appeared to have been extended to later phases—on account, no doubt, of pupils' limited levels of functional development.

Shortly after the *PROMISE* report appeared, the UK Government, through the then Qualifications and Curriculum Authority (QCA), published the so-called 'P-Levels', which were intended to assist teachers in enabling their pupils with learning difficulties to access a broad and balanced curriculum (including music). However, as we shall see, the 'P-Level' for music was flawed in its conception, and observations undertaken as part of the *Sounds of Intent* project (see below) suggest that it has had little practical impact on the design or delivery of the music curriculum. Rather, teachers have learnt to report their pupils' musical experiences, responses and actions against a set of criteria that can at best be described as arbitrary in music-developmental terms.

Resources

The *PROMISE* research (supported by an analysis of a sample of 50 subsequent Ofsted[1] inspection reports, 2000–2005; see Ockelford 2008) suggested that the resources available for the music education of many children and young people with severe or profound learning difficulties were limited—a deficiency that must inevitably have constrained the range of school-based musical experiences that were available to this generation of pupils and students. For example, the prevalence of untuned percussion instruments could only have reinforced the conceptualization of much of the music curriculum within an early years framework, while the domination of 'domestic' music technology mitigated against pupils' active engagement in musical activities. Subsequent observation of a wide range of schools through the *Sounds of Intent* project suggests that items of handheld percussion still tend to fill instrument trays, albeit with examples from a broader diversity of cultures that are now more readily available to teachers. However, specialist music and sound technology does appear to be in more general use than a decade ago, particularly in the context of multisensory environments.

Music in the wider curriculum

The *PROMISE* research and the subsequent Ofsted reports (up to 2005) indicated that the use of music as a medium for the delivery of the wider curriculum—as an agent to enhance learning

---

[1] 'Ofsted' is the *Office for Standards in Education, Children's Services and Skills*, which in England regulates and inspects the care of children and young people, and the education and skills provision for learners of all ages.

throughout the school day—was highly valued and widespread in special schools making provision for pupils with learning difficulties. However, there were no indications that music was systematically conceptualized in this role, nor that general education that used music as a device to promote other learning was coherently linked to music education per se. Yet commonsense suggests that, for pupils whose perception of the world is likely to be fragmented and confusing, a joined-up approach could only have benefited learning and development. Subsequent evidence, for example, from the second author's PhD study (Markou 2010), and that of Cheng (2010), as well as from the *Sounds of Intent* project, suggests that the same position holds true today.

External links

The *PROMISE* research suggested that there were strong links with the wider musical community, and that a good deal of activity was taking place that was reckoned by those involved to have much intrinsic merit for the pupils and students concerned, despite few of the staff having any special training to work with young people with special needs. Moreover, external links seem to have arisen *opportunistically* rather than *strategically*, and there is no evidence, either in the *PROMISE* research or in the later sample of Ofsted reports (Ockelford 2008), that any attempts had been made to relate special events to day-to-day music curricula. Again, evidence from Cheng (2010), suggests that a similar picture may still pertain.

Gauging attainment and progress

The *PROMISE* research found that music coordinators found it easier to conceptualize *extra-musical* outcomes to musical activity with pupils with learning difficulties than purely *musical* attainment and progress. This anomaly was echoed in the comments made by head teachers in relation to music's perceived wider benefits and in the tendency of the Ofsted to focus on the description and analysis of extra-musical (as opposed to musical) activity. The *Sounds of Intent* project (described below) was set up to address this issue, which the researchers considered to lie at the heart of many of the problems associated with music education provision for children and young people with cognitive impairments. It was clear that teachers working in special schools had no sense of the music-developmental paths that their pupils and students were likely to follow, and so had no context in which to assess what they observed and only a limited conception of what 'progress' might mean. Without either of these building blocks in being in place, curriculum design inevitably tended to be ad hoc too.

Music therapy

The provision of music therapy varied considerably across the schools in the *PROMISE* sample. It was reported as being provided on site by 36% of schools,[2] while 19% were aware of some pupils receiving music therapy outside. Although two schools reported offering music therapy to all their pupils, on average, the number of pupils receiving this service was small, equating only to around 2% of the population of children and young people with severe or profound learning difficulties. All the therapists worked with individual pupils, with some undertaking additional work with up to four children or young people at a time, and three taking larger groups.

With regard to the musical content of the sessions, one therapist used improvised music exclusively, five improvised most of the time, and two improvised and used established repertoire in equal measure. As to the style of this repertoire, half the therapists reported using nursery rhymes;

---

[2] Music therapy was mentioned in six (12%) of the 50 Ofsted reports (2000-2005).

two also used folksongs; two, pieces that they had composed; one, pop songs; and one, classical pieces. Only one therapist used recorded music in sessions.

In relation to gauging progress, the therapists gave detailed responses that were largely centred on communication, such as, 'eye contact', 'vocalization', 'language development', 'ability to express emotions through playing', 'awareness of others', and 'turn-taking'. They also mentioned 'increasing confidence', 'enjoyment', 'increased attention span' and 'anticipation of sessions'. These criteria were in many cases identical to those used by music coordinators and head teachers to assess general progress made through music. Other school staff identified similar benefits of music therapy, including various aspects of communication ('developing eye contact', 'non-verbal … communication', 'increasing vocalization and pre-verbal skills', 'developing interpersonal expressive communication', and 'turn-taking') and personal growth ('development of listening and attention', 'increased awareness of self', 'confidence building', 'gaining freedom and independence', and 'making choices'). Again, these closely resembled music coordinators' and head teachers' comments made in relation to music education and progress in other areas.

In summary, the activities that went to make up music therapy sessions with pupils who have learning difficulties displayed a similar eclectic mix to those undertaken in the context of music education—apparently based largely on the personal beliefs and expertise of the practitioner concerned—and many of the perceived benefits of music therapy for pupils with cognitive impairments appeared to be very similar to those ascribed to music education. Yet there is no evidence that music-therapeutic activity or outcomes were typically used to inform other experiential or developmental programmes that involved music, or vice versa. Rather, for the few children who received music therapy, it appeared to be another strand of musical experience, running, at best, in parallel with others.

The relationship between music therapy and music education in provision for children and young people with severe or profound learning difficulties was subsequently the subject of detailed doctoral research by the second author, and is reported below.

Conclusion

The data gathered from the *PROMISE* research project and the sample of 50 Ofsted reports (2000–2005) indicated that there was a widespread recognition of the potential significance of music in the lives of pupils with cognitive impairments and of its power to assist in many areas of their learning and development. While the research was undertaken in England, anecdotal evidence and comments in the (very scarce) literature on the subject suggested that the findings summarized here may well have an international relevance.

While, in a few schools, there is evidence of structured music provision for different age groups, with fruitful links to the wider musical community, the general impression is one of relatively isolated professional activity in music, with schools taking an essentially pragmatic and eclectic approach in the absence of a commonly agreed framework, informed by empirical data, that would set out the musical development of children and young people with complex needs. The *Sounds of Intent* project sought to make good this shortfall.

Towards a model of music education for children and young people with learning difficulties

A key element in the first author's position paper (Ockelford 2000) was the proposition that music education for pupils and students with severe or profound learning difficulties should be conceived as having two distinct strands: activities that are undertaken primarily for their intrinsically musical value ('education *in* music') and those whose main function is to promote wider learning and development ('education *through* music'). Both elements were grounded in the fact that hearing typically starts to develop in the human fetus 4–3 months before birth, and that, by the time they are born, babies may be particularly sensitive to sounds with which they have become familiar in the womb and prefer them to others: their mother's voice, for example, the language she speaks, and certain pieces of music (Lecanuet 1996). Hence those with severe or profound learning difficulties, whose global development may be at a very early stage (as in the first few months of life), may nonetheless be able to process organized sounds relatively effectively: the musical mind may be intact amid a welter of other cognitive challenges. This has implications both for education *in* and *through* music.

Education *in* music: the *Sounds of Intent* project

The model of education *in* music first proposed in Ockelford (1998) had two components: 'listening, responding and reflecting' and 'creating, causing and controlling sounds'. These evolved through substantial further research in what became the *Sounds of Intent* project (reported, for example, in Ockelford et al. 2005; Welch et al. 2009; Cheng et al. 2010; Ockelford et al. 2011; Vogiatzoglou et al. 2011). This sought to map musical development in children and young people with learning difficulties, and to provide a framework to inform the design of curricula suited to their special needs and abilities.

The *Sounds of Intent* research evolved partly in response to the 'P-Levels' (QCA 2001), which outline early learning and attainment for pupils deemed to be functioning 'below' Level 1 on the English National Curriculum. They have eight levels, from 'P1' to 'P8', although the first three levels, corresponding to those with profound needs, are each subdivided into two: P1(i) and P1(ii), P2(i) and P2(ii), and P3(i) and P3(ii). These six descriptors are common across the whole curriculum, with different subject-focused examples added to illustrate some of the ways in which, it is suggested, staff may be able to identify attainment in different subject contexts. From level P4 to P8, the document states that 'it is possible to describe pupils' performance in a way that indicates the emergence of skills, knowledge and understanding in music'—and examples are provided of how this can be achieved. It is claimed that teachers can use the 11 performance descriptions to decide which best fits a pupil over a period of time and in different contexts, and so track his or her 'linear progress' towards attainment at Level 1 of the National Curriculum.

However, the *Sounds of Intent* research team believed this claim to be unsustainable, and they identified a number of serious issues with the 'P-Level' for music. The main problem was the basis on which it was developed: it was unclear what evidence was used to underpin its construction, although it was said to 'draw on effective practice across a range of schools'. But in the absence of a demonstrable, systematically derived, empirical foundation, we were left with an abiding sense of the anecdotal. In relation to music, for example, the following is an exhaustive list of the examples given for levels P1 to P3, in the order in which they occur.[3]

Startles at sudden noise

Becomes still in a concert hall

Becomes excited at repeated patterns of sounds

Turns towards unfamiliar sounds

Looks for the source of music

---

[3] Some examples, which do not in reality pertain to achievement in music (such as 'leading an adult to the CD player), are omitted.

Is encouraged to stroke the strings of a guitar

Relaxes during certain pieces of music but not others

Recognizes a favourite song

Repeatedly presses the keys of an electronic keyboard instrument

Taps piano keys gently and with more vigour

Listens intently when moving across and through a sound beam

Anticipates a loud sound at a particular point in a piece of music

Taps, strokes, rubs or shakes an instrument to produce various effects

We could not imagine how these examples could possibly be thought to be representative when there was no mention (for example) of vocalization or vocal interaction—widely considered to be the bedrock of early music-making and musical communication (see, for instance, Papoušek 1996, p. 58; Trevarthen 2002).

In contrast to the QCA's approach, which attempted to extrapolate developmental concepts 'downwards' from the artificial sociological construct of the National Curriculum, the *Sounds of Intent* team adopted a bottom-up approach, working with a group of practitioners who were active in the field to develop shared interpretations of the different forms and levels of musical engagement that were observed among their pupils and students with severe or profound learning difficulties. Children's and young people's responses, actions, and interactions were carefully noted and encapsulated in short descriptions. (Examples are shown in Table 26.1.)

Table 26.1 Examples of musical engagement observed in children and young people with severe or profound learning difficulties

#	Observation	R	P	I
1	**A** sits motionless in her chair. Her teacher approaches and plays a cymbal with a soft beater, gently at first, and then more loudly, in front of her and then near to each ear. A does not appear to react	✓		
2	**R** is lying in the 'Little Room' (a small, resonant environment, with soundmakers suspended within easy reach), vocalizing in an almost constant drone. Occasionally a sudden movement of her right arm knocks her hand against a bell. Each time, she smiles and her vocalizing briefly turns into a laugh	✓	✓	
3	**M**'s music therapy session begins—as ever—with the 'Hello' song. And as ever, he makes no discernible response			✓
4	**B** startles and then smiles when someone drops a tray of cutlery in the dining room	✓		
5	**T** brushes her left hand against the strings of guitar that someone is holding near to her. There is a pause and then she raises her hand and brushes the strings again, and then again		✓	

Table 26.1 (Continued) Examples of musical engagement observed in children and young people with severe or profound learning difficulties

#	Observation	R	P	I
6	**Y** usually makes a rasping sound as he breathes. He seems to be unaware of what he is doing, and the rasping persists, irrespective of external stimulation. His class teacher has tried to see whether Y can be made aware of his sounds by making them louder (using a microphone, amplifier, and speakers), but so far this approach has met with no response		✓	
7	**G**'s teacher notices that he often turns his head towards her when she sings to him, but she has never noticed him turn towards other sounds	✓		
8	**W** giggles when people repeat patterns of syllables to her such as 'ma ma ma ma ma', 'da da da da da', or 'ba ba ba ba ba'	✓		
9	**J**'s short, sharp vocalizations are interpreted by his teachers and carers to mean that he wants someone to vocalize back			✓
10	**K** gets very excited when she hears the regular beat on the school's drum machine	✓		
11	**U** loves 'call and response' games and joins in by making his own sounds			✓
12	**C** copies simple patterns of vocalization—imitating the ups and downs of her speech and language therapist's voice			✓
13	**S** waves her hand more and more vigorously through an ultrasonic beam, creating an ever wider range of swirling sounds		✓	
14	**N** often vocalizes in response to vocal sounds that are made close to him, although he does not seem to copy what he hears			✓
15	**Z** loves the sound of the bell tree and, when it stops, she rocks in her chair which staff interpret as a gesture for 'more'	✓		
16	**D** has been able to make a wide range of vocal sounds since he started school, but recently he has begun to make more melodious vowel sounds, which he repeats in short sequences		✓	
17	**L** hums distinct patterns of notes and repeats them. Her favourite pattern sounds rather like a playground chant, and her music teacher notices that she repeats it from one day to the next, though not always starting on the same note		✓	

(continued)

Table 26.1 (Continued) Examples of musical engagement observed in children and young people with severe or profound learning difficulties

#	Observation	R	P	I
18	**F** cries whenever she hears the 'Goodbye' song. It only takes the first two or three notes to be played on the keyboard for her to experience a strong emotional reaction	✓		
19	**H** enjoys copying simple rhythms on an untuned percussion instrument. Now he is started making his own rhythms up too, and he flaps his hands with delight when someone else copies what he is doing			✓
20	**E** just laughs and laughs when people imitate her vocalisations			✓
21	**V** vocalizes to get his therapist to make a sound—it does not matter what, he just seems to relish having a vocal response			✓
22	**I** always gets excited in the middle of the 'Slowly/ Quickly' song, anticipating the sudden change of pace	✓		
23	**O** scratches the tambourine, making a range of sounds. Whenever he plays near the rim and the bells jingle, he smiles	✓	✓	
24	**Q**'s eye movements intensify when he hears the big band play	✓		
25	**X** distinctly tries to copy high notes and low notes in vocal interaction sessions			✓
25	**P** has learnt to associate his teacher's jangly bracelet, which she always wears, with her: for him, it seems to be an important part of her identity	✓		

It became evident that it would not be possible to conceptualize their musical development unidimensionally since, for example, a young person's capacity for attending to sounds may well be more advanced than his or her ability to produce them. Therefore, at least two dimensions were required: 'listening and responding', for which the single term 'reactive' ('R') was adopted, and 'causing, creating and controlling', for which the label 'proactive' ('P') was used. In relation to the examples given above, 1, 2, 4, 7, 8, 10, 15, 18, 22, 23, 24 and 26 were considered to be entirely or predominantly 'reactive' and 2, 5, 6, 13, 16, 17 and 23, 'proactive'. However, that left other observations (as in examples 3, 9, 11, 12, 14, 19, 20, 21 and 25) in which listening to sounds and making them occurred in the context of participation with others. It was decided that this form of activity merited the status of a separate dimension, which was termed 'interactive' ('I'). (See Table 26.1.) While the three dimensions R, P, and I have areas of conceptual overlap, the important thing was that they were deemed by practitioners to be *meaningful* and *useful* in terms of categorizing the types of musical engagement that they observed.

Attempts were made to place examples such as those cited above along each of the three dimensions: (i) *reactive* (in response to another), (ii) *proactive* (initiating behaviour without an obvious external prompt), or (iii) *interactive* (with another). Their relative position of each within a dimension was based on its status a necessary developmental precursor or possible successor to another or others. For instance, it was evident that an awareness of sound (as in Example 2) must precede a differentiated response (as in Example 7), which in turn must precede the capacity to anticipate change (Example 22). This heuristic approach was necessary since the evidence available comprised snapshots of *different* children at various stages of development, rather than longitudinal data on the *same* children as they matured, which would have offered greater certainty as to the nature of developmental change. Taking a more exploratory tack, though, was deemed valid as a preliminary step for two reasons: first, since at that stage it was not yet clear what the appropriate data to collect would be; and second, since it was believed that meaningful longitudinal studies of children with complex needs would be likely to last for months if not years. However, it was felt that once an initial model had been developed, this could subsequently be used to inform longer-term empirical work, as well as being informed by it.

As potential sequences of stages of musical engagement emerged, they were mapped onto what is known of 'typical' early musical development (drawing on the established literature in this field, ranging, for example, from Moog 1968/1976; Dowling 1982 and Hargreaves 1986 to Trehub 1990, 2003; Fassbender 1996; Lecanuet 1996; Papoušek 1996; Trevarthen 2002 and Welch 2006) as a way of benchmarking what was being proposed, but without imposing potentially inappropriate constraints, since it was not known just how relevant 'usual' development was to the way in which the musicality of children with complex needs evolves.

A third influence was Ockelford's 'zygonic' theory of musical-structural cognition (for example, 2005, 2010) which seeks to explain how music makes intuitive sense through the (typically non-conscious) recognition of repetition and regularity in the domains of pitch and perceived time: the thinking being that, since such a capacity does not arise in people fully-fledged, it must evolve as a strand in musical development, implying that the theory may provide a useful way of conceptualizing stages within that process of maturation.

A number of attempts were made to draw the three sources of evidence (observations, the findings of 'mainstream' child psychology and zygonic theory) into a single coherent music-developmental framework for young people with complex needs. Different configurations were proposed, discussed and systematically trialled in the field, with practitioners offering qualitative feedback, supplemented with quantitative data gathered by a research assistant. This information enabled the research team iteratively to refine the model, enabling it to capture a wider range of musical behaviours, and enhancing intra- and inter-domain consistency (Welch et al. 2009). Eventually, six fundamental levels of music processing capacity emerged, which offered both an intuitively satisfying and theoretically coherent scheme. These are set out in Table 26.2.

Extending these six levels across the three domains of musical engagement that had been identified gave rise to the following 'headlines' or 'level descriptors' of reactivity, proactivity and interactivity (see Figure 26.1). These were arranged as 18 segments in circular form, which practitioners on the *Sounds of Intent* research team regarded as being the most appropriate metaphor for children's development, ranging from the centre, with its focus on self, outwards, to increasingly wider communities of others.

For ease of reference, levels were ranked from 1–6, each of which could be preceded with an 'R', a 'P', or an 'I', to indicate, respectively, reactive, proactive, or interactive segments. Each was broken down into four more detailed elements, as the examples in Table 26.3 show.

Although this table is regular in appearance, the way that the level descriptors and elements relate to each other within and between the reactive, proactive, and interactive domains is complex. Level descriptors form a hierarchy whereby, within each domain, achievement at higher levels is dependent on the accomplishment of all those that precede. So, for example, in the

Table 26.2 The six levels underpinning the *Sounds of Intent* framework (acronym 'CIRCLE')

Level	Description	Core cognitive abilities
1	Confusion and **C**haos	None: no awareness of sound as a distinct perceptual entity
2	Awareness and **I**ntentionality	An emerging awareness of sound as a distinct perceptual entity and of the variety that is possible within the domain of sound
3	Relationships, Repetition, **R**egularity	A growing awareness of the possibility and significance of *relationships* between the basic aspects of sounds
4	Sounds Forming **C**lusters	An evolving perception of *groups* of sounds, and the relationships that may exist between them
5	Deeper Structural **L**inks	A growing recognition of whole pieces, and of the frameworks of pitch and perceived time that lie behind them
6	Mature Artistic **E**xpression	A developing awareness of the culturally determined 'emotional syntax' of performance (expressed, for example, through *rubato* and dynamics) that articulates the 'narrative metaphor' of a piece

interactive domain, I. 4, 'Engages in musical dialogues, creating and recognizing coherent connections between groups of sounds', could only occur following I. 3, 'Interacts by imitating other's sounds or recognizing self being imitated' and (therefore) after accomplishing I. 2 and I. 1. *Between* domains, there is a broad flow of contingency that runs from reactive to proactive and then to interactive. For instance, in the proactive domain, intentionally making patterns in sound through repetition (P. 3) depends on the capacity to recognize simple patterns in sound (R. 3); while interacting with another or others using sound (I. 2) relies on the ability to cause, create or control sounds intentionally (P. 2), which in turn requires an awareness of sound (R. 2). The pattern of contingencies that links the 72 elements is more intricate. Although in some cases there is a necessary connection between elements at different levels *within* domains (for example, a pupil could not engage in intentional repetition—P. 3. A—before having the wherewithal to make a variety of sounds—P. 2. B) and *between* them (for instance, imitating the sounds made by another——I. 3. A—similarly requires functioning at the level of P. 2. B), this is not always the case. It is perfectly conceivable that a child could intentionally make simple patterns through a regular beat (P. 3. B), for example, before using sounds to symbolize particular people, places or activities (P. 2. D). However, the research team felt that intricacies of this type were an inevitable consequence of the complicated nature of musical development: multi-layered and multi-stranded. At any given time, it was unlikely that the framework would indicate a pupil as being at a particular *point* on a developmental scale, but, rather, having a music-developmental *profile*, incorporating attainment at different levels in relation to a number of different elements.

Education *through* music

The second strand of music education for pupils and students with cognitive impairments proposed in the position paper (Ockelford 2000) was education *through* music, in which it is used as a tool to promote learning and development in a variety of other areas. This notion was developed at some length in Ockelford (2008, pp. 113–145), in which four extra-musical domains of activity were identified, drawing on the findings of the *PROMISE* research:

+ Body awareness and movement
+ Learning

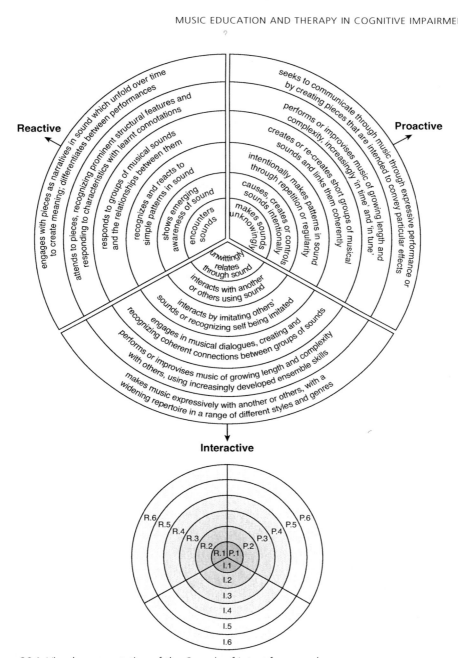

Figure 26.1 Visual representation of the *Sounds of Intent* framework.

Table 26.3 Elements at Levels 1–3 in the reactive, proactive and interactive domains

Reactive domain

Level	R.1	R.2	R.3
Descriptor	**Encounters sounds**	**Shows an emerging awareness of sound**	**Responds to simple patterns in sound**
Element A	Is exposed to a rich variety of sounds	Shows awareness (of a variety) of sounds	Responds to the repetition of sounds
Element B	Is exposed to a wide range of music	Responds differently to sound qualities that differ (e.g. loud/quiet), and/or change (e.g. getting louder)	Responds to a regular beat
Element C	Is exposed to music in different contexts	Responds to sounds increasingly independently of context	Responds to patterns of regular change
Element D	Is exposed to sounds that are linked to other sensory input	Responds to sounds that are linked to other sensory input	Responds to sounds used to symbolize other things

Proactive domain

Level	P.1	P.2	P.3
Descriptor	**Makes sounds unknowingly**	**Makes or controls sounds intentionally**	**Makes simple patterns in sound intentionally**
Element A	Sounds made by life-processes are enhanced and/or involuntary movements are used to make sounds	Makes sounds intentionally, through an increasing variety of means and with greater range and control	Intentionally makes simple patterns through repetition
Element B	Sounds are made or controlled through co-active movements	Expresses feelings through sound	Intentionally makes a regular beat
Element C	Activities to promote sound production occur in a range of contexts	Produces sounds intentionally in a range of contexts	Intentionally makes patterns through change
Element D	Activities to promote sound production are multisensory in nature	Produces sounds as part of multisensory activity	Uses sound to symbolize other things

Interactive domain

Level	1.1	1.2	1.3
Descriptor	**Relates unwittingly through sound**	**Interacts with others using sound**	**Interacts imitating others' sounds or through recognizing self being imitated**
Element A	Co-workers stimulate interaction by prompting with sounds and responding to any sounds that are made	Sounds made by another stimulate a response in sound	Imitates the sounds made by another

(continued)

Table 26.3 (Continued) Elements at Levels 1–3 in the reactive, proactive and interactive domains

Interactive domain

Level	1.1	1.2	1.3
Element B	Co-workers model interaction through sound	Sounds are made to stimulate a response in sound	Shows awareness of own sounds being imitated
Element C	Activity to promote interaction through sound occurs in a range of contexts	Interactions occur increasingly independently of context	Imitates simple patterns in sound made by another
Element D	Some interaction is multisensory in nature	Interaction through sound engages other senses too	Recognizes own patterns in sound being imitated

- Language and communication
- Social interaction.

Body awareness and movement

Children's and young people's awareness of their own physicality, and the control and coordination of a wider range of movements can be nurtured through playing instruments and other sound-makers. Whatever the movement required, the principle is that the pupil or student concerned will be motivated to move in order to produce a sound (implying that he or she is functioning in musical terms at *Sounds of Intent* Level 2 or above).

Music may also provide an 'auditory frame of reference' for movement, whereby the characteristics of a piece they are hearing influence, more or less specifically, accompanying actions. The strongest link between music and movement is found in rhythm, whereby regular changes in sound, which give the impression of a 'pulse', may stimulate a corresponding regularity in movement through the process of 'entrainment' (Clayton et al. 2005). In the domain of pitch, a rise is widely considered to correspond to movement in an upward direction and vice versa. While this correspondence is generally conveyed through the more or less conscious efforts of teachers and others, and appears to be at least in part culturally determined (Zbikowski 2002, p. 71), there is also some evidence that it occurs as a consequence of the natural way that thinking develops (Welch 1991). Either way, it implies the activation of cross-modal connections in the mind (between sound and percepts in another domain), which the *Sounds of Intent* framework suggests may occur from Level 2 onwards.

Learning

Music and other organized sound can be used to promote pupils' and students' acquisition of skills, knowledge and understanding in a number of ways, including:

- Using music and other structured auditory input to enhance sensory information obtained from the environment—for example, by systematically linking auditory to tactile, visual and other sensory experiences.
- Promoting the direct transfer of perceptual and cognitive attributes from musical contexts to other spheres of activity—for example, memory (Overy 1998) and concentration (Bunt 1994, pp. 111ff).
- Isolating selected qualities of sound and treating them as concepts to be manipulated in pursuit of educational goals beyond music—for example, sorting instruments on the basis of the materials from which they are made.

- Regarding pieces of music as potential sources of information about the cultures in which they were created—for example, learning something about Indonesian traditions through playing the gamelan.

Language and communication

Music and other organized sounds, in addition to speech, fulfil a range of symbolic functions in everyday life (such as TV theme tunes, the bells and gongs used in religious ceremonial, door chimes and the referee's whistle in sport)—and sound symbols can be devised especially to augment or replace efforts at receptive or expressive communication (Ockelford 2008, p. 132). For example, a series of sounding objects can function referentially as a kind of 'auditory timetable', informing pupils and students of which activities have been completed, and which are coming next.

Music shares common roots with verbal language in early development (Powers and Trevarthen 2009), and at all stages of the human experience, the two are combined in the form of songs and chants. This affinity can be particularly useful in promoting communication and fostering its development among children who have learning difficulties. Music can provide the motivation to use language, and it can help to structure it, through its characteristic use of repetition (Ockelford 2005).

Social interaction

Music has many different functions in life, many of which are social in nature (Hargreaves and North 1997). Music sessions can offer a unique and secure framework through which many of the skills and disciplines of social interaction (such as listening to others, turn taking, and making a relevant contribution) can be experienced and developed. This is especially true for pupils and students with severe or profound learning difficulties, for whom the intricacies of verbal language and the subtle visual cueing that typically inform face-to-face communication may prove particularly challenging to discern and comprehend.

Music education, music therapy, and the role of wellbeing

The conceptual confusion between music education and music therapy for children and young people with cognitive impairments hinted at in Ockelford (2000) and unearthed in the course of the *PROMISE* project (Welch et al. 2001), was echoed in subsequent research into the musicality of children and young people with septo-optic dysplasia (Pring and Ockelford 2005) and retinopathy of prematurity (Ockelford and Matawa 2009). Here some descriptions of the music *therapy* that was being offered seem to indicate that in reality music *education* was taking place. For example, a 7-and-a-half-year-old visually impaired autistic girl 'works with her music therapist on learning the piano and also a variety of instruments' (Ockelford et al. 2006, p. 32).

Similar examples are sprinkled across the music-therapeutic literature from the last 40 years or so. For example, Nordoff and Robbins describe how some of their young clients learnt 'new activities, new words, new music' and became more responsive to other people (1971, p. 123), how a girl started to develop speech through music therapy (op. cit., pp. 30–31), and how music helped an autistic boy to develop independence skills (p. 105). Similarly, Postacchini et al. (1993) relate how music therapy sessions with a 5-year-old girl with 'severe infantile regression' were considered to improve her movement and use of vision, and assist her in moving from pre-symbolic to symbolic communication. Among the reasons that Bunt sets out for undertaking music therapy with a 9-year-old boy with learning difficulties are 'to help develop auditory awareness and memory' and 'to help develop his ability to share' (1994, p. 105). Similarly, Schwalkwijk (1994, pp. 79ff) discusses the potential role of music therapy in the stimulation of motor and cognitive skills.

But to what extent do these accounts accord with the definitions of music therapy offered by therapists themselves? Bruscia (1987, p. 47), for example, asserts that 'Music therapy is a systematic process of intervention wherein the therapist helps the client to achieve health, using musical experiences and the relationships that develop through them as dynamic forces of change'. Bunt (1994, p. 8), in referring to this definition and others, concludes that 'Music therapy is the use of organized sounds and music within an evolving relationship between client and therapist to support and encourage physical, mental, social and emotional well-being'. When these aims are compared with the descriptions of the music-therapeutic activities cited above, it is evident that some therapists working with children and young people with learning difficulties have diversified from fostering 'well-being' through music, and moved into educational areas such as promoting learning and development, for example (where, as we have seen, music can fulfil a range of functions).

A decade ago, Ockelford (2000) questioned why therapists should have become involved in educational activity. It seemed that potential factors included the unwillingness of those working in music education to work with those with severe or profound learning difficulties. Although, with the increasing inclusion of children and young people with disabilities in mainstream schools, one might have expected the position to have changed in the intervening period, the reality is that those with severest levels of intellectual impairment are still educated in special schools, where, the *Sounds of Intent* research suggests, there are still relatively few music-education specialists working.

The *PROMISE* research and the evidence of the Ofsted inspection reports (2000–2005) suggested that the overlap between the activities that constitute education *in* and *through* music and those that comprise music therapy, identified by Ockelford (2000), continues to exist. The second author's doctoral research (Markou 2010) tackled this issue head on. She tested the speculation, set out in Ockelford's (2000) model, that the key difference lay in the teacher's or therapist's approach (Figure 26.2). The model had suggested that both music education and music therapy promote 'wellbeing', but that this was a more important feature of music therapy. Music education,

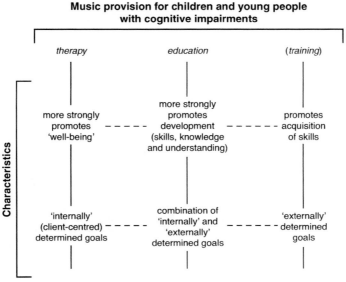

Fig. 26.2 The purported link between music therapy and music education for children and young people with cognitive impairments (after Ockelford, 2000, p. 214).

on the other hand, was more focused on 'development' (of skills, knowledge, and understanding). In parallel with this, therapy was conceived as having more client-centred, 'internally' determined goals, whereas effective music education was thought to balance 'internally' and 'externally' driven objectives.

To test this assertion, Markou asked an equal sample of teachers and therapists working in the field ($N = 96$), 'To what extent does the child play a part in guiding your sessions/lessons?'. The permitted range of responses was from '1 = not at all' to '10 = completely' set out on a Likert scale. The results were as shown in Figure 26.3.

These data suggest that teachers and therapists do indeed tend to differ in the importance they attach to child-centredness. Teachers perceive themselves on average as being slightly more child-centred than not, but with a spread of responses across the entire spectrum ($M = 6.23$, SD = 2.37), whereas therapists believe themselves to be almost entirely child-centred in their work ($M = 7.90$, SD=1.70). The difference is statistically significant, $t(96) = -3.95$, p <0.001. These perceptions tie in with the declared content of the music lessons and therapy sessions, with the majority of teachers and therapists claiming to use both improvised *and* pre-composed songs and instrumental music; 13 teachers using *only* pre-composed instrumental music and 12, *only* pre-composed songs; and 14 therapists using *only* improvised instrumental music and 11, *only* improvised songs (Figure 26.4)—differences that, again, are statistically significant, both for songs $\chi^2(2, N = 98) = 20.31$, p <0.001 and instrumental music $\chi^2(1, N = 98) = 24.27$, p <0.001.

Given the overlap, it is reasonable to ask whether aspects of education and therapy are inextricably linked in effective music provision for children and young people with severe or profound cognitive impairments. For example, one could argue that it would not be possible to engage in

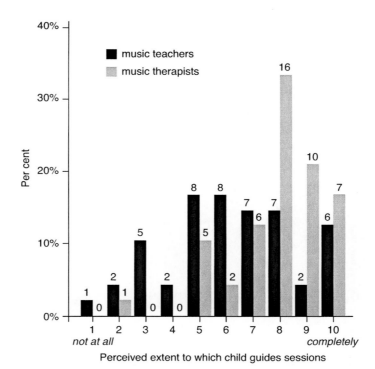

Fig. 26.3 The extent to which children and young people are considered by therapists and teachers to determine the direction of sessions.

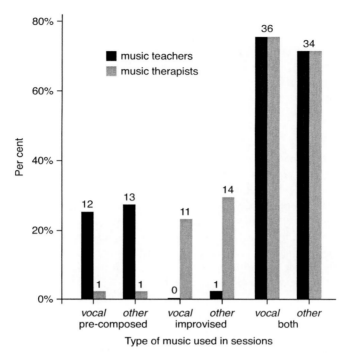

Fig. 26.4 The proportion of improvised and pre-composed vocal and instrumental music that teachers and therapists report using.

music therapy with such pupils and students without, at least to an extent, entering in to educational activity too, since how could they benefit from therapy without some pre-existing skills and understanding (presumably acquired through education, formal or informal)? And is it not reasonable—indeed desirable—to assume that, in many children and young people, skills and understanding will develop in the course of therapy sessions? It seems reasonable to argue that, the greater their technical proficiency, the more effectively children and young people will be able to express themselves in music, and the more likely they will be able to attain, Bunt's state of wellbeing, albeit transiently. Conversely, it seems unimaginable that a child or young person could make educational progress unless he or she had or developed at least some sense of wellbeing in the course of engaging with the curriculum. Hence, is there not inevitably a therapeutic component in education too?

Conclusion

Looking back over the first decade of the twenty-first century, it is pleasing to note that significant progress has been made against the key research objectives set out in Ockelford (2000). The *PROMISE* report investigated the provision that was made for pupils and students with learning difficulties in the England—work that was updated through an analysis of relevant Ofsted reports (2000–2005) (Ockelford 2008). The musical development of children and young people with severe or profound learning difficulties was mapped in great detail as the central focus of the *Sounds of Intent* project, through the collaboration of schools across the UK. Finally, the relationship between education and therapy for this group was elucidated through the second author's doctoral work (Markou 2010).

The authors very much hope that the next decade will see the move from research to impact, as we engage with others to ensure that the academic thinking outlined in this chapter and elsewhere is put to work to influence policy and practice in the field. We believe that the findings of the *Sounds of Intent* research, which is currently coming to fruition through the development of an interactive website, will be key, as it will be freely accessible to all practitioners: therapists, teachers, community musicians, and parents. The information and resources this will make available, combined with its ease of use, should fill in many of the gaps identified in *PROMISE* research, enabling those working with children and young people with severe or cognitive impairments—music specialists and non-specialists alike—to offer a coherent music curriculum throughout school and beyond. The connection between music therapy and education remains as complex as ever, and continues to evolve as forces in the external environment change (see, for example, Darrow and Adamek in press; Jellison in press; McFerran and Elefant in press). Hopefully the *Sounds of Intent* framework will provide a common basis for planning and evaluation, while recognizing that the priorities of delivery may differ. In this respect, it is interesting to observe how, in the last few years, the notion of 'wellbeing', which was previously felt to be the preserve of therapists, is now entering educational discourse much more widely (see, for example White 2007), and it could be that provision for those with the most complex needs will prove a melting pot for new and welcome developments in this respect.

References

Bruscia, K. (1987). *Improvisational Models of Music Therapy*. Springfield, IL: Charles: C. Thomas.

Bunt, L. (1994). *Music Therapy: An Art Beyond Words*. London: Routledge.

Cheng, E. (2010). Musical Behaviours and Development of Children and Young People with Complex Needs: Three Longitudinal Case Studies. Unpublished PhD dissertation, London: Institute of Education.

Cheng, E., Ockelford, A., and Welch, G. (2010). Researching and developing music provision in special schools in England for children and young people with complex needs. *Australian Journal of Music Education*, **2009**(2), 27–48.

Clayton, M., Sager, R., and Will, U. (2005). In time with the music: the concept of entrainment and its significance for ethnomusicology. *European Meetings in Ethnomusicology*, **11**, 3–142.

Darrow, A.-A. and Adamek, M. (in press). Preparing for the future: music students with special educational needs in school and community life. In: G. McPherson and G. Welch (eds.) *The Oxford Handbook of Music Education*, Oxford: Oxford University Press.

Dowling, J. (1982). Melodic information processing and its development. In: D. Deutsch (ed.) *The Psychology of Music*, pp. 413–29. New York: Academic Press.

Fassbender, C. (1996). Infants' auditory sensitivity towards acoustic parameters of speech and music. In: I. Deliège and J. Sloboda (eds.) *Musical Beginnings*, pp. 56–87. Oxford: Oxford University Press.

Hargreaves, D. (1986). *The Developmental Psychology of Music*. Cambridge: Cambridge University Press.

Hargreaves, D. and North, A. (1997). *The Social Psychology of Music*. Oxford: Oxford University Press.

Jellison, J. (in press). Inclusive music classrooms and programmes. In: G. McPherson and G. Welch (eds.) *The Oxford Handbook of Music Education*. Oxford: Oxford University Press.

Lecanuet, J.-P. (1996). Prenatal auditory experiencee. In: I. Deliège and J. Sloboda (eds) *Musical Beginnings*, pp. 3–34. Oxford: Oxford University Press.

Markou, K. (2010). The Relationship between Music Therapy and Music Education in Special School Settings: The Practitioners' Views. Unpublished PhD thesis, London: Roehampton University.

McFerran, K. and Elefant, C. (in press). A fresh look at music therapy in special education. In: G. McPherson and G. Welch (eds.) *The Oxford Handbook of Music Education*. Oxford: Oxford University Press.

Moog, H. (1968/1976). *The Musical Experiences of the Pre-school Child* (C. Clarke, trans.). London: Schott.

Nordoff, P. and Robbins, C. (1971). *Therapy in Music for Handicapped Children*. London: Victor Gollancz.

Ockelford, A. (1998). *Music Moves: Music in the Education of Children and Young People who are Visually Impaired and have Learning Disabilities*. London: Royal National Institute of the Blind.

Ockelford, A. (2000). Music in the education of children with severe or profound learning difficulties: Issues in current UK provision, a new conceptual framework, and proposals for research. *Psychology of Music,* **28**(2), 197–217.

Ockelford, A. (2005). *Repetition in Music: Theoretical and Metatheoretical Perspectives*. London: Ashgate.

Ockelford, A. (2008). *Music for Children and Young People with Complex Needs*. Oxford: Oxford University Press.

Ockelford, A. (2010). Zygonic theory: Introduction, scope, prospects. *Zeitschrift der Gesellschaft für Musiktheorie,* **6**(2), 91–172.

Ockelford, A. and Matawa, C. (2009). *Focus on Music 2: Exploring the Musicality of Children and Young People with Retinopathy of Prematurity*. London: Institute of Education.

Ockelford, A., Welch, G., and Zimmermann, S. (2002). Music education for pupils with severe or profound and multiple difficulties. *British Journal of Special Education,* **29**(4), 178–82.

Ockelford, A., Welch, G., Zimmermann, S., and Himonides, E. (2005). Sounds of intent': mapping, assessing and promoting the musical development of children with profound and multiple learning difficulties. *International Congress Series,* **1282**, 898–902.

Ockelford, A., Pring, L., Welch, G., and Treffert, D. (2006). *Focus on Music: Exploring the Musical Interests and Abilities of Blind and Partially-Sighted Children with Septo-Optic Dysplasia*. London: Institute of Education.

Ockelford, A., Welch, G., Jewell-Gore, L., Cheng, E., Vogiatzoglou, A., and Himonides, E. (2011). *Sounds of Intent*, Phase 2: approaches to the quantification of music-developmental data pertaining to children with complex needs. *European Journal of Special Needs Education,* **26**(2), 177–199.

Overy, K. (1998). Discussion Note: 'Can music really "improve" the mind?. *Psychology of Music,* **26**(1): 97–99.

Papoušek, H. (1996). Musicality in infancy research: biological and cultural origins of early musicality. In: I. Deliège and J. Sloboda (eds), *Musical Beginnings*, pp. 37–55, Oxford: Oxford University Press.

Postacchini, P.L., Borghesi, M., Flucher, B., Guida, L., Mancini, M., Nocentini, P., *et al.* (1993). A case of severe infantile regression treated by music therapy and explored in group supervision. In: M. Heal and T. Wigram (eds.) *Music Therapy in Health and Education*, pp. 26–31. London: Jessica Kingsley.

Powers, N. and Trevarthen, C. (2009). Voices of shared emotion and meaning: Young infants and their mothers in Scotland and Japan, in: S. Malloch and C. trevarthen (eds.) *Communicative Musicality: Exploring the Basis of Human Companionship*, pp. 209–240, (Oxford: Oxford University Press)

Pring, L. and Ockelford, A. (2005). Children with septo-optic dysplasia – musical interests, abilities and provision: the results of a parental survey. *British Journal of Visual Impairment,* **23**(2), 58–66.

Qualifications and Curriculum Authority (2001). *Plannning, Teaching and Assessing the Curriculum for Pupils with Learning Difficulties*. London: QCA.

Schwalkwijk, F. (1994). *Music and People with Developmental Disabilities*. London: Jessica Kingsley.

Trehub, S. (1990). The perception of musical patterns by human infants: the provision of similar patterns by their parents. In: M. Berkley and W. Stebbins (eds.) *Comparative Perception; Vol. 1, Mechanisms*, pp. 429–59, New York: Wiley.

Trehub, S. (2003). Toward a developmental psychology of music, *Annals of the New York Academy of Sciences,* **999**, 402–13.

Trevarthen, C. (2002). Origins of musical identity: evidence from infancy for musical social awareness. In: R. Macdonald, D. Hargreaves and D. Miell (eds.) *Musical Identities*, pp. 21–38, Oxford: Oxford University Press.

Vogiatzoglou, A., Ockelford, A., Welch, G., and Himonides, E. (2011). *Sounds of Intent*: interactive software to assess the musical development of children and young people with complex needs. *Music and Medicine,* **3**(3), 189–195.

Welch, G. (1991). Visual metaphors for sound: a study of mental imagery, language and pitch perception in the congenitally blind. *Canadian Journal of Research in Music Education,* **33** (Special ISME Research Edition).

Welch, G. (2006). The musical development and education of young children. In: B. Spodek and O. Saracho (eds.) *Handbook of Research on the Education of Young Children*, pp. 251–67, Mahwah, NJ: Lawrence Erlbaum Associates.

Welch, G., Ockelford, A., and Zimmermann, S. (2001). *Provision of Music in Special Education ('PROMISE')*. London: Institute of Education and Royal National Institute of the Blind.

Welch, G., Ockelford, A., Carter, F-C., Zimmermann, S., and Himonides, E. (2009). Sounds of Intent: Mapping musical behaviour and development in children and young people with complex needs,' *Psychology of Music*, **37**(3), 348–70.

White, J. (2007). Wellbeing and education: issues of culture and authority. *Journal of Philosophy of Education*, **41**(1), 17–28.

Zbikowski, L. (2002). *Conceptualizing Music: Cognitive Structure, Theory, and Analysis*. New York: Oxford University Press.

Section 5

Everyday Uses

Chapter 27

Music, Subjective Wellbeing, and Health: The Role of Everyday Emotions

Daniel Västfjäll, Patrik N. Juslin, and Terry Hartig

It is widely recognized among both scholars and lay people that music can influence listeners in profound ways. Implicit in the recognition that music can affect listeners is that it may do so in both positive and negative ways. This volume is, of course, mainly concerned with the former possibility.[1]

Music has been linked to health and healing in shamanic traditions for more than 30,000 years (Moreno 1991), long before the music therapy profession developed in the USA after the Second World War. Music (in or as) therapy, active or passive, has now been applied with people with mental health problems, learning difficulties, neurological problems, and physical disabilities in a variety of settings, and music therapy research been conducted in parallel with music therapy practice since the 1950s (for a review, see Wheeler 2009). Such research has mainly focused on responses to music presented for short periods in clinical contexts. In contrast, explorations of the possible long-term benefits of music listening in the normal population have only begun.

Fortunately, the subject of music and health has recently attracted attention from a much wider range of scientific scholars (as evidenced by this volume), which has paved the way for systematic research programmes. Hence, several studies have now documented beneficial (short-term) effects of music listening on subjective wellbeing and physical health outside of clinical contexts (for reviews, see Standley 1995; Pelletier 2004; Hanser 2010; and chapters in the present volume). However, we argue that most studies to date suffer from two limitations that prevent us from drawing more far-reaching conclusions about the implications of music listening for health in the long-term. First, most studies have been conducted in artificial laboratory environments. Hence, it remains unclear whether, or to what extent, such positive effects emerge if the music listening occurs in a real-life situation. Does music have beneficial effects also in the flow of everyday life? Do the effects extend beyond the immediate situation? Are the effects different in any way from effects that can just as easily be obtained through other means, such as guided relaxation exercises?

Second, the mechanisms responsible for the obtained health effects have not yet been elucidated. Some previous accounts have emphasized the roles of 'distraction and competing stimuli' and increases of 'perceived control' in explaining pain relief through music listening (e.g. North and Hargreaves 2008, pp. 305–311), but these explanations can hardly account for the whole gamut of effects documented to date. In fact, most studies of music and health look for simple

---

[1] For a discussion of some of the unfortunate uses of music to achieve negative effects, see Garofalo (2010, pp. 744–9).

links between music and response—thus by-passing any intervening psychological processes. We shall argue below that this is a mistake that seriously limits the applicability of findings from studies of music and health (see also Juslin 2011).

The aim of this chapter is to present a novel approach to music and health that focuses on exploring health benefits within everyday life contexts, with particular consideration of possible underlying mechanisms. The focus is on listening rather than performing, and on public health rather than clinical populations. We attach a central role to emotion in bringing about desired health outcomes, and believe that music may be uniquely suited to managing or regulating emotions and stress in everyday life (see also Thayer 1996; Sloboda and O'Neill 2001; DeNora 2010; Saarikallio in press).

The rest of this chapter is organized into three major sections. First, we explain the background and theoretical basis of the current approach. Then, we illustrate this approach by summarizing a set of empirical studies. Finally, we discuss the implications of the results from these studies for future research on music and health.

Background and theoretical basis

The present approach was based on the following premises:

(1) Although life expectancy is increasing and physical health is improving amongst many social groups in the populations of Western countries, psychological illness (e.g. stress, anxiety, depression) remains at high levels, especially among younger people. Further, some social groups continue to have poor physical health. A surprising conclusion, then, is that although our material living standards are increasing and more and more diseases are preventable or curable in the Western world, mental ill-health is increasing at a global level (Herrman et al. 2005).[2]

(2) Mental ill-health, such as persistent stress and recurrent negative emotions, are signs that an individual is not able to recover adequately from stressors. One way to enhance individual and public health may be to offer better opportunities for recovery—not just by reducing levels of exposure to stressors in the environment, but also by improving possibilities for faster and more complete recovery from stress (Hartig 2004).

(3) One promising avenue to promoting recovery from stress is afforded by culture. Several studies have indicated that cultural activities are positively correlated with health (e.g. Konlaan et al. 2000; Kuhn 2002; Michalos 2005). Still, many of the cultural activities that were surveyed in the investigations (e.g. attending theatres, museums, concerts, cinemas) are not performed frequently. Hence, their cumulative effects on people's long-term health may be less pronounced than the effects of those activities in daily life that occur more frequently, yet with similar short-term effects.

(4) One form of cultural activity occurs frequently, however: music listening. For example, in a survey study featuring a random, representative sample of the Swedish population, 78% of the participants reported that they listened to music *at least* once every day (Juslin et al. 2011). Among the cited motives for listening to music, 'to relax' was the most frequent one.

(5) Insofar as music listening can influence health, it offers a number of advantages. Aside from people with impaired hearing, it is readily available to all parts of society (unlike, for instance, theatre and opera), and it can be tailored to personal taste. Therefore, it may reach those that

---

[2] Notably, the World Health Organization (WHO) defines health as 'a state of complete physical, mental, and social well-being and not merely the absence of disease or infirmity'.

do not normally 'consume' other kinds of culture. Moreover, music can be consumed in many different contexts; it is not tied to a particular time or location. From an intervention point of view, additional advantages include that music is inexpensive, easy to administer, and arguably has few if any negative secondary effects, in contrast to, for instance, prescription drugs and other approaches to addressing stress-related ill-health.

(6) We suggest that music may affect health through the emotions it arouses in listeners (for a recent overview, see Juslin and Sloboda 2010). The notion that music is closely related to emotion is recurrent in numerous aesthetical theories (e.g. Meyer 1956; Langer 1957; Berlyne 1971; Clynes 1977) and evidence that music may arouse emotions comes from several types of measure—self-report, psychophysiology, brain imaging, expression, action tendency, regulation, as well as various 'indirect' measures (e.g. word associations). Findings from survey and experience sampling studies further suggest that emotional responses to music occur frequently enough and for a large enough proportion of the population to be of relevance from a public health perspective (e.g. Juslin et al. 2008).

(7) Results from experimental, observational, and animal studies indicate that emotions are significantly related to physical health (e.g. Kubzansky 2009). Besides the fact that emotions may affect the *subjective wellbeing* of an individual in positive ways, a large body of research has shown that emotions involve *bodily responses* that may influence physical health (e.g. changes in dopamine, serotonin, cortisol, endorphin, and oxytocin levels; see, e.g. van Eck et al. 1996; Fibinger et al. 1984). Long-term health consequences resulting from persistent stress and recurrent negative emotions are well documented in the literature (e.g. depression—cancer, anger—cardiovascular disease; see Davidson et al. 2003, ch. 55–59; Steptoe 1997).

(8) To the extent that music can influence health through its emotional effects, it should be noted that emotional reactions to music can come about in several different ways (Juslin and Västfjäll 2008a,b). Based on a synthesis of the literature, Juslin et al. (2010) postulated seven mechanisms through which music might arouse emotions in listeners (collectively referred to as the BRECVEM framework):

(a) *Brain stem reflexes*, involving 'pre-wired' responses to simple acoustic characteristics of the music, such as loudness and speed (Sokolov 1963);

(b) *Rhythmic entrainment*, related to gradual adjustments of an internal body rhythm (e.g. heart rate) towards an external rhythm in the music (Harrer and Harrer 1977);

(c) *Evaluative conditioning*, related to a regular pairing of a piece of music and other positive or negative stimuli (Blair and Shimp 1992);

(d) *Contagion*, related to internal 'mimicry' of the perceived emotional expression of the music (Lundqvist et al. 2009);

(e) *Visual imagery*, related to visual images of an emotional nature conjured up by the listener while listening to the music (Osborne 1980);

(f) *Episodic memory*, related to specific memories from the listener's past evoked by the music (Baumgartner 1992), and;

(g) *Musical expectancy*, related to the gradual unfolding of the musical structure and its expected or unexpected continuations (Meyer 1956).

Each mechanism has some unique characteristics, and these will influence what kind of emotion the music may arouse (see hypotheses in Juslin et al. 2010). One implication of this framework is that responses to music—just like to responses to a stressor (Lazarus and Folkman 1984)—cannot be understood merely from an analysis of the stimulus: one must understand how the relationship between stimulus and response is *mediated* by mechanisms in the listener.

Depending on the mechanism(s) activated, the response may be completely different (Juslin and Västfjäll 2008a).

(9) Which mechanisms are activated depends, in turn, on a complex interaction between the *listener*, the *music*, and the *situation* (Jørgensen 1988; Gabrielsson 1993; Juslin and Laukka 2004; Hargreaves et al. 2005). Thus, there are no 'pure' effects of music that will invariably occur regardless of the specific listener or situation. The response will depend on factors such as the listener's music preferences and previous experiences, as well as on the specific circumstances of the context (e.g. current activity, other people present, function of the music, features of the physical environment).

The above premises lead us to postulate a conceptual model of music and health, which may be contrasted with the model (implicitly or explicitly) adopted in most research on music and health thus far—especially in research on the use of music in clinical contexts. Figure 27.1a presents the approach adopted in most previous studies in the field. Here, the researcher tries to obtain direct links between pieces of music and physiological reactions. This may appear an obvious way to approach the problem. However, implicit in this approach are certain assumptions which are not borne out by empirical studies. For example, the model appears to assume that: (1) every listener will respond in the same manner to the music, (2) the listener's response depends solely on the music, (3) there is merely one 'causal route' from music to listener response, and (4) the emotions experienced while listening are not relevant in explaining the physiological response.

In contrast, consider Figure 27.1b, which shows the model adopted in the current project. Here, it is assumed that musical experiences occur in a complex interplay between the listener, the music, and the context. Moreover, musical experiences arouse emotions through a number of different psychological mechanisms, which may affect individual listeners differently. The emotions aroused, in turn, involve physiological responses with possible health implications. The important point is that by taking felt emotion and psychological mechanisms into account, one can develop a deeper knowledge of the process, and this knowledge is easier to apply subsequently (with enhanced causal control) in novel contexts (Juslin 2011).

The chief aim of the present research, then, is to explore the psychological and biological mechanisms through which listening to music in everyday life may influence subjective wellbeing and physical health in the general population—particularly effects that are linked to the emotions. Further, we adopt a multi-method approach with regard to both data collection (e.g. surveys, experience sampling, experiments) and measures (subjective experiential self-reports as well as psychophysiological and behavioural measures). It has been observed that self-reports sometimes produce more conservative evidence of beneficial health effects than do behavioural and physiological measures (e.g. Standley 1995).

In the following section, we will summarize selected findings from our initial studies, which have involved the *Experience Sampling Method* (ESM, Conner Christensen et al. 2003), the *Day Reconstruction Method* (DRM, Kahneman et al. 2004), and experimental field studies (West et al. 2000). This is followed by a discussion of the implications of the findings for future research on music and health.

Empirical studies

ESM study

One approach to understanding the relationship between self-reported stress and music listening is to follow participants in their daily lives. This can be achieved through experience sampling studies (Conner Christensen et al. 2003). The ESM involves equipping participants with an

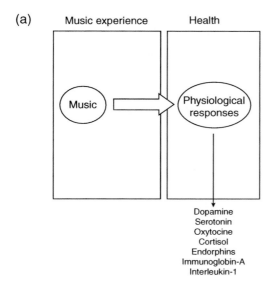

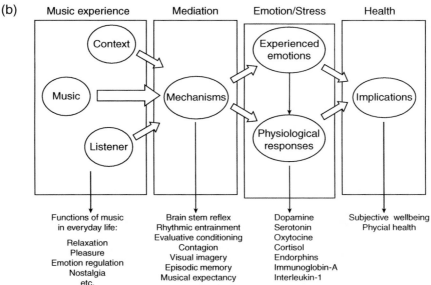

Fig. 27.1 (a) Simple relationship between music experience and health. (b) Sophisticated relationship between music experience and health.

electronic device (e.g. a palmtop) that can be used to verbally probe participants while they are doing various activities.

In a recent ESM study of musical emotions in everyday life (Juslin et al. 2008), we obtained estimates of the occurrence of 14 emotional states in response to music as well as to other stimuli during a 2-week period. The listener sample consisted of 32 college students (aged 20–31 years), of whom 44% played a musical instrument and 31% had some formal music education. These participants carried a palmtop computer that emitted a sound signal seven times a day at random intervals. When signalled, participants were required to complete a questionnaire (with questions about experienced emotions, activities, the situation, and experienced stress) on the palmtop. Results on the prevalence of musical emotions vs. non-musical emotions are provided in detail by Juslin et al. (2008), and only a few key findings will be reiterated here. Self-reported stress was not examined in Juslin et al. (2008), and new data on everyday music listening and stress will be presented here.

Juslin et al. (2008) showed that music occurred in 37% of the random episodes, and in 64% of the music episodes the participants reported that the music influenced their feelings. A comparison of musical with non-musical emotion episodes showed that positive emotions were more common, and negative emotions less common, in musical episodes. However, the prevalence of musical emotions also varied depending on the situation (location and activity) and the participant's personality.

In a new set of analyses of additional data on self-reported stress (measured for each sampled episode) from this study (Västfjäll et al. 2012), we found that self-reported stress was significantly lower in musical ($M = 1.95$) than in non-musical ($M = 2.24$) episodes ($t = 3.3$, $p <0.05$). Hierarchical linear modelling (HLM; Raudenbush and Bryk 2002) allowed us to simultaneously analyse ESM data on the level of a listener's repeated musical emotion episodes over time (level 1) and on the level of the listener (level 2; personality measures). HLM is thus suitable for modelling the complex interactions between the listener, the music, and the situation. A series of HLM analyses were performed in which we assessed stress based on level 1 categories (music present/ not present; situation; place; social setting) and level 2 data ('Big 5' personality measures).

An example of this type of analysis is a simple modification of the effect of music on stress by personality. At level 1, self-reported stress was on average 0.08 scale steps higher in no-music episodes. At level 2, the personality traits neuroticism and extroversion appeared to increase self-reported stress in no-music episodes by 0.02 and 0.01 scale steps, respectively.

Additional, more complex analyses with interactions among level 1 variables (place, activity, social setting) have been performed. Figure 27.2a shows the effects of place on self-reported stress in musical and non-musical episodes. HLM analyses revealed that non-musical episodes were associated with significantly higher stress levels at home, work, and when in others' homes. A similar analysis was performed for activity (Figure 27.2b). Non-musical episodes were associated with significantly higher stress levels when working, travelling, doing housework, and eating dinner.

Participants were further asked what they believed 'caused' their emotion in each episode. However, rather than respond freely—with the risk that the answers would not address any of the possible mechanisms—they could choose from ten alternatives based on previous research. The alternatives included the mechanisms featured in the BRECVEM framework (i.e. *Brain stem responses, Rhythmic entrainment, Evaluative conditioning, Contagion, Visual imagery, Episodic memory, Musical expectancy*) as well as the 'default' mechanism for emotion induction in non-musical contexts, *Cognitive appraisal* (i.e. an evaluation of an event with regard to its implications for the person's goals, in terms of goal congruence, coping potential, compatibility with norms etc.). Each mechanism was carefully explained in a booklet. The alternatives also included 'lyrics', 'other', and 'I don't know', so that participants would not feel forced to select one of the mechanism alternatives.

All of the proposed underlying mechanisms occurred in at least some episodes (Juslin et al. 2010). The most commonly self-reported causes were *emotional contagion, brain stem response*, and *episodic memory*. Moreover, different mechanisms seemed to be related to different musical emotions. For example, *nostalgia-longing* responses often occurred with *episodic memory* rather than with *visual imagery*, whereas the opposite pattern was true of *pleasure-enjoyment* responses.

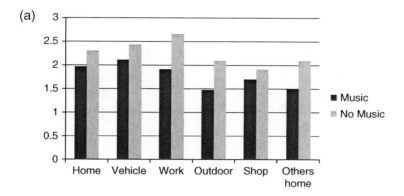

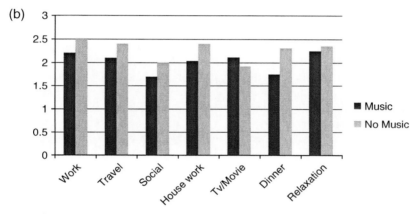

Fig. 27.2 (a) Self-reported stress for various places during musical and non-musical episodes. (b) Self-reported stress for various activities during musical and non-musical episodes.

Although self-reports of the causes of musical emotions must be interpreted with caution, these findings suggest that different mechanisms tend to evoke different emotions.

Given that different psychological mechanisms are related to different musical emotions, it may be asked whether there are differences in self-reported stress depending on the mechanism. Figure 27.3 shows stress intensity as a function of psychological mechanism in episodes where music occurred. As may be seen, mental imagery, emotional contagion, and musical expectancy appear to be related to low self-reported stress. In contrast, cognitive appraisal is related to high stress intensity (it involves situations where music prevented or interfered with goal completion). Cognitive appraisal was related to significantly higher stress levels than musical expectancy, mental imagery, and emotional contagion. It should however be noted that cognitive appraisal was the least commonly reported cause, indicating that listening to music rarely has negative implications for the pursuit of goals in life.

These preliminary findings suggest that different mechanisms indeed may have different effects on stress. This is perhaps not surprising given that different mechanisms may arouse different musical emotions (Juslin and Liljeström 2010). The set of results does, however, suggest that it is important to document the psychological mechanisms underlying the effects of music on health. It should be acknowledged that self-reports on mechanisms have limitations. Participants may

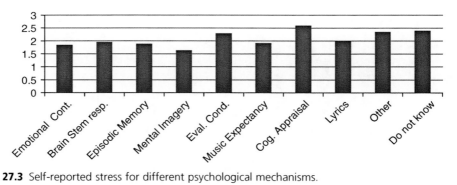

Fig. 27.3 Self-reported stress for different psychological mechanisms.

sometimes have been unaware of the 'true' causes of their emotions. Furthermore, psychological mechanisms that are 'implicit' in nature (conditioning) are likely to be underreported, relative to mechanisms that are more 'salient' in conscious experience (episodic memory). Having said that, the present data render some support to the validity of using self-reports, at least for some mechanisms. For instance, the finding that stress was highest when participants reported that music hindered the pursuit of goals (cognitive appraisal) suggests that participants were at least aware of this psychological mechanism.

Ideally, to make statements about causality the mechanisms should be studied and experimentally varied in a laboratory setting (Juslin and Liljeström 2010), but we believe that field studies of mechanisms also are required. If there are several mechanisms that might induce musical emotions, and their importance varies depending on the situation, then only by sampling a wide variety of real-life situations can we hope to capture all relevant mechanisms and estimate their importance in the real world (Juslin et al. 2010).

Overall, then, the present findings suggest that experienced stress in everyday life is related to music listening, but that the association is contingent on situational and personal characteristics.

DRM study

The experience sampling method provides much information about a sample of moments in the participants' everyday lives. But the ESM is an expensive method, it does not provide information about every single event in the participants' lives, and it places a sometimes heavy burden on the participants (Kahneman et al. 2004).

In another attempt to examine everyday music listening and its relation to self-reported stress and health, we used a hybrid time sampling technique combining features of time-budget measurement and experience sampling. The *Day Reconstruction Method* (DRM) was developed as a less time-consuming alternative to ESM. In this method, participants systematically reconstruct their activities and experiences of the preceding day with procedures designed to reduce recall biases (such as beliefs biasing semantic memory). More specifically, in the DRM participants are first asked to recall what they did the previous day by writing down every activity in a diary, in the form of episodes (e.g. ate breakfast at 07:00, took a shower at 07:15, went to work at 08:00). They are then asked to describe each episode by answering questions about the situation and the emotions experienced (e.g. other people being present or not, experienced stress, feelings of control). Kahneman and colleagues showed that the DRM is able to provide a description similar to what would have been obtained by probing experiences when they happened (i.e. ESM). The obvious advantage is that the DRM imposes a smaller burden on the participant than the ESM. The DRM also makes it possible to gather information about experiences over time in one single setting from a large sample (White and Dolan 2009).

We (Helsing et al. 2012) used the DRM method to investigate: (1) the prevalence of musical emotions in everyday life; (2) the situations, places, and activities in which musical emotions are most likely to be experienced; (3) how often music is actively used as an emotion regulation strategy; and (4) how strongly the occurrence of music and musical emotion regulation are related to overall ratings of stress, wellbeing, and health. We will focus on the last two points here.

A DRM study with 152 women and 55 men, aged 20–77, was performed. Participants came to the laboratory, where the DRM procedure was divided into different parts. First, the participants answered questions about their overall life satisfaction, overall subjective wellbeing, self-perceived health (DUKE Health Profile; Parkerson et al. 1990) and various background variables (e.g. age, gender, life situation, education). In the second part, they were asked to recall the day before and describe each episode in a diary form with regard to activity, time of day, and experienced emotions. The descriptions of experienced emotions were given using scales. The items were carefully selected to include positive, negative, low and high arousal states that were applicable to both everyday experience (tired, happy) and musical experience (pleasant, nostalgic; see Juslin et al. 2008). The third part of the questionnaire featured questions about each episode. These questions concerned, for example, what the participants did, if anyone else was present, how stressed they felt, how much they felt in control of the situation, which emotions they experienced, if they did anything to change how they felt (emotion regulation), and if there was music present in the episode or not. If music was present in the episode, the participant then was asked to answer several questions about the music. These included if the music affected them, how much they liked the music, if they themselves chose the music they heard, their reasons for listening to the music, and where the music came from.

In total 2297 episodes were collected from the participants (the number of episodes per participant ranged from three to 21). Music occurred in 30% of the episodes. In 67% of them, the participants reported that the music influenced their feelings. These findings are very similar to the prevalence estimates obtained in the ESM study by Juslin et al. (2008).

Replicating the finding from the ESM study, almost half of the emotions experienced with music could be characterized as positive (e.g. happy, joyful), about a quarter were arousal states (e.g. inspired-stimulated, strong-energized, tired-low energy, and surprised-astonished) and the remaining quarter were negative (sad, gloomy). A similar distribution was found for non-musical episodes: 43% positive emotions, 30% negative emotions, and 27% arousal states. Statistical tests showed that both positive emotions and arousal emotions were more common in musical episodes than in non-musical ones ($p < 0.001$). Positive emotions were also experienced with stronger intensity in musical episodes ($M = 2.58$) than in non-musical episodes ($M = 2.29$, $t = 4.06$, $p < 0.001$) and arousal states were also more intense in musical episodes ($M = 2.37$) than in non-musical ones ($M = 2.06$; $p < 0.001$).

Participants were also asked to indicate their motives for listening to music from a pre-defined list (see Juslin et al. 2008). The most common motives for listening to music among the participants were *to get energized*, *to relax*, *to affect one's emotions*, *to get some company* and *to pass the time*, all reported by more than 10% of the participants. Other less common motives for music listening were because *other people were playing the music*, the music was *unavoidable*, and because they wanted to *evoke memories*.

Participants also reported on whether or not and to what extent they applied one or more of 25 emotion regulation strategies in each episode. These strategies were reduced to the following six factors through factor analysis: (1) Reappraisal (e.g. 'I controlled my emotions by trying to look at the situation differently'); (2) Suppression (e.g. 'I avoided the cause of the emotion');

(3) Musical emotion regulation (e.g. 'I tried to enhance my emotions by listening to music'); (4) Distraction by activity (e.g. 'I ate something tasty'); (5) Changing circumstances (e.g. 'I changed my environment'); and (6) Social regulation (e.g. 'I talked or spent time with someone, for example a friend or a relative').

In episodes that contained music (both music that affected and did not affect the individuals), the most commonly used emotion regulation strategies were, according to the factors, Reappraisal, Musical emotion regulation, and Social regulation. Statistical tests revealed that the factor Musical emotion regulation was used significantly more often in musical episodes than all the other regulation factors except Reappraisal. In non-musical episodes, Social regulation, Reappraisal, and Suppression were the most frequently used emotion regulation strategies. Overall, these findings suggest, consistent with previous studies (Juslin et al. 2008, 2010), that music represents a major part of everyday life for many people, that listening to music has emotional consequences, and that people use music to enhance their emotional states. Since positive emotions may be linked to better health, we may expect that a higher prevalence of positive musical emotion is related to self-reported health.

To examine the relationship between music and stress, regression analyses were performed with self-reported stress (frequency and mean intensity) as dependent variables and frequency of music and frequency of music reported to affect emotional states as independent variables. Frequency of music was negatively related to both the frequency ($\beta = -0.52$, $p < 0.001$) and mean intensity of stress ($\beta = -0.41$, $p < 0.001$). Looking within the musical episodes, the liked and self-chosen music were related to lower self-reported stress intensity ($\beta_{liked} = -0.93$ and $\beta_{chose} = -0.91$; $p < 0.05$) and stress frequency ($\beta_{liked} = -0.61$ and $\beta_{chose} = -0.33$; $p < 0.05$).

Next, we examined self-reported health. The DUKE Health Profile measures health symptoms during the last 3 months (Parkerson et al. 1990). Four facets (mental, physical, social, and general health) of the DUKE scale were correlated with self-reported emotions. As expected, across all episodes both intensity and frequency of negative emotions were negatively related to general health, whereas frequency and intensity of positive emotions ($r=0.29$, $p < 0.001$) and arousal states ($r = 0.29$, $p < 0.001$) were positively related to general health.

A series of regression analyses examined the relation between self-reported health and music occurrence. No significant relationships were found for the physical and mental health subscales. Music occurrence was significantly related to social health ($\beta = 0.32$, $p < 0.01$). The frequencies of liked ($\beta = 0.78$) and self-chosen music ($\beta = 0.63$) were also linked to higher social health scores ($p < 0.001$). A similar pattern was found for the general health subscale: music occurrence was linked to increased scores ($\beta = 0.20$, $p < 0.01$). The frequencies of liked ($\beta = 0.63$) and self-chosen music ($\beta = 0.61$) were also linked to higher general health scores ($p < 0.01$).

In a final set of regression analyses, we examined the relationships between self-reported stress and health and emotion-regulation strategies. As pointed out by Kubzansky (2009), the emotion-health relationship is often dependent on the success of various emotion regulation strategies. Previous research has documented that music is commonly used for emotion regulation (Juslin and Laukka 2004), but the effectiveness of music as an emotion regulation strategy in real life is relatively little studied. In an attempt to examine this, the frequencies of the six emotion regulation strategies identified earlier were used as predictors in a series of regression analyses with stress, subjective wellbeing, and the four health scales as dependent variables. Table 27.1 summarizes the results. Overall, few significant predictors were identified. Consistent with recent research on the effectiveness of emotion regulation (Augustine and Hemenover 2009), it appears that the frequency of Reappraisal was negatively related to stress and positively to self-reported health, whereas the frequency of Suppression was positively related to stress and negatively to health scores. The Changing circumstances strategy was positively related to stress frequency, and

Table 27.1 Standardized beta weights from regression analyses predicting stress frequency and intensity, wellbeing and health from the frequency of use of different emotion regulation strategies

Dependent variable	Emotion regulation factors[1]					
	R	SU	M	D	C	SO
Stress frequency[a]	−0.13	0.11	−0.39*	−0.13	0.49*	0.04
Stress mean intensity[b]	0.08	0.32*	−0.02	−0.06	0.27	−0.14
SWB[c]	−0.06	−0.18	0.28*	0.12	0.36	0.13
General health[d]	0.24	−0.48*	−0.07	−0.17	0.02	−0.23
Physical health[e]	0.17	−0.39	0.18	−0.06	0.10	0.14
Social health[f]	0.12	−0.15	−0.10	−0.03	−0.17	0.01
Mental health[g]	0.14	−0.35*	−0.05	−0.22*	0.10	−0.29

[1] R = Reappraisal, SU = Suppression, M = Musical emotion regulation, D = Distraction by activity, C = Changing circumstances, SO = Social regulation.

* $p < 0.05$ [e] R^2adj = 0.06

[a] R^2adj = 0.22   [f] R^2adj = 0.04

[b] R^2adj = 0.28   [g] R^2adj = 0.12

[c] R^2adj = 0.01

[d] R^2adj = 0.21

Distraction was negatively related to self-reported mental health. As can be seen in Table 27.1, stress frequency was negatively related to frequency of use of music as an emotion regulation strategy. As expected, there was a positive association between frequency of use of music as an emotion regulation strategy and subjective wellbeing scores. The frequency of musical emotion regulation was not significantly related to any of the health subscales.

Overall, these findings indicate that musical emotion regulation strategies are employed in everyday life, and that they may possibly be as effective as other regulation strategies for some outcomes. However, this type of exploratory correlational analyses on data averaged across situations and individuals does not allow for causal inferences and should thus be interpreted with caution.

Experimental field study: testing a psychophysiological pathway

The ESM and DRM studies suggest that everyday listening may be linked to reduced stress levels. They provide important data on the prevalence of music listening, musical emotions, and musical emotion regulation, but they are limited in that they lack the experimental control needed to draw causal inferences. The ability to draw causal inferences is particularly important when testing putative mechanisms through which music listening may have short-term effects that, cumulatively, engender better health in the long run.

One set of pathways through which psychological stress can come to affect health over the long run involves physiological responses mediated by activation of the hypothalamus–pituitary–adrenal (HPA) axis (Linden et al. 1997). Cortisol concentration in blood or saliva is a marker of HPA activity, and has been found to be responsive to both stressors (increased levels) and opportunities for restoration (decreased levels). Similarly, cortisol increases with negative affect and decreases with positive affect. Consequently, several laboratory studies have used salivary cortisol as an indicator of potential health effects of music (McKinney et al. 1997; Suda et al. 2008). These studies typically experimentally induce stress and find that cortisol levels decrease more rapidly when listening to music in the post stressor phase. However, these studies are limited to the laboratory. Furthermore, they have often used experimenter-selected music intended to evoke a specific emotion or state (Khalfa et al. 2003) or have investigated the effects of specific music programmes (le Roux et al. 2007).

We combined the power of experimental techniques and the ecological validity of field studies in an experimental field study in which 41 full-time employed women were randomly allocated to one of two conditions (Västfjäll et al. 2012). In the experimental condition, 21 participants were asked to bring six pieces of music that they liked to listen to, three relaxing pieces and three energizing, to an initial meeting with the experiment leader. To obtain a description of each piece, they were asked a series of questions: 'What emotion describes your reaction to this piece of music best?'; 'When was the first time you heard this piece of music?'; 'How often do you listen to it now?'; 'What do you think causes this/these emotion/s you feel to the music?'; and 'Why do you usually listen to this piece of music?' They were also asked questions about possible mechanisms responsible for the induced emotion. The questions were based on the BRECVEM framework described in the introduction. Table 27.2 shows the frequency of self-reported mechanisms. An important difference between our earlier sampling studies and this study is that participants only described the causes of emotion (mechanisms) for their own, self-selected music. One could perhaps expect that preferred or 'favourite' music is more contingent on certain mechanisms (e.g. *Episodic memory*). Contrary to this, we see in Table 27.2 that participants report *Emotional contagion* and *Brain stem response* to occur about as frequently as *Episodic memory*. Across participants, energizing and relaxing musical pieces appeared to recruit similar mechanisms. The only significant difference between relaxing and energizing music occurs for *Rhythmic entrainment*.

Based on the musical pieces the participants brought, an additional seven energizing and seven relaxing pieces (chosen from a music library together with each participant) were added and then transferred onto mp3 players, after being reduced to approximately 30 minutes of playing time for each type of music. The participants were then instructed to listen to this music daily for 30 minutes upon arriving home from work for a period of 2 weeks (after an initial week of post-work relaxation periods without music listening). Half of the participants in the music group listened

Table 27.2 Frequency of self-reported mechanisms for self-selected energizing and relaxing music

Mechanism	Music	
	Relaxing	**Energizing**
Episodic memory	28	38
Emotional contagion	27	35
Brain stem response	28	30
Rhythmic entrainment	12	42*
Visual imagery	11	10
Musical expectancy	12	13
Evaluative conditioning	11	11
Other (incl. cognitive appraisal)	18	18
Lyrics	29	22

* = p <0.05 for chi-square test of the relative frequency with which the given mechanism works to produce emotion with relaxing versus energizing music.

to energizing music the first week, and relaxing music the next week. The other half listened to the two music types in the reverse order. Participants were instructed that they must listen to the music during those 30 minutes and that they could also engage in other activities while listening. However, the participants were thoroughly instructed not to sleep, read, watch television, or carry out any other activity that might substantially interfere with the music listening. Participants in the control condition did not listen to music, but were instructed to relax for 30 minutes each day upon arriving home after work. Participants in the control group were also given thorough instructions about the activities that they could do during the relaxation period (knitting, reading a paper, meditating) and examples of what they were not to do during the relaxation period (listen to music, watch TV, play computer games, sleep). Saliva samples for cortisol assays were collected on the Thursday and Friday of each of the three successive weeks of data collection. On each Thursday, samples were collected just before the period spent relaxing with or without music, then just after that period, and then once again just before going to bed. Three samples were then collected the following morning to assess the awakening cortisol profiles. Self-reports concerning stress, experienced emotion, and emotion regulation were collected on each day of the study; however, only preliminary data for the pre- and post-relaxation period cortisol levels will be presented here.

In Figure 27.4, we display the mean cortisol levels measured before and after the relaxation period for the 3 weeks that data were collected. The experimental and control groups had comparable cortisol levels during week 1, when participants in the music condition had not yet started to listen to music. During week 2, cortisol levels declined slightly, with a somewhat larger decline for the musical condition. In week 3, the pre-treatment cortisol levels are higher in both the music and no-music conditions. This effect cannot be attributed to idiosyncratic responses (outliers). Follow-up interviews with participants suggest that this effect is likely due to a cumulative reaction to the demands of the procedure. Nonetheless, a substantial effect of music listening can be seen, such that the average decrease between the pre- and post-test measures is about 9mmol/L in the music condition and only about 1mmol/L in the relaxation condition. The pre-post difference × music condition interaction in week 3 is highly significant ($F_{1,31} = 8.84$, $p < 0.001$).

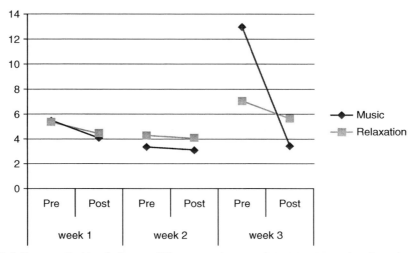

Fig. 27.4 Salivary cortisol levels (in mmol/L) measured pre- and post-treatment (music and relaxation) over 3 weeks.

These preliminary findings suggest that everyday listening to self-selected, preferred music is an effective means of regulating psychophysiological stress. This picture will be elaborated with analyses now underway of self-reported emotions, emotion regulation strategies, self-reported stress, and awakening cortisol profiles.

Experimental field study: addressing a behavioural pathway

Another set of pathways through which psychological stress can come to affect health involves the ways in which people behave in the face of stress. Stress may cause people to eat less healthy food, become less physically active, sleep poorly, and consume more alcohol, tobacco, and other harmful substances. These behavioural effects can increase a person's susceptibility to ill-health over the long run (Steptoe 1997). Accordingly, some approaches to mitigating the negative effects of stress seek to promote healthy behaviours. Some of these behaviours may be doubly beneficial, in that they promote physical fitness as well as take the emotional edge off of stress. Prominent among such behaviours are common forms of exercise such as running and walking (Thayer 1996).

Health behaviors such as running and walking require the availability of a suitable environment. For example, people may prefer to run in a park rather than along city streets (e.g. Bodin and Hartig 2003). Moreover, the emotional and other psychological benefits that people realize from activities such as running and walking may be contingent on the environment in which they are performed. For example, Hartig and colleagues (2003) found that subjects randomly assigned to walk along streets in an area of medium-density urban development following stressful demands showed declines in positive affect and increases in feelings of anger and irritation, while subjects assigned to walk in a nature preserve showed increases in positive affect and declines in anger. The countervailing effects were interpreted in part with regard to the presence versus absence of environmental stressors in the two field settings. Additionally, the nature preserve was seen to have features that promoted versus simply permitted stress recovery.

The final study to be presented here acknowledges the fact that populations today have concentrated in urban areas, and that many people living in those areas have limited access to parks and other outdoor settings where they can run, walk or otherwise perform health-promoting physical activities. The study considered the possibility that music listening with the aid of an mp3 player or other portable device could make exercise in an otherwise relatively stressful urban environment more appealing for exercise (Hartig et al. 2012). The experiment had a within-subjects design. All of the subjects—17 women, 13 men, all university students—completed three 40-minute walks in a Swedish urban centre. The walks followed the same route along streets with heavy vehicular traffic, lighter traffic, and in pedestrian-only zones. On one walk the subjects had no music; they listened to the sounds that are characteristic of the environment. On another walk they listened to pieces of music that they chose from a list which included only fast music. On the remaining walk they listened to pieces of music that they chose from a list with only slow music. The order of music conditions was counterbalanced across the three walks, and equal numbers of subjects completed the walk in each music condition on each day of data collection. This meant that particularities of weather and day of the week were balanced across the music conditions.

The subjects provided data for a variety of measures. Of particular interest here, they provided self-reports of emotion at the half-way point in each walk (an alarm worn around the neck began to vibrate after 20 minutes of walking, prompting them to complete the form and then turn back to the field laboratory). The measures were obtained with the Swedish Core Affect Scale (Västfjäll et al. 2002). We took particular interest in how emotions along the dimensions of activation and valence would vary across the experimental conditions.

The subjects in general reported being somewhat activated; the overall mean was 1.48 on a scale from −4 (low activation) to +4 (high activation). As expected, activation did vary as a function of experimental condition, in that fast music evoked reports of higher activation than slow music ($M = 2.26$ vs. $M = 1.18$; $p < 0.001$). It was for us an open question as to whether or not slow music would evoke a different degree of activation than no-music ($M = 1.01$). The answer proved to be no ($p = 0.48$).

Feelings of activation may help a person to carry on in their physical activity, but from a motivational perspective the more critical issue may be whether the person can anticipate enjoying the activity. We anticipated that the emotional self-reports would have the most positive valence when the walk was done with fast music and the least positive valence when the walk was done without music.

In general, the subjects seemed to be in good spirits; the overall mean for valence was 2.02 on a scale from −4 (low valence) to +4 (high valence). Again, the self-reports varied as a function of the experimental conditions, with the means falling in the expected gradient, with the highest value for the walk with fast music ($M = 2.62$), the next highest value for the walk with slow music ($M = 2.08$) and the lowest for the walk with no music, which nonetheless was regarded as somewhat pleasant ($M = 1.37$). The test of the linear trend indicated that the effect of the music manipulation was large (partial $\eta^2 = 0.50$).

These results speak to the potential utility of today's portable music devices in making a broader range of environments more palatable for everyday physical activities such as walking. This said, we recognize that other aspects of the urban environment, such as exhaust emissions, may remain harmful, even though a person can walk along with a smile on his or her face. And when the music is so engaging and the volume so high that the listener fails to notice an oncoming vehicle, music becomes a hazard to health.

Discussion

Music can influence us in profound ways. Among these, the therapeutic value of music has been appreciated for many years, and music is used in medical practices across different cultures. With scientific evidence mounting that music listening has beneficial effects on emotion, stress, and pain perception, the use of music in the treatment and amelioration of ill health is increasingly accepted (Hanser 2010).

The field of music and health specifically, and culture and health more generally, has witnessed a dramatic increase in the number and quality of empirical studies (as exemplified by this volume). However, we have in this chapter argued that much of the previous research on music and health has had significant limitations, in that: (1) few of the studies have been conducted outside the laboratory, and (2) it has given little attention to the psychological mechanisms that could mediate the effects of music on health. With the research described in this chapter, we have attempted to address those shortcomings, through the study designs chosen and through the measures and analyses used.

Health can be directly influenced by experienced emotions. Leventhal and Patrick-Miller (2000) argued that emotions can be the causes of health states as well as outcomes, and can even be indicators of health. Emotion may not only have a direct impact on health, but may also indirectly motivate various health-related behaviours (Diefenbach et al. 2008). Given that positive emotion is associated with better health and better health behaviours, an important task is to estimate the occurrence of musical emotions in everyday life. In a series of studies employing methodologies where we sampled episodes in the everyday life of our participants (ESM and DRM studies), we found consistently that music occurred in about 1/3 of the episodes. This may seem to be a large proportion of people's everyday activities, but another study using a representative sample of the Swedish population provided a similar estimate (Juslin et al. 2011). Thus, these findings suggest that music is an integral part of many people's lives. This is important from a public health perspective—music may already be providing health benefits to a significant proportion of the population, at low cost relative to other counter measures for stress, and with greater acceptance and more use than other measures.

Importantly, if music is to have a positive effect on health, music listening needs to arouse positive emotions (Leventhal and Patrik-Miller 2000). A consistent finding across our experience sampling studies was that positive emotions dominated when participants were listening to music—especially in situations where the music was self-selected. Furthermore, participants reported lower levels of stress in episodes with music. The experience of positive emotion was inversely correlated with the feeling of stress. In addition, we found that the *frequency* of positive musical emotions was related to self-reported overall health. By sampling episodes over a larger number of participants (~200) than usual for ESM studies, but for only a single day, we found that the recalled occurrence of music and musical emotion for that single day was related to self-reports of health symptoms during the last three months.

Music listening is also used as an overt strategy for changing one's emotional state. Previous research has documented that music is frequently used as an emotion regulation strategy (Juslin and Laukka 2004; Sloboda and O'Neill 2001). However, it is unclear how successful musical emotion regulation is relative to other emotion regulation strategies (Augustine and Hemenover 2009). In the DRM study, we found some correlational evidence that musical emotion regulation is *as* effective, if not more effective, than other common emotion regulation strategies such as reappraisal and suppression.

To follow-up on these findings, we conducted an experimental field study in which participants were asked to listen to self-selected music everyday for a period of 3 weeks. Given that self-selected music likely induces positive emotions and that the procedure required our participants to listen to music every day when returning home from work, we expected stress levels to be lower for these participants than for a control group that did not listen to music. As expected, cortisol levels after the period of relaxation were lower in the music listening group.

Taken together, these findings and others discussed here indicate some of the ways in which music listening can become associated with better health. Music listening is a common and relatively non-costly activity and may therefore represent a powerful and potentially very effective way to increase public health. Music listening as a behaviour is usually intrinsically motivated and may thus be more successful than externally motivated behaviours that have the goal of maintaining or improving health (Diefenbach et al. 2008). We do acknowledge that these findings are preliminary in many respects, and that more research on the link between musical emotion and health is needed. Especially, more research is needed to understand the mechanisms accounting for the effects of music on health. An important implication of the multi-mechanism framework outlined above is that a given piece of music may not actually be the 'same' stimulus for different listeners: How the listener will respond depends on the mechanism activated in the musical event. An understanding of the underlying mechanisms may thus permit practitioners to apply music in a manner that actively manipulates specific mechanisms, so as to achieve predictable effects on subjective wellbeing and health. The present research is only a first step toward elucidating this crucial aspect of the music-health link.

Acknowledgement

This research was supported by the Swedish Research Council.

References

Augustine, A.A. Hemenover, S.H. (2009). On the relative effectiveness of affect regulation strategies: A meta-analysis. *Cognition & Emotion*, **23**, 1181–220.

Baumgartner, H. (1992). Remembrance of things past: Music, autobiographical memory, and emotion. *Advances in Consumer Research*, **19**, 613–20.

Berlyne, D.E. (1971). *Aesthetics and psychobiology*. New York: Appleton Century Crofts.

Blair, M.E. and Shimp, T.A. (1992). Consequences of an unpleasant experience with music: A second-order negative conditioning perspective. *Journal of Advertising*, **21**, 35–43.

Bodin, M. and Hartig, T. (2003). Does the outdoor environment matter for psychological restoration gained through running? *Psychology of Sport and Exercise*, **4**, 141–53.

Clynes, M. (1977). *Sentics: The touch of emotions*. New York: Doubleday.

Conner Christensen, T., Barrett, L.F., Bliss-Moreau, E., Lebo, K., and Kaschub, C. (2003). A practical guide to experience-sampling procedures. *Journal of Happiness Studies*, **4**, 53–78.

Davidson, R.J., Scherer, K.R., and Goldsmith, H.H. (eds.) (2003). *Handbook of affective sciences*. Oxford: Oxford University Press.

DeNora, T. (2010). Emotion as social emergence. Perspectives from music sociology. In: P.N. Juslin and J.A. Sloboda (eds.) *Handbook of music and emotion: Theory, research, applications*, pp. 159–83. Oxford: Oxford University Press.

Diefenbach, M.A., Miller, S.M., Porter, M., Peters, E., Stefanek, M., and Leventhal, H. (2008). Affect and screening for cancer: A self-regulation perspective. In: M. Lewis, J.M. Haviland-Jones, and L. Feldman Barrett (eds.) *Handbook of emotions (3rd edn.)*, pp. 645–60. New York: Guilford Press.

Fibinger, W., Singer, G., Miller, A.J., Armstrong, S., and Datar, M. (1984). Cortisol and catecholamines changes as a function of time-of-day and self-reported mood. *Neuroscience and Biobehavioral Reviews*, **8**, 523–30.

Garofalo, R. (2010). Politics, mediation, social context, and public use. In: P.N. Juslin and J.A. Sloboda (eds.) *Handbook of music and emotion: Theory, research, applications*, pp. 725–54. Oxford: Oxford University Press.

Gabrielsson, A. (1993). Music and emotion. *ESCOM Newsletter*, **4**, 4–9.

Hanser, S.B. (2010). Music, health, and well-being. In P.N. Juslin and J.A. Sloboda (eds.) *Handbook of music and emotion: Theory, research, applications*, pp. 849–77. Oxford: Oxford University Press.

Hargreaves, D.J., MacDonald, R., and Miell, D. (2005). How do people communicate using music? In: D. Miell, R. MacDonald, and D.J. Hargreaves (eds.) *Musical communication*, pp. 1–25. Oxford: Oxford University Press.

Harrer, G. and Harrer, H. (1977). Music, emotion, and autonomic function. In: M. Critchley and R.A. Henson (eds.) *Music and the brain. Studies in the neurology of music*, pp. 202–16. London: William Heinemann.

Hartig, T. (2004). Restorative environments. In: C. Spielberger (ed.) *Encyclopedia of applied psychology (Vol. 3)*, pp. 273–9. San Diego, CA: Academic Press.

Hartig, T., Evans, G. W., Jamner, L. D., Davis, D. S., and Gärling, T. (2003). Tracking restoration in natural and urban field settings. *Journal of Environmental Psychology*, **23**, 109–23.

Hartig, T., Sjöberg, J., Wigren, J., Västfjäll, D., and Juslin, P.N. (2012). *Psychological effects of music listening during a walk in urban surroundings*. Manuscript submitted for publication.

Helsing, M., Västfjäll, D., Juslin, P.N., and Hartig, T. (2012). *Perceived stress, health, and everyday music listening*. Manuscript submitted for publication.

Herrman, H., Saxena, S., and Moodie, R. (eds.) (2005). *Promoting mental health: Concepts, emerging evidence, practice*. Geneva: World Health Organization.

Jørgensen, H. (1988). *Musikkopplevelsens psykologi [The psychology of music experience&cepha_unknown_entity_symbolsetswa_F05D;*. Oslo, Norway: Norsk Musikforlag.

Juslin, P.N. (2011). Music and emotion: Seven questions, seven answers. In: I. Deliège and J. Davidson (eds.) *Music and the mind: Essays in honour of John Sloboda*, pp. 113–35. Oxford: Oxford University Press.

Juslin, P.N. and Laukka, P. (2004). Expression, perception, and induction of musical emotions: A review and a questionnaire study of everyday listening. *Journal of New Music Research, 33,* 217–38.

Juslin, P.N., Eerola, T. and Harmat, L. (2012). *Emotional reactions to music: Exploring underlying mechanisms.* Manuscript submitted for publication.

Juslin, P.N., Liljeström, S., Laukka, P., Västfjäll, D., and Lundqvist, L.O. (2011). Emotional reactions to music in a nationally representative sample of Swedish adults: Prevalence and causal influences. *Musicae Scientiae, 15,* 174–207. (Special Issue on Music and Emotion).

Juslin, P.N., Liljeström, S., Västfjäll, D., Barradas, G., and Silva, A. (2008). An experience sampling study of emotional reactions to music: Listener, music, and situation. *Emotion, 8,* 668–83.

Juslin, P.N., Liljeström, S., Västfjäll, D., and Lundqvist, L.-O. (2010). How does music evoke emotions? Exploring the underlying mechanisms. In: P.N. Juslin and J.A. Sloboda (eds.) *Handbook of music and emotion: Theory, research, applications,* pp. 605–42. Oxford: Oxford University Press.

Juslin, P.N. and Sloboda, J.A. (eds.) (2010). *Handbook of music and emotion: Theory, research, applications.* Oxford: Oxford University Press.

Juslin, P.N. and Västfjäll, D. (2008a). Emotional responses to music: The need to consider underlying mechanisms. *Behavioral and Brain Sciences, 31,* 559–75.

Juslin, P.N. and Västfjäll, D. (2008b). All emotions are not created equal: Reaching beyond the traditional disputes. *Behavioral and Brain Sciences, 31,* 600–21.

Kahneman, D., Krueger, A.B., Schkade, D., Schwarz, N., and Stone, A.A. (2004). A survey method for characterizing daily life experience: The Day Reconstruction Method (DRM). *Science,* 3 December, 1776–80.

Khalfa, S., Dalla Bella, S., Roy, M., Peretz, I., and Lupien, S. J. (2003). Effects of relaxing music on salivary cortisol level after psychological stress. *Annals of the New York Academy of Sciences, 999,* 374–6.

Konlaan, B.B., Bjorby, N., Bygren, L.O.,Weissglas, G., Karlsson,. L.G., and Widmark, M. (2000). Attendence at cultural events and physical exercise and health: A randomized controlled study. *Public Health, 114,* 316–19.

Kubzansky, L.D. (2009). Health and emotion. In: D. Sander and K.R. Scherer (eds.) *Oxford companion to emotion and the affective sciences,* pp. 204–5. Oxford: Oxford University Press.

Kuhn, D. (2002). The effects of active and passive participation in musical activity on the immune system as measured by salivary immunoglobulin A (SlgA). *Journal of Music Therapy, 39,* 30–9.

Langer, S.K. (1957). *Philosophy in a new key.* Cambridge, MA: Harvard University Press.

Lazarus, R.S. and Folkman, S. (1984). *Stress, appraisal, and coping.* New York: Springer.

Leventhal, H. and Patrick-Miller, L. (2000). Emotions and physical illness: Causes and indicators of vulnerability. In: M. Lewis and J.M. Haviland-Jones (eds.) *Handbook of emotions (2nd edn.),* pp. 645–60. New York: Guilford Press.

Linden, W., Earle, T.L., Gerin, W., and Christenfeld, N. (1997). Physiological stress reactivity and recovery: Conceptual siblings separated at birth? *Journal of Psychosomatic Research, 42,* 117–35.

Lundqvist, L.-O., Carlsson, F., Hilmersson, P., and Juslin, P.N. (2009). Emotional responses to music: Experience, expression, and physiology. *Psychology of Music, 37,* 61–90.

McKinney, C.H., Antoni, M.H., Kumar, M., Tims, F.C., and McCabe, P.M. (1997). Effects of guided imagery and music (GIM) therapy on mood and cortisol in healthy adults. *Health Psychology, 16,* 390–400.

Meyer, L.B. (1956). *Emotion and meaning in music.* Chicago, IL: Chicago University Press.

Michalos, A. (2005). Arts and the quality of life: An exploratory study. *Social Indicators Research, 71,* 11–59.

Moreno, J. (1991). The music therapist: Creative arts therapist and contemporary shaman. In: D. Campbell (ed.) *Music physician for times to come,* pp. 167–85. Wheaton, IL: Quest books.

North, A.C. and Hargreaves, D.J. (2008). *The social and applied psychology of music.* Oxford: Oxford University Press.

Osborne, J.W. (1980). The mapping of thoughts, emotions, sensations, and images as responses to music. *Journal of Mental Imagery*, **5**, 133–6.

Parkerson, G.R. Jr, Broadhead, W.E., and Tse, C.-K. J. (1990). The Duke Health Profile: A 17-item measure of health and dysfunction. *Medical Care*, **28**, 1056–72.

Pelletier, C.L. (2004). The effect of music on decreasing arousal due to stress: a meta-analysis. *Journal of Music Therapy*, **41**, 192–214.

Raudenbush, S.W. and Bryk, A.S. (2002). *Hierarchical linear models: Applications and data analysis methods* (2nd edn.). London: Sage.

le Roux, F.H., Bouic, P.J.D., and Bester, M.M. (2007). The effect of Bach's magnificat on emotions, immune, and endocrine parameters during physiotherapy treatment of patients with infectious lung conditions. *Journal of Music Therapy*, **44**, 156–68.

Saarikallio, S. (in press). Music as emotional self-regulation throughout adulthood. *Psychology of Music*.

Sloboda, J.A. and O'Neill, S.A. (2001). Emotions in everyday listening to music. In: P.N. Juslin and J.A. Sloboda (eds.) *Music and emotion: Theory and research*, pp. 415–30. Oxford: Oxford University Press.

Sokolov, E.N. (1963). Higher nervous functions: the orienting reflex. *Annual Review of Physiology*, **25**, 545–80.

Steptoe, A. (1997). Stress and disease. In: A. Baum et al. (eds.) *Cambridge handbook of psychology, health, and medicine*, pp. 147–77. Cambridge: Cambridge University Press.

Standley, J.M. (1995). Music as a therapeutic intervention in medical and dental treatment: Research and clinical applications. In: T. Wigram, B. Saperstone, and R. West (eds.) *The art and science of music therapy*, pp. 3–22. Langhorn, PA: Harwood.

Suda, M., Morimoto, K., Obata, A., Koizumi, H., and Maki, A. (2008). Emotional responses to music: Towards scientific perspectives on music therapy. *NeuroReport: For Rapid Communication of Neuroscience Research*, **19**, 75–78.

Thayer, R.E. (1996). *The origin of everyday moods: Managing energy, tension, and stress*. Oxford: Oxford University Press.

van Eck, M., Berkhof, H., Nicolson, N., and Sulon, J. (1996). The effects of perceived stress, traits, mood states, and stressful events on salivary cortisol. *Psychosomatic Medicine*, **58**, 447–58.

Västfjäll, D., Juslin, P.N., and Liljeström, S. (2012). *Everyday music listening and stress*. Manuscript submitted for publication.

Västfjäll, D., Friman, M., Gärling, T., and Kleiner, M. (2002). The measurement of core affect: A Swedish self-report measure derived from the affect circumplex. *Scandinavian Journal of Psychology*, **43**, 19–31.

Västfjäll, D., Helsing, M., Juslin, P.N., Hartig, T., and Bjälkebring, P. (2012). *Decreased salivary cortisol after everyday listening to preferred music*. Manuscript submitted for publication.

West, S.G., Biesanz, J.C., and Pitts, S.C. (2000). Causal inference and generalization in field settings: Experimental and quasi-experimental designs. In: T.H. Reis and M.C. Judd (eds.) *Handbook of research methods in social and personality psychology*, pp. 40–84. New York: Cambridge University Press.

Wheeler, B.L. (2009). Research and evaluation in music therapy. In: S. Hallam, I. Cross, and M. Thaut (eds.) *Oxford handbook of music psychology*, pp. 515–25. Oxford: Oxford University Press.

White, M. and Dolan, P. (2009). Accounting for the richness of daily activities. *Psychological Science*, **20**(8), 1000–8.

Chapter 28

Epidemiological Studies of the Relationship Between Musical Experiences and Public Health

Töres Theorell and Gunter Kreutz

Introduction

Public health epidemiology aims at scientific descriptions of relationships between life conditions and public health in different groups of people. Such approaches suggest relationships between a given life condition and a specific public health problem. Thus, it can point at life conditions that may be of crucial importance to health. Epidemiology traditionally focuses on risk factors of illness. However, recent approaches also provide opportunities to identify life conditions that may protect against ill health by enhancing immune functions and even actively promote health. Can musical activities and experiences, for example, promote health? We will review recent trends in public health epidemiology with focus on the effects of music on health. Health outcome is defined mainly in a medical context. However, the outcomes that will be covered are both medically defined conditions leading to mortality and morbidity and other outcomes including mental health assessed by means of self-rating questionnaires. Finally, psychophysiological studies are considered which indicate positive and negative health-related processes.

Issues and concepts

Epidemiology refers to the scientific study of distribution of illnesses in population groups and the relationships between possible disease agents and illness risk. Thus musical activities are a matter of epidemiological concern in at least two ways. First, professional musicians are prone to health risks that appear at least in part to originate from the activity itself and the psycho-physiological demands that are associated with it. Second, an even larger group of amateur musicians is believed to benefit in terms of health and wellbeing rather than being exposed to increased health risks through musical practice. It is the latter of these groups that will be in the focus of this chapter.

Musical activities and experiences such as listening to music, singing, dancing, or playing musical instruments, are complex. Even when one of these activities is considered in isolation, there is great variation due to individual and environmental factors influencing a given activity. For example, singing can be performed with little awareness as an everyday ritual during house work or while driving a car, or it can be performed with increasing levels of awareness, sophistication, and skill. From a health perspective, it is important to note that benefits and risks are directly associated with levels of performance demands meaning that any form of assessments need to account for this variations, which are, in addition, prone to sociocultural influences.

How then to disentangle the possible unique contribution of music to health promotion? Does singing or playing music on instruments somehow influence standard epidemiological outcome measures such as longevity (i.e. a statistical measure of the expected length of survival for a member of a group or a population), disability-free life expectancy (i.e. a statistical measure of the expected future period without death or disability for a member of a group or a population), mortality (i.e. the likelihood of death in a group or a population), or morbidity (i.e. the likelihood of health incidence in a group or a population)? To address these questions, it appears important to address conceptual issues from different disciplinary perspectives and to highlight their methodological challenges as well as potentials.

Neurobiological perspective

There is controversy over the existence of music modules in the brain, i.e. brain regions that are specific to processing music (see Chapter 2, this volume). Very briefly, many regions that are activated during music experiences are shared with other processes, such as the emotional brain, motor regions (corresponding to finger activation for instance), and speech-related regions. There is initial evidence showing that music can amplify the activation of brain regions that are relevant in one type of activity and vice versa. For instance, Baumgartner et al. (2006) investigated brain responses to unimodal and bimodal presentations of images and music to healthy participants. Unimodal presentations led to differential activations depending on the visual or auditory modality. These activations were combined and further enhanced in the bimodal condition. The point to be made here is that contextual factors can significantly modulate responses to musical activities in the brain. Therefore, from a neurobiological perspective, it appears difficult from the outset to specify musically-induced public health effects that are independent of situation and contextual influences. However, a recurrent observation is that music experiences may amplify concomitant experiences in other modalities, which can be significant in a health context.

Evolutionary perspective

Music and dance could be regarded as 'social tools' that may have been used throughout the history of mankind (see Mithen 2005) in order to fulfil roles that could be of survival value such as, for example, increasing group cohesion. Benzon (2001) believes that music evolved as a means of 'brain coupling', i.e. a technique to increase the likelihood of cooperation between individuals. Promotion of musical communication may have been enhanced due to evolutionary pressures when human beings were living in small groups in a threatening environment. It was necessary to create tight groups where the members of which would help one another in crisis situations, for instance at night when one of several members had to stay awake and promise to wake the group when dangers were approaching. This may even have been important to evolution in a Darwinistic sense: those who were unable to relate to dance and music may have had a poorer survival chance than others. An illustration of this—albeit speculative—is that only 5% of normal populations could be regarded as 'tone deaf' (Sacks 2007) which means that they are consistently unable to differentiate the high from the low note when these are played randomly in pairs. From these evolutionary backgrounds, epidemiologists should be prepared that music could possibly have public health effects that depend on social contexts.

Physiological perspective

Human music performance requires physical effort. Hundreds of muscles are engaged during singing and also during playing instruments. Singing in groups frequently entails bodily movement and dance. Even listening can induce strong physical activations, for instance when we are moving to dance music or attending a rock concert. Therefore, enhancement of aerobic skill and fitness may be inherent to large parts of musical experience. Vice versa, while performing aerobic exercises, music can act as a motivating stimulus. Some of these effects appear to be exploited in commercial dance and gymnastic studios. In another vein, empirical studies of professional and amateur singers suggest that learning to sing in a controlled way can be associated with a systematic training of breathing technique. Professional singers differ from amateurs as coordination of breathing and cardiovascular functioning is enhanced in the former (Grape et al. 2003). Breathing techniques which were acquired through musical practice could be as effective in other situations as well, producing a transfer effect. It is merely a matter of point of view whether this kind of training effect on muscles should be regarded as specific to music or not ('music specificity'). Thus transfer effects between musical and other domains that could have health implications may or may not be side effects of musical practice.

It must be kept in mind that not all stereotypical concomitants of musical behaviours are unequivocally deemed to be 'good' or 'healthy' practices. To the contrary, for example, histories of some styles of music in Western cultures seem associated with the use of narcotic drugs, cigarette smoking, and other health damaging behaviours. Such concomitant practices may create adverse relationships between some types of music experiences and public health.

Epidemiological studies critically depend on including every individual in a target population. The so-called 'healthy worker effect' describes a bias in occupational health studies to disregard those workers who are not part of the sample due to work-related health problems. This phenomenon can lead to systematic underestimation of health risks in a given population of workers as well as in other populations including amateur or professional musicians. For instance, singers in most choirs will stop participating when they develop illnesses that interfere with their participation, such as lung, voice, and muscle disorders as well as illnesses that reduce energy such as psychiatric, cardiovascular, and metabolic disorders. Therefore, in cross-sectional studies of choir singers may be found healthier than the general population as a result of a 'healthy singer effect'. Thus, other strategies including longitudinal assessments of musical interventions are mandatory to establish their effects on wellbeing and health.

To conclude so far, epidemiological approaches to understanding health implications of musical experiences are subject to a wide array of potentially confounding variables. Thus understanding psychophysiological and immunological implications of musical activities per se appears as important as considerations of the effects of similar activities on the one hand, and variations of life styles that may or may not be associated with specific musical practices on the other. Therefore epidemiological studies can only succeed if sufficient attention is directed at contextual factors of a given musical activity, and if causal relationships can be established by avoiding 'healthy musicians effects'.

Empirical studies

Epidemiological evidence which suggests that music experiences can influence public health is rare, and results must be interpreted with some caution. For example, Hyyppä and Mäki (2001a) used longevity and disability-free life expectancy as dependent measures to compare two groups of people living on the north eastern part of the Finnish Baltic coast. One group belonged to a minority speaking both Swedish and Finnish (Swedish speaking Ostro-Bothnians) and the other group only speaks Finnish. The authors observed that the former group had significantly higher values in both epidemiological variables. Detailed examination revealed that neither genetics nor accepted risk factors were likely to explain this difference. However, singing in a choir belonged to a group of 'social capital' factors that independently and significantly differentiated the two language groups from one another. Social capital is related to the community's cohesiveness. In fact, the authors subsequently showed that social capital factors were strongly related to self-rated health (Hyyppä and Mäki 2001b). These findings suggest that singing in a choir significantly contributes to building social capital, which has direct implications for improved health and longevity.

Konlaan et al. (2000) conducted a cohort study based upon 10609 Swedish men and women aged 25–74. The participants were interviewed in 1982 and 1983 about their living conditions including attendance of cultural activities and health status. Participants were followed-up with regard to survival (regardless of death) until the end of 1996. After adjustment for age, sex, cash buffer, educational standard, long-term disease, smoking, and physical exercise at baseline, it was shown that there was a higher mortality risk for those people who rarely (less than once a week) visited the cinema, concerts, museums, or art exhibitions compared with those visiting them more often. When the association between each one of nine different cultural activities on one hand and survival on the other hand was studied, the relative risks were adjusted for the influence of all the other cultural activities as well as for the demographic and health-related variables listed above. The authors observed that regular visits to concerts significantly predicted survival per se but there was no advantage of regular music-making. Among the strengths of this study was the inclusion of a large, representative cohort, high compliance at baseline (75%) and perfect coverage in public registers which facilitated follow-up assessments. Moreover, several important health factors were controlled in this study. For example, associations between cultural activities and lower health risks could not be explained by the fact that subjects who were ill were also less likely to attend cultural activities—and also more prone to die early. In addition, the observed association remained stable even when variables related to individual socioeconomic background were included in the analysis. Therefore, other explanations than socioeconomic status are needed to explain why cultural participation may be advantageous for public health, in general, and mortality risks, in particular.

The fact that the authors did not find that *performing* music on a regular basis was associated with prolonged life is perhaps not surprising. It may well be that amateur and professional musical activities differ quantitatively and qualitatively in terms of health implications. Future studies, therefore, need to include more detailed information about individual engagement in musical activities.

How often and how intensely do people experience music? Answering basic questions like this one are mandatory to illuminate public health potentials of these experiences and activities. Swedish national surveys (Survey of Living Conditions, ULF) included random selections of participants from the general population from 18–64 years of age. The surveys were based upon large numbers of subjects (approximately 10,000 during each period), while participation rates were in the order of 75% (Kulturrådet 2008). Interview questions addressed—among other variables—visiting concerts as well as performing music (playing an instrument and/or singing in a choir). Surveys were conducted during the years 1982–1983, 1990–1991, 1998–1999 and finally in 2006 (see Table 28.1). To compensate for increasing attrition rates during the last sampling periods, face-to-face interviews were supplemented with telephone interviews. However, statistical differences between face-to-face and telephone data were minimal. The latest data collection year was 2006. During this year 54% of this representative group of the Swedish population reported that they had attended a concert at least once and 8% that they had done so five times during the past 12 months. Fourteen per cent reported that they played an instrument and 6% indicated that they did so at least once a week. Six per cent reported that they regularly sang in a choir, and 3.7% did so once every week or more often. During the 20 years that these surveys have taken place the attendance to concerts has increased. The prevalence of playing an instrument or

Table 28.1a-c Percentage of Swedes (age range 16–84 years) who a) attended concerts, b) played a musical instrument, and c) sang in a choir in their leisure time within several 12-month-periods between 1982 and 2006. Data adapted from Swedish Survey of Living Conditions (ULF)

a) Percentages of Swedes, who attended concerts

	At least once				More than five times			
Year of survey	82–83	90–91	98–99	2006	82–83	90–91	98–99	2006
Total	32.1	38.8	45.8	54.1	6.5	6.0	6.1	6.7
Age range								
16–19	57.3	60.9	61.1	54.3	13.7	11.7	10.1	7.9
20–29	46.9	51.4	57.1	64.1	1.2	8.9	10.1	2.4
30–44	29.6	6.8	47.3	55.7	4.9	4.3	4.4	4.4
45–64	27.8	36.2	44.7	56.6	4.8	5.5	4.2	7.2
65–74	22.4	28.8	35.9	42.9	4.6	5.5	4.2	7.2
75–84	14.1	22.2	5.2	36.2	3.6	3.0	5.2	7.3

b) Percentages of Swedes, who played musical instruments

	At least once				Every week			
Year of survey	82–83	90–91	98–99	2006	82–83	90–91	98–99	2006
Total	17.3	16.0	15.1	13.8	7.7	6.9	6.4	6.3
Age range								
16–19	32.9	27.4	25.8	21.1	20.0	17.6	14.5	10.8
20–29	24.5	20.3	20.0	21.2	10.9	9.4	10.1	12.1
30–44	18.2	17.3	16.4	14.4	7.3	6.6	5.9	6.1
45–64	12.9	14.0	12.8	11.8	5.4	5.4	4.9	3.9
65–74	11.1	9.7	10.5	11.5	4.8	4.1	4.9	4.3
75–84	8.8	8.8	8.8	11.1	3.2	3.1	2.5	5.2

c) Percentages of Swedes, who sang in choir

	At least once				Every week			
Year of survey	82–83	90–91	98–99	2006	82–83	90–91	98–99	2006
Total	5.3	5.5	5.9	5.9	3.5	3.5	3.8	3.7
					More than five times			
Age range								
16–19	12.2	10.5	10.6	10.8	9.1	7.0	7.4	8.3
20–29	6.6	5.5	6.4	6.6	4.5	3.4	4.1	4.4
30–44	4.6	4.7	6.1	5.8	3.0	2.8	3.5	3.2
45–64	4.4	5.0	4.9	4.9	2.7	3.2	3.2	3.0
65–74	4.8	5.7	6.9	4.3	3.2	4.4	5.1	2.6
75–84	2.4	5.1	4.0	7.5	1.4	3.0	2.9	4.6

Table 28.2 Means and standard deviations for 'vitality effect'. Visual analogue scale (VAS)—after minus before, a 10cm horizontal line, degree of tiredness (left)/vitality (right)—of a number of cultural activities lasting for one hour. Number of subjects 29–36

	Mean VAS change	Standard deviation
Engaging theatre	2.76	2.13
One man theatre	2.62	1.90
Music Hall	2.42	1.75
Scottish	2.38	2.08
Theatre	2.07	1.81
Pop group	2.06	2.05
Art lottery	1.73	1.54
Wind players	1.71	2.18
Jazz group[a]	1.67	1.54
Chamber music	1.65	2.37
Chinese theatre[a]	1.10	2.72
Dance group	1.05	2.42
Movie	0.54	2.23

[a] For logistical reasons the sample was divided into halves for these two activities

singing in a choir has remained relatively unchanged during these years—with one important exception, namely among boys and girls from 16–19 years of age. In these age groups there has been a clear decrease in instrument playing and also to some extent in choir singing. Accordingly there is a tendency in the Swedish population that the younger generations are consuming more but producing less music themselves. Both playing musical instruments and singing as well as concert attendance are more common in highly educated groups than in those with lower education. Women sing in a choir more frequently than men while men more often play musical instruments.

On the whole young adults are more active in producing music than older men and women. Active music production decreases with age. However, as can be seen in the Table, in 2006 there is an increase in the reported prevalence of playing an instrument or singing in the oldest age group. This may be due to the increasing popularity of singing in mass media in Sweden (and the other Nordic countries). A parallel trend has been observed in several other countries. Choral singing for elderly is described elsewhere in this volume.

These numbers from Sweden are likely to be typical of the Nordic countries. A survey in the USA is difficult to compare (Chorus America 2009) with Swedish data since the USA survey reported the percentages of households rather than percentages of individuals. In addition the American survey was performed online which means that it is difficult to assess the significance of non-participation. It is possible that the online interview procedure (which requires that the interviewee uses a computer or a mobile telephone) results in an over-representation of subjects with higher education—which is likely to be associated with a higher cultural activity. However, in the American survey an increasing proportion of households with choral singers was reported between the years 2003–2009—from 16% to 18% in adults and from 18% to 23% when adults and children were combined in the households, respectively.

Cultural activities with very few participants are of course likely to have a small total impact on public health and vice versa. According to the Swedish data, 'passive' participation (attending concerts) is very common in the population, however. If this activity does have an impact on individual health it is likely to be a strong factor in public health promotion.

Different phases in life

Growing up

Music experiences differ in their life significance during different ages. It has often been claimed that early music training stimulates general cognitive development. Studies have shown, for instance, that instrument players who started their training early in life have more white matter (corresponding to a higher number of synapses—connections between nerve cells) in their brains than subjects of comparable age. A dose response relationship was even observed—the earlier and the more intensive the training was in the early years, the more white matter there was (Bengtsson et al. 2005). What we need, however, to be sure that there is a causal relationship is a longitudinal study in which both psychological functions and brain development can be followed in comparable groups of children with/without early training. Otherwise it could always be claimed that it is the children that have the most talent—to start with—that also start training earlier and more intensively than others and therefore non-causal associations could arise. An important aspect of this is that it is not only white matter corresponding to motor functions that differentiate the groups, also white matter corresponding to general cognitive functions show these relationships which may indicate that early music training could benefit cognitive development in general. There are two published studies (Costa Giomi 1999; Schellenberg 2004) which have been designed in a scientifically convincing way. They both started with small children in ordinary life conditions. The children were randomized into a group with early music training and a group without such training and cognitive development was followed by means of standardized methods. Both studies showed that indeed the children in the music training group did have a small but significant advantage in IQ development compared to the comparison group. This advantage was decreasing as the follow-up continued. This is an interesting and important clue to be followed in future research. Cognitive functions have been shown increasingly in epidemiological research to be important to public health.

Taking a child development perspective, cognition is not the only thing that matters to health in the long term. Development of social and emotional skills is also important. A famous and scientifically interesting study—large enough and with sufficiently population representative study groups to be labelled epidemiological—which has illustrated this point is the one by Spychiger et al. (2002) in Switzerland. Fifty-two ordinary classes distributed across Switzerland were randomly allocated to 'extra music' or 'no extra music' education with an equal number of classes and pupils in both groups. They were followed for 3 years with repeated observations regarding achievements and behaviour at school. The fact that the pupils in the music classes had slightly less time for language and mathematics was of particular importance in the evaluation. When the results were summed up after 3 years it became evident that not only did the children in the music group have much better cohesiveness in the class room than the other group, they had also managed their language and mathematics achievement at least as well as the other children.

Working age

If we believe that music is different from other cultural activities with regard to effects on health we have to show that the most frequent form of music making—singing individually and in a group—and listening to music differ from other cultural activities with regard to psychological effects. We have studied the immediate psychological effects of 'passive' attendance to cultural (musical as well as other) activities in the work situation during working hours and compared these experiences to psychological effects of the singing lesson and of participating in a choir rehearsal. For these studies we used a visual analogue scale (VAS)—a horizontal 10cm long line on which the participant puts a cross showing 'where he/she is' at that moment with regard to tiredness/vitality. In the left extreme there is maximal tiredness and in the right one maximal vitality. Each subject is asked on each occasion to rate 'tiredness/vitality' before and after the activity. Change is expressed in cm—with a minus sign corresponding to decreased vitality/increased tiredness and vice versa. In the study of 'passive' culture consumption there were ten representative subjects from each one of four large worksites in northern Sweden—altogether 40 subjects. Most of them were 'naïve' with regard to participation in fine culture and represented lower as well as higher social classes. The county organized that a 'culture producer' came to the worksite and create a performance once a week for 3 months. Producers could be theatre groups, music ensembles, art lotteries, and movie shows. The experiment continued for 3 months. Averages were calculated for each participant with regard to 'increase in vitality'.

Average increase in vitality during the different kinds of cultural activities organized at work once a week within the framework of this experiment is presented in Table 28.2.

The four first activities with the highest mean VAS change are all activities with a high degree of interaction between the actors/musicians and the audience. The theatre performances used the audience as active parts in their plays and in the music hall experience as well as the Scottish one, the listeners were clapping hands and moving with the music. At the opposite end, those who looked at the movie in many cases became even more tired during the performance. This is obvious when the relationship between the mean change and its standard deviation is observed since the standard deviation is much larger than the mean in the lower end of the table. Accordingly more 'active' experiences have stronger immediate vitalization effects. This does not mean, however, that the more interactive experiences are more effective in a longer time perspective in promoting health than the more passive ones. This will be an important theme for future research.

How do the vitalization effects of the diverse cultural activities at work relate to specific music activities? Using professional and amateur singers who had been taking singing lessons for at least half a year we performed a small-scale study of the effects of the singing lesson (Grape et al. 2009, 2010) We compared the VAS scores for tiredness/vitality before and after the individual singing. In another study of choir singer beginners the singers were asked to rate their tiredness/vitality before and after a choir rehearsal 4 months after start (Grape et al. 2010). The method used was the same as in the study of cultural activities at work. The singers were all accustomed to these activities. The average increase of vitality after the singing lesson was 1.75 and the average increase in after the choir rehearsal 1.6, in both studies a statistically significant increase. This is in line with another Swedish study of immediate effects of a choir rehearsal on individual singers—with positive feelings increasing and negative feelings decreasing from before to after the rehearsal (Sandgren 2009). However the increases in vitality after the singing lesson and after the choir rehearsal in our own studies are in the medium range in the table of increased vitality after the cultural activities at work. Therefore we have no proof that singing—individually or in a group—has a more pronounced vitalization effect than many other cultural activities with a high degree of human interaction.

Albeit not specific to the musical parts, an unexpected observation in our small-scale study in four worksites illustrates one of the difficulties that may be encountered when cultural activities are introduced through the worksite. The participants were followed during the 3-month period when these cultural activities were offered once a week at the worksites. Standard questionnaires were used for the assessment of mental health before and after the period and blood samples were also taken on these occasions. In general those who had experienced the highest average increase in vitality and joy during the cultural activities were those who had had the most favourable development over time compared to other participants with regard to sleep disturbance and the biological stress marker plasma fibrinogen (Theorell et al. 2009). On the other hand it was also observed that these subjects experienced a worsened social support at work. This may be due to the fact that the participants only comprised a very small part of the total number of employees in these worksites. Therefore, when the most 'positive' participants returned to their workplace they are likely to have encountered jealousy and hostility—particularly if they beamed with joy. An important conclusion from this is that cultural activities at work should be organized in such a way that the majority of workers should have an opportunity to participate. However, it remains to be proven that cultural activity at work can promote a sustained improvement of health. In the same vein, there are no specific proofs that music at work can promote health.

What are the possible mechanisms that could mediate health promoting effects of music in adult subjects? Immediate effects of singing have been shown in several studies. For instance, choir singers have been reported to have an increased saliva content of immunoglobulins after a rehearsal compared to before the rehearsal (Kreutz et al. 2004). In a randomized small-scale study of patients with irritable bowel syndrome (a bowel disease with symptoms that are aggravated by worsened life conditions) we assessed the saliva excretion of testosterone. None of the participants had been singing in a choir but a randomly selected half of the patients were now offered the possibility to sing in a choir once a week during a year. Those randomly allocated to the control group had group activities without singing once a week during a year. Testosterone is important both in men and women for the regeneration of cells and for the body's protection against stress-related disorders and variations in the concentration of saliva reflect variations in blood concentration. It has been shown that the testosterone concentration both in blood and in saliva is related to the general psychosocial situation—when this improves the testosterone excretion increases and vice versa. The saliva excretion was assessed on six occasions during the measurement day, and these assessments were made before start as well as after 6, 9, and 12 months. The findings showed that there was an increased excretion of testosterone in the choir group but not in the comparison group after 6 months (Grape et al. 2010). After 1 year the differences were not so pronounced. Blood samples were collected before start and 1 year later. Plasma fibrinogen concentration, an indicator of long-lasting arousal, was assessed in these samples and the findings indicated a favourable 1-year effect on the choir group relative to the other group (Grape et al. 2009). The results indicate that group singing may stimulate regeneration but also that this effect may depend on context. After 1 year a possible reduction in 'stress level' as reflected in the plasma fibrinogen was also observed. These findings illustrate possible mechanisms that may explain perceived health promoting effects of group singing but much larger studies of representative sample are required for sound conclusions.

According to results recently published by Bygren et al. (2009) a program including self-selected cultural activities once a week for 8 weeks for workers in a municipality had favourable effects on various self-reported aspects of health. Studies of health effects on whole workplaces and with a longer follow-up have not been published, however.

Older age

It is frequently stated that old people can increase their vitality and promote their health by participating in cultural activities. Indirect support could be found in the observational epidemiological studies by Konlaan et al. (2000) and Bygren et al. (2009). Our own group performed an experimental study of elderly living in a service centre in Stockholm. Cultural activities selected on the basis of the elderly's own previous experiences were organized and participants were followed by means of questionnaires, staff ratings, and analyses of the blood concentration of a number of chemical substances. These observations were made before the study started as well as 3 and 6 months after start (Arnetz et al. 1983). Another strictly comparable part of the service centre (with different staff) was selected for comparison. The findings indicated that carbohydrate metabolism (which is influenced by long lasting arousal/stress) as it is reflected in HbA1c concentration as well as indicators of cell regeneration, anabolism, had developed significantly more favourably in the experimental group of elderly compared to the other group. Later, a study was performed of the effects of pictures of fine art on the health of elderly ladies. Such ladies living in a service home for elderly were randomly allocated to a 'art group' or a 'talk group'. The interventions lasted for 4 months. The investigator met the participants once a week during 4 months. In the 'art group' a series of pictures of fine art introduced talks while in the other group talks were regular conversations without art introductions (Wikström 1994). Observations (questionnaires and blood pressure assessments) were made before start as well as 4 and 8 months later. In general there were significantly more favourable effects in the 'art group' than in the other group and these effects lasted longer than the four months of the intervention. For instance, there was significantly more improved coping, better blood pressure development and more improvement in physical health (one example: more decrease in use of laxatives!) in the 'art group'. These experiments were not epidemiological in the sense that the participants were drawn randomly from the population but they were typical of the relatively healthy elderly population living in homes for elderly in Sweden.

In the experimental studies of elderly mentioned above there was no specific music group. Later, however, several studies have indicated that singing in a choir may be of particular importance to health promotion in elderly. The most extensive study published so far is the study by Cohen (2009) whose research group studied 166 elderly living in Washington, New York City, and San Francisco. Those who were willing to participate in singing were randomly assigned to either cultural activity or control group. In New York City and San Francisco other forms of cultural activity took place but in Washington all the three participating centres had choral weekly singing groups which in the end formed a big choir. This went on for 2 years and the participants were followed by means of standard questionnaires. In assessments performed at baseline as well as after 1 and 2 years there were 61 participants in the chorale group and 57 in the control group. Several health indicators showed the same pattern with significantly improved scores (for instance, number of health problems) in the choral and deteriorated scores in the control group. The main difference was particularly pronounced after 2 years. From this study of a representative group of institutionalized elderly it was concluded that organized choir singing could be of particular health promoting value in old age, at least among those who want to sing and have no opportunity to do so without organized help. A large cross-national interview study of elderly chorists in Great Britain and Australia (Clift et al. 2007 and 2008) has explored the potential benefits of active involvement in choral singing. At least six mechanisms were identified as potential explanations of a health promotion effect in this age group: positive affect, focused attention, deep breathing, and social support are four of those. The remaining mechanisms are general mechanisms that are operating in all cultural activities in relation to mental health.

Conclusions

The aim of this review is to point at epidemiological research that may throw light on possible effects of musical activities, passive and active, on public health. The review shows that few studies have been published on the relationship between musical experiences and health in the general population. There is at least initial evidence that cultural participation including musical activities can enhance immunity in individuals. Paradoxically, it may well be that less musical proficiency would mean greater health benefits. However, it is an entirely open issue how and to what extent professional and amateur musicians, singers, and dancers could be affected in terms of their health status at an epidemiological level. Clearly, there are profound methodological differences that must be noted in the development and application of epidemiological approaches as compared to (quasi) experimental studies, or other empirical studies with smaller groups of individuals. For example, whether short-term effects of musical activities have any influence on standard epidemiological measures including longevity, morbidity, or mortality, appears as an important topic of future investigations. However, as we have explicated at the beginning of this chapter, there are both conceptual and methodological problems to be solved in order to arrive at a better understanding of such issues. Therefore, it seems mandatory as one starting point, to include measures of musical participation in larger-scale cohort studies, which are being conducted especially in some countries, which are afflicted with demographic change and aging societies over the next decades until the middle of the century.

Since passive music experience is much more common than active production of music in the general population, the former is more likely to affect larger numbers of people. Since music consumption is extensive in modern society we need more epidemiological studies of health effects. We also need more studies with longitudinal design since cross-sectional studies are difficult to interpret in terms of direction of causality. Finally longitudinal studies health effects of musical activities over longer periods of time are crucial.

References

Arnetz, B., Theorell, T., Levi., L., Kallner, A., Eneroth, P. (1983). An experimental study of social isolation of elderly people: psychoendocrine and metabolic effects. *Psychosomatic Medicine*, **45**, 395–406.

Baumgartner, T, Lutz K, Schmidt, C.F., and Jäncke, L. (2006). The emotional power of music: How music enhances the feeling of affective pictures. *Brain Research*, **1075**, 151–64.

Bengtsson, S.L., Nagy, Z., Skare, S., Forsman, L., Forssberg, H., and Ullén, F. (2005). Extensive piano practicing has regionally specific effects on white matter development. *Nature Neuroscience*, **9**, 1148–50.

Benzon, W. Jr (2001). *Beethoven´s anvil. Music in Mind and Culture*. New York: Basic Books.

Bygren, L.O., Johansson, S-E., Konlaan, B.B., Grjibovski, A.M., Wilkinson, A.V. and Sjöström, M. (2009). Attending cultural events and cancer mortality: A Swedish cohort study. *Arts and Health*, **1**, 64–73.

Bygren, L.O., Weissglas, G., Wikström, B.M., Konlaan, B.B., Grjibovski, A. Karlsson, A.B., *et al.* (2009). Cultural participation and health: a randomized controlled trial among medical care staff. *Psychosomatic Medicine*, **71**, 469–73.

Chorus America (2009). *The Chorus Impact Study. How Children, Adults, and Communities benefit from Choruses*. Washington, DC: Chorus America.

Clift, S., Hancox, G., Morrison, I., Hess, B., Kreutz, G., and Stewart, D. (2007). Choral singing and psychological well-being: Findings from English choirs in a cross-national survey using the WHOGOL-BREF. In: A. Williamon and D. Coimbra (eds.) *Proceedings of the International Symposium on Performance Science*, 25–27 October, Porto. Portugal.

Clift, S., Hancox, G., Morrison, I., Hess, B., Kreutz, G. and Stewart, D. (2008). *Findings from a Cross-National Survey on Choral Singing, Well-being and Health*. Canterbury: Canterbury Christ Church University. Available at: http://www.canterbury.ac.uk/centres/sidney-de-haan-research/ (accessed 3 February 2010).

Cohen, G. (2009). New theories and research findings on the positive influence of music and art on health with ageing. *Arts and Health*, **1**, 48–63.

Costa Giomi, E. (1999). The effects of three years of piano instruction on children´s cognitive development. *Journal of Research In Music Education, 47*, 198–212.

Grape, C., Sandgren, M., Hansson, L-O., Ericson, M. and Theorell, T. (2003). Does singing promote well-being? An empirical study of professional and amateur singers during a singing lesson. Integrative *Physiological and Behavioral Science, 38*, 65–74.

Grape, C., Theorell, T., Wikström, B.M. and Ekman, R. (2009). Choir singing and fibrinogen, VEGF, cholecystokinin and motilin in IBS patients. *Medical Hypotheses, 72*, 223–25.

Grape, C., Wikström, B.M., Hasson, D., Ekman, R. and Theorell, T. (2010). Saliva testosterone increases in choir singer beginners. *Psychotherapy and Psychosomatics, 79*, 196–8.

Hyyppä, M.T. and Mäki, J. (2001a). Why do Swedish-speaking Finns have longer active life? An area for social capital research. *Health Promotion International, 16*, 55–64.

Hyyppä, M.T. and Mäki, J. (2001b). Individual-level relationships between social capital and self-rated health in a bilingual community. *Preventive Medicine, 32*, 148–55.

Konlaan, B.B., Bygren, L.O. and Johansson, S.E. (2000). Visiting the cinema, concerts, museums or art exhibitions as determinant of survival: a Swedish fourteen-year cohort follow-up. *Scandinavian Journal of Public Health, 28*, 174–8.

Kreutz, G., Bongard, S., Rohrmann, S., Hodapp, V. and Grebe, D. (2004). Effects of choir singing or listening on secretory immunoglobulin A, cortisol, and emotional state. *Journal of Behavioral Medicine, 27*, 623–35.

Mithen, S. (2005). *The singing Neanderthals. The Origins of Music, Language and Body.* London: Weidenfeld and Nicholson.

Kulturrådet (Swedish National Arts Council). (2008). *Kulturen i siffror, svenska kulturvanor i ett 30-årsperspektiv (Culture in numbers, Swedish cultural habits en 30 years perspective): 1976-2006,* Stockholm: Kulturrådet number 2008:6.

Sacks, O. (2007). *Musicophilia. Tales of music and the brain.* London: Picador.

Sandgren, M. and Borg, E. (2009). Immediate Effects of Choral Singing on Emotional States: Differences in groups with lower and higher health status. Unpublished.

Schellenberg, E.G. (2004). Music lessons enhance IG. *Psychological Science, 15*, 511–14.

Spychiger, M. (2002). Music education is important – why. In: Matell, G. and Theorell, T. (eds) *Barn och Musik [Children and Music]* Stockholm: Stressforskningsrapporter. (Stress Research Reports, Stress Research Institute, Stockholm University.)

Theorell, T., Hartzell, M., and Näslund, S. (2009). A note on designing evaluations of health effects of cultural activities at work. *Arts and Health, 1*, 89–92.

Wikström, B-M. (1994). *Pleasant guided mental walks via pictures of works of art.* Academic Thesis. Stockholm: Karolinska Institute.

Chapter 29

The Brain and Positive Biological Effects in Healthy and Clinical Populations

Stefan Koelsch and Thomas Stegemann

Introduction

Mounting evidence indicates that making music, dancing, and even simply listening to music activates a multitude of brain structures involved in cognitive, sensorimotor, and emotional processing (Koelsch and Siebel 2005; Zatorre et al. 2007; Koelsch et al. 2010). It has been hypothesized that such activation has beneficial effects on psychological and physiological health, but there is still a lack of systematic high-quality research confirming such hypotheses. To lay out the basis for such research, this chapter focuses on the neural correlates of music-evoked emotions, and their health-related autonomic, endocrinological, and immunological effects. We will start with the question as to how music actually evokes an emotion, and some thoughts on the different routes through which music might evoke emotions.

Mechanisms through which music can evoke emotions

Juslin and Västfjäll (2008) suggested several 'mechanisms' underlying the evocation of emotions with music. These include: (1) *brain stem reflexes* (due to basic acoustic properties of music such as timbre, attack time, and intensity); (2) *evaluative conditioning* (the process of evoking emotion with music that has been paired repeatedly with other positive, or negative, stimuli); (3) *emotional contagion* (where a listener perceives an emotionally relevant feature or expression of the music, and then copies this feature or expression internally); (4) *visual imagery* (where music evokes images with emotional qualities); (5) *episodic memory* (where music evokes a memory of a particular event, also referred to as the 'Darling, they are playing our tune' phenomenon; Davies 1978); and (6) *musical expectancy* (where a specific musical feature violates, delays, or confirms the expectations of listeners, leading to feelings of tension and suspense or release and relaxation).

Additional psychological processes suggested by other researchers include, for example, (7) the *mere exposure effect* which can also contribute to, and modify the liking of music (Moors and Kuppens 2008); (8) *semantic associations* with emotional valence (Fritz and Koelsch 2008); (9) *movement* elicited by music, which can modify emotional states (such as the impetus to move in a depressed individual), even when it is not directly expressive of emotion (Bharucha and Curtis 2008); and (10) *engagement in social activities* (see also the section on the 'the seven Cs' that follows). However, the mechanisms through which music can evoke emotions are still debated, and few empirical studies are available that investigate such mechanisms (reviewed in Juslin and Västfjäll 2008). The next section will provide a review of functional neuroimaging studies on music and emotion, relating the findings where possible to the emotion-evoking mechanisms described above.

Limbic and paralimbic correlates of music-evoked emotions

Functional neuroimaging and lesion studies have shown that music-evoked emotions can modulate activity in virtually all limbic/paralimbic brain structures, that is, in the core structures of the generation of emotions (see Figure 29.1 for an illustration of some limbic/paralimbic brain structures). Because emotions include changes in endocrine and autonomic system activity,

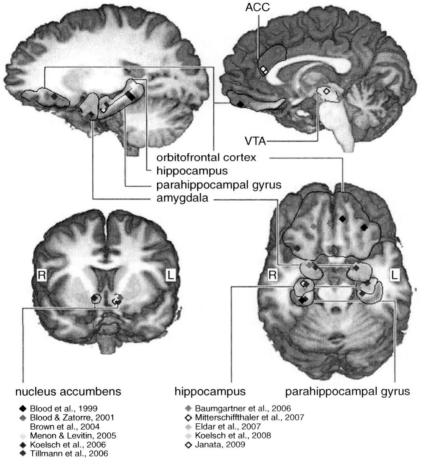

Fig. 29.1 Illustration of some limbic/para-limbic brain structures (amygdala, nucleus accumbens, anterior cingulate cortex [AAC], hippocampus, orbitofrontal cortex, and parahippocampal gyrus). Top: sagittal views (in both images, anterior is left, and superior is upwards). The left image shows a view of the brain slightly lateral of the interhemispheric fissure, the right image shows a view onto the interhemispheric fissure. The bottom left image shows a view from anterior, the slice is slightly anterior of the amygdala. The bottom right image shows a view looking from below (anterior is upwards, the slice is roughly going through the orbitofrontal cortex, the amygdala, and the hippocampus). The diamonds represent music-evoked activity changes in these structures (see main text for details). Note the repeatedly reported activations of amygdala, nucleus accumbens, and hippocampus, reflecting that music is capable of modulating activity in core structures of emotion. From Koelsch (2010).

and because such changes interact with immune system function (Dantzer et al. 2008), music-evoked emotions form an important basis for beneficial biological effects of music, and for possible interventions using music in the treatment of disorders related to autonomic, endocrine, and immune system dysfunction (Koelsch and Siebel 2005; Koelsch 2010; Kreutz et al. Chapter 30, this volume).

Using positron emission tomography (PET), Blood et al. (1999) investigated brain responses related to the valence of musical stimuli. The stimuli varied in their degree of (continuous) dissonance, and were perceived as less or more unpleasant (stimuli with the highest degree of continuous dissonance were rated as the most unpleasant ones). Increasing unpleasantness correlated with regional cerebral blood flow (rCBF) in the (right) parahippocampal gyrus, while decreasing unpleasantness correlated with rCBF in the frontopolar and orbitofrontal cortex, as well as in the (posterior) subcallosal cingulate cortex. No rCBF changes were observed in central limbic structures such as the amygdala, presumably because the stimuli were presented under computerized control without musical expression (which somewhat limits the power of music to evoke emotions).

In another PET experiment, Blood and Zatorre (2001) used naturalistic music to evoke strongly pleasurable experiences involving 'chills' or 'shivers down the spine.' Participants were presented with a piece of their own favourite music (using normal CD recordings; as a control condition, participants listened to the favourite piece of another subject). Increasing chills intensity correlated with rCBF in brain regions thought to be involved in reward and emotion, including the ventral striatum (presumably the nucleus accumbens, NAc; see also next section), the insula, anterior cingulate cortex (ACC), orbitofrontal cortex, and ventral medial prefrontal cortex. The authors also found decreases of rCBF in the amygdala as well as in the anterior hippocampal formation with increasing chills intensity. Thus, activity changes were observed in central structures of the limbic/paralimbic system (e.g. amygdala, NAc, ACC, and hippocampal formation). This was the first study showing modulation of amygdalar activity with music, which was important for two reasons: first, the activity of core structures of emotion processing was modulated by music, which supports the assumption that music can induce 'real' emotions (and not merely illusions of emotions; for details, see Koelsch et al. 2010). Second, it strengthened the empirical basis for music-therapeutic approaches for the treatment of affective disorders such as depression and pathologic anxiety, because these disorders are partly related to dysfunction of the amygdala (in addition, depression has been related to dysfunction of the hippocampus, and the NAc; Drevets et al. 2002; Stein et al. 2007).

An functional magnetic resonance imaging (fMRI) study from Koelsch et al. (2006) showed that activity changes in the amygdala, ventral striatum, and hippocampal formation can be evoked by music even without individuals having intense 'chill' experiences. That study investigated brain responses to joyful instrumental tunes (played by professional musicians) with responses to electronically manipulated, continuously dissonant counterparts of these tunes. Unpleasant music elicited increases in blood-oxygen-level dependent (BOLD) signals in the amygdala, hippocampus, parahippocampal gyrus, and temporal poles (and decreases of BOLD signals were observed in these structures in response to the pleasant music). During the presentation of the pleasant music, increases of BOLD signals were observed in the ventral striatum (presumably the NAc) and the insula (in addition to some cortical structures not belonging to limbic or paralimbic circuits that will not be further reported here). In addition to the mentioned studies from Blood and Zatorre (2001) and Koelsch et al. (2006), several other functional neuroimaging studies (Baumgartner et al. 2006; Ball et al. 2007; Eldar et al. 2007; Koelsch et al. 2008; Lerner et al. 2009) and lesion studies (e.g. Gosselin et al. 2007) showed involvement of the amygdala in emotional responses to music (for reviews see Koelsch 2010; Koelsch et al. 2010).

Most of these studies reported activity changes in the amygdala in response to fearful musical stimuli, but it is important to note that the amygdala is not only a 'fear centre' in the brain, and that the amygdala also plays a role for emotions that we perceive as pleasant (for further details see also Koelsch et al. 2010).

Compared to studies investigating neural correlates of emotion with stimuli other than music (e.g. photographs with emotional valence, or stimuli that reward or punish the subject), the picture provided by functional neuroimaging studies on music and emotion bears a particularly striking feature: The number of studies reporting activity changes within the (anterior) hippocampal formation (Blood and Zatorre 2001; Baumgartner et al. 2006; Koelsch et al. 2006; Eldar et al. 2007; Mitterschiffthaler et al. 2007) is remarkably high. It was previously argued (Koelsch et al. 2010) that the hippocampus plays an important role for the generation of attachment-related *tender positive emotions* (such as joy and happiness), and, in our view, one of the great powers of music is to evoke hippocampal activity related to such emotions (see also next section). The activity changes in the (anterior) hippocampal formation evoked by listening to music are relevant for music therapy because patients with depression or post-traumatic stress disorder (PTSD) show a volume reduction of the hippocampal formation (associated with a loss of hippocampal neurons and blockage of neurogenesis in the hippocampus; Warner-Schmidt and Duman 2006), and individuals with flattened affectivity (i.e. a reduced capability of producing tender positive emotions) show reduced activity changes in the anterior hippocampal formation in response to music (Koelsch et al. 2007). Therefore, it is reasonable to assume that music can be used therapeutically to: (1) re-establish neural activity (related to positive emotion) in the hippocampus, (2) prevent death of hippocampal neurons, and (3) stimulate hippocampal neurogenesis.

Similarly, because the amygdala and the NAc function abnormally in patients with depression, studies showing modulation of activity within these structures motivate the hypothesis that music can be used to modulate activity of these structures (either by listening to or by making music), and thus ameliorate symptoms of depression. However, the scientific evidence for effectiveness of music therapy on depression is surprisingly weak, perhaps due to the lack of high quality studies, and the small number of studies with randomized, controlled trials (see later section 'Effects of music-evoked emotions on endocrine and immune system activity' of this chapter).

From social contact to spirituality: the seven Cs

The previous section illustrated that music can evoke activity in brain structures involved in reward and pleasure (such as the nucleus accumbens), and that music can evoke activity changes in the hippocampus, possibly related to experiences of joy and happiness. This section will provide a summary of explanations as to why music is so powerful in evoking such emotions.

Music making is an activity involving several social functions. In this section, these functions are divided into seven different areas (see also Koelsch 2010). The ability and the need to practice these social functions is part of what makes us human, and emotional effects of engaging in these functions include experiences of reward, joy and happiness (and such effects have important implications for music therapy). Exclusion from the engagement in these functions represents an emotional stressor, and has deleterious effects on health (Cacioppo and Hawkley 2003). Therefore, engaging in such social functions is important for the survival of the individual and thus for the human species. In the following, we will outline the seven different dimensions of social functions.

(1) When we make music, we make *contact* with other individuals. Being in contact with other individuals is a basic need of humans (as well as of numerous other species; Harlow, 1958),

and social isolation is a major risk factor for morbidity as well as mortality (House et al. 1988; Cacioppo and Hawkley 2003). Although no empirical evidence is yet available, we hypothesize that social isolation will result in hippocampal damage and that, on the other hand, contact with other individuals promotes hippocampal integrity.

(2) Music automatically engages *social cognition* (Steinbeis and Koelsch 2009). During music listening, individuals automatically engage processes of mental state attribution ('mentalizing', or 'adopting an intentional stance'), in an attempt to figure out the intentions, desires, and beliefs of the individuals who actually created the music (also often referred to as establishing a 'theory of mind', TOM). A recent fMRI study (Steinbeis and Koelsch 2009) showed that listening to music automatically engages a TOM-network (comprising anterior fronto-median cortex, temporal poles, and the superior temporal sulcus), suggesting that listening to music automatically engages areas dedicated to social cognition in the attempt to understand the composer's intentions.

(3) Music making can engage *co-pathy* in the sense that interindividual emotional states become more homogenous (e.g. reducing anger in one individual, and depression or anxiety in another), thus decreasing conflicts and promoting cohesion of a group (e.g. Huron 2001). With regard to positive emotions, for example, co-pathy can increase the wellbeing of individuals during music making or during listening to music. By using the term co-pathy we refer to the phenomenon that one's own emotional state is affected in the sense that it occurs when one perceives (e.g. observes or hears), or imagines, someone else's affect, and this evokes a feeling in the perceiver which bears strong congruency with what the other individual is feeling (see also Singer and Lamm 2009; see Koelsch et al. 2010, for a differentiation between co-pathy, mimicry, emotional contagion, sympathy, empathic concern, and compassion).

(4) Music always involves *communication* (notably, for infants and young children, musical communication during parent-child singing of lullabies and play-songs is important for social and emotional regulation, as well as for social, emotional, and cognitive development; Trehub, 2003). Neuroscience and behavioural studies have revealed considerable overlap between the neural substrates and cognitive mechanisms underlying the processing of musical syntax and language syntax (Steinbeis and Koelsch 2008; Patel 2007; Koelsch and Siebel 2005). Moreover, musical information can systematically influence semantic processing of language (Koelsch et al. 2004; Steinbeis and Koelsch 2009). It is also worth noting that the neural substrates engaged in speech and song strongly overlap (Callan et al. 2006). Because music is a means of communication, particularly active music therapy (in which patients make music) can be used to train skills of (nonverbal) communication (Hillecke et al. 2005).

(5) Music making also involves *coordination* of actions. This requires individuals to synchronize to a beat, and to keep a beat, a human capability that is unique among primates (although some species, other than non-human primates, are capable of synchronizing movements to an external beat as well; Patel et al. 2009). The coordination of movements in a group of individuals appears to be associated with pleasure (for example, when dancing together), even in the absence of a shared goal (apart from deriving pleasure from concerted movements; see also Huron 2001). The capacity to synchronize movements to an external beat appears to be uniquely human among primates, although other mammals and birds might also possess this capacity (e.g. Patel 2007, 2009). Note that humans are inclined to perceive the participation in inter-individually coordinated movements as pleasurable (Overy and Molnar-Szakacs 2009; Wiltermuth and Heath 2009).

(6) A convincing musical performance by multiple players is only possible if it also involves *cooperation* between players. Cooperation involves a shared goal, and engaging in cooperative

behaviour is an important potential source of pleasure (Rilling et al. 2002). Cooperation between individuals increases inter-individual trust, and increases the likelihood of further cooperation between these individuals. It is worth noting that only humans have the capability to communicate about coordinated activities during cooperation to achieve a joint goal (Tomasello et al. 2005).

(7) As an effect, music leads to increased *social cohesion* of a group (Cross and Morley 2008). A wealth of studies showed that humans have a 'need to belong' (Baumeister and Leary 1995), and a strong motivation to form and maintain enduring interpersonal attachments (Baumeister and Leary 1995). Meeting this need increases health and life expectancy (Cacioppo and Hawkley 2003). Social cohesion also strengthens the confidence in reciprocal care (see also the caregiver hypothesis; Fitch 2005), and the confidence that opportunities to engage with others in the mentioned social functions will also emerge in the future.

Although it should clearly be noted that music can also be used to manipulate other individuals, and to support non-social behaviour (e.g. Brown and Volgsten 2006), music is still special— although not unique—in that it can engage all of these social functions at the same time, which is presumably one explanation for the emotional power of music (for a discussion on the role of other factors, such as sexual selection, for the evolution of music see Huron 2001; Fitch 2005). Therefore, music *does* serve the goal to fulfil social needs (our need to be in contact with others, to belong, to communicate, etc.). In this regard, music-evoked emotions are related to survival functions and to functions that are of vital importance for the individual.

It is also worth mentioning that the experience of engaging in these social functions, along with the experience of the emotions evoked by such engagements, is a spiritual experience (such as the experience of communion; note that neither 'spiritual' nor 'communion' are used here as religious terms). This is perhaps one reason why religious practices usually involve music.

Engaging in social functions during music making evokes activity of the 'reward circuit' (from the lateral hypothalamus via the medial forebrain bundle to the mesolimbic dopamine pathway involving the ventral tegmental area with projection to the NAc) and is immediately perceived as fun. Interestingly, in addition to experiences of mere fun, music making can also evoke attachment-related *tender positive emotions* such as joy and happiness due to the engagement in the mentioned social functions. As mentioned previously, these emotions presumably involve hippocampal activity. That is, music can not only be fun, it can also make people happy. This capacity of music is an important basis for beneficial biological effects of music, and thus for the use of music in therapy. However, as described in the next section, future studies are needed to provide scientific evidence that gives rise to more systematic, more widespread, and more theoretically-grounded applications of music in education and therapy.

Effects of music-evoked emotions on endocrine and immune system activity

So far we have reviewed the mechanisms by which music evokes (real) emotions in human individuals, the neural correlates of such mechanisms, how music-evoked emotions are linked to social functions (the seven Cs), and how this represents evolutionarily adaptive value. In this section, we deal with the effects of music-evoked emotions on the complex interactions between neural activity, autonomic functions, endocrine, and immune system activity. Emotional processes inevitably influence autonomic, endocrine activity (and thus also modulate immune system activity). By virtue of these effects, emotional activity in the brain has potential effects on all organ system of the body.

Several hormones, neurotransmitters, neuropeptides, and other biochemical mediators play a role in the perceptual and emotional processing of music (Boso et al. 2006; Hodges 2010). Numerous studies investigated hormonal effects of music, particularly with regard to the following groups of biochemicals (see also Table 29.1):

1. Hormones and neuropeptides of the hypothalamic–pituitary–adrenal axis (HPA): adrenocorticotropic hormone (ACTH), dehydroepiandrosterone (DHEA), cortisol (a corticosteroid hormone that is crucial for glucose metabolism, inflammation suppression, and stress adaptation), adrenaline (also often referred to as epinephrine), noradrenaline (or norepinephine), and β-endorphin. Note that, although ACTH, cortisol, and adrenaline are hormones that are released during the so-called stress response, these hormones are 'energy hormones' that are also released in non-stressful situations. In this regard, it is important to note that it depends on an individual's situation whether an increase or a decrease of the levels of these hormones is related to beneficial effects (particularly with regard to the level of arousal or stress, and the targeted level of arousal and mood): Early in the morning, for example, an increase in cortisol levels (and the related energization) is beneficial to commence the day. The same holds for lightening up and mobilizing energy when being in a depressed mood. On the other hand, if an individual is chronically stressed and needs relaxation (or needs to get sleep after a stressful day) then a reduction of cortisol levels is beneficial. Thus, an 'optimal basal activity and responsiveness of the stress system (of which the HPA axis is a major part) is essential for a sense of wellbeing, successful performance of tasks, and appropriate social interactions' (Chrousos 2009).

2. Components of the immune system: (a) cytokines such as interleukins, interferon gamma (IFN-γ), and tumour necrosis factor alpha (TNF-α); (b) antibodies such as immunoglobulin A (IgA); (c) natural killer cell (NK cells); and (d) T lymphocytes.

3. Neurotransmitters (particularly dopamine and serotonin).

4. Hormones involved in lactation and social bonding (oxytocin and prolactin).

5. Other parameters such as alpha amylase, atrial natriuretic peptide (ANP), growth hormone, testosterone, and tissue plasminogen activator (t-PA).

In the following, we will review 74 studies investigating effects of music on hormone and immune system activity (see Table 29.1 for a summary; also see Figure 29.2). We will first report findings separately for different emotional parameters (positive emotions, anxiety, and depressed mood).

Studies on positive emotions and biochemicals

Twenty-one studies investigated positive emotion in a broader sense, in healthy individuals and in non-clinical settings (marked with an asterisk in Table 29.1). All of these studies found an increase in positive emotion or mood when participants listened to (mainly classical) music (e.g. VanderArk and Ely 1992; Evers and Suhr 2000; LeRoux et al. 2007), after singing (Beck et al. 2000a,b; Grape et al. 2003; Kreutz et al. 2004), dancing (West et al. 2004; Quiroga et al. 2009), active and receptive music therapy (Burns et al. 2001), receptive music therapy (McKinney et al. 1997a), and active music therapy (Nakayama et al. 2009). Although these studies investigated effects on a variety of endocrine and immune system markers, we will focus here only on those studies that investigated cortisol and IgA, because only very few (n ≤3) studies were available investigating other parameters (thus not providing a sufficient basis for thorough conclusions).

Out of 21 studies, only four studies (VanderArk and Ely 1992; McKinney et al. 1997a; Nater et al. 2006; LeRoux et al. 2007) were randomized controlled trials (RCTs), another four studies (Brownley et al. 1995; Möckel et al. 1995; Grape et al. 2003; West et al. 2004) used a control group

Table 29.1 Overview of studies on effects of music on biochemicals. The table includes studies that investigated the effects of live or recorded music on hormonal or immune parameters, measured using blood, urine, or saliva samples. Only original works were included, and only works of which the full report (English or German) could be retrieved (these studies were also included in our review). Symbols indicate studies that investigated: * = positive emotions; ‡ = anxiety/fear; § = depressed mood; II = perioperative interventions; ¶ = medical interventions; ** = psychiatry. Adapted from Hodges, D. (2010) Psychophysiological measures. In P. Juslin and J. Sloboda (eds.) Handbook of Music and Emotion, pp. 287–8, with permission from Oxford University Press

Adrenaline
Increased: **Kumar et al. 1999; II Migneault et al. 2004; Yamamoto et al. 2003 (fast rhythm music); ‡¶Schneider et al. 2001
Decreased: Conrad et al. 2007; *Möckel et al. 1994
No change: Chlan et al. 2007; ‡¶Escher et al. 1993; *Gerra et al. 1998; *§Hirokawa and Ohira 2003; ‡Wahbeh et al. 2007; ‡II Wang et al. 2002

Adrenocorticotropic hormone (ACTH)
Increased: *Gerra et al. 1998
Decreased: ‡¶Oyama et al. 1983
No change: II Migneault et al. 2004; Conrad et al. 2007; *Evers and Suhr, 2000; *Möckel et al. 1994; ¶Koelsch et al. 2011
Rise of ACTH significant lower than in controls (‡¶Escher et al. 1993)

Alpha amylase
No change: *Nater et al. 2006

Atrial natriuretic peptide (ANP)
Increased: *Möckel et al. 1994; *Möckel et al. 1995

Beta-endorphine
Increased: *Gerra et al. 1998; Goldstein, 1980
Decreased: *McKinney et al. 1997b; ‡Vollert et al. 2003
No change: ‡¶Oyama et al. 1983

Blood glucose
Decreased: Miluk-Kolasa et al. 1996 (normalization after music intervention)
No change: ‡II Nilsson et al. 2005

Chromogranin A (CgA)
Decreased: **Suzuki et al. 2004; **Suzuki et al. 2007

Corticotropin
No change: Chlan et al. 2007

Cortisol
Increase:
*Beck et al. 2000a (solo-singers during performance); *Beck et al. 2000b (choral-singers during performance); *Brownley et al. 1995; *Gerra et al. 1998; *Grape et al. 2003 (in males); Hébert et al. 2005; Müller et al. 1994; *VanderArk and Ely 1992, 1993 (in music majors); *West et al. 2004

(continued)

Table 29.1 (Continued) Overview of studies on effects of music on biochemicals. The table includes studies that investigated the effects of live or recorded music on hormonal or immune parameters, measured using blood, urine, or saliva samples. Only original works were included, and only works of which the full report (English or German) could be retrieved (these studies were also included in our review)

Decrease:
‡Bartlett et al. 1993; *Beck et al. 2000a (solo-singers during rehearsal); *Beck et al. 2000b (choral-singers during rehearsal); *Burns et al. 2001; **Chopra et al. 2007; Clark et al. 2001; **Field et al. 1998; Flaten et al. 2006; Fukui and Yamashita 2003; *Grape et al. 2003 (in females); ¶Koelsch et al. 2011; *Kreutz et al. 2004; ‡ II Leardi et al. 2007; *§Le Roux et al. 2007; ‡Lindblad et al. 2007; *§McKinney et al. 1997a,b; II Miluk-Kolasa et al. 1994; Möckel et al. 1994; Möckel et al. 1995; *‡§Nakayama et al. 2009; ‡II Nilsson 2009a; *Quiroga et al. 2009; Suda et al. 2008; ‡Tornek et al. 2003
No change: ‡§Bittman et al. 2001; Chlan et al. 2007; Conrad et al. 2007; Hucklebridge et al. 2000; ‡**Jeong et al. 2005; ¶Joyce et al. 2001; ‡Knight and Rickard 2001; ‡ II McRee et al. 2003; *Nater et al. 2006; *¶Oyama et al. 1983; ‡Rickard 2004; II Migneault et al. 2004; Rider et al. 1985; Stefano et al. 2004; **Takahashi and Matsushita 2006; ‡Wahbeh et al. 2007; ‡II Wang et al. 2002; Yamamoto et al. 2007
Rise of cortisol significant lower than in controls: ‡¶Escher et al. 1993; Khalfa et al. 2003; ¶Uedo et al. 2004
Decrease of cortisol (postoperative) greater than in controls: ‡II Nilsson et al. 2005
Cortisol remained stable while increasing in controls: ‡¶Schneider et al. 2001
Reduced variability in cortisol values: Shenfield et al. 2003

Dehydroepiandrosterone (DHEA)

No change: ‡§Bittman et al. 2001 (but increased DHEA-to-cortisol ratios); Conrad et al. 2007; ‡Wahbeh et al. 2007
Decreased cortisol-to-DHEA ratio (*§Le Roux et al. 2007)

Dopamine

Decreased: ‡**Jeong et al. 2005; ‡Wahbeh et al. 2007
No change: *§Hirokawa and Ohira 2003

Genetic stress hormone markers

Reversal in 19 of 45 genetic stress hormone markers was demonstrated in participants in a recreational music making programme (Bittman et al. 2005)

Growth Hormone

Increased: Conrad et al. 2007; *Gerra et al. 1998
No change: ‡¶Oyama et al. 1983

Immunoglobulin A (IgA)

Increased: *Beck et al. 2000a; *Beck et al. 2000b; *Burns et al. 2001; Charnetski et al. 1998; Hucklebridge et al. 2000; *Kreutz et al. 2004; Kuhn 2002; *McCraty et al. 1996; Müller et al. 1994; Rider and Weldin 1990
Decreased: ‡Knight and Rickard 2001
No change: ¶Koelsch et al. 2011; ‡II Nilsson et al. 2005

Table 29.1 (Continued) Overview of studies on effects of music on biochemicals. The table includes studies that investigated the effects of live or recorded music on hormonal or immune parameters, measured using blood, urine, or saliva samples. Only original works were included, and only works of which the full report (English or German) could be retrieved (these studies were also included in our review).

Insulin-like growth factor 1 (IGF-1)

Decrease: ‡Wahbeh et al. 2007

Interferon-gamma

No change: ‡§Bittman et al. 2001

Interleukin-1 (IL-1), interleukin-2 (IL-2), interleukin-6 (IL-6), interleukin-10 (IL-10)

Increased: ‡Bartlett et al. 1993 (IL-1)

Decreased: Conrad et al. 2007; Stefano et al. 2004 (IL-6); *Wachi et al. 2007 (IL-10)

No change: ‡§Bittman et al. 2001 (IL-2); Stefano et al. 2004 (IL-1, IL-10)

Lymphokine-activated killer cell activity

Increased: ‡§Bittman et al. 2001

Melatonin

Increased: **Kumar et al. 1999

No change: ‡Wahbeh et al. 2007

Mu opiate receptor expression

Increased: Stefano et al. 2004

Natural killer (NK) cell activity

Increased: ‡§Bittman et al. 2001; *Wachi et al. 2007

Decreased: ‡ II Leardi et al. 2007

No change: *§Hirokawa and Ohira 2003

Neutrophils and lymphocytes

Decreased: Rider and Achterberg 1989

Noradrenaline

Increased: **Kumar et al. 1999; ‡¶Schneider et al. 2001

Decreased: Möckel et al. 1994; Möckel et al. 1995; Yamamoto et al. 2003 (slow rhythm music)

No change: Chlan et al. 2007; Conrad et al. 2007; ‡¶Escher et al. 1993; *Gerra et al. 1998; *§Hirokawa and Ohira 2003; II Migneault et al. 2004; ‡Wahbeh et al. 2007; ‡II Wang et al. 2002

Oxytocin

Increased: *Grape et al. 2003, II Nilsson, 2009b

Prolactin

Increased: *Grape et al. 2003 (in males); ‡ II McRee et al. 2003

Decreased: *Grape et al. 2003 (in females); Möckel et al. 1994

No change: Conrad et al. 2007; *Evers and Suhr, 2000; *Gerra et al. 1998; **Kumar et al. 1999; ‡¶Oyama et al. 1983

(continued)

Table 29.1 (Continued) Overview of studies on effects of music on biochemicals. The table includes studies that investigated the effects of live or recorded music on hormonal or immune parameters, measured using blood, urine, or saliva samples. Only original works were included, and only works of which the full report (English or German) could be retrieved (these studies were also included in our review).

Serotonin (5-HT)

Increased: ‡**Jeong et al. 2005
5-HT content of platelets: Increased to pleasant music; decreased to unpleasant music (*Evers and Suhr, 2000)
No change: **Kumar et al. 1999; ‡Wahbeh et al. 2007

Testosterone

Increased: *Quiroga et al. 2009
Decreased in males and increased in females (Fukui 2001; Fukui and Yamashita 2003)

Tissue plasminogen activator (t-PA)

Decreased: Möckel et al. 1994; Möckel et al. 1995

T lymphocytes (CD3, CD4, CD8, CD16)/B lymphocytes (CD19)

No change: *§Hirokawa and Ohira, 2003; ‡ II Leardi et al. 2007
CD4: CD8-ratio increased (*§Le Roux et al. 2007)

Tumour necrosis factor alpha (TNF-α)

Increased: *Grape et al. 2003 (increased in professionals, decreased in amateurs)

design, and eight further studies used a within-group design (Möckel et al. 1994; Gerra et al. 1998; Beck et al. 2000a,b; Burns et al. 2001; Kreutz et al. 2004; Nakayama et al. 2009; Quiroga et al. 2009). Results of the RCT studies show small (Cohen's $d = 0.31$; VanderArk and Ely 1992) to medium effect sizes (Cohen's $d = 0.62$; McKinney et al. 1997a) with regard to cortisol reduction in the experimental groups. LeRoux and colleagues (2007) found a significant reduction in cortisol

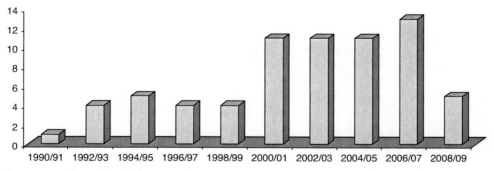

Fig. 29.2 Numbers of published reports on music and biochemicals during the last 20 years. The figure includes studies that investigated the effects of live or recorded music on hormonal or immune parameters, measured using blood, urine, or saliva samples. Only original works were included, and only works of which the full report (English or German) could be retrieved (these studies were also included in our review). See also Table 29.1.

levels in the music group compared to the control group; Nater et al. (2006) did not observe any changes of cortisol. In general, it appears that a decrease in cortisol is found more frequently in response to relaxing slow music, and in music therapy settings, whereas an increase of cortisol levels seems to be observed both when individuals are physically active, when music is perceived as vitalizing, or when individuals are under psychological stress (Gerra et al. 1998; Grape et al. 2003; West et al. 2004).

The results of experiments investigating the antibody IgA as immunological marker appear to be relatively consistent (McCraty et al. 1996; Beck et al. 2000a,b; Burns et al. 2001; Kreutz et al. 2004; three of these studies examined singers, i.e. Beck et al. 2000a,b, and Kreutz et al. 2004): In all five studies, positive emotions were associated with a short-term increase of IgA. However, only McCraty et al. (1996) and Kreutz et al. (2004) used a control-group design (participants acted as their own controls, in the former study participants listened to different styles of music, and in the latter study participants either listened to choral music or sang choral music). The other three studies (Beck et al. 2000a,b; Burns et al. 2001) applied a pre-post design without any control condition or a control group, and should therefore be interpreted with caution. Interestingly, four of these studies (Beck et al. 2000a,b; Burns et al. 2001; Kreutz et al. 2004) also obtained cortisol levels, and consistently reported a decrease of cortisol. Due to the immunosuppressive effects of cortisol (e.g. Bamberger et al. 1996), this lends plausibility to the reported increases in IgA levels.

Anxiety

The potential of music to reduce anxiety is probably one of its most relevant and ubiquitous features in human evolution (e.g. due to the calming effect of lullabies). Such effects are expected to be reflected in biochemicals of the HPA axis, primarily corticotropin-releasing hormone (CRH), ACTH, cortisol, and catecholamines (see also, e.g. Hanser 2010).

Eighteen studies investigated effects of music on anxiety and fear in relation to mainly endocrinological responses (see ‡ in Table 29.1). Seven of the 18 studies on music and anxiety report a subjective reduction of anxiety in the absence of apparent changes in cortisol (Oyama et al. 1983; Knight and Rickard 2001; Wang et al. 2002; McRee et al. 2003; Rickard 2004; Jeong et al. 2005; Wahbeh et al. 2007). Five studies reported a decrease in cortisol, or a reduced rise of cortisol levels (in comparison to a control group) accompanying the reduction of anxiety (Bartlett et al. 1993; Escher et al. 1993; Tornek et al. 2003; Nilsson et al. 2005; Nakayama et al. 2009). Schneider et al. (2001) investigated patients undergoing cerebral angiography and reported that cortisol levels remained stable in the music condition, while levels increased in the control group. Four of these studies were RCTs, but only Schneider et al. (2001) provided sufficient data to calculate an effect size (Cohen's $d = 0.75$, indicating a medium effect size). Again, it seems that a reduction of cortisol tends to occur more often in association with 'relaxing' music (Bartlett et al. 1993, Nilsson et al. 2005; Nilsson 2009a), self selected music (Escher et al. 1993; Leardi et al. 2007), or music therapy (Nakayama et al. 2009). However, note that most of the RCTs (Bittman et al. 2001; Knight and Rickard 2001; Wang et al. 2002; McRee et al. 2003; Jeong et al. 2005) did not find changes of cortisol, or only within-group effects (Lindblad et al. 2007).

Brain structures involved in the generation of (pathological and non-pathological) anxiety include the orbitofrontal cortex and the amygdala (e.g. Milad and Rauch 2007). As reviewed in earlier (in the section 'Limbic and paralimbic correlates of music-evoked emotions') in this chapter, numerous functional neuroimaging studies have shown that activity in these brain structures can be modified by music, lending plausibility to the idea that music can be used in therapeutic applications to ameliorate anxiety.

Depressed mood (in non-psychopathological populations)

Five studies investigated depressed mood or depression as a dependent variable in response to music (see § in Table 29.1; note that depression in terms of an affective disorder is reviewed in the later section 'Depression'). Experimental designs included music therapy group drumming (Bittman 2001), listening to music during physiotherapy (LeRoux et al. 2007), receptive music therapy (McKinney et al. 1997a), weekly active music therapy sessions (Nakayama et al. 2009), and music listening (Hirokawa and Ohira 2003). All except one study (Bittman et al. 2001) reported a reduction of depressed mood (no change was observed in the study from Bittman et al. 2001). These subjective reductions of depressed mood were associated with a decrease of cortisol. However, some of these results have to be interpreted with caution due to small sample sizes (n = 10 in Nakayama et al. 2009), or lack of control groups (Hirokawa and Ohira 2003; Nakayama et al. 2009).

Clinical studies

Thirty-two of the publications included in this review were clinical studies in the sense that they investigated participants with a disorder, or within a clinical setting (the other studies were conducted with healthy individuals).

Music in (peri-)operative interventions

In clinical settings, pain and anxiety call for the application of anxiolytic, analgesic, and anaesthetic drugs. Music has been reported to reduce stress, anxiety, and pain before, during, and after surgery (for review see Nelson 2008; Spintge, Chapter 20, this volume). Correspondingly, four of the nine mentioned studies suggest that listening to music before (Miluk-Kolasa 1994; Leardi et al. 2007), during (Nilsson 2005; Leardi et al. 2007; Koelsch et al. 2011), and after (Nilsson 2005; 2009a) surgery reduces cortisol levels. No significant differences in cortisol levels were found in studies by Wang et al. (2002), McRee et al. (2003), and Migneault et al. (2004).

Stress-reducing effects of music during and before surgical procedures are presumably due to its capacity to engage perceptual, emotional, and cognitive processes. Such processes: (1) interfere with the perception of the noise of the operating theatre, (2) consume attentional resources, and (3) evoke feelings of pleasure and reward (see section 'Limbic and paralimbic correlates of music-evoked emotions' of this chapter for details) which interact with pain and unpleasant affects related to the surgical procedure. It seems likely that emotional effects of music are not the only factor accounting for beneficial biological effects in clinical settings; the exact nature of the different factors that contribute to such effects, as well as their interactions, remain to be specified in future studies.

Other medical interventions

A number of other invasive medical interventions such as cerebral angiography (Schneider et al. 2001), gastroscopy (Escher et al. 1993), colonoscopy (Uedo et al. 2004), dental treatment (Oyama et al. 1983), and circumcision in neonates (Joyce et al. 2001) are also associated with negative feelings (particularly anxiety, worry, and pain). Oyama et al. (1983) reported that music listening before and during dental treatment leads to a significant decrease of anxiety, accompanied by a significant decrease of ACTH. Escher and colleagues (1993) investigated the effect of listening to music during gastroscopy. This study showed the increase of the stress hormones ACTH and cortisol to be significantly lower under the influence of music in contrast to a silence condition. Plasma levels of adrenaline and noradrenaline remained unchanged in both groups. The effect of music played to neonates undergoing circumcision was evaluated by Joyce et al. (2001) in a randomized, double-blind experimental design. Results showed that music had comparable effects on pain management (e.g. cortisol level) as a standard procedure using an analgesic dermal cream.

Schneider et al. (2001) studied the influence of music on the stress reaction of patients during cerebral angiography (a medical imaging technique to visualize the blood vessels in the brain). Patients examined without music showed rising levels of plasma cortisol, indicating high stress levels, whereas cortisol did not change in the music group. Similar results are reported by Uedo et al. (2004), who investigated the effects of listening to music on pain and on salivary cortisol levels in patients undergoing screening colonoscopy. Patients who listened to music during the procedure tended to have lower pain scores. Changes in salivary cortisol levels immediately after colonoscopy were significantly lower in the music intervention group than in the control group. These findings support the notion that music has substantial impact on acute and chronic pain, reflected in changes of stress markers such as cortisol and ACTH.

Dementia

Four studies (Kumar et al. 1999; Suzuki et al. 2004, 2007; Takahashi and Matsushita 2006) investigated the effects of music therapy interventions on psychological and biochemical parameters (cortisol, chromogranin A, catecholamines, melatonin, serotonin, prolactin, and IgA) in patients with Alzheimer's disease and related disorders (ADRD). Only Takahashi and Matsushita (2006) used an RCT, whereas Suzuki and colleagues (2004 and 2007) used a control-group design (and Kumar et al. 1999, used a pre–post comparison without control group). In all studies, psychological and behavioural symptoms improved significantly by the end of the music therapy intervention, although no significant effects were observed on intelligence, and therefore the music-therapeutic treatment did presumably not lead to an amelioration of degenerative cognitive symptoms (Takahashi and Matsushita 2006).

Depression

The scientific evidence for an effectiveness of music therapy on depression is surprisingly weak (for a critical review concerning methods in music therapy research with focus on depression see also Maratos et al. 2008). However, some studies support the notion that music therapy interventions have the potential to alleviate stress responses in depressed patients. An RCT conducted by Field et al. (1998) assessed the effect of listening to popular music on chronically depressed adolescent females (N = 28) in comparison to a silence condition (each 23min). That study (Field et al. 1998) reported that the music group's cortisol values decreased significantly from pre-session to post-session; however, the effect size reveals that this effect is negligible (Cohen's $d = 0.01$). Based on the same paradigm, Tornek and colleagues (2003) investigated the effect of a 20min music listening session on young mothers with depressive symptoms. In one group (exposed to rock music) anxiety scores were decreased after the session, and this decrease was associated with a significant decrease in saliva cortisol levels. The third study (Jeong et al. 2005) investigated the effects of dance movement therapy (DMT) in adolescent girls with mild depression (N = 40; RCT). That study reported an amelioration of negative psychological symptoms (e.g. somatization, depression, anxiety), accompanied by significant changes in serotonin and dopamine levels, but no changes in cortisol levels. These data endorse the hypothesis that DMT has relaxing effects, stabilizes the sympathetic nervous system, and is beneficial in improving the symptoms of mild depression.

Considerably more empirical research is needed to demonstrate the effectiveness of music therapy in patients with depressive disorders. In fact, due to the lack of high-quality studies, there is practically no scientific evidence for beneficial effects of music (and music therapy) in depressive patients. However, as mentioned in an earlier section ('Limbic and paralimbic correlates of music-evoked emotions'), music listening (and presumably even more strongly music-making) seems to be particularly effective in evoking activity changes in the hippocampal formation, a structure that shows functional anomalies and a decreased volume in patients with depression (associated with a loss of hippocampal neurons and blockage of neurogenesis in the hippocampus; Warner-Schmidt and Duman 2006). Hence, it is likely that music can be used to: (1) re-establish neural activity (related to positive emotion) in the hippocampus, (2) prevent death of hippocampal neurons, and (3) stimulate hippocampal neurogenesis in depressive patients. Future neuroscientific studies should therefore investigate whether long-term music therapy in depressed patients leads to functional and structural changes in the hippocampal formation.

Conclusion and unresolved issues

Functional neuroimaging and lesion studies have shown that music-evoked emotions can modulate activity in virtually all limbic/paralimbic brain structures, i.e. in core structures of emotional processing. However, in most studies published in this area so far, the mechanisms through which music evokes emotions remain to be specified. Therefore, future studies should investigate these mechanisms and their neural correlates in order to better understand the emotions evoked by music, as well as their extracerebral biological effects. These extracerebral biological effects include changes in autonomic, hormonal, and immune system activity (thus affecting the activity of all bodily organs). Consequently, music-evoked changes in mood in healthy participants and in individuals with mental or somatic problems are reflected by alterations of autonomic, hormonal, and immunological parameters, and these alterations form the basis of positive biological effects of music. It is important to note that the interaction between central nervous system activity and the internal environment (modulated by autonomic, hormonal, and immune system activity) is heavily influenced by, and partly dependent on, the social interaction with the external environment. Such social interactions are essential for experiences of reward and pleasure, for emotions such as joy and happiness, and for spiritual experiences during music listening and music-making (as well as for their positive biological effects).

A systematic review of studies investigating the effects of music on biochemical processes indicates that music-evoked emotions influence immune and hormonal markers (such as IgA and cortisol), and that music is well-suited to ameliorate symptoms of pain and anxiety in clinical settings. There is lack of quantitative high-quality studies with regard to music therapy and dementia as well as depression; therefore, future studies are needed to provide evidence for the intuitively plausible assumption that music is beneficial in the treatment of these disorders. Future research in these areas should also begin to consider interindividual differences that determine differences in the health-related effects of music, and thus also in the efficacy of music-therapeutic interventions. Moreover, future investigations should shed more light on the musical parameters that modulate autonomic, hormonal, and immune system activity.

Acknowledgements

The authors thank Yu Fukuda and Vienna Doennie for helpful comments on a previous version of this chapter.

References

Ball, T., Rahm, B., Eickhoff, S.B., Schulze-Bonhage, A., Speck, O., and Mutschler, I. (2007). Response properties of human amygdala subregions: evidence based on functional MRI combined with probabilistic anatomical maps. *PLoS ONE*, **2**, e307.

Bamberger, C.M., Schulte, H.M., and Chrousos, G.P. (1996). Molecular determinants of glucocorticoid receptor function and tissue sensitivity to glucocorticoids. *Endocrinology Reviews*, **17**(3), 245–61.

Bartlett, D., Kaufman, D., and Smeltekop, R. (1993). The effects of music listening and perceived sensory experiences on the immune system as measured by interleukin-1 and cortisol. *Journal of Music Therapy*, **30**, 194–209.

Baumeister, R. and Leary, M.R. (1995). The need to belong: Desire for interpersonal attachments as a fundamental human motivation. *Psychological Bulletin,* **117**, 497–529.

Baumgartner, T., Lutz, K., Schmidt, C. F., and Jäncke, L. (2006). The emotional power of music: how music enhances the feeling of affective pictures. *Brain Research*, **1075**, 151–64.

Beck, R J., Cesario, C., Yousefi, A., and Enamoto, H. (2000a). Choral singing, performance perception, and immune systems changes in salivary immunoglubulin A and cortisol. *Music Perception*, **18**, 87–106.

Beck, R.J., Gottfried, T.L., Hall, D. J., Cisler, C.A., and Bozeman, K.W. (2000b). Supporting the health of college solo singers: The relationship of positive emotions and stress to changes in salivary iga and cortisol during singing. *Journal for Learning through the Arts*, **2**(1). Available at: http://www.escholarship.org/uc/item/003791w4 (accessed 15 April 2011).

Bharucha, J.J. and Curtis, M. (2008). Affective spectra, synchronization, and motion: Aspects of the emotional response to music. *Behavioural Brain Sciences*, **31**, 579.

Bittman, B.B., Berk, L.S., Felten, D.L., Westengard, J., Simonton, O.C., Pappas, J., *et al.* (2001). Composite effects of group drumming music therapy on modulation of neuroendocrine-immune parameters in normal subjects. *Alternative Therapies*, **7**, 38–47.

Blood, A. and Zatorre, R.J. (2001). Intensely pleasurable responses to music correlate with activity in brain regions implicated in reward and emotion. *Proceedings of the National Academy of Sciences*, **98**, 11818–23.

Blood, A.J., Zatorre, R.J., Bermudez, P., and Evans, A.C. (1999). Emotional responses to pleasant and unpleasant music correlate with activity in paralimbic brain regions. *Nature Neuroscience*, **2**, 382–7.

Boso, M., Politi, P., Barale, F., and Emanuele, E. (2006). Neurophysiology and neurobiology of the musical experience. *Functional Neurology*, **21**, 187–91.

Brown, S. and Volgsten, U. (eds.) (2006). *Music and manipulation. On the social uses and social control of music*. Oxford: Berghahn.

Brownley, K.A., McMurray, R.G. and Hackney, A.C. (1995). Effects of music on physiological and affective responses to graded treadmill exercise in trained and untrained runners. *International Journal of Psychophysiology*, **19**, 193–201.

Burns, S.J.I., Harbuz, M.S., Hucklebridge, F. and Bunt, L. (2001). A pilot study into the therapeutic effects of music therapy at a cancer help center. *Alternative Therapies*, **7**, 48–56.

Cacioppo, J.T. and Hawkley, L.C. (2003). Social isolation and health, with an emphasis on underlying mechanisms. *Perspectives in Biology and Medicine*, **46**, S39–52.

Callan, D.E., Tsytsarev, V., Hanakawa, T., Callan, A.M., Katsuhara, M., Fukuyama, H., *et al.* (2006). Song and speech: Brain regions involved with perception and covert production. *NeuroImage*, **31**, 1327–42.

Charnetski, C.J., Brennan, F.X., and Harrison, J.F. (1998). Effect of music and auditory stimuli on secretory immunoglobulin A (IgA). *Perceptional and Motor Skills*, **87**, 1163–70.

Chlan, L.L., Engeland, W.C., Anthony, A., and Guttormson, J. (2007). Influence of music on the stress response in patients receiving mechanical ventilatory support: A pilot study. *American Journal of Critical Care*, **16**, 141–5.

Chopra, K.K., Segal, Z.V., Buis, T., Kennedy, S.H., and Levitan, R.D. (2007). Investigating associations between cortisol and cognitive reactivity to sad mood provocation and the prediction of relapse in remitted major depression. *Asian Journal of Psychiatry*, **1**, 33–6.

Chrousos, G.P. (2009). Stress and disorders of stress. *Nature Reviews Endocrinology*, **5**, 374–81.

Clark, L., Iversen, S.D., and Goodwin, G.M. (2001). The influence of positive and negative mood states on risk taking, verbal fluency, and salivary cortisol. *Journal of Affective Disorder*, **63**, 179–87.

Conrad, C., Niess, H., Jauch, K.-W., Bruns, C.J., Hartl, W.H., and Welker, L. (2007). Overture for growth hormone: Requiem for interleukin 6? *Critical Care Medicine*, **35**, 2709–13.

Cross, I. and Morley, I. (2008). The evolution of music: theories, definitions and the nature of the evidence. In: S. Malloch and C. Trevarthen (eds.) *Communicative musicality*, pp. 61–82. Oxford: Oxford University Press.

Dantzer, R., O'Connor, J.C., Freund, G.G., Johnson, R.W., and Kelley, K.W. (2008). From inflammation to sickness and depression: when the immune system subjugates the brain. *Nature Reviews Neuroscience*, **9**, 46–56.

Davies, J.B. (1978). *The psychology of music*. London: Hutchinson.

Drevets, W.C., Price, J.L., Bardgett, M.E., Reich, T., Todd, R.D. and Raichle, M.E. (2002). Glucose metabolism in the amygdala in depression: relationship to diagnostic subtype and plasma cortisol levels. *Pharmacology Biochemistry and Behavior*, **71**, 431–47.

Eldar, E., Ganor, O., Admon, R., Bleich, A. and Hendler, T. (2007). Feeling the real world: limbic response to music depends on related content. *Cerebral Cortex*, **17**, 2828–40.

Escher, J., Höhmann, U., Anthenien, L., Dayer, E., Bosshard, C.H., and Gaillard, R.C. (1993). Musik bei der Gastroskopie [Music during gastroscopy]. *Schweizerische Medizinische Wochenzeitschrift*, **123**, 134–58.

Evers, S. and Suhr, B. (2000). Changes of the neurotransmitter serotonin but not of hormones during short time music perception. *European Archives of Psychiatry and Clinical Neuroscience*, **250**, 144–7.

Field, T., Martinez, A., Nawrocki, T., Pickens, J., Fox, N.A., and Schanberg, S. (1998). Music shifts frontal EEG in depressed adolescents. *Adolescence*, **33**, 109–117.

Fitch, W.T. (2005). The evolution of music in comparative perspective. *Annals of the New York Academy of Sciences*, **1060**, 29–49.

Flaten, M.A., Asli, O., and Simonsen, T. (2006). The effect of stress on absorption of acetominophen. *Psychopharmacology*, **185**, 471–8.

Fritz, T. and Koelsch, S. (2008). The role of semantic association and emotional contagion for the induction of emotion with music. *Behavioural Brain Sciences*, **31**, 579–80.

Fukui, H. (2001). Music and testosterone. A new hypothesis for the origin and function of music. *Annals of the New York Academy of Sciences*, **930**, 448–51.

Fukui, H. and Yamashita, M. (2003). The effects of music and visual stress on testosterone and cortisol in men and women. *Neuroendocrinology Letters*, **24**, 173–80.

Gerra, G., Zaimovic, A., Franchini, D., Palladino, M., Giucastro, G., Reali, N., *et al.* (1998). Neuroendocrine responses of healthy volunteers to 'techno-music': relationships with personality traits and emotional state. *International Journal of Psychophysiology*, **28**, 99–111.

Goldstein, A. (1980). Thrills in response to music and other stimuli. *Physiological Psychology*, **8**, 126–9.

Gosselin, N., Peretz, I., Johnsen, E., and Adolphs, R. (2007). Amygdala damage impairs emotion recognition from music. *Neuropsychologia*, **45**, 236–44.

Grape, C., Sandgren, M., Hansson, L.O., Ericson, M., and Theorell, T. (2003). Does singing promote well-being?—An empirical study of professional and amateur singers during a singing lesson. *Integrative Psychological and Behavioral Science*, **38**, 65–74.

Hanser, S.B. (2010). Music, health, and well-being. In: P.N. Juslin and J.A. Sloboda (eds.) *Handbook of Music and Emotion. Theory, Research, Applications*, pp. 849–77. New York: Oxford University Press.

Harlow, H.F. (1958). The nature of love. *American Psychologist*, **13**, 673–85.

Hébert, S., Beland, R., Dionne-Fournelle, O., Crete, M., and Lupien, S.J. (2005). Physiological stress response to video-game playing: the contribution of built-in music. *Life Sciences*, **76**, 2371–80.

Hillecke, T., Nickel, A., and Bolay, H.V. (2005). Scientific perspectives on music therapy. *Annals of the New York Academy of Sciences*, **1060**, 271–82.

Hirokawa, E. and Ohira, H. (2003). The effects of music listening after a stressful task on immune functions, neuroendocrine responses, and emotional states in college students. *Journal of Music Therapy*, **40**, 189–211.

Hodges, D. (2010). *Psychophysiological measures*. In P. Juslin and J. Sloboda (eds.) *Handbook of Music and Emotion*, pp. 279–312. Oxford: Oxford University Press.

House, J.S., Landis, K.R., and Umberson, D. (1988). Social relationships and health. *Science*, **214**, 540–5.

Hucklebridge, F., Lambert, S., Clow, A., Warburton, D.M., Evans, P.D., and Sherwood, N. (2000). Modulations of secretory immunoglobulin A in saliva: response to manipulation of mood. *Biological Psychology*, **53**, 25–35.

Huron, D. (2001). Is music an evolutionary adaptation? *Annals of the New York Academy of Sciences*, **930**, 43–61.

Jeong, Y., Hong, S., Lee, M.S., Park, M., Kim, Y., and Suh, C. (2005). Dance movement therapy improves emotional responses and modulates neurohormones in adolescents with mild depression. *International Journal of Neuroscience*, **115**, 1711–20.

Joyce, B.A., Keck, J.F., and Gerkensmeyer, J. (2001). Evaluation of pain management interventions for neonatal circumcision pain. *Journal of Pediatric Health Care*, **15**, 105–14.

Juslin, P.N. and Västfjäll, D. (2008). Emotional responses to music: The need to consider underlying mechanisms. *Behavioral and Brain Science*, **31**, 559–75.

Khalfa, P., Dalla Bella, P., Roy, M., Peretz, I., and Lupien, P.J. (2003). Effects of Relaxing Music on Salivary Cortisol Level after Psychological Stresp. *Annals of the New York Academy of Science*, **999**, 374–76.

Knight, W.E.J. and Rickard, N.S. (2001). Relaxing music prevents stress-induced increases in subjective anxiety, systolic blood pressure, and heart rate in healthy males and females. *Journal of Music Therapy*, **38**, 254–72.

Koelsch, S. (2010). Towards a neural basis of music-evoked emotions. *Trends in Cognitive Science*, **14** (3), 131–7.

Koelsch S. and Siebel W.A. (2005). Towards a neural basis of music perception. *Trends in Cognitive Sciences*, **9**, 578–84.

Koelsch, S., Kasper, E., Sammler, D., Schulze, K., Gunter, T.C., and Friederici, A.D. (2004). Music, language, and meaning: Brain signatures of semantic processing. *Nature Neuroscience*, **7**, 511–14.

Koelsch, S., Fritz, T., von Cramon, D.Y., Müller, K., and Friederici, A.D. (2006). Investigating emotion with music: An fMRI study. *Human Brain Mapping*, **27**, 239–50.

Koelsch, S., Remppis, A., Sammler, D., Jentschke, S., Mietchen, D., Fritz, T., *et al.* (2007). A cardiac signature of emotionality. *European Journal of Neuroscience*, **26**, 3328–38.

Koelsch, S., Sammler, D., Jentschke, S., and Siebel, W.A. (2008). EEG correlates of moderate Intermittent Explosive Disorder. *Clinical Neurophysiology*, **119**, 151–62.

Koelsch, S., Siebel, W.A., and Fritz, T. (2010). Functional neuroimaging. In: P. Juslin and J.A. Sloboda (ed.) *Music and Emotion*, pp. 313–46. Oxford: Oxford University Press.

Koelsch, S., Fuermetz, J., Sack, U., Bauer, K., Hohenadel, M., Wiegel, M., *et al.* (2011). Effects of music listening on Cortisol levels and Propofol consumption during spinal anaesthesia. *Frontiers in Auditory Cognitive Neuroscience*, **2**(58), 1–9.

Kreutz, G., Bongard, S., Rohrmann, S., Hodapp, V., and Grebe, D. (2004). Effects of choir singing or listening on secretory immunoglobulin A, cortisol, and emotional state. *Journal of Behavioral Medicine*, **27**, 623–35.

Kuhn, D. (2002). The effects of active and passive participation in musical activity on the immune system as measured by salivary immunoglobulin A (SIgA). *Journal of Music Therapy*, **39**, 30–9.

Kumar, A.M., Tims, F. Cruess, D.G. Mintzer, M.J., Ironson, G., Loewenstein, D., *et al.* (1999). Music Therapy Increases Serum Melatonin Levels in Patients with Alzheimer's Disease. *Alternative Therapies*, **5**, 49–57.

Leardi, S., Pietroletti, R., Angeloni, G., Necozione, S., Ranalletta, G., and Del Gusto, B. (2007). Randomized clinical trial examining the effect of music therapy in stress response to day surgery. *British Journal of Surgery*, **94**, 943–47.

LeRoux, F.H., Bouic, P.J.D., and Bester, M.M. (2007). The Effect of Bach's Magnificat on emotions, immune, and endocrine parameters during physiotherapy treatment of patients with infectious lung conditions. *Journal of Music Therapy*, **44**, 156–68.

Lerner, Y., Papo, D., Zhdanov, A., Belozersky, L., and Hendler T. (2009). Eyes wide shut: amygdala mediates eyes-closed effect on emotional experience with music. *PLoS One*, **4**(7), e6230.

Lindblad, F., Hogmark, A., and Theorell, T. (2007). Music intervention for 5th and 6th graders–effects on development and cortisol secretion. *Stress and Health*, **23**, 9–14.

Maratos, A.P., Gold, C. Wang, X. and Crawford, M.J. (2008). Music therapy for depression. *Cochrane Database Syst. Rev.*, **23**, CD004517.

McCraty, R., Atkinson, M. Rein, G. and Watkins, A.D. (1996). Music enhances the Effect of positive emotional States on Salivary IgA. *Stress Medicine*, **12**, 167–75.

McKinney, C.H., Antoni, M.H., Kumar, M., Tims, F.C., and McCabe, P.M. (1997a). Effects of guided imagery and music (GIM) therapy on mood and cortisol in healthy adults. *Health Psychology*, **16**, 390–400.

McKinney, C.H., Tims, F.C., Kumar, A.M., and Kumar, M. (1997b). The effect of selected classical music and spontaneous imagery on plasma ß-endorphin. *Journal of Behavioral Medicine*, **20**, 85–99.

McRee, L.D. Noble, S., and Pasvogel, A. (2003). Using Massage and Music Therapy to Improve Postoperative Outcomes. *Journal of the Association of periOperative Registered Nurses*, **78**, 433–47.

Migneault, B., Girard, F., Albert, C., Chouinard, P., Boudreault, D., Provencher, D., *et al.* (2004). The effect of music on the neurohormonal stress response to surgery under general anesthesia. *Anesthesia and Analgesia*, **98**, 527–32.

Milad, M.R. and Rauch, S.L. (2007). The role of the orbitofrontal cortex in anxiety disorders. *Annals of the New York Academy of Sciences*, **1121**, 546–61.

Miluk-Kolasa, B., Obminski, Z., Stupnicki, R., and Golec, L. (1994). Effects of music treatment on salivary cortisol in patients exposed to pre-surgical stress. *Experimental and Clinical Endocrinology*, **102**, 118–20.

Miluk-Kolasa, B., Matejek, M., and Stupnicki, R. (1996). The effects of music listening on changes in selected physiological parameters in adult pre-surgical patients. *Journal of Music Therapy*, **33**, 208–218.

Mitterschiffthaler, M.T., Fu, C.H., Dalton, J.A., Andrew, C.M., and Williams, S.C. (2007). A functional MRI study of happy and sad affective states evoked by classical music. *Human Brain Mapping*, **28**, 1150–62.

Möckel, M., Röcker, L., Störk, T., Vollert, J., Danne, O., Eichstädt, H., *et al.* (1994). Immediate physiological responses of healthy volunteers to different types of music: cardiovascular, hormonal and mental changes. *European Journal of Applied Physiology*, **68**, 451–59.

Möckel, M., Störk, T., Vollert, J., Röcker, L., Danne, O., Hochrein, H., *et al.* (1995). Stressreduktion durch Musikhören: Einfluss auf Stresshormone, Hämodynamik und psychisches Befinden bei Patienten mit arterieller Hypertonie und bei Gesunden [Stress reduction through listening to music: effects on stress hormones, haemodynamics and psychological state in patients with arterial hypertension and in healthy subjects]. *Deutsche Medizinische Wochenschrift*, **120**, 745–52.

Moors, A. and Kuppens, P. (2008). Distinguishing between two types of musical emotions and reconsidering the role of appraisal. *Behavioural Brain Sciences*, **31**, 588–9.

Müller, A., Hörhold, N., Bösel, R., Kage, A., and Klapp, B.F. (1994). Einflüsse aktiver Musiktherapie auf Stimmungen und Immunkompetenz psychosomatischer Patienten [The effects of active music therapy on mood and immunocompetence of psychosomatic patients]. *Psychologische Beiträge*, **36**, 198–204.

Nakayama, H., Kikuta, F., and Takeda, H. (2009). A pilot study on effectiveness of music therapy in hospice in Japan. *Journal of Music Therapy*, **46**, 160–72.

Nater, U.M., Abbruzzese, E., Krebs, M., and Ehlert, U. (2006). Sex differences in emotional and psychophysiological responses to musical stimuli. *International Journal of Psychophysiology*, **62**, 300–8.

Nelson, A., Hartl, W., Jauch, K.-W., Fricchione, G.L., Benson, H., Warshaw, A.L., *et al.* (2008). The impact of music on hypermetabolism in critical illness. *Current Opinion in Clinical Nutrition and Metabolic Care*, **11**, 790–4.

Nilsson, U. (2009a). The effect of music intervention in stress response to cardiac surgery in a randomized clinical trial. *Heart and Lung*, **38**, 201–7.

Nilsson, U. (2009b). Soothing music can increase oxytocin levels during bed rest after open-heart surgery: a randomised control trial. *Journal of Clinical Nursing*, **18**, 2153–61.

Nilsson, U., Unosson, M., and Rawal, N. (2005). Stress reduction and analgesia in patients exposed to calming music postoperatively: a randomized controlled trial. *European Journal of Anaesthesiology*, **22**, 96–102.

Overy, K., and Molnar-Szakacs, I. (2009). Being together in time: musical experience and the mirror neuron system. *Music Perception*, **26**, 489–504.

Oyama, T., Hatano, K., Sato, Y., Kudo, M., Spintge, R., and Droh, R. (1983). Endocrine effects of anxiolytic music in dental patients. In: R. Droh and R. Spintge (eds.) *Angst, Schmerz und Musik in der Anästhesie*, pp. 143–46. Grenzach: Editiones Roche.

Patel, A.D. (2007). *Music, Language, and the Brain*. New York: Oxford University Press.

Patel, A.D., Iversen, J.R., Bregman, M.R., and Schulz, I. (2009). Experimental evidence for synchronization to a musical beat in a nonhuman animal. *Current Biology*, **19**, 827–30.

Quiroga Murcia, C., Bongard, S., and Kreutz, G. (2009). Emotional and neurohumoral responses to dancing Tango Argentino: The effects of music and partner. *Music and Medicine,* **1**, 14–21.

Rickard, N.S. (2004). Intense emotional responses to music: a test of the physiological arousal hypothesis. *Psychology of Music*, **23**, 371–88.

Rider, M.S., and Achterberg, J. (1989). Effect of music-assisted imagery on neutrophils and lymphocytes. *Biofeedback and Self-Regulation*, **14**, 247–57.

Rider, M.S., and Weldin, C. (1990). Imagery, improvisation, and immunity. *The Arts in Psychotherapy*, **17**, 211–16.

Rider, M.S., Floyd, J., and Kirkpatrick, J. (1985). The effect of music, imagery, and relaxation on adrenal corticosteroids and the re-entrainment of circadian rhythms. *Journal of Music Therapy*, **22**, 46–58.

Rilling, J., Gutman, D., Zeh, T., Pagnoni, G., Berns, G., and Kilts, C. (2002). A neural basis for social cooperation. *Neuron*, **35**, 395–405.

Schneider, N., Schedlowski, M., Schürmeyer, T.H., and Becker, H. (2001). Stress reduction through music in patients undergoing cerebral angiography. *Neuroradiology*, **43**, 472–76.

Shenfield, T., Trehub, S.E., and Nakata, T. (2003). Maternal singing modulates infant arousal. *Psychology of Music*, **31**, 365–75.

Singer, T. and Lamm, C. (2009). The social neuroscience of empathy. *Annals of the New York Academy of Sciences*, **1156**, 81–96.

Stefano, G.B., Zhu, W., Cadet, P., Salamon, E., and Mantione, K.J. (2004). Music alters constitutively expressed opiate and cytokine processes in listeners. *Medical Science Monitor*, **10**, 18–27.

Stein, M.B., Simmons, A.N., Feinstein, J.S., and Paulus, M.P. (2007). Increased amygdala and insula activation during emotion processing in anxiety-prone subjects. *American Journal of Psychiatry*, **164**, 318–27.

Steinbeis, N. and Koelsch, S. (2008). Shared neural resources between music and language indicate semantic processing of musical tension-resolution patterns. *Cerebral Cortex*, **18**, 1169–78.

Steinbeis, N. and Koelsch, S. (2009). Understanding the intentions behind manmade products elicits neural activity in areas dedicated to mental state attribution. *Cerebral Cortex*, **19**, 619–23.

Suda, M., Moriomoto, K., Obata, A., Koizumi, H., and Maki, A. (2008). Emotional responses to music: towards scientific perspectives on music therapy. *Neuroreport*, **19**, 75–8.

Suzuki, M., Kanamori, M., Nagasawa, S., Tokiko, I., and Takayuki, S. (2007). Music therapy-induced changes in behavioural evaluations, and saliva chromogranin A and immunoglobulin A concentrations in elderly patients with senile dementia. *Geriatrics and Gerontology International*, **7**, 61–71.

Suzuki, M., Kanamori, M., Watanabe, M., Nagasawa, S., Kojima, E., Oosiro, H., and Nakahara, D. (2004). Behavioral and endocrinological evaluation of music therapy for elderly patients with dementia. *Nursing and Health Sciences*, **6**, 11–18.

Takahashi, T. and Matsushita, H. (2006). Long-term effects of music therapy on elderly with moderate/ severe dementia. *Journal of Music Therapy*, **43**, 317–33.

Tomasello, M., Carpenter, M., Call, J., Behne, T., and Moll, H. (2005). Understanding and sharing intentions: the origins of cultural cognition. *Behavioral and Brain Science*, **28**, 675–91; discussion 91–735.

Tornek, A., Field, T., Hernandez-Reif, M., Diego, M., and Jones, N. (2003). Music effects on EEG in intrusive and withdrawn mothers with depressive symptoms. *Psychiatry*, **66**, 234–43.

Trehub, S.E. (2003). The developmental origins of musicality. *Nature Neuroscience*, **6**, 669–73.

Uedo, N., Ishikawa, H., Morimoto, K., Ishihara, R., Narahara, H., Akedo, I., *et al.* (2004). Reduction in salivary cortisol level by music therapy during colonoscopic examination. *Hepato-Gastroenterology*, **51**, 451–53.

VanderArk, S.D. and Ely, D. (1992). Biochemical and galvanic skin responses to music stimuli by college students in biology and music. *Perceptual and Motor Skills*, **74**, 1079–90.

Vollert, J.O., Störk, T., Rose, M., and Möckel, M. (2003). Musik als begleitende Therapie bei koronarer Herzkrankheit [Music accompanying treatment of coronary heart disease]. *Deutsche Medizinische Wochenschrift*, **128**, 2712–16.

Wachi, M., Koyama, M., Utsuyama, M., Bittman, B.B., Kitagawa, M., and Hirokawa, K. (2007). Recreational music-making modulates natural killer cell activity, cytokines, and mood states in corporate employees. *Medical Science Monitor*, **13**, 57–70.

Wahbeh, H., Calabrese, C., and Zwickey, H. (2007). Binaural beat technology in humans: A pilot study to assess psychologic and physiologic effects. *The Journal of Alternative and Complementary Medicine*, **13**, 25–32.

Wang, S.-M., Kulkarni, L., Doslev, J., and Kain, Z.N. (2002). Music and preoperative anxiety: A randomized controlled study. *Anesthesia and Analgesia*, **94**, 1489–94.

Warner-Schmidt, J.L. and Duman, R.S. (2006). Hippocampal neurogenesis: opposing effects of stress and antidepressant treatment. *Hippocampus*, **16**, 239–49.

West, J., Otte, C., Geher, K., Johnson, J., and Mohr, D.C. (2004). Effects of Hatha yoga and African dance on perceived stress, affect, and salivary cortisol. *Annals of Behavioral Medicine*, **28**, 114–18.

Wiltermuth, S.S. and Heath, C. (2009). Synchrony and cooperation. *Psychological Science*, **20**, 1–5.

Yamamoto, M., Naga, S., and Shimizu, J. (2007). Positive musical effects on two types of negative stressful conditions. *Psychology of Music*, **35**, 249–75.

Yamamoto, T., Ohkuwa, T., Itoh, H., Kitoh, M., Terasawa, J., Tsuda, T., *et al.* (2003). Effects of pre-exercise listening to slow and fast rhythm music on supramaximal cycle performance and selected metabolic variables. *Archives of Physiology and Biochemistry*, **111**, 211–14.

Zatorre, R.J., Chen, J.L., and Penhune, V.B. (2007). When the brain plays music: auditory-motor interactions in music perception and production. *Nature Reviews Neuroscience*, **8**, 547–58.

Chapter 30

Psychoneuroendocrine Research on Music and Health: An Overview

Gunter Kreutz, Cynthia Quiroga Murcia, and Stephan Bongard

In this chapter, we examine the influences of musical activities such as listening, singing, or dancing on the endocrine system. The underlying assumption is that psychological processes associated with musical experiences lead to changes in the hormonal systems of brain and body. A brief introduction to general questions of psychoneuroendocrinology as well as to relevant hormonal systems is followed by an overview of empirical studies, which have begun to investigate hormonal responses to musical stimulation and musical activities. The chapter concludes with suggestions for future work that will be derived from initial evidence showing that music can be seen as a psychoactive stimulant inducing physiological effects that are sometimes similar to those produced by pharmacological substances.

How does human experience, thought, and action influence individual health and wellbeing? What are the relationships between psychological aspects such as moods, emotions, and social interactions on the one hand, and prevention, treatment, and therapy of mental and physical disorders on the other? Which mechanisms offer the best explanations of these interactions? These questions are traditionally addressed in disciplines including psychology, neurobiology, endocrinology, immunology, neurology and psychiatry. Interrelated interests in these fields have led to the emergence of a new branch of medical sciences called psychoneuroendocrinology (PNE).

PNE is concerned with the interactions between psychological and behavioural processes on the one hand, and neurohumoral and somatic processes in brain and body on the other (e.g. Campeau et al. 1998). Theories of PNE assert that mental or physical stress can induce releases of hormones and modulations of immune functions. PNE research addresses a wide range of topics ranging from psychiatric illness and syndromes that are associated with (severe) stress experiences (e.g. Vingerhoets and Assies 1991) to more positive experiences such as, the neurobiology of love (e.g. Uvnas-Moberg and Carter 1998). While responses to aversive stimuli appear to have dominated to some extent (e.g. Levine and Coe 1999), in recent years, a general increase of interest in more positively stimulating experimental contexts in relation to health and wellbeing can be observed (e.g. Frederickson 2004; Steptoe et al. 2005).

Hormonal stress responses are mainly regulated by three interrelated systems: the hypothalamic–pituitary–adrenocortical axis (HPA), the sympatho-adrenomedullary system, and the endogenous opioid system (Bongard et al. 2011).

The HPA axis involves brain and peripheral structures: the hypothalamus, the pituitary, and the cortical part of the adrenals. A cascade of activation on this axis is initiated by the release of the corticotropin releasing factor (CRF) from the hypothalamus. CRF leads to subsequent release of adrenocorticotropic hormone (ACTH) and beta (β)-endorphin from the pituitary into the circulation. ACTH then stimulates the synthesis and release of cortisol and to a much lesser extent testosterone from the adrenal cortex (Breedlove et al. 2007). Though usually not considered as part of the HPA, oxytocin is also released in the hypothalamus and pituitary. Research indicates that is able to buffer stress responses (Heinrichs et al. 2003).

The sympatho-adrenomedullary system is part of the sympathetic nervous system which serves numerous functions including the preparation of the organism in regulating and executing fight or flight responses. When this system is activated by physical or psychological stress, norepinephrine is centrally released by the locus coeruleus. Additionally sympathetic innervations of the medulla of the adrenal glands lead to secretion of catecholamines (epinephrine, norepinephrine, dopamine). Since this system operates by nervous stimulation of the andrenal medulla it responses much faster than the HPA which is regulated by hormonal processes.

The third system related to neuroendocrine stress regulation is the endogenous opioid system. This system seems to be directly related to the HPA axis. Pharmacological blockades of opioidergic inhibitory inputs to the hypothalamic neurons specialized in releasing CRF leads to increased ACTH and cortisol concentrations in the blood (Wand and Schumann 1998).

In sum a variation in physical, mental or emotional challenges produces or prevents a complex orchestra of neurohumoral responses. None of the responses is specific to one kind of challenge and their response delays vary to a great deal.

Music psychology and PNE

The field of music psychology encompasses a wide range of musical behaviours (e.g. Thompson 2009). Listening to music is arguably the most widespread musical activity. It is also present in other musical behaviours such as singing, playing musical instruments, or dancing. There is wide agreement that music listening involves different levels of processing (e.g. Deutsch 1999). From the perspective of auditory perception, there are lawful relations between physical sound properties on the one hand, and perceptual phenomena such as pitch, loudness, and duration (e.g. Fastl 2006) as described in the field of psychophysics. At this level, perception of music supposedly relies on similar mechanisms that are required for processing speech and environmental noise. In fact, whether music processing at this or higher levels of cognitive processing is based on patterns of brain activities that can be clearly associated with or dissociated from those activations that are elicited during processing of non-musical, particularly linguistic sound, is a matter of ongoing debates (e.g. Peretz and Hébert 2000; Koelsch and Siebel 2005; Patel 2008).

To date, musical behaviours, in particular, have not been extensively investigated in the context of PNE research (e.g. Bartlett 1996). Perhaps this is not too surprising due to the increasing availability of neuroendocrinological research methods only over the last two to three decades. However, developmental and evolutionary theories to music, for example, suggest that musical stimulation might be effective in social and emotional self-regulation processes (e.g. Wallin et al. 2000). Therefore, it seems likely that musical behaviours should significantly influence neurohumoral processes in the brain and thus may have profound consequences to individual health and wellbeing (see Chapters 2 and 29, this volume).

In a study on health implications of cultural participation (Cohen 2006), elderly individuals who were assigned to cultural activities including singing (n = 77) were found to have fewer doctor visits and experienced less loneliness over a 12-month-period than individuals in a comparison group (n = 64) without cultural interventions. Cohen (2006) argues that 'sense of control' as well as 'social engagement' should be seen as likely mechanisms, which are responsible for the positive outcomes of the interventions. In other words, concepts derived from PNE research are not only needed to explain possible health-related outcomes of cultural interventions, but vice versa it appears that those are well-suited to increase the evidence-base of PNE research. Ultimately,

PNE research should contribute to answering questions including how musical behaviours function as psychological components in processes related to wellbeing and health.

Music as a psychoactive stimulus

Defining music remains a theoretic challenge. In practice, however, there seems less difficulty when effects of musical activity in the context of empirical studies are considered. The important implication is that instead of monolithic uses of the word music, it appears more appropriate to consider psychophysiological responses and behaviours that are under the influence of musically-induced activations within specific experimental contexts. While generalizations appear restricted to those individual experimental contexts, important characteristics of music as a psychoactive stimulus may nevertheless emerge.

Panksepp and Bernatzky (2002) concluded that one key characteristic of musical stimulation of the autonomous nervous system lies in the elicitation of emotions and the modulation of affective states. These authors argue that musically-induced activations involve cortical and subcortical neural networks in the human brain, that are associated with endocrine systems, and homoeostatic changes in these systems. In fact, brain imaging studies have revealed that intensely pleasurable music may activate numerous regions in the midbrain including ventral striatum, amygdalae, and anterior cingulate cortices (Blood and Zatorre 2001). Thus there is emerging indirect evidence that brain circuits of structural and functional relevance to the HPA axis are implicated in emotional processing of music.

Physiological responses to musical activity (predominantly listening) have been reported with respect to a wide range of measures (see Bartlett 1996, for an overview). Since about the mid 1980s of the last century, neurohumoral variables including ACTH, secretory immunoglobulin A (sIgA), cortisol and β-endorphin have been observed in musical tasks. Bartlett (1996) concluded that it was not possible to determine specific effects of music stimulation on neurohumoral responses and that findings need to be interpreted with great caution. For example, patterns of changes that were seen in the context of music showed similarities to other interventions including, for example, relaxation, humour, imagery therapy, meditation, yoga, and mild forms of physical exercise.

Psychophysiological effects of music

Factors influencing the psychophysiological effects of musical activities can be broadly classified as extrinsic and intrinsic. Extrinsic factors entail situation and context of these activities and experiences as well as variables representing individual differences including, for example, personality, preferences, musical expertise, and developmental aspects. Participants in Blood and Zatorre's (2001) positron emission tomography (PET) study listened to personally meaningful music that was perceived as highly pleasurable. These musically-induced sensations were correlated with neural activations (and deactivations) in the midbrain. The authors interpret their findings as responses of the reward system to music in the limbic system. However, unlike other highly rewarding stimuli including sex or opiates, it was not possible to identify specific structural features in the stimuli which unequivocally elicited pleasurable responses. In fact, the same music that induced so-called chills in one listener was used as a control against other musical pieces inducing chills in a different listener. Therefore, it remains unclear which properties of musical sound might be relevant to induce states of intensely pleasurable emotions.

Some authors assume that intrinsic factors of musical materials can be identified, which modulate psychophysiological responses. Berger and Schneck (2003), for example, suggest that musical rhythms may induce physiological adaptation in bodily rhythms and thus may influence oscillatory processes including neuroendocrine activity. Interactions between musical elements (rhythmic structure) and physiological metabolisms could explain sedative effects of music listening which lead to reductions in perceived pain and anxiety. Using a communication model as a starting point, Aldridge (1989) similarly has argued that music may influence neuronal, immunological and endocrine systems. He maintains that because of intrinsic properties music can be effective to modulate homeostasis and vegetative functions.

A comprehensive discussion of intrinsic factors might entail any musical parameters based on pitch, loudness, timing and timbral variations as well as combinations and interactions between these psychophysical properties. However, it appears appropriate to address four aspects here, which appear particularly prominent in the empirical literature, namely musical tempo, consonance, timbre (voice), and loudness. Bernardi and co-workers (1992) assume that musical tempo as measured in beats per minute could systematically influence cardiovascular dynamics. In simplest terms, slow tempi might induce sedation, while fast tempi might induce activation. In light of rather mixes findings concerning cardiovascular responses to music, in general, and to musical tempo, in particular (see Bartlett 1996, for a summary of research), other factors related to the musical structure as well as to the recipient must be accounted for (e.g. Dillman Carpentier and Potter, 2007).

Blood Bermudez and Zatorre (1999) used PET to show that musical excerpts inducing varying degrees of perceived consonance were systematically associated with differential activations in paralimbic and cortical brain areas. Physical characteristics of consonance include sound spectra that are dominated by fusion of partials that are evoked by different parts in a harmonic texture. By contrast, dissonance is characterized by sound spectra in which partials that only approximate integer ratios may give rise to sensations of roughness. However, harmonic spectra and perceived pleasantness ratings of sounds may not necessarily correlate very well. For example, non-linear distortions of musical sounds may be essential, for example, to Rock music and its effects on listeners.

The fetal auditory system is sensitive to sound characteristics of the maternal voice during the last trimester of pregnancy (Parncutt 2009). It is assumed that responsiveness to vocal sound characteristics may become hard-wired within the neural structures that are responsible for auditory processing. Infants are able to extract prosodic cues (pitch patterns) from infant-directed speech, so-called motherese, from the first day after birth (Sambeth 2007). Functional imaging studies in the adult brain further reveal that perception of singing is different from the perception of speech in that the former evokes stronger activations in subcortical regions that are associated with emotional processing (Jeffries et al. 2003). It is not clear yet, however, in what way vocal music may have specific effects on listeners as compared to instrumental music on one hand, and speech on the other.

Physical sound pressure levels and subjective experience of loudness seem both of relevance in relation to psychoneuroendocrinological responses to music in at least two ways. First of all, physical sound energy in and of itself may have significant impact on the human organism. For example, loud music can be equally detrimental to individual wellbeing as is the case for other sound sources with high sound pressure levels—e.g. Zheng and Ariizumi (2007) showed that acute noise bursts led to increases of immune responses, while chronic noise led to suppression of both cellular and humoral immune functions in mice. Second, active control over loudness exposure seems a prerequisite in both clinical and non-clinical studies while measuring psychophysiological responses. In fact, it is not unlikely that in specific contexts, silence may be even more effective than musical sound at all (e.g. Karrer 1999). Finally, Bernardi et al. (2009) observed that increases and decreases of sound volume in musical performances, i.e. crescendi and decrescendo, led to specific modulations of cardiovascular activity with increases associated with crescendi and decreases with decrescendi.

Neuroendocrine and immunological markers

Cortisol

Cortisol is a hormone of the HPA axis. Importantly, changes of levels of cortisol concentrations are associated with psychological and physiological stress. Therefore, it has also been used in music-related studies as a psychophysiological marker in various contexts. For example, listening to classical choral (Kreutz et al. 2004), meditative (Möckel et al. 1994), and folk music (Fukui 2003) has been shown to induce significant reductions of cortisol values in healthy adults, whereas significant increases were noted in listeners who were exposed to Techno (Gerra et al. 1998) and upbeat pop and rock music (Brownley et al. 1995). Yamamoto et al. (2007) studied arousal-mediating effects of pre-selected high-tempo (HT) and low-tempo (LT) music in two experiments which involved stress induction. The two experiments differed in that a 10-minute rest was established between stress induction and music conditions. The authors observed decreases of cortisol levels across stress conditions in response to LT music in Experiment 2 only.

Modulations of cortisol levels in response to music listening appear to be subject to individual differences such as musical expertise. VanderArk and Eli (1993), for instance, showed that in a listening experiment music students responded with increases and biology students with decreases of this hormone. Using participants who are less prone to cognitive influences on music processing and potential endocrine responses, Shenfield et al. (2003) investigated the effects of maternal singing on cortisol levels in 6-month-old infants. Results suggested that infants with initially low levels showed increases and other infants with initially higher levels showed decreases of cortisol (Shenfield et al. 2003).

In clinical contexts, exposure to music has been shown to reduce cortisol levels during medical treatment (e.g. Nilsson et al. 2005; Le Roux et al. 2007). Leardi et al. (2007) compared the effects of New Age music to self-selected music and silence during surgeries involving local or peridural anaesthesia. Individuals in those groups who listened to music showed decreases in cortisol levels, while the controls showed increases. Decreases were more pronounced in follow-up measurements after surgeries in the self-selected than in the New Age music group.

Changes of cortisol can be induced also by musical activities such as singing and dancing. Beck et al. (2000) observed decreases of cortisol of 30% on average in members of a professional chorale during a rehearsal and 37% of increases during a performance of the same group. In a subsequent study, Beck and co-workers (2006) showed that solo singers' satisfaction with performance correlated positively with decreases of cortisol. Grape et al. (2003) were concerned with the effects of singing lessons in small groups of male and female amateur and professional singers. Patterns of changes suggested gender effects as well as effects of musical expertise in these groups. Significant serum cortisol reductions were found in females and increases in males. Re-grouping the data to distinguish professional singers and amateurs showed less pronounced effects albeit decreases in amateurs were still significant. The authors explain their results by differential effects of perceived stress and competitiveness. Music stimulation also had an effect on cortisol levels in the context of tango dancing (Quiroga et al. 2009). These authors observed that the presence of music during dance led to decreases of cortisol levels while a similar effect was not observed in the presence or absence of a dance partner.

In summary, musically induced changes in cortisol were observed across a variety of populations as well as musical activities. While the patterns of changes were mixed, there are initial indications that cortisol concentrations show covariation with psychological measures such as perceived arousal and performance satisfaction. Importantly, such effects extend to clinical populations which implies that music could have, for example, sedative effects where reductions of arousal in patients undergoing medical treatment is needed. However, while short-term modulations as evidenced in the majority of studies are important, little is known about the sustainability of these changes over longer periods of time, because measurement intervals as documented in these studies rarely exceed 15–20 minutes.

Oxytocin

Oxytocin belongs to a class of peptides that is released in the hypothalamus and the posterior part of the pituitary. This hormone has been found to play a fundamental role in social behaviours by increasing trust and social bonding between mother and infant, sexual partners, as well as within social groups (Uvnas-Moberg 1998). Recent research indicates that the administration of oxytocin is potent to buffer subjective and physiological stress responses (Heinrichs et al. 2003; Ditzen et al. 2008).

Grape et al. (2003) observed significant increases of this hormone in both professional and amateur singers after a singing lesson, suggesting a hormonal mechanism for stress reducing effects of singing. In a clinical context, Nilsson (2009) compared effects of music listening during the first day after coronary surgery in groups of patients with and without music stimulation on oxytocin levels. Increases were observed in the former and decreases were found in the latter group of participants. Here the increase of oxytocin might indicate a facilitating effect of music on need for social support and bonding.

Testosterone

Sex hormones, in general, and testosterone, in particular, appear of particular relevance to music. In many cultures music behaviour like dancing, singing and playing an instrument are part of courting behaviour. Particular dancing seems to facilitate intersexual encounters and might initiate mating and reproductive behaviour. Therefore, Charles Darwin (1871) suggests music as originating from sexual selection. Although the precise implications of this hypothesis are unclear, it appears that sex hormones are ideal targets in order to explore the relevance of physiological mechanisms underlying this assumption. Testosterone is a sex hormone which is found in higher concentrations in males and in lower concentrations in females. It is produced in men's testes and to a much less extent in the adrenal cortex of both men and women. Empirical work by Fukui and Yamashita (2003) suggested gender differences in testosterone responses after listening to Japanese folk songs showing that testosterone concentrations decreased in males but not in females. No gender effects were noted in relation to cortisol. In a more recent study, Fukui and Toyoshima (2008) suggest that music stimulation may enhance neurogenesis by means of its modulating effect on steroid secretion, because of its crucial role in neurofunction and regeneration of the nervous system (Hammond et al. 2001). However, there is at present no evidence available to support this hypothesis. In a different vein, Quiroga et al. (2009) found that the presence of a dance partner led to significant increases of testosterone levels in both sexes, while music stimulation alone did not have this effect.

In the perhaps most significant long-term study on the effects of testosterone on musical talent that is available to date, Hassler (1992) compared groups of creatively and performatively talented young musicians with non-musician controls. She observed that optimal levels of testosterone in relation to musical creativity differ for the two sexes. Female composers showed above average and male composers below average testosterone levels in comparison to age-matched controls. These findings suggest that physiologically androgynous individuals are more likely to have higher levels of creativity than individuals that are more in the centre range of testosterone levels with respect to their sex. However, such an interpretation may be premature as, for example, testosterone:oestrogen ratios were not assessed in these studies.

Endorphin

β-endorphin is a hormone which is primarily released in the pituitary gland. It can be measured as serum concentrations in the peripheral vascular system. Increased levels of this hormone are associated with situative stress (Sheps et al. 1995). Conversely, while alleviating effects of music interventions have been found in pain patients (e.g. Mitchell et al. 2007), β-endorphin appears as a plausible physiological marker of such influences. In fact, McKinney et al. (1997) found that music listening in combination with guided imagery led to significant reductions of β-endorphin, while neither music listening nor guided imagery alone had this effect. Gerra et al. (1998) extended these observations by showing that listening to upbeat techno music led to increases of β-endorphin in groups of healthy adults. In the same study, however, individuals who were high in novelty-seeking did not show this response.

Delivering special relaxation music to coronary patients during rehabilitation led to significant decreases of β-endorphin during physical exercises. In addition, systolic blood pressure, anxiety, and worry were also reduced. Conversely, decreases were not significant in patients which performed the exercises without music (Vollert et al. 2003). Music therapy can also be effective before and during surgeries in operating theatres, again with respect to β-endorphin concentrations, anxiety, and pain (Spintge 2000).

In sum, psychophysiological effects of β-endorphin have been consistently observed in experimental contexts, which involved modulation of psychological stress. In some studies music was used to accompany activities including imagination and physical exercise. Only few studies, however, have contributed to assess individual differences in moderating the observed effects.

Secretory immunoglobulin A

Secretory immunoglobulin A (sIgA) is often interpreted as a marker of the local immune system in the upper respiratory tract and as a first line of defence against bacterial and viral infections. Positive affect may lead to increased levels of sIgA (Pressman and Cohen 2005), while chronic stress may be associated with decreased levels (Hennig 1994).

Significant increases of sIgA concentrations were observed across various contexts and populations, for example, in response to listening to relaxation music (Brauchli 1993), easy-listening 'muzak music'(Charnetzki et al. 1998), classical (Wago et al. 2002), and various kinds of dance music (Hucklebridge et al. 2000; Enk et al. 2008). McCraty and co-workers (1996) investigated the effects of music listening and positive emotional state on sIgA in healthy adults. Patterns of results indicated that the combination of specially composed relaxation music and self-induced positive affect led to increases of sIgA concentrations, while Rock and New Age music showed no effects. Similar observations were made in clinical populations (Burns et al. 2001) indicating that mood changes appear to be important components in mediating music listening effects on sIgA.

Other musical activities including singing may induce short-term effects on sIgA. Kuhn (2002) investigated these in adults who were assigned to either one group playing drums or singing, or another group watching a live performance without engagement in playing or singing. There were overall more pronounced effects in those participants involved in active participation. Similarly, Kreutz et al. (2004) found that one hour of rehearsing choral music in an amateur choral society led to significant increases of sIgA at group level. However, no such increase over time was found when the same singers were only listening to choral music that was Mozart's 'Requiem' in this case. Beck et al. (2000) addressed the influences of rehearsal versus public performance in high-achieving choral singers, again observing significant increases of sIgA following these interventions. Moreover, positive correlations between positive emotions, performance satisfaction and physiological changes of sIgA concentrations emerged. In a follow-up study, Beck et al. (2006) showed that positive emotions and subjective wellbeing predicted increases in sIgA in solo singers who were multiply assessed during rehearsing and performing over a 10-week period.

Other neuroendocrine and immunological markers

Evers and Suhr (2000) investigated short-term effects of musical excerpts which were characterized as 'pleasant' (Brahms' symphony no. 3, op. 90) and 'unpleasant' (Penderecki's 'Threnos') on serum concentrations of prolactin, ACTH, and serotonin (5-HT) in healthy adult listeners. The authors observed only significantly reduced concentrations of serotonin under the unpleasant music condition. They interpret this effect as a physiological stress response. Möckel et al. (1994) also used prolactin and, in addition norepinephrine as markers in a similar experimental design which involved listening to contemporary music by Heinz-Werner Henze and meditative music. Prolactin is a hormone that has important regulatory functions during pregnancy. Norepinephrine, by contrast, is a stress hormone which is widely associated with attention, fight-flight responses, and mobilization of physical resources. While prolactin decreased in response to Henze, norepinephrine increased in response to the calmer medidative music.

Hirokawa and Ohira (2003) used a stress induction technique before assessing psychophysiological effects of listening to music which was characterized as 'high-uplifting' (Anderson's 'The Waltzing Cat', Kreisler's 'Liebesfreud' and Satie's 'Picadilly') as opposed to 'low-uplifting' (Albinoni's 'Adagio', Sibelius' 'Swan of Tuonela' and Satie's 'Gnoissiennes'). A number of neuroendocrine and immune markers including natural killer cells, numbers of T lymphocytes, dopamine, norepinephrine and epinephrine were used in pre-post measurements. Although the results were inconclusive, differential trends were observed. These indicated that the low-uplifting music increased a subjective sense of wellbeing that was not reflected in physiological markers, while high-uplifting music led to increases of norepinephrine levels and liveliness, and decreases of depression.

Chromagranin A (CgA) is a marker representing sympathetic-adrenal activity that is also directly, but moderately related to catecholamine secretion and psychosomatic stress (e.g. Omland et al. 2003). Suzuki et al. (2004) investigated the effects of singing and playing musical instruments within a music therapy programme on salivary CgA concentrations in demented patients. The programme delivered over a period of 2 months and involved 16 sessions. The authors observed decreases of salivary CgA concentrations in the music therapy group as compared to controls. Similar findings were reported in a follow-up study (Suzuki et al. 2007) in which the intervention was extended to 3 months.

Conrad et al. (2007) undertook a study, which was designed to assess sedative effects of music stimulation by slow movements of Mozart's piano sonatas in critically ill patients. Application of music significantly reduced the amount of sedative drugs needed to achieve a degree of sedations that was comparable to controls who received a standard therapy. Moreover, in the music group plasma concentrations of growth hormone increased, whereas those of interleukin-6 and epinephrine decreased. In addition, significantly lower levels of blood pressure and heart rate indicated reductions in systemic stress as a consequence of music listening. Findings were interpreted as showing that (sedative) music activates neurohumoral pathways that are associated with psychophysiological sedation.

LeRoux et al. (2007) used a specific psychoimmunological marker called CD4/CD8 ratio to determine physiological influences of music stimulation (J. S. Bach's 'Magnificat') in patients suffering from lung infections. CD4/CD8 indicates the numerical relationship between supporter (CD4) versus suppressor cells (CD8) each of which represent a subpopulation of lymphocytes. During breathing therapy sessions changes of CD4/CD8 rations developed significantly more favourably in the music listening group than in controls. This observation is consistent with the assumption that music stimulation may effectively modulate immune suppression. In a study using a group of healthy adults listening to music, Bartlett et al. (1993) reported that secretion of interleukin-1, which is considered as an important activator of the immune system, was found increased under music stimulation.

In one of the rare studies involving musicians representing different levels of expertise in singing, Grape et al. (2003) used an array of serum concentrations of physiological markers including tumour necrosis factor (TNF-α) as dependent measures to assess responses to singing lesions. TNF-α increases during infections and may also indicate psychophysiological stress. Increases in TNF-α were observed in professional singers, while decreases were found in amateurs.

Bittman and colleagues (2001) studied neuroendocrine and–immune responses to composite drumming based on a music therapy protocol. A total of 60 participants were randomly assigned to a drumming group or to a control group (reading magazines). The authors found, that compared to controls, the percussion session led to increased natural killer cell activity, increased dehydroepiandrosterone-to-cortisol ratio, and increased lymphokine-activated killer cell activity. No changes were observed in plasma cortisol, interleukin 2 or interferon-gamma.

Nuñez et al. (2002) used a standard animal model (male BALB/c mice) to investigate immune responses to cancer development under the influence of sound stress and music stimuli. The rodents were injected with carcinosarcoma cells and sacrificed 8 days after injection. During the experimental phase, mice were allocated randomly to one of four groups who received music, auditory stressor, auditory stressor and music, or nothing (controls) for 5 hours per day. While stress was found to decrease natural killer cell activity and also significantly increase number and percentage of metastatic nodules, a reverse pattern was found in the music group indicating positive immune responses in these rodents to music stimulation. Overall, music appeared to compensate some of the stress responses while showing patterns that were similar to the unstressed group.

Table 30.1 summarizes the above cited research on psychoneuroendocrine responses to musical behaviours. This is one step towards more rigorous evaluations of the available literature.

Conclusions

Empirical approaches over the last two decades have begun to adopt a PNE perspective on the effects of musical stimulation using markers including cortisol, oxytocin, testosterone, endorphin, immunoglobulin A, and others. Although significant effects of musical behaviour on many of these markers have been observed, the development of this research appears compromised by paucity of publications, in general, and methodological issues, in particular. Therefore, empirical evidence, which demonstrates specific influences of musical behaviours at neurohumoral levels, appears limited to date.

In conclusion, patterns of neuroendocrine changes reflecting psychophysiological processes in response to musical interventions are complex, but appear often favourable with respect to health implications. For example, from a psychoneuroendocrinological standpoint, music can be supportive to alleviate physiological effects of stress and unrest and thus can be an effective means as one non-invasive element in psychotherapeutic interventions. However, the available data appear

Table 30.1 Summary of empirical studies using neuroendocrine measures as dependent variables in musical intervention studies

Reference	Sample	Design	Effects
Bartlett et al. (1993)	36 healthy students (17 women, 19 men)	Blood samples before and after (1) listening to selected music followed with expression of 'perceived sensory experience' vs. (2) reading vs. (3) no treatment	Cortisol decreases were shown immediately and after 24 hrs of the listening condition. Interleukin-1 increases were observed only immediately after the listening condition. No changes were observed in the non music conditions
Brauchli (1993)	16 volunteers (5 women, 11 men) with a mean age of 28 (20–52) years	Saliva samples before and after two conditions: (1) optical-acoustic mind machine vs. (2) relaxing music	Both conditions led to decreased cortisol concentrations and increased sIgA levels
VanderArk et al. (1993)	60 college students, 27–41 years old	Blood samples before and after listening to two musical selections. Comparison between (1) music majors vs. (2) biology majors	Cortisol levels were higher for the music majors than for the biology majors after listening to music
Möckel et al. (1994)	20 healthy students (10 women, 10 men) with a mean age of 25 (20–33) years	Blood samples before and after listening to three different examples of music: (1) waltz by J. Strauss, (2) modern classic by H. W. Henze, and (3) meditative music by R. Shankar	Music by Strauss resulted in an increase of atrial natriuretic peptide. After modern music, prolactin values were lowered. Meditative music led to a decrease of cortisol levels, noradrenaline levels and t-PA antigen levels
Brownley et al. (1995)	16 volunteers (12 women, 4 men), 19–28 years old	Blood samples before and after low, moderate and high intensity exercise under three music conditions (1) no music, (2) sedative, and (3) fast	Following high intensity exercise, higher cortisol levels were associated with fast music as compared to no music and sedative music
McCraty et al. (1996)	10 healthy individuals (6 women, 4 men) with a mean age of 41 (range 27–53) years	Saliva samples before and after listening to three music conditions: (1) rock, (2) new age, and (3) designer music, as well as after two control conditions: (4) self-induced positive emotional state in the absence of music, and (5) silence	Only the designer music and the self-induced state of appreciation produced an increase in sIgA levels. The combination of the designer music and the self-induced appreciation produced a much greater immunoenhancement than either of these two conditions alone
McKinney et al. (1997)	28 health adults (24 women, 4 men), with a mean age of 37 years (SD = 6 years)	Blood samples before, after the 13-week and again at a 6-week follow-up period of a guided imagery and music programme. Participants in a wait-list group served as controls	Cortisol levels decreased after 6 biweekly sessions of the guided imagery and music programme. Pretest to follow-up decrease in cortisol was significantly associated with decrease in mood disturbance

Table 30.1 (Continued) Summary of empirical studies using neuroendocrine measures as dependent variables in musical intervention studies

Reference	Sample	Design	Effects
Charnetski et al. (1998)	66 college students (35 women, 31 men) ranging in age from 17 to 40 years.	Saliva samples before and after four conditions: (1) tone/ click presentation, (2) silence, (3) Muzak tape referred to as 'Environmental Music', and (4) radio broadcast comparable in musical style.	Analysis indicated increases in sIgA for the Muzak music condition, but not for any of the other conditions.
Gerra et al. (1998)	16 healthy subjects (8 women, 8 men), age ranging 18 to 19 years	Blood samples before and after two group conditions: listening to (1) techno music vs. (2) classical music Duration: 30min each	Increases in β-endorphin, ACTH, norepinephrine, growth hormone, and cortisol after listening to techno music
Beck et al. (2000)	41 members of a professional chorale (23 women, 18 men) with a mean age of 46 (range 25–62) years	Saliva samples before and after (1) an early rehearsal, (2) a late rehearsal and (3) a public performance of Beethoven's Missa Solemnis	sIgA increased during rehearsals and the performance. Cortisol levels decreased during rehearsals and increased during performance. Performance perception and mood were predictive of changes in levels of sIgA during the performance condition, but the results for the rehearsal conditions were not significant
Evers and Suhr (2000)	20 healthy subjects (9 women, 11 men) with a mean age of 28 (SD = 5) years	Blood samples before and after two random ordered blocks of two pieces of music with either pleasant or unpleasant music. Duration: 10min each	Serotonin (5-HT content of platelets) decreased during the perception of unpleasant music as compared to the perception of pleasant music. This decrease was correlated to the subjective attitude towards the music. Prolactin and ACTH did not change for both the pleasant and the unpleasant music
Hucklebridge et al. (2000)	41 students (31 women, 10 men) with a mean age of 20 years	Saliva samples before and after listening to either a (1) happy vs. an (2) unhappy mood induction music tape, both lasting approximately 30min	Mood induction by music resulted in elevations in sIgA levels and secretion rate and responses were not distinguished by mood valence. No changes in cortisol were observed
Bittman et al. (2001)	60 volunteers (29 women, 31 men)	Blood samples before and after (1) composite group-drumming music therapy intervetion vs. (2) control group	Group drumming led to elevated dehydroepiandrosterone-to-cortisol ratios, increased NK cell activity, and increased lymphokine-activated killer cell activity

(continued)

Table 30.1 (Continued) Summary of empirical studies using neuroendocrine measures as dependent variables in musical intervention studies

Reference	Sample	Design	Effects
Burns et al. (2001)	29 cancer patients, aged 21–68 years	Saliva samples before and after (1) listening to music in a relaxed state vs. (2) active involvement of music improvisation (the playing of percussion instruments)	Results showed increased sIgA in the listening experience and a decrease in cortisol levels in both interventions over a 2-day period
Kuhn (2002)	33 students (28 women, 5 men) with a mean age of 20 years	Saliva samples before and after three conditions: (1) active musical activity (instrument playing and singing), (2) passive listening to live music (3) control group	sIgA concentrations of the active music group showed greater increases than those of the passive and control group
Nuñez et al. (2002)	80 male mice aged between 7–12 weeks	Mice were randomly divided into four experimental groups (1) unstimulated controls, (2) music, (3) auditory stressor, (4) auditory stressor and music	Music reduced the suppressive effects of stress on immune parameters (Thymus and spleen cellularity, peripheral T lymphocyte population, and natural killer cells) in mice and decreased the enhancing effects of stress on the development of lung metastases provoked by carcinosarcoma cells
Fukui and Yamashita (2003)	88 healthy college students (44 males and 44 females) with a mean age of 21 (18–27) years	Saliva samples before and after four conditions: (1) listening to music, (2) listening to music with visual stress (3) visual stress without music, and (4) silence. Duration: 30min each	Music decreased Testosterone in males, whereas it increased Testosterone in females. No gender differences regarding cortisol levels. Cortisol decreased with music and increased under other conditions
Grape et al. (2003)	8 amateur (6 women, 2 men, age 28–53 years) and 8 professional (4 women, 4 men, age 26–49 years) singers	Blood samples before and 30min after a singing lesson. Comparison between (1) amateur vs. (2) professional singers	TNF-alpha increased in professionals after the singing lesson, whereas in amateurs decreased. Levels of prolactin and cortisol increased after the lesson in the group of men and vice versa for women. Oxytocin concentrations increased significantly in both groups after the singing lesson
Hirokawa and Ohira (2003)	24 non-music major college students (15 women, 9 men)	Blood and saliva samples before and after a stressful task, and after a subsequent experimental condition: (1) high-uplifting music, (2) low-uplifting music, and (3) silence. Duration: 20min each	High-uplifting music showed trends of increasing the norepinephrine level. No changes in other variables (sIgA, lymphocyte CD4, CD8. CD16, dompamine) were found

Table 30.1 (Continued) Summary of empirical studies using neuroendocrine measures as dependent variables in musical intervention studies

Reference	Sample	Design	Effects
Shenfield et al. (2003)	34 mothers (*M* = 32 years) and their infants (17 boys, 17 girls; *M* = 6 months, 3 days)	Saliva samples from infants before their mothers began singing and 20min later	Infants with lower baseline levels exhibited modest cortisol increases in response to maternal singing; those with higher baseline levels exhibited modest reductions
Vollert et al. (2003)	15 coronary patients (2 women, 13 men) with a mean age of 62 (SD = 8) years	Blood samples before and after listening to an especially composed relaxation music while training patients' heart-frequency adapted exercises	β-endorphin concentration was found to decrease after listening to music
Kreutz et al. (2004)	31 amateur singers (23 women, 8 men) with a mean age of 57 (29–74) years	Saliva samples before and after two musical conditions: (1) listening vs. (2) singing choral music. Duration: 60min each	Singing led to increases in SIgA. Listening to choral music led to decreases in levels of cortisol
Suzuki et al. (2004)	23 dementia patients (15 women, 8 men) with a mean age of 83 (SD = 6) years	Saliva samples before and after two conditions: (1) music therapy (singing songs and playing percussion Instruments) vs. (2) physical activity. 16 sessions (measures only for sessions 1, 8, 16)	Prior to Music therapy, chromogranin A (CgA) levels before the first session were high compared with those before the 16th session. In addition, after only a week of Music therapy, stress levels were lower, as evidenced by lower CgA levels. Levels of CgA were decreased after each session
Nilsson et al. (2005)	75 patients undergoing open hernia repair surgery	Blood samples during and after surgery. Patients participated in one of three conditions: (1) intraoperative music, (2) postoperative music and (3) silence (control group)	Greater decrease in the level of cortisol in the postoperative music group vs. the control group after 2 hours in the post anaesthesia care unit. There was no difference in sIgA, blood glucose, between the groups
Beck et al. (2006)	10 music majors in a conservatory in an arts college with a mean age of 21 (18–25) years	Saliva samples before and after singers rehearsed and performed repertory in a college conservatory during a 10-week period	Increase in sIgA levels after singing. This effect was mediated by positive emotions of wellbeing and feeling 'high'. Satisfaction with performance correlated significantly with a decrease of cortisol after singing

(continued)

Table 30.1 (Continued) Summary of empirical studies using neuroendocrine measures as dependent variables in musical intervention studies

Reference	Sample	Design	Effects
Leardi et al. (2007)	60 patients undergoing day surgery (30 men and 30 women) with a mean age 65 (range 25–85) years	Blood samples before, during and after surgery. Patients participated in one of three conditions: (1) listening to new age music (2) listening to a choice of music from one of four styles (3) listening to the normal sounds of the operating theatre (control group)	Cortisol levels decreased during operation in both groups who listened to music, but increased in the control group. Postoperative cortisol levels were higher in group 1 than in group 2. Levels of natural killer cells decreased during surgery in groups 1 and 2, but increased in controls. Intraoperative levels of natural killer cells were significantly lower in group 1 than in group 3
LeRoux et al. (2007)	40 patients with lung infections (9 men and 31 women), 40–75 years old.	Blood samples before and after three days of physiotherapy (1) with music ('Magnificant' by J. S. Bach) vs. (2) without music (control group).	Cortisol levels were reduced after the 3rd day of physiotherapy with music, whereas in the control cortisol levels increased. The immunological marker CD4:CD8 ratio increased in the music condition, which impplied less immunological supression.
Suzuki et al. (2007)	16 dementia patients (14 women, 2 men) with a mean age of 85 (SD = 5) years	Saliva samples before and after two group conditions: (1) music therapy vs. (2) control group, at the following three time periods: before the start of the intervention; at the last (25th) session; and 1 month after the end of the intervention	In the music therapy group, the level of salivary CgA after the 25th session was lower than before the intervention, indicating a reduction in stress
Yamamoto et al. (2007)	40 healthy university students (33 women, 7 men) with a mean age of 24 years	Saliva samples before and after four group conditions with vs. without a 10min rest: (1) high-tempo music after a high arousal stressful task, (2) high-tempo music after a low-arousal stressful task, (3) low-tempo music after a high arousal stressful task, (4) low-tempo music after a low-arousal stressful task	Cortisol levels were reduced after task performance including a 10min rest and immediately after low-tempo music exposure, indicating a stress distractive effect under the high arousal stressful task. Other conditions showed no significant differences in cortisol changes
Nilsson et al. (2009)	40 patients (8 women, 32 men) undergoing open-heart surgery, with a mean age of 65 (SD = 9) years	Blood samples at the first postoperative day, before and after 30min and 60min of rest (1) with or (2) without music	In the music group, levels of oxytocin increased significantly in contrast to the control group for which the trend over time was negative, i.e. decreasing values

Table 30.1 (Continued) Summary of empirical studies using neuroendocrine measures as dependent variables in musical intervention studies

Reference	Sample	Design	Effects
Quiroga et al. (2009)	22 amateur tango dancers (11 women, 11 men) with a mean age of 43 (30–56) years	Saliva samples before and after four dance conditions: (1) with partner with music, (2) with partner without music, (3) without partner with music, (4) without partner without music	After tango dancing, decreases of cortisol levels were found with the presence of music, whereas increases of testosterone levels were associated with the presence of a partner

clearly limited with respect to the number of studies, number of participants involved in each study, and a range of methodological aspects. For example, it is not always clear how the musical interventions were constructed. Variables such as familiarity with and liking of the musical materials and activities are rarely systematically assessed, although they are known to have profound psychological influence in many experimental settings which include music stimulation.

These observations of limitations appear even enhanced when subsets such as immunological markers in response to musical activities are considered. Although those represent a particularly important subset of neuroendocrine responses, it is our impression that much more research efforts should be undertaken to ascertain the emerging patterns of changes that were reported in the available literature.

Importantly, sources of musical sound in the environment may have similar effects on the brain such as the same musical sound that is imagined by the listener in the absence of a physical stimulus (e.g. Zatorre and Halpern 2005). The implication is that the sensitivity of the hormonal system to musical activities may well extend to significant influences of even imagined music on hormones and neurotransmitters.

To sum up, psychoneuroendocrine effects of music in the human brain and body are perhaps one of the most fascinating areas of future research. The hormonal system provides direct links between music stimulation, activations in the brain during music processing and emotional responses at both physiological and subjective levels. For example, there is mounting evidence suggesting various roles of music activities in mediating stress responses at hormonal levels. Another promising area can be seen in local immune responses to singing in the upper respiratory pathways.

This initial evidence notwithstanding, basic questions of music emotion research, such as, for instance, the relationship between perceived and felt emotions, need to be examined at hormonal levels. In other words, by understanding how music affects the endocrine system we will increase our knowledge of how music affects emotions. Ultimately, questions of how and why individuals may benefit from music in terms of health and wellbeing must be answered also at that level.

References

Aldridge, D. (1993). The music of the body: music therapy in medical settings. *The Journal of Mind-Body Health*, **9**(1), 17–35.

Aldridge, D. (1989). Music, communication and medicine: Discussion paper. *Journal of the Royal Society of Medicine*, **82**, 743–6.

Bartlett, D.L. (1996). Physiological responses to music and sound stimuli. In D. A. Hodges (ed.) *Handbook of Music Psychology*, pp. 343–85. San Antonio, CA: IMR Press.

Bartlett, D.L., Kaufman, D., and Smeltekop, R. (1993). The effects of music listening and perceived sensory experiences on the immune system as measured by interleukin-1 and cortisol. *Journal of Music Therapy*, **30**(4), 194–209.

Beck, R.J., Cesario, T.C., Youcefi, A., and Enamoto, H. (2000). Choral singing, performance perception, and immune system changes in salivary immunoglobulin A and cortisol. *Music Percpetion*, **18**(1), 87–106.

Beck, R.J., Gottfried, T.L., Hall, D.J., Cisler, C.A., and Bozema, K.W. (2002). Supporting the health of college solo singers: The relationship of positive emotions and stress to changes in salivary IgA and cortisol during singing. *Journal for Learning through the Arts: A Research Journal on Arts Integration in Schools and Communities*, **2**(1), 1–17.

Berger, D.S. and Schneck, D.J. (2003). The use of music therapy as a clinical intervention for physiologic functional adaptation. *Journal of Scientific Exploration*, **17**(4), 687–703.

Bernardi, P., Fontana, F., Pich, E.M., Spampinato, S., and Canossa, M. (1992). Plasma endogeneous opioid levels in acute myocardial infarction patients with and without pain. *European Heart Journal*, **13**, 1074–79.

Bernardi, L., Porta, C., Casucci, G., Balsamo, R., Bernardi, N.F., Fogari, R., et al. (2009). Dynamic Interactions Between Musical, Cardiovascular, and Cerebral Rhythms in Humans. *Circulation*, **119**, 3171–80.

Bittman, B.B., Berk, L.S., Felten, D.L., Westengard, J., Simonton, O.C., Pappas, J., et al. (2001). Composite effects of group drumming music therapy on modulation of neuroendocrineimmune parameters in normal subjects. *Alternative Therapies in Health and Medicine*, **7**(1), 38–47.

Biley, F.C. (2000). The effects on patient well-being of music listening as a nursing intervention: a review of the literature. *Journal of Clinical Nursing*, **9**, 668–77.

Blood, A.J. and Zatorre, R.J. (2001). Intensely pleasurable responses to music correlate with activity in brain regions implicated with reward and emotion. *Proceedings of the National Academy of Sciences*, **98**, 11818–23.

Blood, A.F., Zatorre, R.J., Bermudez, P., and Evans, A.C. (1999). Emotional responses to pleasant and unpleasant music correlate with activity in paralimbic brain regions. *Nature Neuroscience*, **2**(4), 382–7.

Bongard, S., al'Absi, M., and Lovallo, W.R. (2011). Cardiovascular reactivity and health. In: R.A. Wright and G.H.E. Gendolla (eds.) *How motivation affects cardiovascular response: Mechanisms and applications*, pp. 223–241. Washington, DC: American Psychological Association.

Breedlove, S.M., Rosenzweig, M.R., and Watson, N.V. (2007). *Biological Psychology*. Sunderland, MA: Sinauer Associates Inc.

Brauchli, P. (1993). Vergleichsuntersuchung der psychophysiologischen Entspannungseffekte einer optisch-akustischen Mind Machine mit einer Entspannungsmusik. *Zeitschrift für Experimentelle und Angewandte Psychologie*, **40**(2), 179–93.

Brownley, K.A., McMurray, R.G., and Hackney, A.C. (1995). Effects of music on physiological and affective responses to graded treadmill exercise in trained and untrained runners. *International Journal of Psychophysiology*, **19**(3), 193–201.

Bunt, L. (1998). *Musiktherapie: Eine Einführung für psychosoziale und medizinische Berufe*. Weinheim und Basel: Beltz Verlag.

Burns, S.J., Harbuz, M.S., Hucklebridge, F., and Bunt, L. (2001). A pilot study into the therapeutic effects of music therapy at a cancer help center. *Alternative Therapies in Health and Medicine*, **7**(1), 48–56.

Campeau, S., Day, H.E.W., Helmreich, D.L., Kollack-Walker, S., and Watson, S.J. (1998). Principles of psychoneuroendocrinology. *Psychiatric Clinics of North America*, **2**(2), 259–76.

Charnetski, C.J., Brennan, F.X., and Harrison, J.F. (1998). Effect of music and auditory stimuli on secretory Immunoglobulin A (IgA). *Perceptual and Motor Skills*, **87**, 1163–70.

Clift, S. and Hancox, G. (2001). The perceived benefits of singing: findings from preliminary surveys of a university college choral society. *The Journal of the Royal Society for the Promotion of Health*, **121**, 248–56.

Cohen, G. (2006). The impact of professionally conducted cultural programs on the physical health, mental health, and social functioning of older adults. *The Gerontologist*, **46**(6), 726–34.

Conrad, C., Niess, H., Jauch, K.W., Bruns, C.J., Hartl, W., and Welker, L. (2007). Overture for growth hormone: requiem for interleukin-6? *Critical Care Medicine*, **35**(12), 2709–13.

Darwin, C. (1871). *The Descent of Man and Selection in Relation to Sex*. London: John Murray.

Deutsch, D. (ed.) (1999). *The Psychology of Music* (2nd edition). San Diego: Academic Press.

Ditzen, B., Schaer, M., Gabriel, B., Bodenmann, G., Ehlert, U., and Heinrichs, M. (2008). Intranasal oxytocin increases positive communication and reduces cortisol levels during couple conflict. *Biological Psychiatry*, **65**, 728–31.

Dillman Carpentier, F.R. and Potter, R.F. (2007). Effects of music on physiological arousal: explorations into tempo and genre. *Media Psychologogy*, **10**(3), 339–63.

Enk, R., Franzke, P., Offermanns, K., Hohenadel, M., Boehlig, A., Nitsche, I., *et al.* (2008). Music and the immune system. *International Journal of Psychophysiology*, **69**(3), 216.

Evans, D. (2002). The effectiveness of music as an intervention for hospital patients: a systematic review. *Journal of Advanced Nursing*, **37**(1), 8–18.

Evers, S. and Suhr, B. (2000). Changes of the neurotransmitter serotonin but not of hormones during short time music perception. *European Archives of Psychiatry and Clinical Neuroscience*, **250**, 144–7.

Fastl, H. and Zwicker, E. (2006). *Psychoacoustics, Facts and models*. Berlin: Springer.

Fredrickson, B.L. (2004). Gratitude, like other positive emotions, broadens and builds. In: R.A. Emmons and M. E. McCullough (eds.) *The Psychology of Gratitude*, pp. 145–66. New York: Oxford University Press.

Fukui, H. and Yamashita, M. (2003). The effects of music and visual stress on testosterone and cortisol in men and women. *Neuroendocrinology Letters*, **24**, 173–80.

Fukui, H. and Toyoshima, K. (2008). Music facilitates the neurogenesis, regenaration and repair of neurons. *Medical Hypotheses*, **71**, 765–9.

Gembris, H. (2002). Wirkungen von Musik–Musikpsychologische Forschungsergebnisse. In: G. Hofmann and C. Trübsbach (ed.) *Mensch und Musik*, pp. 9–28. Augsburg: Wi ner-Verlag.

Gembris, H. (1985). *Musikhören und Entspannung. Theoretische und experimentelle Untersuchungen über den Zusammenhang zwischen situativen Bedingungen und Effekten des Musikhörens*. Hamburg: Musikalienbuchhandlung Karl Dieter Wagner.

Gerra, G., Zaimovic, A., Franchini, D., Palladino, M., Giucastro, G., Reali, N., et al. (1998). Neuroendocrine responses of healthy volunteers to 'techno-music': relationships with personality trait and emotional state. *International Journal of Psychophysiology*, **28**, 99–111.

Grape, C., Sandgren, M., Hansson, L.O., Ericson, M., and Theorell, T. (2003). Does singing promote well-being? An empirical study of professional and amateur singers during a singing lesson. *Integrative Physiological and Behavioral Science*, **38**(1), 65–74.

Grape, C., Wikström, B-M., Ekman, R., Hasson, D., and Theorell, T. (2010). Comparison between choir singing and group discussion with IBS patients during one year. Saliva testosterone increases in choir singer beginners. *Psychotherapy and Psychosomatic Medicine*, **79**, 196–8.

Gütay, W. and Kreutz, G. (2009). Development of vocal performance in 5th grade children: A longitudinal study of choral class singing. Presentation at the European Society for the Cognitive Sciences of Music (ESCOM), 12–16 August, Jyväskylä, Finland.

Hammond, J., Le Q., Goodyer, C., Gelfand, M., Trifiro, M., and LeBlanc, A. (2001). Testosterone-mediated neuroprotection through the androgen receptor in human primary neurons. *Journal of Neurochemistry*, **77**, 1319–26.

Hassler, M. (1992). Creative musical behavior and sex hormones: musical talent and spatial ability in the two sexes. *Psychoneuroendocrinology*, **17**(1), 55–70.

Hassler M. (2000). Music medicine. A neurobiological approach. *Neuroendocrinology Letters*, **21**, 101–6.

Heinrichs, M., Baumgartner, T., Kirschbaum, C., and Ehlert, U. (2003). Social support and oxytocin interact to suppress cortisol and subjective responses to psychosocial stress. *Biological Psychiatry*, **54**, 1389–98.

Hennig, J. (1994). *Die psychobiologische Bedeutung des sekretorischen Immunglobulin A im Speichel.* Münster, New York: Waxmann.

Hirokawa, E. and Ohira, H. (2003). The effects of music listening after a stressful task on immune functions, neuroendocrine responses, and emotional states in college students. *Journal of Music Therapy*, **40**(3), 189–211.

Horden P. (2000). *Music as Medicine: The History of Music Therapy since Antiquity.* Aldershot: Ashgate.

Hucklebridge, F., Lamber, S., Clow, A., Warburton, D.M., Evans, P.D., and Sherwood, N. (2000). Modulation of secretory immunoglobulin A in saliva: Response to manipulation of mood. *Biological Psychology*, **53**, 25–35.

Jeffries, K., Fritz, J., and Braun, A. (2003). Words in melody: an H2 15O PET study of brain activation during singing and speaking. *Neuroreport,* **14**, 749–54.

Karrer U. (1999). Entspannung durch Musik-Entspannungskassetten? Physiologische Befunde und ihre Aussage. In: K.E.Behne, G. Kleinen, and H. de la Motte-Haber (eds.) *Musikpsychologie Band 14*, pp. 42–51. Göttingen: Hogrefe-Verlag.

Koelsch, S. and Siebel, W.A. (2005). Towards a neural basis of music perception. *Trends in Cognitive Sciences*, **9**(12), 578–84.

Kreutz, G., Bongard, S., Rohrmann, S., Hodapp, V., and Grebe, D. (2004). Effects of choir singing or listening on secretory immunoglobulin A, cortisol and emotional state. *Journal of Behavioral Medicine*, **27**, 623–34.

Kreutz, G. and Lotze, M. (2008). Neuroscience of music and emotion. In: W. Gruhn and F. Rauscher (eds.) *The Neuroscience of Music Education*, pp. 145–69. New York: Nova Publishers.

Krout, R.E. (2007). Music listening to facilitate relaxation and promote wellness: Integrated aspects of our neurophysiological responses to music. *The Arts in Psychoterapy*, **34**, 134–41.

Kuhn, D. (2002). The effects of active and passive participation in musical activity on the immune system as measured by salivary immunoglobulin A (SIgA). *Journal of Music Therapy*, **39**(1), 30–39.

Leardi, S., Pietroletti, R., Angeloni, G., Necozione, S., Ranalletta, G., and Del Gusto, B. (2007). Randomized clinical trial examining the effect of music therapy in stress respnse to day surgery. *British Journal of Surgery*, **94**, 943–7.

Le Roux, F.H., Bouic, P.J.D., and Bester, M.M. (2007). The effect of Bach's Magnificat on emotions, immune, and endocrine parameters during physiotherapy treatment of patients with infectious lung conditions. *Journal of Music Therapy*, **44**(2), 156–68.

Levine, S. and Coe, C.L. (1999). Veränderungen des endokrinen Systems und des Immunsystems durch psychosoziale Faktoren. In: C. Kirschbaum, T. Hellhammer (ed.) *Psychoendokrinologie und Psychoimmunologie*, pp. 435–68. Göttingen: Hogrefe.

Lutgendorf, S.K. and Costanzo, E.S. (2003). Psychoneuroimmunology and health psychology: An integrative model. *Brain, Behavior, and Immunity*, **17**(4), 225–32.

Maranto, C.D. (1993). Applications of music in medicine. In: M. Heal and T. Wigram (ed.) *Music Therapy in Health and Education*, pp. 153–74. London: Jessica Kingsley Publishers.

McCraty, R., Atkinson, M., Rein, G., and Watkins, A.D. (1996). Music enhances the effect of positive emotional states on salivary IgA. *Stress Medicine*, **12**, 167–75.

McKinney, C.H., Tims, F.C., Kumar, A.M., and Kumar, M. (1997). The Effect of Selected Classical Music and Spontaneous Imagery on Plasma B-Endorphin. *Journal of Behavioral Medicine*, **20**(1), 85–99.

Mitschell, L., MacDonald, R., Knussen, C., and Serpell, M. (2007). A survey investigation of the effects of music listening on chronic pain. *Psychology of Music*, **35**(1), 37–57.

Möckel, M., Röcker, L., Störk, T., Vollert, J., Danne, O., Eichstädt, H., et *al.* (1994). Immediate physiological responses of healthy volunteers to different types of music: cardiovascular, hormonal and mental changes. *European Journal of Applied Physiology*, **68**, 451–9.

Nater, U.M., Abbruzzese, E., Kreb,s M., and Ehlert, U. (2006). Sex differences in emotional and psychophysiological responses to musical stimuli. *International Journal of Psychophysiology*, **62**(2), 300–30.

Nilsson U. (2009). Soothing music can increase oxytocin levels during bed rest after open-heart surgery: a randomised control trial. *Journal of Clinical Nursing*, **18**, 2153–61.

Nilsson, U., Unosson, M., and Rawal, N. (2005). Stress reduction and analgesia in patients exposed to calming music. *European Journal of Anaesthesiology*, **22**, 96–102.

Nuñez, M.J., Maña, P., Liñares, D., Rivero, M.P., Balboa, J., Suárez-Quintanilla, J., et al. (2002). Music, immunity and cancer. *Life Sciences*, **71**, 1047–5.

Omland, T., Dickstein, K. and Syversen, U. (2003). Association between plasma chromogranin a concentration and long-term mortality after myocardial infarction. *American Journal of Medicine*, **114**(1), 25–30.

Patel, A. (2008). *Music, Language, and the Brain*. Oxford: Oxford University Press.

Panksepp, J. and Bernatzky, G. (2002). Emotional sounds and the brain: the neuro-affective Foundations of musical appreciation. *Behavioural Processes*, **60**, 133–55.

Parncutt, R. (2009). Prenatal development and the phylogeny and ontogeny of musical behaviour. In: S. Hallam, I. Cross and M. Thaut (eds.) *Oxford handbook of music psychology*, pp. 219–28. Oxford: Oxford University Press.

Pedersen, B.K. and Hoffman-Goetz, L. (2000). Exercise and the immune system: regulation, integration, and adaptation. *Physiological Reviews*, **80**(3), 1055–81.

Peretz, I. and Hébert, S. (2000). Toward a biological account of music experience. *Brain and Cognition*, **42**, 132–34.

Prahl C. (2008). Musiktherapie–Praxisfelder und Vorgehensweise. In: H. Bruhn, R. Kopiez and A.C. Lehmann (eds.) *Musikpsychologie: Das neue Handbuch*, pp. 613–29. Reinbek bei Hamburg: Rowohlt.

Pressman, S.D. and Cohen, S. (2005). Does positive affect influence health? *Psychological Bulletin*, **131**(6), 925–71.

Quiroga Murcia C., Bongard, S. and Kreutz, G. (2009). Emotional and neurohumoral responses to dancing tango argentino: The effects of music and partner. *Music and Medicine*, **1**(1), 14–21.

Rouget, G. (1985). *Music and Trance: A Theory of the Relations between Music and Possession*. Chicago, IL: University of Chicago Press.

Särkämö, T., Tervaniemi, M., Laitinen, S., Forsblom, A., Soinilla, S., Mikkonen, M., et al. (2008). Music listening enhances cognitive recovery and mood after middle cerebral artery stroke. *Brain*, **131**, 866–76.

Sambeth, A.,. Ruohio, K., Alku, P., Fellman, V. and Huotilainen, M. (2007). Sleeping newborns extract prosody from continuous speech. *Clinical Neurophysiology*, **119**(2), 332–41.

Shenfield, T., Trehub, S.E., and Nakata, T. (2003). Maternal singing modulates infant arousal. *Psychology of Music*, **31** (4), 365–75.

Sheps, D.S., Ballenger, M.N., Gent, G., Krittayaphong, R., Dittman, E., Maixner, W., et al. (1995). Psychophysical responses to a speech stressor: correlation of plasma beta-endorphin levels at rest and after psychological stress with thermally measured pain threshold in patients with coronary artery disease. *Journal of the American College of Cardiology*, **25**(7), 1499–503.

Spintge, R. and Droh, R. (1992). *MusikMedizin - Physiologische Grundlagen und praktische Anwendungen*. Stuttgart: Fischer.

Spintge, R. (2000). Musik in Anaesthesie und Schmerztherapie. *Anästhesiologie, Intensivmedizin, Notfallmedizin und Schmerztherapie*, 35, 243–61.

Steptoe, A., Wardle, J., and Marmot, M. (2005). Positive affect and health-related neuroendocrine, cardiovascular, and inflammatory processes. *Proceedings of the National Academy of Sciences*, **102**, 6508–12.

Suzuki, M., Kanamori, M., Watanabe, M., Nagasawa, S., Kojima, O., and Nakahara, D. (2004). Behavioral and endocrinological evaluation of music therapy for elderly patienets with dementia. *Nursing and Health Sciences*, **6**, 11–18.

Suzuki, M., Kanamori, M., Nagasawa, S., Tokiko, I., and Takayuki, S. (2007). Music therapy-induced changes in behavioral evaluations, and saliva chromogranin A and immunoglobulin A concentrations in elderly patients with senile dementia. *Geriatrics and Gerontology*, 7, 61–71.

Thompson, W.F. (2009). *Music, Thought & Feeling: Understanding the Psychology of Music*. New York: Oxford University Press.

Tsao, C., Gordon, T., Maranto, C., Leran, C., and Murasko, D. (1992). The effects of music and biological imagery on immune response. In: C. Maranto (ed.) *Applications of Music in Medicine*, pp. 85–122. Washington, DC: National Association for Music Therapy.

Uvnäs-Moberg, K. (1998). Oxytocin may mediate the benefits of positive Social interaction and emotions. *Psychoneuroendocrinology*, **23**(8), 819–35.

Uvnäs-Moberg, K. and Carter, C.S. (1998). *Is There a Neurobiology of Love?* Proceedings of a Conference Sponsored by the Wenner-Gren Foundation. *Psychoneuroendocrinology* (Special issue). Stockholm, Sweden.

VanderArk, S.D. and Ely, D. (1993). Cortisol, biochemical, and galvanic skin responses to music stimuli of different preference values by college students in biology and music. *Perceptual and Motor Skills*, **77**(1), 227–34.

Vingerhoets, A.J.J.M. and Assies, J. (1991). Psychoneuroendocrinology of stress and emotions: issues for future research. *Psychotherapy and Psychosomatic Medicine*, **55**, 69–75.

Vollert, J.O., Störk, T., Rose, M., and Möckel, M. (2003). Musik als begleitende Therapie bei koronarer Herzkrankheit. *Deutsche Medizinische Wochenschrift*, **128**, 2712–16.

Wago, H., Kimura, M., Inoue, J., Kobayashi, R., and Nakamura, S. (2002). Effects of a listening to Mozart on blood pressure, heart rate, salivary IgA secretion and neutrophil function in healthy college students. *Bulletin of Saitama Medical University College*, **13**, 45–51.

Wallin, B. Merkur, and S. Brown (eds.) (2000). *The Origins of music*. Cambridge, MA: MIT Press.

Wand, G.S. and Schumann, H. (1998). Relationship between plasma adrenocorticotropin, hypothalamic opioid tone, and plasma leptin. *The Journal of Clinical Endocrinology and Metabolism*, **83**, 2138–42.

Yamamoto, M., Shinobu, N., and Shimizu, J. (2007). Positive musical effects on two types of negative stressful conditions. *Psychology of Music*, **35**(2), 249–75.

Zatorre, R.J. and Halpern, A.R. (2005). Mental concerts: Musical imagery and auditory cortex. *Neuron*, 47, 9–12.

Zheng, K.C. and Ariizumi, M. (2007). Modulations of immune functions and oxidative status induced by noise stress. *Journal of Occupational Health*, 2007, **49**(1), 32–8.

Chapter 31

Cross-Cultural Approaches to Music and Health

Suvi Saarikallio

Introduction

Music has been shown to serve as a source of health and wellbeing in cultures around the world (e.g. Gouk 2001; Koen 2009). Yet, to date, little cross-cultural research has been conducted on music and health, and little is known about the universality of the possible health-related meanings and effects of music. This chapter draws together some of the recent literature in order to clarify the role of cultural factors and to discuss possible cross-cultural similarities and differences in how music relates to health and wellbeing. With regards to the concept of health, the chapter mainly focuses on psychological factors and mental health as opposed to other areas such as physiological health or spiritual growth. As regards to the concept of culture, a broad understanding of culture as a set of shared beliefs, values, and practices, as opposed to defining culture as fine arts, for instance, is employed (e.g. Kroeber and Kluckhohn 1952; Griswold 2004).

Music as human behaviour inevitably exists within cultural contexts, and the relevance of contextual factors on musical experience has long been acknowledged, particularly in anthropological and ethnomusicological approaches (e.g. Blacking 1973). The role of culture appears particularly important when studying the effects of music on health and wellbeing: the way we interpret, experience, and react to music is strongly shaped by our personal attributes that are moulded by our social and cultural background. Moreover, culture also plays a role in determining how the relationship between music and health is conceived: whether music-making is considered as an integral element of healing practices or whether the professions of a musician and a healer/doctor are considered as fundamentally separate areas of life. Whether we focus on the health effects of music in clinical settings, everyday life contexts, traditional healing ceremonies, or in a research laboratory, we should acknowledge that musical behaviours and experiences as well as our conceptualizations about the roles and meanings of music in the context of healing are grounded in the surrounding culture.

In addition to exploring the culture-specific characteristics of musical behaviour, it is also important to examine the cross-culturally similar elements in how music is used for healing and improving quality of life. Are there, for example, universal features in the healing aspects of music or in the practices of enhancing wellbeing through music? Answers to such questions seem crucially significant for identifying features that are shared among cultures. They may help us in constructing a better understanding of musical universals, and lay foundations for comprehensive research in the modern world of increasing cross-cultural interaction.

Cognitive and ethnomusicological approaches

The fields of ethnomusicology and cultural anthropology have elaborately focused on exploring the cultural dynamics that underlie potential effects of music on health and wellbeing. A growing area of medical ethnomusicology, in particular, has been interested in health, healing, illness, and disease related to music. A recent Oxford University Press text *The Oxford Handbook of Medical Ethnomusicology* (2009), edited by Benjamin Koen, and the book *Musical Healing in Cultural Contexts* (2001), edited by Penelope Gouk, are both illustrative collections of studies from a variety of cultural contexts showing how music contributes to health and healing within the biological, psychological, emotional, social, and spiritual domains of human life. Ethnomusicological and anthropological approaches both stress the role and importance of cultural factors in understanding musical experience and behaviour, but often the scientific work is limited to case studies within only one cultural context, lacking comparisons between cultures.

Researchers within cognitive musicology and music psychology have investigated the cross-cultural differences and similarities in music perception and cognition, typically focusing on the perception and cognitive processing of musical features such as tonality and harmony (e.g. Harwood 1976; Maher 1976; Kessler et al. 1984; Hargreaves et al. 1986; Krumhansl 2000; Krumhansl et al. 2000; Morrison et al. 2003; Nan et al. 2008). Cross-cultural comparisons have also been conducted on other music-related aspects, such as music-related movement (Himberg and Thompson 2009), and the musical elements of lullabies (Unyk et al. 1992; Trehub et al 1993). Some preliminary cross-cultural comparisons also exist on the perception of emotion in music which has shown that both psychoacoustic features as well as cultural norms are needed to encode and decode musical emotions (Gregory and Varney 1996; Balkwill and Thompson 1999; Gosselin 2009).

Cognitive and ethnomusicological approaches have existed as relatively separate strands of research maintaining their distinct theoretical and methodological profiles. Yet, they could successfully complement each other, as the former provides solid grounds for investigating the cross-cultural similarities and differences in cognitive and emotional processing of music, and the latter offers detailed insight into the cultural characteristics that mediate the music-related healing practices. Finding a shared ground between approaches is obviously challenging due to theoretical, methodological, and ideological differences, but mutual collaboration would certainly be rewarding for cross-cultural research on music and health.

Conceptual and methodological challenges

The body of cross-cultural studies on music and health has remained small, although researchers agree that cultural influences do play a significant role in understanding the possible effects of music on health. Thus, there is a need to ask why. In addition to the abovementioned separation between the relevant approaches, the cross-cultural research on music and health encounters a number of more practical, methodological, and conceptual problems. Since methodological challenges of cross-cultural research in general have been discussed in other volumes (e.g. Davis 2005; Matsumoto and Van de Vijver 2010), this chapter focuses mainly on the discussion of conceptual issues related to the study of music and health.

Conceptual definitions create profound challenges for cross-cultural research: the surrounding culture defines the way people give meaning to and interpret various phenomena, and clear cultural differences exist in how the concepts of 'music' and 'health' are defined. For instance, the Western term 'music' is separated from related concepts such as art and dance. This is reflected in a range of cultural traditions, from public concerts and exhibitions to school curriculums, which all typically treat these art forms separately. Conversely, several Central and Southern African ethnic groups do not use a specific term for music as such but typically merge it together with other forms of art, dance, and performance, under the term 'ngoma' (Janzen 2002). This is reflected, for instance, in the school curriculum in South Africa, which places music under a broader subject of 'Arts and Culture', consisting also of dance, drama, visual arts, media, communication, arts management, and cultural history, with the objective of strengthening understanding of all arts as a comprehensive feature of culture and society (Department of Education 2005).

In addition to defining the boundaries of music, the concept can also be divided into a range of smaller elements such as rhythm or timbre. Alternatively, it may be defined through its various aspects: as a physical phenomenon (sound, vibration), as a psychological phenomenon (experience, behaviour), or as a social phenomenon (group activity, cultural tradition). In order to avoid conceptual misunderstandings, cross-cultural studies need to be particularly cautions about which musical elements (rhythm, harmony, timbre), which related behaviours (listening, playing, dancing), which situations (concerts, everyday life contexts, healing practices), and even which types and genres of music they are focusing on. Moreover, different cultures may even conceptualize specific musical elements in different ways. For instance, to study pitch perception by asking if 'one note is higher than the other' may be problematic across cultures (as it is for young children, who are otherwise able to discriminate pitch). Some cultures conceive pitch through a scale 'dark–bright' instead of 'high–low' (Louhivuori 2009).

It is also difficult to define health across cultures. For example, symptoms that one culture interprets as something that fits within the frames of normal life another culture considers as symptoms of disease (Ruud 1997). Western music therapy has traditionally been based on individualistic, biological, and psychological perspectives, defining health and disease through physiology and/or intrapsychic processes of an individual (e.g. Ruud 1997; Koen et al. 2009). Illness is thus typically considered as something that faces our body or psyche independent of the surrounding social context. This may be significantly different from cultural traditions that are more focused on social dynamics or spirituality. The conceptualizations of illness and wellness have a strong influence on how the role of music is evaluated. In individualistic cultures the role of music in health promotion may be considered from the perspective of personal psychological wellbeing while collectivist cultures may appreciate music's health-effects more in terms of its impact on social behaviour and belonging. Cross-cultural research, therefore, needs to aim for a thorough awareness of the informants' conceptualizations by carefully considering which health-related areas such as mind, body, or social behaviour, are emphasized in the surrounding cultural context.

In addition to the conceptual challenges, some of the practical problems of cross-cultural research might be mentioned briefly. For example, conducting research in cultures outside one's own may require funding for long-distance travel and transport of equipment, foreign language and administration expertise, knowledge regarding foreign administrative structures, as well as understanding norms and traditions to ensure politically and culturally correct communication. In addition, cross-cultural research faces particular methodological concerns, such as arranging identical procedures for experiments in different locations, coping with differences in the reading and writing skills of the participants, in their response styles, and in the ways in which the participants understand their role and relationship to the researchers. It may also be challenging to acquire samples that are representative of the cultural entity that the generalizations are to be made about. In general, as differences between contexts increase so do the number of confounding variables. Moreover, due to the small amount of cross-cultural research there is also often a lack of theoretical background, which makes it difficult to form hypotheses (e.g. Campbell et al. 2004; Liamputtong 2008; Louhivuori 2009.)

Mechanisms that may relate music to psychological wellbeing around the world

Before cross-cultural comparisons can be conducted, there is a need to discuss the basic mechanisms through which music may relate to wellbeing. Broad categorizations about music's functions in society and case studies conducted in separate cultural contexts provide good starting points for understanding the general mechanisms through which music may function as a medium for healing. In the following we shall review some studies that have focused on the effects of music on psychological functioning and mental health.

A general list of music's functions in society can be found in Merriam's *The Anthropology of Music*, from 1964, which presents a typology of 10 different functions related to the emotional, aesthetic, communicative, and society-supporting roles of music. A comparable example is Dissanayake's (2006) classification of the social functions of ritual music, including the display of resources, control of aggression, facilitation of courtship, establishment of social identity, relief from psychological pain, and the promotion of group cooperation. Hargreaves and North's (1999) categorization of the psychological functions of music includes emotional, cognitive, and social domains, with particular emphasis on the effects of music on the formulation and expression of identity, creation and maintenance of interpersonal relationships, and the use of music for mood management. Similarly, Laiho's (2004) review on studies exploring the psychological functions of music in adolescence stresses the importance of music in dealing with emotional experiences, self-identity, personal agency, and interpersonal relationships. A recent discussion by Clayton (2009) about the functions of music from a cross-cultural perspective also underlines similar elements. Clayton argues that music functions as a regulation of an individual's cognitive, physiological, and emotional state, and mediates social behaviour through coordinating action, by managing the relations between self and others, and through symbolically communicating aspects of identity and emotional states. The abovementioned typologies are not specifically focused on health or psychological functioning, but certainly provide valuable starting points for health-related investigations as well. Indeed, the findings are also very much in line with the theoretical models and clinical practices of Western music therapy, which has emphasized music's value especially in facilitating emotional expression and social integration (e.g. Thaut 2005).

Based on the abovementioned categorizations and the literature to be presented in the following paragraphs, at least three psychological aspects seem to be repeatedly connected to the use of music:

+ *Emotional element*: music reflects and evokes emotions, enables expression, experience, and regulation of emotions.

+ *Mental element*: music facilitates introspection, mental work, and personal growth often in relation to altered states of consciousness and spirituality.

+ *Social element*: music strengthens social bonding, belonging, and unity, and strengthens group cohesion and identity.

The *emotional* component can be said to be an inseparable part of music, and experimental studies have shown that music is able to express, communicate and evoke a range of different emotions (e.g. Sloboda and Juslin 2001; Juslin and Laukka 2004). Music seems to be emotionally valuable to people around the world and at different ages: Popular music has been shown to play an important role in the emotional lives of adolescents in a range of countries including the US (Wells 1990; Wells and Hakanen 1991; Hakanen 1994) Japan (Wells et al. 2000), Hong Kong, (Hakanen et al. 1999), Finland (Saarikallio and Erkkilä 2007), and Kenya (Saarikallio 2008), and musical behaviours have been shown to be meaningful for the emotional wellbeing of elderly people in Australia (e.g. Hays and Minichiello 2005; Davidson 2008), Sweden (Laukka 2006), and Germany (Gembris 2008). Recent research has begun to explore the mechanisms through which music is able to reach emotional processing (e.g. Juslin and Västfjäll 2008). The strong influence of music on emotions can partly be explained by music's ability to reach complex emotional structures at a variety of levels: (1) music is able to affect the physiological and nonverbal experiences and reflexes; (2) music reaches memories and the symbolic and referential meanings of the psychodynamic level; and (3) music also influences the cognitive processing of abstract structures (Erkkilä 1996; Juslin and Västfjäll 2008).

The strong effect of music on emotions has unquestionably been demonstrated, so the essential question then is: why are these effects relevant for health? One answer is simply the aesthetic enjoyment provided by music, as it adds to the happiness, satisfaction, and meaning in life. Researchers have proposed that music-related emotions are not necessarily analogous to the so-called utilitarian emotions typical to everyday life, but are better defined as aesthetic emotions, which are detached from pragmatic, self-related concerns and relate instead to concepts such as beauty and awe (Zentner and Schrerer 2008). Another explanation can be related to the increased affective awareness, discussed for instance by Ruud (1997) who proposes that music is able to contribute to an increased 'awareness of feelings', i.e. an ability to experience various emotional nuances, express various degrees of intensity of emotions, and maintain precise concepts about feelings. These kinds of emotional competencies are a key element of emotional intelligence, a set of emotional abilities which have been shown to significantly correlate with various positive health outcomes, such as prosocial behaviour and lower levels of depression (e.g. Salovey et al. 2002; Gohm 2003; Garnefski et al. 2004). Finally, a third possible explanation is related to music's ability to provide access to a person's meaningful emotional experiences and memories, and facilitate the related self-therapeutic processing of personal experiences. It is very likely that the relevance of these three emotion-related aspects—the aesthetic enjoyment, the increased awareness of feelings, and the improved processing of emotional experiences—may notably differ across situational and cultural contexts. Exploration of these aspects presents itself as an interesting new direction for future studies.

When considering the idea that music is able to facilitate emotional processing related to personal experiences, we approach discussion of the *mental element*, which has also been pronounced in studies discussing the health effects of music. Indeed, the emotional and mental elements appear to be strongly interlinked, and a variety of studies have suggested that the importance of music is closely connected to both emotional and self-conceptual processing. For instance, Sloboda et al. (2001) conducted an experience sampling study in which they demonstrated that most of music's functions in every day life were related to memories and emotions. Greasley and Lamont (2006) reported a qualitative study showing that the characteristics of music use included emotional self-regulation and mental work related to internal experiences and memories. In line with these findings, DeNora (1999) concluded that music serves as a resource for self-reflective and autobiographical work and related emotional processing. Findings from non-Western cultures support this notion to some extent. For instance, Roseman (1991, 2009), who studied the Malaysian musical healers in a Temiar village, demonstrated that their practice is based on music's ability to reflect and modify emotions, stimulate sensory excitation and biophysiological transformation, and evoke mental imagination. Respectively, Barz (2009) argued that music is able to enhance the wellbeing of people suffering from HIV/AIDS in Uganda by supporting the emotion-related mental work on their traumatic memories. Furthermore, During (2009), examined the therapeutic dimensions of music in Islamic culture and highlighted that music typically serves as a technology for healing through a process in which the person experiences a modified state of consciousness created by the music and related emotions. According to During, the essential elements contributing to this process include the ability of music to create altered states of consciousness and to influence emotions. The use of music for emotional processing of significant internal experiences may thus be a key element in the enhancement of wellbeing for people around the world.

In addition to the emotional and mental effects, music also seems to have a range of important *social* meanings in different cultures. The fundamental form of social interaction is the communication between mothers and infants, and lullabies are sung to babies in a variety of cultures (Unyk et al. 1992; Trehub et al. 1993). Maternal singing serves as an important means for emotional connection and communication, helping the child to calm down and focus attention (Tafuri and Villa 2002), as well as to express and communicate emotions in an accepting atmosphere of trust, confidence, and playfulness (e.g. Oldfield 1993). A similar bonding effect is also integral to musical behaviour among adults, and in relation to healing and health practices. For instance, Locke and Koen (2009) studied the Lakota hoop dance as a means for social healing emphasized and found that the importance of music is strongly related to strengthening the experience of unity and oneness among human beings. Similarly, During (2009) emphasized the relevance of the communicative element between the performer and the listener in his discussion about the therapeutic dimensions of music in Islamic culture. Comparative notions have also been made by Clayton (2009), who refers to Friedson's (1996) research on the Tumbuka healing practices and Lucas's (2002) work on the musical rituals of Afro-Brazilian religious groups. Based on these and other related examples, Clayton stresses music's importance in creating a sense of communion, group solidarity, togetherness, and unity. These shared experiences are based on music's ability to enhance interpersonal synchronization and entrainment, emotional communication, and expression of social identity (e.g. Clayton 2009; West and Ironson 2009). West and Ironson (2009) argue that the interpersonal entrainment, a sense of finding a shared pulse, is often associated with experiences of ease, relaxation, a heightened sense of awareness, and feelings of unity, and may be an essential element in understanding the effects of music on wellbeing.

Ruud (1997) argues that music's ability to enhance the sense of belonging is also essential for people's wellbeing and quality of life in everyday life contexts. He states that music is able to create a heightened feeling of being included not only in a group of people around us, but also to broader unities including subculture, nationality, ethnicity, or historical era. A substantial amount of research exists concerning the role of music in creation, maintenance, and expression of identity (e.g. Lewis 1995; MacDonald et al. 2002; North and Hargreaves 2008), and the topic of identity has also been studied in non-Western cultures. For instance, the preference for national music styles has been shown to positively correlate with national identity among Brazilians (Ferreira et al. 2007), shared musical hobbies have been considered to be an important element in supporting social identity in a highly multicultural school setting in South Africa (Kivinen 2004), and connection to family and cultural identity has been reported to be an essential reason why music is considered to be meaningful among Kenyans (Saarikallio 2009). Interestingly, recent research has also suggested that music may even connect and unite people across cultures as people may feel closer identification to certain musical subcultures than geographical regions (Boer and Fischer 2009). Moreover, it has been proposed that participation in ethnic arts activities may improve the psychosocial health and wellbeing of immigrants by providing a platform for building favourable intercultural interactions (Fox 2007).

Cross-cultural comparisons

The abovementioned findings illustrate how the three elements—emotional, mental, and social—are recurrently shown to be important for the effects of music on psychological wellbeing irrespective of cultural context. Music's strength as a medium for healing seems to be intrinsically linked to its ability to reflect emotional and mental processes and communicate them among people, functioning at both intrapsychic and interpersonal levels. The abovementioned studies show relatively similar results even though they have been conducted in a variety of cultures. This indicates that the selection of mechanisms through which music functions as a medium for healing may be somewhat comparable in different cultures. Yet, the abovementioned examples are only a starting point for cross-cultural comparisons, providing theoretical suggestions regarding the possible universal elements. Next, let us take a look at some of the cross-cultural comparisons related to these elements.

Boer (2009) conducted a cross-cultural investigation into the psychological functions of music by collecting qualitative data from young adults (mean age 22.56)—222 interviewees from 29 different countries participated in the study. The recruitment of participants from so many countries was made possible by collecting the data through an online survey. The study resulted in a list of seven social psychological functions of music, including: (1) music in the background, (2) memories through music, (3) music as diversion, (4) emotion in music, (5) catharsis through music, (6) music as reflection of self, and (7) social bonding through music. Moreover, the study also showed that some of these functions were more pronounced in some cultures than others: the more individualistic cultures (Western countries) emphasized the emotional and reminiscence function, whereas the more collectivistic cultures (Asian and South-American countries) emphasized the use of music as diversion in social settings, as a means for feeling good, dancing, and entertainment when being with friends and family. However, the social bonding function was not more prevalent in the collectivist subsample compared to the individualistic subsample. Boer's study did not specifically focus on the concept of health or wellbeing, but the findings are illustrative of similar meanings that have been stressed by health researchers, and the study was able to show some interesting cross-cultural differences.

Saarikallio (2009) specifically focused on the psychosocial functions through which music promotes wellbeing in a qualitative interview study. The informants were a small sample (N=14) of young adults (aged between 21–45) from two culturally contrasting countries, Finland and Kenya. Interviews in Finland were conducted in Finnish (the excerpts in this text are translations) and the interviews in Kenya were conducted in English. All participants were from urban areas (cities of Nairobi and Jyväskylä). Despite the small sample, a number of fundamental elements relating music to wellbeing in everyday life were observed. The recurrently emerging themes regarding psychological wellbeing in the descriptions of both Finns and Kenyans were categorized into emotional, personal, and social factors. Interview examples related to the factors are presented in Table 31.1.

The emotional domain consisted of three aspects: (1) entertainment, boredom reduction, and distraction; (2) emotional support, working through worries, getting comfort and acceptance of feelings; and (3) emotional self-expression. The first two aspects included highly similar descriptions from both countries. As regards emotional self-expression, however, Finns talked mostly about listening to music that expressed their feelings whereas Kenyans also talked a lot about singing and dancing along. The personal domain included the following three components: (1) self-identity, memories, and autobiography; (2) spirituality and self-growth; and (3) self-esteem, self-confidence, and capability. The two former aspects were relatively typical among all interviewees, while the last aspect was related to a career as musician, and therefore only mentioned by a couple of participants. The social factors included: (1) social bonding and close interpersonal relationships; (2) connection and belonging to family, relatives, and cultural identity; and (3) unity among all people. The first two aspects were again common for both Finns and Kenyans. However, only the Kenyans talked about the last one, the significance of music in

Table 31.1 Interview excerpts illustrating the different wellbeing-enhancing functions of music

Functions of music	Examples from the interviews
Emotional factors	
1) Entertainment, boredom reduction, and distraction	'I really listen quite a lot while at home, while doing dishes, cleaning, and anything. . . It's nice to have some noise there.' (A woman from Finland)
	'You listen to feel comfortable, to enjoy, when you feel bored and tired.' (A man from Kenya)
2) Emotional support and working through worries	'Music is medicine to the heart. . . Maybe if you pass through hard times then you listen to cassettes, you compose, then you forget all those hardships you passed through. At the end of the day you sleep well, because you, your mind has been sorted through.' (A man from Kenya)
	'When having those low points, it's really been the music that has kept me somewhat together. Perhaps it's so that when you're feeling bad you get some kind of support, since the songs may be melancholic and you dive in the text and in the melody, and you are allowed, you can properly grief then.' (A man from Finland)
3) Emotional self-expression	'When I'm singing alone, most of the time it's for me. When I'm singing by myself, actually, you know, I'm free. That time I'm very free, I can dance the way I want, so I can shout, I can jump, I can do whatever (laughs).' (A woman from Kenya)
	'It depends on your feelings. I think that I listen to music several hours a day, and then, based on your feelings you choose whether it's a bit heavier, or classical, or whatever it is.' (A man from Finland)
Personal factors	
1) Self-identity, memories, and autobiography	'I think listening to music is like watching a photo album. There are so many familiar songs you have listened to and they bring so many memories to you.' (A man from Finland)
	'Because, sometimes. . . musicians will sing about their experiences, other musicians will give an outline before they sing, they say, I'm singing this song because I went through this and that and I got encouragement. So, I've also gone through the same. And so. . . it has helped me to share experiences with others who, through what they went through, they ended up composing songs.' (A woman from Kenya)
2) Spirituality and self-growth	'I often experience therapeutic feelings in relation to spiritual lyrics, so that, it somehow nurtures you soul, that they are not too shallow' (A woman from Finland)
	'Those (songs) which are sacred, they usually give someone a confidence, for example, when some is ill, through listening to those music he can acquire confidence that God is there and He can heal.' (A man from Kenya)
3) Self-esteem, self-confidence, and capability	'After the presentation, I was sitting with my dad waiting for the results to be announced. And sadly, I was last out of about 15 people. And my dad was not too happy and he told me this is what you get for being too proud. You have to sit down, and practice, like the rest. So, after that, I had to prove it to myself that I can do it, so the next year I was given a piece, quite early in the year, so I practiced that piece day and night, day and night, any time I had free time. And when I got to the festival, I actually was the first.' (A man from Kenya)

Table 31.1 (Continued) Interview excerpts illustrating the different wellbeing-enhancing functions of music

Functions of music	Examples from the interviews
Social factors	
1) Social bonding and close interpersonal relationships	'As friends they (choir members) are very important for me. . . and music also. . . So both are very important. They all go together hand in hand. I can not do without friends, and having music without friends it would be like hollow, a gap.' (A woman from Kenya)
	'And sometimes when we are jamming together with other players, hey, do you know this, and then we play, anything, many hours, and we just play them through together and feel sort of unity.' (A woman from Finland)
2) Belonging to family and cultural identity	'When you talk about classical music, I'm more of a spectator, or a third person. Even if I'm the one performing it, because it really does not come from within. But when I go, maybe when I'm with my grandparents and they are singing those traditional African pieces of music and they are doing, I feel part of it, because it comes from where I come from. And I am more in touch with that kind of music.' (A man from Kenya)
	'I really had a strong feeling, after my father and his brother passed away, that now I am the one to continue that (musical) tradition, so that I am the following link in the chain of generations.' (A woman from Finland)
3) Unity among all people	'Most choirs you find, they are not like one tribe. They are different people there who are of different tribes, And a music does a big role, because music is a unison thing that tries to unite people together despite your differences, despite your race, your culture, your tribe, it plays a really big role in uniting people together.' (A woman from Kenya)

uniting nations and ethnic groups, which is rather illustrative of differences between the two countries regarding cultural diversity: Finland is a highly homogenous culture whereas Kenya includes a diversity of over 40 different ethnic groups, with a constant social and political challenge of finding mutual understanding between them. Lastly, in addition to the abovementioned psychosocial elements, the interviews showed that only Kenyans mentioned music also as a possible means for economical wellbeing (e.g. through career and employment) and as a means to build society and educate people (e.g. convincing people to do farming instead of moving to the city and ending up in slums). This is, indeed, a serious observation from the perspective of a cross-cultural study on wellbeing. It reminds us to take into account the fact that that the mental wellbeing, so urgent a concern of modern Western societies, may be overshadowed by more acute problems that threaten the political and economical wellbeing in many other countries.

In addition to finding cross-cultural similarities and differences in the array of health-enhancing functions of music, researchers may also aim to identify more detailed differences in how (e.g. through which type of music, through which music-related behaviours) these functions become realized within specific cultures and contexts. Some examples are described in the following. For instance, Good et al. (2000) investigated cultural differences in the type of music preferred for pain relief. The results showed that the musical choices were significantly related to cultural background, and that, although the majority of participants in each cultural group chose some other types of music, Caucasians most frequently chose orchestra music, African Americans chose jazz music, and Taiwanese chose harp music. The authors pointed out that, for culturally congruent care, healthcare professionals should be aware of these cultural differences in order to provide the most appropriate music for pain relieving purposes. Saarikallio (2008) examined how adolescents in Kenya and Finland regulate mood through music, and reported that, while the regulation occurred in predominantly similar ways, some differences also existed: The Kenyans included dancing and expression of positive emotions as an important part of mood regulation, and preferred jazz and hip hop music in particular, whereas the Finns emphasized the use of music as an entertaining background for other activities, talked more about discharging negative emotions through music, and preferred rock music. Wong (2005) focused on educational settings, and explored the beliefs of 10 music teachers in elementary schools in Vancouver and Hong Kong. The results demonstrated that the music teachers of the two localities held similar cognitive beliefs about the essential elements of music education in general but different beliefs about the value or impact of music education on the wellbeing-related aspects, i.e. music's effects on students' psychological or character development. Olsen (2009) compared healing aspects of shamanistic rituals in two contrasting South-American cultures, and found that both musical and conceptual similarities existed: Singing as well as musical use of a shamanic rattle were employed in both traditions as musical behaviours, and the aims of the rituals in both traditions included mediation of the opposing powers of good and evil, in order to remove the illness-causing object from the patient, and find harmony and balance between the opposite forces.

Concluding comments

The capability of music to enhance health has been appreciated in cultures across the world and throughout history. However, as a manifestation of cultural expression, music typically presents itself in a variety of different forms, and even for different purposes. The cross-cultural approach is particularly useful in finding possible universal elements as well as culture-specific characteristics, and provides a viewpoint from which to understand the meaning of music to mankind. The current chapter has reviewed some of the recent literature exploring the possible meanings of music for promoting psychological wellbeing in different cultures. As a result, it can be suggested that even though the ways may be different, the reasons may be the same: the emotional, mental, and social domains appear recurrently as fundamental elements of the music-related enhancement of psychological wellbeing in a range of cultures. However, clear cultural differences are likely to exist regarding which aspects of these general elements become emphasized in a given cultural context. One possible difference may be that individualistic cultures appreciate music particularly as a means for supporting personal emotional work whereas collectivist cultures appreciate music especially as a form of social enjoyment (see Boer 2009).

Both music and health are concepts that are composed of relatively different components and meanings in different cultures, so the definition of 'musical' practices or the 'health' objectives is not always straightforward in a cross-cultural context. Therefore, cross-cultural study needs particular sensitivity towards the conceptual aspects to make valid comparisons. Different research approaches and methodological paradigms also lead to differences in focus: a cognitive musicologist would perhaps be interested in the psychological reactions of an individual, while an ethnomusicologist would stress the importance of social aspects. Indeed, collaboration among researchers from different fields is highly advantageous for comprehensive and objective results. Interdisciplinary and collaborative approach is beneficial also from a methodological viewpoint: experimental psychologists are specialists in conducting controlled experiments and anthropologists in understanding the key elements to be measured and controlled for.

The current chapter has provided an introductory overview of the cross-cultural approach to music and health. Ironically, the chapter contains the very problem it encourages researchers to overcome: being written by a psychologist it focuses almost solely on aspects of mental health leaving out much of the discussion of music's effects on physiological health or the role of music in spirituality. Nevertheless, the acknowledgement of these disciplinary emphases and limitations is the vital starting point of any comprehensive study or of any interdisciplinary collaboration. The future will bring us conceptually and methodologically challenging but highly intriguing and rewarding years of study as the research within the cross-cultural approach on music and health begins to grow.

References

Balkwill, L.L. and Thompson, W.F. (1999). A cross-cultural investigation of the perception of emotion in music: Psychophysical and cultural cues. *Music Perception*, **17**, 43–64.

Barz, G. (2009). The performance of HIV/AIDS in Uganda: medical ethnomusicology and cultural memory. In: B.D. Koen (ed.) *The Oxford Handbook of Medical Ethnomusicology*, pp. 164–84. New York: Oxford University Press.

Blacking, J. (1973). *How Musical is Man?* Seattle, WA: University of Washington Press.

Boer, D. (2009). Music makes the people come together: social functions of music listening for young people across cultures. Doctoral thesis, Victoria University of Wellington.

Boer, D. and Fishcer, R. (2009). Intercultural bonding through shared music preferences. Paper presented at the 7th Triennial Conference of European Society for the Cognitive Sciences of Music (ESCOM 2009), 12–16 August, Jyväskylä, Finland.

Campbell, R.J., Tirri, K., Ruohotie, P., and Walberg, H. (eds.) (2004). *Cross-cultural Research: Basic Issues, Dilemmas, and Strategies*. Hämeenlinna: Research Centre for Vocational Education, University of Tampere.

Clayton, M. (2009). The social and personal functions of music in cross-cultural perspective. In: S. Hallam, I. Cross, and M. Thaut (eds.) *The Oxford Handbook of Music Psychology*, pp. 35–44. Oxford: Oxford University Press.

Davidson, J.W. (2008). Singing for self-healing, health and wellbeing. *MCA Music Forum*, Feb–Apr, 29–33.

Davis, S.F. (ed.) (2005). *Handbook of Research Methods in Experimental Psychology*. Oxford: Blackwell.

DeNora, T. (1999). Music as a technology of the self. *Poetics: Journal of Empirical Research on Literature, the Media, and the Arts*, **26**, 1–26.

Department of Education (2005). *Revised National Curriculum Statement grades R-9 (schools) policy*, pp. 1–9, 24–25. Pretoria: Department of Education.

Dissanayake, E. (2006). Ritual and ritualization: musical means of conveying and shaping emotion in humans and other animals. In: S. Brown and U. Volgsten (eds.) *Music and Manipulation: On the Social Uses and Social Control of Music*, pp. 31–56. New York: Berghahn.

During, J. (2009). Therapeutic dimensions of music in Islamic culture. In: B.D. Koen (ed.) *The Oxford Handbook of Medical Ethnomusicology*, pp. 361–92. New York: Oxford University Press.

Ember, C.R. and Ember, M. (2009). *Cross-Cultural Research Methods*. Lanham, MD: Alta Mira Press.

Erkkilä, J. (1996). *Musiikki ja tunteet musiikkiterapiassa* [*Music and Emotions in Music Therapy*]. Musiikin emotionaalisten vaikutusten kolmidimensiomalli. Hankasalmi: Havusalmen kirjapaino.

Fox, S. (2007). Arts and acculturation, a possible avenue of inquiry. Paper presented at the Regional Congress of the International Association for Cross-Cultural Psychology, 6–9 July, Mexico City, Mexico.

Friedson, S.M. (1996). *Dancing Prophets: Musical Experience in Tumbuka Healing*. Chicago, IL: University of Chicago Press.

Garnefski, N., Teerds, J., Kraaij, V., Legerstee, J., and Van den Kommer, T. (2004). Cognitive emotion regulation strategies and depressive symptoms: differences between males and females. *Personality and Individual Differences*, **36**, 267–76.

Gembris, H. (2008). Musical activities in the third age. An empirical study with amateur musicians. In: A. Daubney, E. Longhi, A. Lamont, and D.J. Hargreaves (eds.) *Musical Development and Learning*.

Conference Proceedings, 2nd European Conference on Developmental Psychology of Music, pp. 103–8. Hull: GK Publishing, S.

Gohm, C.L. (2003). Mood regulation and emotional intelligence: individual differences. *Journal of Personality and Social Psychology*, **84**(3), 594–607.

Good, M. Picot, B.L., Salem, S.G., Chin, C., Picot, S.F., and Lane, D. (2000). Cultural differences in music chosen for pain relief. *Journal of Holistic Nursing*, **18**(3), 245–60.

Gosselin, N., Fernando, N., Fritz, T., and Peretz, I. (2009). Recognition of musical emotions in Western music by African pygmies. Paper presented at the 7th Triennial Conference of European Society for the Cognitive Sciences of Music, 12–16 August, Jyväskylä, Finland.

Gouk, P. (2001). Introduction. In: P. Gouk (ed.) *Musical Healing in Cultural Contexts*, p. 8. Aldershot: Ashgate.

Greasley, A.E. and Lamont, A. (2006). Music preference in adulthood: Why do we like the music we do? In: M. Baroni, A.R. Addessi, R. Caterina, and M. Costa (eds.) *Proceedings of the 9th International Conference on Music Perception and Cognition*, pp. 960–6. Bologna, Italy: University of Bologna.

Gregory, A.H. and Varney, N. (1996). Cross-cultural comparisons in the affective response to music. *Psychology of Music*, **24**(1), 47–52.

Griswold, W. (2004). *Cultures and Societies in a Changing World*. Thousand Oaks, CA: Pine Forge Press.

Hakanen, E.A. (1994). Emotional use of music by African American adolescents. *Howard Journal of Communications*, **5**(3), 214–22.

Hakanen, E.A., Ying, L.L.S. and Wells, A. (1999). Music choice for emotional use and management by Hong Kong adolescents. *Asian Journal of Communication*, **9**(1), 72–85.

Hargreaves, D.J., Castell, K.C., Crowther, R.D. (1986). The effects of stimulus familiarity on conservation-type responses to tone sequences: A cross-cultural study. *Journal of Research in Music Education*, **34**(2), 88–100.

Hargreaves, D.J. and North, A.C. (1999). The functions of music in everyday life: Redefining the social in music psychology. *Psychology of Music*, **27**(1), 84–95.

Harwood, D.L. (1976). Universals in music: a perspective from cognitive psychology. *Ethnomusicology*, **20**, 521–33.

Hays, T. and Minichiello, V. (2005). The meaning of music in the lives of older people: a qualitative study. *Psychology of Music*, **33**, 437–51.

Himberg, T. and Thompson, M. (2009). Group synchronization of coordinated movements in a cross-cultural choir workshop. Paper presented at the 7th Triennial Conference of European Society for the Cognitive Sciences of Music (ESCOM 2009), 12–16 August, Jyväskylä, Finland.

Janzen, J. (2002). *Ngoma: Discourses of Healing in Central and Southern Africa*. Berkeley, CA: University of California Press.

Juslin, P.N. and Laukka, P. (2004). Expression, perception, and induction of musical emotions: a review and a questionnaire study of everyday listening. *Journal of New Music Research*, **33**(3), 217–38.

Juslin, P.N. and Västfjäll, D. (2008). Emotional responses to music: The need to consider underlying mechanisms. *Behavioral and Brain Sciences*, 31, 559–621.

Kenny, C. and Stige, B. (eds.) (2002). *Contemporary Voices in Music Therapy: Communication, Culture, and Community*. Oslo: Unipub Forlag.

Kessler, E.J., Hansen, C., and Shepard, R.N. (1984). Tonal schemata in the perception of music in Bali and the West. *Music Perception*, **2**, 131–65.

Kivinen, S. (2004). 'You can't do crime if you do music.' Musiikkiharrastuksen vaikutus eteläafrikkalaisen STTEP-musiikkikoulun oppilaiden elämänkuvaan. Unpublished Licenciate thesis, University of Jyväskylä.

Koen, B.D., Barz, G., and Brummel-Smith, K. (2009). Introduction: Confluence of consciousness in music, medicine, and culture. In: B.D. Koen (ed.) *The Oxford Handbook of Medical Ethnomusicology*, pp. 3–17. New York: Oxford University Press.

Kroeber, A.L. and Kluckhohn, C. (1952). *Culture: A Critical Review of Concepts and Definitions.* Vintage Books: New York.

Krumhansl, C.L. (2000). Tonality induction: A statistical approach applied cross-culturally. *Music Perception*, **17**(4), 461–79.

Krumhansl, C., Toivanen, P., Eerola, T., Toiviainen, P., Järvinen, T., and Louhivuori, J. (2000). Cross-cultural music cognition: cognitive methodology applied to North Sami yoiks. *Cognition*, **75**, 1–46.

Laiho, S. (2004). The psychological functions of music in adolescence. *Nordic Journal of Music Therapy*, **13**(1), 49–65.

Laukka, P. (2006). Uses of music and psychological well-being among the elderly. *Journal of Happiness Studies*, **8**(2), 215–41.

Lewis, G.H. (1995). Taste cultures and musical stereotypes: Mirrors of identity? *Popular Music and Society*, **19**(1), 37–58.

Locke, K. and Koen, B.D. (2009). The Lakota hoop dance as medicine for social healing. In: B.D. Koen (ed.) *The Oxford Handbook of Medical Ethnomusicology*, pp. 482–99. New York: Oxford University Press.

Liamputtong, P. (ed.) (2008). *Doing Cross-Cultural Research: Ethical and Methodological Perspectives.* Dordrecht: Springer.

Louhivuori, J. (2009). Kulttuureja vertaileva musiikkispykologia. In: J. Louhivuori and S. Saarikallio (eds.) *Musiikkipsykologia*, p. 369–91. Jyväskylä: Atena.

Lucas, G. (2002). Music Rituals of Afro-Brazilian religious groups within the ceremonies of Congado. *Yearbook for Traditional Music*, **34**, 115–27.

MacDonald, R.A.R., Hargreaves, D.J., and Miell, D.E. (eds.) (2002). *Musical identities*. Oxford: Oxford University Press.

Maher, T.F. (1976). "Need for resolution" ratings for harmonic musical intervals: A comparison between Indians and Canadians. *Journal of Cross-Cultural Psychology*, **7**(3), 259–76.

Matsumoto, D. and Van de Vijver, F.J.R. (eds.) (2010). *Cross-Cultural Research Methods in Psychology* (Cambridge University Press Series: Culture and Psychology). New York: Cambridge University Press.

Merriam, A. (1964). *The Anthropology of Music*. Evanston, IL: Northwestern University Press.

Morrison, S.J., Demorest, S.M., Aylward, E.H., Cramer, S.C., and Maravilla, K.R. (2003). FMRI investigation of cross-cultural music comprehension. *NeuroImage*, **20** (1), 378–84.

Nan, Y., Knösche, T.R., Zysset, S., and Friederici, A.D. (2008). Cross-cultural music phrase processing: an fMRI study. *Human brain mapping*, **29**(3), 312–28.

North, A. and Hargreaves, D. (2008). *The Social and Applied Psychology of Music*. Oxford: Oxford University Press.

Oldfield, A. (1993). Music therapy with families. In: M. Heal and T. Wigram (eds.) *Music therapy in health and education*, pp. 26–54. London: Jessica Kingsley Publishers.

Olsen, D.A. (2009). Shamanism, music and healing in two contrasting South-American cultural areas. In: B.D. Koen (ed.) *The Oxford Handbook of Medical Ethnomusicology*, pp. 331–60. New York: Oxford University Press.

Roseman, M. (1991). *Healing sounds from the Malaysian rainforest. Temiar music and medicine*. Berkeley, CA: University of California Press.

Roseman, M. (2009). A fourfold framework for cross-cultural, integrative research on music and medicine. In: B.D. Koen (ed.) *The Oxford Handbook of Medical Ethnomusicology*, pp. 18–45. New York: Oxford University Press.

Ruud, E. (1997). Music and the quality of life. *Nordic Journal of Music Therapy*, **6**(2), 86–97.

Saarikallio, S. (2008). Cross-cultural investigation of adolescents' use of music for mood regulation. In: *Proceedings of the 10th International Conference on Music Perception and Cognition*, 25–29 August, Sapporo, Japan.

Saarikallio, S. (2009). Cross-cultural investigation of the psychosocial mechanisms through which music promotes wellbeing. Paper presented at the 7th Triennial Conference of European Society for the Cognitive Sciences of Music (ESCOM 2009), 12–16 August, Jyväskylä, Finland.

Saarikallio, S. and Erkkilä, J. (2007). The role of music in adolescents' mood regulation. *Psychology of Music*, **35**(1), 88–109.

Salovey, P., Stroud, L. R., Woolery, A., and Epel, E. S. (2002). Perceived emotional intelligence, stress reactivity, and symptom reports: Further explorations using the trait meta-mood scale. *Psychology and Health*, **17**(5), 611–27.

Sloboda, J.A. and Juslin, P.N. (2001). Psychological perspectives on music and emotion. In: P.N. Juslin and J.A. Sloboda (eds.) *Music and Emotion: Theory and Research*, pp. 71–104. New York: Oxford University Press.

Trehub, S.E., Unyk, A.M., and Trainor, L.J. (1993). Maternal singing in cross-cultural perspective. *Infant Behavior and Development,* **16**(3), 285–95.

Tafuri, V. and Villa, D. (2002). Musical elements in vocalizations of infants aged 2–8 months. *British Journal of Music Education*, **19**(1), 73–88.

Thaut, M.H. (2005). Music in therapy and medicine: from social science to neuroscience. In: M.H. Thaut (ed.) *Rhythm, Music and the Brain: Scientific Foundations and Clinical Applications*, p. 113–36. New York: Taylor and Francis Group.

Trehub, S.E., Unyk, A.M., and Trainor, L.J. (1993). Adults identify infant-directed music across cultures. *Infant Behavior and Development*, **16**(2), 193–211.

Unyk, A.M., Trehub S.A., Trainor, L.J. and Schellenberg, E.G. (1992). Lullabies and simplicity: A cross-cultural perspective. *Psychology of Music,* **20**(1), 15.

Wells, A. (1990). Popular music and emotions: Emotional uses and management. *Journal of Popular Culture*, **24**(1), 105–17.

Wells, A. and Hakanen, E.A. (1991). The emotional use of popular music by adolescents. *Journalism Quarterly*, **68**(3), 445–54.

Wells, A., Hakanen, E.A., and Tokinoya, H. (2000). The emotional use of popular music by Japanese adolescents. In, S. Waksman (ed.) *Popular music: Intercultural interpretations*, pp. 174–81. Bowling Green: Bowling Green State University.

West, T. and Ironson, G. (2009). Effects of music on human health and wellness: Physiological measurements and research design. In: B.D. Koen (ed.) *The Oxford Handbook of Medical Ethnomusicology*, pp. 410–43. New York: Oxford University Press.

Wong, M. (2005). A cross-cultural comparison of teachers' expressed beliefs about music education and their observed practices in classroom music teaching. *Teachers and Teaching: Theory and Practice*, **11**(4), 397–418.

Zentner, M. and Scherer, K. R. (2008). Emotions evoked by the sound of music: Characterization, classification, and measurement. *Emotion*, **8**(4), 494–521.

Chapter 32

The Effects of Background Music on Health and Wellbeing

Susan Hallam

Introduction

Since the advent of recording techniques it has been possible for music to be played at any time, in any place, easily and cheaply. This has led to a proliferation of music in our lives. Commercial companies advise businesses on the best way to utilize music to attract customers, maintain their interest, and encourage them to purchase more; music is used by a range of public services to manipulate behaviour and reduce anxiety or aggressive tendencies; while individuals use music to support a variety of activities in their lives, change their moods, and create particular ambiences in their homes. Music utilized in these ways has come to be referred to as 'background music' distinguishing it from music which is actually listened to, although music which is being listened to or created by one person may be background music to another if s/he happens to be within the same sound location.

The other difficulty in differentiating background music from other forms of music is the way that our attention focus can change from moment to moment. At any one point in time the music in the background might be transformed into the foreground or vice versa (Madsen 1987). Given that these processes are internal it is impossible to establish whether music is in the background or foreground for any individual at any point in time. Even when an individual appears to be actively listening to music they may not be focusing on the music but allowing their thoughts to stray elsewhere. This phenomenon has been explicitly articulated in terms of listening and hearing, the latter seen as essentially passive, a form of reception, while the former involves concentration, focus, or activity on the part of the listener.

Despite the difficulties in distinguishing clear theoretical underpinnings for what might constitute 'pure' background music, in practice, there is a large literature devoted to examining the effects of music on behaviour and cognition, driven by a desire to understand the effect of playing music on the performance of an ongoing task, e.g. studying, driving, exercising, shopping, or eating. In this sense, and for the purpose of the following chapter, background music can be defined as the act of music being played when the music itself is not the main focus for attention. The present chapter will present evidence regarding the effects of background music defined in these terms on behaviour and cognition and will draw conclusions with regard to the subsequent impact on general health and wellbeing.

General responses to background music

Human beings respond to music in a variety of different ways. Responses can be physiological, motor, intellectual, aesthetic, emotional, or related to changes in mood or arousal. No clear patterns have emerged relating to physiological measures, responses to specific elements of background music, and perceived musical experience. The relationships are complex (Salimpoor et al. 2009), although generally music influences physiological arousal in the expected direction, i.e. exciting music leads to increased arousal, calming music the reverse (Abeles and Chung 1996). Music has very powerful effects on our moods and emotions. These responses, as those relating to arousal, are based on 'pre-wired' connections particularly related to the 'primitive' elements of music, e.g. loudness, timbre, pitch, and tempo (Peretz 2010). Emotion may also be aroused when musical expectations are disconfirmed or delayed (Meyer 1956), and in response to particular musical structures, e.g. shivers down the spine, laughter, tears, and lump in the throat (Sloboda 1991).

Preferences and familiarity also affect our responses. Favourite music has been shown to lower subjective feelings of tension whatever its nature, although physiological responses may be in the expected direction (Iwanaga and Moroki 1999). Cognitions also play a mediating role. Music may be linked with particular experiences in our lives evoking pleasant or distressing memories (Robazza et al. 1994) and is also related to identity (MacDonald et al. 2009) so exposure to calming music in a genre which is alien to that identity may increase rather than reduce arousal. For these reasons quite different types of music can change mood in the same direction (Field et al. 1998). Formal music training, perhaps because of its impact on identity, affects responses but there are no clear patterns relating to gender, age, or social class (Abeles and Chung 1996). The complex and interacting nature of the factors which influence responses means that it is difficult to predict the exact effects of any particular piece of music on any individual although there do seem to be some general trends. These will be considered now in relation to health and wellbeing.

Influences on individual responses to background music

While music, clearly, has the potential to have a positive impact on health and wellbeing, impacting as it does on arousal and mood, there are issues arising specific to the nature of background music. The first is whether the individual has selected the music to be played or whether it is imposed by others. Self-selection is likely to lead to a positive impact relating to the specific purpose for which it has been selected. Individuals display considerable metacognitive skills in relation to music and its impact. They seem to know how music can help to achieve the particular aim that they have set for themselves. For instance, Cassidy and MacDonald (2009) found that performance and lived experience in a game-driving task were best when participants selected the background music for themselves. Kotsopoulou and Hallam (2010) have shown that young people recognize the kinds of studying tasks where music will interfere with their success, know what kinds of music will support their learning, and turn music off if they feel that it is interfering. These skills seem to develop over time and are not evident in younger children who believe that they work better if they like the music even where this is not the case (Hallam and Godwin 2000). The evidence to date suggests that individuals have considerable skill in self-selecting background music to meet their particular needs at any specific time, including helping them to relax, making a boring task less tedious, enhancing concentration for a difficult task, or reinforcing a particular mood state, the latter not always in a positive direction.

Secondly, music is closely related to identity (see MacDonald et al. 2009). Music that is selected to be played in the background reflects that identity. Some music, referred to by North and Hargreaves (2008) as 'problem music', can through its lyrics promote attitudes and behaviours which may not be in the best interests of the health and wellbeing of the individual who has selected the music. Perhaps more importantly, this may then affect those with whom they interact, or who may be exposed to the music, for instance younger siblings. Even where music is not considered 'problematic' it may be influential. For instance, there is evidence that the level of playing country music with its focus on problems commonly experienced in everyday life, for instance, relationship difficulties, alcohol abuse, and alienation from work may negatively impact on those who are suicidal. Research in 49 metropolitan boroughs in the USA found that when greater airtime was devoted to country music there was a higher suicide rate even when other factors were taken into account (Stack and Gundlach 1992).

Thirdly, background music can have indirect effects on health and wellbeing through the behaviour it can elicit. If background music influences the nature of our purchasing behaviour, or encourages us to spend more than we can afford this could have an impact on our financial position, our lifestyle and, ultimately, health, and wellbeing.

Fourthly, if background music is imposed whether in a public space, in an on-hold telephone situation, or at home it could, in some cases, cause extreme distress. In a public or telephone situation the individual can take action to remove him or herself from the situation but at home this is more problematic and can lead to legal action being taken to restrain the source. The type of music and whether it is live or recorded is irrelevant here. Classical musicians practising can be as irritating as someone playing loud rock music.

A large survey of people's views of background music played in public places in the UK found that 34% of the general public found it 'annoying', although 36% did not notice it. Older people (45–54-year-olds) were more disturbed (45%) than younger respondents (15–25-year-olds) (21%), as were those of higher socioeconomic status (51%). The group for whom it created real problems were the hard of hearing. Eighty-six per cent reported that it frequently drowned out speech and announcements, this being particularly problematic in restaurants. It also impacted on them in the home when played on radio and TV as people were speaking (National Opinion Poll 1998). The playing of background music in public places also impacts on those working in those environments. A survey, carried out by the UK Noise Association (2007) found that 40% of employees disliked it, 28% tried to ignore it, and only 7% actually liked it. Such is some people's dislike of background music that various pressure groups have been set up to lobby for its removal.

The previous two sections have considered issues relating to general and individual responses to background music. The following sections explore research focusing on the effects of background music on specific populations and in health situations where the use of music has been shown to have an impact on wellbeing.

The use of music to promote the health and wellbeing of children

Perhaps the most striking example of the power of music to impact on health comes from research on babies born prematurely. In comparison with groups not provided with background music, music-exposed groups gain weight, increase food intake, and reduce their length of stay in hospital (e.g. Cassidy and Standley 1995). These effects seem to be maintained across a range of variables including the gestational age of the infant, the volume of the music (within certain parameters), the means of delivery (in a free field or through earphones), and the birth weight of the infant (Standley 2002). Music also contributes to improving the occurrence of quiet sleep states, reduces the extent of crying, and lowers mother anxiety. Improvement seems to occur on a daily basis indicating a cumulative effect (Lai et al. 2006).

If music is played by adults in the home, children may be passive recipients of it. This can lead to marked changes in their behaviour. Several studies have shown that children of primary school age exhibit increased activity levels when exposed to music (Furman 1978) and that fast exciting music has the most dramatic effect, which can be detrimental to good behaviour (Reiber 1965; Ferguson et al. 1994; Hallam and Godwin 2000). These effects seem to be particularly powerful in children with emotional and behavioural difficulties. Relaxing quiet background music can improve behaviour and on-task performance in these children (e.g. Hallam and Price, 1998; Jackson and Owens, 1999) and induces physiological changes including reductions in systolic and diastolic blood pressure, pulse rate, and temperature (Savan 1999).

Use of music to reduce anxiety and increase wellbeing

A frequent use of background music in public places, by organizations and individuals is to manipulate arousal levels and moods. In a review of music's use in hospitals, Standley (1995) identified reducing pain, anxiety, or stress; enhancing the effects of anaesthetic/analgesic drugs or reducing their usage; and reducing the length of hospitalization as the most common applications. Music was found to have a favourable impact on almost all of the medically-related conditions studied, with children responding more positively than adults and infants and females more positively than males. Interestingly, behavioural and physiological measures tended to present more positive outcomes than patients' self-reports.

Calming background music has been shown to have a direct impact on biological indicators of stress such as cortisol (e.g. Flaten et al. 2006) and blood pressure (e.g. Triller et al. 2006), in addition to perceived anxiety (Pelletier 2004), although the level of effectiveness depends on the type of stress, age, the way the music is used, musical preferences, and prior level of musical experience. Numerous studies have indicated that music can help to alleviate stress in patients waiting for treatment. For example, Cooke et al. (2005) found that listening to selected preferred music during the preoperative wait reduced anxiety in day surgery patients. Music can also be effective during some treatments. For instance, children having casts fitted showed less increase in heart rate compared with controls when music was playing (Liu et al. 2007). Similarly, anxiety relating to dental treatment can be reduced through background music (Bare and Dundes 2004). It can also assist in promoting relaxation to aid recovery. For instance, there is a greater impact on reduction in heart rate, respiratory rate, myocardial oxygen demand, and anxiety following heart attacks when music is played in the recovery environment and these effects are maintained over a longer period of time (White 1999).

Older people specifically report that music reduces anxiety and stress levels, increasing thresholds for pain endurance, reducing recovery and shortening convalescent periods after surgical procedures. While active music making plays a crucial role, listening to recorded music is also important providing 'inner happiness, inner contentment and inner peace' (Hays and Minichiello 2005).

Background music can also contribute to alleviating anxiety in pregnancy (e.g. Yang et al. 2009) and stress in childbirth (for a review see McKinney 1990). Music selected to be played by the mother can assist in cuing rhythmic breathing and relaxation, prompt positive associations, and help focus attention on the music as a diversion from pain and hospital sounds (e.g. Hanser et al. 1983), although not all mothers find this use of music appealing (Sammons 1984).

Although research is at an early stage, the ability of music to lower stress and increase feelings of wellbeing seems to be related to improved immune system functioning as measured by levels of salivary immunoglobulin A, an indicator of the ability of the respiratory system to fight off infection. While the most positive effects are related to live music, there is evidence that background music can also have an impact (Charnetski and Brennan 1998).

Given the capacity of music to induce relaxation it is not surprising that it has been shown to be able to induce and improve the quality of sleep. Playing relaxing background music for

45 minutes at the sleep times of 10 to 11-year-olds improved its quality (Tan 2004), while women with sleep disorders over the age of 70 showed decreased time to the onset of sleep, decreases in the number of night time disturbances and improvement in the subjective experience of sleep (Johnson 2003). These findings are supported by a recent meta-analysis of the impact of music-assisted relaxation for sleep in adults and elders with and without sleep problems (de Niet et al. 2009). These findings seem to generalize across cultures (e.g. Deshmukh et al. 2009).

Background music in commercial environments

Unsurprisingly, there has been considerable research on the use of background music in commercial environments (see North and Hargreaves 2008, for a review). The extent to which this impacts on health and wellbeing depends on whether individuals are induced through music to behave in ways that might be detrimental to them. For instance, Milliman (1982) found that when slow music was played in supermarkets it led to customers shopping more slowly and spending more money. Slow music played in a restaurant had a similar effect leading to slower eating and greater expenditure (Milliman 1986). The playing of certain types of music may affect what is bought. For example, Areni and Kim (1993) played classical music and pop music in a wine cellar. They found that although the two different types of music did not lead to customers buying any more wine, classical music led to customers buying more expensive wine. Similarly, providing the right 'fit' of music to products can induce customers into entering shops (see North and Hargreaves 2008, for a review), classical music tending to create an upmarket feel (North et al. 2000a). Once in the shop customers are more likely to make a purchase. Music playing while on hold on the telephone can also sustain customer's patience, relaxing music being the most effective, perhaps because it causes the least offence to the majority of people (North et al. 1999). In all of these cases, the extent to which the induced behaviours impact on health and wellbeing depend on the nature of the products and services on offer and the extent to which they may promote unhealthy behaviours or encourage individuals to spend beyond their means. For instance, spending more in the supermarket or restaurant might lead to health problems associated with being overweight or drinking too much alcohol, while expenditure on computer games may encourage sedentary behaviour. Whether this is actually the case in practice will, of course, depend on the influence of the many other factors which impinge on an individual's behaviour.

Background music at work

Songs have long been utilized to support work related activities, and the advent of recorded music in the twentieth century increased the use of music in the workplace to maintain morale, reduce boredom and fatigue, improve productivity and reduce errors. It is no coincidence that this practice became widespread during the Second World War. The BBC's *Music While You Work* programme continued long after the war effort giving an indication of how successful the cheerful, lively music was in enhancing the moods and productivity of the workers. Subsequent research has supported the effectiveness of music enhancing mood (for a review, see North and Hargreaves 2008), although in some circumstances a positive mood can be detrimental to work performance. For instance, Au et al. (2003) found that when music was used to induce a positive mood in traders on financial markets they lost money, perhaps because it induced risk taking, whereas music that generated a neutral or negative mood led to profits.

Surveys have shown that many people enjoy work more when music is played (e.g. Music Works 2009). The introduction of personalized systems of listening to music has facilitated the individualized selection of preferred music. A survey of employees' use of music on personal players in the office (Haake 2006) established that 80% listened to music at work, on average for 36% of the time. Music most often accompanied routine tasks working alone, word processing, web-surfing, and emailing and was reported to improve concentration and block out unwanted noise. It also reduced stress, enhanced feelings of wellbeing and enhanced the ambience of the work place, providing a topic of conversation with work colleagues. For those doing low-demand tasks music relieved boredom. Disadvantages included music being played too loudly and interfering with the work of others and communication when people were wearing headphones. There may be a role for the use of personal players in open plan offices where the presence of general background noise is a particular problem, reducing performance and job satisfaction, and leading to increased stress and health problems (e.g. Evans and Johnson 2000; Knez and Hygge 2002).

Where personalized listening is allowed there have been significant improvements in perform-ance, enhanced morale, and greater commitment to remain in post, and, overall, a reduction in stress (Oldham et al. 1995; Lesuik 2005) although there are differences between those working on simple or complex tasks (Oldham et al. 1995). Where work is simple and repetitive music reduces boredom but where tasks are complex it can interfere with performance as might be expected on the basis of the Yerkes–Dodson law which suggests that internal arousal levels optimal for particular tasks vary according to task difficulty, the more complex the task the lower the optimal arousal level (Yerkes and Dodson 1908).

Effects of background music in everyday life

Recent studies of self-selected music listening in daily life report that the functions of music listening frequently relate to mood regulating strategies and the support a range of activities. (e.g. Thayer et al. 1994; DeNora 2000; Sloboda et al. 2001; North et al. 2004a; Sloboda et al. 2009). As people listen to music that they like their feelings of wellbeing are usually enhanced (Juslin and Laukka 2004). Individuals apply metacognitive skills when selecting music for mood manage-ment, although there are individual differences, females tending to be more skilled than males (Sloboda 1999; North et al. 2000b). These skills seem to develop through experience of choosing, listening and responding to different music and evaluating its impact on desired outcomes (Batt-Rawden and DeNora 2005).

The generation of positive mood states may also increase altruism. Working with children aged 10–11 years, Hallam et al. (2002) developed short written scenarios where the children could select a course of action which was either altruistic or selfish. More altruistic intentions towards others were reported when calming, relaxing music was being played in the background as opposed to no-music or exciting aggressive music. Similarly, North et al. (2004b) either played pop music which students liked or highly complex computer music which elicited a good deal of annoyance in a gym. As people left the gym they were asked to either sign a petition in support of a fictional sporting charity or distribute leaflets on behalf of the same charity. The pop music affected the distribution of leaflets in a positive manner, although it had no effect on signing the petition.

Not all music generates positive effects on mood and behaviour. Music may contribute to the development of identities which are antisocial in nature, although findings relating to the changes in attitudes towards violence and women following exposure to particular types of rap (Fried 1997) and the relationships between heavy metal music and suicidal thoughts (Stack et al. 1994; Scheel and Westefield 1999), anger (Gowensmith and Bloom 1997), and the increased acceptance of negative attitudes and violence towards women (Lawrence and Joyner 1991) are inconclusive. A study of the perceptions of listeners revealed that very few believed that music affected their actual behaviour (Gardstrom 1999). The direct effects of listening to particular types of music on violent behaviour depend on a range of complex factors and listening is unlikely, of itself, to promote aggression, but for those already predisposed to violence, already holding the views expressed in the music, it may offer support for particular actions.

We also know little about the impact these lyrics may have on the developing identities of those who are exposed regularly from a young age or those who are portrayed negatively. Currently, a quarter of teenage girls in the UK suffer physical violence at the instigation of their boyfriend, while one-third has suffered an unwanted sexual act. The abuse tends not to be reported, partially through fear of the relationship ending, but also because it is seen as 'normal' (Barter et al. 2009). Research needs to address not only whether music affects the behaviour of perpetrators but also the acquiescence of their victims.

Beyond its uses in changing mood and reinforcing identity music can be used to support other activities. For instance, it can support driving where it increases concentration and prevents people falling asleep (Cummings et al. 2001), although it can decrease performance if it disrupts attention (Stutts et al. 2001; Dibben and Williamson 2007). Overall, the effects depend on the nature and complexity of the driving conditions and the nature, speed and intensity of the music (see Sloboda et al. 2009). Music can also support exercise, not necessarily by improving performance per se but by distracting individuals from any discomfort that they are experiencing (e.g. Ferguson et al. 1994; Pujol and Langefield 1999). The evidence from studies of the music selected to accompany exercise has suggested that music of moderate or faster tempo is preferred for higher-intensity exercise (Karageorghis et al. 2006, 2008) supporting the notion that given choice music is selected to create the appropriate mood and arousal level for the activity to be undertaken, leading to more successful outcomes which in turn help to maintain self-esteem and enhance wellbeing.

Conclusions

The playing of music in the background is not new. Music perceived as an art form to be revered and listened to in silence is a relatively recent phenomenon (Goehr 2007). The development of recording techniques has made it possible to play music in a wide variety of environments at little cost, while the introduction of personalized listening devices has provided individuals with the ability to listen to music of their choice whenever they wish. Many clearly learn to utilize music in ways which are beneficial to themselves, but others need support in developing the necessary metacognitive skills. We know relatively little about the ways in which individuals acquire these skills and what factors might affect their acquisition. This is clearly an area for future research.

Music has a very powerful impact on arousal, emotions, and moods and as a result can influence behaviour. The full implications of this are still emerging. While music can be used to positive effect to enhance health and wellbeing this is not always the case, negative effects are frequently found when individuals do not have control of the music and it is a poor 'fit' in relation to their self-perceptions and needs. Walking away can resolve this in many situations but where this is not possible individuals may experience considerable distress.

References

Abeles, H.F. and Chung, J.W. (1996). Responses to music. In: D.A. Hodges (ed.) *Handbook of Music Psychology*, PP. 285–342. San Antonia, CA: IMR Press.

Areni, C.S. and Kim, D. (1993). The influence of background music on shopping behaviour: classical versus top forty music in a wine store. *Advances in Consumer Research,* **20**, 336–40.

Au, K., Chan, F., Wang, D., and Vertinsky, I. (2003). Mood in foreign exchange trading: cognitive processes and performance. *Organizational Behavior and Human Decision Processes,* **91**, 322–38.

Bare, L.C. and Dundes, L. (2004). Strategies for combating dental anxiety. *Journal of Dental Education,* **68**(11), 1172–7.

Barter, C., McCarry, M., Berridge, D., and Evans, K. (2009). *Partner exploitation and violence in teenage intimate relationships.* National Society for Prevention of Cruelty to Children.

Batt-Rawden, K. and DeNora, T. (2005). Music and informal learning in everyday life. *Music Education Research,* **7**, 289–304.

Cassidy, G. and MacDonald, R. (2009). The effects of music choice on task performance : A study of the impact of self-selected and experimenter-selected music on driving game performance and experience. *Psychology of Music,* **33**(2), 357–86.

Cassidy, J.W. and Standley, J.M. (1995). The effect of music listening on physiological responses of premature infants in the MCU. *Journal of Music Therapy,* **32**(4), 208–27.

Charnetski, C.F. and Brennan, F.X. Jr. (1998). Effect of music and auditory stimuli on secretory immunoglobulin A (IgA). *Perceptual Motor Skills,* **87**, 1163–70.

Cooke, M., Chaboyer, W., Schluter, P., and Hiratos, M. (2005). The effect of music on preoperative anxiety in day surgery. *Journal of Advanced Nursing,* **52**(1), 47–55.

Cummings, R., Kopesell, T.D., Moffat, J.M., and Rivara, F.P. (2001). Drowsiness, counter-measures to drowsiness, and the risk of a motor vehicle crash. *Injury Prevention,* **7**, 194–9.

De Niet, G., Tiemens, B., Lendemeijer, B., and Hutschemaekers, G. (2009). Music-assisted relaxation to improve sleep quality: meta-analysis. *Journal of Advanced Nursing,* **65**(7), 1356–64.

DeNora, T. (2000). *Music in Everyday Life.* Cambridge: Cambridge University Press.

Deshmukh, A.D., Sarvaiya, A.A., Seethalakshmi, R., and Nayak, A.S. (2009). The effect of Indian classical music on quality of sleep in depressed patients: A randomized controlled trial. *Nordic Journal of Music Therapy,* **18**(1), 70–8.

Dibben, N. and Williamson, V. (2007). An exploratory survey of in-vehicle music listening. *Psychology of Music,* **35**, 571–89.

Evans, G.W. and Johnson, D. (2000). Stress and open-office noise. *Journal of Applied Psychology,* **85**, 779–83.

Ferguson, A.R., Carbonneau, M.R. and Chambliss, C. (1994). Effects of positive and negative music on performance of a karate drill. *Perceptual Motor Skills,* **78**, 1217–18.

Field, T., Martinez, A. Nawrocki, T., Pickens, J., Fox, N.A. and Schanberg, S. (1998). Music shifts frontal EEG in depressed adolescents. *Adolescence,* **33**(129), 109–16.

Flaten, M.A., Asli, O., and Simonsen, T. (2006). The effect of stress on absorption of acetaminophen. *Psychopharmocology,* **185**(4), 471–8.

Fried, C.B. (1997). Bad rap for rap: Bias in reactions to music lyrics. *Journal of Applied Social Psychology,* **26**(23), 2135–46.

Furman, C.E. (1978). The effect of musical stimuli on the brainwave production of children. *Journal of Music Therapy,* **15**, 108–17.

Gardstrom, S.C. (1999). Music exposure and criminal behavior: Perceptions of juvenile offenders. *Journal of Music Therapy,* **36**(3), 207–21.

Goehr, L. (2007). *Imaginary Museum of Musical Works: an essay in the philosophy of music.* Oxford: Oxford University Press.

Gowensmith, W.N. and Bloom, L.J. (1997). The effects of heavy metal music on arousal and anger. *Journal of Music Therapy,* **1**, 33–45.

Haake, A.B. (2006). *Music-listening practices in workplace settings in the UK.* In M. Baroni, A.R. Addessi, R. Caterina and M. Costa (eds.) *Proceedings of the 9th International Conference on Music Perception and Cognition.* University of Bologna, Bologna, Italy.

Hallam, S. and Godwin, C. (2000). The effects of background music on primary school pupils' performance on a writing task. Paper presented at the annual conference of the British Educational Research Association, University of Wales, Cardiff.

Hallam, S. and Price, J. (1998). Can the use of background music improve the behaviour and academic performance of children with emotional and behavioural difficulties? *British Journal of Special Education*, 25(2), 88–91.

Hallam, S., Price, J., and Katsarou, G. (2002). The Effects of Background Music on Primary School Pupils' Task Performance. *Educational Studies*, 28(2), 111–22.

Hanser, S., Larson, S.C. and O'Connell, A.S. (1983). The effect of music on relaxation of expectant mothers during labor. *Journal of Music Therapy*, 20(2), 50–8.

Hays, T. and Minichiello, V. (2005). The meaning of music in the lives of older people: a qualitative study. *Psychology of Music*, 33, 437–51.

Iwanaga, M., and Moroki, Y. (1999). Subjective and physiological responses to music stimuli controlled over activity and preference. *Journal of Music Therapy*, XXXVI(1), 26–38.

Jackson, J.T. and Owens, J.L. (1999). A stress management classroom tool for teachers of children with BD. *Intervention in School and Clinic*, 35(2), 74–8.

Johnson, J.E. (2003). The use of music to promote sleep in older women. *Journal of Community Health Nursing*, 20(1), 27–35.

Juslin, P.N. and Laukka, P. (2004). Expression, perception and induction of musical emotions: A review and a questionnaire study of everyday listening. *Journal of New Music Research*, 33, 217–38.

Karageorghis, C.I., Jones, L., and Low, D.C. (2006). Relationship between exercise, heart rate and music tempo preference. *Research Quarterly for Exercise and Sport*, 77(2), 240–4.

Karageorghis, C.I., Jones, L. and Stuart, D.P. (2008). Psychological effects of music tempi during exercise. *International Journal of Sports Medicine*, 29(7), 613–19.

Kotsopoulou, A. and Hallam, S. (2010). The perceived impact of playing music while studying: age and cultural differences. *Educational Studies*, 36 (4), 431–40.

Knez, I., and Hygge, S. (2002). Irrelevant speech and indoor lighting: Effects on cognitive performance and self reported affected. *Applied Cognitive Psychology*, 16, 709–18.

Lai, H., Chen, S., Chang, F., Hsieh, M., Huang, H., and Chang, S. (2006). Randomized controlled trial of music during kangaroo care on maternal state anxiety and preterm infants' responses. *International Journal of Nursing Studies*, 43, 139–46.

Lawrence, S. and Joyner, D.J. (1991). The effects of sexually violent rock music on males' acceptance of violence against women. *Psychology of Women quarterly*, 15, 49–63.

Lesuik, T. (2005). The effect of music listening on work performance. *Psychology of Music*, 33(2), 173–91.

Liu, R.W., Mehta, P., Fortuna, S., Armstrong, D.G., Cooperman, D.R., Thompson, G.H., et *al.* (2007). A randomized prospective study of music therapy for reducing anxiety during cast room procedures. *Journal of Pediatric Orthopaedics*, 27(7), 831–3.

MacDonald, R., Hargreaves, D.J., and Miell, D. (2009). Musical identities. In S. Hallam, I. Cross, and M. Thayer (eds.) *Oxford Handbook of Music Psychology*, pp. 462–70. Oxford: Oxford University Press.

Madsen, C.K. (1987). Background music: Competition for focus of attention. In C.K. Madsen and C.A. Prickett (eds.) *Applications of research in music behaviour*, PP. 315–24. Tucaloosa, AL: The University of Alabama Press.

McKinney, C.H. (1990). Music therapy in obstetrics: a review. *Music Therapy Perspectives*, 8, 57–60.

Meyer, L.B. (1956). *Emotion and meaning in music*. Chicago, IL: University of Chicago Press.

Milliman, R.E. (1982). Using background music to affect the behaviour of supermarket shoppers. *Journal of Marketing*, 46, 86–91.

Milliman, R.E. (1986). The influence of background music on the behaviour of restaurant patrons. *Journal of Consumer Research*, 13, 286–9.

Music Works (2009). *Radio in the workplace: Increasing morale and productivity*. Available at: http://www.musicworksforyou.com (accessed 3 January 2010).

National Opinion Poll. (1998). *Muzak: Music to whose ears?* London: Royal National Institute for the Deaf.

North, A.C. and Hargreaves, D.J. (2008). *The social and applied psychology of music*. Oxford: Oxford University Press.

North, A.C., Hargreaves, D.J. and McKendrick, J. (1999). The influence of in-store music on wine selections. *Journal of Applied Psychology, 84*(2), 271–76.

North, A.C., Hargreaves, D.J. and McKendrick, J. (2000a). The effects of music on atmosphere and purchase intentions in a bank and a bar. *Journal of Applied Social Psychology, 30*, 1504–22.

North, A.C., Hargreaves, D.J. and O'Neill, S.A. (2000b). The importance of music to adolescents. *British Journal of Educational Psychology, 70*, 255–72.

North, A.C., Hargreaves, D.J., and Hargreaves, J.J. (2004a). Uses of music in everyday life. *Music Perception, 22*, 41–77.

North, A.C., Tarrant, M., and Hargreaves, D.J. (2004b). The effects of music on helping behaviour: a field study. *Environment and Behavior, 36*, 266–75.

Oldham, G., Cummings, A., Mischel, L., Schmidtke, J. and Zhou, J. (1995). Listen while you work? Quasi-experimental relations between personal-stereo headset use and employee work responses. *Journal of Applied Psychology, 80*(5), 547–64.

Pelletier, C.L. (2004). The effect of music on decreasing arousal due to stress. *Journal of Music Therapy, 41*, 192–214.

Peretz, I. (2010). Towards a neurobiology of musical emotions. In P.N. Juslin and J.A. Sloboda (eds.) *Handbook of Music and Emotion: Theory, Research, Applications,* pp. 99–126. Oxford: Oxford University Press.

Pujol, T.J. and Langefield, M.E. (1999). Influence of music on Wingate Anaerobic Test performance. *Perceptual and Motor Skills, 88*, 292–96.

Reiber, M. (1965). The effect of music on the level of activity of children. *Psychonomic Science, 3*, 325–26.

Robazza, C., Macaluso, C., and D'Urso, V. (1994). Emotional reactions to music by gender, age and expertise. *Perceptual and Motor Skills, 79*, 939–44.

Salimpoor, V.N., Benovoy, M., Longo, G., Cooperstock, J.R. and Zatorre, R. J. (2009). The rewarding aspects of music listening are related to degree of emotional arousal. *PLoS One, 4*(10), e7487.

Sammons, L.N. (1984). The use of music by women during childbirth. *Journal of Nurse-midwifery, 29*, 266–70.

Savan, A. (1999). The effect of background music on learning. *Psychology of Music, 27*(2), 138–46.

Scheel, K.R. and Westefield, J.S. (1999). Heavy metal music and adolescent suicidality: an empirical investigation. *Adolescence, 34*(134), 253–73.

Sloboda, J. (1991). Music structure and emotional response: some empirical findings. *Psychology of Music, 19*(2), 110–20.

Sloboda, J.A. (1999). Everyday uses of music listening: a preliminary study. In S.W. Yi (ed.) *Music, mind and science,* pp. 354–69. Seoul: Western Music Institute.

Sloboda, J.A., O'Neill, S.A. and Ivaldi, A. (2001). Functions of music in everyday life: An exploratory study using the Experience Sampling Method. *Musicae Scientiae,* V, 9–32.

Sloboda, J., Lamont, A., and Greasley, A. (2009). Choosing to hear music: motivation, process, and effect. In S. Hallam, I. Cross, and M. Thayer (eds.) *Oxford Handbook of Music Psychology,* pp. 431–330. Oxford: Oxford University Press.

Stack, S., and Gundlach, J.H. (1992). The effect of country music on suicide. *Social Forces, 71*, 211–18.

Stack, S., Gundlach, J., and Reeves, J.L. (1994). The Heavy Metal Subculture and Suicide. *Suicide and Life-threatening Behaviour, 24*(1), 15–23.

Standley, J.M. (1995). Music as a therapeutic intervention in medical and dental treatment: research and clinical applications. In: T. Wigram, B. Saperstone, and R. West (eds.) *The art and science of music therapy: a handbook,* pp. 3–22. Langhorne, PA: Harwood.

Standley, J.M. (2002). A meta-analysis of the efficacy of music therapy for premature infants. *Journal of Pediatric Nursing, 17*, 107–13.

Stevens, K.M. (1992). My room—not theirs! A case study of music during childbirth. *Australian College of Midwives Inc Journal, 5*(3), 27–30.

Stutts, J.C., Reinfurt, D.W. Staplin, L., and Rodgman, E.A. (2001). *The role of driver distraction in traffic crashes*. Washington, DC: Report prepared for the AAA foundation for traffic safety.

Tan, L.P. (2004). The effects of background music on quality of sleep in elementary school children. *Journal of Music Therapy*, **41**(2), 128–50.

Thayer, R.E., Newman, J.R., and McClain, T.M. (1994). Self-regulation of mood: Strategies for changing a bad mood, raising energy, and reducing tension. *Journal of Personality and Social Psychology*, **67**, 910–25.

Triller, N., Erzen, D., Dub, S., Petrinic-Primozic, M., and Kosnik, M. (2006). Music during bronchoscopic examination: the physiological effects: a randomized trial. *Respiration*, **73**, 95–9.

UK Noise Association (2007). *Year of National Noise Strategy*. Kent: UK Noise Association.

White, J.M. (1999). Effects of relaxing music on cardiac autonomic balance and anxiety after acute myocardial infarction. *American Journal of Critical Care*, **8**(4), 220–30.

Wilson, S. (2003). The effect of music on perceived atmosphere and purchase intentions in a restaurant. *Psychology of Music*, **31**(1), 93–112.

Yang, M., Li, L., Zhu, H., Alexander, I.M., Liu, S., Zhou, W., et *al.* (2009). Music therapy to relieve anxiety in pregnant women on bedrest: A randomized controlled trial. *The American Journal of Maternal/Child Nursing*, **34**(5), 316–23.

Yerkes, R.M. and Dodson, J.D. (1908). The relation of strength of stimulus to rapidity of habit-formation. *Journal of Comparative Neurological Psychology*, **18**, 459–82.

Chapter 33

Pop Music Subcultures and Wellbeing

Adrian C. North and David J. Hargreaves

Introduction

Whereas much of the research on the role of music in promoting wellbeing addresses therapeutic uses, the present chapter concerns a broader and more negative aspect of wellbeing, namely whether pop music subcultures promote self-harming and other factors related to delinquency. Put simply, this chapter considers whether listening to certain forms of pop music is related to a range of behaviours that society deems undesirable. In effect, it represents a greatly condensed version of the extensive review of the field that we published in our 2008 book *The Social and Applied Psychology of Music*. We begin by briefly describing some of the instances where pop music has caused public outrage around the world. From here we address whether there is a relationship between delinquency and an interest in particularly rap and rock music, before briefly noting how an interest in these musical styles is also associated with the commission by young fans of a range of other undesirable behaviours. We then progress to a consideration of another possible consequence of musical taste that, in addition to delinquency, has also caused grave concern, namely self-harming and suicide. Finally, we address whether adolescents can accurately comprehend pop music lyrics, and whether pop music should be censored.

Why is the topic important?

Just one example of why research on music and subcultures is important can be found in Litman and Farberow (1994). They describe how, on 23 December 1985, Ray Belknap and James Vance from Reno, Nevada spent the afternoon drinking beer, smoking cannabis, and listening to the *Stained Class* album by heavy metal band Judas Priest. Belknap had just lost his job and Vance had just quit his, leading to an angry confrontation with his mother. Late in the afternoon, they jumped out of a first-floor window and took a sawn-off shotgun to a nearby churchyard with the intention of fulfilling a suicide pact they had made earlier that afternoon. When they arrived, 18-year-old Ray shouted 'life sucks' put the gun under his chin and pulled the trigger, causing fatal injuries. A few moments later, 20-year-old James did the same, and although he did not die, he did shoot off the lower portion of his face. The boys' parents sued Judas Priest and their record company, claiming that the album their sons had been listening to all afternoon drove them to suicide. One song on the album 'Beyond the realm of death' contained the lyrics, 'He had enough, he couldn't take any more/I have left the world behind/This is my life I'll decide, not you'. Another song, 'Heros end', featured the lyrics, 'Why do you have to die if you're a hero'. The parents later claimed that the suicide attempts resulted from the words, 'Do it' having been recorded backwards into another song on the album *Better by you, better than me*. The parents lost this particular case, but nonetheless this has not stopped countless parents, pressure groups, and politicians from taking pop musicians or their record company to court, or attempting to ban certain albums from public sale. This in turn raises the question of whether pop music has a bad effect on young people.

There is, however, a long history of concerns regarding the potentially negative impact of the arts on young people, dating back to the time of the Ancient Greek philosophers. Plato said in *The Republic*, 'Shall we allow our children to listen to any story anyone happens to make up, and so receive into their minds ideas that are often the very opposite of those we shall think they ought to have when they are adults?'. Plato is, in short, arguing that society should be cautious of the arts, because they could provide messages to young people that society does not believe are good for them. Aristotle went a step further and actually criticized new music in particular, claiming that, 'Any musical innovation is full of danger to the whole state, and ought to be prohibited . . . [since] when modes of music change, the fundamental laws of the state always change with them'. More simply, Aristotle draws a direct line between specifically music and a threat to society.

If one skips forward into the modern era, it is clear that a very large number of new musical innovations have been treated in some way as threatening the wellbeing of society and/or its members. The premiere of Stravinsky's pioneering *Rite of Spring* in Paris in 1913 caused a riot in the theatre. Similarly, the advent of ragtime in the 1910s and 1920s was criticized for supposedly promoting sexuality, and Nazi Germany prohibited jazz on similar grounds (McDonald 1988). In 1953, jukeboxes were outlawed within hearing distance of churches within six counties of Southern Carolina. Local townsfolk were concerned that the rock 'n' roll music played from them may float across the air from a nearby diner and somehow make its way into places of worship. Where widespread societal concern regarding rock 'n' roll really first comes to light, however, is in 1954. At the time, in some parts of American society, the term 'rock "n" roll' was slang for 'sex'. So 'rock "n" roll music' was understood by many people directly as being music about sex. Congresswoman Ruth Thompson argued that it should be illegal to mail such pornographic material, and introduced legislation concerning this. And since the mail was one of the most common ways of distributing and buying music at the time, Thompson's attempt, had it been successful, would have drastically reduced the market for rock 'n' roll music.

If one moves forwards through time, one can clearly see that the types of behaviours that pop musicians have been accused of inciting have become increasing extreme. During his June 1956 television appearance on the *Milton Berle Show*, Elvis Presley performed his new hit song, 'Hound dog'. Video of the performance can be found on several file-sharing websites. The appearance led to outrage, because of Elvis' supposedly sexual dancing, and particularly the immoral effect that this might have on young viewers. The outcry was so strong that, just 3 weeks later, the second time Elvis Presley appeared on coast-to-coast television, he again performed 'Hound dog', this time being forced to wear a tuxedo and to address the song to a basset hound which was sat next to him, wearing a top hat. Elvis later described this as the most embarrassing moment throughout his entire career. Just a few weeks later, Elvis' tour of southern Florida in August 1956 saw his concerts filmed by the FBI for any evidence of sexual dancing.

However, it is interesting to contrast the 1956 reaction to Elvis with the reaction nearly 50 years later to Marilyn Manson. Manson has been accused, although it remains unproven, of inciting a high school shooting, of smoking dried human excrement on stage, of handing out cocaine to the audience, and of attempting to get the audience to pass young female virgins to the front of the stage so the band could have sex with them later. These accusations certainly tell us far more about the attitude of the American Christian right to Manson than they do about his actual behaviour; but they also clearly illustrate an increase in the reprehensibility of the kinds of behaviour that society believes pop music might be able to encourage. Indeed, the degree to which Manson has been criticized can be shown easily with two brief examples. In the 2000 US Presidential campaign, the Democratic Party candidate for the Vice-Presidency, Joe Lieberman, described Manson as, 'Perhaps the sickest act ever promoted by a mainstream record company':

what is remarkable about this is not the quotation itself, but rather the fact that a contender for the American Vice-Presidency would feel it appropriate and necessary to comment on the potential moral impact of a particular pop musician. Similarly, Manson's Florida concerts just a few weeks later were picketed by a Christian protest group who distributed a protest prayer against what they called, 'Those fowl and evil spirits who have brought the music group Marilyn Manson to Orlando', and called on Jesus to help 'So that they cannot sow lies and spread discontent among our youth'. Of course, concern over the potential effects of pop musicians is certainly not restricted to a handful of performers. For instance, in many countries there are concerns over the potentially immoral effects of rap music, and this current concern mirrors worldwide concern throughout the 1970s and 1980s concerning heavy rock. What is just as clear, however, is that, although the degree of hysteria in the 1950s is arguably no greater than in the present day, the nature of the supposed effects of pop music has become more dramatic.

This level of outrage meant that a backlash was inevitable at some point, and can be dated in earnest to 1985 when Tipper Gore, wife of future US Vice-President and Presidential candidate, Al Gore, established the Parents' Music Resource Center (PMRC), reportedly in response to hearing explicit sexual lyrics in the music her daughter listened to. This led to Gore organizing a special meeting with the United States Senate Committee on Commerce Sites and Transportation, which met on 19 September 1985, and resulted in the adoption of the 'Parental Advisory' sticker which is still prevalent today on CDs in many regions in the world. By the year 2000, a total of 19 states within the USA had considered drastic legislation directly targeting CDs that featured the parental advisory sticker. For example, Missouri, Pennsylvania, and Louisiana wanted to make it a crime to sell a CD featuring that sticker to a minor. Pennsylvania also went a step further, attempting to make it illegal for a young person to buy a CD featuring that sticker: if a young male did buy a stickered CD, he would have been sent to work at a rape crisis centre, on the grounds that he must by definition be a threat to women. Ohio tried to allow individual towns to impose their own laws concerned stickered music that would have allowed much stricter restrictions possible. Similarly, the city of Leominster in Massachusetts tried to completely ban sales of stickered albums to all people, rather than just minors.

Nor did nationwide action within the USA stop after the 1985 Senate Committee hearing. 1990 saw the first time that a pop music CD was actually ruled as being legally obscene, namely 2 Live Crew's *Nasty As They Want To Be*. Although the ruling was later overturned, this was only after at least one record store owner had been prosecuted for selling it. 1993 saw massive marches organized by one of the main civil rights bodies in the United States, the National Association for the Advancement of Coloured People, protesting about lawlessness and obscenity in rap music. Similarly, in 1994, the Senate Judiciary Subcommittee on Juvenile Violence met to consider misogyny by male rappers, and self-degradation by female rappers.

There is also a strong business-related element to this issue. Many of the largest music retailers in the USA have stopped selling CDs that feature the parental advisory sticker, in the belief that these are inconsistent with the family market that they target. Many other record stores in the USA will not stock stickered music because of cases where small independent record shops who did sell them were sued. In the year 2000, President Bill Clinton used his final State of the Union address to call for a rating system to be imposed on CDs and video games similar to that imposed on movies. It is worthwhile pointing out also that this issue is not limited to the USA. Australia has considered using an age-based ratings system to restrict access to music. Similarly, in the UK, David Cameron, British Prime Minister at the time of writing, has linked rap music to violence. In June 2006 he commented that, 'I would say to [BBC] Radio 1, do you realise that some of the stuff you play on Saturday nights [i.e. rap] encourages people to carry guns and knives?'. Based on anecdotal evidence, politicians in a great many other countries have voiced concerns over the potential effects of rap music in promoting delinquency or other social ills.

Does the evidence justify societal concerns?

The public debate over the possible negative effects of pop music highlights three major sources of confusion concerning society's response to licentious pop star behaviour and licentious music. First, there is legal confusion. To the best of our knowledge, every attempt to ban a particular piece of music has been overturned later on the grounds of freedom of speech (or similar). This indicates that the legal profession cannot decide which is more important in this issue, public standards of decency or freedom of expression. Secondly, nor have politicians been able to provide clear guidance. Conservatives are typically concerned with standards of law and order, and public decency etc. and so this drives them to disapprove of licentious music and musicians. But conservatives also disapprove of governments meddling with free markets, and as such they appear unsure of whether they should step in. Liberals are just as confused, however. On the one hand is their belief in freedom of speech, but on the other is a desire to protect vulnerable people in society. So should a liberal faced with a suicidal 14-year-old heavy rock fan aim to protect him from the clutches of a potentially manipulative music industry that cares only for profit, or respect the musicians' artistic freedom of expression? Third, there is also considerable artistic confusion. Perhaps the best example of this is when rock guitarist Jimi Hendrix played the Woodstock festival in the late 1960s. Arguably the critical highlight of this lightening rod of countercultural thinking was Hendrix's version of the American national anthem. His use of extensive feedback and other effects in performing the piece was clearly intended as a protest against mainstream American cultural values. At the time, however, many interpreted the performance of the National Anthem as a patriotic act, and congratulated Hendrix for resisting the temptation to 'bow to hippy values'. All this confusion points to one clear conclusion: there is a clear need for psychological evidence. The scientific basis of the discipline means that psychology can provide some definitive answers to the question of whether pop music is 'bad' for young people.

Delinquency

Certainly, many studies in recent years have shown a link between listening to various types of music, particularly rap and rock, and various indicators of 'bad' effects of this. Much of this concern has focused on a large group of studies demonstrating a direct link between exposure to rock and rap music and the likelihood of the individuals concerned engaging in a range of delinquent acts. Wingood et al. (2003), for example, took a group of rap fans and followed them over a 12-month period, measuring the frequency with which they and a control group committed various delinquent acts. People who listened to rap were three times more likely to have hit their teacher over the 12-month period than were fans of other musical styles, and were 2.5 times more likely to have been arrested. Similarly, Wass et al. (1991) found that people in juvenile detention were three times more likely than high school students to list heavy metal as their favourite musical style; and Epstein et al. (1990) found that 96% of their sample of adolescents with behavioural problems listed heavy metal as their favourite musical style.

More generally, an abundance of evidence links liking for particularly rap and rock music with a range of other behaviours and attitudes that society regards as undesirable. For instance, several studies have used experimental methods or evidence of correlations among people in the 'real world' to indicate that exposure to rap or rock is associated with permissive attitudes to violence or the commission of violent acts (e.g. Peterson and Pfost 1989; Johnson et al. 1995);

promiscuous sexual attitudes or a younger age of losing one's virginity (e.g. Strouse and Buerkel-Rothfuss 1987; Strouse et al. 1995); or sexist attitudes towards women (e.g. Hansen and Hansen 1988; Hansen 1989). Indeed, for many, the debate has apparently moved on to consider not so much whether there is a link, but rather to identify who are those members of society most at risk. This work has considered various personality dimensions such as elevated levels of sensation seeking (e.g. McNamara and Ballard 1999) and rebelliousness (e.g. Bleich et al. 1991; Dillmann-Carpentier et al. 2003); and lower levels of conservatism (Glasgow and Cartier 1985; Lynxwiler and Gay 2000; McLeod et al. 2001).

Self-harming

Rather than consider this evidence in detail, we instead move on to consider the potentially negative effect of pop music on young people that is of greatest concern to society, namely whether there is a relationship between musical taste and both suicide and self-harming. Certainly, songs concerning death enjoy disproportionate popularity, relative to songs concerning other topics. Plopper and Ness (1993) considered all the songs that reached the top 40 in the USA, between 1955 and 1991. Of the 9311 songs in question, only 90 concerned death. However, of all the songs that reached the top 10, 25.5% of those about death went on to be number one, whereas only 8.6% of all the songs about other subjects reached number one. Young people do seem to be attracted to music concerning death.

Moreover, a reasonably large body of evidence directly links fans of heavy rock music in particular with a propensity towards suicide, suicidal ideation, and self-harm. Perhaps the first evidence on this came from Australia in 1993, when Martin et al. found that fans of heavy rock were more likely to self-harm, be depressed, and take drugs. What was particularly disturbing about Martin et al.'s results, however, was the prevalence of self-harming and suicidal ideation. Male rock fans were more than twice as likely to self-harm or attempt suicide as other males, and female heavy rock fans were more than four times more likely than other females to self-harm or attempt suicide. Similarly, North and Hargreaves' (2006) study of British undergraduates found that fans of rap and rock had considered and had actually self-harmed more often during the past 2 years than had fans of other musical styles, and were also more likely to have wished that they were dead and to have considered suicide. Furthermore, the extent to which the respondents liked rap and rock music could predict all these measures of self-injurious attitudes/behaviours even when controlling for self-esteem, delinquency, and a measure of participants' conservatism. Scheel and Westefeld (1999) found that, when asked to list their reasons for living, male heavy rock fans had lower scores; and that female heavy rock fans had more suicidal thoughts. Stack et al. (1994) investigated the issue at a broader culture level. They measured interest in heavy rock culture in the whole of the USA by measuring the subscription rates to a magazine devoted to this, namely *Metal Edge*. As subscription rates to *Metal Edge* increased, so also did the suicide rate among 15–24-year-olds (who constitute the core market for heavy rock music). As subscription rates for *Metal Edge* decreased, so also did the suicide rate among 15–24-year-olds. Moreover, there were no relationships between subscription rates to *Metal Edge* and suicide rates amongst any other subgroup of the population (e.g. middle-aged men), only amongst the target audience for heavy rock. In simple terms, it seems that as American adolescents get more interested in heavy rock so they are more likely to kill themselves.

However, the fact that there is a relationship between liking rock music and suicide obviously does not tell us which variable causes which. Indeed, there is a growing body of evidence showing that fans of heavy rock are also more likely to come from 'non-stereotypical families' and experience higher than normal levels of family dysfunction. Maybe it is this family background that triggers an interest in suicide and self-harming and which also draws adolescents towards a musical style that deals with alienation from mainstream society. For instance, Schwartz and Fouts (2003) found that fans of rock generally have greater levels of family disturbance. Stack et al.'s (1994) study of *Metal Edge* subscriptions found that American teenagers' interest in heavy metal was positively related to divorce rates within the USA. Scheel and Westefeld's (1999) study of rock fans' reasons for living found that rock fans were particularly unlikely to cite responsibility to family as a reason for not committing suicide. Martin et al.'s (1993) Australian study found that a smaller percentage of the parents of rock/heavy metal fans were still married compared to pop fans; that a smaller percentage of rock/heavy metal fans had access to their biological father; and that twice as many rock/heavy metal fans than pop fans reported that their family relationship was 'not close'. So perhaps it is a poor family background that in some way leads young people towards self-harm and suicide, and also towards an interest in music that deals with alienation from mainstream society. Rock music may be linked to suicide and self-harming, but might not cause it. And if the music does not cause the problem then the case for censorship and other forms of societal action targeting pop music is weakened considerably.

Moreover, it is not just heavy rock that has been implicated in elevated suicide rates. Stack and Gundlach (1992) argued that the themes of poverty and loneliness commonly found in country and western lyrics might be sufficient to make an already depressed person consider suicide. Consequently, they determined the frequency with which country and western music was played on the radio in 49 cities in the USA, and compared this against the suicide rate amongst whites (but not blacks, i.e. the target audience for country and western music). The researchers found that the more that country and western music was played on the radio, the higher the white suicide rate; and this persisted even when controlling for poverty, geographic location, divorce, and prevalence of gun retailers: any link between rock music and suicide may be no stronger than the link between country music and suicide. Therefore, if one wishes to propose censorship of rock on the grounds that it supposedly encourages suicide, perhaps one should also consider censorship of country music? Furthermore, Stack (2002) considered the relationship between interest in opera and suicide. Stack began by noting that 77 of the 306 (25.2%) operas that are performed with any degree of regularity involve suicide; with well-known examples including *The Flying Dutchman*, *Trovatore*, and *Otello*. Stack notes that these suicides are typically portrayed as morally acceptable reactions to life events, and particularly in reaction to dishonour having being brought upon oneself or one's family. Stack (2002, p. 432) reasoned that, as a consequence of this, 'Drawn to the subculture of honour in opera, opera fans should be more approving than non-fans in the case of suicide involving dishonour'. In confirmation of this, Stack found that his sample of opera fans were indeed 2.37 times more accepting of suicide in the case of dishonour than were non-fans, even when controlling for factors such as church attendance, political conservatism, number of social bonds, and others. Three major predictors of being an opera fan were being female, elderly, and well educated. So, just as young people are arguably particularly vulnerable to any negative effects of rock and should, it has been argued, be protected from it by legislation, so elderly, well-educated women are particularly vulnerable to any negative effects of opera and should also be protected from it by legislation. Of course, the latter seems unlikely, but it is no less logical than using 'parental advisory' stickers to restrict access to certain forms of pop music.

Before moving on, three other pieces of research are relevant to the debate concerning whether rock music can promote suicide. First, North and Hargreaves' (2006) study of British fans of rap and rock who self-harmed investigated a very simple issue. North and Hargreaves argued that if these people's musical tastes were causing their self-injurious behaviour, then the former must have begun at an earlier point in time than the latter. Participants were asked two simple questions, namely, 'When did you first start self-harming?' and, 'When did you first start listening to rock or rap music?'. There was no evidence that the interest in rap or rock pre-dated the onset self-harming. Given this, it is difficult to see how the music could be the cause of the self-harming. Second, Stack (1998) found that the statistical relationship between liking for rock music and suicide disappeared when allowing for rock fans' lower levels of religiosity: in addition to family-related issues, perhaps it is their lack of religious beliefs that leads to the greater level of self-harming among rock fans. Finally, Lacourse et al. (2001) found a link between liking rock and suicide only among females, and even this disappeared when allowing for their higher level of other suicide risk factors, such as feelings of alienation, drug use, and negligent parenting.

Ethical issues mean that only a few experimental studies have investigated the relationship between music and suicide. Nonetheless, three such studies have been carried out, and all fail to find any evidence that music per se can promote self-harming. North and Hargreaves (2005) suggest that any suicide-inducing effects of music on listeners that do exist may be, at least in part, due not to the music itself, but to the message that society sends to young people concerning the negative effect that the music is likely to have on them. Undergraduates were played one of four pop songs. The songs were chosen because the lyrics were arguably ambiguous in terms of whether they promoted or discouraged suicide. For instance, one of the songs, 'Lucky' by Radiohead, features the lyric, 'The head of state/Has called for me . . . by name', which is clearly death-related, although the song then continues to note that, 'But I don't have time for him', which is clearly life-affirming. Similarly, another of the songs, 'My friends' by the Red Hot Chili Peppers, contains the lyric, 'Imagine me taught by tragedy/Release is peace', which is clearly suicide-related, although the lyrics then continue, stating that, 'I heard a little girl/And what she said/Was something beautiful/To give your love/No matter what', which is clearly life-affirming. Before hearing one of the songs, participants were given one of two types of (fictitious) background information concerning it. One group was told that the song had been criticized by protestors, after it had been implicated in the suicide of a young fan of the band in question. However, the second group was told that the song in question had been praised by health professionals for helping vulnerable young people to work through emotional problems. This information had a corresponding influence on ratings of the extent to which the song was perceived by the undergraduates as 'life-destroying versus life-enhancing', whether it made the undergraduates feel happy about themselves, and whether it would make them want to commit suicide if they heard it during difficult emotional times; whether the undergraduates wrote a prose description of the song that was 'life-destroying versus life-enhancing'; and several measures of how the participant felt that someone else of their own age and sex would be affected by the song. In short, telling the participants that society thought that the song was 'life-destroying' caused it to have a negative effect, but telling the participants that society thought that the song could be 'life-enhancing' caused it to have a positive effect. In some cases, of course, pop songs have very unambiguous lyrics (although see the coverage of Leming (1987) below), but North and Hargreaves' findings suggest that where there is some ambiguity then the background information concerning the song provided by society to adolescents can be an important factor in the emotional effect of that song. The pro-censorship activities of protestors against heavy metal, rap, and the like provide just this kind of negative background information, such that they may be exacerbating the very problem they are aiming to eradicate.

Other experimental evidence comes out even more strongly against the notion that music with violent or suicidal content can cause suicide/self-harm. Ballard and Coates (1995) played participants either a heavy metal or rap song which featured one of three types of lyrics, namely non-violent, homicidal, or suicidal. The non-violent rap songs led to higher depression scores than did the more violent rap songs; and there were no effects of either musical style or type of lyric on participants' level of suicidal ideation, anxiety, or self-esteem. Similarly, Rustad et al.

(2003) conducted two experiments in which participants were respectively shown a rock video with or without suicidal content, or listened to rock music with or without suicidal content. In both cases, a subsequent story-writing task (in which participants were asked to describe what was happening in a picture) showed that watching/hearing the suicidal music did indeed raise the salience of suicide for participants. However, there were very few differences between those who had or had not been exposed to suicidal music in terms of measures of negative mood, estimates of the probability that they would experience negative life events, hopelessness, or the acceptability of suicide. In other words, suicidal content in music-primed cognitions related to suicide, but did not affect participants in a way that would increase their actual risk of suicide.

Interpretation of lyrics and masking

As such, the argument that pop music produces effects on young people that society would not like is perhaps not so strong as first appeared. This becomes exacerbated when considering people's poor ability to actually comprehend song lyrics. Konečni (1984) used interviews with musicians to identify short statements where the author of a set of lyrics stated the precise subject matter of those lyrics. Konečni then used these statements to prepare, in effect, a multiple choice test concerning the lyrics, in which participants were asked to state which one of four options was the correct subject matter. The participants selected the correct right answer on only 28% of occasions, which of course is scarcely better than chance. One might argue in response to this that surely adolescents would better understand some of the less ambiguous lyrics heard in pop music. This issue was considered by Leming (1987), who used the song 'Physical' by Olivia Newton John, which features lyrics such as, 'Let's get physical, physical/I want to get physical/Let's get into physical/Let me hear your body talk, your body talk/Let me hear your body talk'. As such, it would seem to be quite transparently a song about sex. When the song was played to teenagers, 36% of them believed that the song was indeed about sex, but another 36% of the sample believed that the song was instead an inducement to take more physical exercise! Another possible objection to the conclusion that people are prone to misinterpreting lyrics is that people are perhaps more accurate in the case of songs that they themselves know well. To address this, Rosenbaum and Prinsky (1987) asked teenagers to name their three favourite songs, and to then state what those three songs were about. One-third of the sample could not even complete the latter task, irrespective of their accuracy, indicating that they had not apparently considered (or at least arrived at a clear conclusion concerning) the subject matter of their favourite music. If a lyric as blatant as Physical's is misinterpreted by a substantial portion of the population, or if a large number of teenagers simply do not know what their favourite music is attempting to communicate then this seriously undermines the argument for censorship. Put simply, a song that glamorizes violence or death may not necessarily be interpreted as doing such by adolescent listeners. It does not mean that lyrics cannot affect listeners, but does suggest that the intended meaning of lyrics will not often be communicated clearly to listeners.

As we saw earlier in the case of Belknap and Vance, some protestors have argued that malicious messages may be inserted into songs that are too quiet to be perceived consciously, or which have been recorded backwards. However, there is no evidence that these masked messages can be interpreted correctly by listeners. Walls et al. (1992) found that masked messages concerning the tempo of the music in question could not influence listeners' beliefs in this respect. Similarly, in one of Vokey and Read's (1985) experiments, participants were presented with backwards statements such as, 'Jesus loves me, this I know' presented without any accompanying background music, but afterwards were unable to state which of five categories of message they had heard (e.g. nursery rhymes, Christianity, Satanism, pornography, and advertising). More simply, participants were unable to determine even the general gist of backwards-masked messages. Indeed, one other experiment has argued that people might only be able to perceive masked messages in music if they are primed to do so by society. Thorne and Himelstein (1984) took several songs that have been criticized frequently by protest groups for featuring masked lyrics. Before the songs were played to people, the researchers provided one of three types of information about them. One group of people were told nothing at all about the music; one group was told that there was a variety of messages hidden in the music via backwards-masking; and a third group was told that the music contained backwards-masked messages concerning specifically Satan. The people who were told nothing about the music did not hear any messages; the people who were told that the music contained a variety of backwards messages did indeed perceive these; and the group who were told to expect backwards messages about Satan did indeed perceive these, but not messages on any other subject. As with North and Hargreaves' (2006) findings discussed earlier, it would seem that it is what society tells adolescents to find hidden in the music that influences what they find hidden, but that backwards-masked or other hidden messages would not otherwise be perceived.

Conclusion

In summary, it would seem that a greater incidence of family dysfunction and personality factors appear to be more probable explanations of why fans of rock might behave in an undesirable manner and why they might also listen to music that reflects their difficult circumstances and disposition. However, we have also seen many examples of individual pieces of evidence that do suggest that there is at least a relationship between music and the kinds of attitudes and behaviours that most societies deem unacceptable. For instance, we have seen that the delinquency and suicide rates are indeed elevated among heavy rock fans: even if the music is not the cause of the undesirable behaviour, nor does this mean that it is acceptable to ignore the latter. We have also seen, more generally, that although a great deal of research (covered elsewhere in this book) has addressed the therapeutic applications of music, there is a growing body of evidence concerning potentially more negative effects that music might have.

If one assimilates the evidence here, three actions seem justifiable. First, both protestors and musicians alike can help. We have seen how the messages that society sends to young people about the music they listen to can influence how they will react to it. This means that we currently have the worst of both worlds in which many societies attach a parental advisory sticker to music, which might itself cause that music to be harmful, but then, nonetheless, allow young people to go ahead and listen to that music anyway. We should either use the sticker to prohibit access to the music, or remove it and eliminate the potential negative effects it might have. Similarly, if certain musical tastes even might be the cause of societal problems there seems to be a case for self-regulation by musicians of the subject matter of their material and the more general subcultures that they promote.

Second, we have also seen evidence concerning how family background might be the factor that drives young people towards self-harming and also an interest in heavy rock. If this is the case then the focus of any intervention ought to be on parenting and family background, rather than music. Finally, it is possible to make the case that rap and rock music in particular are unfairly stigmatized by society. We have already seen evidence linking both country and opera with suicide, and Fried (e.g. 1996) has produced several studies indicating that rap music and rap fans are the subject of negative stereotyping. Indeed, pretend for a moment that the new Marilyn Manson video involved a plotline in which a young man and woman met, leading to the couple having a child. The man then leaves to work overseas, promising the woman that he will return.

Several years pass, and the man eventually returns, but with a different woman upon his arm. The mother of his child is distraught, takes a large dagger, and graphically commits suicide in a pool of her own blood. If that were a Marilyn Manson video it would be banned immediately. However, that brief story is a plot summary of Puccini's *Madame Butterfly*, which is played out nightly on the stage of opera halls around the world. Why is this acceptable in opera and not acceptable in rock music? As the evidence linking both opera and country with suicide demonstrates, society clearly operates a double standard with regard to rock and rap.

References

Ballard, M.E. and Coates, S. (1995). The immediate effects of homicidal, suicidal, and nonviolent heavy metal and rap songs on the moods of college students. *Youth and Society*, **27**, 148–68.

Bleich, S., Zillmann, D., and Weaver, J.B. (1991). Enjoyment and consumption of defiant rock music as a function of adolescent rebelliousness. *Journal of Electronic and Broadcasting Media*, **35**, 351–66.

Dillmann-Carpentier, F., Knobloch, F., and Zillmann, D. (2003). Rock, rap, and rebellion: comparisons of traits predicting selective exposure to defiant music. *Personality and Individual Differences*, **35**, 1643–55.

Epstein, J., Pratto, D., and Skipper, J. (1990). Teenagers, behavioral problems and preferences for heavy metal and rap music: a case study of a Southern middle school. *Deviant Behavior*, **11**, 381–94.

Fried, C.B. (1996). Bad rap for rap: bias in reactions to music lyrics. *Journal of Applied Social Psychology*, **26**, 2135–46.

Glasgow, M.R. and Cartier, A.M. (1985). Conservatism, sensation-seeking and music preferences. *Personality and Individual Differences*, **6**, 393–5.

Hansen, C.H. (1989). Priming sex-role stereotypic event schemas with rock music videos: effects on impression favorability, trait inferences, and recall of a subsequent male-female interaction. *Basic and Applied Social Psychology*, **10**, 371–91.

Hansen, C.H. and Hansen, R.D. (1988). How rock music videos can change what is seen when boy meets girl: priming stereotypic appraisal of social interactions. *Sex Roles*, **19**, 287–316.

Johnson, J.D., Jackson, L.A., and Gatto, L. (1995). Violent attitudes and deferred academic aspirations: deleterious effects of exposure to rap music. *Basic and Applied Social Psychology*, **16**, 27–41.

Konečni, V.J. (1984). Elusive effects of artists' 'messages'. In: W.R. Crozier and A.J. Chapman (eds.) *Cognitive processes in the perception of art*, pp. 71–96. Amsterdam: Elsevier.

Lacourse, E., Claes, M., and Villeneuve, M. (2001). Heavy metal music and adolescent suicidal risk. *Journal of Youth and Adolescence*, **30**, 321–32.

Leming, J. (1987). Rock music and the socialization of moral values in early adolescence. *Youth and Society*, **18**, 363–83.

Litman, R.E. and Farberow, N.L. (1994). Pop-rock music as precipitating cause in youth suicide. *Journal of Forensic Sciences*, **39**, 494–99.

Lynxwiler, J. and Gay, D. (2000). Moral boundaries and deviant music: public attitudes toward heavy metal and rap. *Deviant Behavior*, **21**, 63–85.

Martin, G., Clarke, M., and Pearce, C. (1993). Adolescent suicide: music preference as an indicator of vulnerability. *Journal of the American Academy of Child and Adolescent Psychiatry*, **32**, 530–5.

McDonald, J. (1988). Censoring rock lyrics: a historical analysis of the debate. *Youth and Society*, **19**, 294–313.

McLeod, D.M., Detenber, B.H., and Eveland, W.P. (2001). Behind the third-person effect: differentiating perceptual processes for self and other. *Journal of Communication*, **51**, 678–95.

McNamara, L., and Ballard, M.E. (1999). Resting arousal, sensation seeking, and music preference. *Genetic, Social, and General Psychology Monographs*, **125**, 229–50.

North, A.C. and Hargreaves, D.J. (2005). Labelling effects on the perceived deleterious consequences of pop music listening. *Journal of Adolescence*, **28**, 433–40.

North, A.C. and Hargreaves, D.J. (2006). Problem music and self-harming. *Suicide and Life-Threatening Behavior*, **36**, 582–90.

North, A.C. and Hargreaves, D.J. (2008). *The social and applied psychology of music*. Oxford: Oxford University Press.

Peterson, D.L. and Pfost, K.S. (1989). Influence of rock videos on attitudes of violence against women. *Psychological Reports*, **64**, 319–22.

Plopper, B. and Ness, M. (1993). Death as portrayed to adolescents through top 40 rock and roll music. *Adolescence*, **28**, 793–807.

Rosenbaum, J. and Prinsky, L. (1987). Sex, violence, and rock 'n' roll: youth's perception of popular music. *Popular Music and Society*, **11**, 79–89.

Rustad, R.A., Small, J.E., Jobes, D.A., Safer, M.A., and Peterson, R.J. (2003). The impact of rock videos and music with suicidal content on thoughts and attitudes about suicide. *Suicide and Life-Threatening Behavior*, **33**, 120–31.

Scheel, K.R. and Westefeld, J.S. (1999). Heavy metal music and adolescent suicidality: an empirical investigation. *Adolescence*, **34**, 253–73.

Schwartz, K.D. and Fouts, G.T. (2003). Music preferences, personality style, and developmental issues of adolescents. *Journal of Youth and Adolescence*, **32**, 205–13.

Stack, S. (1998). Heavy metal, religiosity, and suicidal acceptability. *Suicidal and Life-Threatening Behavior*, **28**, 388–94.

Stack, S. (2002). Opera subculture and suicide for honor. *Death Studies*, **26**, 431–7.

Stack, S. and Gundlach, J.H. (1992). The effect of country music on suicide. *Social Forces*, **71**, 211–18.

Stack, S., Gundlach, J., and Reeves, J.L. (1994). The heavy metal subculture and suicide. *Suicide and Life-Threatening Behavior*, **24**, 15–23.

Strouse, J.S. and Buerkel-Rothfuss, N.L. (1987). Media exposure and the sexual attitudes and behaviors of college students. *Journal of Sex Education and Therapy*, **13**, 43–51.

Strouse, J.S., Buerkel-Rothfuss, N., and Long, E.C.J. (1995). Gender and family as moderators of the relationship between music video exposure and adolescent sexual permissiveness. *Adolescence*, **30**, 505–21.

Thorne, S.B. and Himelstein, P. (1984). The role of suggestion in the perception of Satanic messages in rock and roll recordings. *Journal of Psychology*, **116**, 245–8.

Vokey, J.R. and Read, J.D. (1985). Subliminal messages: between the devil and the media. *American Psychologist*, **40**, 1231–9.

Walls, K., Taylor, J., and Falzone, J. (1992). The effects of subliminal suggestions and music experience on the perception of tempo in music. *Journal of Music Therapy*, **29**, 186–97.

Wass, H., Miller, M.D., and Redditt, C.A. (1991). Adolescents and destructive themes in rock music: a follow-up. *Omega: Journal of Death and Dying*, **23**, 199–206.

Wingood, G.M., DiClemente, R.J., Bernhardt, J.M., Harrington, K., Davies, S.L., *et al.* (2003). A prospective study of exposure to rap music videos and African American female adolescents' health. *American Journal of Public Health*, **93**, 437–9.

Chapter 34

Music Listening and Mental Health: Variations on Internalizing Psychopathology

Dave Miranda, Patrick Gaudreau, Régine Debrosse, Julien Morizot, and Laurence J. Kirmayer

The continuum of mental health can range from the most adaptive positive states to the most maladaptive negative conditions. Music listening is an everyday behaviour that can be associated with different levels of mental health. Including optimal wellbeing (Gabrielsson 2010), normative subjective wellbeing (Laukka 2007), and psychopathology (Mulder et al. 2007). This chapter, however, will focus on the role of music listening in psychopathology, which here refers to 'patterns of behaviors, cognitions, and emotions that are abnormal, disruptive, or distressing either to the person or others around the person' (Phares, 2002, p. 2). First, it offers a conceptual framework arguing that music listening may have influences on internalizing psychopathology because: music can involve emotion regulation and coping; songs may have social cognitive influences; and music can have psychotherapeutic effects. Second, it presents a review of the empirical literature according to seven basic methodological strategies (models) that can also be used to design future studies: risk factor; compensatory factor; common cause; mediator; moderator; protective factor; precipitating factor.

Music provides positive experiences and developmental resources that can promote mental health (McPherson 2006; Saarikallio and Erkkilä 2007; Juslin et al. 2008; Miranda and Claes 2009). Nonetheless, in recent years, intriguing relationships have been found between everyday music listening and symptoms of psychopathology—especially in younger populations for whom music may be particularly important (for reviews, see Anderson et al. 2003; Baker and Bor 2008; Brown and Hendee 1989; North and Hargreaves 2008, Chapter 33, this volumes). There is psychometric evidence that symptoms of common mental health problems can strongly correlate with each other and thereby be organized into two broad dimensions: *externalizing psychopathology* (e.g. aggression, antisocial behaviour, drug use) and *internalizing psychopathology* (e.g. depression, anxiety, social withdrawal; Achenbach 1991; Krueger 1999; Krueger et al. 2003; Cicchetti and Cohen 2006). Externalizing behaviours involve socially disruptive mental health problems (e.g. aggression), which actions are mainly oriented 'outwardly' at other individuals, whereas internalizing behaviours involve mental health problems pertaining to individual distress (e.g. depression), which manifestations are primarily oriented 'inwardly' at oneself (Gresham and Kern 2004).

In an overview of the literature on music and mental health, Mulder and collaborators noted that so-called 'non-mainstream' music preferences—those often perceived as more rebellious, for instance metal and rap music—have been more consistently related to externalizing (disruptive)

symptoms than to internalizing (distress) symptoms (Mulder et al. 2007). Still, research on music listening behaviours (e.g. preferences, motivations, reactions) and internalizing psychopathology has received far less attention than has work on the relationship between music preferences (e.g. heavy metal, rap music) and externalizing psychopathology. Researchers' emphasis on externalizing symptoms is pertinent as it addresses societal concerns that exposure to artistic media— such as music—that explore or entertain with deviant, risky, or antisocial material may lead to externalizing problems in some listeners (Anderson and Bushman 2002; North and Hargreaves 2008, Chapter 33, this volume). However, studies of music and externalizing symptoms do not cover the much larger interface between music and mental health.

The importance of internalizing psychopathology

In this chapter, we have adopted the term *internalizing psychopathology* as it cuts across different domains of mental health research, including psychology and psychiatry. It is now well established that several forms of psychopathology (e.g. depression, anxiety, phobia, social withdrawal, suicidal ideation) tend to be correlated and many scholars argue that these correlations reflect underlying biopsychosocial factors, including individual traits or vulnerabilities. This suggests the value of a dimensional system in which everyone can be situated along a continuum, from low to high levels of symptoms (whether in variety, frequency, or seriousness; Hudziak et al. 2008). A dimensional association of common forms of internalized distress has been well documented and labelled 'internalization', 'internalizing problems', 'internalizing spectrum', or 'internalizing psychopathology' (Achenbach 1991; Krueger 1999; Krueger et al. 2003; Cicchetti and Cohen 2006).

Internalizing symptoms, such as depression and anxiety, represent a major public health concern in many societies as they can be associated with significant physical, psychological, social, and economic impacts (e.g. Anthony and Stein 2009; Gotlib and Hammen 2009). For instance, the World Health Organization (WHO) Global Burden of Disease Study identified depression as one of the most burdensome diseases in the world (Murray and Lopez 1996; WHO 2008). Such internalizing symptoms—even when below clinical threshold—can significantly disrupt psychosocial functioning and precipitate full-fledged mood disorders (Lewinsohn et al. 2000). Hence, although small and incremental influences of everyday music listening on internalizing psychopathology should mainly involve subclinical symptoms, these may nevertheless play an important role in mental health outcomes.

Objective of this chapter

This chapter examines the question of whether everyday music listening influences internalizing psychopathology. The rationale for this potential influence stems from two assumptions: *emotion regulation* and *gradual development*. First, in terms of emotion regulation, both music listening and internalizing psychopathology share a core emotional feature. Music can influence human emotions (Juslin and Sloboda 2010) and internalizing psychopathology (or mood disorders) involves impaired emotion regulation (Campbell-Sills and Barlow 2007). Second, in terms of gradual development, both music listening and internalizing symptoms can sometimes qualify as cumulative everyday experiences that may become impactful for many people. Indeed, everyday music listening can be recurrent, ubiquitous, contextualized, associated to daily goals, and have small yet cumulative influences (Sloboda 2010). Likewise, some forms of internalizing psychopathology (e.g. mild to moderate depression) may reflect the cumulative of everyday symptoms (e.g. sad mood, pessimism, demoralization) that do not in themselves attain clinical threshold (e.g. major depressive disorder), but that gradually impair wellbeing (Lewinsohn et al. 2000). Hence, listening to music could influence some of the everyday processes that contribute to the development of internalizing psychopathology.

In this chapter, these assumptions of emotion regulation and gradual development served as guides to a review of the literature examining if everyday music listening may produce small, gradual, and impactful influences on internalizing psychopathology. Of course, performing music, composing music, dancing to music, or other musical activities may also have various relationships with internalizing psychopathology. However, reviewing other musical activities was beyond the scope of this chapter. In what follows, we first present a conceptual framework expanding on the rationale for studying the impact of music listening on mental health. Second, we review the empirical literature according to seven methodological strategies (models) that can also be used to design future studies.

A conceptual framework

Our conceptual framework argues that everyday music listening may have influences on internalizing psychopathology because: (1) music can involve emotion regulation and coping; (2) songs may have social cognitive influences; (3) music can have psychotherapeutic effects.

Emotion regulation and coping through music

Music can involve emotion regulation and coping. There is a wealth of studies demonstrating that music listening induces, influences, and modulates emotions (Juslin and Sloboda 2010). Moreover, there are some theoretical perspectives suggesting that musically-related emotions can be used for everyday self-regulation. For instance, *Mood-management theory* posits that pleasurable consumption of entertaining media may offer resources from which individuals may consciously (or unconsciously) select various stimuli (such as different forms of music) to match their current moods, but also to minimize their negative and maximize their positive moods (Zillmann 1988a, 1988b). Music listening is mostly thought to contribute to quotidian emotion regulation by which one manages advantageous trade-offs between experiencing positive and negative emotions (North et al. 2000; Chamorro-Premuzic and Furnham 2007; Saarikallio and Erkkilä 2007). Internalizing psychopathology often involves impaired emotion regulation (e.g. dysfunctional negative emotional reactivity or inadequate understanding and management of emotions; Campbell-Sills and Barlow 2007). Hence, it is plausible that music may serve as a convenient and accessible everyday resource for emotion regulation that could prevent or reduce internalizing symptoms.

Emotion regulation is thus a central concept for research on music listening (Saarikallio and Erkkilä 2007). Emotion regulation represents a repertoire of processes—whether automatic or controlled and from conscious to unconscious—by which positive and negative emotions are regulated in either adaptive or maladaptive ways (Gross and Thompson 2007). It is thus important to underscore that emotion regulation is multidimensional and that specific dimensions, for instance *reappraisal* and *suppression*, can lead to positive or negative psychosocial outcomes, respectively (Gross and John 2003). These distinctions have important implications for the assumption that emotion regulation represents the core system around which most strategies of self-regulation by music listening gravitate (Saarikallio and Erkkilä 2007). Conceptually, different forms of emotion regulation by music listening can either help or hinder psychological wellbeing. Indeed, there is evidence that the use of media, especially music listening, is associated with both adaptive (e.g. self-reflection) and maladaptive (e.g. rumination) emotion regulation strategies (Greenwood and Long 2009). In sum, music listening may involve both adaptive and maladaptive emotion regulation strategies that should predict less or more internalizing symptoms, respectively.

The effects of music preferences have also been explained by *Uses and gratifications theory*, which posits that individuals are motivated to actively select and use media as a function of their personal dispositions and in order to satisfy different individual, social, and contextual needs (e.g. Katz et al.1973; Rosengren et al. 1985; Roe 1995). On the basis of this theory, it can be argued that emotionally distressed individuals may actively attempt to use music listening to regulate their emotions—a hypothesis that is beginning to receive empirical support (e.g. Chamorro-Premuzic et al. 2009). Furthermore, music listening is often considered to be used purposively as a form of coping strategy for dealing with stress (Arnett 1995; Miranda and Claes 2009). The concept of coping includes diverse conscious strategies used to manage emotions, cognitions, behaviours, and physiological reactions during stressful situations (Compas et al. 2001). Recent work has elaborated a multidimensional model of coping by music listening involving emotion-oriented, problem-oriented, and avoidance/disengagement coping (Miranda and Claes 2009). Still, as it was the case for emotion regulation, different forms of coping are not always adaptive in terms of internalizing symptoms (Compas et al. 2001). In fact, emerging evidence in adolescence shows that both recurrent avoidance/disengagement and emotion-oriented coping by music listening are associated with more internalizing symptoms, whereas problem-oriented coping by music listening is associated with less internalizing symptoms (Miranda and Claes 2009). In other words, adolescents more inclined toward listening to music to forget about their problems (avoidance/disengagement) and/or to manage their emotions (emotion-oriented) felt more depressed, however, those more inclined toward listening to music to find solutions to their problems (problem-oriented) felt less depressed.

Music preferences and social cognitive processes

In addition to the effects of music on emotions, songs with lyrics may influence listeners through social cognitive processes. Lyrics and imagery associated with different music preferences may influence listeners by priming social cognitive schemas. For example, research has shown that repetitive exposure to antisocial lyrics and imagery conveyed by songs can prime antisocial attitudes and behaviours (Anderson et al. 2003). Many songs engage in beautiful and provocative artistic explorations of various negative themes, dramatic scripts, and introspective narratives. For already distressed people, negative and introspective schemas conveyed in their favourite songs may amplify or maintain rumination that contributes to internalizing symptoms (Miranda and Claes 2007). Rumination is known to aggravate internalizing psychopathology because it is 'a mode of responding to distress that involves repetitively and passively focusing on symptoms of distress and on the possible causes and consequences of these symptoms' (Nolen-Hoeksema et al. 2008, p. 400). Indeed, there is evidence that, in times of negative mood, turning to music listening is associated with rumination (Greenwood and Long 2009; for a review on music and rumination, see Garrido 2009). Hence, in distressed individuals, repetitive exposure to preferred 'negative' songs may be detrimental if it fuels their rumination. This may occur by means of some of the emotional mechanisms operating in music. These can involve 'evaluative conditioning' by which music is associated with an environmental stimulus, but also the activation of 'episodic memory' of significant life events (Juslin et al. 2010). Thus, rumination may be facilitated when preferred negative songs are paired to sad events or evoke painful memories. Conversely, these emotional mechanisms in music could also foster mental health improvements. For some individuals, the positive and inspiring social cognitive schemas, associations, or memories conveyed in their favourite songs may prime feelings of solace, positive attitudes, and adaptive self-regulation.

Conceptually, positive social cognitive elements in songs may reduce internalizing symptoms and promote emotional wellbeing (Miranda and Claes 2007, 2008).

In the social context of youth culture, music preferences can also represent musical subcultures (Miranda and Claes 2009). Some of these musical subcultures (e.g. heavy metal) emphasize the artistic exploration of depressive and chaotic themes associated with a sense of loss of meaning or anomie (Scheel and Westefeld 1999; Lacourse et al. 2001; Miranda and Claes 2007, 2008). Repeated exposure to the most negative of these songs could elicit or sustain rumination in distressed music fans. Moreover, peer groups can come together around a shared musical subculture (Miranda and Claes 2009; Selfhout et al. 2009). At times, this may increase exposure to negative songs and facilitate co-rumination among several distressed friends (Miranda and Claes 2009). Co-rumination occurs when friends engage in an excessive conversation about personal problems while concentrating on negative emotions—a cognitive, emotional, and social dynamic that is associated with more internalizing symptoms (Rose 2002). Thus, among distressed friends, repetitive exposure to (or extensive discussions about) their favourite negative songs can be deleterious if it nourishes their co-rumination. This negative outcome may be facilitated by some of music's emotional mechanisms. For instance, 'emotional contagion', by which music (like facial expression and voice) may activate neurological pathways akin to those involved in emotional synchronization between two individuals (as in 'mirror-neurons'; Overy and Molnar-Szakacs 2009; Juslin et al. 2010). Conversely, the same emotional mechanisms mobilized by music could also predict that some individuals' exposure to and discussion about their favourite songs may promote mental health improvements if it encourages social support, shared moments of happiness, identity formation, or other forms of adaptive socialization.

Psychotherapeutic effects of music

Music can have psychotherapeutic effects that may transfer to everyday life. As such, a number of scholars proposed using music as a psychotherapeutic agent or adjunct. Music therapy can be broadly defined as being 'the use of music as an adjunct to the treatment or rehabilitation of individuals to enhance their psychological, physical, cognitive, or social functioning' (American Psychological Association, 2006, p. 603). Positive emotional experiences from music may improve therapeutic processes (e.g. emotional and social learning, cognitive reorientation) and thus strengthen traditional cognitive/behavioural methods and their transfer to everyday goals (Thaut and Wheeler 2010). This may be partially because emotional experiences elicited by music and everyday behaviours share overlapping neurological pathways responsible for positive emotions and motivation (Thaut and Wheeler 2010). Of course, emotions and cognitions have reciprocal influences (Lazarus and Folkman 1984; Gross and Thompson 2007). Thus, positive emotional experiences from music may inspire some persons to appraise life stressors as opportunities for psychological growth (challenge) rather than harm (threat).

Gold et al. (2009) suggest that music therapy with emotional, social, and motivational components may be effective as an adjunct when other types of psychotherapy display limited outcomes. In their meta-analysis of prospective evaluations of music therapy, Gold and collaborators (2009) found a linear dose–effect trend as increasing numbers of music therapeutic sessions predicted less depressive symptoms. These results lend credence to the idea that emotional influences of music might reduce internalizing psychopathology and may be cumulative over time. Therefore, one may ask whether these clinical results are compatible with correlational results in everyday life. As we will discuss later, recent correlational studies have shown that diverse forms of media exposure and musical behaviour can predict either more or less internalizing symptoms (Miranda and Claes 2008; Primack et al. 2009). These results are in keeping with daily follow-up studies using the

Experience Sampling Method, which have indicated that positive and negative emotions coexist in everyday music listening, although the positive ones are much more frequent (Juslin et al. 2008).

Moreover, cognitive neuroscience has demonstrated that music can generate rewards and pleasure by increasing dopaminergic activity in the *nucleus accumbens* and *ventral tegmental* area of the brain (Menon and Levitin 2005). In terms of internalizing symptoms, this finding is promising as one of the core features of depression is *anhedonia*—the loss of motivation and gratification from engaging in what would usually be perceived and felt as pleasurable daily activities. As such, music therapy may be able to influence emotion regulation by means of musical methods that, among other things, promote one's capacity to be gratified by everyday pleasures. This parallel between therapeutic and experimental evidence, suggests that similar self-help mechanisms may occur through everyday music listening.

In sum, the overreaching theoretical implication of this framework is that adaptive patterns of music listening behaviours may reduce daily internalizing symptoms, whereas maladaptive patterns of music listening behaviours may increase daily internalizing symptoms.

Basic methodological strategies

In this section, we discuss seven basic methodological/analytical strategies (models) applicable to the study of music listening and internalizing psychopathology: risk factor; compensatory factor; common cause; mediator; moderator; protective factor; precipitating factor (six of these models were also discussed in the context of music listening and substance use in adolescence (see Miranda et al. in press). These seven models can be used independently or be integrated (e.g. moderated-mediation and mediated-moderation). They are useful to operationalize and test precise empirical hypotheses within larger theories. It must also be highlighted that prospective/longitudinal designs—whether in terms of days, weeks, months, or years—should preferably be employed to fully test these models. These seven strategies are used across diverse areas of research, including developmental psychology, social psychology, personality, and developmental psychopathology (e.g. Rutter 1985; Baron and Kenny 1986; Klein et al. 2002; Cicchetti and Cohen 2006; Wiebe and Fortenberry 2006; Fergusson et al. 2007). In addition to outlining the strategies, we will examine how specific empirical studies are interpretable according to each model.

Search and selection of empirical studies

In the published literature, data that have been collected in everyday life settings are of particular interest because they may have greater ecological validity. The *Experience Sampling Method* generates some of the most ecologically valid data given that it randomly samples everyday life experiences (e.g. Juslin et al. 2008). Unfortunately, these data are still rare in psychology of music. Thus, we focused on correlational studies that used self-reports of everyday life. Self-report data from correlational designs are still the most widely used method to study everyday music listening (Sloboda 2010).

In order to be selected for this literature review, empirical studies had to meet these inclusion criteria: (1) to be published in a peer-reviewed journal; (2) to report empirical results for participants of any age; (3) to have a correlational design with self-report data; (4) to measure any music listening behaviour; and (5) to assess internalizing symptoms broadly defined. Conversely, empirical studies were discarded if they met the following exclusion criteria: (1) clinical samples; (2) specific professional or educational populations; (3) qualitative data and case studies; (4) data from an experimental design, prevention/intervention programme evaluation; (5) musical behaviours related to playing music or dancing to music; and (6) personality traits.

Three databases were exhaustively searched in September 2009: PsycINFO (years 1806–2009), MEDLINE (years 1950–2009), and AARP AgeLine (years 1978–2009). Complementary searches in January 2010 had not yielded any new studies.

The keywords were chosen to cover as much literature as possible on music (e.g. music, music perception) and internalizing psychopathology (e.g. internalizing, depression, anxiety, suicidal ideation, social withdrawal). The combination of keywords generated 1373 abstracts. From these, 40 potential studies were carefully read to see if they fitted inclusion criteria or provided additional references. In all, 16 empirical studies met our inclusion criteria and were included in this literature review (see Table 34.1).

Table 34.1 Characteristics of 16 correlational/self-report studies on everyday music listening and internalizing psychopathology

Studies	Countries	Models	Methods
Burge et al. (2002)	United States	Risk factor Moderator	Cross-sectional design N = 77 high school students (41 males; 36 females) M = 17.5 years of age
Davis and Kraus (1989)	United States	Precipitating factor Protective factor Moderator	Cross-sectional design N1 = 305 undergraduates (112 males; 193 females) N2 = 116 boys in summer camp (M = 13.88 years of age)
George et al. (2007)	Canada	Risk factor Compensatory Moderator	Cross-sectional design N = 358 participants (203 females; 155 males) from university (N = 120) and the community M = 32.9 years of age
Lacourse et al. (2001)	Canada (Quebec)	Risk factor Compensatory factor Common cause/ confounding Moderator	Cross-sectional design N=275 high school students (154 males; 121 females) M=16.22 years of age
Lester and Whipple (1996)	United States	Risk factor Common cause/ confounding	Cross-sectional design N = 93 undergraduates (35 males; 58 females) M = 24 years of age
Martin et al. (1993)	Australia	Risk factor Moderator	Cross-sectional design N = 247 high school students (138 males; 109 females) and final N = 227 M = 14.76 years of age
Miranda and Claes (2007)	Canada (Quebec)	Risk factor Compensatory factor Moderator Common cause/ confounding	Cross-sectional design N = 329 high school students (179 girls; 150 boys) M = 15.34 years of age
Miranda and Claes (2008)	Canada (Quebec)	Risk factor Protective factor Moderator Common cause/ confounding	Longitudinal design N = 311 high school students (166 girls; 145 boys) M = 15.75 years of age

(continued)

Table 34.1 (Continued) Characteristics of 16 correlational/self-report studies on everyday music listening and internalizing psychopathology

Studies	Countries	Models	Methods
Miranda and Claes (2009)	Canada (Quebec)	Risk factor Moderator Compensatory factor Common cause/confounding	Cross-sectional design N = 418 high school students (215 girls; 203 boys) M = 15.74 years of age
Mulder et al. (2007)	Netherlands	Risk factor Common cause/confounding	Cross-sectional design N = 4159 representative high school students (51.5% girls) M = 13.96 years of age
North and Hargreaves (2006)	United Kingdom	Risk factor Common cause/confounding	Cross-sectional design N = 436 non-psychology undergraduates (218 males; 218 females) M = 20.25 years of age
Recours et al. (2009)	France	Risk factor Common cause/confounding	Cross-sectional design N = 321 Metal fans on Internet (49.53% students; 41.74% employed; 282 males; 39 females M = 22.67 years of age
Rentfrow and Gosling (2003)	United States	Correlates	Cross-sectional design N1 = 1704 undergraduates N2 = 1383 undergraduates
Scheel and Westefeld (1999)	United States	Risk factor Moderator	Cross-sectional design N = 121 high school students (44 males; 77 females) N = 113 answered suicidal risk questionnaire M = 17.2 years of age
Thompson and Larson (1995)	United States	Moderator	Cross-sectional design N = 483 child and adolescents (218 males; 218 females) From 9 to 15 years ages
Werner et al. (2006)	United States	Compensatory factor	Cross-sectional design N = college students (181 males; 183 females) M–24.7 years of age

Risk factor model

In a *risk factor model* (Rutter 1985), risk factors (independent variables) can predict an increase in or the occurrence of a given psychopathology (dependent variable). For example, a music listening behaviour predicting higher levels in an internalizing psychopathology could be a potential risk factor.

Thus far, there are no longitudinal studies demonstrating that a music listening behaviour acts as a risk factor for internalizing psychopathology. The longitudinal study of Miranda and Claes (2008) indicated that out of five music preferences (Metal, Soul, Pop, Classical, and Electronic), none were risk factors as they did not predict more depression symptoms in adolescents. Interestingly, their study showed that Metal music (e.g. heavy metal, punk rock)—in which artistic exploration of 'negative' lyrics and imagery are of concern to many adults—was not a risk factor for internalizing symptoms.

Some cross-sectional studies have indicated that different music preferences may be concurrently associated with more internalizing psychopathology. These studies have often considered Metal music as a potential risk factor. For example, Heavy Metal/Rock music predicted more suicidal ideations in adolescents (Burge et al. 2002), heavy metal fans had higher suicidal risk than non-fans in adolescent girls (Scheel and Westefeld 1999), and both Rock and Heavy Metal music correlated with more past suicidal ideation in college students (Lester and Whipple 1996). Rock/Heavy Metal music was associated with more suicidal thoughts and depression in adolescent girls (Martin et al. 1993). Similarly, Metal music was associated with more depression in adolescent girls (Miranda and Claes 2007). Few studies have identified other types of music preferences as potential risk factors. For instance, Rhythmic and Intense music (e.g. hip hop/rap, pop, R&B) correlated with more depression in university and community adult members (George et al. 2007). Also, among adolescents, Mulder et al. (2007) found that 'Exclusive Rock' (i.e. exclusive admirers of heavy metal, punk/hardcore/grunge, gothic, and rock) and 'Omnivores' (i.e. eclectics having diversified music tastes) were music taste groups with more internalizing symptoms. North and Hargreaves (2006) found that what is sometimes labelled as 'Problem music' (e.g. hard rock, hip hop/rap, punk) predicted more suicide ideations in university students.

Other cross-sectional studies have not found concurrent links between music preferences and more internalizing psychopathology. For instance, Recours et al. (2009) recruited fans of Metal music (mostly young men) who participated to Internet forums about this music genre. Their results indicated that these Metal fans had good mental health in terms of anxiety and depression. Moreover, Rentfrow and Gosling (2003) did not find links between music preferences (reflective/complex, intense/rebellious, upbeat/conventional, or energetic/rhythmic) and more depression in two samples of university undergraduates.

Other cross-sectional studies have found that some music listening reactions or motivations can be linked to more internalizing psychopathology. For instance, among adolescents, Martin and collaborators (1993) found that those who felt sadder after listening to music were more depressed and had more suicidal thoughts. Furthermore, Miranda and Claes (2009) reported that avoidance/disengagement coping by music listening was associated with more depression in adolescent girls, and that emotion-oriented coping by music listening was associated with more depression in adolescent boys.

Overall, empirical results suggest that risk factor models involving direct links between music preferences and more internalizing psychopathology receive inconsistent support. Longitudinal evidence, although sparse, suggests that music preferences do not predict more internalizing symptoms. Cross-sectional studies have reported some concurrent links between music preferences (e.g. Metal music) and more internalizing symptoms, mostly in adolescence. Lastly, there are emerging indications that maladaptive music listening reactions (e.g. increase in sadness) and motivations (e.g. avoidance/disengagement coping) may represent potential risk factors for internalizing symptoms.

Compensatory factor model

In a *compensatory factor model* (Fergusson et al. 2007), compensatory factors (independent variables) can predict a decrease in a given psychopathology (dependent variable). They are referred to as 'compensatory' because they offer developmental benefits or gains that may compensate for developmental losses resulting from risk factors of psychopathology. Hence, a music listening behaviour that can predict lower levels of an internalizing psychopathology could represent a compensatory factor for normative development.

The longitudinal study of Miranda and Claes (2008) found that preference for Soul music (e.g. hip hop, R&B, reggae) predicted less depression symptoms in adolescent girls. These authors hypothesized that Soul music's numerous positive lyrics and imagery may have promoted coping, hope, and cultural celebration.

In addition, results of cross-sectional studies also indicated that music preferences may be compensatory factors inasmuch as they are linked to less internalizing psychopathology. For instance, Easy Listening music (e.g. pop, country, soft rock) was linked to less depression in university and community adult members (George et al. 2007). Pop music (e.g. pop rock, dance, pop) and Soul music (e.g. hip hop, rap, R&B, reggae) were associated with less depression in adolescent girls (Miranda and Claes 2007). Pop music was associated with less depression in adolescent girls (Martin et al. 1993). Among adolescents, 'Middle-of-the-Road' (i.e. light listeners of conventional Pop-Dance), 'Rock-Pop' (i.e. listeners of Rock and Pop-Dance), and 'Urban' (i.e. heavy listeners of hip hop, soul/R&B, and reggae) represented music taste groups with less internalizing symptoms (Mulder et al. 2007). Easy Listening music (e.g. vocals, jazz, instrumental) was associated with less past suicidal ideations in college students (Lester and Whipple 1996). In university students, it was found that Upbeat/Conventional music (e.g. pop, soundtracks) was linked to less depression (Rentfrow and Gosling 2003).

Other cross-sectional studies have showed that music listening reactions or motivations can also be linked to less internalizing psychopathology. Werner et al. (2006) reported that experiencing more affective reactions from music correlated with less depression in male college students. Lacourse et al. (2001) showed that vicarious music listening (i.e. 'cathartic' expression of negative emotions) was linked to less suicidal risk in adolescent girls. Miranda and Claes (2009) reported that problem-oriented coping by music listening (i.e. coping oriented at resolving stressful problems) was linked to less depression in adolescent girls.

In sum, there is mounting evidence for a compensatory factor model involving direct links between music listening and less internalizing psychopathology. Longitudinal results suggest that Soul music (e.g. hip hop, R&B, reggae) predicts less internalizing symptoms in adolescence and, as such, may represent a compensatory factor. Cross-sectional results also underscore that music genres inspired by African American cultures (e.g. hip hop, rap, R&B, reggae) and pop music (e.g. conventional pop, pop rock, dance, easy listening) are associated with less internalizing symptoms. Recent evidence also suggests that certain forms of self-regulation through music (e.g. problem-oriented coping) may represent potential compensatory factors against internalizing symptoms, especially in adolescence.

Common cause/confounding model

In a *common cause/confounding model* (Klein et al. 2002; Wiebe and Fortenberry 2006), two associated variables (dependent variables) can share a spurious correlation as a result of sharing a common cause (independent variable). Hence, a music listening behaviour could share a correlation with internalizing psychopathology only because they share a common cause. Once that common cause (confounder) is statistically controlled, the spurious correlation would disappear. Theoretically, a specific risk factor could make individuals more prone to develop both maladaptive musical behaviours and internalizing symptoms, thus creating the needed condition for a confounded association between music and symptoms. The longitudinal study of Miranda and Claes (2008) controlled for confounders (drug use, academic problems, anxiety, antisocial behaviour) in adolescents. Whereas music preferences (Metal, Soul, Pop, Classical, and Electronic) did not predict more depression, Soul music was still able to predict less depression, when the confounders were controlled.

Cross-sectional studies have also provided test of the common cause/confounding model in terms of music preferences and internalizing psychopathology. For instance, among 275 adolescents, Lacourse and collaborators (2001) showed that Heavy metal did not predict suicidal risk when confounders were controlled (e.g. poor family relationship, drug use, alienation/anomie). However, Miranda and Claes (2007) found that after controlling for confounders (drug use, anxiety, academic problems) in adolescent girls, Metal music was still linked to more depression, whereas Pop music (e.g. pop rock, dance, pop) and Soul music (e.g. hip hop, rap, R&B, reggae) were still linked to less depression. After controlling for self-esteem, delinquency, and conservatism, North and Hargreaves (2006) found that so-called 'Problem music' (e.g. hard rock, hip hop/ rap, punk) still predicted suicide ideation in university students. In adolescents, even after controlling for confounders (e.g. quality of social relations with parents and peers), Mulder and collaborators (2007) found that 'Exclusive Rock' and 'Omnivores' music taste groups had more internalizing symptoms, whereas 'Middle-of-the-Road', 'Rock-Pop', and 'Urban' music taste groups had less internalizing symptoms.

In sum, research results indicate that the common cause/confounding model has yet to fully explain all links between music preferences and internalizing psychopathology. Researchers could select more or better confounders in order to support this model. Thus far, however, the literature suggests that some relationships between music listening and internalizing symptoms are not spurious.

Mediator model

In a *mediator model* (Baron and Kenny 1986), a mediating variable (mediator) represents the mechanism that may partly or fully explain why an independent variable predicts a dependent variable. This model can easily be mistaken for the common cause/confounding model, particularly in cross-sectional studies in which all variables are measured concurrently rather than prospectively. The mediator model is better depicted in longitudinal designs in which an antecedent precedes the mediator which is followed by the consequence, thus capturing the unfolding of a causal chain over time. In a full mediation model, the independent variable must first predict the dependent variable, the independent variable must also predict the mediator, the mediator has to predict the dependent variable as well, and lastly, the predictive link between the independent and the dependent variables must become non-significant when the mediator is statistically controlled (Baron and Kenny 1986). For example, a music listening behaviour could be a mediator if it can explain the influence of a risk factor on an internalizing psychopathology. A possible mediation sequence would be that psychological distress predicts maladaptive self-regulation by music listening which in turn predicts more internalizing symptoms (psychological distress → maladaptive emotion regulation or coping by music → internalizing symptoms). Many other mediating mechanisms can be theorized. For instance, preferences for music genres that explore negative themes may predict more internalizing symptoms through the mediating actions of rumination or co-rumination (music genres exploring negative themes → rumination or co-rumination → internalizing symptoms). Unfortunately, to our knowledge, there are no longitudinal studies that have explicitly tested if a mediator model can explain links between music listening and internalizing psychopathology. Such three-wave longitudinal studies would be an important contribution to clarify the causal pathways between music and mental health.

Moderator model

In a *moderator model* (Baron and Kenny 1986), the different levels of a moderating variable (moderator) will change the significance, magnitude, or even valence of the relationship between an independent variable and a dependent variable. This is commonly referred to as an interaction between two independent variables, one of which is defined as the moderator. A music listening behaviour might need to interact with a given moderator (continuous or dichotomous) to exert an influence on internalizing psychopathology. Age and gender are important moderators in the developmental and social psychology of music and may be moderators of the effects of music listening on internalizing psychopathology. For instance, adolescents usually report more music listening than children (Roberts et al. 2009) and adolescent girls usually report more emotion regulation and coping by music listening than their boy counterparts (Miranda and Claes 2009). The longitudinal study of Miranda and Claes (2008) indicated that gender acted as a moderator, in that Soul music (e.g. hip hop, R&B, reggae) predicted less depression only in adolescent girls and not in boys.

Cross-sectional studies on music preferences and internalizing psychopathology have often considered gender as a moderator. One study found that Heavy Metal/Rock music predicted suicidal ideations in adolescent boys, but not in girls (Burge et al. 2002). Still, significant links seem to be found more often in females than males. Rock/Heavy Metal music was associated with more suicidal thoughts and depression in adolescent girls, but not in boys (Martin et al. 1993). Heavy metal fans were identified as having more suicidal risk than non-fans in adolescent girls, but not in boys (Scheel and Westefeld 1999). Lastly, Miranda and Claes (2007) indicated that in adolescent girls, Metal music was linked to more depression, whereas Pop music (e.g. pop rock, dance, pop) and Soul music (e.g. hip hop, rap, R&B, reggae) were associated with less depression. However, their study showed that in adolescent boys, there were no significant links between music preferences and depression.

Other cross-sectional studies have shown that relationships between music listening reactions or motivations and internalizing symptoms can also be moderated by gender. Music listening involving some 'cathartic' expression of negative emotions was associated with less suicidal risk in adolescent girls, but not in boys (Lacourse et al. 2001). Miranda and Claes (2009) found that in adolescent girls, avoidance/disengagement coping by music listening was linked to more depression, whereas problem-oriented coping by music listening was associated with less depression. However, in their subsample of boys, only emotion-oriented coping by music listening was linked to more depression.

Some cross-sectional studies have examined social context as a moderator. In adolescent girls, Metal music was not associated with depression when high school peers had low levels of depression, yet Metal music was associated with more depression when high school peers had high levels of depression (Miranda and Claes 2009). In child and adolescents, affects were more positive when music listening occurred in the company of friends rather than alone or with the family (Thompson and Larson 1995). Surprisingly, studies on music listening and internalizing psychopathology have rarely tested age as a moderator. However, one study indicated that music listening could be linked to loneliness (which we will consider as a proxy for social withdrawal) in college students, but not in adolescents (Davis and Kraus 1989).

In sum, the literature on music listening and internalizing psychopathology supports the usefulness of a moderator model. In terms of music preferences, reactions or motivations; gender seems to be a basic moderator that should be tested on a regular basis. Age and social context are also potentially important moderators that deserve closer empirical scrutiny.

Protective factor model

In a *protective factor model* (Rutter 1985), a protective factor can act as a moderator that can completely buffer or significantly decrease the magnitude of a predictive relationship between a risk factor and a psychopathological symptom. Accordingly, a music listening behaviour that can block or attenuate the predictive link between a risk factor and an internalizing psychopathology could be a protective factor. The longitudinal study of Miranda and Claes (2008) has showed that in adolescent girls, more liking of Soul music (e.g. hip hop, R&B, reggae) completely buffered the positive link between neuroticism (risk factor) and subsequent depression symptoms. Neuroticism predicted more depression in girls with less liking of Soul music, whereas neuroticism did not predict depression in girls with more liking of Soul music. In other words, Soul music was a potential protective factor against depression. Regrettably, we are not aware of any other longitudinal or cross-sectional studies that have explicitly tested if a music listening behaviour could act as a protective factor against a risk factor of internalizing psychopathology.

Precipitating factor model

In a *precipitating (or vulnerability) factor model* (Fergusson et al. 2007), a precipitating factor can also act as a moderator, although this time it significantly increases the magnitude of a predictive relationship between a risk factor and a psychopathological symptom. Thus, a music listening behaviour that can reinforce a predictive link between a risk factor and an internalizing psychopathology could be considered as a precipitating factor. However, longitudinal studies on music listening and internalizing psychopathology have yet to use this model.

We were only able to find one tentative example of a precipitating (or vulnerability) factor model regarding music listening and internalizing psychopathology. Davis and Kraus (1989) conducted a study with college students and adolescent summer campers. Among other things, their study considered whether time devoted to music listening (and media) could act as coping strategies against loneliness (once again we will consider loneliness as a proxy for social withdrawal). Experiencing fewer social contacts can represent a risk factor of loneliness. In this regard, the results of Davis and Kraus (1989) indicated that participants with fewer social contacts experienced even more loneliness if they spent a lot of time listening to music, as compared to participants with fewer social contacts who spent little time listening to music. This may have indicated the presence of a precipitating effect from abundant music listening, which Davis and Kraus called an 'intensification' effect. Therefore, it is possible that abundant music listening is not always a beneficial surrogate companion in times of lack of social contacts. For some individuals, it may exacerbate their social withdrawal, thus compounding the detrimental effects of lack of socialization on their internalizing symptoms.

Conclusion

Music usually evokes positive emotions (e.g. happiness and elation) and provides developmental resources (e.g. emotion regulation and competency; McPherson 2006; Saarikallio and Erkkilä 2007; Juslin et al. 2008; Miranda and Claes, 2009). Our literature review suggests that adaptive and maladaptive music listening behaviours may coexist and—depending on their relative strength or frequency—can lead to less or more internalizing psychopathology, respectively. This notion was grounded in the assumptions of *emotion regulation* and *gradual development* which could underlie the influence of everyday music listening on internalizing symptoms. Internalizing psychopathology could be influenced positively or negatively by cumulative mechanisms in everyday music listening, including emotion regulation, coping strategies, social cognitive effects, and psychotherapeutic effects. We reviewed seven methodological strategies that may capture these mechanisms and effects within longitudinal research designs. There is still a limited number of empirical studies on everyday music listening and internalizing psychopathology. The few available studies are difficult to compare because of methodological differences (e.g. sample, assessment) and the lack of use of explicit models (e.g. examining mediator, moderator, protective, or precipitating factors). Of all music listening behaviours, 'music preference' has been the most studied. However, we believe that much more attention should be given to musical reactions, motivations, and contexts, which are likely to have much greater impact on wellbeing and psychopathology than music preferences.

In sum, there seems to be enough theoretical rationale and empirical evidence to warrant more research on music listening and internalizing psychopathology. In normative development—or through prevention, clinical and educational programmes—the beneficial effects of music should outweigh the detrimental ones. Unfortunately, under certain circumstances and in some vulnerable individuals, maladaptive music listening may increase subclinical internalizing symptoms. Still, longitudinal and cross-sectional studies also suggest that adaptive music listening may decrease subclinical internalizing symptoms. Therefore, it seems that individuals may need to maintain a healthy listening regimen in order to fully benefit from the pleasure, developmental resources, and wellbeing provided by everyday music listening. Understanding these modes of music listening in more details will probably require longitudinal mixed research methods (qualitative and quantitative) that can untangle the complex causal pathways involved.

Acknowledgements

This study was supported in part by a prior scholarship for postdoctoral research from the Fonds Québécois de la Recherche sur la Société et la Culture (FQRSC; years 2008–2010) and by a current postdoctoral fellowship award from the Social Sciences and Humanities Research Council of Canada (SSHRC; years 2010–2012) awarded to the first author. This study was also supported in part by a research grant from the Social Sciences and Humanities Research Council of Canada (SSHRC) awarded to the second author.

References

Achenbach, T.M. (1991). *Manual for the Youth Self-Report and 1991 Profile*. Burlington, VT: University of Vermont, Department of Psychiatry.

American Psychological Association (2006). *APA dictionary of psychology* (G.R. VandenBos, ed.). Washington, DC: APA.

Anderson, C.A. and Bushman, B.J. (2002). The effects of media violence on society. *Science, 295,* 2377–9.

Anderson, C.A., Carnagey, N.L., and Eubanks, J. (2003). Exposure to violent media: The effects of songs with violent lyrics on aggressive thoughts and feelings. *Journal of Personality and Social Psychology, 84,* 960–71.

Arnett, J.J. (1995). Adolescents' uses of media for self-socialization. *Journal of Youth and Adolescence, 24,* 519–33.

Anthony, M.M. and Stein, M.B. (2009). *Oxford handbook of anxiety and related disorders*. Oxford: Oxford University Press.

Baker, F. and Bor, W. (2008). Can music preference indicate mental health status in young people? *Australasian Psychiatry, 16,* 284–8.

Baron, R.M. and Kenny, D.A. (1986). The moderator-mediator variable distinction in social psychology research: Conceptual strategic and statistical considerations. *Journal of Personality and Social Psychology, 51,* 1173–82.

Brown, E.F. and Hendee, W.R. (1989). Adolescents and their music: Insights into the health of adolescents. *Journal of the American Medical Association, 262,* 1659–63.

Burge, M., Goldblat, C., and Lester, D. (2002). Music Preferences and suicidality: A comment on Stack. *Death Studies, 26,* 501–4.

Campbell-Sills, L. and Barlow, D. H. (2007). Incorporating emotion regulation into conceptualizations and treatments of anxiety and mood disorders. In: J.J. Gross (ed.) *Handbook of emotion regulation*, pp. 542–59. New York: Guilford Press.

Chamorro-Premuzic, T. and Furnham, A. (2007). Personality and music: Can traits explain how people use music in everyday life? *British Journal of Psychology,* **98**, 175–85.

Chamorro-Premuzic, T., Gomà-i-Freixanet, M., Furnham, A., and Muro, A. (2009). Personality, self-estimated intelligence, and uses of music: A Spanish replication and extension using structural equation modeling. *Psychology of Aesthetics, Creativity, and the Arts, 3*, 149–55.

Cicchetti, D. and Cohen, D. (2006). *Developmental psychopathology: Theory and method (vol. 1, 2nd ed.).* New York: Wiley.

Compas, B.E., Connor-Smith, J.K., Saltzman, H., Harding-Thomsen, A., and Wadsworth, M.E. (2001). Coping with stress during childhood and adolescence: Problems, progress, and potential in theory and research. *Psychological Bulletin, 127*, 87–127.

Davis, M.H. and Kraus, L.A. (1989). Social contact, loneliness, and mass media use: A test of two hypotheses. *Journal of Applied Social Psychology, 19*, 1100–24.

Fergusson, D.M., Vitaro, F., Wanner, B., and Brendgen, M. (2007). Protective and compensatory factors mitigating the influence of deviant friends on delinquent behaviours during early adolescence. *Journal of Adolescence, 30*, 33–50.

Gabrielsson, A. (2010). Strong experiences with music. In: P.N. Juslin and J.A. Sloboda (eds.) *Handbook of music and emotion: Theory, research, applications*, pp. 547–74. New York: Oxford University Press.

Garrido, S. (2009). Rumination and sad music: A review of the literature and a future direction. In: C. Stevens, E. Schubert, B. Kruithof, K. Buckley and S. Fazio (eds.) *Proceedings of the 2nd International Conference on Music Communication Science (ICoMCS2)*, pp. 20–23. Sydney, Australia: HCSNet, University of Western Sydney.

George, D., Stickle, K., Rachid, F., and Wopnford, A. (2007). The association between types of music enjoyed and cognitive, behavioral, and personality factors of those who listen. *Psychomusicology, 19*, 32–56.

Gold, C., Solli, H.P., Krüger, V., and Lie, S.A. (2009). Dose–response relationship in music therapy for people with serious mental disorders: Systematic review and meta-analysis. *Clinical Psychology Review, 29*, 193–207.

Gotlib, I.H. and Hammen, C.L. (2009). *Handbook of depression (2nd Ed.)*. New York: Guilford Press.

Greenwood, D.N. and Long, C.R. (2009). Mood specific media use and emotion regulation: Patterns and individual differences. *Personality and Individual Differences, 46*, 616–21.

Gresham, F.M. and Kern, L. (2004). Internalizing behavior problems in children and adolescents. In: R.B. Rutherford Jr., M.M. Quinn, and S.R. Mathur (eds.) *Handbook of research in emotional and behavioral disorders*, pp. 262–81. New York: Guilford Press.

Gross, J.J. and John, O.P. (2003). Individual differences in two emotion regulation processes: Implications for affect, relationships, and well-being. *Journal of Personality and Social Psychology, 85*, 348–62.

Gross, J.J. and Thompson, R.A. (2007). Emotion regulation: Conceptual foundations. In: J.J. Gross (ed.) *Handbook of emotion regulation*, pp. 3–24. New York: Guilford Press.

Hargreaves, D.J., North, A.C., and Tarrant, M. (2006). Musical preference and taste in childhood and adolescence. In: G. E. McPherson (ed.) *The child as musician*, pp. 135–54. Oxford: Oxford University Press.

Hudziak, J.J., Achenbach, T.M., Althoff, R.R., and Pine, D.S. (2008). A dimensional approach to developmental psychopathology. In: J.E. Helzer, H.C. Kraemer, R.F. Krueger, H.-U. Wittchen, P.J. Sirovatka and D.A. Regier (eds.) *Dimensional approaches in diagnostic classification: Refining the research agenda for DSM-V*, pp. 101–113. Washington, DC: American Psychiatric Association.

Juslin, P.N., Liljeström, S., Västfjäll, D., Barradas, G., and Silva, A. (2008). An experience sampling study of emotional reactions to music: Listener, music, and situation. *Emotion, 8*, 668–83.

Juslin, P.N., Liljeström, S., Västfjäll, D., and Lundqvist, L.-O. (2010). How does music evoke emotions? Exploring the underlying mechanisms. In: P. N. Juslin and J. A. Sloboda (eds.) *Handbook of music and emotion: Theory, research, applications*, pp. 605–42. New York: Oxford University Press.

Juslin, P.N. and Sloboda, J.A. (2010). *Handbook of music and emotion: Theory, research, applications*. New York: Oxford University Press.

Katz, E., Gurevitch, M., and Haas, H. (1973). On the use of the mass media for important things. *American Sociological Review,* **38**, 164–81.

Klein, D.N., Durbin, C.E., Shankman, S.A., and Santiago, N.J. (2002). Depression and personality. In: I.H. Gotlib and C.L. Hammen (eds.) *Handbook of depression*, pp. 115–40. New York: Guilford Press.

Krueger, R.F. (1999). The structure of common mental disorders. *Archives of General Psychiatry,* **56**, 921–26.

Krueger, R.F., Chentsova-Dutton, Y.E., Markon, K.E., Goldberg, D., and Ormel, J. (2003). A cross-cultural study of the structure of comorbidity among common psychopathological syndromes in the general health care setting. *Journal of Abnormal Psychology,* **112**, 437–47.

Lacourse, E., Claes, M., and Villeneuve, M. (2001). Heavy metal music and adolescent suicidal risk. *Journal of Youth and Adolescence,* **30**, 321–32.

Laukka, P. (2007). Uses of music and psychological well-being among the elderly. *Journal of Happiness Studies,* **8**, 215–41.

Lazarus, R.S. and Folkman, S. (1984). *Stress, appraisal, and coping*. New York: Springer.

Lester, D. and Whipple, M. (1996). Music preference, depression, suicidal preoccupation, and personality: Comment on Stack and Gundlach's papers. *Suicide and Life-Threatening Behavior,* **26**, 68–71.

Lewinsohn, P.M., Solomon, A., Seeley, J.R., and Zeiss, A. (2000). Clinical implications of 'subthreshold' depressive symptoms. *Journal of Abnormal Psychology,* **109**, 345–51.

Martin, G., Clarke, M., and Pearce, C. (1993). Adolescent suicide: Music preference as an indicator of vulnerability. *Journal of the American Child and Adolescent Psychiatry,* **32**, 530–35.

McPherson, G.E. (2006). *The child as musician: A handbook of musical development*. Oxford: Oxford University Press.

Menon, V. and Levitin, D.J. (2005). The rewards of music listening: Response and physiological connectivity of the mesolimbic system. *NeuroImage,* **28**, 175–84.

Miranda, D. and Claes, M. (2007). Musical preferences and depression in adolescence. *International Journal of Adolescence and Youth,* **13**, 285–309.

Miranda, D. and Claes, M. (2008). Personality traits, music preferences and depression in adolescence. *International Journal of Adolescence and Youth,* **14**, 277–98.

Miranda, D. and Claes, M. (2009). Music listening, coping, peer affiliation and depression in adolescence. *Psychology of Music,* **37**, 215–33.

Miranda, D., Gaudreau, P., Morizot, J., and Fallu, J-S. (in press). Can fantasizing while listening to music play a protective role against the influences of sensation seeking and peers on adolescents' substance use? *Substance Use and Misuse.*

Mulder, J., ter Bogt, T., Raaijmakers, Q., and Vollebergh, W. (2007). Music taste groups and problem behaviour. *Journal of Youth and Adolescence,* **36**, 313–24.

Murray, C.J. and Lopez, A.D. (1996). *The global burden of disease*. Cambridge, MA: Harvard University Press.

Nolen-Hoeksema, S., Wisco, B.E., and Lyubomirsky, S. (2008). Rethinking rumination. *Perspectives on Psychological Science,* **3**, 400–24.

North, A.C. and Hargreaves, D.J. (2006). Problem music and self-harming. *Suicide and Life-Threatening Behavior,* **36**, 582–90.

North, A.C. and Hargreaves, D.J. (2008). *The social and applied psychology of music*. Oxford: Oxford University Press.

North, A.C., Hargreaves, D.J., and Hargreaves, J.J. (2004). Uses of music in everyday life. *Music Perception,* **22**, 41–77.

North, A.C., Hargreaves, D.J., and O'Neill. S.A. (2000). The importance of music to adolescents. *British Journal of Educational Psychology, 70*, 255–72.

Overy, K. and Molnar-Szakacs, I. (2009). Being together in time: Musical experience and the mirror neuron system. *Music Perception, 26*, 489–504.

Phares, V. (2002). *Understanding Abnormal Child Psychology*. Hoboken, NJ: Wiley.

Primack, B.A., Swanier, B., Georgiopoulos, A.M., Land, S.R., and Fine, M.J. (2009). Association between media use in adolescence and depression in young adulthood: A longitudinal study. *Archives of General Psychiatry, 66*, 181–8.

Recours, R., Aussaguel, F., and Trujillo, N. (2009). Metal music and mental health in France. *Culture, Medicine, and Psychiatry, 33*, 473–88.

Rentfrow, P.J. and Gosling, S.D. (2003). The Do Re Mi's of everyday life: The structure and personality correlates of music preferences. *Journal of Personality and Social Psychology, 84*, 1236–56.

Roberts, D.F., Henriksen, L., and Foehr, U.G. (2009). Adolescence, adolescents, and media. In: R.M. Lerner and L. Steinberg (eds.) *Handbook of adolescent psychology, 3rd ed. (volume 2): Contextual influences on adolescent development*, pp. 314–44. Hoboken, NJ: Wiley.

Roe, K. (1995). Adolescents' use of socially disvalued media: Towards a theory of media delinquency. *Journal of Youth and Adolescents, 24*, 617–31.

Rose, A.J. (2002). Co-rumination in the friendships of girls and boys. *Child Development, 73*, 1830–43.

Rosengren, K.E., Wenner, L.A., and Palmgreen, P. (1985). *Media gratifications research*. Beverly Hills, CA: Sage.

Rutter, M. (1985). Resiliency in the face of adversity: Protective factors and resistance to psychiatric disorder. *British Journal of Psychiatry, 147*, 598–611.

Saarikallio, A. and Erkkilä, J. (2007). The role of music in adolescents' mood regulation. *Psychology of Music, 35*, 88–109.

Scheel, K.R. and Westefeld, J.S. (1999). Heavy metal music and adolescent suicidality: An empirical investigation. *Adolescence, 34*, 253–73.

Selfhout, M.H.W., Branje, S.J.T., ter Bogt, T.F.M., and Meeus, W.H.J. (2009). The role of music preferences in early adolescents' friendship formation and stability. *Journal of Adolescence, 32*, 95–107.

Sloboda, J.A. (2010). Music in everyday life: The role of emotions. In: P.N. Juslin and J.A. Sloboda (eds.) *Handbook of music and emotion: Theory, research, applications*, pp. 493–514. New York: Oxford University Press.

Thaut, M.H. and Wheeler, B. L. (2010). Music therapy. In: P.N. Juslin and J.A. Sloboda (eds.) *Handbook of music and emotion: Theory, research, applications*, pp. 819–48. New York: Oxford University Press.

Thompson, R.L. and Larson, R. (1995). Social context and the subjective experience of different types of rock music. *Journal of Youth and Adolescents, 24*, 731–44.

Werner, P.D., Swope, A.J., and Heide, F.J. (2006). The music experience questionnaire: Development and correlates. *The Journal of Psychology, 140*, 329–45.

Wiebe, D.J. and Fortenberry, K.T. (2006). Mechanisms relating personality and health. In: M.E. Vollrath (ed.), *Handbook of personality and health*, pp. 137–56. Chichester: Wiley.

World Health Organization (2008). *The global burden of disease: 2004 update*. Geneva: WHO Press.

Zillmann, D. (1988a). Mood management: Using entertainment to full advantage. In: L. Donohew, H.E. Sypher, and E.T. Higgens (eds.) *Communication, social cognition, and affect*, pp. 147–71. Hillsdale, NJ: Erlbaum.

Zillmann, D. (1988b). Mood management through communication choices. *American Behavioral Scientist, 31*, 327–40.

Author Index

Subject Index

Page numbers in italic indicate entries occurring in figure or table captions